To Nikki Condra and the
Social Studies teachers at the
Quartz Hill High School

With best wishes,

Jack Spielberg

# MODERN WORLD HISTORY

# MODERN WORLD HISTORY

## JACKSON J. SPIELVOGEL

*The Pennsylvania State University*

## WEST EDUCATIONAL PUBLISHING

*an International Thomson Publishing company* I(T)P®

Cincinnati ✦ Albany, NY ✦ Belmont, CA ✦ Bonn ✦ Boston ✦ Detroit ✦ Johannesburg ✦ London ✦ Los Angeles ✦ Madrid
Melbourne ✦ Mexico City ✦ New York ✦ Paris ✦ Singapore ✦ Tokyo ✦ Toronto ✦ Washington

## PRODUCTION CREDITS

Team Leader     Robert Cassel
Project Manager     Theresa O'Dell
Production Manager     John Orr
Editors     Lynn Bruton, Phyllis Jelinek,
  Glenda Samples, Pam Starkey
Photo Research     Jan Seidel
Production Editors     Carole Balach, Regan Stilo
Permissions     Elaine Arthur
Illustrators     Lee Anne Dollison, Matthew Thiessen
Copyediting     Mary Berry
Design     Janet Bollow
Composition     Parkwood Composition Service, Inc.
Layout Artist     José Delgado
Maps     Maryland Cartographics and Magellan GeoGraphix
Index     Terry Casey
Cover Design     Janet Bollow
Proofreader     Suzie De Fazio
Prepress Services     Clarinda Company

## PHOTO ACKNOWLEDGMENTS

**Cover** Kandinsky, Wassily. *The Song of the Volga.* 1906. Musée National d'Art Moderne, Paris, France. Giraudon/Art Resource, NY.

**Contents** vii ©Pierre Belzeaux/Photo Researchers, Inc.; **viii** Corbis-Bettmann; **ix (top)** Robert Harding Picture Library, Karachi Museum; **ix (bottom)** detail, National Museum of American Art, Washington, DC/Art Resource, NY; **x** North Wind Picture Archives; **xi (top)** Mary Evans Picture Library; **xi (bottom)** ©The Hulton Getty Picture Collection, Limited/Rischgitz Collection; **xii (top)** Express News/Archive Photos; **xii (bottom)** E. T. Archive; **xiii (top)** Corbis-Bettmann; **xiii (bottom)** Julia Waterflow, Eye Ubiquitous/Corbis; **xiv (top)** Liba Taylor/Corbis; **xiv (bottom)** NASA.

**Introduction** BH1 AP/Wide World Photos; **BH4** © F. Hibon/Sygma; **BH8** ©Dennis Cox/ChinaStock; **BH9** ©The Huntington Library; **BH18** North Wind Picture Archives; **BH22 (top)** Gallery of Prehistoric Art, New York, Scala/Art Resource, NY; **BH22 (bottom)** "Echoes of the Kalabari": Sculpture by Sokari Douglas Camp, "Masquerader with Boat Headdress" 1987, Photograph by Jeffrey Ploskonka, National Museum of African Art, Eliot Elisofon Photographic Archives, Smithsonian Institution; **BH23** Vasily Kandinsky, *Painting with White Border,* (Bild mit weissem Rand). May 1913; Oil on canvas, 140.3 × 200.3 cm (55-1/4 × 78-7/8 inches), The Solomon R. Guggenheim Museum, New York, Photo by Dave Heald ©The Solomon R. Guggenheim Foundation, New York, (FN 37.245).

**Unit Openers** 2 Courtesy of the Arthur M. Sackler Gallery, Smithsonian Institution, Washington, DC; **80** Pablo Picasso, *The Fourteenth of July,* 1901, Solomon R. Guggenheim Museum, New York. Gift, Justin K. Thannhauser, 1964. Photo: David Heald ©The Solomon R. Guggenheim Foundation, New York; **270** Imperial War Museum, London; **412** Jeffrey Dunn/Viesti Associates, Inc.

*(continued following index)*

# ABOUT THE AUTHOR

Jackson J. Spielvogel is associate professor of history at the Pennsylvania State University. He received his Ph.D. from the Ohio State University, where he specialized in Reformation history under Harold J. Grimm. His articles and reviews have appeared in such journals as *Moreana*, *Journal of General Education*, *Archiv für Reformationsgeschichte*, and *American Historical Review*. He has also contributed chapters or articles to *The Social History of the Reformation*, *The Holy Roman Empire: A Dictionary Handbook*, *Simon Wiesenthal Center Annual of Holocaust Studies*, and *Utopian Studies*. His work has been supported by fellowships from the Fulbright Foundation and the Foundation for Reformation Research. His book *Hitler and Nazi Germany* was published in 1987 (third edition, 1996). His book *Western Civilization* was published in 1991 (third edition, 1997). He is the co-author (with William Duiker) of *World History*, published in January 1994 (second edition, 1998). Professor Spielvogel has won five major university-wide teaching awards. During the year 1988–1989, he held the Penn State Teaching Fellowship, the university's most prestigious teaching award. In 1996, he won the Dean Arthur Ray Warnock Award for Outstanding Faculty Member. In 1997, he became the first winner of the Schreyer Institute's Student Choice Award for innovative and inspiring teaching.

## TO DIANE
*whose love and support made it all possible*

# CONTENTS-IN-BRIEF

# CONTENTS-IN-BRIEF

# CONTENTS

# UNIT TWO

## Modern Patterns of World History: The Era of European Dominance (1750 to 1914)
### 80

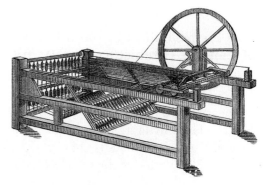

# UNIT TWO

# UNIT THREE

## The Crisis of the Twentieth Century (1914 to 1945)
### 270

# UNIT FOUR

## Toward a Global Civilization: The World Since 1945
### (1945 to Present)
### 412

# UNIT FOUR

# FEATURES

# FEATURES

# MAPS

# ACKNOWLEDGMENTS

I began to teach at age five in my family's grape arbor. By the age of ten, I wanted to know and understand everything in the world so I set out to memorize our entire set of encyclopedia volumes. At seventeen, as editor of the high school yearbook, I chose "Patterns" as its theme.

With that as my early history, followed by twenty-five rich years of teaching, writing, and family nurturing, it seemed quite natural to accept the challenge of writing a world history as I entered that period in life often described as the age of wisdom. Although I see this writing adventure as part of the natural unfolding of my life, I gratefully acknowledge that without the generosity of many others, it would not have been possible.

My ability to undertake a project of this magnitude was in part due to the outstanding teachers that I had as both an undergraduate and graduate student. These included Kent Forster at the Pennsylvania State University and William MacDonald and Harold Grimm at the Ohio State University. These teachers provided me with profound insights into history and also taught me by their example that learning only becomes true understanding when it is accompanied by compassion, humility, and open-mindedness. I am especially grateful to William Duiker and his wife Yvonne for their enormous efforts in helping me to understand and put into perspective the history of the non-Western world. My colleague Arthur Goldschmidt also freely gave of his time to review my efforts.

Thanks to West Publishing Company's comprehensive review process, many teachers took time from their busy schedules to evaluate the different drafts of my manuscript. I am grateful to the following for the innumerable suggestions that have greatly improved my work. I am also grateful to those teachers who provided such outstanding review questions and activities.

Bill Anderson
*Coeur d'Alene High School*
*Coeur d'Alene, ID*

Glenn Anderson
*Apopka High School*
*Apopka, FL*

J. P. Applegate
*Oklahoma State Dept. of Education*
*Oklahoma City, OK*

Simone Arias
*Cleveland State University*
*Cleveland, OH*

Joan Arno
*George Washington High School*
*Philadelphia, PA*

Daniel Berman
*Fox Lane High School*
*Bedford, NY*

Marjorie Bingham
*St. Louis Park High School*
*Minnetonka, MN*

Henry P. Bitten
*Ramapo High School*
*Franklin Lakes, NJ*

Daniel W. Blackmon
*Coral Gables Senior High School*
*Miami, FL*

Janna M. Bremer
*King Philip Regional High School*
*Wrentham, MA*

James A. (Charlie) Brown
*Central Senior High School*
*Little Rock, AR*

Steven L. Buenning
*William Fremd High School*
*Palatine, IL*

Frank Burke
*St. Louis, MO*

Brian Carlson
*Dillard High School*
*Plantation, FL*

Anne Chapman
*Western Reserve Academy*
*Hudson, OH*

Peter J. Cheoros
*Lynwood High School*
*Lynwood, CA*

Timothy C. Connell
*Laurel School*
*Shaker Heights, OH*

Scott Crump
*Bingham High School*
*South Jordan, UT*

Shirley Cruse
*Mayfield High School*
*Las Cruces, NM*

Frank de Varona
*Dade County Public Schools*
*Hialeah, FL*

Linda Dennis
*Cypress Creek High School*
*Houston, TX*

Suzanne Dillard
*Shepton High School*
*Plano, TX*

Robert Doyle
*The Community School*
*Sun Valley, ID*

Felicia C. Eppley
*Lamar High School*
*Houston, TX*

William R. Everdell
*St. Ann's School*
*Brooklyn, NY*

Autumn Farber
*Edmonds School District*
*Lynnwood, WA*

Maggie Favretti
*Scarsdale High School*
*Bronxville, NY*

Helen Crowley Foucault
*Deerfield High School*
*Deerfield, IL*

James Grinsel
*Wausau West High School*
*Wausau, WI*

Gary L. Hammac
*East Central High School*
*San Antonio, TX*

Georgiana Hatch
*Upland High School*
*Upland, CA*

Marilynn Jo Hitchens
*Wheat Ridge High School*
*Wheat Ridge, CO*

Kathryn Hodgkinson
*Berkner High School*
*Richardson, TX*

Richard K. Holloway
*Henry Clay High School*
*Lexington, KY*

Paul A. Horne, Jr.
*Richland County School Dist. No. One*
*Columbia, SC*

Chris Housel
*Centennial High School*
*Boise, ID*

Jean Elliott Johnson
*New York University*
*New York, NY*

Rita Johnson
*Clear Lake High School*
*Houston, TX*

Larry Jones
*Moorpark High School*
*Moorpark, CA*

James T. Jordan
*Scotland High School*
*Laurinburg, NC*

Henry G. Kiernan
*West Morris Regional High School Dist.*
*Chester, NJ*

Ellen Kottler
*Western Senior High School*
*Las Vegas, NV*

Joseph I. Lamas
*G. Holmes Braddock Sr. High School*
*Miami, FL*

Samuel J. Lichterman
*Armstrong High School*
*Plymouth, MN*

Mary Lindquist
*Mercer Island High School*
*Seattle, WA*

Alan Lucibello
*Montville Township High School*
*Montville, NJ*

Sally Lyons
*Lassiter High School*
*Marietta, GA*

Bobette Manees
*Sylvan Hills High School*
*Sherwood, AR*

Silda Mason
*Rio Grande High School*
*Albuquerque, NM*

Steven L. McCollum
*Thomas Jefferson Independent*
*Day School*
*Joplin, MO*

Carrie H. McIver
*San Carlos Summit High School*
*San Diego, CA*

John R. McNamara
*Gilbert High School*
*Gilbert, AZ*

R. J. Olivarez
*Bloomington High School*
*Bloomington, TX*

Brenda Palmer
*Lehigh Senior High School*
*Ft. Myers, FL*

Paul H. Pangrace
*Garrett Morgan Middle School*
*Cleveland, OH*

John S. Pearson
*Thousand Oaks High School*
*Thousand Oaks, CA*

Susan Philippsen
*Simi Valley High School*
*Simi Valley, CA*

Ellen L. Pike
*Lancaster Country Day School*
*Lancaster, PA*

Sheila G. Raihl
*Gadsden Senior High School*
*Anthony, NM*

Arturo V. Rivera
*Cibola High School*
*Yuma, AZ*

Beverly S. Roberts
*Brookwood High School*
*Snellville, GA*

Jeri D. Roberts
*Green Valley High School*
*Henderson, NV*

Esther M. Robinson
*Langham Creek High School*
*Houston, TX*

Heidi Roupp
*Aspen High School*
*Aspen, CO*

Denny L. Schillings
*Homewood-Flossmoor High School*
*Flossmoor, IL*

Rob T. Sears
*Rancho High School*
*N. Las Vegas, NV*

Lawrence A. Spalla
*Trinity Senior High School*
*Washington, PA*

Carol K. Thomson
*Santa Fe High School, North Campus*
*Santa Fe, NM*

John Turnbull
*Chaparral High School*
*Las Vegas, NV*

John Uelmen
*Newbury Park High School*
*Newbury Park, CA*

Martha Van Zant
*Biloxi High School*
*Biloxi, MS*

Nancy L. Webber
*West Charlotte Senior High School*
*Charlotte, NC*

Steve Weiner
*Gateway High School*
*Aurora, CO*

Susan Winslow,
*Montgomery High School*
*Montgomery, TX*

J. Donald Woodruff, Jr.
*Fredericksburg Academy*
*Fredericksburg, VA*

William Zeigler
*El Cajon High School*
*San Diego, CA*

The editors at West Publishing Company have been both helpful and congenial at all times. Their flexible policies allowed the creative freedom that a writer cherishes. I especially wish to thank Clyde Perlee, who encouraged me to undertake this project and taught me so much about the world of publishing. In the early stages of this project, Denis Ralling was always helpful with his insightful analyses and organization of many practical details. Members of the current West team who produced this book constitute a remarkable group of people. Bob Cassel, editor in chief, was a soft-spoken but superb leader whose judgment I grew to trust. John Orr, production manager, had a remarkable sense of timing and direction. To the many people—Theresa O'Dell, Project Manager; Jan Seidel; Pam Starkey; Regan Stilo; Lee Anne Dollison; Matt Thiessen; Phyllis Jelinek—I came to know well through telephone conversations and fax messages, and who provided invaluable editorial assistance, I want to express my deepest gratitude for the efforts they have made on behalf of this book. All of them were as cooperative as they were competent. I am also grateful to Mary Berry for her copyediting skills, Elaine Arthur for obtaining permissions, and Janet Bollow for her magnificent design. In an age when the impersonal has become commonplace, I want to express my appreciation for both the professional and personal relationships that I have shared with the West "family" in California.

Above all, I thank my family for their support. The gifts of love, laughter, and patience from my daughters, Jennifer and Kathryn; my sons, Eric and Christian; and my daughters-in-law Liz and Michele, were invaluable. My wife and best friend, Diane, provided me with editorial assistance, wise counsel, and the loving support that made it possible for me to complete a project of this magnitude. I could not have written the book without her.

**Jackson J. Spielvogel**

# INTRODUCTION
# BECOMING AN HISTORIAN

On August 19, 1991, a group of Soviet leaders opposed to reform arrested Mikhail Gorbachev, the president of the Soviet Union, and tried to seize control of the government. Hundreds of thousands of Russians, led by Boris Yeltsin, the Russian president, poured into the streets of Moscow and Leningrad to resist the rebels. Some army units, sent out to enforce the wishes of the rebels, went over to Yeltsin's side. Within days, the rebels were forced to surrender. This failed attempt to seize power had unexpected results as Russia and a host of other Soviet states declared their independence from the Soviet Union. By the end of 1991, the Soviet Union—one of the largest empires in world history—had come to an end. Quite unexpectedly, a major turning point in world history had been reached.

The sudden collapse of the Soviet Union has been but one of many important events in world history. However, world history is more than just a series of dramatic events—as important as these events are. World history is the story of the human community. It is the story of all of us. That story is a rich and complex one that not only contains dramatic events but also tells how people were ruled, how they lived on a daily basis, how they fought, how they shared ideas, how they looked for the meaning of life, and how they expressed what they felt about the joys and sorrows of this world. The story of world history is the story of politics, economics, and social change, but it is also the story of everyday life, of ideas, of creative arts, of religious insight, and of dreams fulfilled and unfulfilled.

◀ *On August 22, 1991, a crowd of almost 100,000 Russian citizens marched in Red Square, Moscow, to celebrate the collapse of the military coup. Following the attempted coup, who emerged as the president of Russia, and who resigned as president of the USSR?*

## WHAT IS HISTORY?

You may think of history as a boring list of names and dates; an irrelevant record of revolutions and battles; or the meaningless stories of kings, queens, and other rulers. The truth is much more basic. History is simply what happens. History is not just what happens to famous and infamous people but what happens to everyone, including yourself.

We could say that history is everything that has happened since the beginning of time. In this sense, we realize that the age of human beings has been a very brief one compared with the geologic age of Earth, which scientists tell us stretches back for billions of years. During the age of humans, people have spent most of their time simply trying to exist, searching for food and shelter as best they could.

The definition of history as everything that has ever happened, however, is so broad that its use would make it impossible to tell our story. History has a more common meaning: a record of the past. To create this record, historians use documents (what has been recorded or written); artifacts, such as pottery, tools, and weapons; and even artworks. History in this sense really began five thousand to six thousand years ago, when people first began to write and keep records. The period before written records we call *prehistory*.

History could also be defined in a third way, as a special field of study. Herodotus, who lived in Greece in the fifth century B.C., is often regarded as the "father of history" in Western civilization. He was one of the first historians. In his history of the Greek and Persian Wars, Herodotus used evidence, tried to tell a good story, and showed a concern for the causes and effects of events.

In modern times, in the nineteenth and twentieth centuries, history became an academic discipline—a formal field of study that is examined in schools and universities. Leopold von Ranke, a German historian who lived in the nineteenth century, is often regarded as the father of this new kind of history. He created techniques for the critical analysis of documents and began to use formal courses in universities to train new historians. In their college courses, people who want to become professional historians learn not only facts but also methods by which they can analyze those facts

critically and make new discoveries that might change our picture of the past. History is based on factual evidence. Historians, however, try to discover both what happened (the factual evidence) and why it happened. In other words, historians use critical thinking to explain the cause-and-effect relationships that exist among the facts.

All of us are involved in the making of history. Abigail Pafford, a student from Apopka, Florida, was talking to her grandmother when she discovered that her great-grandfather had narrowly avoided one of the most tragic shipping disasters of recent times. Because her great-grandfather had fallen in love, he had not used his ticket for the maiden, and only, voyage of the *Titanic*. That ship struck an iceberg shortly before midnight on April 14, 1912, and sank with a loss of over 1,500 lives. At the time, Pafford's great-grandfather was on his way to San Francisco on another ship with her great-grandmother. Thus, a recorded event that might have been just another piece of information in a textbook—the *Titanic* disaster—is, for Pafford, part of family history.

Alex Haley, the editor of *The Autobiography of Malcolm X*, grew up in Henning, Tennessee, listening to his grandmother tell stories of Kunta Kinte, a family ancestor kidnapped in Africa during the 1700s and taken to America as a slave. Haley's search for his family's history led to his famous book *Roots: The Saga of an American Family*. The book was turned into a television miniseries and became one of the most watched shows of all time. Haley's personal family story had a universal appeal.

You will find, with some investigation, that history has been made by your own family and by the families of your friends. These accumulated experiences have become part of who you are. These experiences help to guide your choices and actions, both personal and public. In turn, your choices and actions then become part of your own children's and grandchildren's history. You are an important link in a chain that stretches back into your ancestors' history and forward into your descendants' future.

In this book, you will be asked to read one account of the history of the world, with a focus on the modern world. You will also be asked to read some of the documents that historians use to create their pictures of the past. Reading the documents will enable you to develop your critical skills and to be an historian yourself. Historians do what students of all ages seek to do—develop the critical skills that enable them to make some sense of human existence. As Socrates, an ancient Greek philosopher, said, "The unexamined life is not worth living." The study of history will give you the tools to examine not only the lives of others but also your own life.

# THEMES FOR UNDERSTANDING WORLD HISTORY

In examining the past, historians often organize their material on the basis of themes that enable them to ask and try to answer basic questions about the past. The following nine themes are especially important. We will meet them again and again in our story.

**Politics and History** The study of politics seeks to answer certain basic questions that historians have about the structure of a society. These questions include the following: How were people governed? What was the relationship between the ruler and the ruled? What people or groups of people held political power? What rights and liberties did the people have? What actions did people take to change their forms of government? The study of politics also includes the role of conflict. Historians examine the causes and results of wars in order to understand the impact of war on human development.

**The Role of Ideas** Ideas have great power to move people to action. For example, in the twentieth century, the idea of nationalism, which is based on a belief in loyalty to one's nation, helped lead to two great conflicts—World War I and World War II. Together these wars cost the lives of over fifty million people. At the same time, nationalism has also led people to work together to benefit the lives of a nation's citizens. The spread of ideas from one society to another has also played an important role in world history.

**Economics and History** A society depends for its existence on meeting certain basic needs. How did the society grow its food? How did it make its goods? How did it provide the services people needed? How did individual people and governments use their limited resources? Did they spend more money on hospitals or on military forces? By answering these questions, historians examine the different economic systems that have played a role in history.

**Social Life** From a study of social life, we learn about the different social classes that made up a society. We also examine how people dressed and found shelter, how and what they ate, and what they did for fun. The nature of family life and how knowledge was passed from one generation to another through education are also part of the social life of a society.

**The Importance of Cultural Developments** We cannot understand a society without looking at its culture, or the common ideas, beliefs, and patterns of behavior that are passed on from one generation to another. Culture includes both high culture and popular culture. High culture consists of the writings of a society's thinkers and the works of its artists. A society's popular culture is the world of ideas and experiences of ordinary people. In an historical sense, the term *popular culture* refers to the ideas and experiences of less educated people, such as peasants and artisans. Although many of these people were illiterate, they passed their culture on orally. Today the media have embraced the term *popular culture* to describe the most current trends and fashionable styles.

**Religion in History** Throughout history, people have sought to find a deeper meaning to human life. How have the world's great religions—such as Hinduism, Buddhism, Judaism, Christianity, and Islam—influenced people's lives? How have those religions spread to create new patterns of culture?

**The Role of Individuals** In discussing the roles of politics, ideas, economics, social life, cultural developments, and religion, we deal with groups of people and forces that often seem beyond the control of any one person.

Mentioning the names of Cleopatra, Queen Elizabeth I, Napoleon, and Hitler, however, reminds us of the role of individuals in history. Decisive actions by powerful individuals have indeed played a crucial role in the course of history. So, too, have the decisions of ordinary men and women who must figure out every day how to survive, protect their families, and carry on their ways of life.

**The Impact of Science and Technology** For thousands of years, people around the world have made scientific discoveries and technological innovations that have changed our world. From the creation of stone tools that made farming easier to the advanced computers that guide our airplanes, science and technology have altered how humans have related to their world.

**The Environment and History** Throughout history, peoples and societies have been affected by the physical world in which they live. They have also made an impact on their world. From the slash-and-burn farming of early societies to the industrial pollution of modern factories, human activities have affected the physical environment and even endangered the very existence of entire societies.

These nine themes will help us to make sense of the past. Of course, these themes do not stand alone. They are connected to one another. Moreover, historians of world history add some special themes that help us to understand our story. In studying world history, we look at the rise, decline, and fall of many civilizations around the world (a civilization, as we will see later, is a complex culture). During much of human history, the most advanced civilizations have been in East Asia or in the Middle East. Only in modern times—in the late nineteenth and early twentieth centuries—did Western civilization dominate the rest of the world. (Western civilization is the civilization of the West—Europe and the Western Hemisphere.) Since the end of World War II, that dominance has gradually faded. In world history, we look at the forces that create civilizations and cause them to fall.

At the same time, world history consists of more than just the study of individual civilizations. From the earliest times, trade served to bring different civilizations into contact with one another. The transmission of religious and cultural ideas soon followed. *World history can be seen in a broad comparative and global framework*, as peoples and countries come into contact, and often into conflict, with one another. In our own time, people often speak of the world as a global village. They mean that the world can be seen as a single community linked by computers, television, and multinational corporations. (After all, an American who travels abroad can now find a McDonald's restaurant in almost every part of the world.)

▲ *Thus far, McDonalds in Moscow has been a capitalist success. Why do you think this very American venture is succeeding in a culture far removed from the United States?*

## HISTORIANS AND THE DATING OF TIME

In recording the past, historians try to determine the exact time when events occurred. World War II in Europe, for example, began on September 1, 1939, when Adolf Hitler sent German troops into Poland. The war in Europe ended on May 7, 1945, when Germany surrendered. By using dates, historians can place events in the order they occurred and try to determine the development of patterns over periods of time.

If someone asked you when you were born, you would reply with a number, such as 1984. In the United States, we would all accept that number without question. Why? The number is part of the dating system followed in the Western world (Europe and the Western Hemisphere). This system refers to dates in relation to the assumed date of the birth of Jesus Christ (the year 1). An event that took place four hundred years before the birth of Jesus is dated 400 B.C. ("before Christ"). Dates after the birth of Jesus are labeled as A.D. These letters stand for the Latin words *anno Domini,* which mean "in the year of the Lord" (or the year of the birth of Jesus Christ). Thus, an event that took place 250 years after the birth of Jesus is written A.D. 250, or "in the year of the Lord 250." It can also be written as 250. Similarly, you would give your birth year as simply 1984 rather than A.D. 1984.

Some historians now prefer to use the abbreviations B.C.E. ("before the common era") and C.E. ("common era") instead of B.C. and A.D. This is especially true of historians who prefer to use symbols that are not so Western or Christian oriented. The dates, of course, remain the same. Thus, 1950 B.C.E. and 1950 B.C. are the same year.

Historians make use of other terms to refer to time. A decade is ten years, a century is one hundred years, and a millennium is one thousand years. The fourth century B.C. is the fourth period of one hundred years counting backward from 1, the assumed date of the birth of Jesus. The first century B.C. covers the years 100 to 1 B.C. Therefore, the fourth century B.C. is the years 400 to 301 B.C. We say, then, that an event in 650 B.C. took place in the seventh century B.C.

The fourth century A.D. is the fourth period of one hundred years after the birth of Jesus. The first period of one hundred years is the years 1 to 100, so the fourth hundred-year period, or the fourth century, is the years 301 to 400. For example, we say that an event in 750 took place in the eighth century. Just as the first millennium B.C. is the years 1000 to 1 B.C., the second millennium A.D. is the years 1001 to 2000.

## SKILLS FOR BECOMING A BETTER HISTORIAN

If you are interested in your friends, your family, and yourself, then you are an historian. The more effective we are as historians, the more fully we find out about and understand ourselves and the people with whom we share this planet. The following pages are intended to show how you can better understand the information presented in this text. Even more important, however, you can become a better historian of events relevant to your life.

To be a better historian, you will want to use skills that professional historians use to evaluate historical information. These skills are effective for more than helping you to understand this textbook and get a better grade in world history class. These techniques will allow you to become a better consumer, a more informed citizen, and a more enlightened human being. The table on page BH–6 summarizes the basic skills we will then examine in detail.

### 1. Understanding Geography as a Key to History

William Shakespeare said, "All the world's a stage." Historians who seek to truly comprehend the events of the past must know something about the stage upon which the drama was being played out. When meeting people for the first time, we usually soon get around to asking where they are from. That is because the environment in which we live greatly influences our development, opportunities, and even belief systems. A Seminole Indian, told he had to leave his land in North Florida at the beginning of the nineteenth century, said, "If suddenly we tear our hearts from the homes around which they are twined, our heartstrings

1. **Understanding Geography as a Key to History**

Understanding where something happened can help you to understand why it happened.

2. **Interpreting Maps**

Reading maps is an effective way to understand a great deal of information in a short time.

3. **Using Time Lines**

Time lines are a simple way of putting information in chronological order.

4. **Reading Charts, Graphs, and Tables**

Charts, graphs, and tables can condense many facts into a more understandable format.

5. **Understanding Cause and Effect**

Developing an awareness of the relationship of cause and effect is an essential historical technique.

6. **Recognizing and Understanding Bias**

All historians bring to their studies bias based upon their backgrounds and life experiences. Learn to recognize bias and account for it.

7. **Identifying Primary and Secondary Sources**

Primary sources are an essential tool for historians, but both primary and secondary sources are important.

8. **Comparing and Contrasting**

Almost everything we know can be described in terms of how it is either similar to or different from something else.

9. **Recognizing Fact versus Opinion**

Facts are information that can be verified as being true or untrue. Opinions are open to dispute.

10. **Analyzing Information—Drawing Inferences**

The ability to reason and reach conclusions based upon evidence is an advanced skill.

11. **Looking at Art as a Key to History**

The fullness of history is sometimes better realized through art than through words.

12. **Studying Economics as a Key to History**

How people distribute and use their resources may be the most powerful indicator of their beliefs, traditions, and actions.

13. **Making Hypotheses and Predicting Outcomes**

By using other social studies techniques, the advanced student historian should be able to predict outcomes based upon evidence presented.

14. **Conducting Research**

Conducting thorough research on a topic involves the skills of a detective.

15. **Writing Research Papers**

The research paper is the culmination of all the social studies skills. It can be the most challenging and rewarding of assignments.

will snap." Native Americans have always strongly felt that people and their environments are intimately connected.

Our modern society is more mobile and more distant from the natural world than were the early cultures of North America. However, we are as closely bound to our environment as they were to theirs. Whether we live in a New York City neighborhood, a farm community in Wisconsin, or a small town in Georgia, we are all products of our surroundings.

Geography is the study of Earth and of our interaction with the environment. There are two basic types of geography: human geography and physical geography. Human geography deals with the various people around the world, including their economic, political, and cultural activities. Physical geography is the study of different regions of the world. It focuses on the climate, resources, and other natural features of these regions. Both types of geography use five basic themes: location, place, people-environment relations, movement, and regions.

**Location** Location refers to where a place is. Absolute location is the exact position of a city, mountain, or river on Earth and is determined by latitudes and longitudes on a map. Latitudes are distances measured by lines drawn on maps or globes to show distance north and south of the equator. Longitudes are distances measured by meridians, or lines drawn on globes or maps to show distances east or west of the prime meridian. The prime meridian is an imaginary line that runs from the North Pole to the South Pole through the Royal Observatory at Greenwich, England. Longitudes and latitudes are both measured in degrees, represented by the symbol °. By using latitudes and longitudes, any place on Earth can be precisely located. For example, look at the world map on page A-7. What city can you find at 39° N latitude and 116° E longitude? Only one city will be found at that specific location.

These absolute locations, however, are probably less helpful to the historian than are relative locations. *Relative location* refers to the location of one place in relation to other places. The absolute location of Beijing, China, which you have just found, does not tell you that Beijing is located on the North China Plain sixty miles from the Yellow Sea and just inside the Great Wall of China. Knowing this relative location helps us to understand why Beijing became an important capital city in Chinese history.

The geographer's theme of location is very useful to the historian. Location helps to show the distribution of climates, vegetation, natural resources, and patterns of human settlement. Where is good farmland? Where are the natural resources that can be used in industries? Answers to these questions help historians to understand where, and even why events take place where they do.

**Place** A place is a particular city, village, or area with certain physical and human characteristics that make it different from other places. A city such as Beijing, for example, has distinct physical characteristics. It has its own landforms, vegetation, climate, and resources. A city also has distinct human characteristics. What are its different social classes? Where do they live in the city? How are the city's streets laid out? What kinds of dwellings have people built? Together, the physical and human characteristics make up a place's identity. Beijing may be similar to other cities, but it is also its own place. This identity, of course, can change through time. This fact makes the theme of place important to an understanding of history.

**People-Environment Relations** The study of interactions between humans and their environment helps us to understand why people are where they are, as well as why their cultures developed the way they did. The physical features of a place affect the way people live. A rich soil, for example, means abundant crops and probably a prosperous society. However, people also alter their environments. By cutting down trees, people convert forests into farmlands. By building cities and roads, they change the landscape. The story of how people relate to their environment becomes an important part of a people's history.

**Movement** The theme of movement encompasses the study of interactions among people located in different places and different environments. Geographers and historians are chiefly concerned with three types of

▲ *Chinese people still commute on bicycles, but for some the bicycle of choice has become a Western high speed model, and the clothing has become highly fashionable, as well.*

movement: migration, transport, and the spread of ideas.

The movements of people have altered patterns of living and changed environments around the world. Migration has been a constant factor in human history. The migration of Europeans, Africans, Latin Americans, and Asians, for example, brought together a variety of talents and cultures that built the United States into a powerful nation. The movement of goods by transport created trading links that have united many peoples into a global trade network and created a truly global economy. The spread of ideas through communication and trade has been important to the development of world history. The spread of Christianity from the Middle East to Europe, for example, helped create a new society. The movements of peoples and goods and the spread of ideas thus have transformed the world.

**Region** Regions are parts of Earth's surface that share one or more characteristics that make them different from other areas. Geographers divide the world into regions to show similarities and differences among areas. Both geographers and historians identify culture regions of Earth that share common characteristics and ways of living that distinguish them from other culture regions. Examples of culture regions are the Middle East, Latin America, Africa, and East Asia.

## 2. Interpreting Maps

Geographers use a number of tools to examine the five basic themes of geography. Their most basic tools are globes and maps. A globe is a spherical representation of Earth. In effect, it is a model of Earth. It is a true map of Earth because it accurately shows both landmasses and bodies of water. Globes are not always practical to use, however. Imagine carrying a globe around with you as a reference tool. Furthermore, the size of a globe limits the amount of detail it can tell us.

More useful to geographers, and to all of us, are maps. Maps are flat representations of Earth. They have a long history. The ancient Egyptians and Babylonians drew maps to show landholdings. The oldest known map is of Mesopotamia around 2300 B.C. It shows an estate in a valley. The Greeks were the first to make a systematic study of the world, which is reflected in the maps they made in the fourth century B.C.

Ptolemy, a Greek man who lived in Egypt around A.D. 150, was the most famous geographer of ancient times. He made a map of the world as it was known at that time, as well as regional maps of Europe, Africa, and Asia. After Ptolemy, the most accurate maps were made by Arab and Chinese scholars until the voyages of Europeans beginning around 1300 enabled Europeans to make more detailed and accurate maps. During the

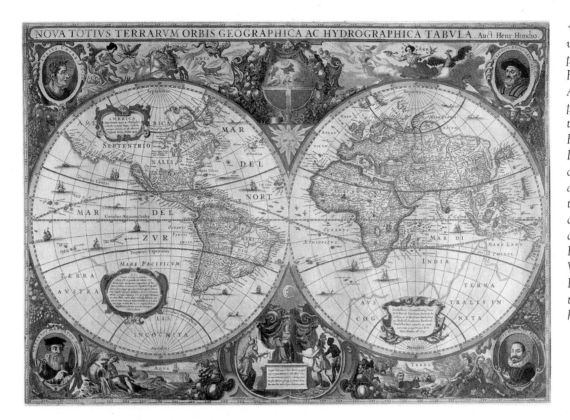

◄ *This beautiful world map was prepared in 1630 by Henricus Hondius. At the corners are portraits of Caesar, the first-century* B.C. *Roman statesman, Ptolemy, the second-century* A.D. *astronomer, Mercator, the sixteenth-century Flemish cartographer, and Hondius himself. Why do you think Hondius included these four figures in his map?*

last five hundred years, mapmakers, who are also called *cartographers*, have mapped almost every inch of Earth. Beginning in the 1980s, photos of Earth taken from space satellites added to the accuracy of maps.

By their very nature, however, maps can never be exact. The basic problem is this: How can mapmakers draw the round surface of a sphere on a flat piece of paper? They cannot—at least, not exactly. A map cannot show the exact shapes of lands and bodies of water for an obvious reason: a map is flat, and Earth's surface is curved. You cannot flatten the surface of a round globe without distorting shapes and sizes. Try to flatten the rind of an orange, and you will see the problem.

Mapmakers try to limit the amount of distortion by using different kinds of map projections. A map projection is a method by which Earth's curved surface is projected onto a flat piece of paper. Different kinds of projections can show accurately either area, shape, distance, or direction. No one map, however, can show all four of these qualities with equal accuracy at the same

time. By looking at a few projections, we can see some of the problems involved in mapmaking.

The most famous map projection in history is the Mercator projection. This projection is the work of a Flemish cartographer, Gerardus Mercator, who lived in the 1500s. The Mercator projection is an example of what mapmakers call a *conformal projection*. It tries to show the true shape of landmasses, but only of limited areas. On the Mercator projection, the shapes of lands near the equator are quite accurate. However, the projection greatly enlarges areas in the polar regions, far away from the equator. Look, for example, at the island of Greenland on the Mercator projection. It appears to be larger than the continent of South America. In fact, Greenland is about one-ninth the size of South America. The Mercator projection, however, was valuable to ship captains. Every straight line on a Mercator projection is a line of true direction, whether north, south, east, or west. Before the age of modern navigational equipment, ship captains were very grateful to Mercator.

The Mollweide projection is an example of an equal-area projection. As you can see in the Mollweide map, equal-area projections distort the shapes of land areas but show land and water areas in accurate proportions. The size of one body of land or water is true in comparison with that of others.

The Robinson projection was created by cartographer Arthur Robinson. In 1988, the National Geographic Society adopted it as its new map projection to portray more accurately the round Earth on a flat surface. As you can see, on the Robinson projection, countries and continents more closely match their true sizes.

### Demonstrating Your Historical Skills

1. Examine the physical map of Poland on page 91. Between 1772 and 1795, Poland was partitioned so often by its neighbors that it ceased to exist as a country until 1919. In 1939 it was again divided, this time by Nazi Germany and the Soviet Union. How can a study of Poland's geography help to explain its recurring problems with its neighbors?

2. Use the following maps to answer questions *a* through *c*: "Early States in Africa" (Chapter 2, Map 3, page 48, "The Industrialization of Europe by 1850" (Chapter 4, Map 1, page 129), and "The States of Eastern Europe and the Former Soviet Union" (Chapter 13, Map 1, page 459).
   (*a*) Identify each of the maps as general purpose or special purpose, and describe the focus of each.
   (*b*) What symbols are used on each map? What do these symbols represent?
   (*c*) Use the scale on the map of the former Soviet republics to determine the distance between the capital of Russia and the capital of Azerbaijan.

### Applying Historical Skills to Your World

1. List the different aspects of your life that are related to the geography of where you live (for example, snow skiing as a hobby for someone from Colorado). How might your life change if you lived in a region of the world that was radically different?

Mercator

Mollweide

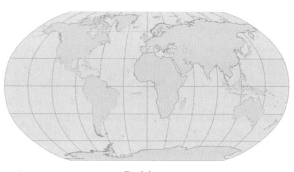

Robinson

2. Make a list of the destinations most frequently visited by you and your family (for example, the grocery store, mall, school, or workplace). Use a road

map to plot the quickest and most efficient way to visit those destinations from your home. Are these the routes you currently use? What factors that are not included on a map do you have to consider when planning a trip?

## 3.  Using Time Lines

In a café in Austin, Texas, the following graffiti can be seen on the wall: "Time is nature's way of keeping everything from happening all at once." If that is true, then time lines are a student's way of avoiding learning everything at once. A time line presents events in chronological order. It is a simple way of comparing events, finding cause-and-effect relationships, and remembering important information.

This text makes use of time lines. Before reading each unit, you should take a few minutes to look at and understand the time line for that unit. The time line provides a chronological framework that should help to make your reading more understandable. The following are some keys to reading time lines:

1.  *Understand the time interval.* Each time line uses its own unit of time, ranging from months to hundreds or even thousands of years. The time interval used can distort your understanding of how closely connected two events were. For example, events might be only a half-inch apart on a time line, but that half-inch could represent five hundred years.

2.  *Note the order of events.* Look carefully at the order in which events are presented on the time line. Also make a mental note of the amount of time between each event.

3.  *Try to make connections in time.* See if you can make connections between one event on the time line and another. Often a cause-and-effect relationship can be demonstrated between different historical occurrences. Ask yourself what other events also occurred during a particular time period.

### Demonstrating Your Historical Skills

Use the following time line to answer these questions:

1.  What is the time interval shown on this time line?

2.  What time period is covered by this time line?

3.  How long was it between the release of *Star Wars: Return of the Jedi* and *Jurassic Park*?

4.  Describe the connections you can make among events on this time line.

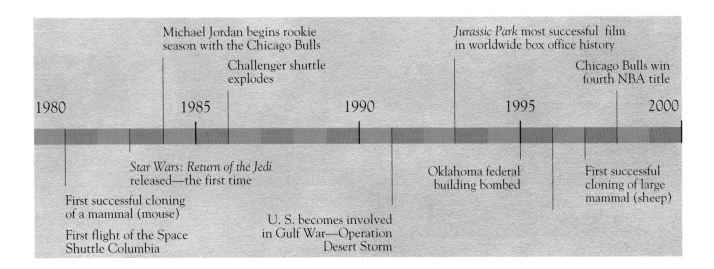

*Applying Historical Skills to Your World*

Using this time line as a reference, create a time line of your own life. Begin with your birth and end with the present year. Fill in the time segments with the events that have been important in your life. Such a time line depicts a chronology of your life. It allows you to place events in the context of their time periods. Where were you when you heard about the Oklahoma City bombing? Do you remember when *Jurassic Park* opened in theaters? What grade were you in when scientists successfully cloned a sheep?

## 4. Reading Charts, Graphs, and Tables

Charts, graphs, and tables, like time lines, are graphic aids that communicate a large amount of information in a simple, straightforward manner. Reading these graphic aids is relatively easy, which is what makes them such useful tools.

Use the following steps to make the best use of any chart, graph, or table:

1. *Determine the type and purpose of the graphic aid.* Is it a graph, chart, or table? Read the title to find out what information is being presented.

2. *Identify the various parts of the graphic aid.* Graphs generally have both horizontal and vertical labels. Charts often show relationships among items. Tables usually have headings explaining the details found within their rows and columns.

3. *Evaluate the data.* Ask yourself what the comparisons and contrasts are between different facts presented. Are relationships revealed within the chart? Does the graph show trends over time? What comparisons can you make?

### Charts

Charts are used to visually display relationships among people, ideas, or organizations. The chart at the top of the next column shows the relationships among the four main ideas of the Buddhist religion. The chart is read from the bottom to the top. You can see that each idea presented is dependent upon, and is an extension of, the previous one.

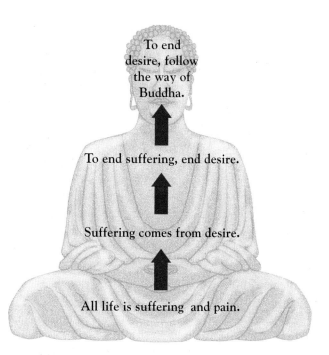

The House of Windsor chart on the next page is another visual representation of information. In this case, the chart shows the succession of the current royal family in Great Britain. Use the chart to determine the following:

1. Who is the current successor to the British throne?

2. What is the relationship of William of Wales to Mark Phillips?

### Graphs

Graphs are a useful way of showing relationships among data, as well as changes over time. The three most common forms of graphs are line graphs, pie graphs, and bar graphs. You have probably used a line graph in math and science classes. It shows changes in information over a period of time.

The pie graph, such as the one on page BH–13 showing the distribution of slaves in the New World, shows proportions relative to the whole. You can see that in this case, a pie graph makes it very easy to identify which regions in the Western Hemisphere had the most and the least percentage of slaves in 1825.

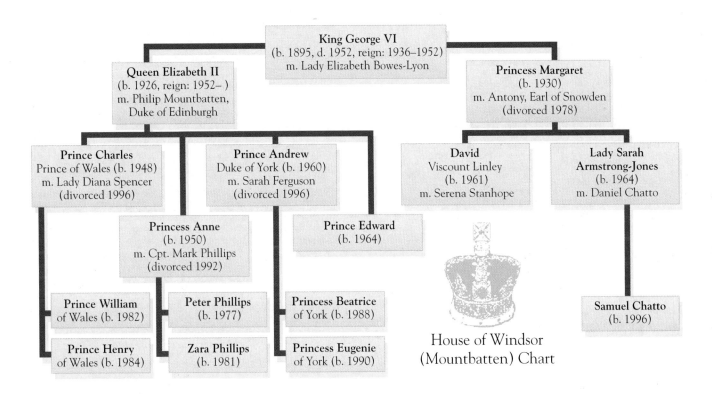

House of Windsor
(Mountbatten) Chart

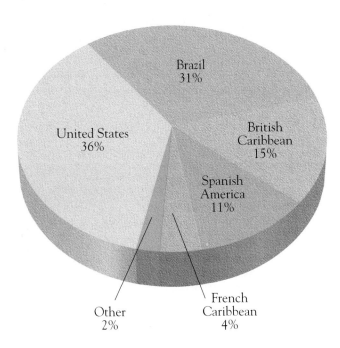

Finally, bar graphs are used for making comparisons among numbers. The bar graph on page BH–14 shows what happened to the Indian population of Central America after the arrival of the Europeans. This bar graph gives a graphic representation of the dramatic drop in the Indian population over a relatively short time.

### Tables

Tables are compact lists of details that have been arranged in rows and columns. Tables are particularly effective for making comparisons. For example, the table on page BH–14 compares a few words in English and some of the Romance languages. The purpose of this table is to demonstrate that English, in some ways, is similar to, and has borrowed from, the Romance languages. A comparison of the five words presented here makes that obvious. The table of population growth in the United States is also helpful in making comparisons. Look at the table on page B–14, and answer the following questions:

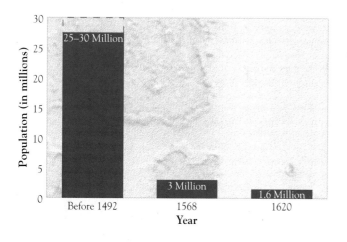

| Projection of the Fifteen Fastest-Growing States in the United States | | |
|---|---|---|
| **State** | **Population in 1995** | **Growth by 2025** |
| California | 31,589,000 | 56% |
| New Mexico | 1,685,000 | 55 |
| Hawaii | 1,187,000 | 53 |
| Arizona | 4,218,000 | 52 |
| Nevada | 1,530,000 | 51 |
| Idaho | 1,163,000 | 50 |
| Utah | 1,951,000 | 48 |
| Alaska | 604,000 | 47 |
| Florida | 14,166,000 | 46 |
| Texas | 18,724,000 | 45 |
| Wyoming | 480,000 | 45 |
| Washington | 5,431,000 | 44 |
| Oregon | 3,141,000 | 39 |
| Colorado | 3,747,000 | 39 |
| Georgia | 7,201,000 | 37 |

*Source: U.S. News & World Report,* November 4, 1996, p. 14.

1. How is the information in this table arranged?

2. What is the difference between the growth rates of California and Texas?

3. Which of the states shown here has the smallest population?

## 5. Understanding Cause and Effect

Understanding why something happened is one of the most important and most difficult tasks of any historian. Without this understanding, history becomes an endless jumble of names and dates, selected at random. The principle of cause and effect enables you to connect actions and ideas with their results. Historians look at an historical event in much the same way as a reporter investigates a story. By asking who, what, why, where, when, and how, the historian begins to understand the actions that resulted in a particular event. What makes this investigative process so complicated is that most events have multiple causes. Historians understand that effects, in turn, can also become causes.

| Similarities between English and Some of the Romance Languages | | | | |
|---|---|---|---|---|
| **English** | **French** | **Spanish** | **Italian** | **Portuguese** |
| *fraternity* | fraternité | fraternidad | fraternità | fraternidade |
| *liberty* | liberté | libertad | libertà | liberdade |
| *society* | societé | sociedad | società | sociedade |
| *possible* | possible | posible | possibile | possível |
| *probable* | probable | probable | probabile | probável |

*Source:* Information from Charles Berlitz, *Native Tongues* (New York: Grossett & Dunlap, 1982), p. 28.

For example, in Chapter 12 (Cold War and a New Order in the West), you will read about the Cold War between the United States and the Soviet Union that began in the 1950s. The heightened tension between the two superpowers was one of the *causes* of a "Red Scare" in the United States. Senator Joseph McCarthy exploited and contributed to this fear of communism through a series of government investigations, searching for supposed communist infiltrators. The *effect* of these actions was not only persecution and censorship, but also an increase in conformity and self-censorship by people afraid of appearing suspicious. Censorship was most noticeable in the entertainment and publishing industries, where many writers and actors were "blackballed," or kept from working because of their political beliefs. This *effect* of the Cold War was in turn one of the *causes* of the rise of a non-conformist counterculture in the 1960s.

When investigating historical events ask yourself how effects may themselves be the causes of further events. During your reading of this text, look for some key words and phrases that may help you make the connection between cause and effect. Some examples follow:

| Words Showing Cause | Words Showing Effect |
| --- | --- |
| contributed to | resulted in |
| resulting from | as a consequence of |
| due to | outcome |
| arising from | product of |
| developed from | consequently |
| owing to | therefore |
| because | leading to |
| brought about by | dependent upon |

### Demonstrating Your Historical Skills

Read the following excerpt from Chapter 13 on the changing role of women since 1960:

> *With early marriage and smaller families, women had more years when they were not raising children. This has contributed to changes in the character of women's employment in both Europe and the United States.*

> *The most important development was the increase in the number of married women working in the workforce. At the beginning of the twentieth century, even working-class wives tended to stay at home if they could afford to do so. In the postwar period, this was no longer the case. In the United States, for example, in 1900, married women made up about 15 percent of the female labor force. By 1990, their number had increased to 70 percent.*

1. What was it that changed in the United States and Europe?

2. What brought about that change?

3. How might that change result in other changes in the United States and Europe?

4. The first sentence mentions early marriage and smaller families in the second half of the twentieth century. What might be some possible causes of that trend?

### Applying Historical Skills to Your World

Think of an important event or turning point in your life. Make a list of the primary and secondary causes that led up to that point. Describe the effects of that event. Have those effects, in turn, become the causes of other events?

## 6. Recognizing and Understanding Bias

You, like all historians, have bias. It is impossible for human beings not to be biased. Bias is the inclinations, predispositions, and prejudices we all have as a result of our upbringing, education, and life experiences. There is nothing inherently wrong with being biased, as long as we don't allow it to prevent us from approaching new situations and people with objectivity and tolerance. However, as an historian, you must learn to recognize and understand bias in your studies. All authors have bias. This does not mean that what they are writing is untrue but simply that they have a point of view.

All historical documents are written by people and, as a result, contain the bias of the author. When you approach any source of information, it is appropriate to maintain a degree of skepticism. Ask yourself if the statements you are reading are dependable and based upon verifiable evidence. What is the author's interest in the topic? Does the author have a particular philosophy or point of view? How would someone with a different background present the information? Finally, examine not only what the document tells you but also what it leaves out.

The following excerpt is a statement by the Soviet government explaining its military intervention in Hungary in 1956:

> The Soviet Government and all the Soviet people deeply regret that the development of events in Hungary has led to bloodshed. On the request of the Hungarian People's Government the Soviet Government consented to the entry into Budapest of the Soviet Army units to assist the Hungarian People's Army and the Hungarian authorities to establish order in the town.

Certainly, the author of this statement, the Soviet government, has a vested interest in the topic as it attempts to justify its military intervention. However, is the statement dependable and based upon an accurate account of events? Since the Hungarian Prime Minister, Imry Nagy, protested the invasion and was arrested shortly after the Soviets took over it would be difficult to conclude that the Hungarian government requested Soviet intervention.

### Applying Historical Skills to Your World

Many teenagers feel that the news media portray them only in a negative light. Select one of your local television news programs and watch it for two weeks. Record each story that involves a young person. How does the media characterization of young people compare with what you know about your generation? How might coverage of teenagers be different if teenagers themselves were making editorial decisions for the media?

## 7. Identifying Primary and Secondary Sources

Primary sources are such things as writings, documents, drawings, and photographs created by participants or observers of an actual historical event. Secondary sources are writings about a historical event after it has occurred, often based upon one or more primary sources. Historians rely on primary sources as the most important tool of their trade. However, both primary and secondary sources serve a useful function.

Primary sources might include diaries, letters, interviews with eyewitnesses, stock inventories, account ledgers, photographs, or any other document that was created by participants of the historical time period in question. Although your textbook includes many primary sources, it is itself a secondary source. It was written after the events described in it occurred, and it was written by someone who did not personally witness these events. Secondary sources, such as textbooks, are useful because they present information in an orderly and understandable context. They are also much more condensed than the primary sources would be. If you were to gather all of the primary sources needed to compile this textbook, you could easily fill your school library.

The following is an example of a primary source. It comes from Chapter 8 and is an Austrian writer's account of the celebration of the beginning of World War I.

> The next morning I was in Austria. In every station placards had been put up announcing general mobilization. The trains were filled with fresh recruits, banners were flying, music sounded, and in Vienna I found the entire city in a tumult. . . . There were parades in the street, flags, ribbons, and music burst forth everywhere, young recruits were marching triumphantly, their faces lighting up at the cheering. . . .
>
> As never before, thousands and hundreds of thousands felt what they should have felt in peace time, that they belonged together. A city of two million, a country of nearly fifty million, in that hour felt that they were participating in world history. . . .

Notice that the author is speaking in the first person as he describes something that is occurring in his own time.

Here is an example from Chapter 8 that describes another aspect of World War I, but is a secondary source:

> These first tanks, used in the Battle of the Somme in 1916, were not very effective. A new model, the Mark

*IV, had more success in November 1917 at the Battle of Cambrai (kam-BRAE). Four hundred tanks spearheaded an advance that drove five miles into the enemy lines, and with relatively few casualties.*

*The French soon followed with their own tanks. They were less effective, however. The Germans were contemptuous of the new tanks and considered them a sign of weakness. However, they, too, finally got around to producing their own tank—the A7V. It was unstable, required a crew of eighteen, and saw little action, however.*

The source of this excerpt is a secondary source, because it was written about tank warfare during World War I by someone who did not participate in or witness that war.

### Demonstrating Your Historical Skills

The following are titles or descriptions of discussions found within this text. Identify them as either primary or secondary sources.

1. You Are There: A Letter to the Shogun, page 258

2. A passage on page 394 written by Rudolph Höss, the commanding officer of a Nazi death camp

3. A description of everyday life for middle-class families written for this textbook, on page 174

4. An excerpt about Ibo tribal society from *Things Fall Apart* by Chinua Achebe on page 528

5. A description of boy soldiers in Africa, compiled from several sources, on page 521

## 8. Comparing and Contrasting

As an historian, one of the most useful ways you have of understanding new information is to compare and contrast it with information with which you are already familiar. Comparing involves examining different events, people, ideas, or facts for similarities. Contrasting is taking those same topics and studying them for differences. You will probably be called upon to compare and contrast frequently in your study of world history.

When comparing and contrasting, it is important first to identify the major characteristics of the two topics you are studying. An effective tool for studying similarities and differences is the Venn diagram. In a Venn diagram of two topics, the overlapping parts of

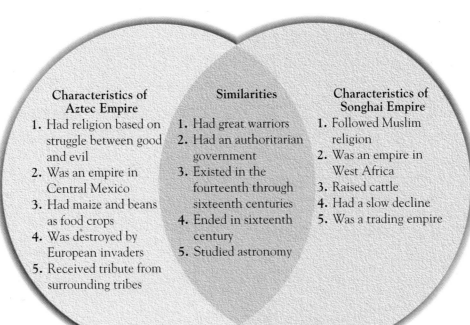

**Characteristics of Aztec Empire**
1. Had religion based on struggle between good and evil
2. Was an empire in Central Mexico
3. Had maize and beans as food crops
4. Was destroyed by European invaders
5. Received tribute from surrounding tribes

**Similarities**
1. Had great warriors
2. Had an authoritarian government
3. Existed in the fourteenth through sixteenth centuries
4. Ended in sixteenth century
5. Studied astronomy

**Characteristics of Songhai Empire**
1. Followed Muslim religion
2. Was an empire in West Africa
3. Raised cattle
4. Had a slow decline
5. Was a trading empire

the two circles represent the similarities of both topics. The remaining part of each circle shows the differences, or what is unique to each topic. This example compares and contrasts the Aztec Empire of Central America with the Songhai Empire of West Africa.

### Demonstrating Your Historical Skills

Read the following biographies of Empress Wu of China (in Chapter 2) and Evita (in Chapter 14). Make a Venn diagram to determine the characteristics of these women that are both the same and different.

### Empress Wu

Wu Zhao was born in 625, the daughter of a Chinese general. Attracted by her beauty, Emperor Tang Taizong chose her to be his concubine when she was only thirteen years old. After his death in 649, she became concubine to the next emperor, Kao Tsung, and bore him four sons and a daughter. Wu Zhao was extremely jealous of the empress and greatly desirous of power. It is said that she strangled her own daughter and then accused the empress, who was childless, of the crime. The emperor chose to accept Wu Zhao's story, deposed the empress, and chose Wu Zhao as his new empress.

Empress Wu was obsessed with power. After her husband's death in 683, she sent one son into exile and ruled with another son. His weakness, however, gave her supreme power. Empress Wu did not hesitate to get rid of officials and even members of her family who stood in her way.

Although she was known for her ruthlessness, Empress Wu was also a capable ruler. She was the first ruler to select graduates of the civil service examinations for the highest positions in government. She forced Korea to become an ally of China, lowered taxes, and patronized the arts. During her last years, her abilities declined, and she was deposed in 705, at the age of eighty. In a country in which women had a low status, Empress Wu had lived a remarkable life.

### Evita

Eva Perón, known as "Evita" to her followers, was one of five children born to a seamstress who lived in poverty in the small town of Los Toldos. As a child, Eva dreamed of being an actress. At age fifteen, she moved to Buenos Aires, Argentina's largest city. She worked in a few theaters and eventually gained fame as a radio soap opera actress.

On January 15, 1944, Eva met Juan Perón, one of the army officers then running the government. She later described the meeting: "I put myself at his side . . . I spoke up as best I could: 'If, as you say, the cause of the people is your own cause, however great the sacrifice I will never leave your side until I die.'" Eva became Juan Perón's mistress and a year later, his wife.

Eva Perón was an important force in her husband's rise to power. Together, they courted the working-class poor with promises of higher wages and better working conditions. Juan Perón, who was elected president in 1946, owed much to the people's adoration of his wife.

As the wife of President Juan Perón, Eva was the first lady of Argentina from 1946 to 1952. She became a tireless champion of the people. She went to the slums of the poor and gave them gifts. She formed a charitable foundation that built hospitals, schools, and orphanages. She also campaigned for women's right to vote and equal pay for equal work.

Eva Perón was ambitious. In 1951, she wanted to be her husband's vice presidential candidate. She backed down, however, after army leaders made it clear that they would never accept Eva Perón in office.

◄ *Evita Perón was adored by the masses, but shunned by Argentina's upper classes. This photograph was taken in 1952, when Perón celebrated the inauguration of his second term as president. Eva Perón died less than one year after this photo was taken.*

## 9. Recognizing Fact versus Opinion

Historians create, evaluate, and use historical statements on the basis of evidence. That evidence, however, is often a combination of facts and opinions. As an historian, you must learn to identify both fact and opinion. A fact is information that can be independently verified as true or untrue. Even incorrect facts are still facts. An opinion is an evaluation, impression, or estimation that is open to dispute. Opinions may or may not be true. They simply cannot be verified.

When reading an historical source, attempt to determine if the statements being made can be proved. If the information in a statement can be verified as being either true or untrue by an independent source, then it is probably a fact. However, if the statement contains phrases that are value judgments based upon the writer's impression of the subject, then the information is probably an opinion.

Read this eyewitness account of a German soldier who fought at the battle of Stalingrad (Chapter 11):

*September 4. We are being sent northward along the front towards Stalingrad. We marched all night and by dawn had reached Voroponovo Station. We can already see the smoking town. It's a happy thought that the end of the war is getting nearer.*

This statement contains a mixture of facts and opinions. That the Germans marched north, and that they reached Voroponovo are facts that can be checked for their accuracy. However, the soldier's statement that the end of the war is getting nearer is an opinion—as it turned out, a misguided opinion.

In Chapter 10, Mao Zedong tells of a coming revolution:

*During my recent visit to Hunan I made a firsthand investigation of conditions in five countries. In a very short time, in China's Central, Southern, and Northern provinces, several hundred million peasants will rise like a mighty storm, like a hurricane, a force so swift and violent that no power, however great, will be able to hold it back.*

Although Mao Zedong no doubt believed that the conditions he witnessed would lead to revolution, his statement is entirely opinion. You would have been able to find many people who would have disagreed with the idea that millions of peasants were about to "rise like a mighty storm." The statement is useful in showing the thinking of Mao Zedong but it cannot be taken as being factual.

### Demonstrating Your Historical Skills

Create your own comparison chart with three columns: "Fact," "Opinion," and "Uncertain." Analyze the information in the quotation from African writer Cyprian Ekwensi that appears in Chapter 15. List each item of information in the appropriate column of your table. After making your list, explain why you put each item where you did. Discuss the items in the "Uncertain" column, and see if there are any that you could move into the "Fact" or "Opinion" columns.

*We have our pride and must do as our fathers did. You see your mother? I did not pick her in the streets. When I wanted a woman I went to my father and told him about my need of her and he went to her father. . . . Marriage is a family affair. You young people of today may think you are clever. But marriage is still a family affair.*

### Applying Historical Skills to Your World

Watch ten commercials on television or look at ten advertisements in a magazine. Place the information from those ads on a blank chart similar to the one in the example you just studied. Are you surprised where the bulk of the information gets placed?

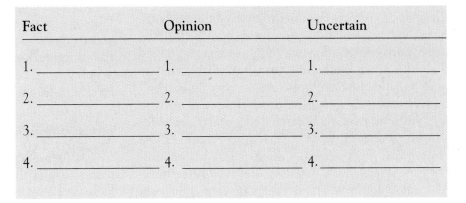

| Fact | Opinion | Uncertain |
|---|---|---|
| 1. _____ | 1. _____ | 1. _____ |
| 2. _____ | 2. _____ | 2. _____ |
| 3. _____ | 3. _____ | 3. _____ |
| 4. _____ | 4. _____ | 4. _____ |

## 10. Analyzing Information— Drawing Inferences

Analyzing information and drawing inferences is a skill you began developing as soon as you were old enough to figure out how to use your television's remote control. Analyzing information requires that you examine and investigate the details and relationships of the facts before you. Often it is useful to separate and study the individual parts of what you are analyzing. Drawing inferences is more difficult. An inference is a conclusion you reach after logically studying the facts. A young child looking at the small, rectangular instrument in her hand may analyze it, without knowing that it is a television remote control, by studying its individual components, such as buttons with numbers and other buttons of different colors. She will eventually draw the inference, after some investigation, that pushing the buttons will result in some corresponding action on the television. The ability to analyze information correctly and make accurate inferences is not only important for the study of history but is essential for success and even, at times, for survival.

You can learn more about inferences from studying information about the Johnstown flood. In the nineteenth century, the small working-class factory town of Johnstown, Pennsylvania, experienced frequent flooding. The people of the town would simply move to the upper floors of their homes until the floodwaters receded. In 1852, a group of wealthy factory owners bought a man-made lake as a private fishing retreat. The lake was created by an earthen dam that had discharge pipes and spillways to relieve pressure when the lake waters rose. Hoping to prevent fish from escaping the lake, the owners eventually removed the discharge pipes and blocked the spillways. On May 3, 1889, heavy rains brought flooding to Johnstown and caused the water in the lake to rise at the rate of six inches an hour. Finally, the dam broke, and twenty million gallons of water came roaring down upon the town at forty miles an hour. Houses, factories, and other buildings were washed away by the deadly torrent. The entire town was thoroughly destroyed. A five-month-old baby miraculously survived after floating seventy-five miles downstream on the floor of an uprooted house. Not everyone was so lucky, however. Over 2,200 people were killed, including at least 99 entire families.

The men who hoped to create an ideal vacation resort had incorrectly analyzed the information about the effects their actions would have on the dam, the lake, and Johnstown. Their inferences were limited only to the consequences that blocking off the dam would have on fishing. It is fortunate that your analyses of this information, and of your textbook, have less dire consequences.

In analyzing the Johnstown flood, you should first list the individual facts relevant to the event. These might include Johnstown's previous history of flooding, the man-made lake and earthen dam, the wealthy owners' desire to create a fishing retreat, the blocking off of the spillways and discharge pipes, and the heavy rains. It is easy to infer that the actions of the lake's owners, along with heavy rains, resulted in the Johnstown flood. However, are you able to draw any inferences about environmental and building regulations in the late nineteenth century? The fact that the lake's owners were able to block off the drainage system would suggest that government regulations were lax or nonexistent at the time. Are you able to make any inferences about the source of energy for the town? Because Johnstown was a factory town with a man-made lake, you might reach the conclusion that it, like many nineteenth-century cities, used water as a source of power. What might you infer about the attitude of the factory owners concerning the working-class people of Johnstown? Their actions might suggest that they gave the town's people very little thought, or at least not as much thought as they gave to creating a lake that was well stocked with fish. This might lead you to make some inferences about class divisions in the nineteenth-century United States, although there is probably not enough information here to reach any broad conclusions.

### Demonstrating Your Historical Skills

In Chapter 13, you will read about the science and technology of the different generations of computers. Here is one small part of that discussion:

*The first electronic computer with stored memory was made in the United States by the IBM Corporation in 1948. The IBM 1401, marketed in 1959, was the first computer used in large numbers in business and industry.*

*All of these early computers, which used thousands of vacuum tubes to function, were large and took up considerable room space. The development of the transistor and then the silicon chip produced a revolutionary new approach to computers. With the invention in 1971 of the microprocessor, a machine that combines the equivalent of thousands of transistors on a single, tiny silicon chip, the road was open for the development of the personal computer. It was both small and powerful.*

Analyze the facts and draw inferences as follows:

1. Make a list of all of the pertinent facts in this passage.

2. Examine these facts, and see if you can find any relationships among them.

3. What can you infer about the differences between computers of the 1950s and those of the 1970s?

4. Can you make any inferences about the sizes of computers?

5. What conclusions might you reach about the future of computers?

### Applying Historical Skills to Your World

Make a list of the people, places, and things that have played major roles in your life thus far (for example, parents, friends, school, place of worship, television, or books). Analyze the influence each has had on you up to this point. Draw some inferences about the effects those influences will have on you as an adult.

## 11. Looking at Art as a Key to History

What makes humans distinct from other animals on this planet? Anthropologists, biologists, and theologians may argue vehemently about the answer to that question, but there is little doubt that the urge for artistic creation is a uniquely human trait. No other creature is able to make abstract representations of reality through painting, sculpture, literature, dance, theater, or architecture. All art is abstract art in that it is a human creation, separate from the material world. Marcel Duchamp, a twentieth-century artist, once painted a picture of a pipe, perfect in every detail, and wrote beneath it, "This is not a pipe." His statement is baffling until you realize that he is, indeed, correct that it is not a pipe but rather a *picture* of a pipe. Duchamp's point was that art is a representation of something else. The ability to make those kinds of representations is something all humans possess. Give any six-year-old a box of chalk and a sidewalk, and you will have immediate proof of that shared trait.

Art is a characteristic we all share as humans, but it is also something that defines us as individuals belonging to a distinct society. Probably no other aspect of human culture reveals more about a people than the culture's artistic creations. For that reason, a good historian will look to art as a key to understanding history.

Each society, in every time, has a complex and unique understanding of the world in which its people live. Historians used to speak of "primitive" and "advanced" cultures. The implication was that primitive cultures were childlike and simplistic, whereas advanced cultures were sophisticated and mature. Good historians, however, now acknowledge that every society, through interaction with its environment, develops complex and elaborate systems of economics, government, philosophy, and self-expression. Studying the products of that self-expression can reveal much about people.

The Paleolithic people of Europe who lived twenty thousand years ago were seemingly simple cave dwellers who hunted game and gathered wild fruits and berries. However, the paintings they left behind in the Lascaux caves of France, as well as statues, such as those found in Ain Ghazal in Jordan, reveal them to be quite sophisticated. The intricate attention to detail and realism in the Lascaux paintings have led many art historians to claim them to be masterpieces of naturalistic art. These expressions of Paleolithic culture reveal much about the people who created them. Animals and hunting played a central role in their lives. The paintings might have been their means of instructing

▲ *The caves at Lascaux, France, are now closed to the public, but the paintings are world famous.*

young hunters. They could also indicate the development of a system of religious belief. The eight plaster statues found in Jordan are among the oldest human-form sculptures ever found. Scientists and museum curators are working together to piece together the story they represent, an intriguing addition to the human story.

By comparison, a twentieth-century painting by the Spanish artist Pablo Picasso, *The Fourteenth of July*, seems more abstract than the cave paintings of Lascaux. However, it, too, reveals something about the culture and time in which it was created. After the invention of the camera, many artists no longer felt compelled to paint strictly realistic pictures. Artists such as Picasso, influenced by Sigmund Freud's developments in psychology, instead began to paint people's "inner" worlds. Picasso also painted his subjects from many points of view, all at the same time. This approach reflected the influence of Albert Einstein's theories about relativity and perception. Thus, although many of Picasso's works seem simplistic, they are in fact complex expressions of the modern world.

## Demonstrating Your Historical Skills

The picture of the African "Masquerader" (right) and the *Painting with White Border* by Kandinsky both are representative of the time periods and cultures from which they came. Examine these two pieces of art to see what they reveal about the contemporary Yoruba culture of Africa and early twentieth-century Europe:

1. What does the artistic workmanship of Sokari Douglas Camp's "Masquerader" tell you about the abilities of modern-day African artists and artisans?

2. What can you infer about the Yoruba culture based on the "Masquerader"?

3. Kandinsky's painting reveals an aversion to realism that did not exist in many earlier works of art. What does Kandinsky's style of painting reveal about changing attitudes toward perception and reality in early twentieth-century Europe?

4. Kandinsky wanted his paintings to elicit strong feelings and emotions. What is your response to the painting? Would Europeans in the 1920s have responded differently? If so, how?

## Applying Historical Skills to Your World

You may think that the appreciation of art is limited only to those who regularly attend museums and art shows. However, we are all surrounded by examples of artistic self-expression. Advertisers regularly employ graphic artists to create billboards, television commercials, and magazine ads. Musicians use artists to design compact disc covers or artistic videos. Tee shirts and posters often display examples of popular art. Using the examples cited or more traditional modern-day paint-

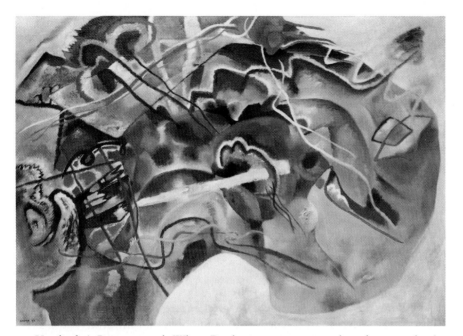

▲ *Kandinsky's* Painting with White Border *is representative of an abstract style of painting that developed in early twentieth-century Europe in response to new technology and new ideas from such diverse fields as photography and psychology.*

ings and sculptures, describe what today's art reveals about modern society.

## 12.  Studying Economics as a Key to History

Economics has been called "the dismal science." Many high school and college students, upon completing an economics course, might wholeheartedly agree that the study of economics is only slightly more interesting than watching toenails grow. Ironically, most of those same students would tell you that getting, keeping, and spending money is of the utmost concern. This attitude is ironic because that is exactly what economics is about.

Of course, economics is about more than just money. It is really about resources. Resources are assets, usually obtained from our environment, that we can use when needed. In the American economic system, the surest way to obtain resources is through the accumulation of money. However, the greatest resource you will ever have is already in your possession. It is you. Your human potential—the ability to

do work, to learn, and to adapt—will be your greatest asset in life. In a very real economic sense, your earning capacity is your primary resource.

All societies have resources. How they accumulate, distribute, and use those resources is central to the study of economics. By studying a country's economic system, historians get a sense of the country's priorities, values, governmental policies, philosophies, and even its religion. Economics is one of the major keys to history.

In Section 4 of Chapter 2 you will read briefly about the Renaissance, or rebirth of European culture, which began in Italy during the fifteenth and sixteenth century. The artists, writers, and scholars of Renaissance Italy became respected and renowned figures in society. Michelangelo's sculptures, Leonardo da Vinci's paintings, and Raphael's frescoes are today considered priceless works of art. However, what would this incredible outburst of artistic creativity have to do with economics?

Because of its geography Italy played a pivotal role in trade between Asia, the Middle East and Europe. Beginning in about the eleventh century Italy experienced an explosion of commercial activity as a result of its role in foreign trade. This in turn gave rise to a wealthy class of merchant families, the most famous of which were the de'Medici.

During the Middle Ages the main patron of artists was the Catholic Church, which commissioned painters and sculptors to create works of art for cathedrals and churches. The subjects of these works, of course, were almost entirely religious. Realism of the human form was not as important as spiritual inspiration. But, with the rise of a new class of wealthy merchants, artists found themselves in demand from new patrons who commissioned works for their elaborate homes and summer villas. The focus of art, while still usually religious, shifted to more earthly beauty. The natural world became a source of inspiration, and the human form was exalted. Patrons wanted portraits of themselves and their families, and artists complied with ever more realistic works.

The world of paint and pallets, so distant from the world of cash and counting houses, experienced one of its most creative periods because of the forces of economics.

### Demonstrating Your Historical Skills

In Chapter 2, you will also read briefly about the development of the feudal system in Europe. After the fall of the Roman Empire, Europe experienced a time of political instability. European peasants faced invasions from Vikings in the north, Magyars in the east, Muslims in the south, and various bandit groups throughout the continent. To provide the basic necessities of life, peasants turned for protection to fighting men. These knights demanded a portion of the peasant's crop for this protection. As these fighting men grew more powerful, they gained control of more land and the peasants who farmed it. Weaker knights gave their allegiance and promises to do battle to stronger nobles, who in turn provided the knights with more land. Soon the peasants found themselves bound to the land, unable to leave without the permission of their lords. These bound peasants were called serfs.

With this background in mind, answer the following questions:

1. What resource did fighting men have to trade for the peasants' crops?

2. What was the main source of wealth in this economic system?

3. What inferences can you draw concerning the effect that this system would have on the development of medieval religion? (Think about the church's need for protection.)

4. Which group was the most economically valuable in this system?

5. Which group had the most political power in this system?

### Applying Historical Skills to Your World

An understanding of economics is essential to your world. For one thing, you probably have more disposable income as a teenager than do most adults. The reason for this is that many teenagers have few or no bills. This frees up a great deal of money for luxury items. It also makes teenagers a powerful economic force in the United States. In what ways do advertisers and retailers pursue the teenage dollar?

Furthermore, economics may affect your belief system. For instance, what is your opinion about raising taxes to pay for better schools? Do you think that college tuition should be lower, or even paid for by state and federal governments? Should the minimum wage be increased? How are your answers influenced by your economic self-interest? In other words, how might someone who is less directly affected by school quality, college tuition, and the minimum wage answer these questions?

## 13. Making Hypotheses and Predicting Outcomes

When was the last time you were looking for an answer and the teacher said, "Just guess"? School is supposed to be about definite answers to specific questions, right? Actually, the great joy and frustration in the study of history is that there are many questions to which there are no definitive answers. Pablo Picasso once said, "Computers are useless. All they do is give you answers." What he meant is that sometimes a well-thought-out question is more important than pages of factual data. Making hypotheses is the process of formulating questions and then coming up with educated guesses about the answers. Predicting outcomes involves using your educated guesses to try to foresee possible future results based upon your past experience.

In Chapter 15, you will read about the decades-long dispute in the Middle East between Israel and its surrounding Arab neighbors. Beginning in the 1970s, a series of events began that seemed to bode well for peace in the region. Egyptian president Anwar Sadat flew to Israel to meet with Israeli officials. Sadat and Israeli prime minister Menachem Begin met with U.S. president Jimmy Carter and signed a peace treaty. Within the next fifteen years, Israel reached an agreement with the Palestine Liberation Organization, which had previously vowed to destroy Israel. More Arab nations began to normalize relations with Israel. At the same time, however, there have been attacks by both sides upon the other. In 1996, Israeli prime minister Yitzak Rabin was assassinated by an Israeli opposed to peace.

From this information you might hypothesize that both Israel and the Arabs have compelling reasons for making peace after decades of war. Educated guesses about those reasons might include the ideas that war is too costly, that both sides are tired of the killing, or that war is preventing both groups from developing and advancing economically and culturally. You might predict that the outcome of this conflict, based upon past events, will be a gradual movement toward peace and more normal relations, periodically interrupted by times of mistrust and tension.

### Demonstrating Your Historical Skills

The following excerpt about popular culture is from Chapter 13:

> Movies and television were the chief vehicles for the spread of American popular culture in the years after World War II. American movies continued to dominate both European and American markets in the next decades. Many American movies make more money in worldwide distribution than they do in the United States. Kevin Costner's Waterworld is but one example of this pattern.
>
> Although developed in the 1930s, television did not become available until the late 1940s. By 1954, there were thirty-two million television sets in the United States as television became the centerpiece of middle-class life. In the 1960s, as television spread around the world, U.S. networks unloaded their products on Europe and the non-Western world at very low prices. Baywatch was the most popular show in Italy in 1996.

See if you can formulate some hypotheses based on the excerpt and predict possible future outcomes:

1. Make a hypothesis, or educated guess, about why American television is so popular in other countries.

2. Hypothesize about the effects that American television has had on the cultures of other countries.

3. Predict the outcome of a continued worldwide demand for American entertainment.

4. Predict the possible future development of television technology.

### Applying Historical Skills to Your World

In the last few decades, the U.S. economy has been moving away from industrial, factory-type jobs toward more service and information-dependent jobs. This has meant that nonskilled, direct-entry jobs are being replaced by positions that require more schooling and training. Make a hypothesis about possible reasons for this change. Make a prediction about the future of the American economy, as well as about the types of jobs that will be available when you enter the labor force.

## 14. Conducting Research

Your textbook contains a great deal of information about a wide variety of topics, but it is not the final word in the study of history. At some point you will be required to go beyond a general discussion of a topic and become more familiar with the specifics of an event. Perhaps there is a subject of particular interest about which you want to know more. In either case, you will need to conduct research.

When you were in fourth grade, a research project was fairly simple and straightforward. You got an encyclopedia, copied down the information about your topic, and put it into your own words. The research project was mostly a matter of rephrasing someone else's words and research. Today, the process is more involved. Not only are you expected to conduct your own research, but the number of sources available is truly staggering. The Information Revolution of the late twentieth century has created a problem that past researchers never would have imagined—too much information. When conducting research, it is helpful to keep a few general questions in mind: Where is the information? How is the information organized? Is the information specific and timely? Is the information credible and reliable?

## Where Is the Information?

You have a wide variety of available resources when conducting research. The most traditional, and probably still the most useful, resource is a library. School and public libraries carry a wide variety of books, newspapers, periodicals, and compact discs of general interest. If you live in a town with a university, you have access to a library that will have a collection targeted toward

more specific topics. Also, most newspapers, historical museums, and large corporations have libraries to which you might be able to gain access with a phone call.

Another possible source of information is the Internet. Using the Internet, you can access libraries, museums, newspapers, and countless home pages from around the world. Even if your school does not yet have Internet access, many copy centers and other businesses offer computers for use by the public on a pay-per-use basis.

You might also try using a computer search service. These services can help find answers to very specific questions, often on a pay-per-use basis. Some examples

▶ *The Internet is an outstanding source of information on myriad subjects. Among the many organizations that have home pages is the Smithsonian Museum in Washington, D.C., "America's Treasure House for Learning."*

include the New York Times Index, Educational Resources Information Center (ERIC), and Social Sciences Citation Index (SSCI).

Finally, people might be your greatest resource. Talk to teachers, librarians, parents, and friends about your research topic. You might find that even if they do not have information for you, they might know someone who does. The telephone and computer e-mail also can assist you in your research. If you are doing research about the 1923 Rosewood tragedy, why not send an e-mail message to John Singleton, the director of the movie *Rosewood*, or to the *St. Petersburg Times*, which first printed the story of the destruction of the small Florida town? If you are researching the effect World War II had on professional football, why not write or call the Football Hall of Fame in Canton, Ohio, for a list of football players from that era who are still alive? Interviewing eyewitnesses and experts can be one of the most effective methods of research.

### How Is the Information Organized?

Whether you are using a library or the Internet, first you have to determine how the information is organized. Most libraries use the Dewey decimal system to organize their collections. This system divides books into general categories and specific subcategories. Ask your librarian for an explanation of this system so that you can save time when doing further research. You will also want to ask about the organization of the library's collection of newspaper articles and periodicals.

Using the Internet can be more confusing, in part because you generally won't have a librarian to guide you. However, access to the Internet can be made easier by the use of search engines. These are programs that allow you to search the Internet for information based on topic, author, title, or key words. Experimentation is the best method of discovering which search engine is most useful to you.

### Is the Information Specific and Timely?

Information is crucial to your research. You want the most specific, up-to-date information available to provide you with the most accurate answers to your questions. General information, such as the type found in encyclopedias, is of little use for the more sophisticated research you are expected to conduct in high school. Whenever possible, you will want to use primary source information. The writings, documents, photographs, and other information produced by actual witnesses and participants of historical events will provide you with the most specific and accurate data. Secondary sources, when used, should come from experts and other reliable sources.

In general, the more up-to-date and recent the information, the better it is for your research. Older information often is proved incorrect by new facts, so it is important that your research be current.

### Is the Information Credible and Reliable?

Finally, your research is only as good as the credibility and reliability of your sources. A dependable source is more likely to result in dependable information. For instance, read the following three statements:

1. The United States is in decline.

2. According to *The Rise and Fall of the Great Powers*, the United States is experiencing decline.

3. Paul Kennedy, professor of history at Yale University, wrote in his book *The Rise and Fall of the Great Powers* that the United States is experiencing economic and military decline relative to its world position just after World War II.

Readers are more inclined to believe the last statement than the other two, because some degree of credibility has been established by the citing of a respected source.

Even established and respected researchers are susceptible to unreliable information, however. Pierre Salinger, a noted freelance journalist, reported that a plane crash in 1996 off the coast of Long Island was caused by a missile attack. It was quickly revealed that the source of his information was a hoax story that had appeared earlier on the Internet.

## 15. Writing Research Papers

Time travel has been a favorite subject of science fiction writers since H. G. Wells wrote *The Time Machine* in the nineteenth century. Although the topic is a favorite with readers and movie audiences, scientists discount the possibility of sending people or objects through time. Historians, however, might disagree with those scientists.

Time travel is as old as human civilization. Through books, music, and art, people have been transporting a treasure trove of ideas, knowledge, and objects of beauty into the future for thousands of years. The information is part of a "Great Conversation" between generations. You are part of that conversation, not only as a recipient but also as a participant. Your creative contribution to the Great Conversation is a well-researched, thoughtfully-written research paper. It is a way of gathering and presenting your insights and observations as an historian.

What is difficult about writing a research paper is that it requires the use of all, or nearly all, of the social studies skills we have covered in this study guide. There is probably nothing that you will do as a student of history that reveals more about you and your abilities than does your research paper. Writing a research paper is a challenging task, but it is by no means impossible.

### Hints for Better Research Papers

When faced with the task of writing a research paper, many students feel like a mountain climber looking up at Mt. Everest. However, follow the example of Edmund Hillary, who was the first man to climb the world's largest mountain: if you divide a task into stages and take it one step at a time, you will find that your goal can be reached. The following are fifteen steps that will help you to create an A+ research paper.

**Knowing Your Topic** Your first task is to know your topic. The most common problem faced by students writing research papers is selecting a topic that is too vague. This leads to frustration and the wasting of many hours of research. For example, if you decide to research "music," you will find thousands of books, and indeed whole libraries, devoted to the topic. If you narrow the topic to "rock music," you will find it somewhat easier to research your topic, but even that topic is too general. A research paper about "the influence of

gospel music on rock and roll" is much more focused and will be immensely easier to research.

Also, make sure that you are researching only one topic. "The influence of gospel music on rock and roll" is a different topic from "the influence of rock and roll on gospel music." Of course, it is possible to narrow your topic too much, but choosing a topic that is too vague is the mistake made by most students.

**Knowing Your Purpose** What is the purpose of your research paper? Are you writing to find out how to do something (or to describe to others how to do something)? Is your paper a report of events that have occurred in a particular time and place? Are you explaining an idea or concept to others? Is the purpose of your paper to persuade or influence your readers on a particular point of view using factual information? A "yes" answer to any of these questions will result in a very different type of research paper.

Perhaps your topic deals with the Brazilian rain forest. A how-to paper might be called "Ecologically Responsible Methods of Harvesting the Resources of the Brazilian Rain Forest." An example of a paper dealing with the reporting of events would be "The First Portuguese Missionaries in the Brazilian Rain Forest." If your purpose were to explain an idea, then you could write on "The Life Cycle of Butterflies in the Canopy of the Brazilian Rain Forest." If you were writing a persuasive paper, "The Need to Protect the Endangered Animals of the Brazilian Rain Forest" might be your topic. Knowing your purpose will determine the direction of your research paper and help to narrow your focus.

**Creating a Working Outline** Once you have chosen a suitably narrow topic and determined your purpose, the next step is to create a working outline. Your outline will help you divide your topic into subtopics and then divide those subtopics into more narrow specifics. The general outline of your paper will include an introduction (where you describe the purpose and topic of your paper), the body (where you write about your topic), and a conclusion (where you summarize the important points of your research paper).

Because you will not have done any research up to

this point, your working outline will probably be somewhat vague. You will most likely end up rearranging the order of subtopics, discarding some, and adding others.

As an example, suppose you decide to do a report on the Holocaust during World War II. You have decided to narrow your focus to the fate of children during the Holocaust and have chosen as your purpose to report on the events that occurred at that time. A working outline might look like this:

The Fate of Children in Nazi Concentration Camps
    I.   Children Sent to Camps
         —different groups, transportation to camps
    II.  Life in the Camps
         —family life, schooling, religious worship, play, creativity
    III. Slave Labor
         —types of jobs, methods of selection
    IV. Death
         —methods, numbers, escapes

**Turning Your Outline into Questions** Once you have a working outline, you can save a great deal of research time by taking the subtopics from that outline and turning them into questions. You will then have a very specific purpose to your research. For example, using the working outline on the fate of children in Nazi concentration camps, you might create the following questions:

▲ What groups were sent to the camps?
▲ When and how were they transported to the camps?
▲ What was life like in the camps?
▲ Did the children attend school?

These and other questions will keep you on track and allow you to make effective use of your research time.

**Finding the Right Sources and Resources** At this point, you are ready to begin your research. You have a topic, a purpose, an outline, and a series of questions in need of answers. Where do you begin your search? The previous section on "Conducting Research" goes into more detail about research. You probably will use your school or local library, the Internet, your family's own books and resources, or a combination of these resources.

You must decide what type of sources you will use. Will your research come from primary or secondary sources (see the earlier discussion)? Most professional researchers use primary source material. You should also rely on primary sources whenever possible. Many students are tempted to use encyclopedias when writing reports. However, encyclopedias should be consulted only for general background, not as sources. It is a rare teacher who can't spot the dry, stilted writing of a report based on encyclopedias.

When you have selected your sources of information, be sure that you understand the method of citation required by your school and teacher. Methods vary, so consult your teacher if you are uncertain. It is essential that you give credit for your information.

**Organizing Your Data** Many methods of note taking are useful for organizing your information. Whether you are using a notebook, note cards, or some other method, the following guidelines will be useful for organizing your data:

1. Always write the information about the source of your notes first. This will allow you to properly cite your source in your paper. Information that does not have bibliographic information cannot be used.

2. Always write your notes in your own words. Days or weeks after you've written your notes, it is easy to forget whether the wording is yours or is from your source.

3. Create an organizational system that helps you retrieve your information easily. Note cards are useful for this purpose, because they allow you to sort by topic and reshuffle as needed.

**Quoting, Paraphrasing, and Plagiarizing** Quoting a source can lend weight and authority to your paper. Using too many quotations, however, implies a lack of confidence in your own words. When quoting, you must use quotation marks and cite the person who made the statement. Sometimes you may want to reword another person's statement or shorten an idea to a few essentials. This is called *paraphrasing*. It is an acceptable practice, as long as you cite the source of the information. What is not acceptable is using other people's words or unique ideas without giving them credit. This practice is both unethical and foolish. Most teachers can tell the difference between the writings of their students and those of established and published authors.

**Writing a Thesis Statement** A thesis statement describes in one or two sentences the topic and purpose of your paper. It is often the last sentence in the introduction. Writing a thorough, carefully thought out thesis statement will help keep your essay focused and keep you on track in your writing. By constantly checking to see if the information in the report supports your thesis, you will know whether each point is essential or extraneous to the research paper.

**Creating a Formal Outline** After doing your research and writing a thesis statement, you are ready to make a formal outline. Many students skip this step, thinking that it is simply more work. This is a mistake. A well-organized outline will make the actual writing of your paper much easier. The subheadings of the outline will become the individual paragraphs of the body of the paper. The specific facts listed become the details that support your thesis. Writing an outline allows you to focus on writing technique, because the actual topics and subtopics will already be prepared.

**Using Graphics** When you pick up a book, newspaper, or magazine, your eyes probably are immediately drawn to the pictures and graphics. The use of pictures, maps, graphs, charts, and other graphics not only enlivens your paper but also helps make your point to the reader. Be sure to give credit to the source of the graphics you use, as you do for other information that was not created by you.

**Writing the Body** The body of your research paper can be said to be the "meat and potatoes" of the paper. It is where you present the information that supports your thesis statement. Many people find it easier to write the body before they actually create the introduction. When writing the body of your paper, be sure that each paragraph deals with no more than one topic. When changing topics, be sure to change paragraphs. Link your paragraphs together with transitional phrases that let your readers have some idea of what is coming next. Once you have written a paragraph for each of the subtopics in your outline, you will have completed the body of the paper. You then will be ready to go back and write the introduction and conclusion.

**Writing the Introduction and Conclusion** An introduction to a research paper is no different than an introduction to someone you've never met before. You are giving the reader an idea of the topic and purpose of the paper—in a sense, explaining "who" your paper is. The introduction will contain the thesis statement and will give the reader an idea of the points you will cover in your paper. Save supporting details and factual evidence for the body of the paper.

The conclusion is your summary of the main points of your research paper. You are restating your argument for the benefit of your readers. Do not introduce any new information in the conclusion. The rule is to tell your readers what you are going to tell them (introduction), tell them (body), and tell them what you just told them (conclusion).

**Writing with Creativity** Writing a research paper is an artistic endeavor that reflects your abilities. You are creating something that did not previously exist. Your paper should be special and unique. It should also be interesting to the reader. If you see the process as a plodding act of boring drudgery, then your writing will be plodding and boring. However, if you are intrigued and excited by your topic, then that sense of enthusiasm will come through in your words.

There are techniques for making your writing more interesting. Try to vary your word choices by using a thesaurus. Use a mixture of sentence lengths so that your writing does not become monotonous. Write in an active voice that avoids the different forms of the verb *to be*. Use vivid, descriptive words and phrases to paint a verbal picture for your readers.

**Writing the Rough Draft and Proofreading** At this point, you should have before you a written research paper. You might think you are done, but you have one more step to take before you have reached the top of the mountain. You have written only the rough draft. You must now proofread your paper for errors in spelling, grammar, and style. Have someone read your rough draft and give you suggestions. See if you have chosen the best order for the presentation of your facts.

**Writing the Final Draft** Now you are ready to revise your research paper on the typewriter or word processor. Make all of your final changes. Make sure that the format meets the teacher's requirements. Some students like to use plastic covers or binders for their reports, but many teachers find them cumbersome. You have written a well-researched, creative, and original paper. Let it stand on its own merits.

# BACKGROUND TO MODERN WORLD

◄ *These life-size statues made of plaster and bitumen date from 6500 B.C. and were discovered in 1984 in Ain Ghazal, near Amman, Jordan. They are among the oldest statues ever found of the human figure. Archaeologists are studying the sculptures to try to understand their purpose and their meaning.*

**B.C.**

| 3000 | 1800 | 1600 | 1400 | 1200 | 1000 | 800 | 600 | 400 | 200 |
|------|------|------|------|------|------|-----|-----|-----|-----|

**The Middle East and India**

3000–1800 B.C. Sumerian civilization

3000–1500 B.C. Harappan civilization

1000–586 B.C. Hebrew civilization

**East Asia**

1766–1122 B.C. Shang dynasty in China

1122–221 B.C. Zhou dynasty in China

**Africa and the Americas**

**The Mediterranean World and Europe**

800–338 B.C. World of the Greek city-states

2700–1085 B.C. Flowering of Egyptian civilization

753 B.C.–A.D. 500
Roman Republic and Empire

# HISTORY: THE WORLD TO A.D. 1800

## (PREHISTORY TO A.D. 1800)

Around 3000 B.C., civilizations began to emerge in four different areas of the world—western Asia, Egypt, India, and China—and to give rise to the great empires of the ancient world. By the beginning of the first millennium A.D., however, the great states of the ancient world were mostly in decline or at the point of collapse. On the ruins of these ancient empires, new patterns of civilization began to take shape between 400 and 1500. At the same time, new civilizations were also beginning to appear in a number of other parts of the world—in Japan, in Southeast Asia, in Africa, and across the Atlantic in the Americas. All of these states were increasingly linked by trade into the first "global civilization."

Beginning in the late fifteenth century, a new force entered the world scene in the form of a revived Europe. This new Europe made an impact on the rest of the world as voyages of exploration led Europeans into new areas of the world. Within the European world, ideas of democracy, based on older models, also began to emerge.

## UNIT OUTLINE

CHAPTER 1
**The First Civilizations and the Rise of Empires (Prehistory to A.D. 500)**

CHAPTER 2
**The Emergence of New World Patterns (400 to 1800)**

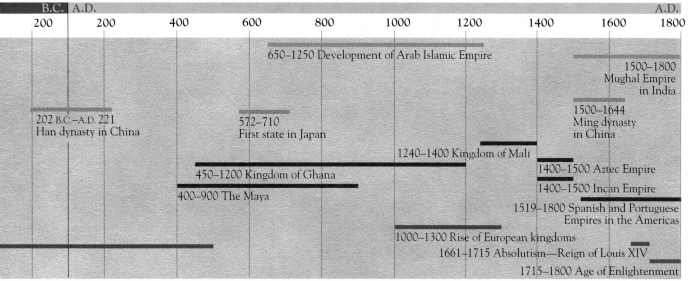

| | | | | | | | | | |
|---|---|---|---|---|---|---|---|---|---|
| B.C. | A.D. | | | | | | | | A.D. |
| 200 | 200 | 400 | 600 | 800 | 1000 | 1200 | 1400 | 1600 | 1800 |

650–1250 Development of Arab Islamic Empire

1500–1800 Mughal Empire in India

202 B.C.–A.D. 221 Han dynasty in China

572–710 First state in Japan

1500–1644 Ming dynasty in China

1240–1400 Kingdom of Mali

450–1200 Kingdom of Ghana

1400–1500 Aztec Empire

400–900 The Maya

1400–1500 Incan Empire

1519–1800 Spanish and Portuguese Empires in the Americas

1000–1300 Rise of European kingdoms

1661–1715 Absolutism—Reign of Louis XIV

1715–1800 Age of Enlightenment

3

# THE FIRST CIVILIZATIONS

In the winter of 1849, a daring young Englishman made a difficult journey into the deserts and swamps of southern Iraq. He moved south down the banks of the river Euphrates while braving high winds and temperatures that reached 120 degrees Fahrenheit. The man, William Loftus, led a small expedition in search of the roots of civilization. As he said, "From our childhood we have been led to regard this place as the cradle of the human race."

Guided by native Arabs into the southernmost reaches of Iraq, Loftus and his small group of explorers were soon overwhelmed by what they saw. Loftus wrote, "I know of nothing more exciting or impressive than the first sight of one of these great piles, looming in solitary grandeur from the surrounding plains and marshes." One of these "piles" was known to the natives as the mound of Warka. The mound contained the ruins of the ancient city of Uruk, one of the first real cities in the world and part of the world's first civilization.

Southern Iraq, known to ancient peoples as Mesopotamia, was one of four areas in the world where civilization began. (A civilization is a complex culture in which large numbers of human beings share a number of common elements.) The other three areas were Egypt, India, and China. From the beginnings of the first civilizations around 3000 B.C., there was an ongoing movement toward the creation of larger states with more sophisticated systems of control.

This process reached a high point in the first millennium B.C. Between 1000 and 500 B.C., the Assyrians and Persians created empires that included either large areas of or all of the ancient Middle East and Egypt. The conquests of Alexander the Great and his Greek army in the fourth century B.C. created an even larger, if short-lived, empire that soon divided into four kingdoms. Later, the western portion of these kingdoms, as well as the Mediterranean world and much of western Europe, fell subject to the mighty empire of the Romans. At the same time, much of India became part of the Mauryan Empire. Finally, in the last few centuries B.C., the rulers of China created a unified Chinese Empire.

▲ *These are Sumerian ruins at Uruk, formerly the site of the ziggurat, or stepped tower, of Warka.*

# AND THE RISE OF EMPIRES

## (PREHISTORY TO A.D. 500)

### THE WORLD TO 1800

| FIRST CIVILIZATIONS AND RISE OF EMPIRES | 500 | 1800 |
| --- | --- | --- |
| 3500 B.C. | | A.D. 1800 |

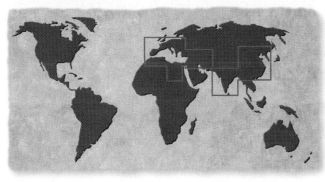

## QUESTIONS TO GUIDE YOUR READING

1. What were the major achievements of early humans during the Paleolithic and Neolithic Ages?

2. What contributions did the Code of Hammurabi and the spiritual ideas of the Hebrews make to civilization?

3. What importance did Siddhartha Gautama and Confucius have to the civilizations of India and China?

4. What was the *polis*, or city-state, and how did the important city-states of Athens and Sparta differ?

5. What political contributions did the Greeks and Romans make to Western civilization?

6. What contributions did the ideas of Christianity make to the development of Western civilization?

## OUTLINE

1. THE FIRST HUMANS (PREHISTORY TO 3500 B.C.)

2. THE FIRST CIVILIZATIONS: THE PEOPLES OF WESTERN ASIA AND EGYPT (3500 TO 500 B.C.)

3. THE FIRST CIVILIZATIONS: ANCIENT INDIA AND CHINA (3000 B.C. TO A.D. 500)

4. THE CIVILIZATION OF THE GREEKS (1900 TO 133 B.C.)

5. THE WORLD OF THE ROMANS (600 B.C. TO A.D. 500)

## THE FIRST HUMANS (PREHISTORY TO 3500 B.C.)

Historians rely mostly on documents, or written records, to create their pictures of the past. However, an account of prehistory—the period before written records—depends upon the work of archaeologists and anthropologists. These investigators rely on the scientific analysis of human remains to construct their theories about the development of early human beings.

The term *Paleolithic Age* is used to designate the early period of human history from approximately 2,500,000 to 10,000 B.C., in which humans used simple stone tools. (*Paleolithic* is Greek for "Old Stone.") For hundreds of thousands of years, during the Paleolithic Age, human beings lived in small communities, seeking to survive by hunting, fishing, and gathering in an often hostile environment. Over a long period of time, Paleolithic people learned how to create more sophisticated tools; how to use fire; and how to adapt to, and even change, their physical environment. Paleolithic

▲ *Nomadic Paleolithic people followed the migration of animals in order to provide food and other necessities for their families. Can you imagine hunting mammoths with the primitive tools used by these early humans?*

people were primarily nomads (people who moved from place to place) who hunted animals and gathered wild plants for survival. Nevertheless, they created a human culture that included sophisticated cave paintings.

The agricultural revolution of the Neolithic Age dramatically changed human patterns of living. The term *Neolithic Age* is used to designate the period of human history from 10,000 to 4,000 B.C. (*Neolithic* is Greek for "New Stone.") The growing of food on a regular basis and the taming of animals made it possible for humans to stop their nomadic ways of living. People began to stay in one place and form more permanent settlements. These organized communities gradually gave rise to more complex human societies.

These more complex human societies, which we call the first civilizations, emerged around 3000 B.C. in the

river valleys of Mesopotamia, Egypt, India, and China. An increase in food production in these regions led to a significant growth in human population and to the rise of cities. Efforts to control the flow of water for farming also led to organized governments in these new urban civilizations. The emergence of civilizations was a dramatic new chapter in the story of world history.

❋ **SECTION REVIEW** ❋

1. **Recall:**
   (*a*) Describe the Paleolithic people.
   (*b*) How did the agricultural revolution of the Neolithic Age affect its people?

2. **Think Critically:**
   (*a*) How might a rise in food production lead to the rise of cities?
   (*b*) How might the need to control the flow of water encourage people to organize a government?

## THE FIRST CIVILIZATIONS: THE PEOPLES OF WESTERN ASIA AND EGYPT (3500 TO 500 B.C.)

The peoples of Mesopotamia and Egypt built the first civilizations. They developed cities and struggled with the problems of organized states. They invented writing to keep records, and they created literature. They constructed monumental buildings to please their gods, give witness to their powers, and preserve their cultures for all time. They developed new political, military, social, and religious structures to deal with the basic problems of human existence and organization.

These first civilizations left detailed records that allow us to view how they struggled with three of the fundamental problems that humans have thought about: the nature of human relationships, the nature of the universe, and the role of divine forces in that universe. Although later peoples would provide different

◄ *The "Royal Standard" of Ur, a box from c. 2700 B.C., depicts a royal celebration following a military victory. The panels show the king and his court as well as the spoils of victory. How does this method of recording historic events compare to the way events are recorded today?*

answers from those of the Mesopotamians and Egyptians, it was they who first posed the questions, gave answers, and wrote them down.

## Civilization in Mesopotamia: The Law Code of Hammurabi

The first states in Mesopotamia were city-states (cities that came to have political and economic control over the surrounding countryside) created by the Sumerians, a people whose origins remain a mystery. By 3000 B.C., the Sumerians had established a number of independent city-states in southern Mesopotamia. As the number of Sumerian city-states grew and the city-states expanded, new conflicts arose. City-state fought city-state for control of land and water. Because the Sumerian city-states were located on the flat land of Mesopotamia, they were open to invasion. Thus, some leaders were able to create empires. (An empire is a large political unit or state, usually under a single leader, that controls many peoples or territories.)

In 1792 B.C. a new empire came to control much of Mesopotamia. Leadership came from Babylon, a city-state north of Akkad, where Hammurabi had come to power. He had a well-disciplined army of foot soldiers who carried axes, spears, and copper or bronze daggers.

Hammurabi divided his opponents and defeated them one by one. He gained control of Sumer and Akkad, thus creating a new Mesopotamian kingdom. After his conquests, Hammurabi called himself "the sun of Babylon, the king who has made the four quarters of the world subservient."

Hammurabi, the man of war, was also a man of peace. He built temples, defensive walls, and irrigation canals. He encouraged trade and brought an economic revival. After his death in 1750 B.C., however, a series of weak kings were unable to keep Hammurabi's empire united. It finally fell to new invaders.

Hammurabi is best remembered for his law code, a collection of 282 laws. For centuries, laws had regulated people's relationships with one another in the lands of Mesopotamia. Hammurabi's collection provides considerable insight into social conditions in Mesopotamia and touches on almost every aspect of everyday life there.

The Code of Hammurabi was based on a system of strict justice (see "You Are There: Justice in Mesopotamia"). Penalties for criminal offenses were severe and varied according to the social class of the victim. A crime against a member of the upper class (a noble) by a member of the lower class (a commoner) was punished more severely than the same offense against a member of the lower class. Moreover, the

**Map 1.1   Ancient Mesopotamia**

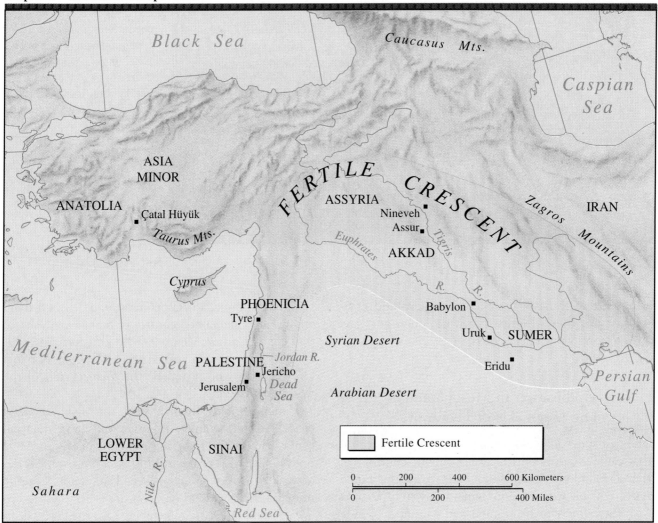

principle of retaliation ("an eye for an eye, tooth for a tooth") was a fundamental part of this system of justice. This principle and other Mesopotamian ideas would find their way into the Hebrew civilization.

The law code encouraged the proper performance of work with what we would call consumer protection laws. Builders were held responsible for the buildings they constructed. If a house collapsed and caused the death of the owner, the builder was put to death. If the collapse caused the death of the son of the owner, the son of the builder was put to death. If goods were

destroyed by the collapse, they had to be replaced and the house itself rebuilt at the builder's expense.

The largest category of laws in the Code of Hammurabi focused on marriage and the family. Parents arranged marriages for their children. After marriage, the two parties signed a marriage contract. Without this contract, no one was considered legally married.

Society in Mesopotamia was **patriarchal;** that is, it was dominated by men. Hammurabi's code makes it clear that women had far fewer privileges and rights in marriage than did men. A woman's place was in the

# YOU ARE THERE

## Justice in Mesopotamia

*Although there were earlier Mesopotamian law codes, the Code of Hammurabi is the most complete. The law code emphasizes the principle of retribution ("an eye for an eye") and punishments that vary according to social status. Punishments could be severe, as these examples show.*

**The Code of Hammurabi**

25: If fire broke out in a free man's house and a free man, who went to extinguish it, cast his eye on the goods of the owner of the house and has appropriated the goods of the owner of the house, that free man shall be thrown into that fire.

196: If a free man has destroyed the eye of a member of the aristocracy, they shall destroy his eye.

198: If he has destroyed the eye of a commoner or broken the bone of a commoner, he shall pay one mina of silver.

199: If he has destroyed the eye of a free man's slave or broken the bone of a free man's slave, he shall pay one-half his value.

◀ *The Code of Hammurabi was the most famous, though not the first, early Mesopotamian law code. The upper section of this stone monument shows Hammurabi standing in front of the seated sun god Shamash, who orders the king to record the law. The actual code is inscribed on the lower portion. Do you think the Code of Hammurabi could be enforced today?*

1. Explain the principle of retribution.

2. According to the Code of Hammurabi, what was most highly valued in Mesopotamian society? What was the least valued? Explain your answers.

3. What is the guiding principle in the American criminal justice system? How does this compare with Hammurabi's justice?

home, and failure to fulfill her expected duties was grounds for divorce. If a wife was not able to bear children or tried to leave home to engage in business, her husband could divorce her. Furthermore, a wife who was a "gadabout, . . . neglecting her house [and] humiliating her husband," could be drowned.

Fathers ruled their children as well as their wives. Obedience was expected: "If a son has struck his father, he shall cut off his hand." If a son committed a serious enough offense, his father could disinherit him. Obviously, Hammurabi's law code covered almost every aspect of people's lives. A code of laws is an important step in the development of civilization.

## New Centers of Civilization: The Hebrews

By 1500 B.C., much of the creative impulse of the Mesopotamian and Egyptian civilizations was beginning to decline. By 1200 B.C., a power vacuum had emerged in western Asia that allowed a number of small states to emerge and flourish for a short while. All these states were eventually overshadowed by the rise of the great empires of the Assyrians and Persians.

The Assyrian Empire was the first to unite almost all of the ancient Middle East. Even larger, however, was the Persian Empire of the "Great Kings" of Persia. Persian rule was not only efficient but also tolerant. Conquered peoples were allowed to keep their own religions, customs, and methods of doing business. The many years of peace that the Persian Empire brought to the Middle East aided trade and the general well-being of its peoples.

It is no wonder that many peoples expressed their gratitude for being subjects of the Great Kings of Persia. The Hebrews were one of these peoples—a people who created no empire but nevertheless left an important legacy. In Judaism, the Hebrews developed a world religion that influenced the later religions of Christianity and Islam. The spiritual heritage of the Hebrews is one of the basic pillars of Western civilization.

### The History of the Hebrews

The Hebrews were a nomadic people, organized in tribes. They followed a lifestyle based on grazing flocks

**Map 1.2    Ancient Palestine**

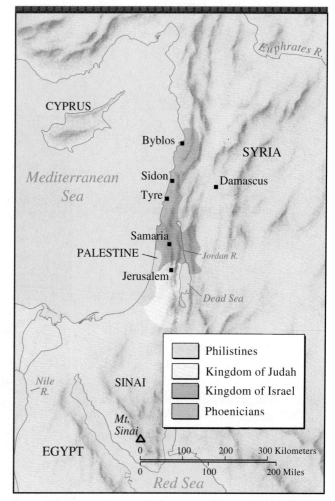

and herds rather than farming. According to tradition, because of drought, the Hebrews migrated to Egypt. There they were enslaved until Moses led his people out of Egypt, probably in the first half of the thirteenth century B.C. The Hebrews then wandered for many years in the desert until they entered Palestine (possibly around 1220 B.C.). They became involved in a lengthy conflict with people who were already settled there. Around 1000 B.C., under the pressure of this ongoing struggle, the Hebrews established a monarchy.

The creation of a monarchy was not easy. However, by the time of King Solomon, who ruled from about 971 to 931 B.C., the Hebrews had established control

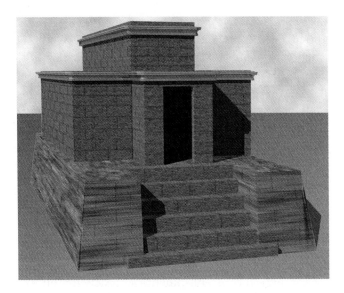

▲ *Solomon's temple, as seen in this artist's rendering, dominated the walled city of ancient Jerusalem. The temple is said to be one of Solomon's greatest accomplishments during his reign. Why was the temple given such a prominent location in the city, and why was it such an important part of the Hebrew lifestyle?*

over all of Palestine and had made Jerusalem into the capital of a united kingdom, known as Israel. Solomon did even more to strengthen royal power. He expanded the government and army, as well as encouraged trade. Solomon is best known for his building projects, of which the most famous was a temple in the city of Jerusalem. The Hebrews viewed the temple as the symbolic center of their religion and of the Hebrew kingdom itself. Under Solomon, ancient Israel was at the height of its power.

After Solomon's death, tension between the northern and southern Hebrew tribes led to the creation of two separate kingdoms—a northern Kingdom of Israel and a southern Kingdom of Judah. Both kingdoms eventually fell to the large empires of the Assyrians and the Persians. However, the people of Judah survived, eventually becoming known as the Jews and giving their name to Judaism, the religion of Yahweh, the Jewish God. Judaism became a stateless religion, based on the belief that God was not fixed to one particular land but instead was creator and lord of the whole world.

## CONNECTIONS
### TO OUR WORLD

**Conflict in Palestine**   In 1948, an independent Jewish state known as Israel was established in an area known as Palestine. The Arab neighbors of the new state were outraged, because 90 percent of the people in Palestine were Arab Muslims. An invasion of the new state of Israel by its Arab neighbors failed. However, conflict between Arabs and Israelis over Palestine continues to this day. In 1964, an Arab organization called the Palestine Liberation Organization was founded. Its goal is to bring about an independent Arab state of Palestine.

Conflict between Jews and other peoples in Palestine has a very long history. When the Hebrews entered Palestine around 1220 B.C., after their enslavement in Egypt, they found other peoples who were already settled there. One of these peoples was the Philistines (FIL-eh-steenz). For over two centuries, Hebrews and Philistines fought over control of much of Palestine.

This struggle made a strong impact on the Hebrews. By 1020 B.C., after a series of defeats, the Hebrews found themselves on the verge of being conquered by the Philistines. In desperation, the Hebrews decided to form a solid united front by giving up their loose tribal organization and choosing one of their members—Saul—as king. At first, Saul was very successful. He organized a small army and went on the offensive against the Philistines. Around 1000 B.C., however, Saul and his army experienced disaster when they dared to meet the Philistines on an open plain. The army was disastrously defeated, Saul's sons were killed, and Saul committed suicide. David, the next king of the Hebrews, was more successful. During his reign, the Hebrews defeated the Philistines and established control over all of Palestine. Although later the Hebrews were conquered and scattered by the Assyrians, Persians, and Romans, for centuries Palestine remained the Promised Land in the minds of many Jews.

## The Spiritual Dimensions of the Hebrews

According to the Hebrews, there was only one God, called Yahweh, who was the creator of the world and everything in it. God ruled the world. All peoples, whether they knew it or not, were his servants. Moreover, God had created nature but was not in nature. The stars, moon, rivers, wind, and other natural phenomena were not gods, as other ancient peoples believed, but God's handiwork. All of God's creations could be admired for their awesome beauty, but not worshipped as gods.

This powerful creator of the universe, however, was not removed from the life he had created. God was just and good, and he expected goodness from his people. If they did not obey his will, they would be punished. He was also a God of mercy and love: "The Lord is gracious and compassionate, slow to anger and rich in love. The Lord is good to all; he has compassion on all he has made."[1] Each person could have a personal relationship with this powerful being.

The covenant, law, and the prophets were three special aspects of the Hebrew religious tradition. The Hebrews believed that during the exodus from Egypt, when Moses led his people out of bondage into the promised land, a special event occurred. God made a **covenant,** or contract, with the tribes of Israel. The Hebrews promised to obey Yahweh and follow his law. In return, Yahweh promised to take special care of his chosen people, "a peculiar treasure unto me above all people."

This covenant between Yahweh and his chosen people could be fulfilled, however, only by Hebrew obedience to the law of God. Most important were the moral concerns that stood at the center of the law. These Ten Commandments, as they are called, spelled out God's ideals of behavior: "You shall not murder. You shall not commit adultery. You shall not steal."[2] God gave the Hebrews true freedom to follow his moral standards voluntarily. If people chose to ignore the good, then suffering and evil would follow.

The Hebrews believed that certain religious teachers, called **prophets,** were sent by God to serve as his voice to his people (see "Our Literary Heritage: The Words of the Prophets"). The golden age of prophecy began in the mid-eighth century B.C. and continued during the time when the Hebrews were threatened by Assyrian conquerors. The "men of God," or prophets, went through the land warning the Hebrews that they had failed to keep God's commandments and would be punished for breaking the covenant: "I will punish you for all your iniquities." Amos prophesied the fall of the northern Kingdom of Israel to Assyria. Twenty years later, Isaiah said that the Kingdom of Judah, too, would fall.

Out of the words of the prophets came new concepts that enriched the Hebrew tradition. The prophets embraced a concern for all humanity. All nations would someday come to the God of Israel: "all the earth shall worship thee." This vision included the end of war and the establishment of peace for all the nations of the world. In the words of the prophet Isaiah: "He will judge between the nations and will settle disputes for many people. They will beat their swords into plowshares and their spears into pruning hooks. Nation will not take up sword against nation, nor will they train for war anymore."[3]

The prophets also cried out against social injustice. They condemned the rich for causing the poor to suffer. They denounced luxuries as worthless, and they threatened Israel with prophecies of dire punishments for these sins. The prophets said that God's command was to live justly, share with one's neighbors, care for the poor and the unfortunate, and act with compassion. When God's command was not followed, according to the prophets, the community was threatened. These words of the Hebrew prophets became a source for universal ideals of social justice.

The Hebrew religion was unique among the religions of western Asia and Egypt. The most dramatic difference was the Hebrews' belief that there was only one God for all peoples (**monotheism**). Furthermore, in virtually every religion in ancient Mesopotamia and Egypt, only priests (and occasionally rulers) had access to the gods and their desires. In the Hebrew tradition, God's wishes, though communicated to the people through a series of prophets, had all been written down. No Jewish spiritual leader could claim that he alone knew God's will. This knowledge was open to anyone who could read Hebrew.

## OUR LITERARY HERITAGE

# The Words of the Prophets

*The Hebrew prophets warned the Hebrew people that they must obey God's commandments or face being punished for breaking their covenant with God. These selections from the prophets Isaiah (eye-ZAY-uh) and Amos make clear their belief that God's punishment would fall upon the Hebrews for their sins.*

### Isaiah 3:14–17, 24–26

The Lord enters into judgment against the elders and leaders of his people: "It is you who have ruined my vineyard; the plunder from the poor is in your houses. What do you mean by crushing my people and grinding the faces of the poor?" declares the Lord, the Lord Almighty. The Lord says, "The women of Zion are haughty, walking along with outstretched necks, flirting with their eyes, tripping along with mincing steps, with ornaments jingling on their ankles. Therefore the Lord will bring sores on the heads of the women of Zion; the Lord will make their scalps bald. . . ." Instead of fragrance there will be a stench; instead of a sash, a rope; instead of well-dressed hair, baldness; instead of fine clothing, sackcloth; instead of beauty, branding. Your men will fall by the sword, your warriors in battle. The gates of Zion will lament and mourn; destitute, she will sit on the ground.

### Amos 3:1–2

Hear this word the Lord has spoken against you, O people of Israel—against the whole family I

▲ *The Ark of the Covenant, as depicted in this mosaic, was in Solomon's Temple before it was destroyed and played an important role in Jewish worship. What other symbols do you know of that are important in different religions?*

brought you up out of Egypt: "You only have I chosen of all the families of the earth; therefore I will punish you for all your sins."

1. What did Isaiah say were the sins of the Hebrew people?

2. Relate the punishments prophesied by Isaiah to the errors of the people. What kind of people did God desire the Hebrews to be?

Moreover, the demands of the Hebrew religion (the need to obey God) encouraged a separation between Jews and their non-Jewish neighbors. Unlike most other peoples of the Middle East up to that time, Jews would not accept the gods of their conquerors or neighbors and be made part of a community. To remain faithful to the demands of their God, they might even have to refuse loyalty to political leaders. These religious convictions frequently created serious conflicts for Jews.

## SECTION REVIEW

1. **Locate:**
   (*a*) Mesopotamia,   (*b*) Babylon,   (*c*) Akkad,
   (*d*) Sumer,   (*e*) Palestine,   (*f*) Jerusalem,
   (*g*) Kingdom of Israel

2. **Define:**
   (*a*) patriarchal,   (*b*) covenant,   (*c*) prophets,
   (*d*) monotheism

3. **Identify:**
   (*a*) Hammurabi,   (*b*) Code of Hammurabi,
   (*c*) Hebrews,   (*d*) King Solomon,   (*e*) Yahweh

4. **Recall:**
   (*a*) How would you describe Persian rule?
   (*b*) List three accomplishments of King Solomon.

5. **Think Critically:** Hammurabi established his code; the Hebrews agreed to a covenant. What are the advantages and disadvantages of living under such systems?

## 3

# THE FIRST CIVILIZATIONS: ANCIENT INDIA AND CHINA (3000 B.C. TO A.D. 500)

Western Asia and Egypt were not the only places where civilizations first emerged. In the fertile river valleys of India and China, intensive farming made it possible to support large groups of people. The people in these regions were able to develop the organized societies that we associate with civilization.

## Ancient India

After its conquest of India in the 1850s, Great Britain began to build a series of railroads to connect the far-flung lands of its new colony. While building on the floodplain of the Indus River in the 1850s, British engineers realized the need for a strong foundation bed for their railroad tracks. Lacking sufficient quantities of stone, they found another solution. Lying nearby were the ruins of ancient, deserted cities. Why not pull down the walls and use the old bricks? By plundering the old ruins, the British laid the foundation bed for hundreds of miles of railroad tracks. Trains still travel on these tracks today.

**Map 1.3   The Indian Subcontinent**

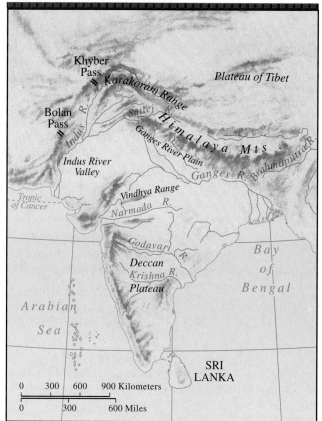

One of the plundered sites was known as Harappa—the name of a nearby village. In the 1920s, archaeologists discovered that Harappa and a number of other ruins were sites of once-vibrant cities. Indeed, they were all part of a vast civilization in India that had flourished between 3000 and 1500 B.C. and had covered far more territory than the early civilizations of Mesopotamia and Egypt.

The first civilization in India—known as Harappan or Indus civilization—that arose in the Indus River valley during the fourth millennium B.C. was based in two major cities, Harappa and Mohenjo-Daro. Harappan civilization made significant political and social achievements for some two thousand years. Internal decline then weakened the civilization, and the invasion of the Aryans finally brought its end around 1500 B.C.

The Aryans were an Indo-European–speaking people who established political control throughout all of India and created a new Indian civilization. A rigid caste system—a system in which people were clearly divided into distinct classes—became a chief feature of the new Indian civilization.

There were five major castes in Indian society in ancient times. The priestly class, whose members were known as the Brahmins, was usually considered to be at the top of the social scale. They were in charge of the religious ceremonies that were such an important part of Indian society. The second caste was the Kshatriyas, or the warriors. The third-ranked caste in Indian society was the Vaisyas, or commoners. The Vaisyas were usually the merchants who engaged in commerce.

Below these three castes were the Sudras and the Untouchables, who made up the great bulk of the Indian population. Most Sudras were peasants, artisans, or people who worked at other forms of manual labor. They had only limited rights in society. The Untouchables were at the lowest level and, in fact, not even considered a real part of the caste system. The Untouchables were given menial, degrading tasks that other Indians would not accept, such as collecting trash and handling dead bodies. They probably made up about 5 percent of the total population of ancient India. The life of the Untouchables was extremely difficult. They were not considered human, and their very presence was considered harmful to members of the other classes. No Indian would touch or eat food handled by an Untouchable.

Technically, these caste divisions were absolute. Individuals supposedly were born, lived, and died in the same caste, and throughout most of Indian history caste divisions remained strict. Members were generally not allowed to marry or share meals outside their caste.

Two of the world's great religions, Hinduism and Buddhism, began in India. Hinduism was an outgrowth of the religious beliefs of the Aryan peoples who invaded and settled in India. Early Hindus believed in the existence of a single force in the universe, a form of ultimate reality or God, called **Brahman.** It was the duty of the individual self—called the **Atman**—to seek to know this ultimate reality. By doing so, the self would merge with Brahman after death.

By the sixth century B.C., another new concept—**reincarnation**— had also appeared in Hinduism. Reincarnation is the belief that the individual soul is reborn in a different form after death. After a number of existences in the earthly world, the soul reaches its final goal in a union with the Great World Soul, or Brahman. According to Hinduism, all living beings seek to achieve this goal. Important to this process is the idea of **karma,** or the force of a person's actions in this life in determining his or her rebirth in a next life. What people do in their lives determines what they will be in the next life.

Buddhism was the product of one man, Siddhartha Gautama, one of the great figures of ancient India. Born around 563 B.C., Siddhartha Gautama is better known as the Buddha. In his lifetime he gained thousands of devoted followers. People would come to him seeking to know more about him. They asked, "Are you a god?" "No," he answered. "Are you an angel?" "No." "Are you a saint?" "No." "Then what are you?" Buddha replied, "I am awake." The religion of Buddhism began with a man who claimed that he had awakened and seen the world in a new way. His simple message of achieving wisdom created a new spiritual philosophy that came to rival Hinduism. Both Buddhism and Hinduism began in India. Both were crucial to the civilization that flourished in India. The two

flourishing of the arts. Indian civilization was extensive. Eventually, in the form of Hinduism and Buddhism, it spread to China and Southeast Asia.

## Ancient China

Of the great civilizations mentioned so far, China was the last to come into full flower. By the time the Shang dynasty began to display the first signs of emerging as an organized state, the societies in Mesopotamia, Egypt, and India had already reached an advanced level of civilization. Not enough is known about the early stages of any of these civilizations to allow us to determine why some developed earlier than others. One likely reason for China's late arrival was its virtual isolation from the other emerging centers of culture

▼ *Qin Shi Huangdi's Tomb, an elaborate underground palace complex, was built by order of the powerful First Emperor of Qin. An army of life-sized soldiers and horses made of terra cotta was fashioned to accompany the emperor on his journey to the afterlife. What does this tomb tell you of the emperor's view of death?*

▲ *Siddhartha, the Buddha, assumes the lotus position called* padmasana *in this fifth-century limestone sculpture. Beneath him, figures representing his first five students gather to hear Buddha's teaching, symbolized by the wheel in the center. The image was found in Sarnath, where Siddhartha preached his first sermon.*

religions have continued to influence the ways of the people who have lived in India for thousands of years.

For most of the time between 325 B.C. and A.D. 500, India was a land of many different states. Two major empires, however, were able to create large, unified Indian states. The Mauryan Empire in northern India lasted from 324 to 183 B.C. The Gupta Empire flourished from A.D. 320 until the invasion of the Huns reduced its power in the late fifth century. Both empires experienced strong central government and a

**Map 1.4    The Han Empire**

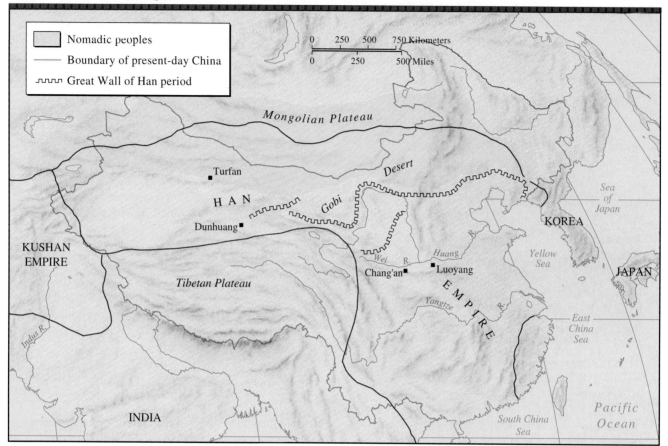

elsewhere in the world. Basically, China was forced to develop on its own.

The Shang dynasty (about 1750 to 1122 B.C.) created the first flourishing Chinese civilization. Under the Shang, China developed organized government, a system of writing, and advanced skills in the making of bronze vessels. During the Zhou dynasty (1122 to 256 B.C.), China began to adopt many of the features that were to characterize Chinese civilization for centuries. Especially important politically was the "mandate of Heaven," which, it was believed, gave kings a divine right to rule (divine right is the belief that rulers receive their power directly from God). The family also emerged as a powerful economic and social unit.

After two hundred years of civil war, a new dynasty, known as the Qin, created a new era of Chinese unity.

However, the First Qin Emperor was also the last of his dynasty. A new dynasty—the Han—then established a vast empire that lasted over four hundred years (202 B.C. to A.D. 221). During the glory years of the Han dynasty, China extended the boundaries of its empire far into the sands of central Asia and southward along the coast of the South China Sea into what is modern-day Vietnam. Chinese culture appeared to be unrivaled. Its scientific and technological achievements also were unsurpassed (see "The Role of Science and Technology: Papermaking in Han China").

One reason for China's striking success was that unlike other civilizations during this time, China was able to fend off the danger from nomadic peoples along its northern frontier. By the end of the second century B.C., however, the presence of the Xiongnu

## THE ROLE OF SCIENCE AND TECHNOLOGY
# Papermaking in Han China

塘漂竹斬

◀ *This drawing shows some of the steps involved in Chinese papermaking. After workers collected bamboo, it was stripped of its leaves and soaked. Later, it was reduced to pulp, formed into sheets on mesh frames, and dried.*

▲ *A modern artisan demonstrates the ancient art of papermaking, invented in the Han dynasty.*

The ancient Chinese were a remarkably inventive people. They were responsible for four inventions that were crucial to the development of modern technology: the magnetic compass, paper, printing, and gunpowder. How to make paper was one of their early discoveries.

The oldest piece of paper found in China dates from the first century B.C. Made from hemp fibers, it was thick, rough, and useless for writing. That was not a problem for the ancient Chinese, however, because they preferred to write on bamboo or silk.

Around A.D. 100 paper that had writing on it began to appear. By this time, the Chinese had figured out how to make paper of better quality. After soaking hemp or linen rags in water, they were mixed with potash and mashed into a pulp. A frame with a fine bamboo mesh was lowered into this vat of pulp. The frame was then

removed, together with a thin sheet of pulp. Any extra water was removed. As seen in the illustration, the sheets of paper were then hung up to dry.

The art of papermaking spread eastward from China beginning in the seventh century A.D. First India and then the Arab world developed the technique. The Arab cities of Baghdad, Damascus, and Cairo (KIE-ROE) all had large papermaking industries. Paper was shipped from these centers to the West, but Europeans did not begin their production of paper until the twelfth century.

1. Why was Chinese papermaking called an art?

2. What is remarkable about the beginning of European production of paper?

was becoming a threat, and tribal warriors began to nip at the borders of the empire. While a dynasty was strong, the problem was manageable. When internal difficulties began to weaken the unity of the state, however, China became vulnerable to the threat from the north and entered a time of troubles.

The civilization of China is closely tied to Confucius, a philosopher who lived in the sixth century B.C. Confucius traveled the length of China observing events and seeking employment as a political counselor. He had little success in his job search and instead became a teacher to hundreds of students who sought his wise advice. He taught by asking questions and expected much of his students. As he said: "Only one who bursts with eagerness do I instruct; only one who bubbles with excitement, do I enlighten." Some of his students became ardent disciples of their teacher and recorded his sayings, which eventually became the guiding principles for the Chinese Empire. For thousands of years, Chinese children studied Confucian ideas. Also for thousands of years—until the twentieth century—Confucius's ideas continued to influence the ways of the Chinese people.

## 🌸 SECTION REVIEW 🌸

1. **Locate:**
   (*a*) Indus River valley,
   (*b*) South China Sea   (*c*) Han Empire

2. **Define:**
   (*a*) Brahman,   (*b*) Atman,   (*c*) reincarnation,
   (*d*) karma

3. **Identify:**
   (*a*) Harappan civilization,   (*b*) Aryans,
   (*c*) Siddhartha Gautama,   (*d*) Shang dynasty,
   (*e*) Zhou dynasty,   (*f*) mandate of Heaven,
   (*g*) Han dynasty,   (*h*) Confucius

4. **Recall:**
   (*a*) Which two of the world's greatest religions originated in India? Describe the source of each religion.
   (*b*) List two characteristics of the Mauryan and Gupta Empires.

5. **Think Critically:**
   (*a*) Why might China have developed later than other civilizations?
   (*b*) Both Siddhartha Gautama and Confucius traveled widely and became teachers. What similarities do you see in their philosophies as described in this section?

# THE CIVILIZATION OF THE GREEKS (1900 TO 133 B.C.)

During the Zhou dynasty in China, another great civilization took form on the northern shores of the Mediterranean Sea. The political and cultural achievements of ancient Greece were equal to any of the civilizations that came before it. These achievements would make a significant impact on the rest of the ancient world.

In 431 B.C., war erupted in Greece as two very different Greek states—Athens and Sparta—fought for domination of the Greek world. Strengthened by its democratic ideals, Athens felt secure behind its walls. In the first winter of the war, the Athenians held a public funeral to honor those who had died in battle. On the day of the ceremony, the citizens of Athens joined in a procession. The relatives of the dead wailed for their loved ones.

As was the custom in Athens, one leading citizen was asked to address the crowd. On this day it was Pericles who spoke to the people. He talked about the greatness of Athens and reminded the Athenians of the strength of their political system. "Our constitution," Pericles said, "is called a democracy because power is in the hands not of a minority but of the whole people. When it is a question of settling private disputes, everyone is equal before the law. Just as our political life is free and open, so is our day-to-day life in our relations with each other. . . . Here each individual is interested not only in his own affairs but in the affairs of the state as well."

**Map 1.5    Classical Greece**

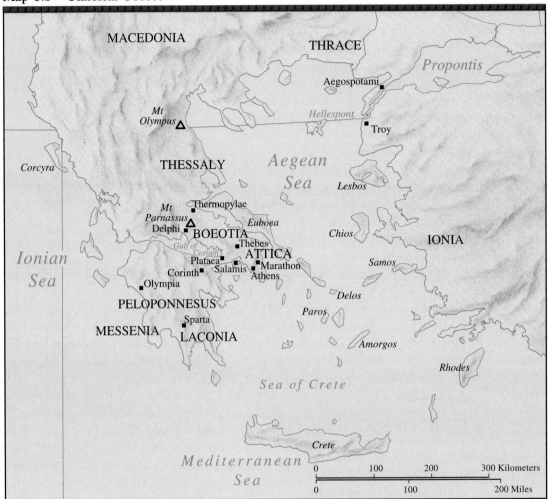

In this famous Funeral Oration, Pericles gave voice to the ideal of democracy and the importance of the individual. The Greeks laid the intellectual foundations of Western civilization. They asked some basic questions about human life that we still ask today: What is the nature of the universe? What is the purpose of human life? What is our relationship with divine forces? What is a community? What is a state? What is true education? What is truth itself, and how do we realize it? The Greeks not only gave answers to these questions but also created a system of logical, analytical thought in order to examine them. We in the Western world still regard this system of thought as worthwhile.

## The World of the Greek City-States

By the eighth century B.C., the city-state, or what the Greeks called a **polis,** became the central focus of Greek life. Our word *politics* is derived from the Greek word *polis*. In a physical sense, the polis was a town, city, or even a village, along with its surrounding countryside. The town, city, or village served as the central point where the citizens of the polis could meet for political, social, and religious activities. The central meeting point was usually a hill, such as the Acropolis at Athens. An **acropolis** (usually the upper fortified part of a city or town) served as a place of refuge during an attack and sometimes came to be the religious center on which temples and public buildings were built. Below the acropolis would be an **agora,** an open place that served both as a place where citizens could assemble and as a market.

City-states varied greatly in size, from a few square miles to a few hundred square miles. They also varied in population. Athens had a population of over 300,000 by the fifth century B.C. Most city-states were much smaller, consisting of only a few hundred to several thousand people.

The polis was, above all, a community of citizens who shared a common identity and common goals. As a community, the polis consisted of citizens with political rights (adult males), citizens with no political rights (women and children), and noncitizens (slaves and resident aliens). All citizens of a polis had rights, but these rights were coupled with responsibilities. The Greek philosopher Aristotle argued that a citizen did not just belong to himself or herself. According to Aristotle, "we must rather regard every citizen as belonging to the state." However, the loyalty that citizens had to their city-states also had a negative side. City-states distrusted one another. The division of Greece into fiercely patriotic independent units helped to bring about its ruin.

In the seventh and sixth centuries B.C., many Greek states fell under the control of tyrants. They were not necessarily oppressive or wicked, as our word *tyrant* implies. Greek tyrants were rulers who seized power by force and who were not subject to the law. Support for the tyrants came from the new rich who made their money in trade and industry, as well as from poor peasants who were in debt to landholding aristocrats (an upper-class person whose wealth is based on land and whose power is passed on from one generation to another). Both groups were tired of the domination of their city-states by the aristocrats.

Tyrants gained power and kept it by using mercenaries, or hired soldiers. Once in power, the tyrants built new marketplaces, temples, and walls. These constructions glorified the city but, more important, increased the tyrants' own popularity. Tyrants also favored the interests of merchants and traders. By the end of the sixth century B.C., tyrants fell out of favor.

Greeks believed in the rule of law, and tyranny (the rule by tyrants) made a mockery of that ideal.

Although tyranny did not last, it did play an important role in Greek history. The rule of the tyrants had ended the rule of the aristocrats in many city-states. The end of tyranny opened the door to new and more people in government and, in some Greek city-states, to the development of **democracy** (rule of the many). Other city-states remained committed to rule by an **oligarchy** (rule by the few). We can see the differences in how Greek city-states were governed by examining the two most famous and most powerful Greek city-states, Sparta and Athens.

### Sparta

Like other Greek city-states, Sparta was faced with the need for more land. Unlike other Greek states, which solved their problem by sending people out to new colonies, Sparta conquered the neighboring state of Messenia despite its larger size and population. After the conquest of Messenia around 740 B.C., Sparta made the Messenians, although greatly outnumbered by them (7 to 1), their serfs. Known as helots, these serfs were forced to work the land for the benefit of the Spartans. In the seventh century B.C., the Messenians revolted. Sparta crushed the revolt, but the struggle was so long and hard that the Spartans made a decision. They would create a military state so that their warriors could control Messenia for ages to come.

After 600 B.C., the Spartans transformed their state into a military camp. The lives of Spartans were rigidly organized and tightly controlled (thus, our word *spartan,* meaning "highly self-disciplined"). After a childhood of military discipline (see "Young People in Greece: The Spartan and Athenian Models"), Spartan males were enrolled in the army for regular military service at age twenty. Although allowed to marry, they continued to live in the military barracks. All meals were eaten in public dining halls with fellow soldiers. Meals were simple; the famous Spartan black broth consisted of a piece of pork boiled in blood, salt, and vinegar. A visitor who ate the black broth in a public mess once remarked that he now understood why Spartans were not afraid to die. At thirty, Spartan males

## YOUNG PEOPLE IN GREECE

# The Spartan and Athenian Models

Spartans and Athenians were both Greeks, but they had very different political systems. They also differed on how to raise their young people.

In Sparta, boys were trained to be soldiers. At birth, each child was examined by state officials, who decided whether the child was fit to live. Those who were judged unfit were left in the open on a mountainside to die. Boys judged to be fit were taken from their mothers at the age of seven and put under control of the state. They lived in military-style barracks, where they were subjected to harsh discipline to make them tough and mean. Their education stressed military training and obedience to authority. The Greek historian Plutarch (PLOO-tark) gave a vivid description of the handling of young Spartans:

*After they were twelve years old, they were no longer allowed to wear any undergarments, they had one coat to serve them a year; their bodies were hard and dry, with but little acquaintance of baths; these human indulgences they were allowed*

◄ *In Sparta girls and boys were trained to be athletes, as is shown in this bronze statue, which was part of a vase lid. How might the lives of girls raised in Athens have differed from those raised in Sparta?*

*only on some few particular days in the year. They lodged together in little bands upon beds made of the rushes which grew by the banks of the river Eurotas, which they were to break off with their hands with a knife. . . .*

*[Spartan boys were also encouraged to steal their food.] They stole, too, all other meat they could lay their hands on, looking out and watching all opportunities, when people were asleep or more careless than usual. If they were caught, they were not only punished with whipping, but hunger, too, being reduced to their ordinary allowance, which was but very slender, and so contrived on purpose, that they might set about to help themselves, and be forced to exercise their energy and address. This was the principal design of their hard fare.*

were allowed to vote in the assembly and live at home, but they stayed in the army until the age of sixty.

While their husbands remained in military barracks until age thirty, Spartan women lived at home. Because of this separation, Spartan women had greater freedom of movement and greater power in the household than was common elsewhere in Greece. Spartan women were expected to exercise and remain fit to bear and raise healthy children. Many Spartan women upheld

the strict Spartan values, expecting their husbands and sons to be brave in war. The story is told that as a Spartan mother was burying her son, an old woman came up to her and said, "You poor woman, what a misfortune." "No," replied the other, "because I bore him so that he might die for Sparta and that is what has happened, as I wished." Another Spartan woman, as she was handing her son his shield, told him to come back carrying his shield or be carried on it.

## YOUNG PEOPLE IN GREECE

# The Spartan and Athenian Models, continued

Basically, the Spartan system worked. Spartan males were known for their toughness and their meanness. They were also known as the best soldiers in all of Greece.

Spartan girls received an education similar to that of the boys. Girls, too, underwent physical training, including running, wrestling, and throwing the javelin. The purpose was clear: to strengthen the girls for their roles as healthy mothers. Like the boys, they exercised naked in public, an activity considered shocking to other Greeks.

Well-to-do Athenian citizens raised their children very differently. Athenian children were carefully nurtured by their mothers until the age of seven. At seven, a boy of the upper class was turned over to a male servant, known as a pedagogue, who became the child's constant companion until his late teens. The pedagogue, who was usually a slave, accompanied the child to school. He was also responsible for teaching his charge good manners. He could punish the child with a birch rod to impose discipline.

The purpose of an education for upper-class Athenian boys was to create a well-rounded person. To that end, a boy had three teachers. One taught him reading, writing, and arithmetic. Another taught physical education, a necessity to achieve the ideal of a sound mind in a sound body. A third taught him music, which consisted of playing the lyre (a stringed instrument) and singing. To Greeks, music was considered an important way to create balance and harmony. Education ended at eighteen, when an Athenian male formally became a citizen.

Formal education in ancient Athens was only for boys. Girls of all classes remained at home, as their mothers did. Their mothers taught them how to run a home, which included how to spin and weave—all activities expected of a good wife. Only in some wealthy families did girls learn to read, write, and even play the lyre.

1. Describe a Spartan upbringing.

2. Compare a well-educated Spartan boy with a well-educated Athenian.

3. Does your education today incorporate any Spartan and/or Athenian ideas? Which ones?

The Spartan government was headed by two kings, who led the Spartan army on its campaigns. A group of five men, known as the ephors, were elected each year and were responsible for the education of youth and the conduct of all citizens. A council of elders, composed of the two kings and twenty-eight citizens, all of whom were required to be over the age of sixty, decided on the issues that would be presented to an assembly. This assembly, which consisted exclusively of male citizens, did not debate. It only voted on the issues put before it by the council of elders.

To make their new military state secure, the Spartans turned their backs on the outside world. Foreigners, who might bring in new ideas, were discouraged from visiting Sparta. Furthermore, except for military reasons, Spartans were not allowed to travel abroad, where they might pick up new ideas that might be dangerous to the stability of the state. Likewise, Spartan citizens were discouraged from studying philosophy, literature, or the arts—subjects that might encourage new thoughts. The art of war was the Spartan ideal. All other arts were frowned upon.

### Athens

By 700 B.C., Athens had become a unified polis on the peninsula of Attica. Early Athens was ruled by a king. By the seventh century B.C., however, Athens had become an oligarchy when it fell under the control of its aristocrats. They owned the best land and controlled political life by means of a council of nobles, assisted by a board of nine archons (rulers). Although there was an assembly of all the citizens, it had few powers.

Near the end of the seventh century B.C., Athens faced political turmoil because of serious economic problems. Many Athenian farmers found themselves sold into slavery when they were unable to repay their debts to their aristocratic neighbors. Over and over, there were cries to cancel the debts and give land to the poor. Athens seemed on the verge of civil war.

The ruling Athenian aristocrats reacted to this crisis in 594 B.C. by giving full power to Solon, a reform-minded aristocrat, to make changes. Solon canceled all land debts and freed people who had fallen into slavery for debts. He refused, however, to take land from the rich and give it to the poor. Solon's reforms, though popular, did not solve the problems of Athens. Aristocrats were still powerful, and poor peasants could not get land. It was not until 508 B.C. that another reformer, Cleisthenes, gained the upper hand.

Cleisthenes, first of all, created a new council of five hundred that supervised foreign affairs and the treasury and proposed the laws that would be voted on by the assembly. The Athenian assembly, composed of all male citizens, was given final authority to pass laws after free and open debate. The assembly of citizens now had the central role in the Athenian political system. Thus, the reforms of Cleisthenes had created the foundations for Athenian democracy.

Under Pericles, who was a dominant figure in Athenian politics between 461 and 429 B.C., Athenian democracy flourished. This period of Athenian and

▲ *The Parthenon, which was built between 447 and 432 B.C., still stands on the Acropolis in Athens. Its classical beauty and symmetry symbolize the power and wealth of the Athenian Empire.*

Greek history, which historians have called the Age of Pericles, saw the height of Athenian power and the brilliance of Athens as a civilization.

In the Age of Pericles, the Athenians became deeply attached to their democratic system. The will of the people was expressed in the assembly, which consisted of all male citizens over eighteen years of age. In the mid-fifth century B.C., that was probably a group of about forty-three thousand. Meetings of the assembly were held every ten days on a hillside east of the Acropolis. Not all attended, and the number present seldom reached six thousand. The assembly passed all laws, elected public officials, and made final decisions on war and foreign policy. Anyone could speak, but usually only respected leaders did so.

Pericles also expanded the involvement of Athenians in their democracy. He made lower-class citizens eligible for public offices that formerly had been closed to them. By paying officeholders, including those who served on the large Athenian juries, he made it possible for poor citizens to take part in public affairs. Pericles believed that Athenians should be proud of their democracy (see "You Are There: Pericles Speaks to the Athenian People").

A large body of city officials ran the government on a daily basis. Ten officials, known as generals, were the

YOU ARE THERE

# Pericles Speaks to the Athenian People

*In his* History of the Peloponnesian War, *the Greek historian Thucydides presented his account of the speech given by Pericles to honor the Athenians killed in the first campaigns of the Great Peloponnesian War. It is a magnificent, idealized description of the Athenian democracy at its height.*

**Thucydides, *History of the Peloponnesian War***

Our constitution is called a democracy because power is in the hands not of a minority but of the whole people. When it is a question of settling private disputes, everyone is equal before the law; when it is a question of putting one person before another in positions of public responsibility, what counts is not membership in a particular class, but the actual ability which the man possesses. No one, so long as he has it in him to be of service to the state, is kept in political obscurity because of poverty. And, just as our political life is free and open, so is our day-to-day life in our relations with each other. We do not get into a state with our next-door neighbor if he enjoys himself in his own way, nor do we give him the kind of black looks which, though they do no real harm, still do hurt people's feelings. We are free and tolerant in our private lives; but in public affairs we keep to the law. This is because it commands our deep respect. . . .

Here each individual is interested not only in his own affairs but in the affairs of the state as

◄ *For Pericles, shown here, the democratic system that prevailed in Athens was of major importance, and he worked diligently to increase participation in civic affairs. During his rule, the Athenian empire flourished and grew. Do you think leaders can be both democratic and imperialistic?*

well: even those who are mostly occupied with their own business are extremely well-informed on general politics—this is a peculiarity of ours: we do not say that a man who takes no interest in politics is a man who minds his own business; we say that he has no business here at all. . . . Taking everything together then, I declare that our city is an education to Greece.

1. How was Athens "an education to Greece"?

2. What does Pericles say are the rights and responsibilities of Athenian citizens?

3. Would an ideal Athenian citizen make a good modern-day American citizen? Why or why not?

---

overall directors of policy. The generals could be reelected, making it possible for individual leaders to play an important political role. Pericles, for example, was elected to the generalship thirty times between 461 and 429 B.C. The Athenians, however, also devised the practice of **ostracism** to protect themselves against overly ambitious politicians. In this practice, members of the assembly could write on a broken pottery frag-

## CONNECTIONS
### AROUND THE WORLD

**Rulers and Gods**   All of the world's earliest civilizations believed that there was a close connection between rulers and gods. In Egypt, pharaohs were considered gods whose role was to maintain the order and harmony of the universe in their own kingdoms. In Mesopotamia, India, and China, rulers were thought to rule with divine assistance. Kings were often seen as rulers who derived their power from the gods and who were the agents or representatives of the gods. Many Romans certainly believed that their success in creating an empire was a visible sign of divine favor. As one Roman stated, "We have overcome all the nations of the world, because we have realized that the world is directed and governed by the gods."

The rulers' supposed connection to the divine also caused them to seek divine aid in the affairs of the world. This led to the art of divination, or an organized method to figure out the intentions of the gods. In Mesopotamian and Roman society, divination took the form of examining the livers of sacrificed animals or the flights of birds to determine the will of the gods. The Chinese used oracle (ORE-eh-cul) bones to receive advice from the gods. The Greeks divined the will of the gods by use of the oracle, a sacred shrine dedicated to a god or goddess who revealed the future. Underlying all of these practices was a belief in a supernatural universe; that is, a world in which divine forces were in charge and in which humans were dependent for their own well-being on those divine forces. It was not until the Scientific Revolution of the modern world that many people began to believe in a natural world that was not governed by spiritual forces.

ment (*ostrakon*) the name of a person they considered harmful to the city. A person who received at least six thousand votes was banned from the city for ten years.

Under Pericles, Athens became the leading center of Greek culture. New temples and statues soon made vis-

ible the greatness of Athens. Art and architecture flourished. Pericles boasted that Athens had become the "school of Greece." The achievements of three Athenian philosophers—Socrates, Plato, and Aristotle—have been especially important to Western culture.

## The Greek Love of Wisdom

**Philosophy** (an organized system of thought) is a Greek word that means "love of wisdom." Early Greek philosophers were concerned with the development of critical or rational thought about the nature of the universe and the place of divine forces in it. Socrates, Plato, and Aristotle remain to this day three of the greatest philosophers of the Western world.

Because he left no writings, we know about Socrates only from his pupils. Socrates was a stonemason, but his true love was philosophy. He taught a number of pupils, although not for pay, because he believed that the goal of education was only to improve the individual. He made use of a teaching technique with his students that is still known by his name. The **Socratic method** of teaching uses a question-and-answer approach to lead pupils to see things for themselves by using their own reason. Socrates believed that all real knowledge is already present within each person. Only critical examination is needed to call it forth. This was the real task of philosophy, because "the unexamined life is not worth living." This belief in the individual's ability to reason was an important contribution of the Greeks.

Socrates questioned authority, and this soon led him into trouble. Athens had had a tradition of free thought and inquiry, but defeat in war changed the Athenians. They no longer trusted open debate and soul-searching. Socrates was accused and convicted of corrupting the youth of Athens by teaching them to question and think for themselves. An Athenian jury sentenced him to death.

One of Socrates' students was Plato, considered by many the greatest philosopher of Western civilization. Unlike his master Socrates, who did not write down his thoughts, Plato wrote a great deal. He set out his ideas of government in his work entitled *The Republic*. Based on his experience in Athens, Plato had come to distrust the workings of democracy. It was obvious to him that individuals could not achieve a good life unless they lived in a just and rational state.

Plato's search for the just state led him to construct an ideal state in which people were divided into three basic groups. At the top was an upper class of philosopher-kings: "Unless either philosophers become kings in their countries or those who are now called kings and rulers come to be sufficiently inspired with a genuine desire for wisdom; unless, that is to say, political power and philosophy meet together . . . there can be no rest from troubles . . . for states, nor for all mankind."[4] The second group in Plato's ideal were those who showed courage. They would be the warriors who protected society. All the rest made up the masses, who were people driven not by wisdom or courage but by desire. They would be the producers of society—the artisans, tradespeople, and farmers. Contrary to common Greek custom, Plato also believed that men and women should have the same education and equal access to all positions.

Plato established a school at Athens known as the Academy. One of his pupils, who studied there for twenty years, was Aristotle. Aristotle's interests lay in analyzing and classifying things based on observation and investigation. His interests were wide ranging. He wrote works on an enormous number of subjects, including ethics, logic, politics, poetry, astronomy, geology, biology, and physics. Until the seventeenth century, science in the Western world remained largely based on Aristotle's thinking.

Like Plato, Aristotle wanted an effective form of government that would rationally direct human affairs. Unlike Plato, he did not seek an ideal state but tried to find the best form of government by analyzing existing governments. For his *Politics*, Aristotle looked at the constitutions of 158 states and found three good forms of government: monarchy, aristocracy, and constitutional government. Based on his examination, however, he warned that monarchy can easily turn into

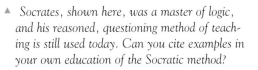

▲ *Socrates, shown here, was a master of logic, and his reasoned, questioning method of teaching is still used today. Can you cite examples in your own education of the Socratic method?*

tyranny, aristocracy into oligarchy, and constitutional government into radical democracy or anarchy. He favored constitutional government as the best form for most people.

The civilization of the ancient Greeks was the principal source of Western culture. Socrates, Plato, and Aristotle established the foundations of Western philosophy. Western literary forms are largely derived from Greek poetry and drama.

The Greek notions of harmony, proportion, and beauty have remained the touchstones for all subsequent Western art and architecture. A rational method of inquiry, so important to modern science, was conceived in ancient Greece. Many political terms are Greek in origin. So are concepts of the rights and duties of citizenship, especially as they were conceived in Athens, the first great democracy the world had seen.

## ❀ SECTION REVIEW ❀

1. **Locate:**
   (*a*) Greece,   (*b*) Athens,   (*c*) Sparta,
   (*d*) Attica

2. **Define:**
   (*a*) polis,   (*b*) acropolis,   (*c*) agora,
   (*d*) democracy,   (*e*) oligarchy,   (*f*) ostracism,
   (*g*) philosophy,   (*h*) Socratic method

3. **Identify:**
   (*a*) Aristotle,   (*b*) Solon,   (*c*) Cleisthenes,
   (*d*) Age of Pericles,   (*e*) Socrates,   (*f*) Plato,
   (*g*) *The Republic*

4. **Recall:**

(*a*) What were the roles of the Spartan kings, assembly, and council of elders?

(*b*) List two ways in which Pericles involved the Athenians in government.

(*c*) According to Socrates, what was the task of philosophy?

(*d*) List the three basic groups in Plato's ideal state.

(*e*) List Aristotle's three "good forms of government."

5. **Think Critically:** Plato divided society into three basic groups when describing an ideal state. If you were to describe an ideal state, what basic groups would you choose? Why?

## THE WORLD OF THE ROMANS (600 B.C. TO A.D. 500)

The Greeks made a strong impact on the Romans, who did not hesitate to borrow their ideas and culture. Early Roman history is filled with legendary stories that tell of the heroes who made Rome great. One of the best known is the story of Horatius at the bridge. Threatened by attack from the neighboring Etruscans, Roman farmers abandoned their fields and moved into the city of Rome, where they would be protected by the city's walls. One weak point in the Roman defense was a wooden bridge over the Tiber River. On the day of the Etruscan attack, Horatius was on guard at the bridge. A sudden attack by the Etruscans caused many Roman troops to throw away their weapons and run. Horatius acted promptly, urging them to make a stand at the bridge in order to protect Rome. As a last resort, he challenged the Roman troops to destroy the bridge while he made a stand at the outer end to give them more time.

At first, the Etruscans held back, astonished at the sight of a single defender. Soon, however, they threw their spears at the lone figure who barred their way. Horatius caught the spears on his shield and held his ground. The Etruscans advanced on foot, ready to overwhelm the sole figure. However, the Roman soldiers had used the extra time to bring down the bridge. When Horatius heard the sound of the bridge crashing into the river behind him, he dove, fully armed, into the water and swam, despite the arrows that fell around him. He safely reached the other side. Rome had been saved by the courageous act of a Roman who knew his duty and was determined to carry it out.

Courage, duty, determination—these were common words to many Romans, who believed that it was their mission to rule nations and peoples. Whereas the Greeks had excelled in philosophy and the arts, the Romans were practical people. Their strength lay in government, law, and engineering. They knew how to govern people, make laws, and build the roads that took them to the ends of the known world. Throughout their empire, they carried their political institutions, their law, their building skills, and their Latin language. Even after the Romans were gone, those same gifts continued to play an important role in the civilizations that came after them.

### The Roman State

In law and politics, as in conquest, the Romans were practical. They did not try to build an ideal government but instead fashioned political institutions in response to problems as they arose. The

◀ *This bronze figure of a legionnaire shows him in full battle dress at the height of the Roman Empire during the second century A.D. Here, his armor is constructed of metal bands that overlap each other. Roman legionnaires were both courageous and resolute in their duty. What differences are immediately visible between Greek hoplite forces and Roman legionnaires?*

◄ *In this mosaic found in the ruins of Pompeii, a wealthy Roman woman is pictured at her dressing table. Several female slaves help her dress, while others carry refreshments in for her.*

Romans had a distrust of kingship and of one sole ruler, so they devised a sophisticated system of government.

The chief executive officers of the Roman Republic were the **consuls** and **praetors.** Two consuls, chosen every year, ran the government and led the Roman army into battle. In 366 B.C., a new office, that of the praetor, was created. The praetor was in charge of civil law (law as it applied to Roman citizens). As the Romans' territory expanded, they added another praetor to judge cases in which one or both people were noncitizens.

The Roman **Senate** came to hold an especially important position in the Roman Republic. It was a select group of about three hundred landowning men who served for life. At first, its only role was to advise government officials. However, the advice of the Senate was not taken lightly, and by the third century B.C. it had the force of law.

The Roman Republic had a number of popular assemblies. By far the most important was the **centuriate assembly.** Organized by classes based on wealth, it was fixed in such a way that the wealthiest citizens always had a majority. The centuriate assembly elected the chief officials and passed laws. However, another assembly, the council of the plebs, came into being in 471 B.C. as a result of internal struggle.

This conflict arose as a result of the division of early Rome into two groups—the **patricians** and the **plebeians.** The patricians were great landowners, who became Rome's ruling class. Only they could be consuls, other officials, and senators. The considerably larger numbers of less wealthy landholders, craftspeople, merchants, and small farmers were called plebeians. They, too, were citizens, but they did not have the same rights as the patricians. Both patricians and plebeians could vote, but only the patricians could be elected to governmental offices. Patricians and plebeians were forbidden to marry each other. Plebeians fought in the Roman army. As a result, they thought that they deserved both political and social equality with the patricians.

The rivalry between the patricians and plebeians dragged on for hundreds of years, but it led to success for the plebeians. A popular assembly for plebeians only, called the **council of the plebs,** was created in 471 B.C. New officials, known as **tribunes of the plebs,** were given the power to protect plebeians. A new law allowed marriages between patricians and plebeians. In the fourth century B.C., plebeians were permitted to become consuls. Finally, in 287 B.C., the council of the plebs received the right to pass laws for all Romans.

The struggle between the patricians and the plebeians had a significant impact on the development of the Roman state. Plebeians could hold the highest offices of state, they could intermarry with the patricians, and they could pass laws that were binding on the entire Roman community. By 287 B.C., all Roman citizens were supposedly equal under the law. In reality, however, a select number of wealthy patrician and plebeian families formed a new senatorial ruling class that came to dominate the political offices. The Roman Republic had not become a democracy.

## Roman Law

One of Rome's chief gifts to the Mediterranean world of its day and to later generations was its system of law. The Twelve Tables of 450 B.C. was Rome's first code of laws. It was a product of a simple farming society, however, and proved inadequate for later Roman needs. Nevertheless, from the Twelve Tables the Romans developed a system of civil law that applied only to Roman citizens.

As Rome expanded, Romans became involved in problems involving both Romans and non-Romans, as well as problems involving only non-Romans. The Romans found that although some of their rules of civil law could be used in these cases, special rules were often needed. These rules gave rise to a body of law known as the law of nations, defined by the Romans as "that part of the law which we apply both to ourselves and to foreigners." The Romans came to identify their law of nations with natural law, or universal law based on reason. This enabled them to establish standards of justice that applied to all people.

These standards of justice included principles that we would immediately recognize. A person was regarded as innocent until proven otherwise. People accused of wrongdoing were allowed to defend themselves before a judge. A judge, in turn, was expected to weigh evidence carefully before arriving at a decision. These principles lived on long after the fall of the Roman Empire.

## From Republic to Empire

According to tradition, Rome became a republic in 509 B.C. Between 509 and 264 B.C., the expansion of this city led to the union of almost all of what is today Italy under Rome's control. Even more dramatic is the fact that between 264 and 133 B.C., Rome expanded to the west and east and became master of the Mediterranean Sea. Rome's republican institutions, however, proved inadequate for ruling an empire.

After a series of bloody civil wars, Augustus created a new order that began the Roman Empire. Between A.D. 14 and 180, the Roman Empire experienced a lengthy period of peace and prosperity. Trade flourished, and the provinces were ruled in an orderly fashion. There was, however, an enormous gulf between rich and poor. The upper classes enjoyed lives of great leisure and luxury in their villas and on their vast estates (see "Focus on Everyday Life: The Banquets of the Rich"). Many small farmers became dependent on the huge estates of their wealthy neighbors. In the cities, many poor citizens worked in shops and markets. There were also thousands of unemployed who depended on the emperor's handouts of grain to survive.

The Roman Empire was one of the largest empires in antiquity. Using their practical skills, the Romans made achievements in law, government, language, and engineering that were passed on and that became an important part of Western civilization. The Romans also preserved the intellectual heritage of the Greek world.

After A.D. 200, however, a slow transformation of the Roman world took place. Invasions by Germanic peoples hastened this process and brought an end to the Western Roman Empire in 476. Many aspects of the Roman world would continue. However, a new civilization, which we will examine in Chapter 2, was emerging in western Europe that would usher in yet another stage in the development of human society. A

## FOCUS ON EVERYDAY LIFE
# The Banquets of the Rich

*Wealthy Roman homes contained a formal dining room, the scene of the dinner parties that were the chief feature of Roman social life. The banquet usually consisted of three courses: the appetizers, main course, and dessert. As the following menu from a cookbook by Apicius illustrates, each course included an enormous variety of unusual foods. Banquets lasted an entire evening. They were accompanied by entertainment provided by acrobats, musicians, dancers, and even poets. People usually ate reclining on couches. It was not considered improper for diners to vomit after each course so they could have room enough for the next course. Naturally, the diet of lower-class Romans was much different. It consisted of the basics: bread, olives, and grapes. Poorer Romans ate little meat.*

▲ *This painting gives an idea of how lavish the Roman banquets of the rich could be. The poor in the Roman Empire served, while the rich enjoyed their wealth.*

### A Sample Banquet Menu

#### Appetizers
Jellyfish and eggs
Sow's udders stuffed with salted sea urchins
Patina of brains cooked with milk and eggs
Boiled tree fungi with peppered fish-fat sauce
Sea urchins with spices, honey, oil, and egg sauce

#### Main Course
Fallow deer roasted with onion sauce and rue
Jericho dates, raisins, oil, and honey
Boiled ostrich with sweet sauce
Turtle dove boiled in its feathers
Roast parrot
Dormice stuffed with pork and pine kernels
Ham boiled with figs and bay leaves, rubbed with
honey, baked in pastry crust
Flamingo boiled with dates

#### Dessert
Fricassee of roses with pastry
Stoned dates stuffed with nuts and pine kernels
fried in honey
Hot African sweet-wine cakes with honey

1. What does the wide variety of foods suggest about the geographical location of Rome?

2. Explain the differences in the diets of the rich and the poor. Do those differences still exist today?

**Map 1.6    The Roman Empire from A.D. 14 to 117**

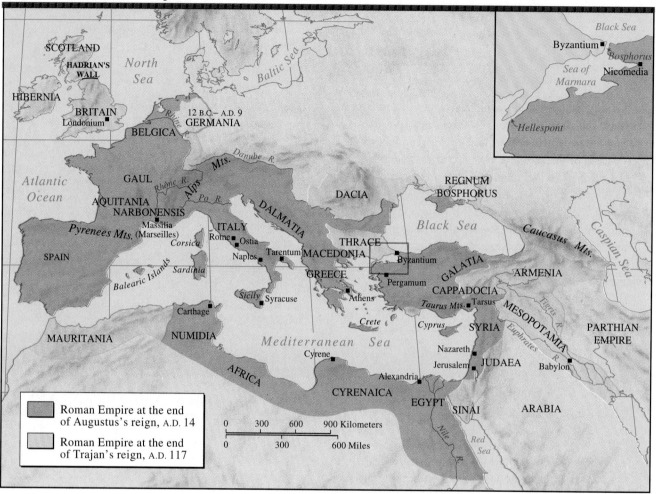

major factor in the transformation of the Roman Empire was the growth of Christianity.

## The Development of Christianity

Jesus—a Palestinian Jew—grew up in Galilee, in the Roman Empire. His message was simple. He told his fellow Jews that he did not plan to harm their traditional religion: "Do not think that I have come to abolish the Law or the Prophets; I have not come to abolish them but to fulfill them."[5] According to Jesus, what was important was not strict adherence to the letter of the law but the transformation of the inner person: "So

in everything, do to others what you would have them do to you, for this sums up the Law and the Prophets."[6] God's command was a simple one: to love God and one another: "Love the Lord your God with all your heart and with all your soul and with all your mind and with all your strength. The second is this: Love your neighbor as yourself."[7] In the Sermon on the Mount (see "Our Literary Heritage: The Sermon on the Mount"), Jesus voiced the ethical concepts—humility, charity, and love toward others—that would form the basis for the value system of medieval Western civilization.

Some people welcomed Jesus as the Messiah, who would save Israel from oppression and establish God's

▶ *This fresco showing Christ and his disciples was found in the catacombs of Rome and then transferred to the Church of San Lorenzo in Milan. Through the work of these disciples, particularly Paul of Tarsus, Christianity grew to be the dominant religion in the Roman Empire and in Europe.*

kingdom on Earth. However, Jesus spoke of a heavenly kingdom, not an earthly one: "My kingdom is not of this world."[8] As a result, he disappointed the radicals. He also alienated conservative religious leaders, who believed Jesus was undermining respect for traditional Jewish religion. To the Roman authorities of Palestine, Jesus was a potential revolutionary who might lead Jews into a revolt against Rome. Therefore, Jesus found himself denounced by the leadership on all sides and was given over to the Roman authorities. The Roman leader Pontius Pilate ordered his crucifixion. That did not solve the problem, however. Loyal followers of Jesus believed that he had overcome death and come back to life. He was called *Christos*, or "the anointed one," and hailed as the savior who had come to reveal the secrets of personal immortality.

The basic values of Christianity differed markedly from those of the Greco-Roman world. The Romans, however, did not pay much attention to the Christians, whom they regarded at first as simply members of another sect of Judaism. The structure of the Roman Empire itself aided the growth of Christianity. Christian missionaries, including some of Jesus' original twelve disciples or apostles, used Roman roads to travel throughout the empire in spreading the gospel (or the "good news").

As time passed, however, the Roman attitude toward Christianity began to change. The Romans tolerated other religions except when they threatened public order or public morals. Many Romans came to view Christians as harmful to the Roman state, especially because Christians held their meetings in secret. The Romans persecuted Christians in the first and second centuries, but never on a regular basis. Persecution began during the reign of Nero in the first century. The emperor blamed the Christians for a fire that destroyed much of Rome. He accused them of arson and subjected them to cruel deaths. In the second century, Christians were largely ignored as harmless. The occasional persecution of Christians by the Romans in the first and second centuries did nothing to stop the growth of Christianity. In fact, the persecution served to strengthen Christianity in the second and third centuries by forcing it to become more organized.

Christianity grew slowly in the first century, took root in the second, and by the third had spread widely. Why was Christianity able to attract so many followers? First, the Christian message had much to offer the

## OUR LITERARY HERITAGE

# The Sermon on the Mount

*The four Gospels of the New Testament are sacred books to Christians, but they are also great literature and an important part of the literary heritage of Western civilization. Written originally in Greek, they were later translated into Latin. Jesus' Sermon on the Mount is taken from the Gospel of Saint Matthew. As these excerpts illustrate, in the Sermon Jesus emphasized humility, charity, love for others, and a belief in the inner being and a spiritual kingdom superior to this material world. These values and principles were not those of classical Greco-Roman civilization as seen in the words and deeds of its leaders. Thus, they were an important part of Christianity's appeal to the poor and powerless.*

**The Gospel According to Saint Matthew**

Now when he saw the crowds, he went up on a mountainside and sat down. His disciples came to him, and he began to teach them saying:
Blessed are the poor in spirit: for theirs is the kingdom of heaven.
Blessed are those who mourn: for they will be comforted.
Blessed are the meek: for they will inherit the earth.
Blessed are those who hunger and thirst for righteousness: for they will be filled.

Blessed are the merciful: for they will be shown mercy.
Blessed are the pure in heart: for they will see God.
Blessed are the peacemakers: for they will be called sons of God.
Blessed are those who are persecuted because of righteousness: for theirs is the kingdom of heaven. . . .

You have heard that it was said, "Eye for eye, and tooth for tooth." But I tell you, Do not resist an evil person. If someone strikes you on the right cheek, turn to him the other also. . . .
You have heard that it was said, "Love your neighbor, and hate your enemy." But I tell you, Love your enemies and pray for those who persecute you. . . .
Do not store up for yourselves treasures on earth, where moth and rust destroy, and where thieves break in and steal. But store up for yourselves treasures in heaven, where moth and rust do not destroy, and where thieves do not break in and steal. For where your treasure is, there your heart will be also. . . .
No one can serve two masters. Either he will hate the one and love the other, or he will be devoted to the one and despise the other. You cannot serve both God and money.

Roman world. The promise of salvation, which Christians believed was made possible by Jesus' death, made a strong impact on a world full of suffering and injustice. Christianity gave life a meaning and purpose beyond the simple material things of everyday reality. Second, Christianity seemed familiar. It was viewed by some as another mystery religion, offering immortality as the result of the sacrificial death of a savior-god. At the same time, it offered more than the other mystery religions did. Jesus had been a human figure who was easy to relate to. Moreover, Christianity did not require a painful or expensive initiation rite, as other mystery religions did. Initiation was by baptism—a purification by water—by which one entered into a personal

## OUR LITERARY HERITAGE

## The Sermon on the Mount, continued

Therefore I tell you, do not worry about your life, what you will eat or drink; or about your body, what you will wear. Is not life more important than food, and the body more important than clothes? Look at the birds of the air; they do not sow or reap or store away in barns, and yet your heavenly Father feeds them. Are you not much more valuable than they? . . . So do not worry, saying, What shall we eat? or What shall we drink? or What shall we wear? For the pagans run after all these things, and your heavenly Father knows that you need them. But seek first his kingdom and his righteousness, and all these things will be given to you as well.

1. What are the ideals of early Christianity?

2. How do Christian values differ from the principles of classical Greco-Roman civilization?

▲ *This illustrated page from an early Bible, c. A.D. 700, shows Saint Matthew. What features indicate that he is considered a saint?*

relationship with Jesus Christ. In addition, Christianity gave new meaning to life and offered what the Roman state religions could not—a personal relationship with God.

Finally, Christianity fulfilled the human need to belong. Christians formed closely knit communities in which people could express their love by helping one another and offering assistance to the poor, the sick, widows, and orphans. Christianity satisfied the need to belong in a way that the huge Roman Empire could never do.

Christianity proved attractive to all classes, but especially to the poor and powerless. The promise of eternal life was for all—rich, poor, aristocrats, slaves,

▶ *The importance of baptism as a Christian rite of initiation is represented in this illustration of Clovis, a Frankish King. Clovis had long resisted Christianity, until, on the verge of losing an important battle, he cried out, "Jesus Christ, if you shall grant me victory over these enemies, I will believe in you and be baptized." After he had uttered these words, the enemy began to flee, and Clovis became a Christian.*

men, and women. As Paul stated in his Epistle to the Colossians: "And [you] have put on the new self. . . . Here there is no Greek nor Jew . . . barbarian, Scythian, slave or free, but Christ is all, and is in all."9 Although Christianity did not call for revolution, it stressed a sense of spiritual equality for all people.

In the third century, some emperors began new persecutions of the Christians, but their schemes failed to work. Christianity had become too strong to be blotted out by force. In the fourth century, Christianity prospered as never before after the emperor Constantine became the first Christian emperor. Although he was not baptized until the end of his life, in 313 Constantine issued the Edict of Milan, which proclaimed official tolerance of Christianity. Under Theodosius, who ruled from 378 to 395, it was made the official religion of the Roman Empire. Christianity had triumphed.

## ❀ SECTION REVIEW ❀

1. **Locate:**
   (*a*) Rome,    (*b*) Roman Empire

2. **Define:**
   (*a*) consuls,   (*b*) praetors,   (*c*) Senate,
   (*d*) centuriate assembly,   (*e*) patricians,
   (*f*) plebeians,   (*g*) council of the plebs,
   (*h*) tribunes of the plebs

3. **Identify:**
   (*a*) Twelve Tables,   (*b*) Jesus,   (*c*) Pontius Pilate,
   (*d*) Constantine

4. **Recall:**
   (*a*) Name three basic rights that the plebeians had acquired by 287 B.C.
   (*b*) What did radicals, conservative religious leaders, and Roman authorities think of Jesus?

**5. Think Critically:** Imagine you are a patrician. Explain why you believe patricians should maintain their privileged position and why plebeians should not gain equal rights.

## Conclusion

The first civilizations that emerged in Mesopotamia, Egypt, India, and China all shared a number of basic characteristics. Each developed in a river valley that provided the food needed to maintain a large population. In each civilization a part of the population was able to live in cities, which became centers for political, economic, social, cultural, and religious development. All of these early civilizations established some kind of organized government bureaucracy to meet the needs of the growing population. Armies were created for protection and to gain land and power. A new social structure based on economic power arose. Kings, priests, and warriors formed an upper class. There also existed a large group of free people (farmers and artisans) and, at the very bottom of the social scale, a class of slaves.

The new urban civilizations were also characterized by important religious and cultural developments. Because the gods were often seen as crucial to a community's success, a class of priests arose whose job it was to regulate relations with the gods. Writing was also a significant development. Rulers, priests, merchants, and artisans used writing to keep records and create new literary forms. Monumental buildings also occupied a prominent place in the new cities.

From the beginnings of the first civilizations around 3000 B.C., there was a movement toward the creation of empires. The Assyrians, Persians, and later Alexander the Great created large empires that included either large areas of or all of the ancient Middle East. Later, western Asia, as well as the Mediterranean world and much of western Europe, fell subject to the mighty empire of the Romans. At the same time, much of India became part of the Mauryan Empire. Finally, in the last few centuries B.C., the Qin and Han dynasties of China created a Chinese Empire.

The achievements of the Greeks and Romans were especially important in the later development of Western civilization. Greek political ideas and practices, especially those of the rights and duties of citizens in a democracy, became an important model. Greek philosophy, drama, and art established cultural standards for later Western societies. A rational method of inquiry, so important to modern science, was devised in ancient Greece. The Romans not only preserved the intellectual heritage of the Greeks but also developed political institutions and principles of law that became an important part of Western civilization. Spiritual ideals and ethical concepts derived from the Hebrews and Christianity provided the basis for the value system of Western civilization.

## Notes

1. Psalms 145:8–9.
2. Exodus 20:13–15.
3. Isaiah 2:4.
4. Plato, *The Republic*, trans. F. M. Cornford (New York, 1945), pp. 178–179.
5. Matthew 5:17.
6. Matthew 7:12.
7. Mark 12:30–31.
8. John 18:36.
9. Colossians 3:10–11.

# CHAPTER 1 REVIEW

## USING KEY TERMS

1. According to the Hebrews, God made a _____ with the tribes of Israel.
2. In a _____ society, women have fewer privileges and rights than men.
3. The Hebrews believed that God communicated through religious teachers called _____.
4. The belief in one God, rather than many gods, is called _____.
5. Some Greek city-states were committed to government by many, a _____, while others ruled by _____, which means rule by a few.
6. The upper fortified part of a Greek city, the _____, served as a place of refuge during an attack.
7. The central focus of ancient Greek life was known as the _____.
8. Athenians devised the practice of _____ to protect themselves against overly ambitious politicians.
9. Greek citizens assembled in an open area called an _____ that also served as a market.
10. _____ is a Greek word that means "love of wisdom."
11. The _____ uses a question-and-answer format that trains pupils to see things for themselves by using their own reasoning.
12. Cases of civil law were applied to citizens and noncitizens of Rome by judges who were called _____.
13. Officials of Rome who were to protect the power of the less wealthy landholders, craftspeople, merchants, and small farmers were called _____.
14. During the Roman Republic, two _____ led the army and directed the government.
15. By the third century B.C. the Roman _____ determined the laws of the Republic.
16. Early Hindus believed it was the duty of the individual self, the _____, to seek to know the ultimate reality called _____.
17. _____ were Roman citizens who wanted political and social equality with the wealthy _____.
18. The _____ was organized in such a way that the wealthiest citizens always had a majority.
19. A popular assembly for the less wealthy Roman citizens was created after hundreds of years of struggle and was named the _____.
20. _____ is the belief that the individual soul is reborn in a different form after death.
21. _____ is the Hindu idea that what people do in their lives determines what they will be in the next life.

## REVIEWING THE FACTS

1. Upon what do archaeologists and anthropologists rely to construct their theories about the development of early human beings?
2. What is the meaning of *neolithic* in the Greek language?
3. What are three fundamental problems that humans have thought about through the ages?
4. For what is Hammurabi best remembered?
5. After Solomon's death, what two separate Hebrew kingdoms were created?
6. What is the probable cause for the relatively slow development of civilization in China?
7. What role did tyrants play in the development of Greek history?
8. What caused the Spartans to create a military state?
9. Why were the Romans considered practical people?
10. Who were the patricians and plebeians and why were they in conflict with each other?
11. According to Jesus Christ, what was God's simple command?

# CHAPTER 1 REVIEW

## THINKING CRITICALLY

1. What kinds of things might a civilization with a well-developed writing system be able to do that a society without writing could not?
2. Restate in your own words the meaning of William Loftus's phrase, "the cradle of civilization."
3. What did the value of responsibility mean to the ancient Greeks?
4. How must the Spartans' distrust of the outside world have shaped their society?
5. Analyze the important beliefs common to Judaism and Christianity and explain why they appealed to those living in the Roman Empire.
6. Why did early civilizations typically develop in river valleys and build social structures based on economic power?

## APPLYING SOCIAL STUDIES SKILLS

1. **Government:** Compare and contrast laws in the code of Hammurabi with laws in the American legal system. Are the rights of individuals treated differently in these two codes? Explain your answer.
2. **Geography:** Identify at least four ways in which the geography of Mesopotamia affected the development of civilization in that region.
3. **Government:** Choose a partner—one of you will take the role of Pericles, the other the role of Plato. List the major arguments each of you would make in describing the perfect government.
4. **Religion in History:** Explain why the ethical monotheism of Christianity appealed to Romans and why persecution did not stop Christianity's spread.

## MAKING TIME AND PLACE CONNECTIONS

1. What conditions in modern society contribute to making us more separate from and ignorant of nature than early humans were?
2. Compare and contrast the commandments spelled out in the covenant between Yahweh and his chosen people, the Hebrews, with those of the Ten Commandments received by Moses in the Bible. Do you suppose similar commandments existed in other religions? What social purpose do such commandments fulfill?
3. In its search for security, Sparta turned its back on the outside world. Does an isolated modern state, such as North Korea, face the same problems? What are the problems?
4. If you could choose a teacher from ancient Greece, who would you choose to study with— Socrates, Plato, or Aristotle? Explain why.
5. Identify a modern struggle for power between the rich and middle-class people, and compare it to the struggle between the patricians and plebeians in Rome. What general inferences can you make about the impact of such struggles on history?

## BECOMING AN HISTORIAN

**Understanding and Interpreting Maps:** Examine Map 1.1, Ancient Mesopotamia.

1. What information does the key provide? What symbols are used to represent cities?
2. How far is it from Babylon to Jerusalem? From the Zagros Mountains to the Taurus Mountains?
3. Determine the approximate length of the Euphrates and Tigris Rivers. Compare this map with other maps in this text. Are they similar or different in their layout and in the types of information they provide? In what different ways may maps be used to communicate information?

# THE EMERGENCE OF

By A.D. 400, the great states of the ancient world that we examined in Chapter 1 were in decline or even at the point of collapse. On the ruins of these ancient empires, new patterns of civilization began to take shape between 400 and 1500. In some cases, these new societies—such as the Tang dynasty in China and the Guptas in India—were built on the political and cultural foundations of earlier states. In other cases, new states—such as the new European civilization and the Arabic societies of the Middle East—built on elements of earlier civilizations while moving in different directions. In the meantime, new civilizations were also beginning to appear in other parts of the world—in Japan, in Southeast Asia, in Africa, and across the Atlantic in the Americas.

By 1500, a revived Europe began the voyages of exploration that led Europeans into new areas of the world. One explorer was the Portuguese navigator Ferdinand Magellan, who was convinced that he could find a sea passage to Asia through the New World to the west. On August 10, 1519, Magellan set sail on the Atlantic with five ships and a Spanish crew of 277 men. After a stormy and difficult crossing of the Atlantic, Magellan's fleet moved down the coast of what is today South America in search of the elusive strait, or sea passage, that would take him through America. His Spanish ship captains thought he was crazy:

▲ *When Magellan passed by the tip of South America, he and his men had no idea they were entering the 10,000-mile-wide Pacific Ocean. Of the 277 men who accompanied Magellan, only eighteen returned to Spain. How do you think they were greeted and treated upon their return?*

"The fool is obsessed with his search for a strait," one remarked. "On the flame of his ambition he will crucify us all."

At last, in October 1520, Magellan found an opening in the land. He passed through a narrow waterway (later named the Strait of Magellan) and emerged into an unknown ocean, which he called the Pacific Sea. Magellan reckoned that it would then be a short distance to the Spice Islands of the East. He was badly mistaken. Week after week he and his crew sailed on across the Pacific as their food supplies dwindled. According to one account, "When their last biscuit had gone, they scraped the maggots out of the casks, mashed them and served them as gruel. They made cakes out of sawdust soaked with the urine of rats—the rats themselves, as delicacies, had long since been hunted to extinction." At last they reached the Philippines (named after King Philip of Spain by Magellan's crew), where Magellan was killed by the natives. Magellan is still remembered as the first person to sail around the world.

European adventurers such as Magellan launched a new era, not only for Europe but also for the peoples of Asia, Africa, and the Americas. The voyages of these Europeans marked the beginning of a process that led to radical changes in the political, economic, and cultural lives of the entire non-Western world after 1500.

# NEW WORLD PATTERNS

## (400 TO 1800)

## QUESTIONS TO GUIDE YOUR READING

1. What were the chief features of the new patterns of civilization in the Americas, the Middle East, and Africa between 400 and 1500?

2. What were the chief features of the civilizations in Asia between 400 and 1500?

3. What were the chief features of European civilization in the Middle Ages?

4. What were the major developments in European history between 1500 and 1700?

5. What were the basic issues in the struggle between king and Parliament in seventeenth-century England? How did Parliament put an end to the divine-right theory of kingship in England?

6. What was the importance of the Scientific Revolution and the Enlightenment?

## OUTLINE

## NEW PATTERNS OF CIVILIZATION IN THE AMERICAS, THE MIDDLE EAST, AND AFRICA

Between 400 and 1500, new patterns of civilization appeared in the Americas, the Middle East, and Africa. In the Americas and Africa, new civilizations were beginning to emerge. In the Middle East, a new society was built on earlier civilizations but moved in new directions.

### Early American Civilizations

Around 5000 B.C., farming settlements began to appear in river valleys and upland areas in both Central and South America. Shortly after, organized communities

41

## SPORTS AND CONTESTS

# The Deadly Games of Central America

Most Mayan cities contained a ball court. Each of these courts usually consisted of a rectangular space surrounded by walls with highly decorated stone rings. The contestants tried to drive a solid rubber ball through these rings. Ball players, usually two or three on a team, used their hips to propel the ball (hands and feet were not allowed). Players donned helmets, gloves, and knee and hip protectors made of hide to protect themselves against the hard rubber balls. Because the stone rings were placed twenty-seven feet above the ground, it took considerable skill to score a goal.

The exact rules of the game are unknown, but we do know that it was more than a sport. The ball game had a religious meaning. The ball court was a symbol of the world, and the ball represented the sun and the moon. Apparently, it was also believed that playing the game often would produce better harvests. The results of the game were deadly. The defeated players were sacrificed in ceremonies held after the end of the game. Sim-

◀ *Players wore stone yokes like this one on one hip to provide some protection during the ball games. The yoke in this picture was made in the fifth century B.C. near Veracruz, Mexico. Why do you think the yokes were decorated?*

ilar courts have been found at sites throughout Central America, as well as present-day Arizona and New Mexico.

1. Why was great skill required of athletes who played the Mayan ball game?

2. Explain the symbolism of the Mayan ball game.

3. What other sporting events that you have read about resulted in death for the losing participant?

located along the coast of the Gulf of Mexico and the western slopes of the central Andes Mountains began the long march to civilization. The Maya and Aztecs were especially successful in developing advanced and prosperous civilizations. Both cultures built elaborate cities with pyramids, temples, and palaces. Both the Aztecs and the Maya were **polytheistic** (believed in many gods) and practiced human sacrifice as a major part of their religions (see "Sports and Contests: The Deadly Games of Central America"). Mayan civiliza-

tion collapsed in the ninth century. The Aztecs fell to Spanish invaders in the sixteenth century.

In the fifteenth century, another remarkable civilization—that of the Inca—flourished in South America. The Inca Empire was carefully planned and regulated, which is especially evident in the extensive network of roads that connected all parts of the empire. However, the Inca, possessing none of the new weapons of the Spaniards, fell eventually to the foreign conquerors.

## SPORTS AND CONTESTS

# The Deadly Games of Central America, continued

▲ *Throughout Mesoamerica, a dangerous game was played on courts such as this one from Mayan ruins in modern-day Guatemala. What was the importance of these ball games?*

While the Maya, Aztecs, and Inca were developing their civilizations, the peoples of North America were creating a remarkable number of different cultures. Inuits, Mound Builders, Anasazi, Plains Amerindians, and Iroquois all developed flourishing societies that responded in their own unique ways to the environmental conditions that they faced.

All of these societies in the Americas developed in apparently total isolation from their counterparts elsewhere in the world. This lack of contact with other human beings deprived them of access to developments taking place in Africa, Asia, and Europe. They did not know of the wheel, for example. Also, their written languages were not as sophisticated as those in other parts of the world.

In other respects, however, the cultural achievements of the early societies in the Americas were the equal of those realized elsewhere. When the first European explorers arrived in the Americas at the beginning of the sixteenth century, they described much

**Map 2.1    The Heartland of Mesoamerica**

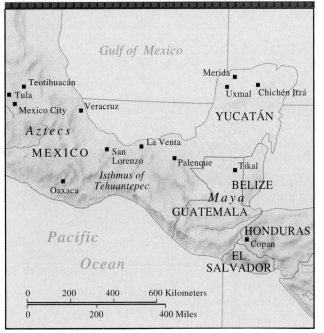

that they observed in glowing terms. Bernal Díaz, who accompanied Hernan Cortés on his expedition to Mexico in 1519, could not believe his eyes when he saw the city of Tenochtitlán in central Mexico: "When we beheld so many cities and towns on the water, and other large settlements built on firm ground, and that broad causeway running so straight and perfectly level to the city of Tenochtitlán, we were astonished because of the great stone towers and temples and buildings that rose up out of the water." To some of the soldiers, "all these things seemed to be a dream."

One development that the peoples of the Americas lacked, however, was the knowledge of firearms. In a few short years, tiny bands of Spanish explorers armed with these weapons were able to conquer the magnificent civilizations of the Americas and turn them into ruins.

Even before the Spanish conquest of the Americas, during the height of the Mayan civilization, another new civilization was emerging in the Middle East.

## The World of Islam

In the seventh century, a new force arose in the Arabian peninsula and spread rapidly throughout the Middle East. This new force was a new religion called Islam, which means "submission to Allah," and was the

▶ *The Aztec ruler Moctezuma initially welcomed Cortés and his army to his royal court, a decision he came to regret. Why did the Spaniards so completely destroy Aztec cities and vestiges (traces) of their culture?*

◄ *During Ramadan, the holy month of Islam, Muslims fast from dawn to sunset, and observance of Ramadan is considered one of the "five pillars" of the Islamic faith. This Persian miniature shows a festive group of Muslims celebrating the end of Ramadan.*

work of a man named Muhammad. He was born in 570 in Mecca, a small town of about three thousand people located in the desert lands of the Arabian peninsula. Mohammad's father died when he was not yet one and his mother when he was only five. He was raised by relatives, from whom he learned how to buy, sell, and transport goods. Intelligent and hardworking, he became a capable merchant. He married, had children, and seemed to have a happy and rewarding life.

Muhammad, however, was not content. Deeply disturbed by problems in Meccan society, he spent days on end in a nearby cave, praying and meditating. According to tradition, one night in 610, while Muhammad was deep in meditation, an angelic voice called out, "Recite!" A frightened Muhammad replied, "What shall I recite?" The voice responded, "In the name of thy Lord the Creator, who created mankind from a clot of blood, recite!" The voice then began to speak about the nature of God. Over a period of time, Muhammad memorized everything the voice revealed and began to preach these words to others: "Allah will bring to nothing the deeds of those who disbelieve. . . . As for the faithful who do good works and believe in what is revealed to Muham-

mad—which is the truth from their Lord—He will forgive them their sins and ennoble their state. . . . As for those who are slain in the cause of Allah, . . . He will admit them to the Paradise He has made known to them." Words such as these would later be gathered together to form the Quran (Koran), the sacred book of Islam, the religion founded by Muhammad.

Muhammad's life changed the course of world history. At the time of his birth, old empires that had once ruled the entire Middle East were only a memory. The region was now divided into many separate states. The people worshiped many different gods. Within a few decades of Muhammad's death, the Middle East was united once again. Arab armies marched westward across North Africa and eastward into Mesopotamia and Persia, creating a new empire that stretched from Spain to the Indus valley. Arab rule also brought with it a new religion and a new culture—that of Islam.

Islamic beliefs had a powerful impact in all areas occupied by Arab armies, but the Arab Empire failed to last. Internal struggles led first to its decline and then to its destruction at the hands of the Mongols in 1258. Still, the Arab conquest left a powerful legacy. The

## Map 2.2    The Expansion of Islam

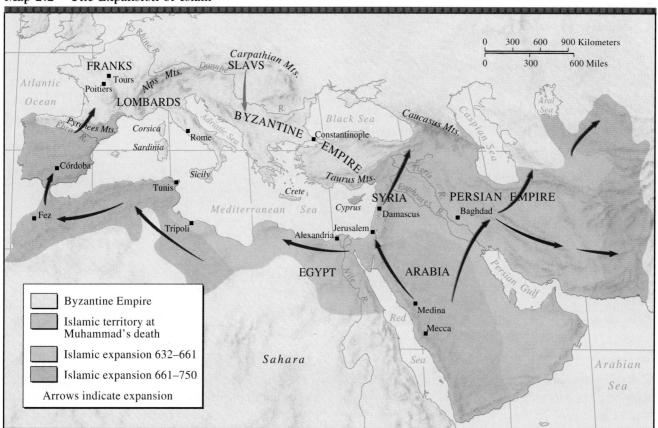

appeal of Islam remained strong throughout the Middle East and extended into areas not occupied by Arab armies, such as Africa, India, and Southeast Asia.

## Early Civilizations in Africa

In 1871, the German explorer Karl Mauch began to search South Africa's Central Plateau for the colossal stone ruins of a legendary lost civilization. In late August, he found what he had been looking for. He wrote in his diary: "Presently I stood before it and beheld a wall of a height of about 20 feet of granite bricks. Very close by there was a place where a kind of foot-path led over rubble into the interior. Following this path I stumbled over masses of rubble and parts of walls and dense thickets. I stopped in front of a tower

like structure. Altogether it rose to a height of about 30 feet." Mauch was convinced that "a civilized nation must once have lived here." Like many other nineteenth-century Europeans, however, Mauch was equally convinced that the Africans who had lived there could never have built such splendid structures like the ones he had found at Great Zimbabwe. Mauch and other archaeologists believed that Great Zimbabwe must have been the work of "a northern race closely akin to the Phoenician and Egyptian." It was not until the twentieth century that Europeans could overcome their prejudices and finally admit that Africans south of Egypt had indeed developed advanced civilizations with spectacular achievements.

Thanks to the dedicated work of a generation of archaeologists, anthropologists, and historians, we now have a much better understanding of the evolution of

▲ *Great Zimbabwe was once the capital of a prosperous state in southern Africa. Its thirty-foot-high walls, shown here, were the first in Africa to be built without mortar. Why would Europeans have difficulty accepting this proof that advanced civilization existed at Zimbabwe?*

human societies in Africa than we did a few decades ago. The mastery of agriculture gave rise to three early civilizations in Africa: Egypt, Kush, and Axum. Later, new states emerged in different parts of Africa, some of them strongly influenced by the spread of Islam. Ghana, Mali, and Songhai were three flourishing trading states in West Africa. Zimbabwe, which emerged around 1300, played an important role in the southern half of Africa. The continent was also an active participant in emerging regional and global trade with the Mediterranean world and across the Indian Ocean. Although the state-building process in sub-Saharan Africa was still in its early stages when the ancient civilizations of India, China, and Mesopotamia were flourishing, in many respects the new African states were as impressive and sophisticated as their counterparts elsewhere in the world.

## CONNECTIONS
### TO OUR WORLD

**The Conflict between Sunnites and Shi'ites**   In 1990, a brutal and bloody war erupted between Iran and Iraq. Border disputes were one cause of the war, but religious differences were another.

Both Iranians and Iraqis are Muslims. The Iranians are largely Shi'ites. Although the Iraqi people are mostly Shi'ites, the ruling groups in the country are Sunnites, or Sunni Muslims. During the war, Iran hoped to defeat Iraq by appealing to the Shi'ite majority in Iraq for support. The attempt largely failed, however.

The clash between Shi'ites and Sunnites goes back to the seventh century. The Shi'ites believed that only the descendants of Ali, Muhammad's son-in-law, were the true leaders of Islam. Sunnites, however, were those Muslims who claimed that only descendants of the Umayyad dynasty were the true leaders. Over the years, Shi'ites developed their own body of law, which differed from that of the Sunnite majority. Most Muslims remained Sunnites, although Shi'ites form majorities in both Iran and Iraq. Shi'ite minorities also continue to exist in Turkey, Syria, Lebanon, India, Pakistan, and east Africa. The success of the Iranian Revolution in 1978–1979, led by the Ayatollah Khomeini, resulted in a noticeable revival of Shi'ism in Iran and in parts of the Islamic world adjacent to Iran. In August, 1979, Khomeini established an Islamic Revolutionary Guard Corps. Its job was to train Shi'ite militants from many countries in the methods of terrorism.

Because of a lack of written records, we know little about early African society and culture. We do know that the relationship between king and subjects was often less rigid in African society than in other civilizations. Family, and especially the **lineage group** (a community of extended family units), was the basic unit in

**Map 2.3    Early States in Africa**

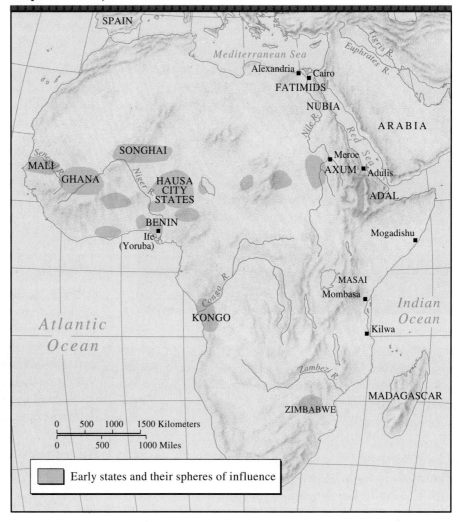

African society. Religious beliefs in many African societies focused on various gods, nature spirits, the role of diviners, and the importance of ancestors. Africans produced a distinctive culture with a rich heritage in wood carving, sculpture, music, and architecture.

In the fifteenth century, a new factor came to affect Africa. Fleets from Portugal began to probe southward along the coast of West Africa. At first the sponsors of these fleets were in search of gold and slaves. However, when Portuguese ships rounded the southern coast of Africa by 1500, they began to seek to dominate the trade of the Indian Ocean as well. The new situation posed a threat to the peoples of Africa, whose new states would be severely tested by the demands of the Europeans.

❀    **SECTION REVIEW**    ❀

1. **Locate:**
   (*a*) Gulf of Mexico,    (*b*) Mecca,
   (*c*) Arabian peninsula,    (*d*) Axum

2. **Define:**
   (*a*) polytheistic,    (*b*) lineage group

3. **Identify:**
   (*a*) Inca,   (*b*) Tenochtitlán,   (*c*) Muhammad,
   (*d*) Quran,   (*e*) Great Zimbabwe

4. **Recall:**
   (*a*) How did isolation affect the American societies?
   (*b*) What led to the fall of the Arab Empire?
   (*c*) List three things the Portuguese sought from Africa in the fifteenth century.

5. **Think Critically:** Mauch and other archaeologists believed Africans were incapable of building a great civilization. How might this attitude have affected foreign relations between European and African nations? Why?

## CIVILIZATION IN SOUTH, SOUTHEAST, AND EAST ASIA (400 TO 1500)

The peoples of Africa were not the only ones to confront a new threat from Europe at the beginning of the sixteenth century. When the Portuguese sailed across the Indian Ocean, they sought to reach India. In India, a new empire capable of rivaling the great Mauryan Empire was in the throes of creation.

### Civilization in South and Southeast Asia

By 500, the Gupta dynasty, which had ruled northern India since 320, had begun to collapse. Northern India fell into chaos. For the next five hundred years, India was divided into a large number of small kingdoms. Fighting among these states became a way of life. Indian poems of the period tell of combat between Indian kings that was carried on by warrior bands seated on elephants and in chariots and armed with lances, swords, and bows and arrows. When a king won, he and his warriors collected their loot, returned to the palace, and celebrated. Colossal banquets were served, according to one poet, "by beautiful women decked in fine jewels and sweet smiles." Eating never

## CONNECTIONS
### TO OUR WORLD

**The Clash Between Hindus and Muslims**   On December 7, 1992, a mob of Hindu militants in India sacked a Muslim mosque in the town of Ayodhya, in northern India. For years, militant Hindus had demanded that this Muslim mosque, built on a Hindu holy site that had once been occupied by a Hindu temple, should be destroyed. The mosque had been constructed in the seventeenth century, but was no longer used to any great extent.

When the government failed to meet the militants' demands, the Hindu demonstrators pulled down the mosque and began to erect a Hindu temple at the site. These actions in turn led to clashes between Hindus and Muslims throughout the country. In neighboring Pakistan as well, Muslim rioters destroyed a number of Hindu shrines.

Since 1982, the tensions between Hindus and Muslims in India have continued to grow. Recently, a militant Hindu political party led by Balasaheb Thackeray, who calls himself the "Hitler of Bombay," has called for a new Indian state that would only meet the interests of the Hindu majority. This conflict between Hindus and Muslims has been a feature of life in India for over a thousand years.

The invasion of India by Muslim forces began in the eighth century. At the end of the tenth century, however, Muslim invaders became more numerous and more deadly. One Muslim conqueror of northern India, Mahmud of Ghazni, delighted in destroying Hindu places of worship. His army once massacred 50,000 Hindus who had gathered in a Hindu holy city. Other Muslim conquerors after Mahmud continued his destructive example. Stones from demolished Hindu temples were often used to build mosques. The fanatacism of these early Muslim conquerors angered Hindus and helped create the bitter rivalries that have lasted in India to this day.

▲ *This enormous temple at Angkor Wat in Cambodia was built by the Khmer people and then buried under jungle growth for centuries. It was dedicated to Hindu mythology.*

seemed to end. One poet described how a participant felt: "By eating flesh day and night, the edges of my teeth became blunt like the plowshare after plowing dry land." When a king lost, his deeds were remembered in poetry and song.

Indian poets gave advice to those who wanted to follow a military career: "When you see a fight, rush to the front, divide your enemy's forces, stand before them, and get your body scarred by the deep cuts of their swords; thus your fame is pleasant to the ear, not your body to the eye. As for your enemies, when they see you, they turn their backs, and with bodies whole and unscarred, they are pleasant to the eye, not so their shame to the ear." One king, who was injured in the back when he retreated, was so ashamed he starved himself to death.

Beginning in the eleventh century, much of northern India was conquered by Turkish people from the northwest, who established some sense of order. Turk-

ish dynasties were set up in many areas. These dynasties brought Islamic religion and civilization to India, adding yet another religion to this land of many religions. The new faith caused serious conflict between its followers and the Hindu majority.

Situated at the crossroads between two oceans and two great civilizations, Southeast Asia has long served as a bridge linking peoples and cultures. Despite the central position that Southeast Asia occupied in the ancient world, complex societies were slow to take form in the region. When they did begin to appear, they were strongly influenced by the older civilizations of neighboring China and India. In Vietnam, the Chinese imposed their culture by conquest. Elsewhere, merchants and missionaries brought Indian influence. Whatever the means, all the young states throughout the region—Vietnam, Angkor, Thailand, the Burmese kingdom of Pagan, and several states on the Malay peninsula and Indonesian archipelago—were heavily

**Map 2.4    Asia in the Middle Ages**

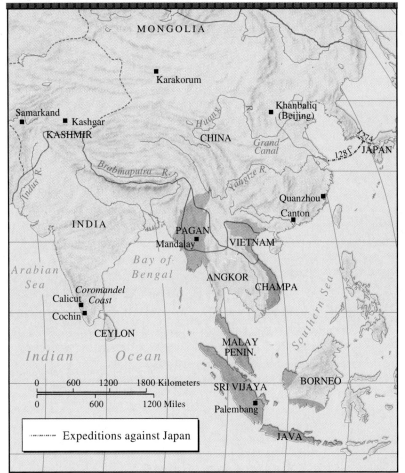

affected by foreign ideas and adopted them as a part of their own cultures. At the same time, the Southeast Asian peoples, like the Japanese, put their own unique stamp on the ideas that they adopted. The result was a region marked by cultural richness and diversity, yet rooted in the local culture.

## Golden Ages in East Asia

In 1266, the Mongol emperor of China, Khubilai Khan, demanded that the Japanese pay tribute to China or face invasion. When the Japanese refused, the Great Khan sent a force of thirty thousand warriors to teach the Japanese a lesson. Bad weather forced the emperor's forces to retreat. It was not until 1281 that the Great Khan was prepared to try again. This time he sent a force of two fleets, consisting of 4,400 ships carrying almost 150,000 warriors. The Japanese appeared to be doomed. On August 15, however, just as the Great Khan's forces were preparing to land, the sky darkened. A massive typhoon struck, battering the Mongol fleet and killing thousands. One Korean observer wrote: "The bodies of men and broken timbers of the vessels were heaped together in a solid mass so that a person could walk across from one point of land to another on the mass of wreckage." Those warriors who made it to shore were cut down by the Japanese defenders. To the Japanese, this was a sign of divine aid. They called the storm a "divine wind"

# BIOGRAPHY

## Empress Wu

▲ *This painting of Empress Wu was done during the Tang dynasty and shows how powerful the Empress was. How does the artist convey her power in such a simple painting?*

Wu Zhao (WOO CHOW) was born in 625, the daughter of a Chinese general. Attracted by her beauty, Emperor Tang Taizong chose her to be his concubine when she was only thirteen years old. After his death in 649, she became concubine to the next emperor, Kao Tsung, and bore him four sons and a daughter. Wu Zhao was extremely jealous of the empress and greatly desirous of power. It is said that she strangled her own daughter and

then accused the empress, who was childless, of the crime. The emperor chose to accept Wu Zhao's story, deposed the empress, and chose Wu Zhao as his new empress.

Empress Wu was obsessed with power. After her husband's death in 683, she sent one son into exile and ruled with another son. His weakness, however, combined with the support of the army, gave her supreme power. Empress Wu did not hesitate to get rid of officials and even members of her family who stood in her way.

Although she was known for her ruthlessness, Empress Wu was also a capable ruler. She was the first ruler to select graduates of the civil service examinations for the highest positions in government. She forced Korea to become an ally of China, lowered taxes, and patronized the arts. During her last years, her abilities declined, and she was deposed in 705, at the age of eighty. In a country in which women had a low status, Empress Wu had lived a remarkable life. She is still known as one of the strongest leaders in China's history.

1. In your own words, tell the story of how Wu Zhao become empress of China.

2. What qualities of character enabled Empress Wu to hold on to her power?

3. What do you find most remarkable about the life of Empress Wu?

4. Empress Wu used many unethical methods to obtain and keep a position of power, and yet she improved the quality of life for many of her subjects. Explain why you would favor either an ethical, ineffective ruler or an unethical, effective ruler.

(*kamikaze*) and became convinced that they would always be protected from foreign invasion.

This great confrontation between the ancient and well-established civilization of China and the newly emerged Japanese state was but one of the events in East Asia between 400 and 1500. Between 581 and 1644, five different dynasties ruled China (see "Biography: Empress Wu"). During the thousand years of these five dynasties, China advanced in many ways. Industry and trade grew in size and technological capacity. In the countryside a flourishing agriculture supported China's economic prosperity. In addition, Chinese society achieved a high level of development and stability. The civil service of government officials provided for a stable government bureaucracy and an avenue of upward mobility that was virtually unknown elsewhere in the world. China's achievements were unsurpassed and made it a civilization that was the envy of its neighbors and of the world. China also influenced other states in the region, including Japan.

Few societies in Asia historically have been as isolated as Japan. Cut off from the mainland by 120 miles of ocean, the Japanese had little contact with the outside world during most of their early development. However, once the Japanese became acquainted with Chinese culture, they were quick to take advantage of the opportunity. In the space of a few decades, the young state adopted many features of Chinese society and culture and thereby introduced major changes into the Japanese way of life. Nevertheless, while early Japanese rulers tried to create a centralized political system like that of China, the power of great landowners in Japan ensured a weak central authority. The result was a society that was able to make use of ideas imported from beyond its borders without endangering customs, beliefs, and institutions inherited from the past.

## ❀   SECTION REVIEW   ❀

1. **Locate:**
   (*a*) Southeast Asia,   (*b*) Japan

2. **Identify:**
   (*a*) Khubilai Khan

3. **Recall:**
   (*a*) Describe the state of India from 500 to 1000.
   (*b*) Name two accomplishments of the Turkish rule over northern India.
   (*c*) List three ways China advanced between 581 and 1644.

4. **Think Critically:** Southeast Asia was located between two great empires: India and China. In developing as a culture, what were the advantages and disadvantages of this geographical position?

# EUROPEAN CIVILIZATION IN THE MIDDLE AGES

In 800, Charlemagne, the king of a Germanic people known as the Franks, journeyed to Rome to help Pope Leo III, head of the Catholic Church. The pope was barely clinging to power in the face of rebellious Romans. On Christmas Day, Charlemagne, his family, and a host of visitors crowded into Saint Peter's Basilica to attend mass. According to a Frankish writer, all were surprised when, "as the king rose from praying before the tomb of the blessed apostle Peter, Pope Leo placed a golden crown on his head." In keeping with ancient tradition, the people in the church shouted, "Long life and victory to Charles Augustus, crowned by God the great and peace-loving Emperor of the Romans."

It appeared that the Roman Empire in the West had been reborn, and Charles had become the first Roman emperor since 476. However, this "Roman emperor" was actually a German king, and he had been crowned by the head of the Western Christian Church. In truth, the coronation of Charlemagne was a sign not of the rebirth of the Roman Empire but of the emergence of a new European civilization that came into being in western Europe after the collapse of the Western Roman Empire.

This new civilization—European civilization—was formed by the coming together of three major ele-

▲ *This miniature painting shows Pope Leo III placing a crown on Charlemagne's head while church officials watch. What did this occasion symbolize for the church and the state?*

ments: the Germanic peoples who moved in and settled the Western Roman Empire, the legacy of the Romans, and the Christian Church. By 800, this new European civilization was taking shape. Increasingly, Europe would become the center of what we call Western civilization. European civilization emerged and developed during a period that historians call the Middle Ages or the medieval period. It lasted from about 500 to 1500. To historians who first used the title, the Middle Ages was a middle period between the ancient world and the modern world.

After the death of Charlemagne, the Carolingian Empire that he had established soon began to disintegrate. With the collapse of the Carolingian Empire, new forms of political institutions began to develop in Europe. The **feudal system** put power into the hands of many different lords, who came to constitute a powerful group of nobles that dominated the political, economic, and social life of Europe. Quietly and surely within this world of castles, however, kings gradually began to extend their powers. Although they could not know it then, their actions laid the foundations for the European kingdoms that have dominated the European political scene ever since. One of these kingdoms—England—created political institutions that

ultimately had a strong impact in the formation of the democratic political system of the United States.

# England in the High Middle Ages (1000 to 1300)

On October 14, 1066, an army of heavily armed knights under William of Normandy landed on the coast of England and soundly defeated King Harold and the Anglo-Saxon foot soldiers. William was crowned king of England at Christmastime in London. He then began the process of combining Anglo-Saxon and Norman institutions to create a new England. Many of the Norman knights were given parcels of land, known as **fiefs,** from the new English king. William made all nobles swear an oath of loyalty to him as sole ruler of England. He also insisted that all people owed loyalty to the king.

In the twelfth century, the power of the English monarchy was greatly enlarged during the reign of Henry II, from 1154 to 1189. The new king was especially successful in strengthening the power of the royal courts of law. Henry expanded the number of criminal cases to be tried in the king's court. He also devised means for taking property cases from local courts to the royal courts. Henry's goals were clear: expanding the power of the royal courts expanded the king's power. Moreover, because the royal courts were now found throughout England, a body of common law (law that was common to the whole kingdom) began to replace the different law codes that often varied from place to place.

## The Magna Carta

Many English nobles came to resent the ongoing growth of the king's power and rose in rebellion during the reign of King John. At Runnymeade in 1215, John was forced to put his seal on the Magna Carta (the Great Charter) of feudal liberties. The Magna Carta was, above all, a feudal document. It conferred more rights to the nobility than the commoners. Feudal custom had always recognized that the relationship

▲ *The tapestry of Bayeux, a detail of which is shown here, chronicles the invasion of England by the Norman French. How many medieval weapons can you identify in this scene?*

between king and his knights—vassals—was based on mutual rights and obligations. The Magna Carta gave written recognition to that fact. The document was used in later years to strengthen the idea that a monarch's power was limited, not absolute.

Some provisions of the Magna Carta, however, came to have greater significance because of the way they were later interpreted. One stands out. Chapter 39 read: "No free man shall be taken or imprisoned or dispossessed, or outlawed, or banished, or in any way destroyed, nor will we go upon him, nor send upon him, except by the legal judgment of his peers or by the law of the land." In 1215, the label of "free man" applied to less than half of the English population. Later, however, this statement was applied to all. In the fourteenth century it gave rise to trial by jury. Its emphasis on the need to abide by the "law of the land"

in legal proceedings against a free person also came to mean a guarantee of "due process of law."

### The Beginnings of Parliament

During the reign of Edward I, an important institution in the development of representative government—the English Parliament—also emerged. At first the word *parliament* referred to the king's Great Council, which was made up of the king's officials, nobles, and bishops. However, because of his need for money, in 1295 Edward I invited two knights from every county and two residents from each town to meet with the Great Council to consent to new taxes. This was the first official Parliament.

The English Parliament came to be composed of two knights from every county, two people from every

**Map 2.5    Europe in the High Middle Ages**

## Europe in the High and Late Middle Ages

town, the nobles, and the bishops. Eventually, nobles and church lords formed the House of Lords; knights and townspeople formed the House of Commons. The Parliaments of Edward I granted taxes, discussed politics, and passed laws. Although it was not yet the important body it would eventually become, the English Parliament nevertheless had clearly emerged as an institution by the end of the thirteenth century. The law of the English kingdom would be determined not by the king alone but by king and Parliament together. Much conflict, and even open war, would ensue before Parliament gained the primary political power it has today in England.

In the twelfth century, William Fitz-Stephen spoke of London as one of the noble cities of the world: "It is happy in the healthiness of its air, in the Christian religion, in the strength of its defences, the nature of its site, the honor of its citizens, the modesty of its women; pleasant in sports; fruitful of noble men." To Fitz-Stephen, London offered a number of opportunities and pleasures: "practically anything that man may need is brought daily not only into special places but even into the open squares, and all that can be sold is loudly advertised for sale." (See "Focus on Everyday Life: The Lifestyle of the European Peasants.")

# FOCUS ON EVERYDAY LIFE
## The Lifestyle of the European Peasants

The lifestyle of the peasants in Europe was simple. Their cottages had wood frames surrounded by sticks, with the spaces between them filled with straw and rubble and then plastered over with clay. Roofs were simply thatched. The houses of poorer peasants consisted of a single room. Others, however, had at least two rooms—a main room for cooking, eating, and other activities and another room for sleeping. There was little privacy in a medieval household. A hearth in the main room was used for heating and cooking. However, because there were few or no windows and no chimney, the smoke created by fires in the hearth went out through cracks in the walls or, more likely, through the thatched roof.

Though simple, a peasant's daily diet was adequate when food was available. The basic staple of the peasant diet, and of the medieval diet in general, was bread. Women made the dough for the bread. The loaves were usually baked in community ovens, which were owned by the lord of the manor. Peasant bread was highly nutritious because it contained not only wheat and rye but also barley, millet, and oats. These ingredients gave the bread its dark appearance and very heavy, hard texture. Numerous vegetables from the household gardens; cheese from cow's or goat's milk; nuts and berries from woodlands; and fruits, such as apples, pears, and cherries, added to the peasant's diet. Chickens provided eggs and sometimes meat. Peasants usually ate meat only on the great feast days, such as Christmas, Easter, and Pentecost.

Grains were important not only for bread but also for making ale. In northern European coun-

▲ *A peasant's life was one of harsh labor, and the kind of work peasants performed changed each season and month by month. Here a flock of sheep is being taken out to pasture. One woman is milking a cow while another churns butter. What season is shown here? How can you tell?*

(continued)

## FOCUS ON EVERYDAY LIFE
# The Lifestyle of the European Peasants, continued

tries, ale was the most common drink of the poor. If records are accurate, enormous quantities of ale were consumed. A monastery in the twelfth century records a daily allotment to the monks of three gallons a day. Peasants in the field probably consumed even more. This high consumption of alcohol might help to explain the large number of accidental deaths recorded in medieval court records.

1. How were the peasants' homes constructed? Do they sound comfortable to you? Compare the construction to that of your home.

2. Why were grains important?

3. Compare your diet with that of medieval peasants.

Sporting events and leisure activities were available in every season of the year. In winter, for example, "when the great fen, or moor, which waters the walls of the city on the north side, is frozen, many young men play upon the ice; some, striding as wide as they may, do slide swiftly." To Fitz-Stephen, "every convenience for human pleasure is known to be at hand" in London.

One would hardly know from his cheerful description that London and other European medieval cities faced overcrowded conditions, terrible smells from rotting garbage, and the constant threat of epidemics and fires.

The rise of cities was but one aspect of the new burst of energy and growth that characterized European civilization in the High Middle Ages (the period from 1000 to 1300). New farming practices, the growth of trade, and the rise of cities—all accompanied by a growing population—created a vigorous European society. Strong leadership by the popes, combined with new aspects of religious life, made the Catholic Church a forceful presence in every area of life. The new energy of European society was also evident in a burst of intellectual and artistic activity. The intellectual revival led to new centers of learning in the universities and to the use of reason to develop new ways of thought in theology. The High Middle Ages witnessed an explosion of building in medieval Europe (see "Our Artistic

◄ *This illustration captures the activity of a French medieval town. Tailors, furriers, a barber, and a grocer are seen working in their shops. Craftspeople worked in ground-level rooms and lived upstairs, above their shops. How does this scene compare to a suburban mall?*

# OUR ARTISTIC HERITAGE
## The Gothic Cathedral

▶ *Notre Dame in Paris is one of the largest Gothic cathedrals in Europe and stands as one of the great architectural and artistic triumphs of the High Middle Ages. This view from the east shows the graceful span of the flying buttresses that allow room for the windows set in the stone framework. What other features of Gothic architecture are shown here?*

Begun in the twelfth century and brought to perfection in the thirteenth, the Gothic cathedral remains one of the greatest artistic triumphs of the High Middle Ages. Soaring skyward, almost as if to reach Heaven, it was a fitting symbol for medieval people's preoccupation with God.

Two basic innovations of the twelfth century made Gothic cathedrals possible. The combination of ribbed vaults and pointed arches replaced the barrel vault of Romanesque churches and enabled builders to make Gothic churches higher than Romanesque churches. The use of pointed arches and ribbed vaults created an impression of upward movement, a sense of weightless upward thrust as

▶ *Chartres is an exception among French Gothic cathedrals because most of its windows are original ones, and each of the windows in Chartres has its own story to tell. Some windows present the lives of saints, while others portray the daily activities of medieval town life. This window presents scenes from the life of Christ. Some people believe that the stained glass windows served as teachers for the illiterate. Do you agree or not?*

if reaching to God. Another technical innovation, the flying buttress—basically a heavy, arched pier (a supporting part) of stone built onto the outside of the walls—made it possible to distribute the weight of the church's vaulted ceilings outward

*(continued)*

## OUR ARTISTIC HERITAGE
# The Gothic Cathedral, continued

and down. This eliminated the heavy walls needed in Romanesque churches to hold the weight of the massive barrel vaults. Gothic cathedrals were built, then, with thin walls that were filled with magnificent stained glass windows, which created a play of light inside that varied with the sun at different times of the day. The preoccupation with colored light in Gothic cathedrals was not accidental. Natural light was believed to be a symbol of the divine light of God.

The Gothic style was a product of northern France. By the mid-thirteenth century, however, French Gothic architecture had spread to England, Spain, and Germany—virtually all of Europe. Its most brilliant examples were the French cathedrals in Paris (Notre Dame), Reims (REEMZ), Amiens (am-YAHN), and Chartres (SHART).

A Gothic cathedral was the work of an entire community. All classes contributed to its construction. Money was raised from wealthy townspeople who had profited from the new trade and industries, as well as from kings and nobles. Master masons, who were both architects and engineers, designed the cathedrals. They drew up the plans and supervised the construction. Stonemasons and other craftspeople were paid a daily wage and provided the skilled labor to build the cathedrals. The building of cathedrals often became highly competitive as communities vied with one another to build the highest tower. Most important, a Gothic cathedral symbolized the chief preoccupation of a medieval Christian community: its dedication to a spiritual ideal. As we have observed before, the largest buildings of an era reflect the values of its society. The Gothic cathedral, with its towers soaring toward Heaven, bears witness to an age when most people believed in a spiritual world.

1. What innovations made the Gothic cathedrals possible?

2. What does the Gothic cathedral tell us about medieval values and medieval science?

3. How was the entire community involved in building the cathedral?

4. What did the Gothic cathedral symbolize?

---

Heritage: The Gothic Cathedral"). Growth and optimism seemed to characterize the High Middle Ages.

European society in the fourteenth and early fifteenth centuries (the Late Middle Ages), however, was challenged by an overwhelming number of disastrous forces. Devastating plague (the Black Death), a decline in trade and industry, seemingly constant warfare, political instability, the decline of the church, and even the spectacle of two popes condemning each other as the Antichrist all seemed to overpower Europeans. It should not be surprising, then, that much of the art of the time showed the Four Horsemen of the Apocalypse—Death, Famine, Pestilence, and War—described in the New Testament book of Revelation. No doubt, to some people it appeared that the last days of the world were at hand. In the course of the fifteenth century, however, Europe began to experience a revival or rebirth of civilization.

❀    SECTION REVIEW    ❀

1. **Define:**
   (*a*) feudal system,    (*b*) fiefs

2. **Identify:**
   (*a*) Charlemagne,    (*b*) Pope Leo III,    (*c*) William of Normandy,    (*d*) Henry II

3. **Recall:**
   (*a*) What three major elements contributed to the formation of European civilization?
   (*b*) Explain how Henry II strengthened the monarchy's power.

4. **Think Critically:**
   (*a*) How did the Magna Carta interpret the relationship between the monarchy and the vassals?
   (*b*) How was European civilization in the High Middle Ages different from that of the Late Middle Ages?

## REBIRTH, REFORM, AND CRISIS: STATE BUILDING IN EUROPE (1500 TO 1700)

Between 1350 and 1550, Italian intellectuals believed that they were living in a new age. This new age, based on a rebirth of the culture of the Greeks and Romans, came to be known as the Renaissance. The Renaissance, which began in Italy, was a period of transition as well as a continuation of the economic, political, and social trends that had begun in the High Middle Ages. It was also a new age in which intellectuals and artists proclaimed a new vision of humankind and raised fundamental questions about the value and importance of the individual. Of course, intellectuals and artists wrote and painted for the upper classes. The brilliant intellectual, cultural, and artistic accomplishments of the Renaissance were really products of and for the elite. The ideas of the Renaissance did not have a broad base among the masses of the people.

The Renaissance did, however, raise new questions about medieval traditions. In advocating a return to the early sources of Christianity and criticizing current religious practices, the intellectuals known as humanists aroused fundamental issues about the Catholic Church, which was still an important institution. In the sixteenth century, the intellectual revolution of the fifteenth century gave way to a religious renaissance that touched the lives of people, including the masses, in new and profound ways.

## The Reformation

On April 18, 1520, a lowly monk stood before the emperor and princes of Germany in the city of Worms. He had been called before this gathering to answer charges of heresy—charges that could threaten his very life. The monk was shown a pile of his books and asked if he wished to defend them all or reject a part. Courageously, Martin Luther defended them all. He asked to be shown where any part was in error on the basis of "Scripture and plain reason." The emperor was outraged by Luther's response and made his own position clear the next day: "Not only I, but you of this noble German nation, would be forever disgraced if by our negligence not only heresy but the very suspicion of heresy were to survive. After having heard yesterday the obstinate defense of Luther, I regret that I have so long delayed in proceeding against him and his false teaching. I will have no more to do with him." Luther's appearance at Worms set the stage for the beginning of the Protestant Reformation.

The movement begun by Martin Luther when he made his dramatic stand quickly spread across Europe. Within a short time, new Protestant churches were attracting supporters all over Europe. Although seemingly helpless to stop the new churches, the Catholic Church also underwent a religious rebirth and managed to revive its fortunes. By the mid-sixteenth century, the religious division had produced two militant faiths—Calvinism and Catholicism—that were prepared to do combat for the souls of the faithful. An age of religious passion would soon be followed by an age of religious warfare.

◄ *Martin Luther is shown at the far left in this painting, while the prince, Elector John Frederick of Saxony, takes center stage. Other reformers surround the German prince. Why do you think the artist chose to put the prince in the foreground, not Luther?*

One of the responses to these crises was a search for order. Many states satisfied this search by extending monarchical power and creating absolutism, or absolute monarchy. **Absolutism** meant that the ultimate authority in the state rested in the hands of monarchs, who claimed that they received their power from God. Absolutism was most evident in France during the flamboyant reign of Louis XIV, regarded by some as the perfect embodiment of an absolute monarch. In his

▼ *Louis XIV, shown here, had a clear vision of himself as absolute monarch and had no intention of sharing his power with anyone. What effect do you think his views on monarchical government had on the landed aristocracy and the educated middle class in France?*

## Crisis in Europe and the Emergence of Absolutism

The religious upheavals of the sixteenth century had left Europeans sorely divided and led to a series of wars that dominated much of European history from 1560 to 1650. Wars, revolutions, economic crises, and social crises all haunted Europe. Indeed, the ninety-year period from 1560 to 1650 was an age of crisis in European life.

**Map 2.6   Europe in the Seventeenth Century**

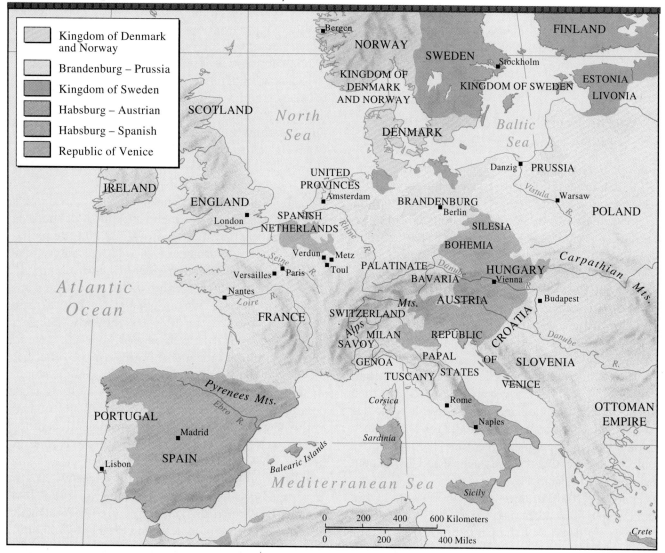

Kingdom of Denmark and Norway

Brandenburg – Prussia

Kingdom of Sweden

Habsburg – Austrian

Habsburg – Spanish

Republic of Venice

memoirs, duc de Saint-Simon, who had firsthand experience of French court life, said that Louis was "the very figure of a hero, so imbued with a natural majesty that it appeared even in his most insignificant gestures and movements." The king's natural grace gave him a special charm as well: "He was as dignified and majestic in his dressing gown as when dressed in robes of state, or on horseback at the head of his troops." Louis excelled at exercise and was never affected by the weather: "Drenched with rain or snow, pierced with cold, bathed in sweat or covered with dust, he was always the same." He spoke well and learned quickly. His self-control was evident: "He did not lose control of himself ten times in his whole life, and then only with inferior persons." However, even absolute monarchs had imperfections, and Saint-Simon had the courage to point them out: "Louis XIV's vanity was without limit or restraint" and led to his "mistakes of judgment in matters of importance."

Absolute monarchy was also set up in Austria, Prussia, and Russia. It was not the only response to crisis in the seventeenth century, however. In western Europe, the Dutch Republic successfully resisted monarchy. Moreover, England created a system in which monarchs were limited by the power of a parliament. However, it took two revolutions before the English Parliament achieved this goal.

## The English Revolutions of the Seventeenth Century

At the core of the English revolutions of the seventeenth century was a struggle between king and Parliament that turned into an armed conflict to determine the roles that king and Parliament should play in governing England. The struggle over this political issue, however, was complicated by a deep and profound religious controversy.

With the death of Queen Elizabeth I in 1603, the Tudor dynasty came to an end. The Stuart line of rulers began with the accession to the throne of Elizabeth's cousin, the king of Scotland, who became James I of England. James understood little about the laws and customs of the English. He believed in the **divine right of kings.** That is, he believed that kings receive their power directly from God and are responsible to no one except God. Parliament, however, did not think much of the divine right of kings. Over time, Parliament had come to assume that king or queen and Parliament together ruled England.

Then, too, the Puritans (those Protestants in England inspired by Calvinist ideas) did not like the king's strong defense of the Church of England. The Puritans were officially members of the Church of England. However, they were Calvinists by conviction, and they wished to reform the Church of England by making it even more Protestant. Many of England's gentry, mostly well-to-do landowners below the level of the nobility, had become Puritans. The Puritan gentry formed an important part of the House of Commons, the lower house of Parliament. It was not wise to alienate this group.

The conflict that had begun during the reign of James came to a head during the reign of his son Charles I. Charles believed as strongly in divine-right monarchy as his father had. In 1628, Parliament passed

a Petition of Right, which the king was supposed to accept before being granted any taxes. This petition prohibited taxes without Parliament's consent. At first Charles accepted the petition. Later, he changed his mind, realizing that it put limits on the king's power.

Religious differences also added to the hostility between Charles I and Parliament. Charles tried to impose more ritual on the Church of England. To the Puritans, this was a return to Catholic practices. When Charles tried to force the Puritans to accept his religious policies, thousands of them went to the "howling wildernesses" of America instead.

Complaints grew until England finally slipped into a civil war in 1642 between the supporters of the king (known as the Cavaliers or Royalists) and the parliamentary forces. Parliament proved victorious, due largely to the New Model Army of Oliver Cromwell, the only real military genius of the war. The New Model Army was made up chiefly of more extreme Puritans, known as the Independents, who believed they were doing battle for God. As Cromwell wrote in one of his military reports: "Sir, this is none other but the hand of God; and to Him alone belongs the glory." We might give some credit to Cromwell as well, because his soldiers were well disciplined and trained in the new military tactics of the seventeenth century.

The victorious New Model Army lost no time in taking control. Cromwell purged Parliament of any members who had not supported his forces. What was left—the so-called Rump Parliament—then had Charles I executed on January 30, 1649. Parliament next abolished the monarchy and the House of Lords, and it declared England a republic or commonwealth. However, Cromwell and his army found it difficult to work with the Rump Parliament and finally dispersed it by force. As the members of Parliament departed, he shouted after them: "It is you that have forced me to do this, for I have sought the Lord night and day that He would slay me rather than put upon me the doing of this work." With the certainty of one who is convinced he is right, Cromwell had destroyed both king and Parliament. He then set up a military dictatorship.

After Cromwell's death, the army leaders decided that military rule was no longer desirable. They restored the Stuart monarchy in the person of Charles

◄ *This painting shows the execution of King Charles I. A woman faints at the bottom when the executioner displays the king's head. At the top left is a portrait of the king. Who followed Charles I as England's ruler?*

II, the son of Charles I. The restoration of the monarchy did not mean, however, that the work of the English Revolution was undone. Parliament kept much of the power it had won and continued to play an important role in government. The principle that Parliament must give its consent to taxation was also accepted. However, Charles continued to push his own ideas, some of which were clearly out of step with many of the English people.

Charles was sympathetic to Catholicism. Moreover, his brother James, heir to the throne, did not hide the fact that he was a Catholic. Parliament's suspicions about the brothers' Catholic leanings were therefore aroused when Charles took the bold step of suspending the laws that Parliament had passed against Catholics and Puritans after the restoration of the monarchy. Parliament would have none of it and forced the king to back down on his action. Driven by a strong anti-Catholic sentiment, Parliament then passed a Test Act. This act specified that only Anglicans (as members of the Church of England were called) could hold military and civil offices.

The accession of James II to the crown brought a new crisis for England. James was an open and devout Catholic. His attempt to promote Catholic interests made religion once more a cause of conflict between king and Parliament. Contrary to the Test Act, James

named Catholics to high positions in the government, army, navy, and universities. He issued a Declaration of Indulgence, which suspended all laws excluding Catholics and Puritans from office.

Parliamentary outcries against James's policies stopped short of rebellion, however. Members knew that James was an old man and that his successors were his Protestant daughters Mary and Anne, born to his first wife. However, when a son was born to James's second wife, also a Catholic, the possibility of a Catholic monarchy loomed large. A group of prominent English noblemen invited the Dutch leader, William of Orange, husband of James's daughter Mary, to invade England. William and Mary raised an army and "invaded" England in 1688 while James, his wife, and their infant son fled to France. With almost no bloodshed, England had undergone a "Glorious Revolution." This revolution was not over the issue of whether there would be monarchy but rather over who would be monarch.

The events of 1688 were only the first stage of the Glorious Revolution. Early the next year, Parliament offered the throne to William and Mary, who accepted it, along with a Bill of Rights. The Bill of Rights set forth Parliament's right to make laws and levy taxes. It also made it impossible for kings to oppose or do without Parliament by stating that standing armies could be raised only with the consent of Parliament. The rights of citizens to keep arms and have a jury trial were also confirmed. The Bill of Rights helped to fashion a system of government based on the rule of law and a freely elected Parliament. Thus it laid the foundation for a limited or constitutional monarchy.

Many historians have viewed the Glorious Revolution as the end of the seventeenth-century struggle between king and Parliament. By deposing one king and establishing another, Parliament had destroyed the divine-right theory of kingship (William was, after all, king by grace of Parliament, not God). Parliament had also asserted its right to be part of the government. Parliament did not have complete control of the government. However, it now had the right to participate in governing. Over the next century, it would gradually prove to be the real authority in the English system of constitutional monarchy.

## Political Thought: Responses to Revolution

The seventeenth-century concerns with order and power were reflected in the political thought of the time. The English revolutions of the seventeenth century prompted very different responses from two English political thinkers—Thomas Hobbes and John Locke. Hobbes was alarmed by the revolutionary upheavals in seventeenth-century England and wrote a work on political thought—known as the *Leviathan*—that tried to deal with the problem of disorder.

Hobbes claimed that before society was organized, human life was "solitary, poor, nasty, brutish, and short." Humans were guided not by reason and moral ideals but by a ruthless struggle for self-preservation. To save themselves from destroying one another, people agreed to form a state, which Hobbes called "that great Leviathan to which we owe our peace and defense." This state agreed to be ruled by an absolute ruler with unlimited power. Subjects may not rebel. If they do, they must be crushed. To Hobbes, such absolute power was needed to preserve order in society.

◀ *Peter Hoadley painted this cameo portrait of the new English rulers William of Orange and his wife Mary. How does this painting compare to the portrait of Louis XIV on page 62?*

John Locke, who wrote a political work called *Two Treatises of Government*, viewed the exercise of political power quite differently from Hobbes and argued against the absolute rule of one person. Unlike Hobbes, Locke believed that before society was organized, humans lived in a state of equality and freedom rather than a state of war.

In this state of nature, humans had certain inalienable natural rights—to life, liberty, and property. Like Hobbes, Locke did not believe all was well in the state of nature. People found it difficult to protect these natural rights, so they agreed to establish a government to ensure the protection of their rights. This was a contract of mutual obligations. Government would protect the rights of people, whereas the people would act reasonably toward government. However, if a government broke this contract—if a monarch, for example, failed to live up to the obligation to protect the natural rights—the people might form a new government. Locke's ideas proved important to both Americans and French in the eighteenth century. The ideas were used to support demands for constitutional government, the rule of law, and the protection of rights. Locke's ideas can be found in the American Declaration of Independence and the U.S. Constitution.

## ❀   SECTION REVIEW   ❀

1. **Locate:**
   (a) Prussia,   (b) Austria

2. **Define:**
   (a) absolutism,   (b) divine right of kings

3. **Identify:**
   (a) Martin Luther,   (b) Louis XIV,   (c) James I

(*d*) Charles I,   (*e*) Oliver Cromwell,   (*f*) Charles II,   (*g*) James II,   (*h*) William and Mary of Orange

4. **Recall:**
   (*a*) List three actions of Cromwell that led to the establishment of his military dictatorship.
   (*b*) How does James II's treatment of the Test Act and Declaration of Indulgence show his support for Catholicism?
   (*c*) Describe the "Glorious Revolution."

5. **Think Critically:** Do you agree with the political views of Hobbes and Locke? Explain why or why not.

## NEW HORIZONS: EXPLORATION AND NEW WORLD PATTERNS (1500 TO 1800)

At the end of the fifteenth century, Europeans burst upon the world scene. The process began with the modest ventures of the Portuguese ships that sailed southward along the West African coast in the mid-fifteenth century. It quickened with the voyages of Christopher Columbus to the Americas under the Spanish flag. Soon a number of other European states had entered the scene. By the end of the eighteenth century, they had created a global trade network dominated by Western ships and Western power (see "The Role of Science and Technology: Sea Travel in an Age of Exploration and Expansion" on page 69).

In less than three hundred years, the European "age of exploration" changed the shape of the world. In some areas, such as the Americas and the Spice Islands, the movement led to the destruction of local civilizations and the establishment of European colonies. In other areas, such as Africa and mainland Southeast Asia, it left native regimes intact but had a strong impact on local societies and regional trade patterns. European expansion affected Africa with the dramatic expansion of the slave trade. The Dutch built a trade empire based on spices in the Indonesian archipelago, and trade increased in Southeast Asia. Most societies

### CONNECTIONS AROUND THE WORLD

**A Population Explosion**   Between 1700 and 1800, many areas in the world experienced a population explosion. In Europe, China, India, and the Muslim world, the number of people grew dramatically. Europe, for example, went from 120 million people to almost 200 million by 1800; China, from less than 200 million to 300 million during the same period.

Four factors were important in causing this population explosion. First, better growing conditions affected wide areas of the world and enabled people to produce more food. Second, by the eighteenth century, people had begun to develop immunities to epidemic diseases. The spread of people by ship after 1500 had led to devastating epidemics. For example, the arrival of Europeans in Mexico led to smallpox, measles, and chicken pox among a native population that had no immunities to European diseases. In 1500, between 11 and 20 million people lived in the area of Mexico; by 1650, only 1.5 million remained. By 1750, however, plagues and epidemic diseases were no longer as devastating in Europe, India, China, and the Middle East.

A third factor in population increase came from new food sources. The use of American food crops, such as sweet potatoes in China, corn in Africa and Europe, and the potato in northern Europe and Russia, provided new sources of nutrition. Finally, the use of new weapons based on gunpowder allowed states to control larger territories and ensure a new degree of order. Less violence led to fewer deaths.

in that region, however, were still based on farming. One historian has described the period as the beginning of an "age of Western dominance."

The age of European exploration also affected other areas of the world, such as East Asia, South Asia, and

▲ *In this Indian painting, Akbar, Babur's grandson, leads an attack from his war elephant. What was used to construct the bridge that the elephants are using?*

the Middle East. South Asia and the Middle East felt the European influence most keenly, because the stated objective of many European adventurers was to bring an end to Muslim domination of the Indian Ocean trade network. However, the Islamic world was able to handle the challenge.

## The Muslim Empires

At the beginning of the sixteenth century, India was still divided into a number of kingdoms. To the north of India, in present-day Afghanistan, lived a military adventurer named Babur. Babur began with a pitifully small following. He described these people this way: "The greater part of my followers (about 250 men) were on foot with sandals on their feet, clubs in their hands, and long frocks over their shoulders." After seizing Kabul in 1504, Babur increased his forces, armed them with the new firearms, and expanded his vision to the lands of India. With a force of eight thousand, but now armed with artillery, he destroyed the forces of the Lodi (the dynasty in power) ruler of North India. (Twenty thousand of the latter's army of fifty thousand were left dead on the battlefield.) Nine months later, Babur's army faced yet another Indian prince with a considerably larger army. Babur rallied his forces with

## THE ROLE OF SCIENCE AND TECHNOLOGY
# Sea Travel in an Age of Exploration and Expansion

Europeans could not have made their sea voyages without a certain level of knowledge and technology, much of which was acquired from the Arabs. First, they needed to know where they could sail. In the thirteenth and fourteenth centuries, Arab navigators and mathematicians had drawn detailed charts, known as *portolani*. They gave details on the shape of coastlines and distances between ports. These charts proved to be of great value for voyages in European waters. The *portolani* had a weakness, however: they were drawn on a flat scale and took no account of the curvature of Earth. Thus, they were of little value for longer, overseas voyages. Only as sailors began to move beyond the coasts of Europe did they gain information about the actual shape of Earth. By the

*Long distance voyages were made possible by the development of this ship, the caravel. What special attributes of the caravel made these far-reaching ocean journeys possible?*

The use of multiple masts was pioneered by the Chinese in the fourteenth century.

The triangular lateen sail that allowed the ship to sail into the wind originated in the Muslim world.

The sails were made of different weights of cloth or canvas for different types of winds.

The deep-sea rudder posted on the stern was invented by the Chinese and transmitted to Europe via trade with the Muslims.

*(continued)*

## THE ROLE OF SCIENCE AND TECHNOLOGY
# Sea Travel in an Age of Exploration and Expansion, continued

end of the fifteenth century, cartography—the art and science of mapmaking—had reached the point where Europeans had fairly accurate maps of the known world.

Moreover, Europeans had developed remarkably seaworthy ships. European shipmakers had learned how to build ships large enough and strong enough to sail in any waters. They had also figured out how to combine the use of lateen sails (triangular sails) with a square rig. This enabled them to build ships mobile enough to sail against the wind and to engage in naval warfare. The ships were also large enough to mount heavy cannon and carry a substantial amount of goods over long distances.

Europeans had also learned new navigational techniques from the Arabs. Previously, sailors had used their knowledge of the position of the North Star to figure out their latitude—how far north or south of the equator they were. Below the equator, however, this technique was useless. New naviga-

◀ *The Hispano-Moorish astrolabe shown here is from 1068. Why were better navigational aids needed by European sailors in the fifteenth and sixteenth centuries?*

tional aids, such as the compass and the astrolabe (also perfected by the Arabs), gave them the confidence to explore the high seas. The compass showed in what direction a ship was moving. The astrolabe used the sun or a star to ascertain a ship's latitude.

1. What two contributions of the Arabs made sailing easier for the Europeans?

2. What two advances made by the end of the fifteenth century caused sea exploration to increase?

3. Which one advance discussed in this feature do you feel was the most important for early explorers? Explain your answer.

the following words: "Let us, then, with one accord, swear on God's holy word, that none of us will even think of turning his face from this warfare, nor desert from the battle and slaughter that ensues, till his soul is separated from his body." Babur's troops responded with enthusiasm and won yet another decisive victory. "Towards evening," Babur wrote later, "the confusion was complete, and the slaughter was dreadful. The fate of the battle was decided . . . I ordered the [enemy leader] to be flayed alive." With his victories, Babur created a great Muslim empire—the Mughal Empire—in India.

Meanwhile, Europeans had been trying for hundreds of years to weaken the forces of Islam. In the sixteenth century, European fleets had had some success in taking control of the spice trade from Muslim shippers. Even this success, however, did not cripple the power of Islam.

In fact, during Europe's age of exploration, between 1500 and 1800, the world of Islam experienced new life with the rise of three great Muslim empires. Known as the Ottomans, the Safavids, and the Mughals, these three powerful Muslim states dominated the Middle East and the South Asia subcontinent. They brought stability to a region that had been in turmoil for centuries. This stability, however, lasted for only about two centuries. By 1800, much of India and the Middle East had come under severe European pressure and had returned to a state of anarchy. The Ottoman Empire itself had entered a period of gradual decline.

The Muslim empires, however, were not the only states that were able to resist the first outward thrust of European expansion. Further to the east, the mature civilizations in China and Japan successfully faced a similar challenge from European merchants and missionaries.

## The East Asian World

Between 1500 and 1800, China experienced one of its most glorious eras. The empire expanded, and Chinese culture earned the admiration of many European visitors. China seemed unchanging. In reality, however, it was beginning to experience a great deal of change.

So, too, was Japan. Vigorous new leadership at the beginning of the seventeenth century kept the traditional Japanese system alive for almost another 250 years. However, underneath the surface of stability, major changes were also taking place in Japanese society. One of the factors that quickened the pace of change in both China and Japan was contact with the West.

When Christopher Columbus sailed from southern Spain in August 1492, he was seeking a route to China and Japan. He did not find it, but others soon did. In 1514, Portuguese ships arrived on the coast of South China. Thirty years later, a small group of Portuguese merchants became the first Europeans to set foot on the islands of Japan.

At first the new arrivals were welcomed (see "You Are There: The Japanese Discover Firearms"). Several nations established trade relations with Japan and China. Christian missionaries were active in both countries. However, European success was short-lived. During the seventeenth century, most of the merchants and missionaries were forced to leave. From that time until the beginning of the nineteenth cen-

tury, neither Japan nor China was much affected by events taking place outside the region.

Chinese and Japanese leaders had adopted their "closed country" policy to keep out foreign ideas and protect native values and institutions. In one respect, the policy worked. Both countries were able to resist the fate of many Asian societies during the period. Both the Japanese and Chinese societies were changing, however, and by the early nineteenth century were quite different from what they had been three hundred years earlier. Under these conditions, both countries were soon forced to face a new challenge from the aggressive power of an industrializing Europe.

## SECTION REVIEW

1. **Locate:**
   (*a*) Indian Ocean,   (*b*) China

2. **Identify:**
   (*a*) Babur

3. **Recall:**
   (*a*) What was the state of India and the Middle East in 1800?
   (*b*) Why did the Chinese and Japanese adopt their "closed door policy"?

4. **Think Critically:** In what ways might the "age of exploration" have led to the "age of western dominance"?

### 6

## TOWARD A NEW HEAVEN AND A NEW EARTH: AN INTELLECTUAL REVOLUTION IN THE WEST

In 1633, the Italian scientist Galileo was put on trial by the Catholic Church for maintaining that the sun was the center of the universe and that the Earth moved around the sun. Galileo, who was sixty years old and in

## YOU ARE THERE

# The Japanese Discover Firearms

◀ *The first Portuguese traders to Japan landed there by accident. This late sixteenth-century painting is a Japanese account of that first landing at Nagasaki. What features seem out of place or curious to you?*

*The Portuguese brought firearms to Japan in the sixteenth century. In this selection, the* daimyo *of a small island off the southern tip of Japan receives an explanation of how to use the new weapons. Obviously, he is fascinated by the results.*

### A *Daimyo* Lord Describes How to Use a Firearm

There are two leaders among the traders. In their hands they carried something two or three feet long, straight on the outside with a passage inside, and made of a heavy substance. The inner passage runs through it although it is closed at the end. At its side, there is an opening which is the passageway for fire. Its shape defies comparison with any-

thing I know. To use it, fill it with powder and small lead pellets. Set up a small target on a bank. Grip the object in your hand, compose your body, and closing one eye, apply fire to the opening. Then the pellet hits the target squarely. The explosion is like lightning and the report like thunder. Bystanders must cover their ears. This thing with one blow can smash a mountain of silver and a wall of iron. If one sought to do mischief in another man's domain and he was touched by it, he would lose his life instantly. . . . Lord Tokitaka saw it and thought it was the wonder of wonders. He did not know its name at first nor the

*(continued)*

## YOU ARE THERE

# The Japanese Discover Firearms, continued

details of its use. Then someone called it "iron-arms. . . ."

Disregarding the high price of the arms, Tokitaka purchased from the aliens two pieces of the firearms for his family treasure. As for the art of grinding, sifting, and mixing of the powder, Tokitaka let his retainer learn it. Tokitaka occupied himself, morning and night, and without rest in handling the arms. As a result, he was able to convert the misses of his early experiments into hits—a hundred hits in a hundred attempts.

1. Who introduced firearms to Japan in the sixteenth century?

2. Considering the description of the firearm the Portuguese brought, what do you think we would call it today?

3. In the last paragraph, what does the term *aliens* refer to?

---

ill health, was kept waiting for two months before he was tried and found guilty of **heresy** (the holding of religious doctrines different from the official teachings of the church) and disobedience. Completely shattered by the experience, Galileo condemned his supposed errors: "With a sincere heart I curse and detest the said errors contrary to the Holy Church, and I swear that I will nevermore in future say or assert anything that may give rise to a similar suspicion of me." Legend holds that when he left the trial room, Galileo muttered to himself: "And yet it does move!" (referring to the Earth).

Galileo was but one of the scientists of the seventeenth century who set the Western world on a new path known as the Scientific Revolution. The Scientific Revolution brought to Europeans a new way of viewing the universe and their place in it.

## The Scientific Revolution

The Scientific Revolution was a major turning point in modern civilization. In the Scientific Revolution, the Western world overthrew the medieval worldview and arrived at a new conception of the universe. The universe was now seen as having the sun at the center and the planets as material bodies revolving around the sun in elliptical orbits. The world was seen as infinite rather than finite. With the changes in the conception of "heaven" came changes in the conception of "Earth."

The work of Francis Bacon and René Descartes left Europeans with the idea of the separation of mind and matter and the belief that by using only reason, people could, in fact, understand and dominate the world of nature. The development of a scientific method (a way to examine nature built upon the use of organized experiments and thorough observation) furthered the work of scientists. The creation of scientific societies spread the results of the Scientific Revolution. Although churches resisted the new ideas, nothing was able to halt the replacement of the traditional ways of thinking with new ones. This was the time of a fundamental break with the past.

## The Enlightenment

The eighteenth-century Enlightenment was a movement of intellectuals who were greatly impressed with the achievements of the Scientific Revolution. One of

▶ *Louis XIV formally recog-nized the French Academy in 1666, at which time the organi-zation became the French Royal Academy of Sciences. In this painting, Louis is seated and Minister Colbert and members of the academy gather around the king. What advantages and dis-advantages might have resulted from the king's patronage?*

the favorite words of these intellectuals was *reason*, by which they meant the application of the scientific method to the understanding of all life. They believed that all institutions and all systems of thought were subject to the rational, scientific way of thinking if people would only free themselves from past, worthless traditions, especially religious ones. These thinkers believed that if scientists could discover the natural laws regulating the world of nature, they as thinkers, too, could use reason to find the laws that governed human society. They hoped that in doing so, they could make progress toward a better society than the one they had inherited. *Reason, natural law, hope, progress*—these were common words to the thinkers of the Enlightenment.

### The Philosophes and Their Ideas

The intellectuals of the Enlightenment were known by the French term **philosophes.** They were not all French, and few were philosophers in the strict sense of the term. They were literary people, professors, jour-nalists, economists, political scientists, and above all,

social reformers. They came from both the nobility and the middle class. A few even had lower-middle-class origins. The Enlightenment was a truly international movement, but most of the leaders of the Enlighten-ment were French. The French philosophes influenced intellectuals elsewhere and created a movement that touched the entire Western world.

To the philosophes, the role of philosophy was to change the world, not just discuss it. As one writer said, the philosophe is one who "applies himself to the study of society with the purpose of making his kind better and happier." To the philosophes, reason was scientific method. Reason meant an appeal to facts. A critical spirit based on reason was to be applied to everything, including religion and politics.

The philosophes often disagreed as well. The Enlightenment spanned almost an entire century, and it evolved over time. Each succeeding generation became more radical as it built upon the contributions of the previous one. A few people, however, dominated the landscape completely. We might best begin our sur-vey of the ideas of the philosophes by looking at two French giants: Montesquieu and Voltaire.

The baron de Montesquieu came from the French nobility. His most famous work, *The Spirit of the Laws*, was published in 1748. In this comparative study of governments, Montesquieu tried to apply the scientific method to the social and political arena to find the "natural laws" that governed the social and political relationships of human beings.

Montesquieu found three basic kinds of governments: (1) republics, which are suitable for small states; (2) despotism, which is appropriate for large states; and (3) monarchy, which is appropriate for moderate-size states. Montesquieu used England as an example of monarchy. His analysis of England's constitution led to his most lasting contribution to political thought—the importance of checks and balances created by means of a **separation of powers.** He believed that England's system was based on this separation of the executive, legislative, and judicial powers. Each power limited and controlled the other, which in turn provided the greatest freedom and security for the state. The translation of Montesquieu's work into English made it available to American philosophes, who took its principles and worked them into the U.S. Constitution.

The greatest figure of the Enlightenment was François-Marie Arouet, known simply as Voltaire. He was from a prosperous middle-class family in Paris. Although he studied law, he wished to be a writer and achieved his first success as a playwright. Voltaire wrote an almost endless stream of pamphlets, novels, plays, letters, essays, and histories. His writings brought him both fame and wealth.

Voltaire was especially well known for his criticism of Christianity and his strong belief in religious toleration. He fought against religious intolerance in France. In 1763, he penned his *Treatise on Toleration*, in which he reminded governments that "all men are brothers under God."

Throughout his life, Voltaire championed **deism,** a system of thought that denies the interference of the

◄ *François-Marie Arouet, Voltaire, was well known for his support of religious tolerance. He was also a prolific writer of poetry, history, and plays, both comedies and tragedies.*

creator in the laws of the universe. Most other philosophes shared this religious outlook. Deism was built upon the idea of the world as a machine. In this view, a mechanic (God) had created the universe. To Voltaire and most other philosophes, the universe was like a clock. God was the clockmaker who had created it, set it in motion, and allowed it to run according to its own natural laws.

### The Later Enlightenment

By the late 1760s, a new generation of philosophes came to maturity. The most famous of these later philosophes was Jean-Jacques Rousseau. The young Rousseau wandered through France and Italy, where he held various jobs. Eventually he made his way to Paris, where he was introduced into the circles of the philosophes. He never really liked the life of the cities, however, and often withdrew into long periods of solitude.

Rousseau's political beliefs were set out in two major works. In his *Discourse on the Origins of the Inequality of Mankind*, Rousseau argued that people had adopted laws and government in order to preserve their private property. In the process, they had become enslaved by government. What, then, should people do to regain their freedom?

In his famous work *The Social Contract*, published in 1762, Rousseau found an answer in the concept of the social contract. In a social contract, an entire society agreed to be governed by its general will. If any individuals wished to follow their own self-interests, they should be forced to abide by the general will. "This means nothing less than that he will be forced to be free," said Rousseau, because the general will represented what was best for the entire community. Thus, liberty was achieved by being forced to follow what was best for each individual.

Another important work by Rousseau was *Emile,* one of the Enlightenment's most important works on education. Written in the form of a novel, the work was really a general discussion "on the education of the natural man." Rousseau's basic concern was that education should foster, rather than restrict, children's natural instincts. Rousseau's own experiences had shown him the importance of the emotions. What he sought was a balance between heart and mind, between emotions and reason.

Rousseau did not necessarily practice what he preached, however. His own children were sent to orphanages, where many children at the time died at a young age. Rousseau also viewed women as "naturally" different from men: "to fulfill her functions, . . . [a woman] needs a soft life to suckle her babies. How much care and tenderness does she need to hold her family together." To Rousseau, women should be educated for their roles as wives and mothers by learning obedience and the nurturing skills that would enable them to provide loving care for their husbands and children. Not everyone in the eighteenth century agreed with Rousseau, however.

### The Rights of Women

For centuries, male intellectuals had argued that the nature of women made them inferior to men and made male domination of women necessary. Female thinkers in the eighteenth century, however, provided suggestions for improving the condition of women. The strongest statement for the rights of women in the eighteenth century was advanced by the English writer Mary Wollstonecraft. She is seen by many as the founder of modern European **feminism** (the movement for women's rights).

In *Vindication of the Rights of Women,* Wollstonecraft pointed to two problems in the views of women that were held by such Enlightenment thinkers as Rousseau. She noted that the same people who argued that women must obey men also said that a system of government based on the arbitrary power of monarchs over their subjects was wrong. Wollstonecraft pointed out that the power of men over women was equally wrong. Moreover, she argued that the Enlightenment was based on an ideal of reason in all human beings. If women have reason, then they, too, are entitled to the same rights that men have. Women, Wollstonecraft declared, should have equal rights with men in education, as well as in economic and political life.

## ❀ SECTION REVIEW ❀

1. **Define:**
   (*a*) heresy,   (*b*) philosophes,   (*c*) separation of powers,   (*d*) deism,   (*e*) feminism

2. **Identify:**
   (*a*) Galileo,   (*b*) Montesquieu,   (*c*) *The Spirit of the Laws,*   (*d*) Voltaire,   (*e*) Rousseau,   (*f*) Mary Wollstonecraft

3. **Recall:**
   (*a*) What was the new view of the universe during the Scientific Revolution?
   (*b*) According to the philosophes, what was the role of philosophy? What was the role of reason?
   (*c*) What did Mary Wollstonecraft believe women were entitled to?

4. **Think Critically:** Montesquieu, Voltaire, and Rousseau developed philosophies on government. In your experience, whose philosophy do you find most important? Why?

## Conclusion

Between 400 and 1500, new patterns of civilization emerged after the collapse of the great empires of the ancient world. During this period of over one thousand years, a number of forces were at work in human society. In India and China, new civilizations began to emerge on the ruins of the old. In the Middle East, the rise of Islam led to a sudden burst of energy in the region and the spread of Arab power into North Africa and the Indian subcontinent. In the meantime, organized communities were beginning to emerge in new areas of the world—in Japan, in Southeast Asia, and in Africa. In some cases, such civilizations appeared as the result of a spread of ideas and technology brought by trade or conquest. In other instances, however, these civilizations developed independently, as in the Americas.

Beginning in the late fifteenth century, a new force entered the world scene in the form of a revived Europe. Western civilization, of course, had a long tradition, tracing back to the Greeks. It had declined as an influential force, however, after the fall of Rome in the fifth century. In the Middle Ages, new forces led gradually to the emergence of a dynamic new European civilization by the end of the fifteenth century.

The period of European history in the early modern era (1500 to 1800) was marked by the Scientific Revolution, which emphasized the power of human beings to dominate nature. After the breakdown of Christian unity in the Reformation, Europeans also engaged in a vigorous period of state building that resulted in the creation of strong monarchies in western and central Europe. In England, however, a struggle between king and Parliament led to a system of limited monarchy.

The rise of the European states had an immediate, as well as a long-term, impact on the rest of the world. The first stage began with the discovery of the Americas by Christopher Columbus in 1492. These voyages and those that followed—collectively known as the age of exploration—led Europeans into new areas of the world. European ships took the lead in developing new patterns of world trade. Some historians have labeled the period the beginning of an era of Western dominance.

# CHAPTER 2 REVIEW

## USING KEY TERMS

1. A person who believes in many gods is

   _____ .

2. The belief that the monarch receives power directly from God is called the

   _____ .

3. _____ refers to the political system in which ultimate authority rests with the monarch.

4. Mary Wollstonecraft is considered by many to be the founder of modern European

   _____ .

5. Montesquieu believed that _____ should bring about checks and balances of one branch of government over another.

6. _____ is a philosophy that says God does not interfere with the natural laws of the universe.

7. The intellectuals, or thinkers, of the Enlightenment were generally called

   _____ .

8. The parcels of land given to Norman Knights after William of Normandy defeated King Harold of England were known as _____ .

9. The basic unit in the African society was the family, especially the _____ (a community of extended family units).

10. The _____ was a political institution that put power into the hands of many different lords, who came to constitute a powerful group of nobles in Europe.

11. Galileo was tried and found guilty for teaching _____, religious doctrines different from the official teachings of the church.

## REVIEWING THE FACTS

1. Describe the city of Tenochtitlán that Hernan Cortés found on his expedition to Mexico in 1519.

2. What is the Quran and how was it created?

3. What three early civilizations in Africa were founded on a mastery of agriculture?

4. Why were the early civilizations of Southeast Asia marked by cultural richness and diversity?

5. What prevented the conquest of Japan by the Mongols?

6. What prevented in Japan the creation of a strong centralized political system like that of China?

7. How did Henry II increase the power of the English monarchy?

8. The Renaissance was a rebirth of the ideas of which ancient civilizations?

9. In his response to Charles V at Worms, what did Martin Luther say was the sole basis for Christian beliefs?

10. What impact did the Glorious Revolution have on the theory of divine right?

11. What three great Muslim empires flourished between 1500 and 1800?

12. What was the Enlightenment?

13. How did Montesquieu arrive at his idea that a good political system must have a separation of powers?

14. What is deism?

15. Why were the written languages of the Mayas, Aztecs, and Incas considered less sophisticated than those in other parts of the world during the fifteenth century?

16. What one act was said to be the emergence of a new European civilization that came into being in western Europe after the collapse of the Western Roman Empire?

17. According to the text, what two militant faiths were produced from the religious division that took place in the mid-sixteenth century?

## THINKING CRITICALLY

1. How did the lineage group system ensure that the values of African societies would be continued?

2. Why was it relatively easy for Islam to penetrate into India in the eleventh century?

3. Louis XIV was "quite willing to pay the price of being a strong ruler." What did this mean for him? Did he have to make sacrifices in his personal life? How do public figures today have to pay the price for their popularity?

4. In what ways might the histories of China and Japan have been different if these countries had been more receptive to the ideas of foreign visitors?

5. Discuss Rousseau's belief that if any individual is determined to pursue his own self-interest at the expense of the common good, "he will be forced to be free." Do you agree or disagree with Rousseau's ideas? Why?

## APPLYING SOCIAL STUDIES SKILLS

1. **Geography:** Study Map 2.2. Explain how the geography of the Mediterranean basin may have both helped and hindered the spread of Islam.

2. **Government:** Compare and contrast the sharing of power between the king and Parliament in England during the thirteenth century and the balance of power between the Congress and President in the government of the United States today.

3. **Government:** What similarities are there between the extension of political power in the British Parliament in the seventeenth century and the growth of women's suffrage (right to vote and participate in government) that took place nearly three hundred years later? What steps do groups need to take to be able to achieve political power?

4. **Sociology:** How do you think the new ideas of the Scientific Revolution and the Enlightenment were received by the average person in the seventeenth and eighteenth centuries? How might you react to scientific discoveries that undermine present ideas of life and the universe? Use a specific example of some recent scientific discovery in your answer.

## MAKING TIME AND PLACE CONNECTIONS

1. When did the first civilizations appear in Central America? What was happening in the Fertile Crescent at this time?

2. Read the Bill of Rights (the first ten amendments to the American Constitution). Compare and contrast it with the Magna Carta that was signed by King John in 1215.

3. What is a major difference between European civilization in the High Middle Ages and in the Late Middle Ages?

4. In the eighteenth century, feminists worked to achieve equality with men in scientific and cultural endeavors. How have the goals of feminists today expanded beyond these original objectives?

## BECOMING AN HISTORIAN

**Analyzing Information and Drawing Inferences:** What are two historical interpretations of the meaning of the crowning of Charlemagne by Pope Leo in 800? Which one does the author claim and how does it determine the direction of his narrative?

**Comparing and Contrasting:** Compare and contrast the ideas of John Locke and Thomas Hobbes about government and society. Which of these thinkers do you believe was closest to being correct in his ideas? Explain why you believe this.

**Art as a Key to History:** You have been commissioned to write an account of the role of science in our lives. Write an essay that will help people five hundred years from now understand how science is a part of our civilization at the beginning of the twenty-first century.

# MODERN PATTERNS OF WORLD HISTORY:

## UNIT TWO

▶ *Pablo Picasso's 1901 painting,* The Fourteenth of July, *celebrates Bastille Day. Happy crowds gather to celebrate their national holiday, many in red, white, and blue.*

| 1755 | 1760 | 1765 | 1770 | 1775 | 1780 | 1785 | 1790 | 1795 | 1800 | 1805 | 1810 | 1815 | 1820 | 1825 | 1830 | 1835 |
|------|------|------|------|------|------|------|------|------|------|------|------|------|------|------|------|------|

**Africa** — ● 1808 Slave trade declared illegal in Great Britain
1831 French seizure of Algeria ●

**India and the Middle East** — 1820–1870 Decline of Ottoman Empire in the Middle East

**East Asia and Southeast Asia**

**Europe and the Western Hemisphere** — 1776–1783 The American Revolution
1810–1822 Latin American movements for independence
1789–1799 The French Revolution

# THE ERA OF EUROPEAN DOMINANCE

## (1750–1914)

The period of world history from 1750 to 1914 was characterized, above all, by three major developments: the French Revolution, the growth of industrialization, and Western domination of the world. The three developments were, of course, directly interconnected. The French and Industrial Revolutions became two of the major forces for change in the nineteenth century as they led Western civilization into the political and industrial era that has characterized the modern world. At the same time, the Industrial Revolution created the technological means, including the new weapons, by which the Western world achieved domination of much of the rest of the world by 1900.

Between 1870 and 1914, Western civilization expanded into all of the Americas, as well as Australia. Most of Africa and Asia was divided into European colonies or spheres of influence. Two major events explain this remarkable expansion: (1) the migration of many Europeans to other parts of the world because of population growth and (2) the revival of imperialism, which was made possible by the West's technological advances.

## UNIT OUTLINE

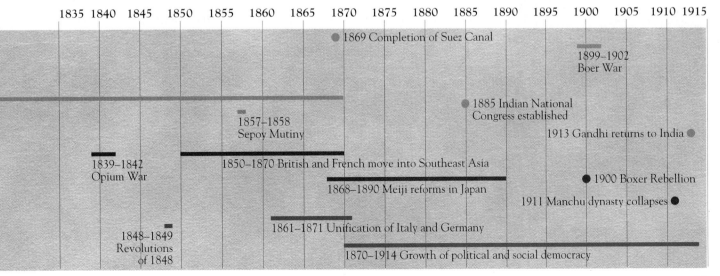

1835 1840 1845 1850 1855 1860 1865 1870 1875 1880 1885 1890 1895 1900 1905 1910 1915

1869 Completion of Suez Canal

1899–1902 Boer War

1885 Indian National Congress established

1857–1858 Sepoy Mutiny

1913 Gandhi returns to India

1839–1842 Opium War

1850–1870 British and French move into Southeast Asia

1868–1890 Meiji reforms in Japan

1900 Boxer Rebellion

1911 Manchu dynasty collapses

1848–1849 Revolutions of 1848

1861–1871 Unification of Italy and Germany

1870–1914 Growth of political and social democracy

# ON THE EVE OF A NEW WORLD ORDER

## (1750 TO 1815)

**3**

On the morning of July 14, 1789, a Parisian mob of some 8,000 men and women in search of weapons streamed toward the Bastille (bah-STEE[uhl]), a royal armory filled with arms and ammunition. The Bastille was also a state prison. Although it contained only seven prisoners at the time, in the eyes of those angry Parisians it was a glaring symbol of the government's despotic policies. The armory was defended by the Marquis de Launay (mar-KEE de loe-NAE) and a small garrison of 114 men. The attack began in earnest in the early afternoon. After three hours of fighting, de Launay and the garrison surrendered. Angered by the loss of ninety-eight of its members, the victorious mob beat de Launay to death, cut off his head, and carried it aloft in triumph through the streets of Paris. When King Louis XVI was told about the fall of the Bastille by the duc de La Rochefoucauld-Liancourt, he exclaimed, "Why, this is a revolt." "No, Sire," replied the duke, "It is a revolution."

The French Revolution began a new age in European political life. The eighteenth century was the final phase of Europe's old order. That old order, still largely based on farming, was dominated by kings and landed aristocrats. We have read about the new intellectual order that emerged in the Scientific Revolution and Enlightenment. At the same time, economic, social, and political patterns were also beginning to change. These changes heralded the emergence of a new order.

A key factor in the emergence of a new world order was the French Revolution. The French Revolution saw the destruction of the old political order in France. The new order that emerged was based on individual rights, representative institutions, and a concept of loyalty to the nation rather than the monarch. The revolutionary upheaval of the era, especially in France, created new political ideals, summarized in the French revolutionary slogan, "Liberty, Equality, and Fraternity." These ideals transformed France and then spread to other European countries and to the rest of the world.

◄ *The guillotine, which was used for the first time in 1792, symbolizes the horror and the reality of the French Revolution. The American Revolution may have served as a model for the French Revolution, but there were many differences between them.*

## ERA OF EUROPEAN DOMINANCE

A NEW WORLD ORDER

| 1750 | 1815 | |
|---|---|---|
| 1750 | | 1914 |

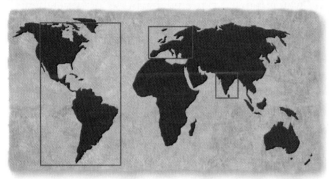

## QUESTIONS TO GUIDE YOUR READING

1. How was European society organized in the eighteenth century?

2. What do we mean by the term *enlightened absolutism?* To what extent was enlightened absolutism practiced in Prussia, Austria, and Russia in the eighteenth century?

3. What were the causes and results of the Seven Years' War?

4. What were the chief characteristics of Latin American society?

5. What caused the American Revolution, and what did it accomplish?

6. What were the long-term and immediate causes of the French Revolution?

7. What were the major events of the French Revolution from 1789 to 1799?

8. What were Napoleon's achievements? Why did his empire collapse?

## THE OLD ORDER AND THE EMERGENCE OF NEW PATTERNS

In the eighteenth century in Europe, economic changes that would have a strong impact on the rest of the world began to occur. The new patterns included rapid population growth, a dramatic increase in food production, the beginnings of an industrial revolution, and an expansion of worldwide trade.

### New Economic Patterns

Europe's population began to grow noticeably around 1750. The total European population was probably around 120 million in 1700. It expanded to 140 million by 1750 and grew to 190 million by 1790. A falling death rate was probably the most important cause of population growth. Why did the death rate decline?

83

More food and better transportation of available food supplies led to a better diet and relief from the famines that had previously been so common. Also of importance in lowering death rates was the disappearance of bubonic plague.

Agricultural practices and methods improved in the eighteenth century—especially in Britain, parts of France, and the Low Countries. Food production increased as more land was farmed, yields per acre increased, and climate improved. Especially important were the moderate summers that provided more ideal growing conditions. Also important to the increased yields was the spread of new vegetables, including two important American crops, the potato and maize (Indian corn). Both had been brought to Europe from the Americas in the sixteenth century.

In European industry in the eighteenth century, the most important product was textiles. Most were still produced by traditional methods. In the cities, artisans produced finished goods in their guild workshops. In the countryside, peasants added to their incomes by spinning raw materials (mostly wool and flax) into yarn and then weaving it into cloth on simple looms. This was a system known as a **cottage industry,** because spinners and weavers did their work on spinning wheels and looms in their own homes, or cottages. A cottage industry was truly a family enterprise; women and children could spin while men wove on the looms.

In the course of the eighteenth century, the demand for cotton clothes, which were less expensive than woolens and linens, increased dramatically. However, the traditional methods of the cottage industry could not keep up with the growing demand. This situation led British cloth manufacturers to develop new methods and new machines. Richard Arkwright invented a "water frame," powered by horse or water, which spun yarn much faster than cottage spinning wheels could. The resulting abundance of yarn, in turn, led to the development of mechanized looms. These were invented in the 1780s but were not widely adopted until the early nineteenth century (see Chapter 4). Already at the end of the eighteenth century, however, rural workers realized that the new machines meant the end of their cottage industries and began to call for the destruction of the machines (see "You Are There: The Attack on New Machines").

In the eighteenth century, overseas trade boomed. This trade expansion led to the emergence of a global economy. Patterns of trade connected Europe, Africa, the Far East, and North and South America. One trade pattern centered on the gold and silver that went to Spain from the South American part of the Spanish

▶ *During the eighteenth century, Dieppe was a modern port city. Trade was carried on with the French colonies throughout the Americas from this busy commercial center. How does this city compare to Italian city-states made wealthy by trade?*

# YOU ARE THERE

## The Attack on New Machines

At the end of the eighteenth century, the use of simple machines brought changes to the traditional cottage industry of cloth making. This selection is taken from a petition of English wool workers to manufacturers. The petition asks that machines (Scribbling-Machines) no longer be used to prepare wool for spinning.

◄ This illustration of a wool carding, or Scribbling-Machine, shows two men doing the work that had been done by twelve to make the same amount of woolen cloth. Carefully examine this illustration and explain how the machine worked.

### The Leeds Woolen Workers' Petition

The Scribbling-Machines have thrown thousands of your petitioners out of work. . . . We therefore request that you pay attention to the following facts:

The number of Scribbling-Machines extending about seventeen miles south-west of LEEDS, exceed all belief, being no less than *one hundred and seventy!* and as each machine will do as much work in twelve hours, as ten men can in that time do by hand, and they working night and day, one machine will do as much work in one day as would otherwise employ twenty men. . . .

Twelve men are thrown out of work for every single machine used; and as it may be supposed the number of machines in all the other quarters together, nearly equal those in the South-West, full four thousand men are left without work. . . . We wish to propose a few questions to those who would plead for the further use of these machines:

How are those men, thus thrown out of work to provide for their families. . . . Some say, Begin and learn some other business.—Suppose we do, who will maintain our families, while we undertake the difficult task; and when we have learned it, how do we know we shall be any better for all our pains; for by the time we have served our second apprenticeship, another machine may arise, which may take away that business also; . . .

But what are our children to do; are they to be brought up in idleness? Indeed as things are, it is no wonder to hear of so many executions; for our parts, though we may be thought illiterate men, our conceptions are, that bringing children up to industry, and keeping them employed, is the way to keep them from falling into those crimes, which an idle habit naturally leads to.

1. What arguments were used by the English wool workers to get rid of their new Scribbling-Machines?

2. Do these arguments sound familiar? In what ways?

**Map 3.1    Global Trade Patterns of the European States in the Eighteenth Century**

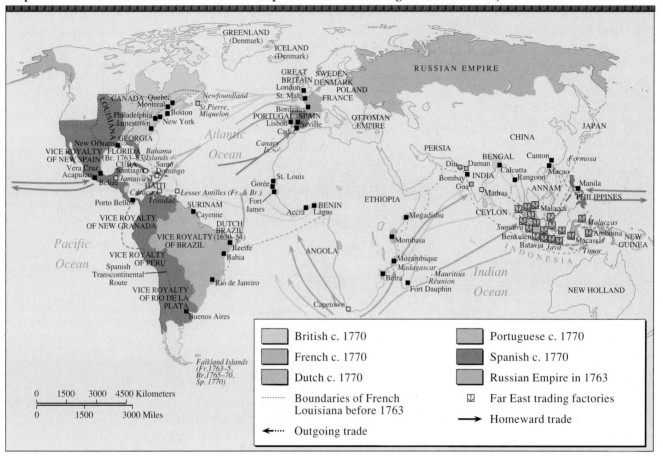

Empire. Much of this gold and silver made its way to Britain, France, and the Dutch Republic, where it was traded for manufactured goods. British, French, and Dutch merchants in turn used their profits to buy tea, spices, silk, and cotton goods from China and India to sell in Europe.

Another important trade pattern involved the plantations of the Americas. The plantations were worked by African slaves and produced tobacco, cotton, coffee, and sugar—all products in demand by Europeans.

In a third pattern of trade, British merchant ships carried British manufactured goods to Africa, where they were traded for a cargo of slaves. The slaves were then shipped to Virginia and paid for by tobacco. The tobacco in turn was shipped back to Britain.

Overseas trade created enormous prosperity for some European countries. By 1700, Spain, Portugal, and the Dutch Republic were increasingly overshadowed by France and England. These two nations built very profitable colonial empires in the course of the eighteenth century. After 1763, however, when France lost much of its overseas empire, Britain emerged as the world's strongest overseas trading nation. London became the world's greatest port.

## European Society in the Eighteenth Century

The pattern of Europe's social organization, first established in the Middle Ages, continued well into the

◄ *This market scene in Turin, Italy, shows the diversity that existed in towns. Communities, then as now, were composed of diverse social groups, with a wide range of incomes and occupations. How many different activities and vendors can you identify in this painting?*

eighteenth century. Society was still divided into the traditional **orders,** or social groups also known as *estates*. Governments helped to maintain these divisions. In Prussia, for example, a law forbade marriage between noble males and middle-class females. Nevertheless, some forces of change were at work in this traditional society. Enlightenment reformers argued that the idea of an unchanging social order based on special privileges was hostile to the progress of society. Despite these ideas, however, it would not be until the revolutionary upheavals at the end of the eighteenth century that the old order would finally begin to disintegrate.

Because society was still mostly rural in the eighteenth century, the peasantry made up the largest social group, about 85 percent of Europe's population. There were rather wide differences within this group, however, especially between free peasants and serfs. In eastern Germany, eastern Europe, and Russia, serfs remained tied to the lands of their noble landlords. In contrast, peasants in Britain, northern Italy, the Low Countries, Spain, most of France, and some areas of western Germany were largely free. Legally free peas-

ants, however, still had burdens. Many owned little or no land. Peasants who did own land still owed a variety of dues and fees to local aristocrats. All these payments were deeply resented.

The nobles, who made up about two or three percent of the European population, played a dominating role in society. Being born a noble automatically guaranteed a person a place at the top of the social order, with all of the special privileges and rights of that position. Nobles, for example, were exempt from many forms of taxation. Nobles also played important roles in military and government affairs. Since medieval times, landed aristocrats had been military officers. The tradition remained that nobles made the most natural, and thus the best, officers. Eighteenth-century nobles also held most of the important offices in the administrative machinery of state and controlled much of the life of their local districts.

Townspeople were still a distinct minority of the total population except in the Dutch Republic, Britain, and parts of Italy. At the end of the eighteenth century, about one-sixth of the French population lived in towns of 2,000 or more. The biggest city in Europe was

London, with its 1,000,000 inhabitants, whereas Paris had about 600,000 people. Altogether, Europe had at least twenty cities in twelve countries with populations over 100,000.

In many cities in western Europe and even central Europe, a small group of very wealthy people known as the patricians continued to control their communities. Just below the patricians stood an upper crust of the middle classes: nonnoble officeholders; bankers; merchants; and important professionals, including lawyers. Another large urban group was the lower middle class, made up of master artisans, shopkeepers, and small traders. Below this group were the laborers, or working classes. Urban communities also had a large group of unskilled workers who were employed as servants, maids, and cooks at pitifully low wages.

Eighteenth-century cities experienced high death rates, especially among children, because of filthy living conditions, polluted water, and a lack of sewers. One observer compared the stench of Hamburg to an open sewer that could be smelled for miles around. Overcrowding became a problem as peasants moved to urban areas in search of work. Because they lacked skills, however, the peasants found few jobs. The result was a serious problem of poverty in the eighteenth century (see "Focus on Everyday Life: The Homeless in Eighteenth-Century Europe").

## Political Change: Enlightened Absolutism in the Eighteenth Century

Enlightenment thought had some impact on the political life of European states in the eighteenth century. The philosophes believed in natural rights for all people. These included equality before the law; freedom of religious worship; freedom of speech and press; and the right to assemble, hold property, and pursue happiness. As the American Declaration of Independence expressed, "We hold these truths to be self-evident, that all men are created equal; that they are endowed by their creator with certain unalienable rights; that among these are life, liberty and the pursuit of happiness."

How were these natural rights to be established and preserved? Most philosophes believed that people needed to be ruled by an **enlightened ruler.** What, however, made rulers enlightened? They must allow religious toleration, freedom of speech and press, and the rights of private property. They must nurture the arts, sciences, and education. Above all, enlightened rulers must obey the laws and enforce them fairly for all subjects. Only strong monarchs could bring the enlightened reforms society needed. According to the philosophes, then, reforms should come from above (from absolute rulers) rather than from below (from the people).

Many historians once assumed that a new type of monarchy emerged in the later eighteenth century, which they called **enlightened absolutism.** Did Europe's rulers, however, follow the advice of the philosophes and become enlightened rulers? To answer this question, we can examine three states—Prussia, Austria, and Russia—where philosophes tried to influence rulers to bring enlightened reforms.

### Prussia: The Army and the Bureaucracy

Two able Prussian kings, Frederick William I and Frederick II, made Prussia into a major European power in the eighteenth century. Frederick William I strove to maintain a highly efficient bureaucracy of civil service workers. The bureaucracy had its own code, in which the supreme values were obedience, honor, and service to the king as the highest duty. As Frederick William asserted: "One must serve the king with life and limb, and surrender all except salvation. The latter is reserved for God. But everything else must be mine."

Frederick William's other major concern was the army. By the end of his reign, he had doubled the army's size. Although Prussia was tenth in physical size and thirteenth in population in Europe, it had the fourth largest army after France, Russia, and Austria. The nobility or landed aristocracy known as Junkers, who owned large estates with many serfs, were the officers in the Prussian army. These officers, too, had a strong sense of service to the king or state. As Prussian nobles, they believed in duty, obedience, and sacrifice. The Prussian army, because of its size and reputation as one of the best armies in Europe, was the most important institution in the state.

## FOCUS ON EVERYDAY LIFE

# The Homeless in Eighteenth-Century Europe

Poverty was a highly visible problem in eighteenth-century Europe, both in cities and in the countryside. In Venice, licensed beggars made up 3 to 5 percent of the population. Beggars without licenses may have constituted as much as 13 to 15 percent of the population. Beggars in Bologna, Italy, were estimated at 25 percent of the population. In France and Britain by the end of the century, an estimated 10 percent of the people depended on charity or begging for their food.

Earlier in Europe, the homeless poor had been viewed as blessed children of God. Helping them was a Christian duty. By the eighteenth century, however, there had been a drastic change in attitude. Charity to poor beggars, it was argued, simply encouraged their idleness and led to crime. A French official stated, "Beggary is the apprenticeship of crime; it begins by creating a love of idleness which will always be the greatest political and moral evil. In this state the beggar does not long resist the temptation to steal." Private charities, such as the religious Order of Saint Vincent de Paul and the Sisters of Charity, worked hard to help the poor. However, they were soon overwhelmed by the increased numbers of homeless in the eighteenth century.

Some "enlightened" officials argued that the state should become involved in the problem, but in most countries people had mixed feelings about poverty. Since the sixteenth century, homelessness and begging had been considered crimes. In the eighteenth century, French authorities rounded up the homeless and beggars and put them in jail for eighteen months as an example to others. The authorities accomplished little by this process, however, because many people had no work. In

▲ Homelessness and poverty were serious problems of eighteenth-century Europe. This illustration shows homeless people seeking food at a shelter in London, England. How does the artist convey the difference between those working in the shelter and those seeking help?

the 1770s, the French tried to use public works projects, such as road building, to give people jobs, but not enough money was provided to accomplish much. The problem of poverty remained as a

(continued)

## FOCUS ON EVERYDAY LIFE
# The Homeless in Eighteenth-Century Europe, continued

serious blemish on the quality of eighteenth-century life. Societies today are still wrestling with this issue.

**1.** Describe the attitudes people had toward the homeless in eighteenth-century France.

**2.** How do those attitudes compare with attitudes toward the homeless in the United States today?

▼ *Frederick II was a well-educated, reform-minded ruler. In this painting, he is shown at his royal retreat Sans-Souci at Potsdam.*

Frederick II, or Frederick the Great, was one of the best educated and most cultured monarchs in the eighteenth century. He was well versed in Enlightenment thought and even invited Voltaire to live at his court for several years. A believer in the king as the "first servant of the state," Frederick the Great was a dedicated ruler. He, too, enlarged the Prussian army (to 200,000 men) and kept a strict watch over the bureaucracy.

For a time, Frederick seemed quite willing to make enlightened reforms. He abolished the use of torture except in treason and murder cases. He also granted a limited freedom of speech and press, as well as complete religious toleration. However, he kept Prussia's rigid social structure intact. He kept serfdom alive and avoided any additional reforms.

### The Austrian Empire of the Habsburgs

The Austrian Empire had become one of the great European states by the beginning of the eighteenth century. It was difficult to rule, however, because it was a sprawling empire composed of many different nationalities, languages, religions, and cultures. Empress Maria Theresa worked to centralize the Austrian Empire in order to strengthen the power of the Austrian state. She was not open to the wider reform calls of the philosophes. However, her successor was.

## Map 3.2   Europe in 1763

Joseph II was determined to make changes. He believed in the need to sweep away anything standing in the path of reason. As he said, "I have made Philosophy the lawmaker of my empire, her logical applications are going to transform Austria." Joseph's reform program was far reaching. He abolished serfdom, eliminated the death penalty, and established the principle of equality of all before the law. Joseph produced drastic religious reforms as well, including complete religious toleration. Altogether, Joseph II issued 6,000 decrees and 11,000 laws in his effort to change Austria.

Joseph's reform program largely failed, however. He alienated the nobles by freeing the serfs. He alienated the church by his religious reforms. Even the serfs were

unhappy, because they were unable to make sense of the drastic changes in Joseph's policies. Joseph realized his failure when he wrote his own epitaph for his gravestone: "Here lies Joseph II who was unfortunate in everything that he undertook." His successors undid many of his reforms.

### Russia under Catherine the Great

In Russia, Peter the Great was followed by six weak successors who were put in power and deposed by the palace guard. After the last of these six successors, Peter III, was murdered by a group of nobles, his

▲ *Catherine favored reform, but not at the expense of her own power. This portrait by Dmitry Levitsky shows her in legislative dress in the Temple of Justice. Why might she have preferred this setting, rather than one that shows her wearing a royal gown and crown in her palace?*

German wife emerged as ruler of all the Russians. Catherine II, or Catherine the Great, was an intelligent woman who was familiar with the works of the philosophes and seemed to favor enlightened reforms. She invited the French philosophe Denis Diderot to Russia and, when he arrived, urged him to speak frankly "as man to man." He did so, outlining a far-reaching program of political and financial reform. However, Catherine was skeptical about what she felt were his impractical theories that "would have turned everything in my kingdom upside down." She did consider the idea of a new law code that would recognize the principle of the equality of all people in the eyes of

the law. In the end, however, she did nothing because she knew that her success depended upon the support of the Russian nobility. In 1785, she gave the nobles a charter that exempted them from taxes.

Catherine's policy of favoring the landed nobility led to even worse conditions for the Russian peasants, and eventually to rebellion. Led by an illiterate Cossack (a Russian warrior), Emelyan Pugachev, the rebellion spread across southern Russia. The rebellion soon faltered, however. Pugachev was captured, tortured, and executed. The rebellion collapsed completely, and Catherine responded by effecting even greater measures against the peasantry. All rural reform was halted. Serfdom was even expanded into newer parts of the empire.

Above all, Catherine proved to be a worthy successor to Peter the Great in her policies of territorial expansion westward into Poland and southward to the Black Sea. Russia spread southward by defeating the Turks. Russian expansion westward occurred at the expense of neighboring Poland. In three partitions of Poland, Russia gained about 50 percent of the Polish territory.

Of the rulers we have discussed, only Joseph II sought truly radical changes based on Enlightenment ideas. Both Frederick II and Catherine II liked to talk about enlightened reforms, and they even attempted some. However, they never took the reforms seriously. To Frederick II and Catherine II, maintaining the existing system took priority over reform. Actually, all three rulers were chiefly guided by a concern for the power and well-being of their states. In the final analysis, heightened state power in Prussia, Austria, and Russia was not used to undertake enlightened reforms. Rather, it was used to collect more taxes, and thus to create armies, to wage wars, and to gain more power. In the next section, we shall look at the wars.

## ❀    SECTION REVIEW    ❀

1. **Locate:**
   (*a*) the Dutch Republic,   (*b*) Prussia,
   (*c*) Russia,   (*d*) Austria,
   (*e*) Black Sea

2. **Define:**
   (*a*) cottage industry,   (*b*) orders,   (*c*) enlightened ruler,   (*d*) enlightened absolutism

3. **Identify:**
   (*a*) water frame,   (*b*) global economy,   (*c*) the peasantry,   (*d*) patricians,   (*e*) philosophes, (*f*) Junkers

4. **Recall:**
   (*a*) What was the main reason for the rapid growth of population in eighteenth-century Europe?
   (*b*) Name two results of the increased demand for cotton clothing.
   (*c*) What were the three values of the Prussian civil service workers' code during the reign of Frederick William I?
   (*d*) How did Catherine II become ruler of Russia?

5. **Think Critically:** Compare and contrast the reforms of Joseph II of Austria with those of Frederick II of Prussia and Catherine II of Russia.

# CHANGING PATTERNS OF WAR: GLOBAL CONFRONTATION

The philosophes condemned war as a foolish waste of life and resources in stupid quarrels of no value to humankind. Despite their words, the rivalry among states that led to costly struggles remained unchanged in the European world of the eighteenth century. Europe consisted of a number of self-governing, individual states that were chiefly guided by the self-interest of the ruler.

The eighteenth-century monarchs were concerned with the **balance of power,** the idea that states should have equal power in order to prevent any one from dominating the others. This desire for a balance of power, however, did not imply a desire for peace. Large armies created to defend a state's security were often used to

conquer new lands as well. As Frederick the Great of Prussia remarked, "The fundamental rule of governments is the principle of extending their territories."

## War of the Austrian Succession

Between 1715 and 1740, it seemed that Europe did want peace. In 1740, however, a major war broke out over the succession to the Austrian throne. When the Austrian emperor Charles VI died, he was succeeded by his daughter, Maria Theresa. King Frederick II of Prussia took advantage of the succession of a woman to the throne of Austria by invading Austrian Silesia (sie-LEE-zhee-uh). France then entered the war against its traditional enemy Austria. In turn, Maria Theresa made an alliance with Great Britain, which feared that the French were growing too powerful on the European continent. The Austrian succession had rapidly produced a worldwide war.

The War of the Austrian Succession (1740 to 1748) was fought in three areas of the world. In Europe, Prussia seized Silesia while France occupied the Austrian Netherlands. In the Far East, France took Madras in India from the British. In North America, the British captured the French fortress of Louisbourg at the entrance to the St. Lawrence River. By 1748, all parties were exhausted and agreed to stop. The peace treaty guaranteed the return of all occupied territories to their original owners except for Silesia. Prussia's refusal to return Silesia meant another war, at least between the two central European powers of Prussia and Austria.

## The Seven Years' War (1756 to 1763): A Global War

Maria Theresa refused to accept the loss of Silesia. She rebuilt her army while working diplomatically to separate Prussia from its chief ally, France. In 1756, Austria achieved what was soon labeled a **diplomatic revolution.** French-Austrian rivalry had been a fact of European diplomacy since the late sixteenth century. However, two new rivalries now replaced the old one: the rivalry of Britain and France over colonial empires, and

**Map 3.3    The Seven Years' War**

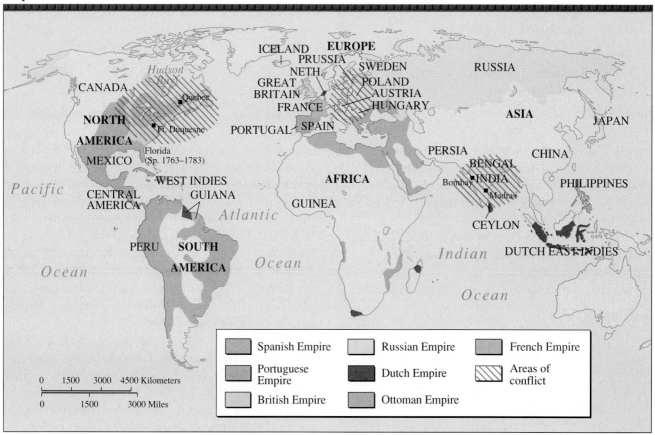

the rivalry of Austria and Prussia over Silesia. France abandoned Prussia and allied with Austria. Russia, which saw Prussia as a major threat to Russian goals in central Europe, joined the new alliance with France and Austria. In turn, Britain allied with Prussia. This diplomatic revolution of 1756 led to another world-wide war. The war had three major areas of conflict: Europe, India, and North America.

Europe witnessed the clash of the two major alliances: the British and Prussians against the Austrians, Russians, and French. With his superb army and military skill, Frederick the Great of Prussia was able for some time to defeat the Austrian, French, and Russian armies. His forces were under attack from three different directions, however, and were gradually worn

down. Frederick faced disaster until Peter III, a new Russian tsar who greatly admired Frederick, withdrew Russian troops from the conflict and from the Prussian lands that the Russians had occupied. This withdrawal created a stalemate and led to the desire for peace. The European war ended in 1763. All occupied territories were returned to their original owners, while Austria officially recognized Prussia's permanent control of Silesia.

The struggle between Britain and France in the rest of the world had more decisive results. Known as the Great War for Empire, it was fought in India and North America. The French had returned Madras to Britain after the War of the Austrian Succession, but the struggle in India continued. The British ultimately won out, not because they had better forces but because they were more persistent. With the Treaty of Paris in 1763, the French withdrew and left India to the British.

By far, the greatest conflicts of the Seven Years' War took place in North America. Both the French and British colonial empires in the New World consisted of large parts of the West Indies and the North American continent. On the tropical islands of the West Indies, both the British and the French had set up plantations. These were worked by African slaves and produced tobacco, cotton, coffee, and sugar.

On the North American continent, the French and British colonies were set up in different ways. French North America (Canada and Louisiana) was run by the French government as a vast trading area. It was valuable for its fur, leather, fish, and timber. However, the French state was unable to get its people to move to North America, so its colonies were thinly populated.

British North America had come to consist of thirteen colonies on the eastern coast of the present United States. Unlike the French colonies, the British colonies were thickly populated, containing about 1.5 million people by 1750. They were also prosperous. The thirteen colonies were supposedly run by the British Board of Trade, the Royal Council, and Parliament, but the colonies actually had legislatures that tended to act independently. Merchants in port cities such as Boston, Philadelphia, New York, and Charleston did not want the British government to run their affairs.

Both the North American and West Indian colonies of Britain and France provided raw materials for the mother countries while buying the latter's manufactured goods. Navigation acts regulated what could be taken from and sold to the colonies. In keeping with the economic ideas of that time, the system was supposed to provide a balance of trade favorable to the mother country, at the expense of the colonies.

The British and French fought over two primary areas in North America. One consisted of the waterways of the Gulf of St. Lawrence, which were protected by the fortress of Louisbourg and by forts that guarded French Quebec (kwi-BEK) and French traders. The other area that was fought over was the unsettled Ohio River valley. The French began to move down from

Canada and up from Louisiana to establish forts in the Ohio River valley. This French activity threatened to cut off the British settlers in the thirteen colonies from expanding into this vast area. The French were able to gain the support of the Indians. As traders and not settlers, the French were viewed by the Indians with less hostility than the British were viewed.

At first, the French scored a number of victories. However, British fortunes were revived by the efforts of William Pitt the Elder, Britain's prime minister. Pitt was convinced that the French colonial empire would have to be destroyed in order for Britain to create its own colonial empire. Pitt's policy focused on doing little in the European theater of war while putting resources into the colonial war, especially through the use of the British navy. The French had more troops in North America, but not enough naval support. The defeat of French fleets in major naval battles gave the British an advantage, because the French could no longer easily reinforce their garrisons.

A series of British victories soon followed. In 1759, British forces under General Wolfe defeated

▲ *Benjamin West painted this scene of General Wolfe, the British commander who successfully led his troops against the French at the Battle of Quebec. Do you think this is a realistic scene of the general's death?*

the French under General Montcalm on the Plains of Abraham, outside Quebec. Both generals died in the battle. The British went on to seize Montreal (MAWN-tree-ahl), the Great Lakes area, and the Ohio River valley. The French were forced to make peace. By the Treaty of Paris, they transferred Canada and the lands east of the Mississippi to England. Their ally Spain transferred Spanish Florida to British control. In return, the French gave their Louisiana territory to the Spanish. By 1763, Great Britain had become the world's greatest colonial power.

## ❀ SECTION REVIEW ❀

1. **Locate:**
   (*a*) Silesia,    (*b*) Madras,    (*c*) West Indies,
   (*d*) St. Lawrence River,    (*e*) Louisiana,
   (*f*) Ohio River,    (*g*) Quebec,
   (*h*) Montreal

2. **Define:**
   (*a*) balance of power,    (*b*) diplomatic revolution

3. **Identify:**
   (*a*) Maria Theresa,    (*b*) Frederick the Great,
   (*c*) Peter III,    (*d*) Treaty of Paris,    (*e*) William Pitt the Elder

4. **Recall:**
   (*a*) Summarize the events that caused the War of the Austrian Succession.
   (*b*) Name the countries in the two major alliances during the Seven Years' War.
   (*c*) Why was the Great War for Empire fought?
   (*d*) Name two of the three groups that officially ran the thirteen British colonies in North America.
   (*e*) Over what two geographical areas did the British and French fight in North America?

5. **Think Critically:** How does the conflict between the British and the French in North America illustrate Frederick the Great's remark that "the fundamental rule of governments is the principle of extending their territories"? Why did each country's pursuit of this principle lead to war?

## COLONIAL EMPIRES AND REVOLUTION IN THE WESTERN HEMISPHERE

As we have seen, the colonial empires in the Western Hemisphere were an important part of the European economy in the eighteenth century. The colonies had also been involved in the conflicts of the European states. Despite their close ties to their European mother countries, the colonies of Latin America and British North America were developing in ways that sometimes differed significantly from those of Europe.

### The Society of Latin America

In the sixteenth century, Portugal came to dominate Brazil while Spain established an enormous colonial empire in the New World that included Central America, most of South America, and parts of North America. Within the lands of Central America and South America, a new civilization arose, which we call Latin America.

Latin America was a multiracial society. Already by 1501, Spanish rulers permitted intermarriage between Europeans and native American Indians, whose offspring became known as the **mestizos.** In addition, another group of people was brought to Latin America—the Africans. Over a period of three centuries, possibly as many as 8 million slaves were brought to Spanish and Portuguese America to work the plantations. Africans also contributed to Latin America's multiracial character. **Mulattoes**—the offspring of Africans and Europeans—joined mestizos and other descendants of Europeans, Africans, and native Indians to produce a unique society in Latin America.

### *Economic Foundations*

Both the Portuguese and the Spanish sought ways to profit from their colonies in Latin America. One source of wealth came from the abundant supplies of gold and silver. Most of the Latin American gold and silver wound up being sent to Europe. Little remained in the New World to benefit those whose labor had produced it.

The pursuit of gold and silver offered fantastic financial rewards. However, farming proved to be a more long-lasting and rewarding source of prosperity for Latin America. A noticeable feature of Latin American agriculture was the dominating role of the large landowner. Both Spanish and Portuguese landowners created immense estates, which left the Indians either to work on the large estates or to work as poor farmers on marginal lands. This system of large landowners and dependent peasants has remained one of the lasting features of Latin American society.

Trade provided another avenue for profit. Latin American colonies became sources of raw materials for Spain and Portugal. Gold, silver, sugar, tobacco, diamonds, animal hides, and a number of other natural products made their way to Europe. In turn, the mother countries supplied their colonists with manufactured goods. Both Spain and Portugal closely regulated the trade of their American colonies to keep others out. By the beginning of the eighteenth century, however, both the British and the French had become too powerful to be kept out of the lucrative Latin American markets.

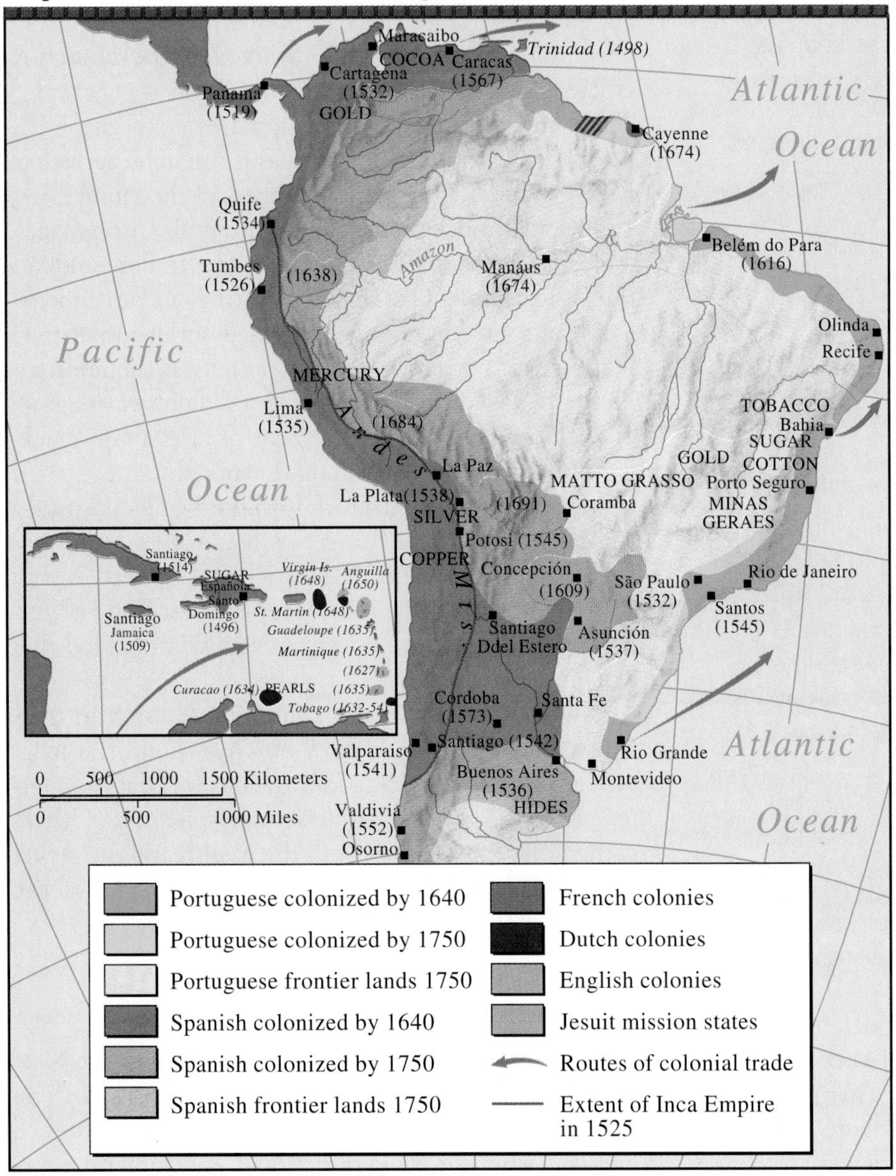

### The State and Church in Colonial Latin America

Portuguese Brazil and Spanish America were colonial empires that lasted over three hundred years. The difficulties of communication and travel between the New World and Europe made the attempts of the Spanish and Portuguese monarchs to provide close regulation of their empires virtually impossible. As a result, colonial officials in Latin America had much freedom in carrying out imperial policies. The most

**Map 3.4   Latin America in the Eighteenth Century**

| | |
|---|---|
| Portuguese colonized by 1640 | French colonies |
| Portuguese colonized by 1750 | Dutch colonies |
| Portuguese frontier lands 1750 | English colonies |
| Spanish colonized by 1640 | Jesuit mission states |
| Spanish colonized by 1750 | Routes of colonial trade |
| Spanish frontier lands 1750 | Extent of Inca Empire in 1525 |

## CONNECTIONS
### TO OUR WORLD

**Large Landowners in Brazil**    In April 1997, Brazilian police in the northern state of Pará opened fire on landless peasants who were seeking to settle on land that had not been used for decades. One local landowner admitted that property owners had paid police to clear away the settlers. Although police claimed that the peasants had fired first, a video filmed at the scene revealed that police officers had opened fire as soon as they arrived. Many of the victims were killed by a single shot in the head or back of the neck.

In Brazil, the wealthiest 2 percent of landowners own 20 percent of the land, more than the combined areas of England, France, Germany, and Spain. Almost 65 percent (or hundreds of millions of acres) of that land is not used. At the same time, more than 50 percent of Brazilian peasants farm less than 3 percent of the land. A Landless Workers Movement has emerged, whose goal is to organize peasants to occupy and settle unused lands.

The enormous gap between a small elite of landowners and a mass of peasants who hold very little land has a long history in Brazil. After the creation of a colony in Brazil in the 1500s, Portuguese kings awarded enormous grants of land to Portuguese settlers who became the ruling class. Leading families in Brazil today, many of them descendants of the original landowners, keep their landed estates even though they are so large that they are unable to farm all of the land. Millions of peasants are left without land and with little hope for a decent life.

important posts of the colonial government were kept in the hands of Europeans.

From the beginning of their conquest of the New World, Spanish and Portuguese rulers were determined to Christianize the native peoples. This policy gave the Catholic Church an important role to play in the New World—a role that added considerably to church power. Catholic missionaries—especially the Dominicans, Franciscans, and Jesuits—fanned out to different parts of the Spanish Empire.

To make their efforts easier, missionaries brought Indians together into villages where the natives could be converted, taught trades, and encouraged to grow crops. A German tourist in the eighteenth century commented, "The road leads through plantations of sugar, indigo, cotton, and coffee. The regularity which we observed in the construction of the villages reminded us that they all owe their origin to monks and missions. The streets are straight and parallel; they cross each other at right angles; and the church is erected in the great square situated in the center."[1] Their missions enabled missionaries to control the lives of the Indians. In turn, the missions served to keep the Indians as docile members of the empire.

The Catholic Church built hospitals, orphanages, and schools. Monastic schools taught Indian students the basic rudiments of reading, writing, and arithmetic. The Catholic Church also provided outlets other than marriage for women. One such outlet was the nunnery. Nunneries were places of prayer. Women in religious orders, however—many of them of aristocratic background—often lived well and worked outside their establishments by running schools and hospitals. Indeed, one of these nuns, Sor Juana Inés de la Cruz (WAHN-uh eh-NAZE de la KROOZ), was one of seventeenth-century Latin America's best-known literary figures. She wrote poetry and prose and urged that women be educated.

The legacies left to the church by the rich in their wills enabled the Catholic Church to build the magnificent cathedrals that adorn the cities of Latin America. Even today, the architectural splendor of these cathedrals reminds us of both the wealth and the power that the Catholic Church exercised in some of the colonial empires of the New World.

## British North America

In the eighteenth century, Spanish power in the New World was increasingly challenged by the British. (The United Kingdom of Great Britain came into existence in 1707, when the governments of England and Scot-

◄ *This sixteenth-century church in Trinidad, Paraguay, was built by Guarani Indians. The two finely hewn stone cherubs carved into this block wall demonstrate the Indians' accomplished skills as stone workers. Why was the church one of the first buildings to be erected when the Spanish created towns in the New World?*

land were united. The term *British* came into use to refer to both the English and the Scots.) In eighteenth-century Britain, the king or queen and the Parliament shared power, with Parliament gradually gaining the upper hand. The king or queen chose ministers who were responsible to the Crown and who set policy and guided Parliament. Parliament had the power to make laws, levy taxes, pass the budget, and indirectly influence the ministers of the king or queen.

The eighteenth-century British Parliament was dominated by a landed aristocracy divided into two groups: the peers (who sat for life in the House of Lords) and the landed gentry (who were elected to the House of Commons). The two groups had much in common. Both were landowners, and they frequently intermarried. The deputies to the House of Commons were chosen from the towns and counties not by popular voting but by election by holders of property. These

▶ *Sor Juana Inés de la Cruz was denied admission to the University of Mexico because she was a woman. As a result of this rejection, she chose to enter a convent where she could write poetry and plays. Do you think she would have had different opportunities in England or France? Why or why not?*

Map 3.5    North America, 1700–1803

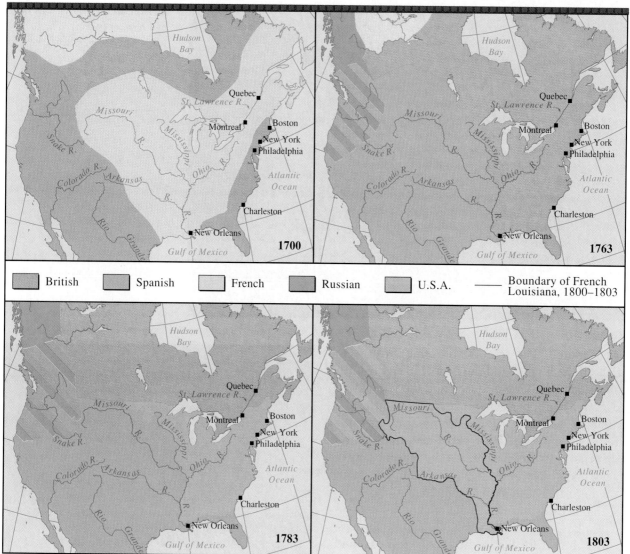

landowners tended to elect the same members of the leading landed gentry families over and over again.

In 1714, a new dynasty—the Hanoverians—was established when the last Stuart ruler, Queen Anne, died without an heir. The crown was offered to the nearest relatives, Protestant rulers of the German state of Hanover. Because the first Hanoverian king (George I) did not speak English, and neither the first nor the second George knew the British system very

well, their chief ministers were allowed to handle Parliament. Robert Walpole served as prime minister from 1721 to 1742 and pursued a peaceful foreign policy. However, growing trade and industry led to an ever-increasing middle class that favored expansion of trade and world empire. These people found a spokesman in William Pitt the Elder, who became prime minister in 1757. He expanded the British Empire by acquiring Canada and India in the Seven Years' War.

### The American Revolution

At the end of the Seven Years' War in 1763, Great Britain had become the world's greatest colonial power. In North America, Britain controlled Canada and the lands east of the Mississippi River. After the Seven Years' War, British leaders wanted to get new revenues from the colonies to pay for the expenses the British army had amassed in defending the colonists and to cover war costs. An attempt to levy new taxes by the Stamp Act of 1765 led to riots. The act was quickly repealed.

In the course of the eighteenth century, significant differences had arisen between the Americans and the British. Both peoples shared the same property requirement for voting—voters had to possess a property that could be rented for at least 40 shillings a year. In Britain, this meant that fewer than 20 percent of all adult males had the right to vote. In the colonies, where there was an enormous group of independent farmers, over 50 percent of adult males could vote.

The Americans and British also had different ideas of empire. The British viewed their empire as a single entity, with Parliament as the supreme authority throughout. Only Parliament could make laws for all the people in the empire, including the American colonists. The Americans, in contrast, had their own representative assemblies. To them, neither king nor Parliament should interfere in their internal affairs. American colonists believed strongly that no tax could be levied without the consent of an assembly whose members actually represented the people.

Crisis followed crisis in the 1770s. To counteract British actions, the colonies organized the First Continental Congress, which met in Philadelphia in September 1774. Outspoken members urged colonists to "take up arms and organize militias." When a British army tried to stop rebel mobilization in Massachusetts, fighting erupted in Lexington and Concord between colonists and redcoats in April 1775.

The colonists did not rush headlong into rebellion and war. It was more than a year after the fighting in Lexington and Concord before the decision was made to declare independence from the British Empire. On July 4, 1776, the Second Continental Congress approved a Declaration of Independence written by Thomas Jefferson. A stirring political document, the Declaration of Independence declared the colonies to be "free and independent states absolved from all allegiance to the British Crown." The war for American independence had formally begun.

The war against Great Britain was a great gamble. Britain was a strong European military power with enormous financial resources. The Americans had formed the Continental Army with George Washington as commander in chief. Compared with the British forces, however, it was made up of undisciplined amateurs who agreed to serve for only a short time.

Of great importance to the colonies' cause was support by foreign countries who were eager to gain revenge for earlier defeats at the hands of the British. The French supplied arms and money to the rebels from the beginning of the war. French officers and soldiers also served in Washington's army. The defeat of the British at Saratoga in October 1777 finally led the French to grant diplomatic recognition to the American state. When Spain and the Dutch Republic entered the war against Great Britain, the British were faced with war against much of Europe, as well as against the Americans.

When the army of General Cornwallis was forced to surrender to combined American and French forces under Washington at Yorktown in 1781, the British decided to end the war. The Treaty of Paris, signed in 1783, recognized the independence of the American colonies and granted the Americans control of the western territory from the Appalachians to the Mississippi River.

### The Birth of a New Nation

The thirteen American colonies had gained their independence, but a fear of concentrated power and concern for their own interests caused them to have little enthusiasm for establishing a united nation with a strong central government. The Articles of Confederation, the American nation's first constitution, were ratified in 1781, but did little to provide for a strong central government. A movement for a different form of national government soon arose. In the summer of 1787, fifty-five

▲ *The* Signing of the Declaration, *painted by John Trumbull, shows John Adams, Roger Sherman, Robert Livingston, Thomas Jefferson, and Benjamin Franklin standing in front of John Hancock, who was president of the Second Continental Congress. Why is this painting so important to American history?*

delegates met in Philadelphia to revise the Articles of Confederation. The convention's delegates—who were wealthy, politically experienced, and well educated—decided instead to devise a new Constitution.

The proposed Constitution created a central government that was superior to the governments of the individual states. The national government was given the power to levy taxes, raise a national army, regulate trade, and create a national currency. The central or federal government was divided into three branches, each with some power to check the working of the others. A president would serve as the chief executive with the power to execute laws, veto the legislature's acts, supervise foreign affairs, and direct military forces. The second branch of government would consist of a Senate elected by the state legislatures and a House of Representatives elected directly by the people. A Supreme Court and other courts "as deemed necessary"

by Congress provided the third branch of government. They would enforce the Constitution as the "supreme law of the land."

According to the constitutional convention, the new Constitution would have to be approved by conventions of elected delegates in nine of the thirteen states before it would take effect. The Constitution was approved, but by a slim margin. Important to its success was a promise to add a Bill of Rights to the Constitution. In March 1789, the new Congress enacted the first ten amendments to the Constitution, which have been known ever since as the Bill of Rights. These amendments guaranteed freedom of religion, speech, press, petition, and assembly. They gave Americans the right to bear arms and to be protected against unreasonable searches and arrests. They guaranteed trial by jury, due process of law, and the protection of property rights. Many of these rights were derived from the

▲ *John Trumbull, an American artist and an aide to George Washington, painted this twelve-by-eighteen-foot scene of Lord Cornwallis (in the center) surrendering to George Washington (just left of the U.S. flag).*

natural rights philosophy of the eighteenth-century philosophes and the American colonists. Is it any wonder that many European intellectuals saw the American Revolution as the embodiment of the Enlightenment's political dreams?

## ❀  SECTION REVIEW  ❀

1. **Locate:**
   (*a*) Portugal,   (*b*) Brazil,   (*c*) Spain,
   (*d*) Central America,   (*e*) South America,
   (*f*) Mississippi River

2. **Define:**
   (*a*) mestizos,   (*b*) mulattoes

3. **Identify:**
   (*a*) Dominicans,   (*b*) Sor Juana Inés de la Cruz,
   (*c*) House of Commons,   (*d*) Hanoverians,
   (*e*) Robert Walpole,   (*f*) Stamp Act of 1765,
   (*g*) First Continental Congress,   (*h*) Articles of
   Confederation,   (*i*) Federalists

4. **Recall:**
   (*a*) What was the role of Africans in Latin American society?
   (*b*) Name two sources of profit for the Portuguese and the Spanish in Latin America.
   (*c*) What country challenged Spanish power in the New World?
   (*d*) How did the system of representative government in Britain differ from the one in the colonies?

(*e*) What was the major accomplishment of the Second Continental Congress?

(*f*) What was the main difference between the Articles of Confederation and the Constitution?

5. **Think Critically:** Analyze the role of the Catholic Church in colonial Latin America.

# TOWARD A NEW POLITICAL ORDER: THE FRENCH REVOLUTION BEGINS

The year 1789 witnessed two far-reaching events: the beginning of a new United States of America and the beginning of the French Revolution. Compared with the American Revolution, the French Revolution was more complex, more violent, and far more radical. It tried to create both a new political order and a new social order.

## Background to the French Revolution

The French Revolution has often been seen as a major turning point in European political and social history. The institutions of the Old Regime were destroyed. A new order emerged, which was based on individual rights, representative institutions, and a concept of loyalty to the nation rather than the monarch. The causes of the French Revolution include both long-range problems and immediate, precipitating forces.

The long-range causes of the French Revolution are to be found in the condition of French society. Before the Revolution, French society was based on inequality. France's population of 27 million was divided, as it had been since the Middle Ages, into three orders, or estates.

The First Estate consisted of the clergy and numbered about 130,000 people. These people owned approximately 10 percent of the land. Clergy were exempt from the *taille* (taw-YEE), France's chief tax. They were also radically divided. The higher clergy,

stemming from aristocratic families, shared the interests of the nobility. The parish priests were often poor and from the class of commoners.

The Second Estate was the nobility, composed of about 350,000 people who nevertheless owned about 25 to 30 percent of the land. The nobility played an important, and even a crucial, role in French society in the eighteenth century. They held many of the leading positions in the government, the military, the law courts, and the higher church offices. The nobles sought to expand their power at the expense of the monarchy. Many nobles said they were defending liberty by resisting the arbitrary actions of the monarchy. They also sought to keep their control over positions in the military, church, and government. Moreover, nobles still possessed privileges, including tax exemptions, especially from the *taille*.

The Third Estate, or the commoners of society, made up the overwhelming majority of the French population. The Third Estate was divided by vast differences in occupation, level of education, and wealth. The peasants, who alone constituted 75 to 80 percent of the total population, were by far the largest segment of the Third Estate. They owned about 35 to 40 percent of the land. However, their landholdings varied from area to area, and over half of the peasants had little or no land on which to survive. Serfdom no longer existed on any large scale in France, but French peasants still had obligations to their local landlords that they deeply resented. These **relics of feudalism,** or aristocratic privileges, were obligations that survived from an earlier age. They included the payment of fees for the use of village facilities such as the flour mill, community oven, and winepress, as well as tithes (voluntary contributions) to the clergy.

Another part of the Third Estate consisted of skilled craftspeople, shopkeepers, and other wage earners in the cities. In the eighteenth century, a rise in consumer prices that was greater than the increase in wages left these urban groups with a decline in buying power. Simply their struggle for survival led many of these people to play an important role in the Revolution, especially in Paris.

About 8 percent of the population, or 2.3 million people, made up the bourgeoisie, or middle class, who

▲ *This painting by French artist Jacques Louis David captures the drama and tension of the Third Estate meeting held in the tennis court of the Jeu de Paume. Do you think the nobility and clergy believed that the Third Estate would react so vehemently to their actions?*

owned about 20 to 25 percent of the land. This group included merchants, bankers, and industrialists who benefited from the economic prosperity after 1730. The bourgeoisie also included professional people—lawyers, holders of public offices, doctors, and writers. Members of the middle class were unhappy with the privileges held by nobles. At the same time, members of the middle class shared a great deal with the nobility. By obtaining public offices, wealthy middle-class individuals could enter the ranks of the nobility. During the eighteenth century, 6,500 new noble families were created.

Moreover, both aristocrats and members of the bourgeoisie were drawn to the new political ideas of the Enlightenment. Both groups were increasingly upset with a monarchical system resting on privileges and on an old and rigid social order. The opposition of these elites to the old order ultimately led them to drastic action against the monarchical regime.

The French monarchy handled the new social realities and problems poorly. Specific problems in the 1780s made things worse. Despite economic expansion for fifty years, the French economy had periodic crises. Bad harvests in 1787 and 1788 and a slowdown in manufacturing led to food shortages, rising prices for food, and unemployment in the cities. The number of poor, estimated by some at almost one-third of the population, reached crisis proportions on the eve of the Revolution.

The immediate cause of the French Revolution was the near collapse of government finances. The French government continued to spend enormous sums on costly wars and court luxuries. It had spent large amounts to help the American colonists against Britain. On the verge of a complete financial collapse, the government of Louis XVI was finally forced to call a meeting of the Estates-General. This was the French parliament, and it had not met since 1614. The Estates-General was composed of representatives from the three orders of French society. The First Estate (the clergy) and the Second Estate (the nobility) had about 300 delegates each. The Third Estate had almost 600 delegates, most of whom were lawyers from French towns. In order to fix France's financial problems, most members of the Third Estate wanted to set up a constitutional government that would abolish the fiscal privileges of the church and nobility.

## The Destruction of the Old Regime

The meeting of the Estates-General opened at Versailles on May 5, 1789. It was troubled from the start with a problem of voting. Traditionally, each estate would vote as a group and have one vote. That meant that the First and Second Estates could outvote the Third Estate two to one. The Third Estate demanded that each deputy have one vote. With the help of a few nobles and clerics, that would give the Third Estate a majority. When the king declared he was in favor of each estate's having one vote, the Third Estate reacted quickly. On June 17, 1789, it called itself a National Assembly and decided to draw up a constitution. Three days later, on June 20, the deputies of the Third Estate arrived at their meeting place, only to find the doors locked. They then moved to a nearby indoor tennis court and swore (hence, the name **Tennis Court Oath**) that they would continue to meet until they had

produced a French constitution. Louis XVI prepared to use force against the Third Estate.

The common people, however, saved the Third Estate from the king's forces. On July 14, a mob of Parisians (puh-REE-zhunz) stormed the Bastille and proceeded to dismantle it, brick by brick. Paris was abandoned to the rebels. Louis XVI was soon informed that he could no longer trust the royal troops. Royal authority had collapsed. Louis XVI could enforce his will no more. The fall of the Bastille had saved the National Assembly.

At the same time, popular revolutions broke out throughout France, both in the cities and the countryside. A growing hatred of the entire landholding system, with its fees and obligations, led to a popular uprising. Peasants decided to take matters into their own hands. Peasant rebellions took place throughout France and became part of the Great Fear, a vast panic that spread like wildfire through France in the summer of 1789. The fear of invasion by foreign troops that would support the French monarchy encouraged the formation of citizens' militias. The greatest impact of the peasant revolts and the Great Fear was on the National Assembly meeting in Versailles.

One of the first acts of the National Assembly was to destroy the relics of feudalism, or aristocratic privileges. On the night of August 4, 1789, the National Assembly voted to abolish the rights of landlords, as well as the fiscal privileges of nobles and clergy. On August 26, the National Assembly adopted the Declaration of the Rights of Man and the Citizen (see "You Are There: Declaration of the Rights of Man and the Citizen"). This charter of basic liberties began with a ringing affirmation of "the natural and imprescriptible rights of man" to "liberty, property, security, and resistance to oppression." It went on to affirm the destruction of aristocratic privileges by proclaiming freedom and equal rights for all men, access to public office based on talent, and an end to exemptions from taxation. All citizens were to have the right to take part in the making of laws. Freedom of speech and press were coupled with the outlawing of arbitrary arrests.

The declaration also raised another important issue. Did its ideal of equal rights for all men also include women? Many deputies insisted that it did, provided

▲ *With the fall of the Bastille, the French Revolution was truly underway. This prison in Paris, a symbol of royal oppression, was completely dismantled by angry commoners. How does the artist convey the confusion and frenzy of this moment?*

that, as one said, "women do not hope to exercise political rights and functions." Olympe de Gouges, a playwright, refused to accept this exclusion of women from political rights. Echoing the words of the official declaration, she penned a Declaration of the Rights of Woman and the Female Citizen, in which she insisted that women should have all the same rights as men

(see "You Are There: Declaration of the Rights of Woman and the Female Citizen"). The National Assembly ignored her demands.

In the meantime, Louis XVI had remained quiet at Versailles. He did refuse, however, to accept the decrees on the abolition of feudalism and the Declaration of Rights. On October 5, thousands of Parisian

## YOU ARE THERE

# Declaration of the Rights of Man and the Citizen

*One of the important documents of the French Revolution, the Declaration of the Rights of Man and the Citizen, was adopted in August 1789 by the National Assembly. Here is an excerpt:*

### Declaration of the Rights of Man and the Citizen

The representatives of the French people, organized as a national assembly, considering that ignorance, neglect, and scorn of the rights of man are the sole causes of public misfortunes and of corruption of governments, have resolved to display in a solemn declaration the natural, inalienable, and sacred rights of man, so that this declaration, constantly in the presence of all members of society, will continually remind them of their rights and their duties; . . . Consequently, the National Assembly recognizes and declares, in the presence and under the auspices of the Supreme Being, the following rights of man and citizen:

1. Men are born and remain free and equal in rights; social distinctions can be established only for the common benefit.
2. The aim of every political association is the conservation of the natural and imprescriptible rights of man; these rights are liberty, property, security, and resistance to oppression. . . .
4. Liberty consists in being able to do anything that does not harm another person. . . .
6. The law is the expression of the general will; all citizens have the right to concur personally or through their representatives in its formation; it must be the same for all, whether it protects or punishes.

◄ *This woodcut shows the figure of Equality holding the Declaration of the Rights of Man and the Citizen. Compare and contrast this figure with the Statue of Liberty that was given to the United States by France.*

7. No man can be accused, arrested, or detained except in cases determined by the law, and according to the forms which it has prescribed. . . .
10. No one may be disturbed because of his opinions, even religious, provided that their public demonstration does not disturb the public order established by law.
11. The free communication of thoughts and opinions is one of the most precious rights of man: every citizen can therefore freely speak, write, and print. . . .
16. Any society in which guarantees of rights are not assured nor the separation of powers determined has no constitution.

1. According to this document, what are the natural (or imprescriptible) rights of man?
2. According to this document, can a person be arrested or otherwise "disturbed" because of his religious beliefs?
3. How do the rights listed in number 2 of the document compare to the rights listed in the Bill of Rights?

# YOU ARE THERE

# Declaration of the Rights of Woman and the Female Citizen

*Olympe de Gouges (a pen name for Marie Gouze) argued that the Declaration of the Rights of Man and the Citizen did not apply to women. Thus, she composed her own Declaration of the Rights of Woman and the Female Citizen in 1791. Here is an excerpt:*

**Olympe de Gouges, *Declaration of the Rights of Woman and the Female Citizen***

. . . Believing that ignorance, omission, or scorn for the rights of woman are the only causes of public misfortunes and of the corruption of governments, the women have resolved to set forth in a solemn declaration the natural, inalienable, and sacred rights of woman in order that this declaration, constantly exposed before all the members of the society, will ceaselessly remind them of their rights and duties. . . .

1.  Woman is born free and lives equal to man in her rights. Social distinctions can be based only on the common utility.
2.  The purpose of any political association is the conservation of the natural and imprescriptible rights of woman and man; these rights are liberty, property, security, and especially resistance to oppression. . . .
4.  Liberty and justice consist of restoring all that belongs to others; thus, the only limits on the exercise of the natural rights of woman are perpetual male tyranny; these limits are to be reformed by the laws of nature and reason. . . .
6.  The law must be the expression of the general will; all female and male citizens must contribute either personally or through their representatives to its formation; it must be the

▲ *In the days of the French Revolution, women took an active role in the politics of Paris, a role that had previously been denied to them. In this picture a group of women are discussing the decrees of the National Convention. Why do you think it suddenly became possible for women to march in the streets and to conduct their own protests?*

same for all: male and female citizens, being equal in the eyes of the law, must be equally admitted to all honors, positions, and public employment according to their capacity and without other distinctions besides those of their virtues and talents.

7.  No woman is an exception; she is accused, arrested, and detained in cases determined by law. Women, like men, obey this rigorous law. . . .

*(continued)*

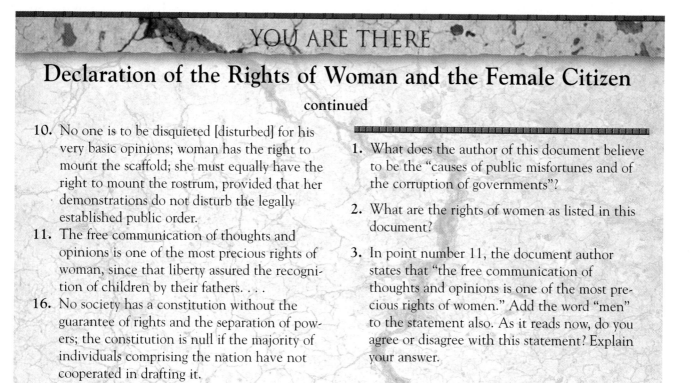

## YOU ARE THERE

# Declaration of the Rights of Woman and the Female Citizen

### continued

10. No one is to be disquieted [disturbed] for his very basic opinions; woman has the right to mount the scaffold; she must equally have the right to mount the rostrum, provided that her demonstrations do not disturb the legally established public order.

11. The free communication of thoughts and opinions is one of the most precious rights of woman, since that liberty assured the recognition of children by their fathers. . . .

16. No society has a constitution without the guarantee of rights and the separation of powers; the constitution is null if the majority of individuals comprising the nation have not cooperated in drafting it.

1. What does the author of this document believe to be the "causes of public misfortunes and of the corruption of governments"?

2. What are the rights of women as listed in this document?

3. In point number 11, the document author states that "the free communication of thoughts and opinions is one of the most precious rights of women." Add the word "men" to the statement also. As it reads now, do you agree or disagree with this statement? Explain your answer.

women—described by one eyewitness as "detachments of women coming up from every direction, armed with broomsticks, lances, pitchforks, swords, pistols and muskets"—marched to Versailles and forced the king to accept the new decrees. The crowd now insisted that the royal family return to Paris. On October 6, the king did so. As a goodwill gesture, he brought along wagonloads of flour from the palace stores. The royal family and the supplies were escorted by women armed with pikes, some of which held the severed heads of the king's guards. The women sang, "We are bringing back the baker, the baker's wife, and the baker's boy" (the king, queen, and their son). The king became a virtual prisoner in Paris.

Because the Catholic Church was seen as an important pillar of the old order, it, too, was reformed. Most of the lands of the church were seized. A new Civil Constitution of the Clergy was put into effect. Both bishops and priests were to be elected by the people and paid by the state. The French government now controlled the church. Many Catholics became enemies of the Revolution.

The National Assembly completed a new constitution, the Constitution of 1791, which set up a limited monarchy. There was still a king, but a Legislative Assembly was to make the laws. The Legislative Assembly was to consist of 745 representatives chosen in such a way that only the more affluent members of society would be elected.

By 1791, the old order had been destroyed. However, many people—including Catholic priests, nobles, lower classes hurt by a rise in the cost of living, and radicals who wanted more drastic solutions—opposed the new order. The king also made things difficult for the new government. He sought to flee France in June 1791. He almost succeeded but was recognized, captured, and brought back to Paris. In this unsettled situation, with a seemingly disloyal monarch, the new Leg-

**A National Holiday**   The French Revolution gave rise to the concept of the modern nation-state. With the development of the modern state came the celebration of one day a year as a national holiday—usually called Independence Day. The national holiday is a day that has special significance in the history of each nation-state.

In France, the fall of the Bastille on July 14, 1789, has been celebrated ever since as the beginning of the French nation-state. Independence Day in the United States is on July 4. On July 4, 1776, the Second Continental Congress approved the Declaration of Independence. In Norway, people celebrate Constitution Day as a national holiday on May 17. On that day in 1814 Norway received a constitution, even though it did not gain its independence from Sweden until 1905.

Most Latin American countries became independent of Spain or Portugal in the early nineteenth century. Their independence days reflect this. Mexico celebrates its Independence Day on September 16 with a colorful festival. On September 16, 1810, a crowd of local people attacked Spanish authorities in a small village near Mexico City. They were crushed, but that action eventually led to Mexico's independence from Spanish control in 1821.

Most nations in Africa and Asia received their independence from Western colonial powers after World War II. India celebrates Independence Day on August 15. On that day in 1947 India received its independence from the British Empire.

islative Assembly held its first session in October 1791. France's relations with the rest of Europe soon led to the downfall of Louis XVI.

Over time, some European leaders began to fear that revolution would spread to their countries. The kings of Austria and Prussia even threatened to use force to restore Louis XVI to full power. Insulted by this threat,

the Legislative Assembly declared war on Austria in the spring of 1792. The French fared badly in the initial fighting. A frantic search for scapegoats began. One observer noted, "Everywhere you hear the cry that the king is betraying us, the generals are betraying us, that nobody is to be trusted; . . . that Paris will be taken in six weeks by the Austrians . . . we are on a volcano ready to spout flames." [2]

Defeats in war, coupled with economic shortages at home in the spring of 1792, led to new political demonstrations, especially against the king. In August, radical political groups in Paris organized a mob attack on the royal palace and Legislative Assembly. They took the king captive and forced the Legislative Assembly to suspend the monarchy and call for a National Convention, chosen on the basis of universal male suffrage, to decide on the future form of government. (Under a system of universal male suffrage, all adult males had the right to vote.) The French Revolution was about to enter a more radical stage.

❀   **SECTION REVIEW**   ❀

1. **Locate:**
   (a) Paris,   (b) Versailles

2. **Define:**
   (a) relics of feudalism,   (b) Tennis Court Oath

3. **Identify:**
   (a) *taille*,   (b) bourgeoisie,   (c) Estates-General,
   (d) Bastille,   (e) Olympe de Gouges,
   (f) National Assembly

4. **Recall:**
   (a) Name and describe the group of people who made up the majority of the French population.
   (b) Give two causes of discontent in French society before the revolution.
   (c) What prompted Louis XVI to call a meeting of the Estates-General for the first time in 175 years?
   (d) What was the Great Fear?
   (e) What was one of the main affirmations of the Declaration of the Rights of Man and the Citizen?

(*f*) Why did many Catholics become enemies of the Revolution?

5. **Think Critically:** Why did the kings of Austria and Prussia want to restore Louis XVI to full power?

# FROM RADICAL REVOLUTION TO THE AGE OF NAPOLEON

In September 1792, the newly elected National Convention began its sessions. It was dominated by lawyers, professionals, and property owners. Two-thirds of its deputies were under age forty-five. Almost all had had political experience as a result of the Revolution. Almost all distrusted the king. It was therefore no surprise that the National Convention's first major step was to abolish the monarchy and establish a republic. On January 21, 1793, the king was executed, and the destruction of the Old Regime was complete. There could be no turning back. However, the execution of the king created new enemies for the Revolution, both at home and abroad. A new crisis was at hand.

The local government in Paris—known as the Commune—had a number of working-class leaders who wanted radical change. Led by Georges Danton (DAW[n]-TOE[n]), the Commune put constant pressure on the National Convention to adopt ever more radical positions. Moreover, the National Convention itself still did not rule all France. Peasants in western France, as well as many people in France's major cities, refused to accept the authority of the National Convention.

A foreign crisis also loomed large. The execution of the king had outraged the royalty of most of Europe. An informal coalition of Austria, Prussia, Spain, Portugal, Britain, the Dutch Republic, and even Russia took up arms against France. The French armies began to fall back. By late spring of 1793, the coalition was poised for an invasion of France. If successful, both the Revolution and the revolutionaries would be destroyed, and the Old Regime would be reestablished.

▲ *Maximilien Robespierre, shown in this portrait, was executed on July 28, 1794, in the same way that he had ordered thousands of others to their deaths—by guillotine. Many considered France to be the most civilized country in the world at the time. Why do you think its leaders felt it was necessary to conduct a nationwide Reign of Terror?*

## The Radical Revolution

To meet these crises, the National Convention gave broad powers to a special committee of twelve known as the Committee of Public Safety. It came to be dominated by Maximilien Robespierre (ROBEZ-PIR), the leader of a political group known as the Jacobins (JACK-uh-bunz). For a twelve-month period, from 1793 to 1794, the Committee of Public Safety took control of France.

### A Nation in Arms

To save the republic from its foreign enemies, the Committee of Public Safety decreed a universal mobilization of the nation on August 23, 1793:

*Young men will fight, young men are called to conquer. Married men will forge arms, transport military baggage and guns and will prepare food supplies. Women, who at long last are to take their rightful place in the revolution and follow their true destiny, will forget their futile tasks: their delicate hands will work at making clothes for soldiers; they will make tents and they will extend their tender care to shelters where the defenders of the Patrie will receive the help that their wounds require. Children will make lint of old cloth. It is for them that we are fighting: children, those beings destined to gather all the fruits of the revolution, will raise their pure hands toward the skies. And old men, performing their missions again, as of yore, will be guided to the public squares of the cities where they will kindle the courage of young warriors and preach the doctrines of hate for kings and the unity of the Republic.*[3]

In less than a year, the French revolutionary government had raised an army of 650,000; by September 1794, it numbered 1,169,000. The Republic's army was the largest ever seen in European history. It pushed the allies invading France back across the Rhine and even conquered the Austrian Netherlands.

The French revolutionary army was an important step in the creation of modern nationalism (devotion to one's country). Previously, wars had been fought between governments or ruling dynasties by relatively small armies of professional soldiers. The new French army was the creation of a people's government. Its wars were now people's wars. When dynastic wars became people's wars, however, warfare became more destructive. The wars of the French revolutionary era opened the door to the total war of the modern world (see Chapter 8).

### The Reign of Terror

To meet the crisis at home, the National Convention and the Committee of Public Safety set in motion the **Reign of Terror.** Under this system, revolutionary courts were set up to protect the revolutionary Republic from its internal enemies. In the course of nine months, 16,000 people were killed under the blade of the guillotine—a revolutionary device for the quick and efficient separation of heads from bodies. The true number of the Reign of Terror's victims was probably closer to 30,000. Most executions were held in places that had openly rebelled against the authority of the National Convention. The Committee of Public Safety held that this bloodletting was only temporary. Once the war and domestic crisis were over, the true republic would follow, and the Declaration of the Rights of Man and the Citizen would be fully realized.

Revolutionary Armies were set up to bring rebellious cities back under the control of the National Convention. Lyons had rebelled against the National Convention during a time when the Republic was in peril. The Committee of Public Safety decided to make an example of that city. Soon, 1,880 citizens of Lyons had been executed. When guillotining proved too slow, cannon fire and grapeshot (a cluster of small iron balls) were used to blow condemned men into open graves. A German observed:

◄ *The French National Convention created its own revolutionary army to help protect France from its foreign enemies. In this painting, citizens are enthusiastically signing up at the recruitment table, and they receive money in return for enrolling. Why was it necessary for France to recruit a new army?*

*Whole ranges of houses, always the most handsome, burnt. The churches, convents, and all the dwellings of the former patricians were in ruins. When I came to the guillotine, the blood of those who had been executed a few hours beforehand was still running in the street . . . I said to a group of citizens that it would be decent to clear away all this human blood. Why should it be cleared? one of them said to me. It's the blood of aristocrats and rebels. The dogs should lick it up.*[4]

## The Reaction

By the summer of 1794, the French had largely defeated their foreign foes. There was less need for the Reign of Terror, but it continued nonetheless. Robespierre, who had become very powerful, was obsessed with ridding France of all the corrupt. Many deputies in the National Convention who feared Robespierre decided to act. They gathered enough votes to condemn him, and Robespierre was guillotined on July 28, 1794.

After the death of Robespierre, a reaction set in as more moderate middle-class leaders took control. The Reign of Terror came to a halt. The National Convention reduced the power of the Committee of Public Safety. Churches were allowed to reopen for public worship. In addition, a new constitution was created in August 1795 that reflected the desire for more stability. Five directors—the Directory—acted as the executive authority.

The period of the Revolution under the government of the Directory (1795 to 1799) was an era of corruption and graft as people reacted against the sufferings and sacrifices that had been demanded in the Reign of Terror. Some people made fortunes in property by taking advantage of the republic's severe money problems. At the same time, the government of the Directory was faced with political enemies. Royalists who desired the restoration of the monarchy continued their plots. The hopes of radicals were revived by continuing economic problems. The Directory, which was unable to find a real solution to the country's economic problems and was still carrying on the wars left from the Committee of Public Safety, increasingly relied on the military to maintain its power. This led to a coup d'etat (KOO-DAE-TAW) (violent overthrow of a government) in 1799 in which the successful and popular military general Napoleon Bonaparte (BOE-nuh-PART) was able to seize power.

## The Age of Napoleon

Napoleon dominated both French and European history from 1799 to 1815. He was born in 1769 in Corsica, only a few months after France had annexed the island. The young Napoleon received a royal scholarship to study at a military school in France. When the Revolution broke out in 1789, Napoleon was a lieutenant. The Revolution and the European war that followed gave him new opportunities, and Napoleon rose quickly through the ranks. At the age of only twenty-five, he was made a brigadier general by the Committee of Public Safety. Two years later, he was made commander of the French armies in Italy, where he won a series of victories. He returned to France as a conquering hero. After a disastrous expedition to Egypt, Napoleon returned to Paris, where he took part in the coup d'etat that led to his control of France. He was only thirty years old at the time.

With the coup d'etat of 1799, a new form of the republic—called the **consulate**—was proclaimed. It was hardly a republic. As first consul, Napoleon controlled the entire government. He appointed members of the government bureaucracy, controlled the army, conducted foreign affairs, and influenced the legislature. In 1802, Napoleon was made consul for life. Two years later, he had himself crowned as Emperor Napoleon I.

One of Napoleon's first moves at home was to establish peace with the oldest enemy of the Revolution, the Catholic Church. In 1801, Napoleon made an agreement with the pope. The agreement recognized Catholicism as the religion of a majority of the French people. In return, the pope agreed not to ask for the return of the church lands seized in the Revolution. With this agreement, the Catholic Church was no longer an enemy of the French government. At the same time, those who had bought church lands during the Revolution became avid supporters of the Napoleonic regime.

Napoleon's most long-lasting domestic achievement was his codification of the laws. Before the Revolution, France did not have a single set of laws but rather almost 300 different legal systems. During the Revolution, efforts were made to prepare a single code of laws for the entire nation. However, it remained for Napoleon to bring the work to completion in the famous Civil Code (or Code Napoléon). This code preserved most of the revolutionary gains by recognizing the principle of the equality of all citizens before the law, the right of the individual to choose a profession, religious toleration, and the abolition of serfdom and feudalism. Property rights continued to be carefully protected, and the interests of employers were safeguarded by outlawing trade unions and strikes.

The rights of some people were strictly curtailed by the Civil Code, however. During the radical phase of the French Revolution, new laws had made divorce an easy process for both husbands and wives and had allowed all children (including daughters) to inherit property equally. Napoleon's Civil Code undid these laws. Divorce was still allowed, but the Civil Code made it more difficult for women to obtain. Women were now "less equal than men" in other ways as well. When they married, their property was brought under the control of their husbands. In lawsuits they were treated as minors, and their testimony was regarded as less reliable than that of men.

Napoleon also developed a powerful, centralized administrative machine. He worked hard to develop a bureaucracy of capable officials. Early on, the regime showed that it cared little whether the expertise of officials had been gained in royal or revolutionary bureaucracies. Promotion, whether in civil or military offices, was to be based not on rank or birth but on ability only. This principle of a government career open to individual talents was, of course, what the middle class had wanted before the Revolution.

In his domestic policies, then, Napoleon both destroyed and preserved aspects of the Revolution. Liberty had been replaced by Napoleon's despotism, but the Civil Code preserved the equality of all citizens before the law. The concept of careers open to talents was also a gain of the Revolution that he preserved.

▲ *This idealistic portrait of Napoleon was painted by Baron Gros. Napoleon had an amazing ability to seize public attention, and he was a master at political propaganda.*

### Napoleon's Empire

When Napoleon became consul in 1799, France was at war with a second European coalition of Russia, Great Britain, and Austria. Napoleon realized the need for a pause in the war and achieved a peace treaty in 1802. However, the peace did not last. War was renewed in 1803 with Britain, which was soon joined by Austria, Russia, and Prussia in the Third Coalition. In a series of battles from 1805 to 1807, Napoleon's Grand Army defeated the Austrian, Prussian, and Russian armies. This gave Napoleon the opportunity to create a new European order.

Map 3.6    Napoleon's Grand Empire

From 1807 to 1812, Napoleon was the master of Europe. His Grand Empire was composed of three major parts: the French Empire, dependent states, and allied states. The French Empire was the inner core of the Grand Empire. The French Empire consisted of an enlarged France extending to the Rhine in the east and including the western half of Italy north of Rome. Dependent states were kingdoms under the rule of Napoleon's relatives. These came to include Spain,

Holland, the kingdom of Italy, the Swiss Republic, the Grand Duchy of Warsaw, and the Confederation of the Rhine (a union of all German states except Austria and Prussia). Allied states were those defeated by Napoleon and forced to join his struggle against Britain. The allied states included Prussia, Austria, Russia, and Sweden.

Within his empire, Napoleon sought to spread some of the principles of the French Revolution, including legal equality, religious toleration, and economic freedom. In the inner core and dependent states of his Grand Empire, Napoleon tried to destroy the old order. The nobility and clergy everywhere in these states lost their special privileges. Napoleon decreed equality of opportunity with offices open to talents, equality before the law, and religious toleration. This spread of French revolutionary principles was an important factor in the development of liberal traditions in these countries.

Napoleon hoped that his Grand Empire would last for centuries, but it collapsed almost as rapidly as it had been formed. Two major reasons help to explain this: the survival of Great Britain and the force of nationalism.

### The European Response

Britain's survival was primarily due to its sea power. As long as Britain ruled the waves, it was almost invulnerable to military attack. Napoleon hoped to invade Britain, but he could not overcome the British navy's decisive defeat of a combined French-Spanish fleet at Trafalgar in 1805. To defeat Britain, Napoleon turned to his Continental System, the aim of which was to stop British goods from reaching the European continent to be sold there. By weakening Britain economically, Napoleon would destroy its ability to wage war. However, the Continental System failed. Allied states resented it. Some began to cheat and others, to resist. Then, too, new markets in the Middle East and in Latin America gave Britain new outlets for its goods. Indeed, by 1809–1810, British overseas exports were at near-record highs.

A second important factor in the defeat of Napoleon was **nationalism.** The spirit of French nationalism had made possible the mass armies of the revolutionary and Napoleonic eras. However, Napoleon's spread of the principles of the French Revolution beyond France indirectly brought a spread of nationalism as well. The French aroused nationalism in two ways. First, they were hated as oppressors. This hatred stirred the patriotism of others in opposition to the French. Second, the French showed the people of Europe what nationalism was and what a nation in arms could do. It was a lesson not lost on other peoples and rulers. A Spanish uprising against Napoleon's rule, aided by British support, kept a French force of 200,000 pinned down for years.

The beginning of Napoleon's downfall came in 1812 with his invasion of Russia. The refusal of the Russians to remain in the Continental System left Napoleon with little choice but to invade. He knew the risks in invading such a large country. However, he also knew that if the Russians were allowed to challenge the Continental System unopposed, others would soon follow suit. In June 1812, a Grand Army of more than 600,000 men entered Russia. Napoleon's hopes for victory depended on a quick defeat of the Russian armies. The Russian forces, however, refused to give battle. They retreated for hundreds of miles while burning their own villages and countryside to keep Napoleon's army from finding food. When the troops of the Grand Army arrived in Moscow, they found the city ablaze. Lacking food and supplies, Napoleon abandoned Moscow and made a retreat across Russia in terrible winter conditions. Only 40,000 out of the original army managed to arrive back in Poland in January 1813.

This military disaster led other European states to rise up and attack the crippled French army. Paris was captured in March 1814. Napoleon was soon sent into exile on the island of Elba, off the coast of Italy. Meanwhile, the Bourbon monarchy was restored to France in the person of Louis XVIII, brother of the executed king. Napoleon then escaped from Elba and returned to Paris. He thus had one last period of rule, called the One Hundred Days, from March to June 1815. At the battle of Waterloo, Napoleon's One Hundred Days ended in bloody defeat. He was exiled to St. Helena, a small and forsaken island in the south Atlantic. Only his memory would continue to haunt French political life.

## ❋   SECTION REVIEW   ❋

1. **Locate:**
   (*a*) Rhine River,   (*b*) Lyons, (*c*) Corsica,
   (*d*) Trafalgar,   ( *e*) Moscow,   (*f*) Elba,
   (*g*) Waterloo

2. **Define:**
   (*a*) Reign of Terror,   (*b*) consulate,
   (*c*) nationalism

▲ *Napoleon's defeat in Russia was a disaster for French troops, and it marked the beginning of a new European coalition that joined forces against France.*

3. **Identify:**
   (*a*) National Convention,   (*b*) Georges Danton,
   (*c*) Committee of Public Safety,   (*d*) guillotine,
   (*e*) Robespierre,   (*f*) the Directory,
   (*g*) Napoleon Bonaparte,   (*h*) the Grand Empire,
   (*i*) the Continental System

4. **Recall:**
   (*a*) What was the first action taken by the National Convention in 1792?
   (*b*) Name three of the countries in the European coalition in 1793. What was the purpose of this coalition?
   (*c*) Why were over 1,800 citizens of Lyons executed?
   (*d*) Describe one of the changes in French governmental policy after the death of Robespierre.
   (*e*) How did Napoleon gain control of France?
   (*f*) What was Napoleon's most long-lasting domestic achievement?

5. **Think Critically:** How was the awakening of nationalism both a benefit and a detriment for France?

## Conclusion

At the beginning of the eighteenth century, the old order remained strong everywhere in Europe. Nobles, clerics, towns, and provinces all had privileges. Monarchs sought to enlarge their bureaucracies. In this way, they could raise taxes to support large standing armies. The existence of these armies led to wars on a worldwide scale. Indeed, the Seven Years' War could be viewed as the first world war. The wars changed little in Europe. However, British victories enabled Great Britain to emerge as the world's greatest naval and colonial power.

Everywhere in Europe, increased demands by governments for taxes to support these wars led to attacks on the old order and a desire for change that was not met by the ruling monarchs. At the same time, a growth in population, as well as changes in finance, trade, and industry, created tensions that undermined the foundations of the old order. The inability of the monarchs to deal with these changes led to a revolutionary outburst at the end of the eighteenth century that marked the beginning of the end for the old order.

The revolutionary era of the late eighteenth century brought dramatic political changes. Revolutions, beginning in North America and continuing in France, were movements based on the people as the source of political power and on the principles of liberty and equality. Liberty meant, in theory, freedom from arbitrary power, as well as the freedom to think, write, and worship as one chose. Equality meant equality in rights, although it did not include the equality of men and women.

The French Revolution created a modern revolutionary concept. No one had foreseen or consciously planned the upheaval that began in 1789. After 1789, however, revolutionaries knew that the proper use of mass uprisings could overthrow unwanted governments. The French Revolution became the classic political and social model for revolution in the modern world. A new era had begun, and the world would never again be the same.

## Notes

1. Quoted in E. Bradford Burns, *Latin America: A Concise Interpretative History*, 4th ed. (Englewood Cliffs, N.J., 1986), p. 62.
2. Quoted in William Doyle, *The Oxford History of the French Revolution* (Oxford, 1989), p. 184.
3. Quoted in Leo Gershoy, *The Era of the French Revolution* (Princeton, N.J., 1957), p. 157.
4. Quoted in Doyle, *The Oxford History of the French Revolution*, p. 254.

# CHAPTER 3 REVIEW

## USING KEY TERMS

1. In the Americas, the offspring of European and American natives were called _____.
2. The _____ theory was an approach to prevent one country from being militarily dominant.
3. An important step in the radicalization of the French Revolution was the development of the _____ by the Committee of Public Safety.
4. French _____ aroused patriotism in nations opposed to France.
5. A(n) _____ allowed religious toleration, freedom of speech and press, and the right to own property.
6. The offspring of Europeans and Africans were referred to as _____.
7. A new type of monarchy called _____ was influenced by reform-minded philosophes.
8. After the members of the Third Estate were locked out of their meeting place, they moved outdoors, where they took the _____.
9. In 1799 Napoleon proclaimed a new form of government called the _____.
10. A _____ was a family enterprise in which spinners and weavers did their work at home.
11. The payment of fees to the local lord in France for the use of village facilities was an example of _____.
12. Empress Maria Theresa of Austria caused a _____ in her successful attempt to separate Russia from its chief ally, France.
13. European society in the eighteenth century was divided into _____ or estates.

## REVIEWING THE FACTS

1. What is considered the start of the French Revolution?
2. What was probably the most profitable goods item traded in the New World in the eighteenth century?
3. What was the function of the nobility in traditional European society?
4. What rights were considered natural rights by the philosophes?
5. Was Catherine the Great of Russia truly an enlightened monarch? Why or why not?
6. What was the major cause of the Seven Years' War?
7. Explain how Spain benefited from its trading pattern with Latin America.
8. When was the American Declaration of Independence signed by the American colonists?
9. Name two far-reaching events that took place in 1789.
10. Define the three orders or estates that existed in French society prior to the French Revolution.
11. What was the Tennis Court Oath?
12. What happened to the Declaration of the Rights of Woman and the Female Citizen?
13. Who opposed the new order brought about by the Constitution of 1791?
14. How did the French Revolution lead to war with Austria?
15. What is the importance of the Battle of Waterloo?

## THINKING CRITICALLY

1. The French revolutionary slogan was "Liberty, Equality, and Fraternity." In a short paragraph, explain what each of these words meant in revolutionary France.
2. What two technological advancements helped to increase productivity in the textile industry? Explain how productivity was increased.
3. Why were the British policies toward North America more likely to establish permanent settlements than the equivalent French policies?
4. Review the section of the chapter that discusses the

# CHAPTER 3 REVIEW

characteristics of the U.S. Constitution. Then, refer to what the textbook says about John Locke, Montesquieu, Rousseau, and Voltaire. How did the ideas of these philosophes influence the Constitution?

5. How could Louis XVI have avoided the initial events of the French Revolution? What could he have done to make things turn out differently?

6. From 1789 to 1812, France was governed by many different types and systems of government. Which is most effective—government of one, a few, or a larger group? Why?

7. Why did Napoleon choose to make peace with the Catholic Church as one of his first moves after taking power?

## APPLYING SOCIAL STUDIES SKILLS

1. **Geography:** On a blank map of the world, indicate the three main patterns of worldwide trade activity that developed as a result of the European colonization of the Americas.

2. **Sociology:** Describe the problems of city living in the eighteenth century.

3. **Political Science:** Compare and contrast the Declaration of Independence and the Universal Declaration of the Rights of Man and Citizen.

4. **Political Philosophy:** What characteristics would make a ruler today "enlightened"?

## MAKING TIME AND PLACE CONNECTIONS

1. During the sixteenth and seventeenth centuries, transatlantic transportation was slow and uncertain. It often took more than 60 days to get an answer from Spain to a question posed by a local governor in the Americas. What effect could this have on the practice of politics?

2. Read the excerpt from the United States Declaration of Independence in the section, "Political Change: Enlightened Absolutism in the Eighteenth Century." Then, develop a statement of your own, indicating your beliefs about the nature of government.

3. Frederick the Great remarked, "the fundamental rule of government is the principle of extending their territories." Do governments today follow this principle? If so, what is the result?

4. Locate a map of the Americas that shows the present location of colonies on the continent. Locate one French colony in North America, and one in South America.

## BECOMING AN HISTORIAN

1. **Drawing Inferences:** Write a dialogue that might have taken place between Napoleon and one of the anti-Napoleonic rulers of your choice. Napoleon should take the position of establishing his Grand Empire based on the principles of the French Revolution. His counterpart should be able to point out any contradictions between Napoleon's actions and the principles proclaimed by the French Revolution.

2. **Making Hypotheses:** Napoleon was enormously popular during his time as leader of France. Acting as an historian, based on the information in this chapter and any other information available to you, develop a hypothesis as to why he was so popular.

3. **Writing Research Papers:** Write an essay analyzing the importance of French assistance to the American colonists in their rebellion against Britain.

4. **Making a Hypothesis:** The French Revolution has been studied as a model of how a revolution can develop over time. Do your own analysis by developing a time line containing all the events that you feel are of importance. Then form a hypothesis that could apply to other revolutions.

# THE BEGINNINGS OF MODERNIZATION:

In the fall of 1814, hundreds of foreigners began to converge on Vienna, the capital city of the Austrian Empire. Many of these foreigners were members of European royalty—kings, archdukes, princes, and their wives—accompanied by their political advisors and scores of servants. Their congenial host was the Austrian emperor Francis I, who never tired of providing Vienna's guests with concerts, glittering balls, sumptuous feasts, and an endless array of hunting parties. One participant remembered, "Eating, fireworks, public illuminations. For eight or ten days, I haven't been able to work at all. What a life!" Of course, not every waking hour was spent in pleasure during this gathering of notables, known to history as the Congress of Vienna. These people were also representatives of all the states that had fought Napoleon, and their real business was to arrange a final peace settlement after almost ten years of war.

The French Revolution and the age of Napoleon had unleashed powerful forces for change, which were halted for a while after the defeat of Napoleon. However, the new forces of change had become too powerful to be contained forever. This was especially true of the forces of nationalism and liberalism, products of the revolutionary upheaval that began in France. The forces of change called forth revolts and revolutions that at times shook Europe in the 1820s and 1830s and led to widespread revolutions in 1848. Some of the revolutions were successful; most were not. Within twenty-five years, however, many of the goals sought by the liberals and nationalists during the first half of the nineteenth century were achieved.

The Industrial Revolution unleashed yet another set of forces for change at the beginning of the nineteenth century. By transforming the economic and social structure of Europe, the Industrial Revolution led the world into the industrialization that has been such a powerful feature of the modern world. The forces unleashed by two revolutions—the French Revolution and the Industrial Revolution—made it impossible to return to the old Europe and began what historians like to call the modern European world.

▶ *This painting records a meeting of the Congress of Vienna. In this elegant setting aristocratic negotiators from around Europe gathered to work out the treaties that ensured peace in Europe for almost one hundred years.*

# INDUSTRIALIZATION AND NATIONALISM

## (1800 TO 1870)

### ERA OF EUROPEAN DOMINANCE

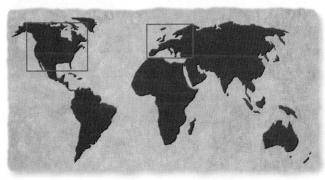

| | INDUSTRIALIZATION | | |
|---|---|---|---|
| 1800 | AND NATIONALISM | 1870 | |
| 1800 | | | 1914 |

## QUESTIONS TO GUIDE YOUR READING

1. What were the basic features of the new industrial system created by the Industrial Revolution?

2. How did the early Industrial Revolution affect the growth of cities, the living and working conditions of industrial workers, the family, and the role of women?

3. What did the Congress of Vienna and the Concert of Europe try to accomplish?

4. What caused the revolutions of 1848, and why did they fail?

5. What were the roles of Count Camillo di Cavour and Count Otto von Bismarck in the unification of their countries? What role did war play in the two unification movements?

6. What were the major features of the cultural movements known as romanticism and realism?

## OUTLINE

## THE INDUSTRIAL REVOLUTION AND ITS IMPACT

The Industrial Revolution led to an enormous leap in industrial production. Coal and steam replaced wind and water as new sources of energy and power to drive labor-saving machines. In turn, these machines led to new ways of organizing human labor as factories replaced shop and home workrooms. During the Industrial Revolution, Europe saw a shift from an economy based on farming and handicrafts to an economy based on manufacturing by machines and industrial factories.

It took decades for the Industrial Revolution to spread, but it was truly revolutionary in the way it changed Europeans and the world itself. Large numbers of people moved from the countryside to cities to work in the new factories. Impersonal life in the cities replaced the closeness of life in the country. A revolution in transportation also occurred with the use of railroads and steamboats. New products now moved quickly around the world, and new patterns of living emerged. Finally, the Industrial Revolution changed how people related to nature. This development ultimately created

123

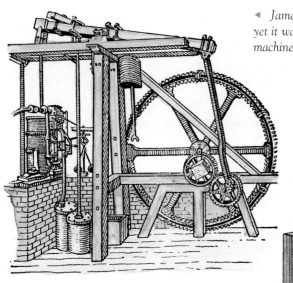

◄ *James Watt's steam engine seems simple compared to modern-day equipment, yet it was revolutionary. Examine this diagram carefully and explain how this machine worked.*

▼ *James Hargreaves's spinning jenny changed the way yarn was made, and this basic machine contributed significantly to the factory system of manufacture. How did this one machine change the way of life for many working-class families in Britain?*

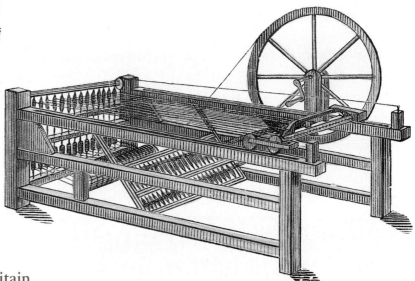

an environmental crisis that in the twentieth century has finally been recognized as a danger to human existence itself.

## The Industrial Revolution in Great Britain

The Industrial Revolution began in Great Britain in the 1780s. One important factor in producing the Industrial Revolution was the change in agricultural practices in the eighteenth century (see Chapter 3). These new practices led to a dramatic increase in food production. British agriculture could now feed more people at lower prices with less labor. Even ordinary British families could use some of their income to buy manufactured goods. At the same time, with more abundant food supplies, population grew in the second half of the eighteenth century. This provided a pool of surplus labor for the new factories of the emerging British industry.

As we saw in Chapter 3, the traditional methods of the cottage industry could not keep up with the growing demand for cotton clothes throughout Britain and its vast colonial empire. This problem led British cloth manufacturers to seek new ways to increase production. In so doing, these individuals produced the Industrial Revolution.

### Changes in Textile Production

Already in the eighteenth century, Great Britain had surged ahead in the production of cheap cotton goods using the methods of cottage industry. The invention of the flying shuttle by John Kay made weaving on a loom even faster. This invention, however, created shortages of yarn until James Hargreaves's spinning jenny, perfected by 1768, allowed spinners to produce yarn in greater quantities. Edmund Cartwright's loom, powered by water and invented in 1787, then made it possible for the weaving of cloth to catch up with the spinning of yarn. It was now more efficient to bring workers to the machines and have them work in factories placed next to rivers and streams, the sources of power for many of these early machines. Workers and their families came to live in the new towns that rapidly grew up around the factories.

What pushed the cotton industry to even greater heights was the invention of the steam engine. In the 1760s, a Scottish engineer, James Watt, built an engine powered by steam that could pump water from mines three times as quickly as previous engines had. In 1782, Watt developed a rotary engine that could turn a shaft and thus drive machinery. Steam power could now be used to spin and weave cotton. Before long, cotton mills using steam engines were found all over Britain. Because steam engines were fired by coal, they did not need to be located near rivers.

British cotton cloth production increased dramatically. In 1760, Britain had imported 2.5 million pounds of raw cotton, which was farmed out to cottage industries. In 1787, the British imported 22 million pounds of cotton. Most of it was spun on machines. By 1840, 366 million pounds of cotton were imported annually, much of it from the U.S. South, where it was grown by slaves. By this time, cotton cloth was Britain's most valuable product, and it was produced mainly in factories.

The price of yarn was but one-twentieth of what it had been. Even by using its cheapest labor, India could not compete in quality or quantity with Britain. British cotton goods sold everywhere in the world. In Britain itself, the availability of cheap cotton cloth made it possible for millions of poor people to wear underclothes. These garments had previously been worn only by the rich, who alone could afford underwear made with expensive linen cloth. New cotton work clothing that was tough, comfortable to the skin, and yet inexpensive and easily washable became common. Even the rich liked the colorful patterns of cotton prints and their light weight for summer use.

### Other Technological Changes

The steam engine was crucial to Britain's Industrial Revolution. It depended for fuel on coal, a substance that seemed then to be unlimited in quantity. The success of the steam engine led to a need for more coal and, thus, to an expansion in coal production. In turn, new processes using coal aided the development of the iron industry.

The British iron industry changed dramatically during the Industrial Revolution. Britain had always had large resources of iron ore. At the beginning of the eighteenth century, however, the basic process of producing iron had changed little since the Middle Ages.

A better quality of iron came into being in the 1780s, when Henry Cort developed a system called **puddling.** In this process, coke, which was derived from coal, was used to burn away impurities in pig iron (crude iron) and produce an iron of high quality. A boom then ensued in the British iron industry. In 1740, Britain produced 17,000 tons of iron. By 1852, it produced almost 3 million tons—more than the rest of the world combined.

In turn, the new high-quality iron was used to build new machines and new industries. Most noticeable were the new means of transportation—steamboats and railroads (see "The Role of Science and Technology: The Railroad"). The railroad was important to the success of the Industrial Revolution. The needs of railroads for coal and iron led to more growth in those industries. Building railways also created new jobs for farm laborers and peasants. Moreover, less expensive transportation led to lower-priced goods, thus creating larger markets. More sales meant more factories and more machinery. Business owners could reinvest their profits in new equipment, thereby adding to the growth of the economy. This type of regular, ongoing economic growth came to be seen as a basic feature of the new industrial economy.

### The New Factories

The factory was also important to the Industrial Revolution. From its beginning, the factory created a new labor system. Factory owners wanted to use their new machines constantly. Thus, workers were forced to work regular hours and in shifts to keep the machines producing at a steady rate. Early factory workers, however, came from rural areas, where they were used to a different pace of life. Peasant farmers worked hard, especially at harvest time, but they were also used to periods of inactivity.

Early factory owners, therefore, had to create a system of work discipline in which employees became used to working regular hours and doing the same work over and over. One early industrialist said that his aim was "to make the men into machines that cannot err." Of course, such work was boring, and factory owners got tough to achieve their goals. They issued detailed

## THE ROLE OF SCIENCE AND TECHNOLOGY
# The Railroad

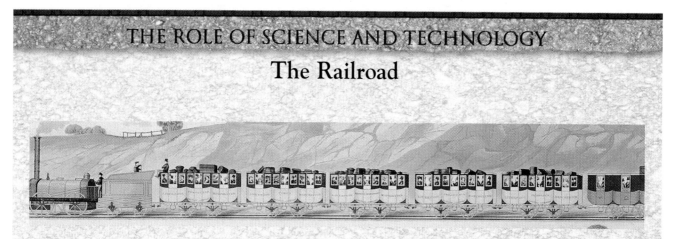

▲ *When they were first developed, railroads were used primarily for carrying passengers. Second- and third-class travelers ride in open cars like those shown in this illustration. First-class passengers were transported in covered cars.*

In 1804, Richard Trevithick tested the first steam-powered locomotive on a rail line in southern Wales. The locomotive pulled ten tons of iron and seventy people at five miles per hour. Better locomotives soon followed. The engines built by George Stephenson and his son Robert proved superior, and it was in their workshops in Newcastle upon Tyne that the locomotives for the first modern railways in Britain were built. George Stephenson's locomotive, called the *Rocket*, was used on the first public railway line. The line opened in 1830 and extended thirty-two miles from Liverpool to Manchester. The *Rocket* sped along at sixteen miles per hour while pulling a forty-ton train.

Within twenty years, locomotives were able to reach fifty miles per hour, an incredible speed to pas-

regulations. For example, adult workers were fined for being late and were dismissed for more serious misconduct, especially for being drunk. The loss of one's job could be disastrous for adults. Child workers, however, did not care if they were fired, so they were disciplined more directly—often by beating. In one crucial sense the early industrialists were successful. As the nineteenth century wore on, the second and third generations of workers came to view a regular working week as a natural way of life. It was, of course, an attitude that made possible Britain's incredible economic growth in that century.

By the mid-nineteenth century, Great Britain had become the world's first and richest industrial nation. Britain was the "workshop, banker, and trader of the world." It produced one-half of the world's coal and manufactured goods. Its cotton industry alone in 1850 was equal in size to the industries of all other European countries combined.

## The Spread of Industrialization

Beginning in Great Britain, the Industrial Revolution spread to the rest of Europe at different times and speeds during the nineteenth century. First to be industrialized on the Continent were Belgium, France, and the German states. In these states, governments were especially active in encouraging the development of industrialization. For example, the governments set up technical schools to train engineers and mechanics. They also bore much of the cost of building roads,

# THE ROLE OF SCIENCE AND TECHNOLOGY
## The Railroad, continued

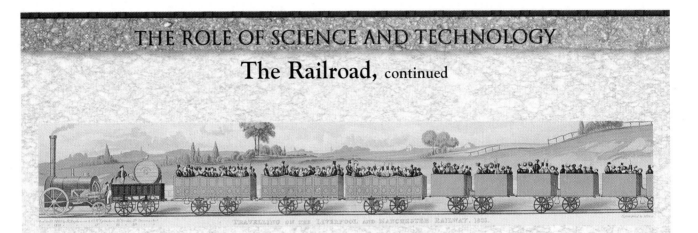

sengers. During the same period, new companies formed to build additional railroads as the infant industry proved to be not only technically but also financially successful. In 1840, Britain had almost 2,000 miles of railroads. By 1850, 6,000 miles of railroad track crisscrossed much of that country.

The railroad was a perfect symbol of the rapid and dynamic economic growth that came with the Industrial Revolution. The railroad's ability to transport goods and people at dramatic speeds was also a visible reminder of a new sense of power. When railway engineers pierced mountains with tunnels and spanned chasms with breathtaking

bridges, people had a sense of power over nature that had not been felt before in civilization.

1. How fast did the locomotive used on the first public railway travel?

2. Do you think the *Rocket* was worthy of its name by today's standards? By the standards of the 1800s?

3. How do you think the invention of the railroad changed life in England?

---

canals, and railroads. By 1850, a network of iron rails had spread across Europe.

There was also an Industrial Revolution in North America, in the new nation of the United States. In 1800, six out of every seven American workers were farmers, and there were no cities with more than 100,000 people. By 1860, the population had grown from 5 million in 1800 to 30 million people. Nine U.S. cities had populations over 100,000, and only 50 percent of U.S. workers were farmers. Between 1800 and 1860, the United States had experienced an industrial revolution and the growth of cities that went with it.

Unlike Britain, the United States was a large country. Thousands of miles of roads and canals were built to link east and west. The steamboat made transporta-

tion easier on the Great Lakes, Atlantic coastal waters, and rivers. The steamboat was especially important to the Mississippi River valley; by 1860, a thousand steamboats plied that river.

Most important of all in the development of an American transportation system was the railroad. It began with 100 miles of track in 1830. By 1860, more than 27,000 miles of railroad track covered the United States. This revolution in transportation turned the United States into a single massive market for the manufactured goods of the Northeast.

Labor for the growing number of factories in the Northeast came chiefly from the farm population. Many of the workers in the new textile and shoe factories of New England were women. Indeed, women

▶ *This engraving of a cotton factory shows the number of machines that could be tended by just a few workers. In order to maximize production and profitability, work was organized into shifts. Do you think it was easy for workers to adjust to working set hours in factories like this one? Why or why not?*

made up more than 80 percent of the workers in the large textile factories. Factory owners sometimes sought entire families, including children, to work in their mills. One mill owner ran this advertisement in a newspaper in Utica (YOOT-i-kuh), New York: "Wanted: A few sober and industrious families of at least five children each, over the age of eight years, are wanted at the Cotton Factory in Whitestown. Widows with large families would do well to attend this notice."

## The Social Impact of the Industrial Revolution

The Industrial Revolution drastically changed the social life of Europe and the entire world in the nineteenth and twentieth centuries. This change was already evident in the first half of the nineteenth century in the growth of cities and the emergence of new social classes.

### Growth of Population and Cities

A growth in population had already begun in the eighteenth century, but it became dramatic in the nineteenth century. In 1750, European population stood at an estimated 140 million. By 1800, it had increased to 187 million. By 1850, the population had almost doubled since 1750, to 266 million. The key to this growth was a decline in death rates. Wars and major epidemic diseases, such as smallpox and plague, became less frequent. This led to a drop in the number of deaths. Because of an increase in the food supply, more people were better fed and more resistant to disease. Famine largely disappeared from western Europe, although there were some exceptions. Ireland, for example, experienced a great catastrophe, the Great Potato Famine, caused by overdependence on a single crop— the potato.

Ireland was one of the most oppressed areas in western Europe. Its mostly Catholic peasant population rented land from mostly absentee British Protestant landlords, whose chief concern was collecting their rents. Irish peasants lived in mud huts in desperate poverty. They grew potatoes, a nutritious and relatively easy-to-grow crop that produced three times as much food per acre as grain. The cultivation of the potato gave Irish peasants a basic staple that enabled them to survive and even expand in numbers. Between 1781 and 1845, the Irish population doubled, from four million to eight million. In the summer of 1845, a fungus that turned the potato black devastated the potato

## Map 4.1   The Industrialization of Europe by 1850

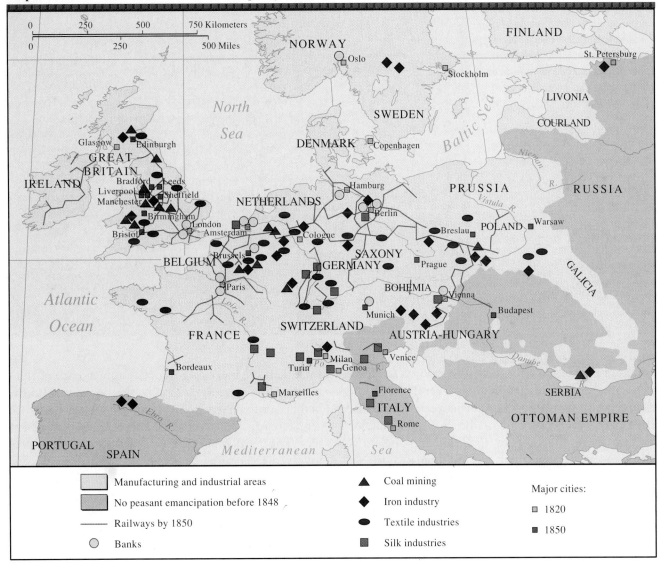

crop in Ireland. Between 1845 and 1851, the Great Famine decimated the Irish population. Over one million people died of starvation and disease, and almost two million emigrated to the United States and Britain. Of all the European nations, only Ireland had a declining population in the nineteenth century.

Elsewhere in Europe, cities and towns grew dramatically in the first half of the nineteenth century. The growth was directly related to industrialization. By 1850, especially in Great Britain and Belgium, cities were rapidly becoming home to many industries. With the steam engine, factory owners did not need water power and could locate their plants in cities, to which people flocked from the country to find work. The workers came on the new railroads.

In 1800, Great Britain had one major city, London, with a population of 1 million, and six cities with populations between 50,000 and 100,000. Fifty years later,

▶ *Inner-city housing for the poor was too often overcrowded, filthy, and unhealthy. This drawing of a London slum shows the railroad viaducts that cut through the area. How did the railroad contribute to the pollution that existed in these neighborhoods?*

London's population had swelled to 2,363,000. There were nine cities with populations over 100,000 and eighteen cities with populations between 50,000 and 100,000. Over 50 percent of the British population lived in towns and cities by 1850. Urban populations also grew on the Continent, but less dramatically.

The rapid growth of cities in the first half of the nineteenth century led to pitiful living conditions for many of the inhabitants. Eventually, these conditions led to the rise of urban reformers who called upon city governments to clean up their cities. As we shall see in Chapter 5, their calls would be heeded and produce better living conditions in the second half of the nineteenth century.

### New Social Classes: The Industrial Middle Class

The rise of industrial capitalism (a capitalist system based on industrial production rather than trade, as in commercial capitalism) produced a new middle-class group—the industrial middle class. The **bourgeois,** or middle-class person, was not new. The bourgeoisie (middle class) had existed since the emergence of cities in the Middle Ages. Originally, the bourgeois was the burgher or town dweller, who may have been active as a merchant, official, artisan, lawyer, or person of letters. The term *bourgeois* came also to include people involved in industry and banking, as well as professionals, such as lawyers, teachers, doctors, and government officials. At the lower end of the economic scale were master craftspeople and shopkeepers.

The new industrial middle class was made up of the people who built the factories, bought the machines, and figured out where the markets were. Their qualities included initiative; vision; ambition; and often, of course, greed. One cotton manufacturer said, "Getting of money . . . is the main business of the life of men." This was not an easy task, however. The opportunities for making money were great, but the risks were also tremendous.

Members of the industrial middle class sought to separate themselves from the working classes below them. In the first half of the nineteenth century, the industrial working class was actually a mixture of different groups. In the course of the nineteenth century, however, factory workers came to form the majority of the working class.

### New Social Classes: The Industrial Working Class

Industrial workers faced wretched working conditions. Work hours ranged from twelve to sixteen hours a day, six days a week, with a half-hour for lunch and dinner. There was no security of employment and no minimum wage. The worst conditions were in the cotton mills, where temperatures were especially harmful. One report noted that "in the cotton-spinning work, these creatures are kept, fourteen hours in each day, locked up, summer and winter, in a heat of from eighty to eighty-four degrees." Mills were also dirty, dusty, dangerous, and unhealthy. Reformers were especially critical of the treatment of married women. One reported, "We have repeatedly seen married females, in the last stage of pregnancy, slaving from morning to night beside these never-tiring machines, and when . . . they were obliged to sit down to take a moment's ease, were fined by the manager."

Conditions in the coal mines were also harsh. Although steam-powered engines were used to lift coal from the mines to the top, inside the mines men still bore the burden of digging the coal out. Horses, mules, women, and children hauled coal carts on rails to the lift. Dangerous conditions, including cave-ins, explosions, and gas fumes (called "bad air"), were a way of life. The cramped conditions in mines—tunnels were often only three or four feet high—and their constant dampness led to deformed bodies and ruined lungs.

Both children and women worked in large numbers in early factories and mines (see "Young People in the Industrial Revolution: Child Labor"). By 1830, women and children made up two-thirds of the cotton industry's workforce. However, the number of children declined under the Factory Act of 1833, which set nine as the minimum age for employment. Children between nine and thirteen could work only eight hours a day; those between thirteen and eighteen, could work twelve hours.

As the number of children employed declined, their places were taken by women. Women made up 50 percent of the labor force in textile (cotton and woolen)

▲ *Saltaire, shown here, was considered a model textile town. It was built near Bradford, England, by Titus Salt in 1851. Why would a factory owner have developed an entire town around his mill?*

factories before 1870. They were mostly unskilled labor and were paid half or less than half of what men received. Excessive working hours for women were finally outlawed in 1844.

The employment of children and women was in large part carried over from an earlier pattern. Husband, wife, and children had always worked together in cottage industry. Thus, it seemed perfectly natural to continue this pattern. Men who moved from the countryside to industrial towns and cities took their wives and children with them into the factory or into the mines. The desire for this family work often came from the family itself. The factory owner Jedediah Strutt was opposed to employing children under age ten but was forced by parents to take children as young as seven.

The Factory Acts that limited the work hours of children and women also led to a new pattern of work. Men were expected to earn most of the family income by working outside the home. Women, in contrast, took over daily care of the family and performed low-paying jobs, such as laundry work that could be done in the home. Working at home for pay made it possible for women to continue to help with family survival.

## YOUNG PEOPLE IN THE INDUSTRIAL REVOLUTION
### Child Labor

▶ *Small children were often employed in textile mills, and they were carefully supervised to ensure that they worked hard. Why do you think there were no laws to protect children from this kind of exploitation?*

Children had been an important part of the family economy in preindustrial times. They worked in the fields or carded and spun wool at home with the growth of cottage industry. In the Industrial Revolution, however, child labor was exploited. The owners of cotton factories in England found child labor very helpful. Children had a delicate touch as spinners of cotton. Their smaller size

### Early Socialism

In the first half of the nineteenth century, the pitiful conditions found in the slums, mines, and factories created by the Industrial Revolution gave rise to a movement known as socialism. Early socialism was largely the product of intellectuals who believed in the equality of all people and who wanted to replace competition with cooperation in industry. To later socialists, especially the followers of Karl Marx, such ideas were merely impractical dreams. The later socialists, in contempt of the earlier theorists, labeled them **utopian socialists.** The term has lasted to this day.

Robert Owen, a British cotton manufacturer, was one utopian socialist. He believed that humans would show their true natural goodness if they lived in a cooperative environment. At New Lanark in Scotland, Owen transformed a squalid factory town into a flourishing, healthy community. He also tried to create a cooperative community at New Harmony, Indiana, in the United States in the 1820s. However, fighting within the community eventually destroyed Owen's dream.

## YOUNG PEOPLE IN THE INDUSTRIAL REVOLUTION

### Child Labor, continued

made it easier for them to move under machines to gather loose cotton. Furthermore, they were more easily trained to factory work.

Discipline was often harsh. A report from a British parliamentary inquiry into the condition of child factory workers in 1838 stated:

*It is a very frequent thing at Mr. Marshall's [at Shrewsbury] where the least children were employed (for there were plenty working at six years of age), for Mr. Horseman to start the mill earlier in the morning than he formerly did; and provided a child should be drowsy, the overlooker walks round the room with a stick in his hand, and he touches that child on the shoulder, and says, "Come here." In a corner of the room there is an iron cistern; it is filled with water; he takes this boy, and takes him up by the legs, and dips him over head in the cistern, and sends him to work for the remainder of the day. . . .*

*What means were taken to keep the children to their work?—Sometimes they would tap them over the head, or nip them over the nose, or give them a pinch of snuff, or throw water in their faces, or pull them off where they were, and job them about to keep them waking.*

The same inquiry also reported that in some factories, children were often severely flogged (beat with a rod or whip) to keep them at work.

Children represented a cheap supply of labor. In 1821, 49 percent of the British people were under twenty years of age. Hence, children made up a large pool of laborers. They were paid only about one-sixth to one-third of what a man was paid. In the cotton factories in 1838, children under the age of eighteen made up 29 percent of the total workforce. In cotton mills, children as young as age seven worked twelve to fifteen hours per day, six days a week.

1. What kind of working conditions did children face in the factories during the early Industrial Revolution?

2. Why did factory owners permit such conditions and such treatment of children?

---

### ❀  SECTION REVIEW  ❀

1. **Define:**
   (*a*) puddling,
   (*b*) bourgeois,
   (*c*) utopian socialists

2. **Identify:**
   (*a*) steam engine,
   (*b*) Great Famine,
   (*c*) Factory Act of 1833,
   (*d*) Karl Marx

3. **Recall:**
   (*a*) What economic shift was experienced in Europe during the Industrial Revolution?
   (*b*) Why were railroads important to the success of the Industrial Revolution?

4. **Think Critically:** In what ways must the growth of the Industrial Revolution have changed the way families lived?

# REACTION AND REVOLUTION: THE GROWTH OF NATIONALISM, 1815 TO 1848

After the defeat of Napoleon, European rulers moved to restore much of the old order. This was the goal of the great powers—Great Britain, Austria, Prussia, and Russia—when they met at the Congress of Vienna in September 1814 to arrange a final peace settlement. The leader of the congress was the Austrian foreign minister, Prince Klemens von Metternich (MET-ur-NIK), who claimed that he was guided at Vienna by the **principle of legitimacy.** This meant that the lawful monarchs were restored to their positions of power in order to keep peace and stability in Europe. This had already been done in France with the restoration of the Bourbon monarchy.

In fact, however, the principle of legitimacy was largely ignored elsewhere. At the Congress of Vienna, the great powers all grabbed lands to add to their states. In doing so, they believed that they were forming a new balance of power that would keep any one country from dominating Europe.

The peace arrangements worked out at the Congress of Vienna were a victory for conservative rulers, who wanted to contain the forces of change unleashed by the French Revolution. Those like Metternich believed in the ideology known as **conservatism.** Most conservatives at that time favored obedience to political authority and believed that organized religion was crucial to order in society. Moreover, they hated revolutions and were unwilling to accept the liberal demands for either individual rights or representative

**Map 4.2    Europe after the Congress of Vienna**

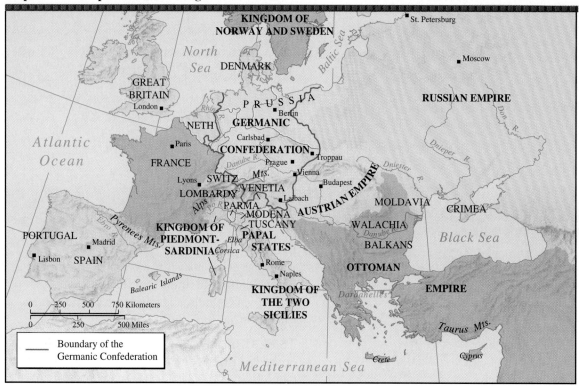

governments. After 1815, the political philosophy of conservatism was supported by hereditary monarchs, government bureaucracies, landowning aristocracies, and churches, be they Protestant or Catholic. The conservative forces were dominant after 1815.

One method used by the great powers to maintain the new status quo was the Concert of Europe. Great Britain, Russia, Prussia, and Austria (and later France) agreed to meet at times in conferences to discuss their common interests and to take steps that would maintain the peace in Europe. Eventually, the great powers adopted a **principle of intervention.** This was the right of the great powers to send armies into countries where there were revolutions in order to restore legitimate monarchs to their thrones. Britain refused to agree to the principle, arguing that the great powers should not interfere in the internal affairs of other states. Austria, Prussia, Russia, and France ignored the British and used military forces to crush revolutions in Spain and Italy, as well as to restore legitimate (and conservative) monarchs to their thrones.

### Revolutionary Outbursts

Between 1815 and 1830, conservative governments throughout Europe worked to maintain the old order. However, powerful forces for change—known as **liberalism** and nationalism—were also at work.

Liberalism owed much to the Enlightenment of the eighteenth century and the American and French Revolutions at the end of that century. Liberals had different opinions at times, but they all agreed that liberalism was the idea that people should be as free from restraint as possible.

Liberals came to hold a common set of political beliefs. Chief among them was the protection of civil liberties, or the basic rights of all people. The civil liberties included equality before the law and freedom of assembly, speech, and press. All of these freedoms

*Prince Klemens von Metternich, shown in this formal portrait, was both a powerful and persuasive politician. He was a dominant member of the Congress of Vienna and one of the main supporters of legitimacy and intervention.*

should be guaranteed by a written document, such as the American Bill of Rights. Most liberals wanted religious toleration for all, as well as separation of church and state. Liberals also demanded the right of peaceful opposition to the government both from within and from outside, and the making of laws by a representative assembly (legislature) elected by qualified voters. Many liberals believed, then, in a constitutional monarchy or constitutional state (rule by a constitution). They believed that written constitutions would guarantee the rights they sought to preserve.

Liberals were not democrats, however. They thought that the right to vote and hold office should be open only to men of property. Liberalism, then, was tied to middle-class men, and especially industrial middle-class men, who wanted voting rights for themselves so that they could share power with the landowning classes. The liberals feared mob rule and had little desire to let the lower classes share that power.

Nationalism was an even more powerful force for change in the nineteenth century than was liberalism. Nationalism arose out of an awareness of being part of a community that has common institutions, traditions, language, and customs. This community is called a *nation.* The chief political loyalty of individuals should be to the nation rather than to a dynasty, city-state, or other political unit.

Nationalism did not become a popular force for change until the French Revolution. From then on, nationalists came to believe that each nationality should have its own government. Thus, the Germans, who were not united, wanted national unity in a Ger-

▶ *On July 25, 1830, Charles X dissolved the French legislative chamber and suspended freedom of the press. The reaction of the Parisians was immediate, and Charles X was overthrown. This painting shows a scene from the July 1830 revolution when students, former soldiers, and middle-class citizens joined together to demand a republic. The attempt to stop these rebels was feeble and short-lived.*

man nation-state with one central government. Subject peoples, such as the Hungarians, wanted the right to establish their own governments rather than be subject to the emperor of the Austrian Empire.

Nationalism, then, was a threat to the existing political order. A united Germany, for example, would upset the balance of power set up at Vienna in 1815. At the same time, an independent Hungarian state would mean the breakup of the Austrian Empire. Conservatives feared such change and thus tried hard to repress nationalism.

Beginning in 1830, the forces of change—liberalism and nationalism—began to break through the conservative domination of Europe. In France, liberals overthrew the Bourbon monarch Charles X in 1830 and established a constitutional monarchy. Political support for the new monarch, Louis-Philippe (LOO-ee fi-LEEP), came from the upper middle class.

Liberals played an important role in the 1830 revolution in France, but nationalism was the chief force in three other revolutions the same year. The Belgians, who had been annexed to the Dutch Republic in 1815, rebelled and created an independent state. Revolutions

in Poland and Italy were much less successful. Russian forces crushed the attempt of Poles to free themselves from foreign domination. Austrian troops marched into Italy and crushed revolts in a number of Italian states.

## The Revolutions of 1848

Despite the liberal and nationalist successes in France and Belgium, the conservative order still dominated much of Europe. However, the forces of liberalism and nationalism continued to grow. In 1848, these forces of change erupted once more.

As before, revolution in France was once again the spark for revolution in other countries. Severe economic problems beginning in 1846 brought untold hardship in France to the lower middle class, workers, and peasants. At the same time, members of the middle class clamored for the right to vote. As the government of Louis-Philippe refused to make changes, opposition grew. The monarchy was finally overthrown on February 24, 1848. A group of moderate and radical republicans (people who wanted to set up a republic) set up a provisional (temporary) government. They called for the election by **universal male suffrage** (all adult men could vote) of a Constituent Assembly that would draw up a new constitution.

The provisional government also set up national workshops to provide work for the unemployed. From March to June, the number of unemployed enrolled in the national workshops rose from 6,100 to almost 120,000. This emptied the treasury and frightened the moderates, who reacted by closing the workshops on June 21. The workers refused to accept this decision and poured into the streets. Four days of bitter and bloody fighting by government forces crushed the working-class revolt. Thousands were killed, and 11,000 prisoners were sent to the French colony of Algeria in northern Africa.

The new constitution, ratified on November 4, 1848, set up a republic, called the Second Republic. The Second Republic had a single legislature elected by universal male suffrage. A president, also chosen by universal male suffrage, served for four years. In the elections for the presidency held in December 1848, Charles Louis Napoleon Bonaparte, the nephew of the famous French ruler, won a resounding victory. Within four years, President Napoleon would become Emperor Napoleon (see later in this chapter).

News of the 1848 revolution in France led to upheaval in central Europe as well (see "You Are There: Revolutionary Excitement"). The Vienna settlement in 1815 had recognized the existence of thirty-eight independent German states (called the Germanic Confederation). Austria and Prussia were the two great powers, whereas the other states varied in size. In 1848, cries for change led many German rulers to promise constitutions, a free press, jury trials, and other liberal reforms. In Prussia, King Frederick William IV agreed to establish a new constitution and work for a united Germany.

The governments of all the German states allowed elections by universal male suffrage for deputies to an all-German parliament called the Frankfurt Assembly. Its purpose was to fulfill a liberal and nationalist dream—the preparation of a constitution for a new united Germany. However, the Frankfurt Assembly failed to achieve its goal. The members had no real

## CONNECTIONS
### TO OUR WORLD

**Russian Troops in Hungary**   On November 1, 1956, Imry Nagy, leader of Hungary, declared Hungary a free nation and promised new elections. Fearing that these elections would mean the end of Communist rule in Hungary, Nikita Khrushchev, leader of the Soviet Union, reacted dramatically. On November 4, 200,000 Soviet (mostly Russian) troops and 4,000 Soviet tanks invaded Budapest, Hungary's capital city. An estimated 50,000 Hungarians died on that day. Nagy fled but was later arrested and executed. The Hungarian Revolution of 1956 had failed.

To Hungarians who knew their country's history, the use of Russian troops to crush their independence had an all-too-familiar ring. In 1848, Louis Kossuth had led a revolt that forced Hungary's Austrian rulers to grant Hungary its own legislature and a separate national army. Nevertheless, the Austrians remained unwilling to give up their control of Hungary. Austrian armies, however, had little success in defeating Hungarian forces fighting for their country's independence. In April 1849, the Hungarian legislature declared Hungary a republic. Kossuth was made the new president. Unable to subdue the Hungarians, the Austrian government asked the Russians for help. Tsar Nicholas I of Russia, who feared revolution anywhere, gladly agreed to help. A Russian army of 140,000 men crushed the Hungarian forces, and Kossuth fled abroad. The Hungarian Revolution of 1848–1849 had failed.

means of forcing the German rulers to accept the constitution they had drawn up. German unification was not achieved. The revolution had failed.

The Austrian Empire also had its problems and needed only the news of the revolution in Paris to erupt in flames in March 1848. The Austrian Empire was a **multinational state,** or collection of different peoples, including Germans, Czechs, Magyars (Hungarians), Slovaks, Romanians, Slovenes, Poles, Croats,

## YOU ARE THERE
# Revolutionary Excitement

▶ *In 1848, Austrian students joined the revolutionary civil guard that took control of Vienna and demanded that the emperor call an assembly to draft a constitution. The revolt was short-lived. By 1849, the emperor and his powers were restored. This painting depicts students planning the 1848 actions.*

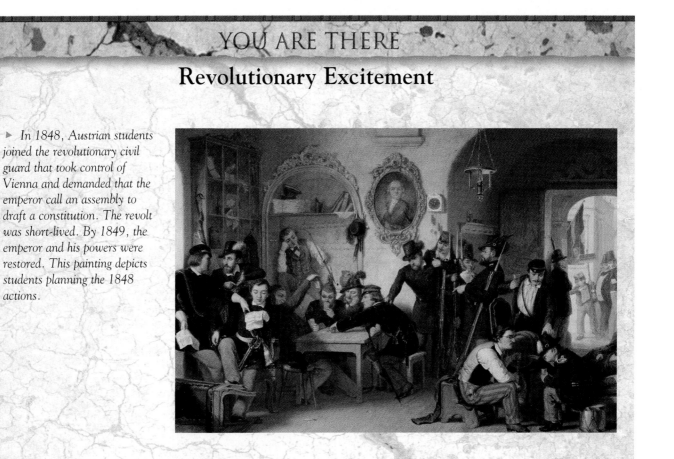

*The excitement with which German liberals and nationalists received the news of the revolution in France and their own expectations for Germany are captured well in this selection from the* Reminiscences *of Carl Schurz (SHOOurTS). After the failure of the German revolution of 1848, Schurz went to the United States, where he fought in the Civil War and became secretary of the interior.*

**Carl Schurz,** *Reminiscences*
One morning, toward the end of February, 1848, I sat quietly in my attic-chamber, working hard at my tragedy of "Ulrich von Hutten" [a sixteenth-century German knight], when suddenly a friend rushed breathlessly into the room, exclaiming: "What, you sitting here! Do you not know what has happened?"

Serbians, and Italians. Only the Habsburg emperor provided a common bond. The Germans, though only a quarter of the population, played a leading role in the governing of the Austrian Empire. The Hungarians, however, wanted their own legislature.

In March, demonstrations in the major cities led to the dismissal of Metternich, the Austrian foreign minister, who fled abroad. In Vienna, revolutionary forces took control of the capital and demanded a liberal constitution. Hungary was given its own legislature and a

## YOU ARE THERE

# Revolutionary Excitement, continued

"No; what?"

"The French have driven away Louis Philippe and proclaimed the republic."

I threw down my pen—and that was the end of "Ulrich von Hutten." I never touched the manuscript again. We tore down the stairs, into the street, to the market-square, the accustomed meeting-place for all the student societies after their midday dinner. Although it was still forenoon, the market was already crowded with young men talking excitedly. . . . We were dominated by a vague feeling as if a great outbreak of elemental forces had begun, as if an earthquake was impending of which we had felt the first shock, and we instinctively crowded together. . . .

The next morning there were the usual lectures to be attended. But how profitless! The voice of the professor sounded like a monotonous drone coming from far away. What he had to say did not seem to concern us. At last we closed with a sigh the notebook and went away, pushed by a feeling that now we had something more important to do—to devote ourselves to the affairs of the fatherland. . . . Certain ideas and catchwords worked themselves to the surface, which expressed more or less the feelings of the people. Now had arrived in Germany the day for the establishment of "German Unity," and the founding of a great, powerful national German Empire. In the first line the meeting of a national parliament. Then the demands for civil rights and liberties, free speech, free press, the right of free assembly, equality before the law, a freely elected representation of the people with legislative power . . . the word democracy was soon on all tongues, and many, too, thought it a matter of course that if the princes should try to withhold from the people the rights and liberties demanded, force would take the place of mere petition. Of course the regeneration of the fatherland must, if possible, be accomplished by peaceable means. Like many of my friends, I was dominated by the feeling that at last the great opportunity had arrived for giving to the German people the liberty which was their birthright and to the German fatherland its unity and greatness, and that it was now the first duty of every German to do and to sacrifice everything for this sacred object.

1. Why were Schurz and other Germans so excited about the revolution in France?

2. Were the German students willing to fight for their freedom?

3. Schurz states that "it was now the first duty of every German to do and to sacrifice everything for this sacred project." The sacred project was freedom and liberty. Would you be willing to sacrifice everything for your freedom and liberty? Why or why not?

separate national army. In Bohemia, the Czechs began to clamor for their own government as well.

Austrian officials had made concessions to appease the revolutionaries, but they were determined to reestablish their firm control. As did officials in France and the German states, the Austrian officials welcomed the divisions between radical and moderate revolutionaries and played upon the middle-class fear of a working-class social revolution. In June 1848, Austrian military forces crushed the Czech rebels in Prague. By the end of October, the rebels had been crushed in Vienna. However, it was only with the help of a Russian army of 140,000 men that the Hungarian revolution was finally crushed in 1849. The revolutions in the Austrian Empire had failed.

So, too, did the revolutions in Italy. The Congress of Vienna had set up nine states in Italy, including the kingdom of Sardinia in the north; the kingdom of the Two Sicilies (Naples and Sicily); the Papal States; a handful of small states; and the northern provinces of Lombardy and Venetia (vi-NEE-shuh), which were now part of the Austrian Empire. In 1848, a revolt broke out against the Austrians in Lombardy and Venetia. Revolutionaries in other Italian states also took up arms and sought to create liberal constitutions. By 1849, however, the Austrians had reestablished complete control over Lombardy and Venetia. The old order also prevailed in the rest of Italy.

Throughout Europe in 1848, popular revolutions had brought about the formation of liberal constitutions and liberal governments. Moderate, middle-class liberals and radical workers were soon divided over their aims, though, and authoritarian regimes were soon reestablished. However, the forces of nationalism and liberalism were by no means dead.

## ❀ SECTION REVIEW ❀

1. **Locate:**
   (*a*) Vienna,   (*b*) Prague

2. **Define:**
   (*a*) principle of legitimacy,   (*b*) conservatism,
   (*c*) principle of intervention,   (*d*) liberalism,
   (*e*) universal male suffrage,   (*f*) multinational state

3. **Identify:**
   (*a*) Congress of Vienna,   (*b*) American Bill of Rights,   (*c*) Charles Louis Napoleon Bonaparte, (*d*) the Germanic Confederation

4. **Recall:**
   (*a*) Why was nationalism a threat to the existing order in nineteenth-century Europe?

(*b*) Why did liberal forces who won political rights from the rule of monarchs typically lose their power after a relatively few years?

5. **Think Critically:** How may social and economic changes forced on Europe by the Industrial Revolution have contributed to the spread of liberalism?

# NATIONAL UNIFICATION AND THE NATIONAL STATE, 1848 TO 1871

The revolutions of 1848 had failed. Within twenty-five years, however, many of the goals sought by the liberals and nationalists during the first half of the nineteenth century were achieved. Italy and Germany became nations, and many European states were led by constitutional monarchs.

## Breakdown of the Concert of Europe

The growth of nationalism produced dramatic changes in two European countries by 1871: both Italy and Germany became unified. They were able to do so because of the breakdown of the system created by the Concert of Europe. The Crimean (krie-ME-uhn) War played a crucial role in the breakdown.

The Crimean War was the result of a long-standing struggle between Russia and the Ottoman Empire. The Ottoman Empire had long been in control of much of southeastern Europe (an area known as the Balkans). By the beginning of the nineteenth century, however, the Ottoman Empire was in decline, and its authority over its territories in southeastern Europe began to weaken. As a result, European states began to take an active interest in the disintegration of the "sick man of Europe," as they called the Ottoman Empire. Russia was especially interested in expanding its power into Ottoman lands in the Balkans and gaining access to the Dardanelles and thus, the Mediterranean Sea.

**Map 4.3   The Unification of Italy**

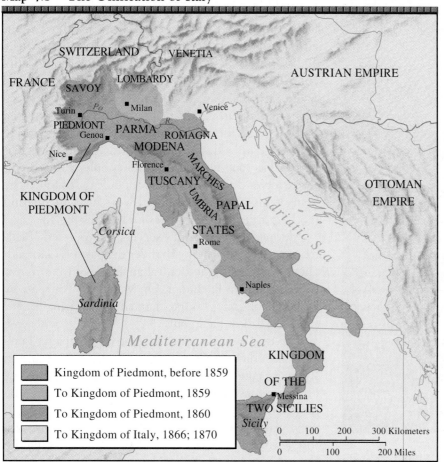

Kingdom of Piedmont, before 1859
To Kingdom of Piedmont, 1859
To Kingdom of Piedmont, 1860
To Kingdom of Italy, 1866; 1870

agreed to allow Moldavia and Walachia to be placed under the protection of all the great powers.

The Crimean War destroyed the Concert of Europe. Austria and Russia had been the two chief powers maintaining the status quo in the first half of the nineteenth century. They were now enemies, because Austria, which had its own interests in the Balkans, had refused to support Russia in the Crimean War. A defeated and humiliated Russia withdrew from European affairs for the next twenty years. Austria was now without friends among the great powers. This new international situation opened the door for the unification of both Italy and Germany.

## National Unification: Italy

In 1850, Austria was still the dominant power on the Italian peninsula. After the failure of the revolution of 1848 to 1849, more and more Italians saw the northern Italian state of Piedmont, ruled by the royal house of Savoy, as their best hope to achieve the unification of Italy. It was doubtful, however, that the little state could unify Italy, or so it seemed, until King Victor Emmanuel II named Count Camillo di Cavour as his prime minister in 1852.

Cavour was a dedicated political leader. As prime minister, he pursued a policy of economic expansion that increased government revenues and enabled Piedmont to equip a large army. Cavour, however, knew that Piedmont's army was not strong enough to beat the Austrians. He would need help. Consequently, he made an alliance with the French emperor Louis Napoleon and then provoked the Austrians into

Such a move would make Russia the major power in eastern Europe and would enable the Russians to challenge British naval control of the eastern Mediterranean. Other European powers feared Russian ambitions and had their own interest in the decline of the Ottoman Empire.

When the Russians invaded the Turkish provinces of Moldavia and Walachia (wah-LAE-kee-uh), the Ottoman Turks declared war on Russia on October 4, 1853. In the following year, on March 28, Great Britain and France, fearful of Russian gains, declared war on Russia. The Crimean War, as the conflict came to be called, was poorly planned and poorly fought. Heavy losses caused the Russians to sue for peace. By the Treaty of Paris, signed in March 1856, Russia

▲ *This painting shows Giuseppe Garibaldi arriving in Sicily on May 11, 1860. Compare and contrast the development of Spain, France, and England with Italy, and explain why it took Italy so long to unify. Was unification due solely to the efforts of leaders such as Garibaldi and Cavour?*

raised an army of 1,000 volunteers called Red Shirts because of the color of their uniforms. Garibaldi's forces landed in Sicily, where a revolt had broken out against the Bourbon king of the Two Sicilies. By the end of July 1860, most of Sicily was under Garibaldi's control. In August, Garibaldi and his forces crossed over to the mainland and began a victorious march up the Italian peninsula. Naples, and with it the kingdom of the Two Sicilies, fell in early September. Everywhere he went, Garibaldi was hailed by the Italians as a great hero. One reporter wrote: "The people threw themselves forward to kiss his hands, or at least, to touch the hem of his garment. Children were brought up, and mothers asked on their knees for his blessing."

Alarmed by Garibaldi's success, Cavour sent Piedmontese forces to the south. Ever the patriot, Garibaldi chose not to fight another Italian army but to turn over his conquests to Piedmont. On March 17, 1861, a new kingdom of Italy was proclaimed under King Victor Emmanuel II of Piedmont.

The task of unification was not yet complete, however. Venetia in the north was still held by Austria, and Rome was under the control of the pope, supported by French troops. In the Austro-Prussian War of 1866, the new Italian state became an ally of Prussia. The Italian army was defeated by the Austrians, but Prussia's victory left the Italians with Venetia. In 1870, during the Franco-Prussian war (see "National Unification: Germany"), French troops withdrew from Rome. The Italian army then annexed Rome on September 20, 1870. Rome became the new capital of the united Italian state.

## National Unification: Germany

After the failure of the Frankfurt Assembly to achieve German unification in 1848 and 1849, German nationalists focused on Austria and Prussia as the only two states powerful enough to unify Germany. Austria was a large multinational empire, however, and it feared the creation of a strong German state in central Europe. Consequently, more and more Germans looked to Prussia for leadership in the cause of German unification.

invading Piedmont in 1859. In the early stages of fighting, it was mostly French armies that defeated the Austrians in two major battles. A peace settlement gave the French Nice and Savoy, which they had been promised for making the alliance. Lombardy was given to Piedmont. Cavour's success caused nationalists in some northern Italian states (Parma, Modena, and Tuscany) to overthrow their governments and join their states to Piedmont.

Meanwhile, in southern Italy, a new leader of Italian unification had arisen. Giuseppe Garibaldi (joo-SEP-ee GAR-uh-BAWL-dee), a dedicated Italian patriot,

## Map 4.4   The Unification of Germany

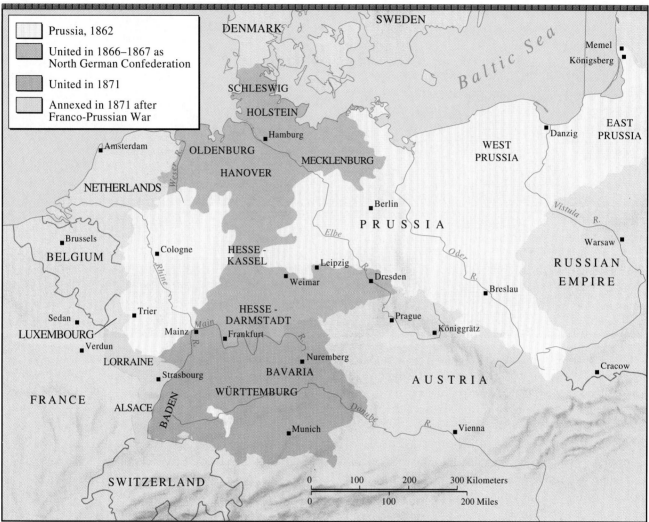

In the course of the nineteenth century, Prussia had become a strong and prosperous state. Its government was authoritarian. The Prussian king had firm control over both the government and the army. Prussia was also known for its **militarism,** or glorification of the military.

In the 1860s, King William I tried to enlarge the Prussian army. When the Prussian legislature refused to levy new taxes for the proposed military changes, William I appointed a new prime minister, Count Otto von Bismarck (BIZ-MARK). Bismarck ignored the leg-

islative opposition to the military reforms. He argued instead that "Germany does not look to Prussia's liberalism but to her power. . . . Not by speeches and majorities will the great questions of the day be decided—that was the mistake of 1848–1849—but by iron and blood."[1] Bismarck proceeded to collect the taxes and strengthen the army. From 1862 to 1866, Bismarck governed Prussia by simply ignoring the parliament. In the meantime, opposition to his domestic policy led Bismarck to follow an active foreign policy, which led to war and German unification. Bismarck has often

▲ *On January 18, 1871, a new German Empire was formally established at a ceremony held in the Hall of Mirrors in Versailles. Bismarck is shown at the foot of the throne as William I is named Emperor William I of the Second German Empire. Why do you think Bismarck is the central figure in the painting, not the emperor?*

been seen as the ultimate realist. He was the foremost nineteenth-century practitioner of **realpolitik**—the "politics of reality," or politics based on practical matters rather than on theory or ethics. Bismarck was also open about his strong dislike of anyone who opposed him. He said one morning to his wife, "I could not sleep the whole night; I hated throughout the whole night."

Bismarck's first war was against Denmark and was fought over the duchies (DUTCH-eez) of Schleswig (SHLESS-WIG) and Holstein (HOLE-STINE). Bismarck persuaded the Austrians to join Prussia in declaring war on Denmark on February 1, 1864. The Danes, who were quickly defeated, surrendered Schleswig and Holstein to the victors. Austria and Prussia then agreed to divide the administration of the two duchies. Prussia took Schleswig, and Austria administered Holstein. However, Bismarck used the joint administration of the two duchies to create friction with the Austrians and goad them into a war on June 14, 1866.

The Austrians proved to be no match for the well-disciplined Prussian army. The Prussians, with a superior network of railroads, could mass troops quickly. At Königgrätz (kuh-NIK-grats) (or Sadowa [zah-DOE-vuh]) on July 3, the Austrian army was decisively defeated. Prussia now organized the German states north of the Main River into a North German Confederation. The southern German states, which were largely Catholic, feared Protestant Prussia. However, they also feared France, their western neighbor. As a result, they agreed to sign military alliances with Prussia for protection against France.

Bismarck and King William I had achieved a major goal by 1866. Prussia now dominated all of northern

Germany, and Austria had been excluded from any role in German affairs. However, problems with France soon arose. Bismarck realized that France would never be content with a strong German state to its east because of the potential threat to French security. At the same time, Napoleon III, the French ruler, was in need of a diplomatic triumph to offset his serious domestic problems. In 1870, Prussia and France became embroiled in a dispute over the candidacy of a relative of the Prussian king for the throne of Spain. Bismarck took advantage of the misunderstandings between the French and Prussians to goad the French into declaring war on Prussia on July 15, 1870 (the Franco-Prussian War).

The French proved to be no match for the better led and better organized Prussian forces. The southern German states honored their military alliances with Prussia and joined the war effort against the French. The Prussian armies advanced into France. At Sedan, on September 2, 1870, an entire French army and Napoleon III himself were captured. Paris finally surrendered on January 28, 1871, and an official peace treaty was signed in May. France had to pay 5 billion francs (about $1 billion) and give up the provinces of Alsace (al-SASS) and Lorraine (luh-RANE) to the new German state. The loss of these territories left the French burning for revenge.

Even before the war had ended, the southern German states had agreed to enter the North German Confederation. On January 18, 1871, Bismarck and 600 German princes, nobles, and generals filled the Hall of Mirrors in the palace of Versailles, twelve miles outside Paris. The words "Long live His Imperial Majesty, the Emperor William!" rang out, and the assembled guests took up the cry. William I of Prussia had been proclaimed kaiser (KIE-zur), or emperor, of the Second German Empire (the first was the medieval Holy Roman Empire). German unity had been achieved by the Prussian monarchy and the Prussian army. The authoritarian and militaristic values of Prussia were triumphant in the new German state. With its industrial resources and military might, the new state had become the strongest power on the Continent. A new European balance of power was at hand.

## Nationalism and Reform: Great Britain, France, the Austrian Empire, and Russia

While Italy and Germany were being unified, other states in Europe were also experiencing changes. Great Britain managed to avoid the revolutionary upheavals of the first half of the nineteenth century. In 1815, Great Britain was governed by the aristocratic landowning classes that dominated both houses of Parliament. However, in 1832, to avoid the revolutionary turmoil on the Continent, Parliament passed a Reform Bill that increased the numbers of male voters, chiefly members of the industrial middle class. By joining the industrial middle class to the landed interest in ruling Britain, Britain avoided revolution in 1848.

In the 1850s and 1860s, the liberal parliamentary system of Britain made both social and political reforms that enabled the country to remain stable. One of the other reasons for Britain's stability was its continuing economic growth. After 1850, middle-class prosperity was at last coupled with some improvements for the working classes as well. Real wages for laborers increased more than 25 percent between 1850 and 1870. The British feeling of national pride was well reflected in Queen Victoria, whose reign from 1837 to 1901 was the longest in English history. Victoria had nine children and, when she died at age eighty-one, thirty-seven great-grandchildren. Her sense of duty and moral respectability reflected the attitudes of her age, which has ever since been known as the Victorian Age.

In France, events after the revolution of 1848 moved toward the restoration of the monarchy. Four years after his election as president, Louis Napoleon returned to the people to ask for the restoration of the empire. Ninety-seven percent responded with a yes vote. On December 2, 1852, Louis Napoleon assumed the title of Napoleon III. (The first Napoleon had abdicated [renounced the throne] in favor of his son, Napoleon II, on April 6, 1814.) The Second Empire had begun.

The government of Napoleon III was clearly authoritarian. As chief of state, Napoleon III controlled the armed forces, police, and civil service. Only he could introduce legislation and declare war. The Legislative

▲ *Louis Napoleon took the title of Napoleon III on December 2, 1852, and served as an authoritarian monarch until 1870. Why do you think the French people strongly supported an imperial government during these years?*

Corps gave an appearance of representative government, because the members of this group were elected by universal male suffrage for six-year terms. However, they could neither initiate legislation nor affect the budget.

The first five years of Napoleon III's reign were a spectacular success. He took many steps to expand industrial growth. Government subsidies helped to fos-ter the rapid construction of railroads, as well as harbors, roads, and canals. The major French railway lines were completed during Napoleon's reign. Iron production tripled. In the midst of this economic expansion, Napoleon III also carried out a vast rebuilding of the city of Paris. The old Paris of narrow streets and walls was destroyed and replaced by a modern Paris of broad boulevards, spacious buildings, public squares, an underground sewage system, a new public water supply, and gaslights. The new Paris served a military purpose as well. Broad streets made it more difficult for would-be rebels to throw up barricades and easier for troops to move rapidly through the city in the event of revolts.

In the 1860s, as opposition began to mount, Napoleon III began to liberalize his regime. He gave the Legislative Corps more say in affairs of state, including debate over the budget. In a vote in May 1870, on whether to accept a new constitution that might have begun a parliamentary regime, the French people gave Napoleon another resounding victory. This triumph was short-lived, however. War with Prussia in 1870 brought Napoleon's expulsion, and a republic was proclaimed.

As we have seen, nationalism was a major force in nineteenth-century Europe. However, one of Europe's most powerful states—the Austrian Empire—was a multinational empire that had been able to frustrate the desire of its ethnic groups for independence. After the Habsburg rulers had crushed the revolutions of 1848 and 1849, they restored centralized, autocratic government to the empire. Austria's defeat at the hands of the Prussians in 1866, however, forced the Austrians to make concessions to the fiercely nationalistic Hungarians.

The result was the **Ausgleich,** or Compromise, of 1867. This compromise created the dual monarchy of Austria-Hungary. Each part of the empire now had its own constitution, its own legislature, its own government bureaucracy, and its own capital (Vienna for Austria and Budapest for Hungary). Holding the two states together were a single monarch (Francis Joseph was both Emperor of Austria and King of Hungary) and a common army, foreign policy, and system of finances. In domestic affairs, the Hungarians had become an independent nation. The Ausgleich, however, did not satisfy the other nationalities that made up the multinational Austro-Hungarian Empire.

At the beginning of the nineteenth century, Russia was overwhelmingly rural, agricultural, and autocratic. The Russian tsar was still regarded as a divine-right monarch with unlimited power. The Russian imperial autocracy, a government based on soldiers, secret police, repression, and censorship, had withstood the revolutionary fervor of the first half of the nineteenth century. The Russian army had even crushed revolutions elsewhere in Europe. However, defeat in the Crimean War in 1856 led even staunch conservatives to realize that Russia was falling hopelessly behind the western European powers. Tsar Alexander II decided to make serious reforms.

Serfdom was the largest problem in tsarist Russia. On March 3, 1861, Alexander issued his **emancipation** (to set free from bondage) edict (see "You Are There: Emancipation—Serfs and Slaves"). Peasants were now free to own property and marry as they chose. However, the new land system was not that helpful to the peasants. The government provided land for the peasants by buying it from the landlords. The landowners, however, often kept the best lands. The Russian peasants soon found that they did not have enough good land to support themselves.

Furthermore, the peasants were not completely free. The state paid the landowners for the land given to the peasants. In turn, the peasants were expected to repay the state in long-term installments. To ensure that the payments were made, peasants were placed in village communes, or communities called **mirs.** The commune was responsible for the land payments to the government. Because the village communes were responsible for the payments, they did not want the peasants to leave their land. Emancipation of the serfs, then, led not to a free, landowning peasantry but to an unhappy, land-starved peasantry that largely followed the old ways of farming.

Alexander II attempted other reforms as well, but he soon found that he could please no one. Reformers wanted more and rapid change. Conservatives thought that the tsar was trying to destroy the basic institutions of Russian society. When a group of radicals assassinated Alexander II in 1881, his son and successor, Alexander III, turned against reform and returned to the old methods of repression.

## The Growth of the United States

The U.S. Constitution, ratified in 1789, committed the United States to two of the major forces of the first half of the nineteenth century, liberalism and nationalism. National unity did not come easy, however. Bitter conflict erupted between the Federalists and the Republicans over the power of the federal government in relation to the states. Led by Alexander Hamilton, the Federalists favored a financial program that would establish a strong central government. The Republicans, guided by Thomas Jefferson and James Madison, feared a strong central government as a danger to popular liberties. These early divisions ended with the War of 1812 against the British. A surge of national feeling at that time served to cover over the nation's divisions.

The election of Andrew Jackson as president in 1828 opened a new era in American politics. Jacksonian democracy introduced mass democratic politics. Property qualifications for voting were dropped. By the 1830s, the right to vote had been extended to almost all adult white males.

By the mid-nineteenth century, the issue of slavery had become a threat to American national unity. Like the North, the South had grown dramatically in population during the first half of the nineteenth century. Unlike the situation in the North, however, the South's economy was based on growing cotton on plantations, chiefly by slave labor. Although the importation of slaves had been banned in 1808, there were four million African American slaves in the South by 1860, compared with one million in 1800. The cotton economy and plantation-based slavery were closely related. The South was determined to maintain them. At the same time, the growth of a movement in the North to end slavery (**abolitionism**) challenged the southern way of life.

As opinions over slavery grew more divided, compromise became less possible. Abraham Lincoln said in a speech in Illinois in 1858 that "this government cannot endure permanently half slave and half free."

## YOU ARE THERE

# Emancipation—Serfs and Slaves

▶ *Alexander II freed the serfs on March 3, 1861, but this action did little to end their poverty. This photograph taken in 1870 shows a family huddled together in their one-room home. Based on the visual evidence in this photo, how do you think the living conditions of Russian serfs compared to living conditions of slaves in the United States?*

*The United States and Russia shared a common feature in the 1860s. Both still had large enslaved populations (the Russian serfs were virtually slaves). The leaders of both countries issued emancipation proclamations within two years of each other.*

### The Imperial Decree, March 3, 1861

By the grace of God, we, Alexander II, Emperor and Autocrat of all the Russias, King of Poland, Grand Duke of Finland, etc., to all our faithful subjects, make known:

We thus came to the conviction that the work of a serious improvement of the condition of the peasants was a sacred inheritance bequeathed to us by our ancestors, a mission which, in the course of events, Divine Providence called upon us to fulfill. . . .

In virtue of the new dispositions above mentioned, the peasants attached to the soil will be invested within a term fixed by the law with all the rights of free cultivators. . . .

At the same time, they are granted the right of purchasing their close, and, with the consent of the proprietors, they may acquire in full property

When Lincoln was elected president in November 1860, the die was cast. Lincoln carried only 2 of the 1,109 counties in the South. On December 20, 1860, a South Carolina convention voted to repeal ratification

(withdraw formal approval) of the Constitution of the United States. In February 1861, six more southern states did the same, and a rival nation—the Confederate States of America—was formed. In April, fighting

## YOU ARE THERE

# Emancipation—Serfs and Slaves, continued

the arable lands and other appurtenances [right of ways] which are allotted to them as a permanent holding. By the acquisition in full property of the quantity of land fixed, the peasants are free from their obligations towards the proprietors for land thus purchased, and they enter definitely into the condition of free peasants-landholders.

### The Emancipation Proclamation, January 1, 1863

Now therefore, I, Abraham Lincoln, President of the United States, by virtue of the power in me vested as Commander-in-Chief of the Army and Navy of the United States in time of actual armed rebellion against the authority and government of the United States, and as a fit and necessary war measure for suppressing such rebellion, do, on this 1st day of January, A.D. 1863, and in accordance with my purpose to do so, . . . order and designate as the States and parts of States wherein the people thereof, respectively, are this day in rebellion against the United States the following, to wit:

Arkansas, Texas, Louisiana, . . . Mississippi, Alabama, Florida, Georgia, South Carolina, North Carolina, and Virginia. . . .

And by virtue of the power for the purpose aforesaid, I do order and declare that all persons held as slaves within said designated States and parts of States are, and henceforward shall be free; and that the Executive Government of the United States, including the military and naval authorities

▲ *President Lincoln believed that the Emancipation Proclamation was an "act of justice" and a military necessity. Do you think Tsar Alexander II saw the Imperial Decree as an act of justice? As a military necessity? Why or why not?*

thereof, will recognize and maintain the freedom of said persons.

1. Compare and contrast the Emancipation Proclamation of Abraham Lincoln and the Imperial Decree of Alexander II. How are they similar? How are they different?

erupted between North and South (the Union and the Confederacy).

The American Civil War (1861 to 1865) was an extraordinarily bloody struggle. Over 600,000 soldiers died, either in battle or from deadly infectious diseases spawned by filthy camp conditions. Over a period of four years, the Union states gradually wore down the South. Moreover, what had begun as a war to save the

Union became a war against slavery. On January 1, 1863, Lincoln's Emancipation Proclamation declared most of the nation's slaves "forever free" (see "You Are There: Emancipation—Serfs and Slaves"). The surrender of Confederate forces on April 9, 1865, meant that the United States would be "one nation, indivisible." National unity had prevailed in the United States.

## The Emergence of a Canadian Nation

By the Treaty of Paris in 1763, Canada—or New France, as it was called—passed into the hands of the British. By 1800, most Canadians favored more freedom from British rule. However, there were also serious differences among the colonists. Upper Canada (now Ontario) was mostly English speaking, whereas Lower Canada (now Quebec) was dominated by French Canadians. Increased immigration to Canada after 1815 also fueled the desire for self-government. After two short rebellions against the government broke out in Upper and Lower Canada in 1837 and 1838, the British moved toward change. In 1840, the British Parliament formally joined Upper and Lower Canada into the United Provinces of Canada, but without granting self-government.

The head of Upper Canada's Conservative Party, John Macdonald, became a strong voice for self-government. The British government, fearful of American designs on Canada, finally gave in. In 1867, Parliament passed the British North American Act, which established a Canadian nation—the Dominion of Canada—with its own constitution. John Macdonald became the first prime minister of the Dominion. Although Canada now possessed a parliamentary system and ruled itself, foreign affairs were still in the hands of the British government.

### ❀ SECTION REVIEW ❀

1. **Locate:**
   (a) Crimean peninsula, (b) Balkans,
   (c) Dardanelles, (d) Budapest, (e) Alsace,
   (f) Lorraine

2. **Define:**
   (a) militarism, (b) realpolitik, (c) Ausgleich,
   (d) emancipation, (e) mirs, (f) abolitionism

3. **Identify:**
   (a) Count Camillo di Cavour, (b) Giuseppe Garibaldi, (c) Franco-Prussian war, (d) Count Otto von Bismarck, (e) Queen Victoria, (f) Legislative Corps, (g) Francis Joseph, (h) Tsar Alexander II, (i) Emancipation Proclamation, (j) British North American Act

4. **Recall:**
   (a) How did the Crimean War destroy the Concert of Europe?
   (b) What action by Giuseppe Garibaldi made him unique among most national leaders?
   (c) How was Great Britain able to avoid revolutions that occurred in many parts of Europe in 1848?
   (d) Why didn't the distribution of land to the peasants by the Russian government enable them to support themselves?
   (e) What was the difference between the basis for the economy of the North and that of the South in the United States before the Civil War?

5. **Think Critically:** How did the existence of a common enemy help bring about the unification of Germany?

## CULTURAL LIFE: ROMANTICISM AND REALISM IN THE WESTERN WORLD

At the end of the eighteenth century, a new intellectual movement, known as romanticism, emerged to challenge the ideas of the Enlightenment. The Enlightenment had stressed reason as the chief means for discovering truth. The romantics emphasized feelings, emotion, and imagination as sources of knowing.

▲ *The Houses of Parliament in London burned in 1834 and were replaced with new buildings in the neo-Gothic style. What features of Gothic architecture do you see in these tall, graceful buildings that overlook the Thames River?*

## The Characteristics of Romanticism

The romantics stressed emotion and sentiment. They believed that these inner feelings were only understandable to the person experiencing them. In their novels, romantic writers created figures who were often misunderstood and rejected by society, but who continued to believe in their own worth through their inner feelings.

Romantics also valued individualism, or the belief in the uniqueness of each person. The desire of romantics to follow their inner drives to know themselves led them to rebel against middle-class conventions. They grew long hair and beards and wore outrageous clothes to express their uniqueness.

Many romantics had a passionate interest in the past. They revived medieval Gothic architecture and adorned European countrysides with pseudomedieval castles. Grandiose neo-Gothic (built in the Gothic style of the Middle Ages) cathedrals, city halls, parliamentary buildings, and even railway stations were built in many European cities. Literature, too, reflected a love of the past. The novels of Walter Scott became European best-sellers in the first half of the nineteenth century. *Ivanhoe*, in which Scott tried to evoke the clash between Saxon and Norman knights in medieval England, became one of his most popular novels. In focusing on their nations' past, romantic writers created national literature and reflected the nineteenth century's fascination with nationalism.

Many romantics had a deep attraction to the exotic and unfamiliar. This attraction gave rise to so-called Gothic literature. Chilling examples are Mary Shelley's *Frankenstein* in Britain and Edgar Allen Poe's short stories of horror in the United States. Some romantics even sought the unusual in their own lives by exploring their dreams and nightmares and seeking altered states of consciousness.

The romantics loved poetry, which they viewed as the direct expression of the soul. Romantic poetry gave full expression to one of the most important characteristics of romanticism—its love of nature. This is especially evident in the poetry of William Wordsworth, the foremost English romantic poet of nature. His

▲  *Edgar Allen Poe quickly gained international fame for his short stories, including the* Fall of the House of Usher. *This illustration captures the horror and excitement of the story.*

experience of nature was almost mystical as he claimed to receive "authentic tidings of invisible things":

> *One impulse from a vernal wood*
> *May teach you more of man,*
> *Of Moral Evil and of good,*
> *Than all the sages can.* [2]

Romantics believed that nature served as a mirror into which humans could look to learn about themselves.

The worship of nature also caused Wordsworth and other romantic poets to be critical of eighteenth-century science, which, they believed, had reduced nature to a cold object of study. To Wordsworth, the scientists' dry, mathematical approach left no room for the imagination or for the human soul. The poet who left to the world "one single moral precept," Wordsworth said, did more for the world than did scientists, who were soon forgotten. The monster created by Frankenstein in Mary Shelley's Gothic novel was a symbol of the danger of science's attempt to conquer nature. Many romantics were convinced that the emerging industrialization would cause people to become alienated from their inner selves and the natural world around them.

Like the literary arts, the visual arts and music were also deeply affected by romanticism (see "Our Artistic Heritage: The Romantic Vision"). To many romantics, music was the most romantic of the arts, because it enabled the composer to probe deeply into human emotions. Music historians have called the nineteenth century the age of romanticism. One of the greatest composers of all time, Ludwig van Beethoven (BAE-TOE-vun), was the bridge between the classical and romantic periods in music. At first, Beethoven's work was still largely within the classical framework of the eighteenth century. His style differed little from that of Wolfgang Amadeus Mozart and Franz Joseph Haydn. However, with his Third Symphony, the *Eroica*, Beethoven broke through to the elements of romanticism. His use of powerful melodies to create dramatic intensity led one writer to say that "Beethoven's music opens the flood gates of fear, of terror, of horror, of pain, and arouses that longing for the eternal which is the essence of romanticism." [3]

One of the great figures of the romantic period was Franz Liszt (LIST), who was born in Hungary. Liszt, a child prodigy, established himself as an outstanding concert pianist by the age of twelve. Between the ages of thirteen and fifteen, Liszt embarked on a series of concert tours throughout France, England, and Switzerland. His performances and his dazzling personality

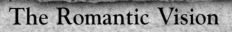

# OUR ARTISTIC HERITAGE

## The Romantic Vision

◀ Man and Woman Gazing at the Moon *shows the romantic, mystical view of nature held by German artist Caspar David Friedrich. Does the artist give more emphasis to the two humans or to the tree? Explain your answer.*

Romantic artists shared at least two common features. First, to them, all art was a reflection of the artist's inner feelings. A painting should mirror the artist's vision of the world and be the instrument of the artist's own imagination. Second, romantic artists deliberately rejected classicism. The romantics abandoned classical coldness and reason for warmth and emotion.

The early life experiences of the German painter Caspar David Friedrich (FREE-drik) left him with a lifelong preoccupation with God and nature. Friedrich painted many landscapes, but with an interest that went beyond the mere natural details. His portrayal of mountains shrouded in mist, gnarled trees bathed in moonlight, and the stark ruins of monasteries surrounded by withered trees all conveyed a feeling of mystery. For

Friedrich, nature was a revelation of divine life. As is exemplified in the painting *Man and Woman Gazing at the Moon*, he liked to depict one or two solitary figures gazing upon a natural scene with their backs to the viewer. His human figures were overwhelmed by the grandeur of nature, but they expressed the human desire to lose themselves in the universe. To Friedrich, art depended upon the use of an imagination that could be achieved only through inner vision. He advised artists: "Shut your physical eye and look first at your picture with your spiritual eye, then bring to the light of day what you have seen in the darkness."

Eugène Delacroix (DELL-uh-KrWAW) was one of the most famous French romantic painters. His

*(continued)*

# OUR ARTISTIC HERITAGE

## The Romantic Vision, continued

▲ *Eugène Delacroix often chose the exotic and unknown, North Africa and the Near East, as subjects for his paintings. Women of Algiers, shown here, is typical in that regard. The painting also reflects Delacroix's interest in light and color. Can you tell from which direction the light comes into the room? How did the artist convey that to the viewer?*

paintings showed two chief characteristics: a fascination with the exotic and a passion for color. Both are visible in his *Women of Algiers*. This portrayal of the world of the harem in exotic North Africa is significant for its use of light and its patches of interrelated color. In Delacroix, drama and movement combined with a daring use of color. Many of his works reflect his own belief that "a painting should be a feast to the eye."

1. What were the two common features shared by romantic artists?

2. How did the artist Friedrich view nature?

3. What do you think the phrase "a painting should be a feast to the eye" means?

made him a famous figure. Liszt has been called the greatest pianist of all time.

## A New Age of Science

The Scientific Revolution had created a modern, rational approach to the study of the natural world. For a long time, only the educated elite understood its importance. With the Industrial Revolution, however, came a renewed interest in basic scientific research. By the 1830s, new discoveries in science led to many practical benefits that affected all Europeans. Science came to have a greater and greater impact on European life.

In biology, the Frenchman Louis Pasteur (pass-TUR) discovered the germ theory of disease, which was crucial to the development of modern scientific medical practices. In chemistry, the Russian Dmitri Mendeleev (duh-MEE-tree MEN-duh-LAE-uf) in the 1860s classified all the material elements then known on the basis of their atomic weights. In Great Britain, Michael Faraday (FAR-uh-DAY) put together a primitive generator that laid the foundation for the use of electricity.

The dramatic material benefits often provided by science and technology led Europeans to have a growing faith in science. This faith, in turn, undermined

▲ The Stonebreakers *by Gustave Courbet, an artist of the realist school, represents a complete break with the mystical and imaginative qualities of the romantic period. These two life-size figures are engaged in hard, manual labor, but the artist does not try to draw the viewer into the painting or gain our sympathy for them. We are simply observers of the scene. Why do you think this work was initially rejected by French art critics as too harsh?*

the religious faith of many people. It is no accident that the nineteenth century was an age of increasing secularization. For many people, truth was now to be found in science and the concrete material existence of humans. No one did more to create a picture of humans as material beings that were simply part of the natural world than Charles Darwin.

In 1859, Charles Darwin published *On the Origin of Species by Means of Natural Selection.* The basic idea of this book was that each kind of plant and animal had evolved over a long period of time from earlier and simpler forms of life. Darwin called this principle **organic evolution.**

How did this natural process work? According to Darwin, in every species, "many more individuals of each species are born than can possibly survive." This results in a "struggle for existence." Darwin believed that some organisms were more adaptable to the environment than others, a process that Darwin called **natural selection.** He describes the natural selection process as follows:

*Owing to this struggle [for existence], variations, however slight . . . , if they be in any degree profitable to the individuals of a species, in their infinitely complex relations to other organic beings and to their physical conditions of life, will tend to the preservation of such individuals, and will generally be inherited by the off-spring.*[4]

In other words, the organisms that were selected for survival through this natural process—those that had characteristics that favored their preservation—were the organisms that survived. (This is called "survival of the fittest.") The unfit did not survive. The fit, in turn, propagated. In this way they passed on the variations that enabled them to survive until, according to Darwin, a new, separate species emerged.

In *The Descent of Man*, published in 1871, Darwin argued that human beings had animal origins. Humans, he believed, were not an exception to the rule governing other species.

Darwin's ideas raised a storm of controversy. Some people objected that Darwin's theory made human beings ordinary products of nature rather than unique beings. Others were bothered by his idea of life as a mere struggle for survival. "Was there a place in the Darwinian world for moral values?" they asked. Many people also condemned Darwin for denying God's role in creation. Gradually, however, many scientists and other intellectuals came to accept Darwin's theory.

## Realism

The belief that the world should be viewed realistically, a view frequently expressed after 1850, was closely related to the scientific outlook. In politics, Bismarck had practiced the "politics of reality." Realism became a movement in the literary and visual arts as well. The literary realists of the mid-nineteenth century rejected romanticism. They wanted to write about ordinary characters from actual life rather than romantic heroes in exotic settings. They also tried to avoid emotional language by using precise description. Thus, they preferred to write novels rather than poems.

The leading novelist of the 1850s and 1860s, the French Gustave Flaubert (floe-BEH[uh]R), perfected the realist novel. His *Madame Bovary* was a straightforward, critical, description of small-town life in France. The British novelist Charles Dickens became very successful with his realistic novels focusing on the lower

and middle classes in Britain's early Industrial Age. In such novels as *Oliver Twist* and *David Copperfield*, Dickens's descriptions of the urban poor and the brutal life they led were vividly realistic.

In art, too, realism became dominant after 1850. Realist artists sought to show the everyday life of ordinary people and the world of nature with photographic realism. The French became leaders in realist painting.

Gustave Courbet was the most famous artist of the realist school. Courbet loved to portray scenes from everyday life. His subjects were factory workers, peasants, and the wives of saloon keepers. "I have never seen either angels or goddesses, so I am not interested in painting them," Courbet said. One of his famous works, *The Stonebreakers*, painted in 1849, shows two roadworkers engaged in the deadening work of breaking stones to build a road. There were those who objected to Courbet's "cult of ugliness" and who found his scenes of human misery scandalous. To Courbet, however, no subject was too ordinary, too harsh, or too ugly to be interesting.

## ❊ SECTION REVIEW ❊

1. **Define:**
   (*a*) organic evolution,
   (*b*) natural selection

2. **Identify:**
   (*a*) *Ivanhoe*,   (*b*) *Frankenstein*,
   (*c*) *On the Origin of Species by Means of Natural Selection*,   (*d*) realism

3. **Recall:**
   (*a*) How was romanticism different from the ideas of the Enlightenment?
   (*b*) Why were romantic poets critical of eighteenth-century science?

4. **Think Critically:** Many political, economic, and social injustices existed during the nineteenth century. How do you think this may have contributed to both the ages of romanticism and realism?

## Conclusion

In 1815, a conservative order had been reestablished throughout Europe, and the great powers worked to maintain it. However, the waves of revolution in Europe in the first half of the nineteenth century made it clear that the forces of nationalism and liberalism, brought into being by the French Revolution and strengthened by the spread of the Industrial Revolution, were still alive and active.

Between 1850 and 1871, the national state became the focus of people's loyalty. Wars were fought to create unified nation-states, and reforms at home served to make the nation-state the center of attention. Nationalism became a powerful force of change during the first half of the nineteenth century, but its triumph came only after 1850. Tied at first to middle-class liberals, by the end of the nineteenth century nationalism had great appeal to the broad masses as well.

In 1870, however, not all peoples had achieved their national dreams. Large minorities, especially in the empires controlled by the Austrians, Ottoman Turks, and Russians, had not achieved the goal of establishing their own national states. Moreover, nationalism also changed in the course of the nineteenth century. Liberal nationalists had believed that unified nation-states would preserve individual rights and lead to a great community of European peoples. Rather than unifying people, however, the nationalism of the late nineteenth century divided people as the new national states competed bitterly with one another after 1870.

Europeans, however, were hardly aware of nationalism's dangers in 1870. The spread of the Industrial Revolution and the wealth of technological achievements convinced many Europeans that they stood on the verge of a new age of progress.

## Notes

1. Louis L. Snyder, ed., *Documents of German History* (New Brunswick, N.J., 1958), p. 202.
2. William Wordsworth, "The Tables Turned," *Poems of Wordsworth*, ed. Matthew Arnold (London, 1963), p. 138.
3. Quoted in Siegbert Prawer, ed., *The Romantic Period in Germany* (London, 1970), p. 285.
4. Charles Darwin, *On the Origin of Species*, vol. 1 (New York, 1872), pp. 77, 79.

# CHAPTER 4 REVIEW

## USING KEY TERMS

1. _____ was the movement to end slavery in the United States.
2. At the Congress of Vienna in 1814, the _____ became the guiding political principle for the great powers.
3. _____ means that all adult men have the right to vote.
4. A political philosophy that concentrates on practical matters, rather than on theory or ethics, is called _____.
5. The process invented by Henry Cort to produce high quality iron is called _____.
6. The basic idea of Charles Darwin's book, *On the Origin of Species* was the principle of _____.
7. Obedience to political authority, emphasis on organized religion to maintain the social order, and resistance to the ideas of individual rights and representative government are characteristics of _____.
8. The _____ class included merchants, artisans, officials, lawyers, industrialists, bankers, teachers, doctors, and shopkeepers.
9. Traditional Russian peasant communal villages were called _____.
10. The _____, or Compromise, of 1867, created the dual monarchy of Austria-Hungary.
11. Charles Darwin believed that some organisms were able to adapt better to the environment than others, a process he called _____.
12. A state that is made up of many different peoples, such as the Austrian Empire, is called a _____.
13. A(n) _____ justified the use of military forces to crush popular revolts in Spain and Italy.
14. _____ was the name given by Marxists to men who believed that cooperation could replace competition in industry.
15. A(n) _____ edict by Russian Tsar Alexander II allowed peasants to own property and marry as they chose.
16. The glorification of war and the military is called _____.
17. _____ is the idea that people should be as free from restraint as possible.

## REVIEWING THE FACTS

1. What new sources of energy became important in the early Industrial Revolution?
2. In what ways did the economy of Europe shift during the Industrial Revolution?
3. Name three important inventors in England and their inventions.
4. What was the cause of the famine in Ireland between 1845 to 1851?
5. What four nations were prepared to use military forces to crush revolts in other nations?
6. Which countries were involved in the Crimean War? Why did the war break out?
7. Who are the two men most responsible for the unification of Italy?
8. Who is the man who united Germany?
9. What were the provisions of the British Reform Bill in 1832?
10. Why did Great Britain pass the British North America Act in 1867?

## THINKING CRITICALLY

1. Why is liberalism thought to be an outgrowth of the Enlightenment?
2. Describe the importance of the railroads in spurring the Industrial Revolution in Great Britain.
3. Explain why the agricultural revolution in the late eighteenth century led to dramatic population growth in Europe.
4. Who supported the ideology of conservatism? Why would these groups support conservatism?

# CHAPTER 4 REVIEW

5. In what way did the Crimean War indirectly contribute to the unification of Italy and Germany?
6. Compare and contrast Cavour and Bismarck. In your opinion, who was the greater statesman?
7. Trace the conflict over national unity in the United States from 1789 to 1865. In what ways were the twin principles of liberalism and nationalism involved?

## APPLYING SOCIAL STUDIES SKILLS

1. **Economics:** Consult Map 4.1 on page 129. In 1815, Prussia was the weakest of the great powers. By 1871, Germany was a more powerful nation than France. Does this map provide any clues as to why this was now so? In 1815, Russia was perhaps the most powerful of the great powers; by 1870, it had become the weakest. Does this map provide any clues as to why this had occurred?
2. **Geography:** Consult Map 4.2 on page 134 (Europe after the Congress of Vienna). Which nation dominated the Balkan Peninsula? What is the largest nation in the North German Plain? How many nations occupy the northern portion of Italy?
3. **Government:** Compare the motives for Alexander II's emancipation of the serfs with Abraham Lincoln's motives for the Emancipation Proclamation in 1862.
4. **Government:** Contrast the relationship between the British Prime Minister and Parliament with that of Otto von Bismarck to the Prussian Reichstag.

## MAKING TIME AND PLACE CONNECTIONS

1. Why would the Soviet Union name the space station which they sent up to orbit the Earth the *Mir*?

2. How has nationalism influenced the former Yugoslavia? The former Soviet Union? The former Czechoslovakia? Spain? Great Britain? Belgium? Ireland? Refer to at least two countries in your answer. Give examples within your own community, or from recent news, of expressions of nationalism.
3. In what ways are Camillo di Cavour and Giuseppe Garibaldi similar to Simon Bolivar and Jose de San Martin?

## BECOMING AN HISTORIAN

1. **Charts, Graphs, Tables:** Construct charts showing (1) British imports from 1760 to 1840; (2) European population growth from 1750 to 1850; and (3) the population of Ireland from 1781 to 1851.
2. **Compare and Contrast:** Compare the portrait of Prince Metternich (p. 135) with that of Emperor Napoleon III (p. 146). How does each portrait reflect the political philosophies of each statesman?
3. **Compare and Contrast:** Compare the photograph of Russian peasants (p. 148) with Courbet's *The Stonebreakers* (p. 155). Decide whether these works are romantic or realist and explain why.
4. What similarities are there between *The July Revolution in Paris* (p. 136), *Austrian Students in the Revolutionary Civil Guard* (p. 138), and *Garibaldi Arrives in Sicily* (p. 142)? Why might *Garibaldi Arrives in Sicily* be considered romantic?
5. **Art as a Key to History:** How do Caspar David Friedrich's *Man and Woman Gazing at the Moon* (p. 153) and Eugène Delacroix's *Women of Algiers* (p. 154) represent different facets of romanticism?
6. Compare the view of the world pictured in Caspar David Friedrich's *Man and Woman Gazing at the Moon* (p. 153) with that of Gustave Dore's drawing *Over London By Rail* (p. 130). Would you regard Dore as a romantic or a realist?

5

In the late nineteenth century, Europe witnessed a dynamic age of material prosperity. With new industries, new sources of energy, and new goods, the Second Industrial Revolution dazzled Europeans and led them to believe that their material progress meant human progress. Scientific and technological achievements, many believed, would solve all human problems. The doctrine of progress became widely accepted, and this period has often been labeled an age of progress.

Out of the new urban and industrial world created by the rapid economic changes of the nineteenth century emerged a mass society late in the century. A mass society meant improvements for the lower classes, who benefited from the extension of voting rights, a better standard of living, and mass education.

A mass society also brought mass leisure. New work patterns established the concept of the weekend as a distinct time of recreation and fun. New forms of mass transportation—railroads and streetcars—enabled even workers to make brief trips to amusement parks. Coney Island was only eight miles from central New York City; Blackpool, in England, was a short train ride from nearby industrial towns. With their Ferris wheels and other daring rides that threw young

men and women together, amusement parks offered a whole new world of entertainment. Thanks to the railroad, seaside resorts, once the preserve of the wealthy, became accessible to more people for weekend visits. This accessibility disgusted one upper-class seaside resort regular, who described the new "day-trippers": "They swarm upon the beach, wandering about with apparently no other aim than to get a mouthful of fresh air." Enterprising entrepreneurs in resorts like Blackpool, however, welcomed the masses of new visitors and built for them piers laden with food, drink, and entertainment.

The coming of mass society also created new roles for the governments of the European nation-states, which now fostered national loyalty, created mass armies, and took more responsibility for public health and housing in their cities. By 1870, the national state had become the focus of Europeans' lives. Within the nation-state political democracy grew as the right to vote was extended to all adult males. With political democracy came a new mass politics and a new mass press. Both would become regular features of the twentieth century.

▲ *Ferris wheels like this one built for the 1893 Columbian Exposition in the United States were very popular with young people. How have amusement parks changed over the past century?*

# STATE IN THE WESTERN WORLD

## (1870 TO 1914)

ERA OF EUROPEAN DOMINANCE

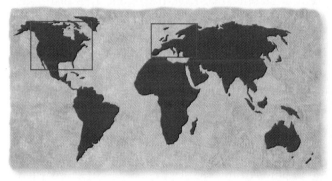

MASS SOCIETY AND THE NATIONAL STATE
| 1870       1914 |
| 1800       1914 |

## QUESTIONS TO GUIDE YOUR READING

1. What was the Second Industrial Revolution? What was its impact on European society?

2. What were the chief ideas of Karl Marx?

3. What do we mean by the phrase *mass society*? What were the chief features of this mass society?

4. How did the position of women change between 1870 and 1914?

5. What domestic problems did the United States, Canada, and the European nations face between 1870 and 1914?

6. What were the issues behind the international crises that occurred in the late nineteenth and early twentieth centuries?

7. What do we mean by the phrase *modern consciousness*? How did the modern consciousness begin to emerge between 1870 and 1914 in the sciences, psychology, and the arts?

## OUTLINE

1. THE GROWTH OF INDUSTRIAL PROSPERITY

2. THE EMERGENCE OF MASS SOCIETY

3. THE NATIONAL STATE

4. TOWARD THE MODERN CONSCIOUSNESS: INTELLECTUAL AND CULTURAL DEVELOPMENTS

## THE GROWTH OF INDUSTRIAL PROSPERITY

After 1870, Europeans virtually worshiped progress. At the heart of this belief in progress was the stunning material growth produced by what historians have called the Second Industrial Revolution. The first Industrial Revolution had given rise to textiles, railroads, iron, and coal. In the Second Industrial Revolution, steel, chemicals, electricity, and petroleum led the way to new industrial frontiers.

### New Products and New Patterns

The first major change in industry between 1870 and 1914 was the substitution of steel for iron. New methods for shaping steel made it useful in the building of lighter, smaller, and faster machines and engines, as well as railways, ships, and weapons. In 1860, Great Britain, France, Germany, and Belgium produced 125,000 tons of steel. By 1913, the total was an astounding 32 million tons.

Electricity was a major new form of energy that proved to be of great value. It could be easily converted into other forms of energy, such as heat, light, and

▲ *This picture from* The Illustrated London News *in 1897 shows the changes in transportation that occurred during the reign of Queen Victoria. Compare the scenes on the left, which date from 1837, with those on the right, which date from 1897. What major changes in transportation do you think will occur between 2000 and 2060?*

in entire areas to be tied into a single, common source of power.

Electricity gave birth to a whole new series of inventions. The creation of the lightbulb by Thomas Edison in the United States and Joseph Swan in Great Britain opened homes and cities to electric lights. A revolution in communications began when Alexander Graham Bell invented the telephone in 1876 and Guglielmo Marconi (mar-KOE-nee) sent the first radio waves across the Atlantic in 1901. Electricity was also put to use in transportation. By the 1880s, streetcars and subways powered by electricity had appeared in major European cities. This development allowed cities to grow even larger, as it enabled workers to get to factories and wealthy people to live in suburbs. Electricity also transformed the factory. Conveyor belts, cranes, and machines could all be powered by electricity and be located anywhere. With electric lights, factories could remain open twenty-four hours a day. Thanks to electricity, all countries could now enter the Industrial Age.

The development of the internal combustion engine, fired by oil and gasoline, provided a new source of power in transportation. This engine, in which fuel is burned inside the engine itself, gave rise to ocean liners with oil-fired engines, as well as to the airplane and the automobile (see "The Role of Science and Technology: The Automobile"). In 1903, at Kitty Hawk, North Carolina, the Wright brothers made the first flight in a fixed-wing plane powered by a gasoline engine. In 1919, the first regular passenger air service was established.

Industrial production grew at a rapid pace at this time because of the greatly increased sales of manufactured goods. An increase in real wages for workers after 1870, combined with lower prices for manufactured goods because of reduced transportation costs, made it easier for Europeans to buy consumer products. In the cities, the first department stores began to sell a whole new range of consumer goods made possible by the development of the steel and electrical industries. Sewing machines, clocks, bicy-

motion. Also, electricity moved easily through space by means of wires. The British scientist Michael Faraday produced the first electric generator in 1831, but it was not until the 1870s that the first practical generators of electrical current were developed. By 1910, however, hydroelectric power stations and coal-fired steam-generating plants enabled homes and factories

# THE ROLE OF SCIENCE AND TECHNOLOGY
## The Automobile

Of all the new forms of transportation created in the Industrial Revolution, the automobile affected more people on a daily basis than any other. There were early experiments with steam-powered automobiles, but they did not work very well. It was the invention of the internal combustion engine, a unit in which fuel is burned inside the engine itself, that made the automobile possible.

A German engineer, Gottlieb Daimler (GAWT-leeb DIME-lur), invented a light engine in 1886. In 1889, Daimler and Wilhelm Maybach (MIE-bawk) produced an automobile powered by a two-cylinder gasoline engine that reached a speed of ten miles per hour. However, it was another German, Karl Benz, who went on to design a four-wheeled vehicle that became the basis for the modern automobile. It took time, however, for the automobile to catch on. Early cars, such as the Benz, were handmade and expensive. Only the rich could afford to try one, and only several hundred were sold between 1893 and 1901. Their slow speed, fourteen miles per hour, was a problem, too. It prevented early models from being able to climb steep hills.

It was an American, Henry Ford, who revolutionized the car industry. Ford used an assembly line to mass-produce his Model T, beginning in 1908. Before Ford's use of the assembly line, it took a group of workers twelve hours to build a single car. On the assembly line, the same number of workers could build a car in an hour and a half. By cutting production costs, Ford lowered the price of the automobile. A Model T cost $850 in 1908 but only $360 by 1916.

Large numbers of people could now buy an automobile. By 1916, Ford's factories were producing 735,000 cars a year. By 1925, Ford's Model T

▲ *This automobile, a 1914 Ford Model T, was a symbol for the 1920s. Why do you think this car gained popularity so quickly?*

cars made up half of the automobiles in the world. By 1927, when the Ford company decided to discontinue its Model T line, over 18 million of these cars had been built.

---

1. Who is credited with designing the vehicle that became the basis for our modern-day car?

2. Who revolutionized the car industry? How did he do it?

3. What effect do you think the automobile had on the development of society?

cles, electric lights, and typewriters were bought in great quantities.

In the Second Industrial Revolution, manufacturing plants became larger, especially in the iron and steel, machinery, heavy electrical equipment, and chemical industries. Factory owners also streamlined production as much as possible. The development of precision tools enabled manufacturers to produce interchangeable parts, which in turn led to the creation of the assembly line for production. The assembly line was first used in the United States to produce small weapons and clocks. It had moved to Europe by 1850. In the last half of the nineteenth century, it was used in manufacturing sewing machines, typewriters, bicycles, and automobiles.

Not all nations benefited from the Second Industrial Revolution. Between 1870 and 1914, Germany replaced Great Britain as the industrial leader of Europe. Moreover, by 1900, Europe was divided into two economic zones. Great Britain, Belgium, France, the Netherlands, Germany, the western part of the Austro-Hungarian Empire, and northern Italy made up an advanced industrialized core that had a high standard of living, decent systems of transportation, and relatively healthy and educated peoples. Another part of Europe was still largely agricultural. This was the backward and little industrialized area to the south and east, consisting of southern Italy, most of the Austro-Hungarian Empire, Spain, Portugal, the Balkan kingdoms, and Russia. These countries provided food and raw materials for the industrial countries.

## Toward a World Economy

The Second Industrial Revolution, combined with the growth of steamships and railroads, fostered a true world economy. By 1900, Europeans were receiving beef and wool from Argentina and Australia, coffee from Brazil, iron ore from Algeria, and sugar from Java. European capital was also invested abroad to develop railways, mines, electrical power plants, and banks. Of course, foreign countries also provided markets for the manufactured goods of Europe. With its capital, industries, and military might, Europe dominated the world economy by the beginning of the twentieth century.

## Organizing the Working Classes

Before 1870, capitalist factory owners were largely free to hire workers on their own terms based on market forces. Early efforts by workers to fight for improved working conditions and reasonable wages had largely failed. Real change for the industrial working class came only with the development of **Socialist** parties and Socialist trade unions. These emerged after 1870, but the theory of public ownership of the means of production that made them possible had been developed earlier by Karl Marx.

In 1848, there appeared a short treatise entitled *The Communist Manifesto,* written by two Germans, Karl Marx and Friedrich Engels. Marx and Engels were appalled at the horrible conditions in factories. They blamed the system of industrial capitalism for these conditions and described a new socialist order—a new social system. One form of Marxist socialism was eventually called communism (see Chapter 8).

Marx believed that all of world history was a "history of class struggles." According to Marx, oppressor and oppressed have "stood in constant opposition to one another" throughout history. One group of people—the oppressors—owned the means of production and thus had the power to control government and society. Indeed, government itself was but an instrument of the ruling class. The other group, which depended upon the owners of the means of production, were the oppressed.

In the industrialized societies of Marx's day, the class struggle continued. According to Marx, "society as a whole is more and more splitting up into two great hostile camps, into two great classes directly facing each other: Bourgeoisie and Proletariat." The **bourgeoisie**—the middle class—were the oppressors. The **proletariat**—the working class—were the oppressed. Marx predicted that the struggle between the bourgeoisie and the proletariat would finally break into open revolution with the violent overthrow of the bourgeoisie by the proletariat. For a while the proletariat would form a dictatorship in order to organize the means of production. However, because social classes themselves arose from the economic differences that had been abolished, a classless society would be the end result.

## Map 5.1    The Industrial Regions of Europe by 1914

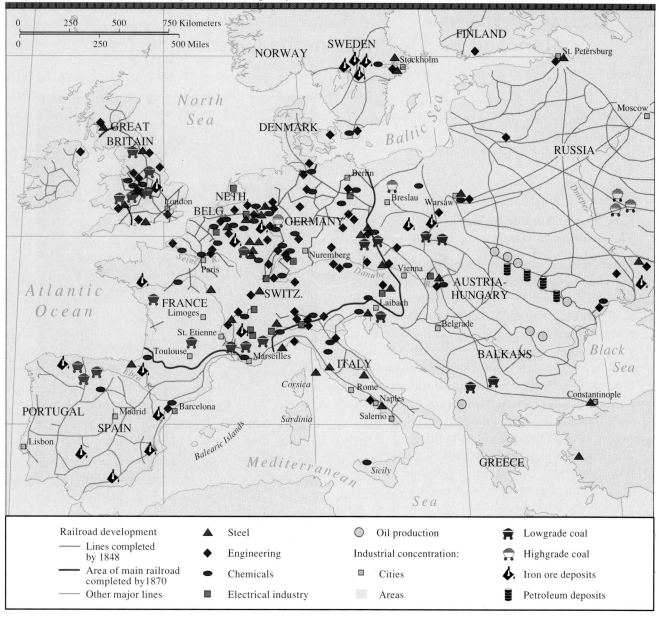

| Railroad development | | Steel | Oil production | Lowgrade coal |
|---|---|---|---|---|
| —— Lines completed by 1848 | ◆ | Engineering | Industrial concentration: | Highgrade coal |
| —— Area of main railroad completed by 1870 | ● | Chemicals | ▫ Cities | Iron ore deposits |
| —— Other major lines | ■ | Electrical industry | ░ Areas | Petroleum deposits |

The state—itself an instrument of the bourgeois interests—would wither away (see "You Are There: Marx and Engels Proclaim the Classless Society").

In time, Marx's ideas were picked up by working-class leaders who formed socialist parties. Most important was the German Social Democratic Party (SPD), which emerged in 1875. Under the direction of its two Marxist leaders, Wilhelm Liebknecht (LEEP-next) and August Bebel (BEA-buhl), the SPD spoke of revolution while organizing itself as a mass political party

## YOU ARE THERE

# Marx and Engels Proclaim the Classless Society

*In* The Communist Manifesto, *Karl Marx and Friedrich Engels projected the creation of a classless society as the final end product of the struggle between the bourgeoisie and the proletariat.*

### Karl Marx and Friedrich Engels, *The Communist Manifesto*

When, in the course of development, class distinctions have disappeared, and all production has been concentrated in the whole nation, the public power will lose its political character. Political power, properly so called, is merely the organized power of one class for oppressing another. If the proletariat during its contest with the bourgeoisie is compelled, by the force of circumstances, to organize itself as a class, if, by means of a revolution, it makes itself the ruling class, and, as such, sweeps away by force the old conditions of production, then it will, along with these conditions, have swept away the conditions for the existence of class antagonisms and of classes generally, and will thereby have abolished its own supremacy as a class.

In place of the old bourgeois society, with its classes and class antagonisms, we shall have an association, in which the free development of each is the condition for the free development of all. . . .

The Communists disdain to conceal their views and aims. They openly declare that their ends can be attained only by the forcible overthrow of all existing social conditions. Let the ruling classes tremble at a Communist revolution. The proletarians have nothing to lose but their chains. They have a world to win.

Workingmen of all countries, unite!

▲ *Many workers joined working-class parties and socialist groups to try to improve their situations in factories and mines and at home. This German poster proclaims "Proletarians of the World, Unite!" Can you understand the banners that join the feet of the workers?*

1. Do you agree with Marx's definition of political power? Why or why not?

2. Do you think Marx's idea of a classless society is realistic? Why or why not?

## CONNECTIONS
### TO OUR WORLD

**May Day**   On May 1, 1997, parades and demonstrations took place around the world. Mexican workers poured into the streets of Mexico City to denounce the North American Free Trade Agreement (NAFTA). Workers believed it was the cause of the decline in their wages. In Seoul, Korean workers hurled rocks at police to protest government corruption in South Korea. In Berlin and Leipzig, union workers marched to protest high unemployment in Germany. In Beijing, workers filled Tiananmen Square to praise workers at the beginning of a three-day vacation. In Japan, two million workers attended rallies across the country. Fifteen thousand workers marched in the streets of San Salvador to demand that the government pass laws that would benefit the workers of El Salvador.

Why did these marches and demonstrations occur around the world on May 1? In the nineteenth century, the growth of socialist parties in Europe led to a movement to form an international organization. The purpose of this organization was to strengthen the position of socialist parties against international capitalism. In 1889, leaders of various socialist parties formed the Second International, a loose association of national groups. Its first action was to declare May Day (May 1) an international labor day to be marked by strikes and mass labor demonstrations. Although the Second International no longer exists, workers around the world still observe May Day.

competing in elections for the Reichstag (the German parliament). Once in the Reichstag, SPD delegates worked to pass laws that would improve the condition of the working class. Despite government efforts to destroy it, the German Social Democratic Party continued to grow. When it received four million votes in the 1912 elections, it became the largest single party in Germany.

Socialist parties also emerged in other European states. In 1889, leaders of the various socialist parties joined together and formed the Second International, an association of national socialist groups that would fight against capitalism worldwide. (The First International had failed in 1872.) The Second International took some common actions. May Day (May 1), for example, was made an international labor day. However, differences often caused great disorder at its meetings.

One issue that divided international socialism was nationalism. Karl Marx had believed that "the working men have no country" and that workers of all countries would unite against capitalists everywhere. In truth, workers often had strong patriotic feelings. Nationalism remained a much more powerful force than socialism.

Marxist parties were also divided over their goals. Pure Marxists thought that capitalism would be overthrown in a violent revolution. Other Marxists (called **revisionists**) rejected the revolutionary approach and argued that the workers must continue to organize in mass political parties and even work with other parties to gain reforms. As workers received the right to vote, they were in a better position than ever to achieve their aims by working within democratic systems. Revisionists believed that evolution by democratic means, not revolution, would achieve the desired goal of socialism. This idea of evolutionary socialism was especially popular in western Europe, where political rights gave workers the hope of ultimate success.

Another force working for evolutionary rather than revolutionary socialism was the development of trade unions. In Great Britain, unions won the right to strike in the 1870s. Soon after, the masses of workers in factories were organized into trade unions in order to use the instrument of the strike. By 1900, there were two million workers in British trade unions; by 1914, there were almost four million. By 1914, German trade unions, with their three million members, became the second largest group of organized workers in Europe. Trade unions in the rest of Europe had varying degrees of success. By the beginning of World War I, however, they had made considerable progress in bettering both the living and the working conditions of the laboring classes.

## ❀ SECTION REVIEW ❀

1. **Define:**
   (*a*) Socialist,   (*b*) bourgeoisie,   (*c*) proletariat,
   (*d*) revisionists

2. **Identify:**
   (*a*) Second Industrial Revolution,   (*b*) *The Communist Manifesto*,   (*c*) German Social Democratic Party (SPD),   (*d*) evolutionary socialism,   (*e*) trade unions

3. **Recall:**
   (*a*) What advantage did electric power and internal combustion engines offer over the steam engine?
   (*b*) How did interchangeable parts make the assembly line possible?

4. **Think Critically:**
   (*a*) What similarities can you see between the steamships and railroads that fostered a true world economy in the nineteenth century and the impact the Internet will have on our global economy today?
   (*b*) For what reasons may people think of society in terms of class structure? What impact may these classifications have on people's lives and society in general?

## THE EMERGENCE OF MASS SOCIETY

The new urban and industrial world led to the emergence of a mass society by the late nineteenth century. For the lower classes, a mass society brought voting rights, an improved standard of living, and elementary education. Mass society had other features as well. Governments fostered national loyalty and created mass armies. A mass press worked to sway popular opinion. To understand this mass society, we need to examine certain aspects of its structure.

## The New Urban Environment

In the course of the nineteenth century, more and more people came to live in cities. In 1800, city dwellers made up 40 percent of the population in Britain, 25 percent in France and Germany, and only 10 percent in eastern Europe. By 1914, urban residents had increased to 80 percent of the population in Britain, 45 percent in France, 60 percent in Germany, and 30 percent in eastern Europe. The size of cities also expanded, especially in industrialized countries. Between 1800 and 1900, London's population grew from 960,000 to 6,500,000. Berlin's population increased from 172,000 to 2,700,000 in the same years.

Urban populations grew so fast mainly because of the vast migration from rural areas to cities. Lack of jobs and lack of land drove people from the countryside to the city. There they found jobs in factories and, later, in service trades and professions. Cities also grew faster in the second half of the nineteenth century because living conditions improved so much that more people could survive there longer.

In the 1840s, a number of urban reformers, such as Edwin Chadwick in England and Rudolf Virchow in Germany, had pointed to filthy living conditions as the chief cause of deadly epidemic diseases in the cities. Cholera (KAW-lur-uh), for example, had ravaged Europe in the early 1830s and 1840s, especially in the overcrowded cities. Following the advice of reformers, city governments created boards of health to improve the quality of housing. City medical officers and building inspectors were authorized to inspect dwellings for public health hazards. New building regulations required running water and an internal drainage system for all new buildings.

Essential to the public health of the modern European city was the ability to bring clean water to it and to expel sewage from it. The need for fresh water was met by a system of dams and reservoirs that stored the water and by aqueducts and tunnels that carried it from the countryside to the city and into individual dwellings. Gas heaters in the 1860s, and later electric heaters, made regular hot baths available to many people. The treatment of sewage was also improved by building mammoth underground pipes that carried raw

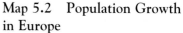

Map 5.2   Population Growth in Europe

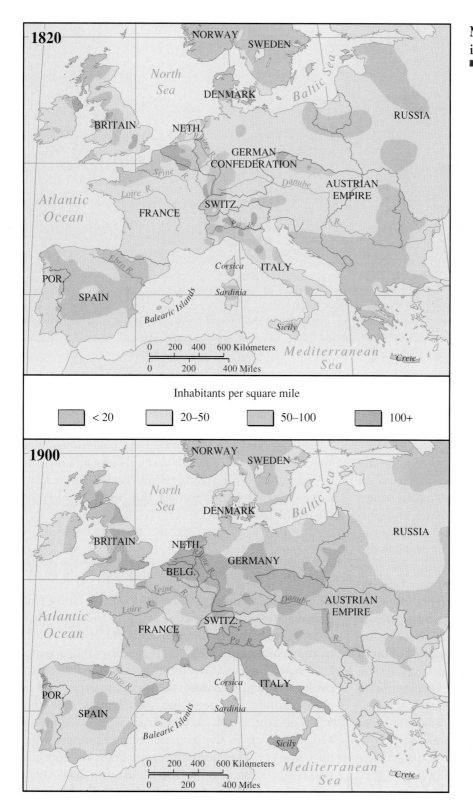

► *This 1912 photograph shows the grim reality of working-class housing in the East End of London. In most cases these rows of houses had no lawns or trees to break the drab monotony of the streets.*

sewage far from the city for disposal. The city of Frankfurt, Germany, began its program for sewers with a lengthy public campaign featuring the slogan "from the toilet to the river in half an hour."

Middle-class reformers who criticized the unsanitary living conditions of the working class also focused on housing needs. Overcrowded, disease-ridden slums were viewed as dangerous not only to physical health but also to the political and moral health of the entire nation. Early efforts to attack the housing problem followed the middle-class, liberal belief in the power of private, or free, enterprise. Liberal reformers believed that the building of model dwellings that could be rented at a reasonable price would force other private landlords to raise their housing standards. A fine example of this approach was the work of Octavia Hill, a practical-minded British housing reformer who believed that workers and their families were entitled to happy homes.

As the number and size of cities continued to grow, however, governments by the 1880s came to the conclusion that private enterprise could not solve the housing crisis. In 1890, a British Housing Act gave power to local town councils to build inexpensive housing for the working classes. London and Liverpool were the first communities to take advantage of their new powers. Germany was doing the same by 1900. Obviously, the liberal belief that the government that governs least governs best had simply proved untrue in this situation. More and more, governments were moving into new types of activity that they would never have touched earlier.

## The Social Structure of Mass Society

At the top of European society stood a wealthy elite that made up only 5 percent of the population while controlling between 30 and 40 percent of the wealth. In the course of the nineteenth century, landed aristocrats had joined with the most successful industrialists, bankers, and merchants (the wealthy upper middle class) to form this new elite. Members of this elite, whether aristocratic or middle class in background, became leaders in the government and military. Marriage also served to unite the two groups. Daughters of business tycoons gained titles, and aristocratic heirs gained new sources of cash. For example, when the

American Consuelo Vanderbilt married the British duke of Marlborough, the new duchess brought $10 million to her husband.

The middle classes consisted of a variety of groups. Below the upper middle class was a middle group that included lawyers, doctors, and members of the civil service, as well as the business managers, engineers, architects, accountants, and chemists created by industrial expansion. Beneath this solid and comfortable middle group was a lower middle class of small shopkeepers, traders, and prosperous peasants. The members of this group provided goods and services for the classes above them.

Standing between the lower middle class and the lower classes were new groups of white-collar workers who were the product of the Second Industrial Revolution. They were the traveling salespeople, bookkeepers, telephone operators, department store salespeople, and secretaries. Although they were little better paid than skilled workers, these white-collar workers were often committed to middle-class ideals.

The middle classes shared a certain style of life—one whose values tended to dominate much of nineteenth-century society. The members of the middle class liked to preach their worldview both to their children and to the upper and lower classes of their society. This was especially evident in Victorian Britain, often considered a model of middle-class society. The European middle classes believed in hard work, which was open to everyone and guaranteed to have positive results. They were also regular churchgoers who believed in the good conduct associated with traditional Christian morality. The middle class was concerned with the right way of doing things, which gave rise to such best-selling books as *The Habits of Good Society* and *Don't: A Manual of Mistakes More or Less Prevalent in Conduct and Speech.*

Below the middle classes on the social scale were the working classes of European society, who made up almost 80 percent of the European population. Many of the members of these classes were landholding peasants, farm laborers, and sharecroppers, especially in eastern Europe. The urban working class consisted of many different groups, including skilled artisans and semiskilled laborers. Skilled artisans worked in such

trades as cabinetmaking and printing. Semiskilled laborers included carpenters and many factory workers, and they earned wages that were about two-thirds the wages of highly skilled workers. At the bottom of the urban working class were the unskilled laborers. They were the largest group of workers and included day laborers and large numbers of domestic servants. One out of every seven employed persons in Great Britain in 1900 was a domestic servant. Most domestic servants were women.

Urban workers experienced an improvement in the material conditions of their lives after 1870. For one thing, cities created better living conditions. A rise in real wages, accompanied by a decline in many consumer costs, made it possible for workers to buy more than just food and housing. Workers now had money for more clothes and even leisure at the same time that strikes were leading to ten-hour workdays and Saturday afternoons off.

## The Experiences of Women

In 1800, women were largely defined by family and household roles. They remained legally inferior and economically dependent. In the course of the nineteenth century, women struggled to change their status.

### Women and Work: New Job Opportunities

During much of the nineteenth century, working-class groups upheld the belief that women should remain at home to bear and nurture children and not be allowed in the industrial workforce. Working-class men argued that keeping women out of industrial work would ensure the moral and physical well-being of families. In reality, however, when their husbands were unemployed, women had to do low-wage work at home or labor part-time in sweatshops to support their families.

The Second Industrial Revolution opened the door to new jobs for women. The growth of larger industrial plants and the expansion of government services created a wide number of service and white-collar jobs. The high demand for white-collar workers at relatively low wages coupled with a shortage of male workers led employers to hire women. Big businesses and retail shops needed clerks, typists, secretaries, file clerks, and salesclerks. The expansion of government services created opportunities for women to be secretaries and telephone operators, as well as to take jobs in the fields of health and social services. Compulsory (legally required) elementary education created a need for more teachers. The development of hospital services opened the way for an increase in nurses.

Many of the new white-collar jobs were by no means exciting. The work was routine and, except for teaching and nursing, required few skills. However, these jobs had real advantages for the daughters of the middle classes and especially the upward-aspiring working classes. For some middle-class women, the new jobs offered freedom from the domestic patterns expected of them. Most of the new jobs, however, were filled by working-class women who saw their chance to escape from the "dirty" work of the lower-class world.

▲ *The Second Industrial Revolution created many new jobs for women. This illustration of a 1904 Paris telephone exchange shows that most of the telephone operators were women, and a woman was employed as a secretary as well. How have jobs for women changed since the early 1900s?*

### Marriage and the Family

Many people in the nineteenth century admired the ideal expressed in Alfred, Lord Tennyson's (TENN-i-sun) *The Princess*, published in 1847:

> *Man for the field and woman for the hearth:*
> *Man for the sword and for the needle she:*
> *Man with the head and woman with the heart:*
> *Man to command and woman to obey.*

This view of the sexes was still popular in the nineteenth century, largely because of the impact of the Industrial Revolution on the family. As the chief family wage earners, men worked outside the home. Women were left with the care of the family, work for which they were paid nothing. Of course, the ideal did not always match reality, especially for the lower classes. A need for extra income often drove lower-class women to do low-wage work.

For most women, marriage was viewed as the only honorable and available career throughout most of the nineteenth century. The middle class glorified the ideal of women in the home. For most women, however, marriage was a matter of economic necessity. The lack of meaningful work and the lower wages paid to women for their work made it difficult for single women to earn a living. Most women chose to marry.

The family was the central institution of middle-class life. Men provided the family income, and women focused on household and child care. At the same time, by reducing the number of children in the family, mothers could devote more time to child care and domestic leisure (see "Young People in Victorian Britain: Middle-Class Children"). The decline in the number of children born to the average woman was the most significant development in the modern family and was already evident in the nineteenth century. This decline in the birthrate was tied to improved economic conditions, the rise of birth control, and abortion. In 1882 in Amsterdam, Dr. Aletta Jacob founded Europe's first birth control clinic.

▲ Many Happy Returns of the Day *depicts a middle-class family celebrating a little girl's birthday. Grandparents, parents, and children are all enjoying the festivities. How does this birthday gathering compare to parties you have attended?*

Women in working-class families were accustomed to hard work. Daughters in working-class families were expected to work until they married. Even after marriage, they often did piecework at home to support the family. For the children of the working classes, childhood was over by the age of nine or ten, when children became apprentices or were employed in odd jobs.

Between 1890 and 1914, however, family patterns among the working class began to change. High-paying jobs in heavy industry and improvements in the standard of living made it possible for working-class families to depend on the income of husbands alone. By the early twentieth century, some working-class mothers could afford to stay at home, following the pattern of middle-class women. At the same time, working-class families also aspired to buy new consumer products, such as sewing machines, clocks, bicycles, and cast-iron stoves.

Working-class families also followed the middle classes in having fewer children. As child labor laws and compulsory education took children out of the workforce and into schools, children were seen as

dependents rather than wage earners. At the same time, strikes and labor agitation led to laws that reduced work hours to ten hours per day by 1900 and eliminated work on Saturday afternoons. Working-class parents now had more time to spend with their children and often developed closer emotional ties with them.

### The Movement for Women's Rights

Modern European feminism, or the movement for women's rights, had its beginnings during the French Revolution, when some women advocated equality for women based on the doctrine of natural rights. In the 1830s, a number of women in the United States and Europe argued for the right of women to divorce and own property. At the time, it was difficult for women to secure divorces, and property laws gave husbands almost complete control over the property of their wives. The early efforts were not very successful, however. Women did not gain the right to own property until 1870 in Britain, 1900 in Germany, and 1907 in France.

The fight for property rights was only a beginning for the women's movement, however. Some middle- and upper-middle-class women fought for and gained access to universities, and others sought entry into occupations dominated by men. The first occupation to which women gained access was teaching. Medical training was largely closed to women, so they sought alternatives in nursing. A nursing pioneer in Germany was Amalie Sieveking, who founded the Female Association for the Care of the Poor and Sick in Hamburg. Even more famous was the British nurse Florence Nightingale. Her efforts during the Crimean War (1854 to 1856), combined with those of Clara Barton in the U.S. Civil War (1861 to 1865), transformed nursing into a profession of trained, middle-class "women in white."

## YOUNG PEOPLE IN VICTORIAN BRITAIN

# Middle-Class Children

The new middle-class ideal of the family home had an impact on child raising and children's play in the nineteenth century. People believed that children were entitled to a long childhood in which they were involved in activities with other children their own age. The early environment in which they were raised, it was thought, would determine how they turned out. Mothers were seen as the most important force in protecting children from the harmful influences of the adult world. The father remained the symbol of authority. Children were taught to please their parents, whom they should both love and fear.

New children's games and toys, including mass-produced dolls for girls, appeared in middle-class homes. However, games and toys were not only for fun but also for instruction. One advice manual

▶ *This painting shows well-dressed girls playing a form of picture lotto, a game that continues to be popular with children today. Based on what you have read in your text, do you think boys would have played this game? Why or why not?*

By the 1840s and 1850s, the movement for women's rights had entered the political arena as women called for equal political rights. Many feminists believed that the right to vote was the key to all other reforms to improve the position of women. The British women's movement was the most active in Europe. The Women's Social and Political Union, founded in 1903 by Emmeline Pankhurst and her daughters (see "Biography: The Pankhursts"), used unusual publicity stunts to call attention to its demands. Its members pelted government officials with eggs, chained themselves to lampposts, burned railroad cars, and smashed the windows of department stores on fashionable shopping streets. Suffragists had one basic aim: the right of women to full citizenship in the nation-state (see "Our Literary Heritage: *A Doll's House*—One Woman's Cry for Freedom" on p. 191).

Before World War I, the demands for women's rights were being heard throughout Europe and the United States. However, only in Norway and some U.S. states did women actually receive the right to vote before 1914. It would take the dramatic upheaval of World War I before male-dominated governments gave in on this basic issue.

## YOUNG PEOPLE IN VICTORIAN BRITAIN

# Middle-Class Children, continued

stated that young children should learn checkers because it "calls forth the resources of the mind in the most gentle, as well as the most successful manner." Puzzles of maps and of the kings of England helped prepare boys for their future careers. Paper patterns for making dolls' clothes prepared girls for their future homemaking roles.

The sons of the middle-class family were expected to follow careers like those of their fathers, so they were kept in school until the age of sixteen or seventeen. Sports were used in the schools to "toughen" boys up. Their leisure activities centered around military concerns and character building. This combination was especially evident in the creation of the Boy Scouts in Great Britain in 1908. The Boy Scouts provided recreation for boys between twelve and eighteen years of age. Adventure was combined with the discipline of earning merit badges and ranks. In this way, the Boy Scouts instilled ideals of patriotism and self-sacrifice. Many men viewed activities like those offered by the Boy Scouts as a way of counteracting the possible dangers that female domination of the home posed for boys. As one scout leader wrote, "The REAL Boy Scout is not a sissy. He adores his mother but is not hitched to her apron strings."

There was little organized recreational activity of this kind for girls. Robert Baden-Powell, founder of the Boy Scouts, did encourage his sister to establish a girls' division of the Boy Scouts. Agnes Baden-Powell made clear the goal of the girls' group when she stated that "you do not want to make tomboys of refined girls. The main object is to give them all the ability to be better mothers and guides to the next generation."

1. What were the parents' roles in middle-class Britain?

2. What was the purpose of the Boy Scouts?

3. What was the purpose of the girls' division of the Boy Scouts?

4. Are the ideals stated here for parents, boys, and girls still evident in our society today?

## Education in an Age of Mass Society

Mass education was a product of the mass society of the late nineteenth and early twentieth centuries. Being educated in the early nineteenth century had meant attending a secondary school or possibly even a university. In secondary schools, students received a classical education based on the study of Greek and Latin. Secondary and university educations were primarily for the elite or the wealthier middle class.

Between 1870 and 1914, most Western governments began to set up state-financed primary schools that required both boys and girls between the ages of six and twelve to attend. States also took responsibility for training teachers by setting up teacher-training schools.

Why did Western nations make this commitment to mass education? One reason was industrialization. In the first Industrial Revolution, unskilled labor was able to meet factory needs. The new firms of the Second Industrial Revolution, however, needed skilled labor. Mass education gave industrialists the trained workers they needed. Both boys and girls with elementary educations now had new job possibilities beyond their vil-

# BIOGRAPHY
## The Pankhursts

Emmeline Pankhurst recalled that her determination to fight for women's rights stemmed from a childhood memory: "My father bent over me, shielding the candle flame with his big hand and I heard him say, somewhat sadly, 'What a pity she wasn't born a lad.'" Eventually, Pankhurst and her daughters became suffragists; they marched and fought for the right of women to vote.

The struggle was often violent. "They came in bruised, hatless, faces scratched, eyes swollen, noses bleeding," one of the Pankhurst daughters recalled. The women were often arrested for damaging property or disturbing the peace. Once in jail, the Pankhursts, like other suffragists, went on hunger strikes. This was a potentially dangerous action. The government allowed prison authorities to force-feed hunger strikers by pouring liquids

▶ *This black and white photo shows a confident, smiling Emmeline Pankhurst with daughters, Christábel and Adela. They are joined by Mrs. Pethick Lawrence, another suffragist. Why do you think it took so long for women to be granted the right to vote?*

lages or small towns. These included white-collar jobs in railways, post offices, banking firms, and the teaching and nursing fields.

The chief motive for mass education, however, was political. Giving more people the right to vote created a need for better-educated voters. Even more important, however, was the fact that primary schools instilled patriotism. As people lost their ties to local regions and even to religion, nationalism gave them a new faith. Furthermore, children in schools were taught a single national language, which brought greater national unity.

National values, then, determined what was taught in the elementary schools. Reading, writing, arithmetic, national history (especially history geared to a patriotic view), geography, literature, and some singing and drawing were taught in most primary schools. Often, boys and girls were separated. Girls learned domestic skills such as sewing, washing, ironing, and cooking, all necessary for providing a good home for a husband and children. Boys acquired some practical skills, such as carpentry, and even had some military drill. Most of the elementary schools also taught the middle-class virtues of hard work, thrift, cleanliness,

# BIOGRAPHY

## The Pankhursts, continued

into their stomachs "through a rubber tube clamped to the nose or mouth."

Neither jail nor abusive treatment could stop the Pankhursts, however. When Emmeline, a strong-willed woman with a flair for public speaking, was arrested and jailed in 1908, she informed her judges, "If you had the power to send us to prison, not for six months, but for six years, or for our lives, the Government must not think they could stop this agitation. It would go on!" It did go on, and women in Britain eventually received the right to vote.

The Pankhursts reacted to their success by taking on new causes. Emmeline became active in moral issues until her death in 1928. Her eldest daughter, Christábel, became an ardent evangelical Christian. She moved to the United States and settled in California, where she died in 1959. Sylvia, Emmeline's second daughter, worked for social reform in London's working-class slums and became one of the founders of Britain's Communist Party. She moved to Ethiopia to fight against the Italian invasion of that African country. At the time of her death in 1956, she was the editor of the chief English-language newspaper in Ethiopia. Throughout their careers, the Pankhursts remained firmly committed to their ideals.

1. What was Emmeline Pankhurst's early memory that fueled her determination to fight for women's rights?

2. Were the Pankhursts' actions successful?

3. Would you be willing to go through the things the Pankhursts suffered for something you believe in? Why or why not?

4. Can you identify an individual, or individuals, who is fighting today for social causes against strong opposition? Would you be willing to join in the fight? Why or why not?

and respect for the family. For most students, elementary education led to apprenticeship and a job.

Compulsory elementary education created a demand for teachers. Most of them were women. Many men saw the teaching of children as a part of women's "natural role" as nurturers of children. Moreover, females were paid lower salaries, which in itself was a strong incentive for governments to set up teacher-training schools for women. The first female colleges were really teacher-training schools. It was not until the beginning of the twentieth century that women were permitted to enter male-dominated universities.

The most immediate result of mass education was an increase in literacy, or the ability to read. In Germany, Great Britain, France, and the Scandinavian countries, adult illiteracy was almost eliminated by 1900. Where there was less schooling, the story was very different. Adult illiteracy rates were 79 percent in Serbia and Russia, for example.

With the increase in literacy after 1870 came the rise of mass newspapers, such as the *Evening News* (1881) and the *Daily Mail* (1896) in London. Millions of copies were sold each day. Known as the yellow press in the United States, these newspapers were all written

# SPORTS AND CONTESTS

## The New Team Sports

Sports were by no means a new activity in the late nineteenth century. Soccer games had been played by peasants and workers, and these games were often bloody or even deadly. In the late nineteenth century, sports became strictly organized. The English Football Association (founded in 1863) and the American Bowling Congress (founded in 1895), for example, provided strict rules and officials to enforce them.

The new sports were not just for leisure or fun. Like other forms of middle-class recreation, they were intended to provide excellent training, especially for youth. The participants not only could develop individual skills but also could acquire a sense of teamwork useful for military service. These characteristics were already evident in the British public schools in the 1850s and 1860s.

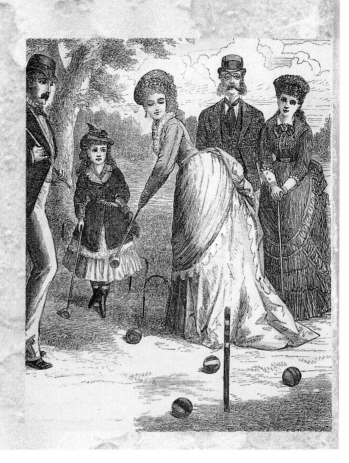

▶ *Croquet was especially popular in the 1870s because both men and women could play. Croquet is still played competitively in Britain and in the United States.*

in an easily understood style. They were also sensational, as they provided lurid details of crimes, gossip, and sports news.

## Leisure in an Age of Mass Society

With the Industrial Revolution came new forms of leisure. Work and leisure became opposites as leisure came to be viewed as what people do for fun after work. In fact, the new leisure hours created by the industrial system—evening hours after work, weekends, and a week or two in the summer—largely determined the forms of the new mass leisure.

New technology created new experiences for leisure, such as the Ferris wheel at amusement parks. The subways and streetcars of the 1880s meant that even the working classes could make their way to athletic games, amusement parks, and dance halls. Likewise, railroads could take people to the beaches on weekends.

The upper and middle classes had created the first market for tourism. As wages went up and workers were given paid vacations, however, tourism, too, became another form of mass leisure. Thomas Cook was a British pioneer of mass tourism. Cook found that by renting special trains, lowering prices, and increasing the number of passengers, he could make substan-

## SPORTS AND CONTESTS

### The New Team Sports, continued

Such schools as Harrow and Loretto placed organized sports at the center of education. At Loretto, for example, education was supposed to instill "First—Character. Second—Physique. Third—Intelligence. Fourth—Manners. Fifth—Information."

The new team sports rapidly became professionalized as well. In Britain, soccer had its Football Association in 1863. In the United States, the first national association to recognize professional baseball players was formed in 1863. By 1900, the National League and the American League had complete control over professional baseball. Subways and streetcars made possible the building of stadiums where thousands could attend. Thus, mass spectator sports became a big business. In 1872, 2,000 people watched the British Soccer Cup finals. By 1885, the crowd had increased to 10,000 and by 1901, to 100,000. Spectator sports even reflected class differences. Upper-class soccer teams in Britain viewed working-class teams as vicious and inclined to "money-grubbing, tricks, sensational displays, and utter rottenness."

The sports cult of the late nineteenth century was mostly for men, who believed that females were not particularly suited for "vigorous physical activity." Nevertheless, it was permissible for middle-class women to play such "easy" sports as croquet and lawn tennis. Eventually, some sports began to appear at women's colleges and girls' public schools in England.

1. What did sports offer middle-class men of the late nineteenth century?

2. Why do you think spectator sports became such a big business?

3. Compare the educational goals at your school with those at Loretto. What are the differences? the similarities?

tial profits. By the late nineteenth century, team sports had also developed into yet another form of mass leisure (see "Sports and Contests: The New Team Sports").

The new forms of popular leisure drew masses of people and mostly served to provide entertainment and distract people from the realities of their work lives. The new mass leisure was quite different from earlier forms of popular culture. The earlier festivals and fairs had been based on community participation. The new forms of mass leisure were standardized for largely passive mass audiences. Amusement parks and professional sports teams were, after all, big businesses organized to make profits.

### ❀ SECTION REVIEW ❀

1. **Identify:**
   (a) white-collar jobs,   (b) the Women's Social and Political Union,   (c) Thomas Cook

2. **Recall:**
   (a) What forces drove people from the countryside to the cities in the nineteenth century?
   (b) What problems did the urban poor encounter in the cities?
   (c) In what way did the Second Industrial Revolution open the door to new jobs for women?

(d) Why was marriage a matter of economic necessity for most women during the nineteenth century?

(e) Why did many European states provide mass education in the nineteenth century?

**3. Think Critically:**

(a) Why do many people still believe that the "government that governs least governs best"?

(b) Why may it not have been reasonable for European middle classes to believe that hard work was open to everyone and would guarantee positive results?

# THE NATIONAL STATE

Throughout much of the Western world by 1870, the national state had become the focus of people's loyalties. Only in Russia, eastern Europe, the Austro-Hungarian Empire, and Ireland did national groups still struggle for independence.

## The United States

Four years of bloody civil war had preserved American national unity, but the old South had been destroyed. One-fifth of the adult white male population in the South had been killed, and four million black slaves had been freed. The Thirteenth Amendment to the U.S. Constitution in 1865 abolished slavery. The Fourteenth and Fifteenth Amendments later gave citizenship to blacks and guaranteed black males the right to vote. However, new state laws in southern states soon stripped blacks of their right to vote. By the end of the 1870s, supporters of white supremacy were back in power everywhere in the South.

Between 1860 and 1914, the United States made the shift from an agrarian to an industrial nation. American heavy industry stood unchallenged in 1900. In that year, the Carnegie (KAR-nuh-gee) Steel Com-

pany alone produced more steel than did Great Britain's entire steel industry. As in Europe, industrialization in the United States led to urbanization. Whereas 20 percent of Americans lived in cities in 1860, over 40 percent did in 1900.

By 1900, the United States had become the world's richest nation. Yet serious problems remained. In 1890, the richest 9 percent of Americans owned an incredible 71 percent of all the wealth. Labor unrest over unsafe working conditions and regular cycles of devastating unemployment led workers to organize. By the turn of the century, the American Federation of Labor had emerged as labor's chief voice, but it lacked real power. In 1900, its members were only 8.4 percent of American workers.

During the Progressive Era after 1900, the reform of many features of American life became a key issue. Under President Theodore Roosevelt (ROE-zuh-vult), the federal government began to regulate corrupt industrial practices. President Woodrow Wilson created a graduated federal income tax. Like European states, the United States was slowly adopting policies that increased the power of the central government.

At the end of the nineteenth century, the United States began to expand abroad. The Samoan (suh-MOE-un) Islands in the Pacific became the first important U.S. colony. By 1887, U.S. settlers had gained control of the sugar industry on the Hawaiian Islands. As more Americans settled in Hawaii, they sought to gain political power. When Queen Liliuokalani (li-LEE-uh-WOE-kuh-LAWN-ee) tried to strengthen the power of the monarchy in order to keep the islands for the native peoples, the U.S. government sent U.S. Marines to "protect" American lives. The queen was deposed, and Hawaii was annexed by the United States in 1898.

The defeat of Spain by the United States in the Spanish-American War in 1898 encouraged the United States to extend its empire by acquiring Cuba, Puerto Rico, Guam, and the Philippine Islands. Although the Filipinos (FILL-uh-PEEN-ohz) hoped for independence, the United States refused to grant it. As President William McKinley said, the United States had the duty "to educate the Filipinos and uplift and Christianize them," a remarkable statement in view of the fact that for centuries, most Filipinos had been Roman Catholics. It took three years and 60,000 troops to pacify the Philippines and establish U.S. control. By the beginning of the twentieth century, the United States had an empire.

## Canada

Canada, too, faced problems of national unity between 1870 and 1914. At the beginning of 1870, the Dominion of Canada had four provinces: Quebec, Ontario, Nova Scotia (SKOE-shuh), and New Brunswick. With the addition of two more provinces in 1871—Manitoba and British Columbia—the Dominion of Canada extended from the Atlantic to the Pacific.

Real unity was difficult to achieve, however, because of the distrust between the English-speaking and French-speaking peoples of Canada. Wilfred Laurier (lor-ee-A), who became the first French-Canadian prime minister in 1896, was able to reconcile Canada's two major groups. During his administration, industrialization boomed and immigrants from Europe helped to populate Canada's vast territories.

## Western Europe: The Growth of Political Democracy

By 1871, Great Britain had a working two-party parliamentary system. For the next fifty years, Liberals and Conservatives alternated in power at regular intervals. Both parties were led by a ruling class composed of aristocratic landowners and upper-middle-class businesspeople. The Liberals and Conservatives competed with each other in passing laws that expanded the right to vote. Reform Acts in 1867 and 1884 expanded the number of adult males who could vote. By the end of World War I (1918), all males over age twenty-one and women over age thirty could vote. At the beginning of World War I (1914), political democracy was well established in Britain. Social welfare measures for the working class soon followed.

The Liberals in Great Britain were disturbed by two developments. First, trade unions grew, and they began to favor a more radical change of the economic system. Second, in 1900 the Labour party, which dedicated

itself to the interests of the workers, emerged. The Liberals held the government from 1906 to 1914 and soon perceived that they would have to create a program of social welfare or else lose the support of the workers. Therefore, the Liberals voted for a series of social reforms. The National Insurance Act of 1911 provided benefits for workers in case of sickness and unemployment. Additional laws provided a small pension for those over age seventy and compensation for those injured in accidents while at work.

In France, the collapse of Louis Napoleon's Second Empire left the country in confusion. In 1875, a new constitution created a republic. The new government had an upper house, or Senate, elected indirectly and a lower house, or Chamber of Deputies, chosen by universal male suffrage. The powers of the president, who was chosen by the legislature for seven years, were deliberately left vague. The premier (or prime minister) led the government. He and his ministers were responsible not to the president but to the Chamber of Deputies. This principle of **ministerial responsibility,** or the idea that a prime minister is responsible to the popularly elected legislative body and not to the executive officer, is a crucial one for a democracy.

The French Constitution of 1875 was meant to be temporary, but the republic—France's Third Republic—lasted sixty-five years. France failed to develop a strong parliamentary system, however. The existence of a dozen political parties forced the premier to depend upon a coalition of parties to stay in power. Regular changes of government plagued the Third Republic. Nevertheless, by 1914, the French Third Republic commanded the loyalty of most French people.

Italy had emerged by 1870 as a united state. It believed that it was now a great power. Its internal weaknesses, however, made that a poor claim. Italy had little sense of community because of the great gulf that separated a poverty-stricken south from an industrializing north. Constant turmoil between labor and industry undermined the social fabric. The Italian government was unable to deal with these problems because of the widespread corruption among government officials. The grant of universal male suffrage in 1912 did little to correct the widespread corruption and weak government.

**Map 5.3    Europe in 1871**

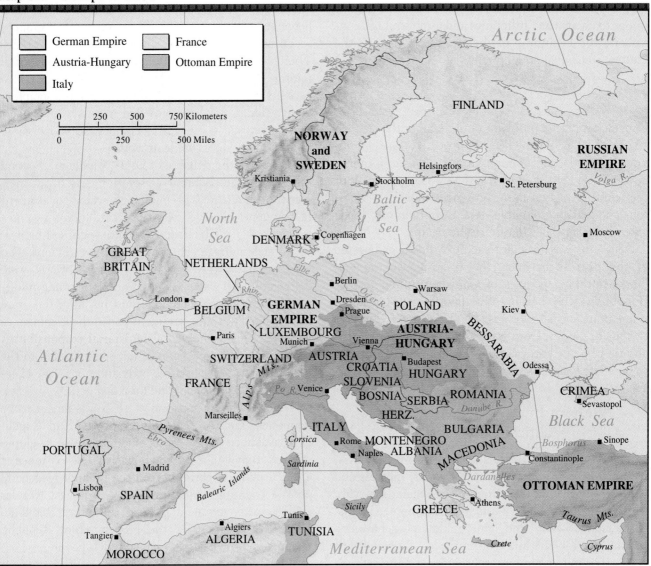

## Central and Eastern Europe: Persistence of the Old Order

Germany, Austria-Hungary (or the Austro-Hungarian Empire), and Russia pursued policies that were quite different from those of the western European nations. Germany and Austria-Hungary had legislative bodies and elections by universal male suffrage, but powerful monarchies and conservative social groups remained strong. In Russia, the old system of autocracy was barely touched by the winds of change.

The constitution of the new imperial Germany begun by Bismarck in 1871 provided for a two-house legislature. The lower house of the German parliament, known as the Reichstag, was elected on the basis of universal male suffrage, but it did not have ministerial responsibility. Ministers of government were responsible not to the parliament but to the emperor. The emperor also commanded the armed forces and controlled foreign policy and the government bureaucracy. As chancellor (or prime minister), Bismarck worked to keep Germany from becoming a democracy.

During the reign of Emperor William II, from 1888 to 1918, the new imperial Germany continued as an authoritarian state. By the end of William's reign, Germany had become the strongest military and industrial power on the Continent. Cities had mushroomed in number and size. However, these rapid changes caused divisions in German society. With the expansion of industry and cities came demands for a real democracy. Conservative forces—especially the landowning nobility and big industrialists, two of the powerful ruling groups in imperial Germany—tried to block the movement for democracy by supporting a strong foreign policy. Expansion abroad, they believed, would not only increase their profits but also divert people's attention from democracy.

A new, radical right-wing political movement added to the tensions in German society. Groups such as the Pan-German League stressed strong German patriotism and favored expansion abroad as a way to unite all classes. These groups were also anti-Semitic and blamed Jews for destroying national community.

After the creation of the dual monarchy of Austria-Hungary in 1867, the Austrian part received a constitution that in theory set up a parliamentary system with ministerial responsibility. However, Emperor Francis Joseph largely ignored ministerial responsibility by ruling by decree when the parliament was not in session.

The problem of the various nationalities remained a troublesome one. The German minority that governed Austria felt increasingly threatened by the Czechs, Poles, and other Slavic groups within the empire. Representatives of these groups in the parliament agitated for their freedom, which led the government to ignore the parliament and rely on imperial decrees to govern. Austria-Hungary had not solved its minorities problem.

In Russia, the assassination of Alexander II in 1881 convinced his son and successor, Alexander III, that reform had been a mistake. Alexander III lost no time

▲ *In this political cartoon, Emperor William II relaxes on his throne made of cannonballs and artillery, while Bismarck bids him good-bye. The woman, who represents Germany, watches this scene with serious concern about the future.*

in persecuting both reformers and revolutionaries. When Alexander III died in 1894, his weak son and successor, Nicholas II, began his rule believing that the absolute power of the tsars should be preserved: "I shall maintain the principle of autocracy just as firmly and unflinchingly as did my unforgettable father."[1] Conditions were changing, however, and the tsar's approach was not realistic.

Industrialization progressed rapidly in Russia after 1890. By 1900, Russia had become the fourth largest producer of steel behind the United States, Germany, and Great Britain. With industrialization came factories, an industrial working class, and socialist parties, including the Marxist Social Democratic Party and the Social Revolutionaries. Repression soon forced both parties to go underground and be revolutionary. The Social Revolutionaries worked to overthrow the tsarist autocracy by terrorism. They tried to assassinate government officials and members of the ruling dynasty.

▶ *Nicholas II, the last tsar of Russia, is shown here with his wife Alexandra. Why do you think all the men in this photograph are wearing military uniforms?*

The growing opposition to the tsarist regime finally exploded into revolution in 1905.

The defeat of the Russians by the Japanese in 1904/1905 (see Chapter 7) brought to Russia severe economic suffering, especially massive food shortages. As a result, on January 9, 1905, a massive procession of workers went to the Winter Palace in St. Petersburg to present a petition of grievances to the tsar. Troops foolishly opened fire on the peaceful demonstration, killing hundreds. This "Bloody Sunday" caused workers to call strikes and forced Nicholas II to grant civil liberties and create a **Duma,** or legislative assembly. Real constitutional monarchy proved short-lived, however. Already by 1907, the tsar had curtailed the power of the Duma, and he fell back on the army and bureaucracy to rule Russia.

## International Rivalry and the Coming of War

Between 1871 and 1914, Europeans experienced a long period of peace. There were wars, but none involved the great powers. In Germany, Bismarck had realized

that the emergence in 1871 of a unified Germany as the most powerful state on the Continent had upset the balance of power established at Vienna in 1815. Fearing a possible anti-German alliance led by its new enemy, France, Bismarck made a defensive alliance with Austria-Hungary in 1879. In 1882, this German–Austro-Hungarian alliance added a third partner, Italy, which was angry with the French over competing claims in North Africa. The Triple Alliance of 1882— Germany, Austria-Hungary, and Italy—committed the three powers to a defensive alliance against France. At the same time, Bismarck maintained a separate treaty with Russia and tried to remain on good terms with Great Britain.

When Emperor William II fired Bismarck in 1890 and took over direction of Germany's foreign policy, he embarked upon an activist policy dedicated to enhancing German power. He wanted, as he put it, to find Germany's rightful "place in the sun." One of the changes he made in Bismarck's foreign policy was to drop the treaty with Russia. The ending of that alliance brought France and Russia together. In 1894, the two powers concluded a military alliance. During

**Map 5.4   The Balkans in 1878**

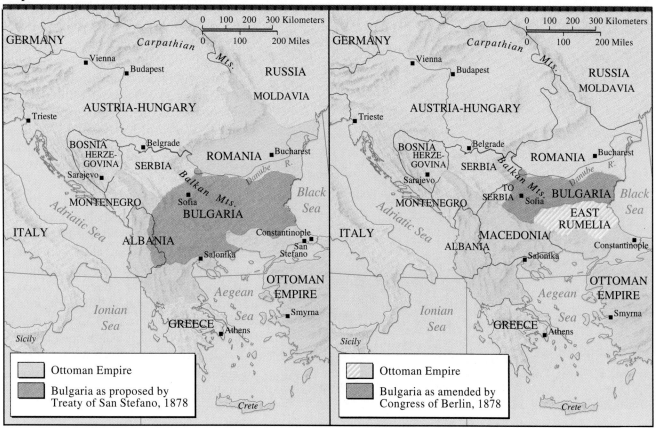

Ottoman Empire
Bulgaria as proposed by Treaty of San Stefano, 1878

Ottoman Empire
Bulgaria as amended by Congress of Berlin, 1878

the next ten years, German policies abroad caused the British to draw closer to France. By 1907, an alliance of Great Britain, France, and Russia—known as the Triple Entente (awn-TAWNT)—stood opposed to the Triple Alliance of Germany, Austria-Hungary, and Italy. Europe was dangerously divided into two opposing camps that became more and more unwilling to compromise. A series of crises in the Balkans between 1908 and 1913 set the stage for World War I.

## The Ottoman Empire and Nationalism in the Balkans

The Ottoman Empire was severely troubled by the hopes of its subject peoples in the Balkans for their freedom. Corruption and inefficiency had so weakened

the Ottoman Empire that only the efforts of the great European powers, who feared one another's designs on the empire, kept it alive.

In the course of the nineteenth century, the Balkan provinces of the Ottoman Empire gradually gained their freedom, although the rivalry in the region between Austria-Hungary and Russia complicated the process. Greece was made an independent kingdom in 1830 after its successful revolt. In 1875, several peoples in the Balkans revolted. The Ottomans crushed the revolts, but the Russians came to the aid of their fellow Slavs in the Balkans by declaring war on Turkey. After Russia's defeat of the Turks, the great powers met at the Congress of Berlin in 1878 and recognized Romania, Serbia, and Montenegro (MAWN-tuh-NEE-GROE) as independent states. Bulgaria gained autonomous status

▲ *This illustration shows the Ottoman army, disorganized and beaten, in a hasty retreat. Well-armed and well-supplied Bulgarian forces continue the pursuit. What modern weaponry do you see in this illustration?*

ported the Serbs and opposed the action of Austria-Hungary. Backed by the Russians, the Serbs prepared for war against Austria-Hungary. At this point, Emperor William II demanded that the Russians accept the annexation of Bosnia and Herzegovina by Austria-Hungary or face war with Germany. Weakened from their defeat in the Russo-Japanese War in 1904/1905, the Russians were afraid to risk war, and they backed down. Humiliated, the Russians vowed revenge.

In 1912, Serbia, Bulgaria, Montenegro, and Greece organized the Balkan League and defeated the Ottomans in the First Balkan War. When the victorious allies were unable to agree on how to divide the conquered Ottoman provinces of Macedonia (MASS-uh-DOE-nee-uh) and Albania, a second Balkan War erupted in 1913. Greece, Serbia, Romania, and the Ottoman Empire attacked and defeated Bulgaria. As a result, Bulgaria obtained only a small part of Macedonia. Most of the rest was divided between Serbia and Greece. The two Balkan wars left the inhabitants embittered and created more tensions among the great powers.

Serbia's desire to create a large Serbian kingdom remained unfulfilled. The Serbians blamed Austria-Hungary for their failure. Austria-Hungary was convinced that Serbia was a mortal threat to its empire and must at some point be crushed. As Serbia's chief supporters, the Russians were angry and determined not to back down again in the event of a confrontation with Austria-Hungary or Germany in the Balkans. The allies of Austria-Hungary and Russia were also determined to be more supportive of their respective allies in another crisis.

By the beginning of 1914, two armed camps viewed each other with suspicion. An American in Europe observed: "The whole of Germany is charged with electricity. Everybody's nerves are tense. It needs only a spark to set the whole thing off." The European age of progress was about to come to a bloody end.

under Russian protection. The other Balkan territories of Bosnia and Herzegovina (HERT-suh-go-VEE-nuh) were placed under the protection of Austria-Hungary. These gains, however, did not still the forces of Balkan nationalism.

In 1908, Austria-Hungary took the drastic step of annexing the two Slavic-speaking territories of Bosnia and Herzegovina. Serbia was outraged because the annexation dashed the Serbians' hopes of creating a large Serbian kingdom that would include most of the southern Slavs. The Russians, with their mission to protect their fellow Slavs and their own desire to gain access to the eastern Mediterranean through the Bosphorus and Dardanelles (DARD-un-ELZ), sup-

**Map 5.5 The Balkans in 1913**

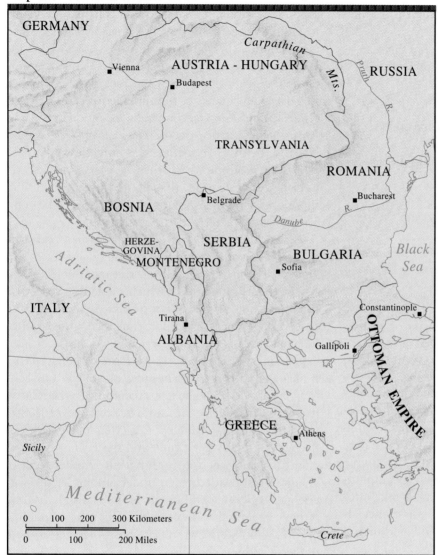

⚜ SECTION REVIEW ⚜

1. **Locate:**
   (*a*) Great Britain,  (*b*) St. Petersburg,
   (*c*) Romania,  (*d*) Serbia,  (*e*) Montenegro,
   (*f*) Bosnia,  (*g*) Herzegovina,
   (*h*) Bulgaria

2. **Define:**
   (*a*) ministerial responsibility,  (*b*) Duma

3. **Identify:**
   (*a*) Progressive Era,  (*b*) Spanish-American War,
   (*c*) The National Insurance Act,  (*d*) the Constitution of 1875,  (*e*) Reichstag,  (*f*) Pan-German League,  (*g*) The Triple Alliance,  (*h*) The Triple Entente,  (*i*) The Balkan League

**4. Recall:**

(*a*) What situation made the achievement of true unity in Canada difficult?

(*b*) What problems did the existence of German minorities in many European nations create?

**5. Think Critically:**

(*a*) Why is it often difficult for people to join together to create a nation when some are poor while others are wealthy?

(*b*) Why may inconclusive wars lead to further conflicts?

# TOWARD THE MODERN CONSCIOUSNESS: INTELLECTUAL AND CULTURAL DEVELOPMENTS

Before 1914, many people in the Western world continued to believe in the values and ideals that had been put forth by the Scientific Revolution and the Enlightenment. *Reason, science,* and *progress* were still important words to Europeans. The idea that human beings could improve themselves and build a better society seemed to be proved by a rising standard of living, urban improvements, and mass education. Such products of modern technology as electric lights and automobiles reinforced the popular prestige of science. It was easy to think that the human mind could understand the universe.

Between 1870 and 1914, however, radically new ideas challenged these optimistic views and opened the way to a modern consciousness. The real impact of many of these ideas was not felt until after World War I. Before 1914, however, these ideas created a sense of confusion and anxiety that would become even more pronounced after the war.

## The Emergence of a New Physics

Science was one of the chief pillars supporting the optimistic view of the world that many westerners shared in the nineteenth century. Science, which was supposedly based on hard facts and cold reason, offered a certainty of belief in the orderliness of nature. Many believed that by applying already known scientific laws, humans could arrive at a complete understanding of the physical world and an accurate picture of reality.

Throughout much of the nineteenth century, westerners believed in a mechanical conception of the universe that was based on the classical physics of Isaac Newton. In this perspective, the universe was viewed as a giant machine in which time, space, and matter were objective realities that existed independently of those observing them. Matter was thought to be composed of solid material bodies called atoms.

Albert Einstein (INE-STINE), a German-born patent officer working in Switzerland, questioned this view of the universe. In 1905, Einstein published his special theory of relativity, which stated that space and time are not absolute but rather relative to the observer. Neither space nor time had an existence independent of human experience. As Einstein later explained to a journalist, "It was formerly believed that if all material things disappeared out of the universe, time and space would be left. According to the relativity theory, however, time and space disappear together with the things."[2] Moreover, matter and energy reflected the relativity of time and space. Einstein concluded that matter was nothing but another form of energy. This idea led to an understanding of the vast energies contained within the atom. It also led to the Atomic Age and to uncertainty. To some, a relative universe—unlike Newton's universe—seemed to be a universe without certainty.

## Sigmund Freud and the Emergence of Psychoanalysis

At the turn of the century, Sigmund Freud (FROID), a Viennese doctor, put forth a series of theories that undermined optimism about the rational nature of the human mind. Freud's thought, like the new physics, added to the uncertainties of the age. His major ideas were published in 1900 in *The Interpretation of Dreams*.

According to Freud, human behavior was strongly determined by the unconscious—by past experiences

▲ *Sigmund Freud was a major intellectual leader of the nineteenth century. His theories about the unconscious state and human behavior served as a foundation for much of twentieth-century psychoanalysis.*

and internal forces of which people were largely unaware. For Freud, human behavior was no longer truly rational but rather instinctive or irrational. He argued that painful and unsettling experiences were repressed, or blotted from conscious awareness. They still continued to influence behavior, however, because they had become part of the unconscious. Repression began in childhood. Freud devised a method—known as **psychoanalysis**—by which a psychotherapist and patient could probe deeply into the memory of the patient. In this way, they could retrace the chain of repressed thoughts all the way back to their childhood

origins. If the patient's conscious mind could be made aware of the unconscious and its repressed contents, the patient's conflict could be resolved and the patient healed.

The full importance of Sigmund Freud's thought was not felt until after World War I. In the 1920s, his ideas gained worldwide acceptance. Freudian terms, such as *unconscious* and *repression,* became new standard vocabulary words. Psychoanalysis, pioneered by Freud, developed into a major profession, especially in the United States.

## Social Darwinism and Racism

In the second half of the nineteenth century, scientific theories were sometimes applied inappropriately to achieve desired results. For example, Charles Darwin's principle of organic evolution was applied to the social order in what came to be known as **Social Darwinism.** The most popular exponent of Social Darwinism was the British philosopher Herbert Spencer. He argued that societies were organisms that evolved through time from a struggle with their environments. Social progress came from "the struggle for survival" as the "fit"—the strong—advanced while the weak declined. Some prominent businessmen used Social Darwinism to explain their success. To them, the strong and fit—the able and energetic—had risen to the top; the stupid and lazy had fallen by the wayside.

The ideas of Darwin were also applied to human society in a radical way by nationalists and racists. In their pursuit of national greatness, extreme nationalists often insisted that nations, too, were engaged in a "struggle for existence" in which only the fittest (the strongest) survived. The German general Friedrich von Bernhardi (burn-HARD-ee) argued in 1907, "War is a biological necessity of the first importance, . . . since without it an unhealthy development will follow, which excludes every advancement of the race, and therefore all real civilization. War is the father of all things."[3]

Biological arguments were also used to defend racism. Perhaps nowhere was the combination of extreme nationalism and racism more evident and more dangerous than in Germany. One of the chief exponents of German racism was Houston Stewart Chamberlain (CHAME-bur-lun), a Briton who became a German citizen. He believed that modern-day Germans were the only pure successors of the Aryans, who were portrayed as the original creators of Western culture. According to Chamberlain, the Aryan race, under German leadership, must be prepared to fight for Western civilization and save it from the assaults of such lower races as Jews, Negroes, and Orientals. Chamberlain singled out Jews as the racial enemy who wanted to destroy the Aryan race.

## Anti-Semitism: Jews within the European Nation-State

Near the end of the nineteenth century, a revival of racism combined with extreme nationalism to produce a new right-wing political movement aimed primarily at the Jews. Of course, anti-Semitism was not new to European civilization. Since the Middle Ages, the Jews had been portrayed as the murderers of Christ and subjected to mob violence. Their rights had been restricted, and they had been physically separated from Christians in areas of cities known as ghettos.

In the nineteenth century, Jews were increasingly granted legal equality in many European countries. Many Jews now left the ghetto and became assimilated into the cultures around them. Many became successful as bankers, lawyers, scientists, scholars, journalists, and stage performers. In 1880, for example, Jews made up 10 percent of the population of Vienna, Austria, but 39 percent of its medical students and 23 percent of its law students.

These achievements were only one side of the picture, however, as is evident from the Dreyfus (DRIE-fus) affair in France. Alfred Dreyfus, a Jew, was a captain in the French general staff. Early in 1895, a secret military court found him guilty of selling army secrets and condemned him to life imprisonment on Devil's Island. During his trial, right-wing mobs yelled, "Death to the Jews." Soon after the trial, however, evidence emerged that pointed to Dreyfus's innocence. Another officer, a Catholic aristocrat, was more obviously the traitor. The army refused a new trial, however. A wave of public outrage forced the government to hold a new trial and pardon Dreyfus in 1899.

In the 1880s and 1890s in Germany and Austria-Hungary, new parties arose that used anti-Semitism to win the votes of people who felt threatened by the new economic forces of the times. However, the worst treatment of Jews at the turn of the century occurred in eastern Europe, where 72 percent of the entire world Jewish population lived. Russian Jews were forced to live in certain regions of the country. Persecutions and **pogroms** (organized massacres of helpless people) were widespread. Hundreds of thousands of Jews decided to emigrate to escape the persecution.

Many Jews went to the United States. Some (probably about 25,000) moved to Palestine, which became home for a Jewish nationalist movement called **Zionism.** For many Jews, Palestine, the land of ancient Israel, had long been the land of their dreams. A key figure in the growth of political Zionism was Theodor Herzl (HERT-sul), who stated in his book *The Jewish State* (1896), "The Jews who wish it will have their state." Settlement in Palestine was difficult, however, because it was then part of the Ottoman Empire, which was opposed to Jewish immigration. Nevertheless, 1,000 Jews moved to Palestine in 1900. Although 3,000 Jews went annually to Palestine between 1904 and 1914, the Zionist dream of a homeland in Palestine still remained only a dream on the eve of World War I.

## Literature and the Arts: Toward Modernism

Between 1870 and 1914, many writers and artists rebelled against the traditional literary and artistic styles that had dominated European cultural life since the Renaissance. The changes that they produced have since been called **modernism.**

Throughout much of the late nineteenth century, literature was dominated by **naturalism.** Naturalists accepted the material world as real and felt that literature should be realistic. They believed that by addressing social problems, writers could contribute to an objective understanding of the world (see "Our Literary Heritage: *A Doll's House*—One Woman's Cry for Freedom"). The naturalists portrayed characters caught in the grip of forces beyond their control.

# OUR LITERARY HERITAGE

## A Doll's House—One Woman's Cry for Freedom

Henrik Ibsen was a Norwegian writer who took a strong interest in social issues, including a woman's place in the home and society. Most women probably tried to conform to the nineteenth-century middle-class ideal of women as housewives and mothers. However, an increasing number fought for the rights of women. The following selection is taken from Act III of Henrik Ibsen's play A Doll's House (1879). The character, Nora Helmer, declares her freedom from the control of her husband, Torvald, over her life.

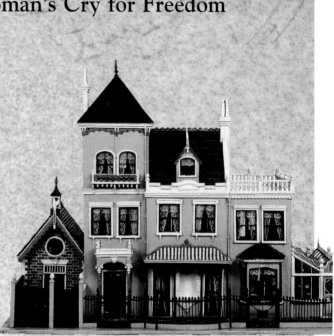

▲ This Victorian doll house was made in England in 1889. In what ways do you think it mirrors the lives of middle-class women at this time? Do you think this doll house was a child's toy? Why or why not?

▲ This painting by American artist Thomas Eakins symbolizes the lonely, confining role assigned to women during the late nineteenth century. If you were to draw a woman in her modern-day role, what would you include? How would she be dressed?

### Henrik Ibsen, A Doll's House

NORA: Yes, it's true, Torvald. When I was living at home with father, he told me his opinions and mine were the same. If I had different opinions, I said nothing about them, because he would not have liked it. He used to call me his doll-child and played with me as I played with my dolls. Then I came to live in your house.

HELMER: What a way to speak of our marriage!

NORA (Undisturbed): I mean that I passed from father's hands into yours. You arranged everything

(continued)

## OUR LITERARY HERITAGE

# A *Doll's House*—One Woman's Cry for Freedom, continued

to your taste and I got the same tastes as you; or pretended to—I don't know which—both, perhaps; sometimes one, sometimes the other. When I look back on it now, I seem to have been living here like a beggar, on hand-outs. I lived by performing tricks for you, Torvald. . . . I must stand quite alone if I am ever to know myself and my surroundings; so I cannot stay with you.

HELMER: You are mad! I shall not allow it! I forbid it!

NORA: It's no use your forbidding me anything now. I shall take with me only what belongs to me; from you I will accept nothing, either now or later. . . .

HELMER: Forsake your home, your husband, your children! And you don't consider what the world will say.

NORA: I can't pay attention to that. I only know that I must do it.

HELMER: This is monstrous! Can you forsake your holiest duties?

NORA: What do you consider my holiest duties?

HELMER: Need I tell you that? Your duties to your husband and children.

NORA: I have other duties equally sacred.

HELMER: Impossible! What do you mean?

NORA: My duties toward myself.

HELMER: Before all else you are a wife and a mother.

NORA: That I no longer believe. Before all else I believe I am a human being, just as much as you are—or at least that I should try to become one. I know that most people agree with you, Torvald, and that they say so in books. But I can no longer be satisfied with what most people say and what is in books. I must think things out for myself and try to get clear about them.

1. Why would many nineteenth-century middle-class women have had a problem with Nora's ideas?

2. What do you think Nora would have said to those women?

The novels of the French writer Émile Zola provide a good example of naturalism. Zola used a backdrop of the urban slums and coalfields of northern France to show how alcoholism and different environments affected people's lives. He wrote *Rougon-Macquart* (ROO-zhawn), a 20-volume series of novels on the history of a family. Zola maintained that the artist must analyze and dissect life as a biologist would a living organism.

At the turn of the century, a new group of writers, known as the **symbolists,** reacted against naturalism. The symbolists were primarily interested in writing

poetry and were strongly influenced by the ideas of Freud. They believed that an objective knowledge of the world was impossible. The external world was not real but only a collection of symbols that reflected the true reality of the individual human mind. Art, the symbolists believed, should function for its own sake instead of serving, criticizing, or seeking to understand society.

The period from 1870 to 1914 was one of the most fertile in the history of art. Since the Renaissance, the task of artists had been to represent reality as accurately as possible. By the late nineteenth century, artists were seeking new forms of expression. **Impressionism** was a movement that began in France in the 1870s, when a group of artists rejected the studios and went out into the countryside to paint nature directly. Camille Pissarro, one of impressionism's founders, expressed what these artists sought:

> *Do not define too closely the outlines of things; it is the brush stroke of the right value and color which should produce the drawing. . . . The eye should not be fixed on one point, but should take in everything, while observing the reflections which the colors produce on their surroundings. Work at the same time upon sky, water, branches, ground, keeping everything going on an equal basis. . . . Don't proceed according to rules and principles, but paint what you observe and feel. Paint generously unhesitatingly, for it is best not to lose the first impression.*[4]

Pissarro's suggestions are evident in the work of Claude Monet (moe-NAE). As seen in *Impression, Sunrise,* Monet was especially enchanted with water. He painted many pictures in which he sought to capture the interplay of light, water, and sky.

▲ *Claude Monet had a long, prolific career as an artist. As shown in* Impression, Sunrise, *Monet tried to capture the moment that the sun rose, using light playing on both the water and the atmosphere. How does this compare to* The Stonebreakers, *seen in Chapter 4?*

◄ *This painting of several of France's leading writers of the late nineteenth century shows a serious, thoughtful group. Paul Verlaine and Arthur Rimbaud, the first two on the left, were among the group of symbolist poets. Do you think these poets relied heavily on allusions? Why or why not?*

▲  *In van Gogh's* The Starry Night, *the sky is painted as a series of swirling forms far above and yet dominating the village below. Why do some art critics believe that van Gogh was more interested in color than form?*

By the 1880s, a new movement, known as **post-impressionism,** arose in France but soon spread to other European countries. A famous post-impressionist was the tortured and tragic figure Vincent van Gogh (GOE), who, in a fit of anger, cut off his own ear. For van Gogh, art was a spiritual experience. He was especially interested in color and believed that it could act as its own form of language. Van Gogh maintained that artists should paint what they feel. In his *Starry Night,*

he painted a sky alive with whirling stars that overwhelmed the huddled buildings in the village below.

By the beginning of the twentieth century, the idea that the task of art was to represent reality had lost much of its meaning. This was especially true in the visual arts. Perhaps the most important factor in the decline of realism in painting was the spread of photography to the mass markets. Photography had been invented in the 1830s. It became popular and wide-

## OUR ARTISTIC HERITAGE

# Modern Art and Architecture

▲ *Kandinsky used color freely in* Painting with White Border, *believing that color would appeal directly to the human soul and heart. He also tried to eliminate representational objects from his paintings. Do you think he was successful? Why or why not?*

One of the most outstanding features of modern art is the attempt of the artist to avoid "visual reality." By 1905, one of the most important figures in modern art was just beginning his career. Pablo Picasso was from Spain but settled in Paris in 1904. He painted in a remarkable variety of styles. He created a new style, called cubism, that used geometric designs as visual stimuli to recreate reality in the viewer's mind. In his paintings, Picasso attempted to view the human form from many sides. In this aspect he seems to have been influenced by the theory of relativity, which was becoming popularized at the time.

The modern artist's flight from visual reality reached a high point in 1910 with the beginning of abstract painting. Vasily Kandinsky, a Russian who worked in Germany, was one of the founders of abstract expressionism. As is evident in his *Painting with White Border,* Kandinsky and the other abstract expressionists sought to avoid visual reality altogether. Kandinsky believed that art should speak directly to the soul. To do so, it must use only line and color.

Modernism in the arts revolutionized architecture and gave rise to a new principle known as functionalism. Functionalism was the idea that buildings, like the products of machines, should be functional or useful; they should fulfill the purpose for which they were built. All unnecessary ornamentation was to be stripped away.

The United States was a leader in the new architecture. The country's rapid urban growth and lack of any architectural tradition allowed for new building methods, especially in the relatively new city of Chicago. The Chicago School of the 1890s, led by Louis H. Sullivan, used reinforced concrete, steel frames, and electric elevators in building skyscrapers virtually free of external ornamentation. One of Sullivan's most successful pupils was Frank Lloyd Wright. Wright's private houses, built chiefly for wealthy patrons, were geometric structures with long lines and overhanging

*(continued)*

## OUR ARTISTIC HERITAGE
## Modern Art and Architecture, continued

◀ Frank Lloyd Wright's homes and buildings quickly won him international fame. The houses he designed seem to be natural extensions of their surroundings. What elements from this house, Fallingwater, do you see in current ranch-house style homes?

roofs. The interiors had large open spaces and included cathedral ceilings, built-in furniture, and built-in lighting features. Wright pioneered the modern American house.

1. Describe *abstract expressionism*.

2. Describe *functionalism*.

3. From the descriptions given here, do you think you would find paintings done in the style of cubism or abstract expressionism more interesting to view? Explain your answer.

spread after George Eastman created the first Kodak camera in 1888. Now anyone could take a photograph that looked exactly like the subject.

Artists came to realize that their strength was not in mirroring reality (which the camera could do) but in creating reality. The visual artists, like the symbolist writers of the time, sought meaning in individual consciousness. Between 1905 and 1914, this search for individual expression created modern art (see "Our Artistic Heritage: Modern Art and Architecture").

At the beginning of the twentieth century, developments in music paralleled those in painting. Expressionism in music was a Russian creation. It was the product of the composer Igor Stravinsky (struh-VIN-skee) and the Ballet Russe (RUSS), the dancing company of Sergei Diaghilev (ser-GAE dee-AWG-uh-LEFF). Together they revolutionized the world of

music with Stravinsky's ballet, *The Rites of Spring*. When it was performed in Paris in 1913, the savage and primitive sounds and rhythms of the music and dance caused a near riot from an audience outraged at its audacity.

## ❀ SECTION REVIEW ❀

1. **Locate:**
   (*a*) Ottoman Empire

2. **Define:**
   (*a*) psychoanalysis,   (*b*) Social Darwinism,
   (*c*) pogroms,   (*d*) Zionism,   (*e*) modernism,
   (*f*) naturalism,   (*g*) symbolists,
   (*h*) impressionism,   (*i*) post-impressionism

3. **Identify:**
(*a*) theory of relativity, (*b*) *The Interpretation of Dreams,* (*c*) the Dreyfus affair, (*d*) Vincent van Gogh

4. **Recall:**
(*a*) How did German general Friedrich von Bernhardi support his idea that "War is a biological necessity . . ."?
(*b*) How have biological arguments been used to defend racism?

5. **Think Critically:** Why are times of political and economic change often associated with a time of artistic change?

## Conclusion

The Second Industrial Revolution helped create a new material prosperity that led Europeans to believe they had ushered in a new age of progress. A major feature of this age was the emergence of a mass society. The lower classes in particular benefited from the right to vote, a higher standard of living, and new schools that provided them with some education. New forms of mass transportation, combined with new work patterns, enabled large numbers of people to enjoy weekend trips to amusement parks and seaside resorts, as well as to participate in new mass leisure activities.

By 1870, the national state had become the focus of people's lives. Liberal and democratic reforms made possible greater participation in the political process, although women were still largely excluded from political rights. After 1871, the national state also began to expand its functions beyond all previous limits. The enactment of public health and housing measures, designed to curb the worst ills of urban living, were an example of how state power could be used to benefit the people.

The period between 1870 and 1914 was also a time of great anxiety. International rivalries and the creation of mass armies increased the tensions among the major powers. At the same time, scientists, writers, and artists began to question traditional ideas about the nature of reality and thus frightened many people. By 1914, many people had a sense of unease about the direction society was headed.

## Notes

1. Quoted in Shmuel Galai, *The Liberation Movement in Russia, 1900–1905* (Cambridge, 1973), p. 26.
2. Quoted in Arthur E. E. McKenzie, *The Major Achievements of Science,* vol. 1 (New York, 1960), p. 310.
3. Friedrich von Bernhardi, *Germany and the Next War,* trans. Allen H. Powles (New York, 1914), pp. 18–19.
4. Quoted in John Rewald, *History of Impressionism* (New York, 1961), pp. 456–458.

# CHAPTER 5 REVIEW

## USING KEY TERMS

1. _____ is a method by which a therapist and a patient probe for repressed experiences.
2. Marxists who believed their goals could be achieved by peaceful, democratic evolution were called _____.
3. Palestine became home for the Jewish nationalist movement known as _____.
4. Karl Marx referred to the middle class as the _____.
5. The _____ is the Russian Legislative Assembly.
6. _____ was a movement that attempted to paint both what was observed and what was felt.
7. Literary and artistic styles that rejected traditional styles were called _____.
8. A group of writers who believed that art was for art's sake, not for criticizing society, were the _____.
9. The development of _____ parties and trade unions helped workers in their struggle to achieve better pay and working conditions.
10. A literary style that portrayed individuals caught up in forces beyond their control was _____.
11. The principle by which a prime minister is directly answerable to a popularly elected representative body is _____.
12. Marx called the workers the _____ and predicted their struggles would result in revolution.
13. Herbert Spencer, a believer in _____, argued that social progress came from the advancement of the strong while the weak declined.
14. Vincent van Gogh's painting was a spiritual experience in the style of _____.
15. Russian Jews were massacred in _____ in eastern Europe.

## REVIEWING THE FACTS

1. List one invention of Michael Faraday, Thomas Alva Edison, and Guglielmo Marconi.
2. What three factors enabled Europe to dominate the world by 1914?
3. Who wrote *The Communist Manifesto?*
4. Who were the two leaders of the German Social Democratic Party?
5. What new jobs for women were created by the Second Industrial Revolution?
6. What was the most significant development in family life in the nineteenth century? Why did this change occur?
7. What purposes were served by the the institution of compulsory education?
8. What was the yellow press?
9. What was the Pan-German League?
10. Which were the two revolutionary socialist parties of Russia?
11. What was Albert Einstein's greatest contributions to science?
12. Who was Alfred Dreyfus and what was his significance?
13. What was a pogrom? Where did pogroms occur in the early twentieth century?
14. Who was Theodore Herzl?

## THINKING CRITICALLY

1. Why are interchangeable parts so important in manufacturing?
2. Describe in your own words Marx' ideas about history and social classes.
3. Why was revisionist, or evolutionary, socialism more powerful in western Europe than in eastern Europe?
4. How did liberals such as Octavia Hill go about reforming urban housing? How is this approach consistent with their liberal philosophy?

5. Why did the average number of children per family drop during the nineteenth century?

6. In what ways did the Crimean War and American Civil War unintentionally promote feminism?

7. Why did women come to dominate the teaching profession?

8. Was the Revolution of 1905 in Russia a success or a failure? Explain your answer.

9. Explain how the Congress of Berlin helped create conditions that eventually led to the outbreak of World War I in 1914.

10. What was the difference between the approach to manufacturing automobiles between Karl Benz and Henry Ford? Which man had the better approach?

## APPLYING SOCIAL STUDIES SKILLS

1. **Sociology:** Proportionately, did London or Berlin grow more in the nineteenth century? How did you reach your conclusion?

2. **Sociology:** Was wealth in the United States more or less evenly distributed in 1890 than in Europe? Please explain your reasoning.

3. **Government:** Draw a diagram showing the structure of the government for the United States, Great Britain, France, and Germany in 1914. In your opinion, which government is the most democratic? The least democratic? Explain.

4. **Geography:** Consult Map 5.3 on page 182 "Europe in 1871." Militarily, what would be Germany's greatest problem in the event of war?

## MAKING TIME AND PLACE CONNECTIONS

1. Compare the British Conservative, Liberal, and Labour parties of 1914 with the present U.S. Democratic and Republican parties. Identify their common characteristics.

2. At the turn of the century, how did the United States approach urban problems compared to that of Great Britain and Germany?

3. In what ways have the problems facing Canada not changed since the time of Sir Wilfred Laurier?

4. What is your response to the scene between Helmer and Nora in *A Doll House?*

## BECOMING AN HISTORIAN

1. **Charts, Graphs, Tables:** Construct a graph showing urban population growth in Britain, France, Germany, and eastern Europe between 1800 and 1914. Does this graph support or not support the text generalization that Europe had developed two economic zones?

2. **Making Inferences:** Which of the following schools or movements had their roots more in realism than romanticism? Why? (1) Naturalism, (2) Symbolism, (3) Impressionism, (4) Post-Impressionism, (5) Expressionism, (6) Cubism, (7) Abstract Expressionism, (8) The Chicago School of Architecture.

3. **Primary and Secondary Sources:** Classify the following features as either primary or secondary sources, and explain why: (1) The Pankhursts (p. 176), (2) *A Doll's House*—One Woman's Cry for Freedom (p. 191), and (3) Modern Art and Architecture (p. 195).

4. **Analyzing Information:** Interpret the cartoon "Bismarck and William II" (p. 183). What is the message of the cartoon? Why is William portrayed as he is? What is the meaning of the props in his hand?

5. **Art as a Key to History:** Compare Claude Monet's "Impression, Sunrise" (p. 193) with Vincent van Gogh's "The Starry Night" (p. 194). Why is Monet's painting described by art historians as impressionist while van Gogh's painting is described as post-impressionist?

6. Listen to a recording of Igor Stravinsky's "The Rite of Spring." How does Stravinsky try to achieve musically the effect that Kandinsky tried to achieve visually through painting?

# THE HIGH TIDE OF IMPERIALISM:

**6**

In 1841, the Scottish doctor and missionary David Livingstone began a series of journeys that took him through much of central and southern Africa. His travels were not easy. Much of his journey was done by foot, canoe, or mule. He suffered at times from rheumatic fever, dysentery, and malaria. He survived an attack by armed warriors and a mutiny by his own servants. Back in Great Britain, his exploits made Livingstone a national hero. People jammed into lecture halls to hear him speak of Africa's beauties. As the *London Journal* reported, "Europe had always heard that the central regions of southern Africa were bleak and barren, heated by poisonous winds, infested by snakes . . . [but Livingstone spoke of] a high country, full of fruit trees, abounding in shade, watered by a perfect network of rivers." Livingstone also tried to persuade his listeners that Britain needed to send both missionaries and merchants to Africa. Combining Christianity and commerce, he said, would achieve civilization for Africa.

During the nineteenth and early twentieth centuries, Western colonialism spread throughout much of the non-Western world. A few powerful Western states—namely, Great Britain, France, Germany, Russia, and the United States—competed for markets and raw materials for their expanding economies. By the end of the nineteenth century, virtually all of the peoples of Asia and Africa were under colonial rule.

Western states sought colonies chiefly to enhance their wealth and power. Some had other goals, such as bringing Western values and institutions to the peoples of Asia and Africa. One result of this colonial process was the beginnings of the westernization of the societies of Asia and Africa. Another result was the rise of nationalism, borrowed from the West. Anticolonist elements in Asia and Africa used the idea of nationalism in their struggles to reassert the rights of native peoples to control their own destinies. By the first quarter of the twentieth century, the revolt against colonial rule had begun to spread throughout much of Asia and Africa. Nowhere, however, had it yet succeeded.

Only in Latin America had resistance to Europeans been successful in the nineteenth century. National movements for independence in South and Central America led to new states by the 1820s and 1830s. However, even these new states found themselves economically dependent on Europe and the United States.

◄ *This portrait of David Livingstone shows him in the continent that he grew to love, Africa. Do you think it was difficult for him to convince his fellow Englishmen about the beauties of Africa and of the African people?*

# AN AGE OF WESTERN DOMINANCE

## (1800 TO 1914)

### ERA OF EUROPEAN DOMINANCE

| 1800 | HIGH TIDE OF IMPERIALISM | 1914 |
| --- | --- | --- |
| 1800 | | 1914 |

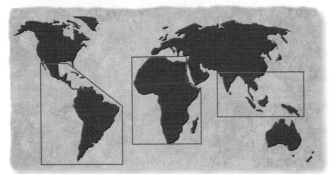

## QUESTIONS TO GUIDE YOUR READING

1. What were the major causes of the new imperialism after 1880?

2. What general principles of rule did Europeans follow in their colonial empires?

3. What economic policies were followed by the colonial nations? Who benefited from these policies?

4. How did nationalism affect the colonial peoples of Asia and Africa?

5. What was the nature of British rule in India?

6. How did Latin American nations achieve their independence?

7. What domestic problems did Latin American nations face in the nineteenth century?

## OUTLINE

### 1

## THE SPREAD OF COLONIAL RULE: SOUTHEAST ASIA

In the nineteenth century, a new phase of Western expansion into Asia and Africa began. European nations began to view Asian and African societies as a source of industrial raw materials and a market for Western manufactured goods. No longer were Western gold and silver traded for cloves, pepper, tea, and silk. Now the products of European factories were sent to Africa and Asia in return for oil, tin, rubber, and the other resources needed to fuel European industries.

### The New Imperialism

Beginning in the 1880s, European states began an intense scramble for overseas territory. **Imperialism,** or the extension of one nation's power over other lands, was not new. Europeans had set up colonies in North and South America and trading posts around Africa and the Indian Ocean by the sixteenth century. However, the imperialism of the late nineteenth century, called the "new imperialism" by some, was different from the earlier European imperialism. The new imperialism was more rapid and more dominating. Earlier, European states had been content, especially in Africa and Asia, to set up a few trading posts where they could carry on trade and even some missionary activity. Now they sought nothing less than direct control over vast territories.

Why did Westerners begin this mad scramble for colonies after 1880? No doubt, there was a strong economic motive. Capitalist states in the West sought both markets and raw materials such as rubber, oil, and tin for their industries. Moreover, Europeans wanted to be sure they could get these raw materials and set up reliable markets. To do so, they wanted more direct control of the areas where the raw materials and markets were found.

The issue was not simply an economic one, however. As we saw with the new system of alliances described in Chapter 5, European nation-states were involved in heated rivalries. As European affairs grew tense, states sought to gain colonies abroad in order to gain an advantage over their rivals. Colonies were also a source of national prestige. Once the scramble for colonies began, failure to enter the race was seen as a sign of weakness. To some, in fact, a nation could not be great without colonies. One German historian wrote that "all great nations in the fullness of their strength have the desire to set their mark upon barbarian lands and those who fail to participate in this great rivalry will play a pitiable role in time to come."[1]

Then, too, imperialism was tied to Social Darwinism and racism. Social Darwinists believed that in the struggle between nations, the fit are victorious and survive. Superior races must dominate inferior races by military force to show how strong they are. One British professor argued in 1900, "The path of progress is strewn with the wrecks of nations; traces are everywhere to be seen of the [slaughtered remains] of inferior races. Yet these dead people are, in very truth, the stepping stones on which mankind has arisen to the higher intellectual and deeper emotional life of today."[2]

Some Europeans took a more religious and humanitarian approach to imperialism. They argued that Europeans had a moral responsibility to civilize ignorant people, which they called the "white man's bur-

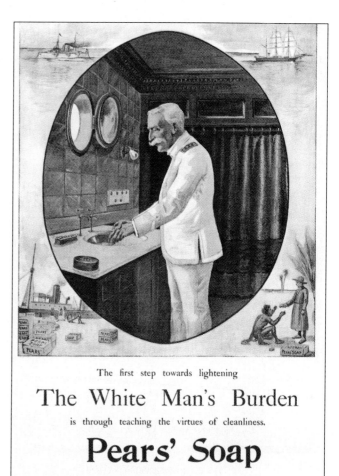

The first step towards lightening

# The White Man's Burden

is through teaching the virtues of cleanliness.

# Pears' Soap

is a potent factor in brightening the dark corners of the earth as civilization advances, while amongst the cultured of all nations it holds the highest place—it is the ideal toilet soap.

▲ *This advertisement for Pears' Soap clearly communicates the Europeans' view of their responsibility toward other peoples and cultures. To which groups in English society would this ad have appealed?*

den." They believed that the advanced nations of the West should help the backward nations of Asia and Africa. To some, this meant bringing the Christian message to the "heathen masses." To others, it meant bringing the benefits of Western democracy and capitalism to the societies of the East. Either way, many Westerners believed that their governments were bringing civilization to the primitive peoples of the world.

**Map 6.1   Colonial Southeast Asia**

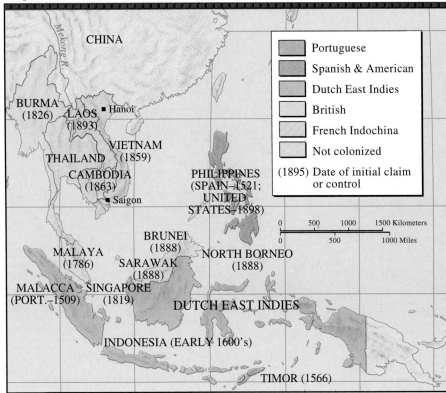

life and activity; and it would be difficult to name a place on the face of the globe with brighter prospects or more present satisfaction."[3]

During the next few decades, the British advance into Southeast Asia continued. At the beginning of the nineteenth century, Great Britain had received the right to trade with the kingdom of Burma (modern Myanmar). A few decades later, Britain sought a more direct presence in the area to protect the eastern flank of its possessions in India. It also sought a land route through Burma into South China. Although the difficult terrain along the frontier between Burma and China caused this effort to fail, British activities in Burma led to the collapse of the Burmese monarchy. Britain soon established control over the entire country.

## The Colonial Takeover in Southeast Asia

In 1800, only two societies in Southeast Asia were ruled by Europeans: the Spanish Philippines and the Dutch East Indies. By 1900, virtually the entire area was under colonial rule.

The process began with Great Britain. After the Napoleonic Wars (see Chapter 3), the British agreed with the Dutch to abandon British claims to lands in the East Indies in return for a free hand in the Malay peninsula. In 1819, Britain under Sir Stamford Raffles founded a new British colony on a small island at the tip of the peninsula. Called Singapore (city of the lion), it had previously been used by Malay pirates to raid nearby shipping. In the new age of steamships, Singapore soon became a major stopping point for traffic on a route to or from China. Raffles was proud of his new city and wrote to a friend in England, "Here all is

The British advance into Burma was watched nervously by France, which had some missionaries operating in Vietnam. The French missionaries were persecuted by the local authorities, who viewed Christianity as a threat to Confucian doctrine. However, Vietnam failed to stop the Christian missionaries. Vietnamese internal rivalries divided the country into two separate governments, in the north and the south.

France was especially alarmed at the British attempt to gain a monopoly of trade in South China. To stop this, the French government decided in 1857 to force the Vietnamese to accept French protection. A naval attack launched in 1858 was not a total success, but the French did succeed in forcing the Vietnamese ruler to cede territories in the Mekong River delta. The French occupied the city of Saigon (sie-GAWN) and, during the next 30 years, extended their control over the rest of the country. In 1884, France completed its conquest of Vietnam. It seized the city of Hanoi and made the Vietnamese

▶ *This Chinese painting shows the French navy attacking a Vietnamese fort on the Red River. The Manchu court sent forces to help the Vietnamese fight the French, but to no avail.*

Empire a French **protectorate** (a political unit that depends on another state for its protection).

In the 1880s, France extended "protection" over neighboring Cambodia, Annam, Tonkin, and Laos. By 1900, France included all of its new possessions in a new Union of French Indochina.

After the French conquest of Indochina, Thailand was the only remaining free state on the Southeast Asian mainland. During the last quarter of the nineteenth century, British and French rivalry threatened to place Thailand, too, under colonial rule. However, two remarkable rulers, King Mongkut (known to theatergoers as the king in *The King and I*) and his son King Chulalongkorn, acted to prevent colonial rule. Both introduced Western learning and maintained friendly relations with the major European powers. In 1896, Britain and France agreed to maintain Thailand as an independent buffer state between their possessions in Southeast Asia.

One final conquest in Southeast Asia occurred at the end of the nineteenth century. In 1898, during the Spanish-American War, U.S. naval forces under Commodore George Dewey (DOO-ee) defeated the Spanish fleet in Manila Bay. President William McKinley

decided that the moral thing to do was to turn the Philippines into an American colony to prevent the area from falling into the hands of the Japanese. In fact, the islands gave the United States a convenient jumping-off point for trade with China.

This mixture of moral idealism and desire for profit was reflected in a speech given in the Senate in January 1900 by Senator Albert Beveridge of Indiana:

*Mr. President, the times call for candor. The Philippines are ours forever. And just beyond the Philippines are China's unlimited markets. We will not retreat from either. We will not abandon an opportunity in the Orient. We will not renounce our part in the mission of our race, trustee, under God, of the civilization of the world. And we will move forward to our work . . . with gratitude for a task worthy of our strength, and thanksgiving to Almighty God that He has marked us as His chosen people, henceforth to lead in the regeneration of the world.*[4]

The Filipinos, who had been fighting the Spaniards for their freedom, did not agree with the American senator. Under the leadership of Emilio Aguinaldo (AWG-ee-NAWL-DOE), guerrilla forces fought bitterly against U.S. troops to establish their independence. However, the United States won its first war against guerrilla forces in Asia. Aguinaldo was captured and resistance collapsed in 1901. President McKinley had his stepping-stone to the rich markets of China.

## Colonial Regimes in Southeast Asia

Western powers governed their new colonial empires with policies known as either indirect or direct rule. As we have seen, the chief goal of the Western nations was to exploit the natural resources of these lands and open up markets for their own manufactured goods. Sometimes that goal could be realized most easily through cooperation with local political elites. In these cases, **indirect rule** was used. In other words, local rulers were allowed to maintain their positions of authority and status in a new colonial setting. However, indirect rule was not always possible, especially when local elites resisted the foreign conquest. In such cases, the local elites were removed from power and replaced with a new set of officials brought from the mother country. This system is called **direct rule.**

In Southeast Asia, colonial powers, wherever possible, tried to work with local elites. This made it easier to gain access to a region's natural resources. Indirect rule also lowered the cost of government, because Western powers had to train fewer officials. Moreover, indirect rule had less effect on local culture. One example of indirect rule was in the Dutch East Indies. Officials of the Dutch East India Company allowed local landed aristocrats in the Dutch East Indies to control local government. These local elites maintained law and order and collected taxes in return for a payment from the Dutch East India Company.

Indirect rule, then, was convenient and cost less, but it was not always feasible. Local resistance to the colonial conquest made such a policy impossible in some places. In Burma, the staunch opposition by the monarchy caused Great Britain to abolish the monarchy and administer the country directly through its colonial government in India.

In Indochina, France used both direct and indirect rule. It imposed direct rule on the southern provinces in the Mekong delta, which had been ceded to France as a colony after the first war in 1858 to 1860. The northern parts of Vietnam, seized in the 1880s, were governed as a protectorate. The emperor still ruled from his palace in Hue, but he had little power. France adopted a similar policy in Cambodia and Laos, where local rulers were left in charge with French advisors to counsel them.

To justify their conquests, Western powers had spoken of bringing the blessings of advanced Western civilization to their colonial subjects. Many colonial powers, for example, spoke of introducing representative institutions and educating the native peoples in the democratic process. However, many westerners came to fear the idea of native peoples (especially educated ones) being allowed political rights. The westerners were afraid that the native peoples would be too likely to demand full participation in the government, or even want national independence.

Whether they used indirect or direct rule, colonial regimes in Southeast Asia were slow to create democratic institutions. The first legislative bodies were made up almost entirely of European residents in the colonies. When representatives from the local people were allowed to take part, the people chosen were always wealthy and conservative in their political views. When Southeast Asians began to complain, colonial officials gradually extended the right to vote to more people. However, the colonial officials also warned that education in democratic institutions must come before voting rights.

At the same time, colonial officials adopted a cautious attitude toward educational reform. Western powers had said that their civilizing mission included the introduction of Western school systems. However, colonial officials soon discovered that educating the native peoples could backfire. Often there were few jobs for highly trained lawyers, engineers, and architects in colonial societies. Thus, it might be dangerous to have large numbers of educated people without jobs. These people might take out their frustrations on the colonial regime. By the mid-1920s, many colonial governments in Southeast Asia began to limit education to a small elite. As one French official noted, educating the natives meant "one rebel more."

▶ *Resistance against colonial governments was not tolerated, and dissidents were punished harshly. This 1907 photograph shows Vietnamese prisoners awaiting trial for plotting against the French.*

Colonial powers were also not always eager to foster economic development. As we have seen, their chief goals were to gain a source of inexpensive raw materials and to keep markets for manufactured goods. For this reason, the colonial powers did not want their colonists to develop their own industries. Thus, colonial policy stressed the export of raw materials—teak wood from Burma; rubber and tin from Malaya; spices, tea, coffee, and palm oil from the East Indies; and sugar from the Philippines. In many cases, this policy led to some form of plantation agriculture, in which peasants worked as wage laborers on plantations owned by foreign investors.

Some industrial development did take place in Southeast Asia, however, largely to meet the needs of Europeans and local elites. Cities like Rangoon in Burma and Saigon in French Indochina grew rapidly, because they were centers of manufacturing. Textile plants, cement and brick works, and factories for bicycles and automobiles were set up.

Colonial policy was often harmful in urban areas. Most industrial and commercial businesses were owned and managed by Europeans or, in some cases, by Indian or Chinese merchants. In Saigon, for example, even the manufacture of the traditional Vietnamese fish sauce was under Chinese ownership.

In the countryside, these economic changes hurt the natives and benefited their colonial masters. Plantation owners kept the wages of their workers at poverty levels in order to increase profits. Conditions on plantations were often so unhealthy that thousands died. In addition, high taxes levied by colonial governments to pay for their administrative costs were a heavy burden for poor peasants.

Colonial rule did bring some benefits to Southeast Asia. It led to the beginnings of a modern economic system. The development of an export market helped to create an entrepreneurial class in rural areas. In the Dutch East Indies, for example, small growers of rubber, palm oil, coffee, tea, and spices began to share in the profits of the colonial enterprise. Even then, however, most of the profits were taken back to the colonial mother country, and peasants fleeing to cities found few jobs. Many were left with seasonal employment, with one foot on the farm and one in the factory. The old world was being destroyed while the new one had yet to be born.

## Resistance to Colonial Rule

Many subject peoples were quite unhappy with being governed by Western powers. At first, resistance came

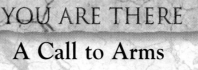

## A Call to Arms

◀ *Vietnamese attempts to regain homelands were not only unsuccessful, they were futile. This drawing shows trained and well-armed French troops in action against their Vietnamese opponents.*

*In 1862, the Vietnamese emperor ceded three provinces in southern Vietnam to the French. In outrage, many patriotic Vietnamese military officers and government officials appealed to their fellow Vietnamese to rise up and resist the foreigners. The following lines were written in 1864.*

### An Appeal to Vietnamese Citizens to Resist the French

This is a general proclamation addressed to the
   scholars and the people. . . .
Our people are now suffering through a period of
   anarchy and disorder. . . .
Let us now consider our situation with the French
   today.

We are separated from them by thousands of
   mountains and seas.
By hundreds of differences in our daily customs.
Although they were very confident in their copper
   battleships surmounted by chimneys,
Although they had a large quantity of steel rifles
   and lead bullets,
These things did not prevent the loss of some of
   their best generals in these last years, when they
   attacked our frontier in hundreds of battles. . . .
You, officials of the country,
Do not let your resistance to the enemy be
   blunted by the peaceful stand of the court,
Do not take the lead from the three subjected
   provinces and leave hatred unavenged.

*(continued)*

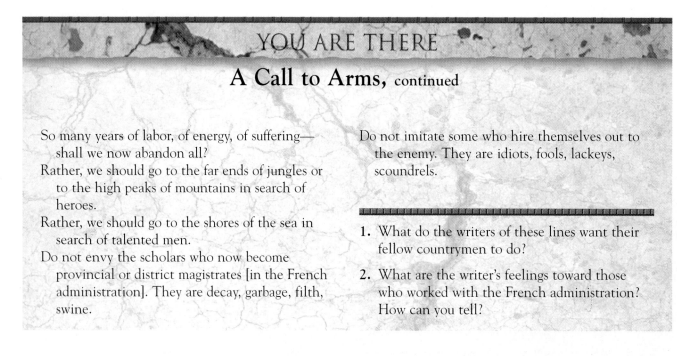

## YOU ARE THERE

## A Call to Arms, continued

So many years of labor, of energy, of suffering—
shall we now abandon all?
Rather, we should go to the far ends of jungles or
to the high peaks of mountains in search of
heroes.
Rather, we should go to the shores of the sea in
search of talented men.
Do not envy the scholars who now become
provincial or district magistrates [in the French
administration]. They are decay, garbage, filth,
swine.

Do not imitate some who hire themselves out to
the enemy. They are idiots, fools, lackeys,
scoundrels.

1. What do the writers of these lines want their
fellow countrymen to do?

2. What are the writer's feelings toward those
who worked with the French administration?
How can you tell?

from the existing ruling class. In Burma and Vietnam, for example, the resistance to Western domination came from the monarchs themselves. After the emperor in Vietnam had agreed to French control of his country, a number of civilian and military officials set up an organization called Can Vuoug (Save the King). They fought against the French without the emperor's help (see "You Are There: A Call to Arms").

Sometimes resistance to Western control went beyond the elite. When this occurred, it most commonly took the form of peasant revolts. Rural rebellions were not uncommon in traditional Asian societies as a means of expressing peasant discontent with high taxes, official corruption, debt, or famine in the countryside. Under colonial rule, conditions often got worse as peasants were driven off the land to make way for plantation agriculture. Angry peasants then vented their anger at the foreign invaders. For example, in Burma, the Buddhist monk Saya San led a peasant uprising against the British colonial regime many years after the regime had completed its takeover.

These early resistance movements, however, were overcome by Western power, and they failed. At the beginning of the twentieth century, a new kind of resistance began to emerge that was based on the force of nationalism. The leaders were often a new class that had been created by colonial rule: westernized intellectuals in the cities. In many cases, this new urban middle class—composed of merchants, clerks, students, and professionals—had been educated in Western-style schools. A few had spent time in the West. They were the first generation of Asians to understand the institutions and values of the West. Many spoke Western languages, wore Western clothes, and worked in jobs connected with the colonial regimes.

At first, many of the leaders of these movements did not focus clearly on the idea of nationhood but simply tried to defend the economic interests or religious beliefs of the natives. In Burma, for example, the first expression of modern nationalism came from students at the University of Rangoon. They formed an organization to protest against official persecution of the Buddhist religion and British lack of respect for local religious traditions. The students called themselves *Thakin* (meaning "Lord" or "Master," thus showing their demand for the right to rule themselves). They protested against British arrogance and failure to observe local customs in Buddhist temples. Only in the 1930s, however, did these resistance movements begin to demand national independence.

## ❀ SECTION REVIEW ❀

1. **Locate:**
   (*a*) Indian Ocean,   (*b*) Dutch East Indies,
   (*c*) Singapore,   (*d*) Burma,   (*e*) Vietnam,
   (*f*) Cambodia,   (*g*) Thailand,   (*h*) Philippines,
   (*i*) Laos

2. **Define:**
   (*a*) imperialism,   (*b*) protectorate,
   (*c*) indirect rule,   (*d*) direct rule

3. **Identify:**
   (*a*) new imperialism,   (*b*) buffer state,
   (*c*) Spanish-American War,   (*d*) Can Vuoug,
   (*e*) Saya San

4. **Recall:**
   (*a*) What economic forces drove the movement of European nations to the new imperialism?
   (*b*) How did the ideas of Social Darwinism support the new imperialism?
   (*c*) Why did imperialist nations want to consolidate their control over nations they dominated?
   (*d*) What advantages were provided by indirect rule to imperial nations?
   (*e*) Why did imperial powers often oppose education for dominated peoples?

5. **Think Critically:** Why did natives of dominated lands, who had been educated and lived in Western nations, often lead their homelands in revolt against imperialist nations?

## EMPIRE BUILDING IN AFRICA

Before 1800, Europeans had shown little interest in taking complete control of African territory. The slave trade, the main source of European profit in Africa during the eighteenth century, was carried on by using African rulers and merchants who cooperated for profits. Disease, lack of transportation, and an unhealthy climate all served to keep Europeans out of Africa on any permanent basis.

Gradually, however, Europeans took a greater interest in Africa. Before 1880, they controlled little of the African continent directly. European rule was limited to the fringes of Africa, such as Algeria, the Gold Coast, and South Africa. Between 1880 and 1900, however, a mad scramble for African territory took place. Fed by intense rivalries among themselves, Great Britain, France, Germany, Belgium, and Portugal placed virtually all of Africa under European rule.

## The Growing European Presence in West Africa

By 1800, the slave trade, which had particularly affected West Africa, was beginning to decline. One reason was the growing outrage in Western countries over the sale and exploitation of human beings. In 1808, both Great Britain and the United States declared the slave trade illegal. Other European countries eventually followed suit. In the meantime, the demand for slaves began to decline in the Western Hemisphere. Slavery was abolished in the United States in 1865 and in Cuba and Brazil fifteen years later. By the 1880s, slavery had been abolished in all major countries of the world.

The decline of the Atlantic slave trade did not lead to fewer Europeans in West Africa, however. Europe's interest in other forms of trade actually increased as slavery declined. Europeans sold textiles and other manufactured goods in exchange for such West African natural resources as peanuts, timber, hides, and palm oil.

Encouraged by this growing trade, European governments began to push for a more permanent presence along the coast. During the first decades of the nineteenth century, the British set up settlements along the Gold Coast and in Sierra Leone (see-ER-uh lee-OWN). The latter became a haven for freed slaves. When British ships captured illegal slave ships, they freed the slaves and brought them to Sierra Leone. The United States created a homeland for its freed slaves in Liberia. Founded in 1822, Liberia became an independent state in 1850. Its capital city, Monrovia, was named after President James Monroe.

▶ *The first ships passed through the Suez Canal in 1869. It is still an important strategic site, and it is Egypt's largest revenue producer.*

The growing European presence in West Africa led to increasing tensions with African governments in the area. British efforts to increase trade with the state of Ashanti, for example, led to conflict in the 1820s. For a long time, most African states were able to maintain their independence. However, by the 1870s, European power had grown too great. In 1874, Great Britain stepped in and annexed the coastal states as the first British colony of Gold Coast. At about the same time, Britain established a protectorate over warring tribal groups in Nigeria. The French also moved into West Africa. By 1900, France had added the huge area of French West Africa to its colonial empire. This left France in control of the largest part of West Africa.

## North Africa

Egypt had been part of the Ottoman Empire, but as Ottoman rule declined, the Egyptians sought their independence. In 1805, an officer named Muhammad Ali seized power and established a separate Egyptian state. During the next thirty years, Muhammad Ali introduced a series of reforms to bring Egypt into the modern world. He modernized the army, set up a public school system, and helped to create a small industrial sector. Refined sugar, textiles, munitions, and even ships were among the products manufactured.

Muhammad Ali's new army also made it possible to extend Egyptian authority southward into the Sudan and across the Sinai peninsula into Arabia.

The growing economic importance of the Nile valley in Egypt, along with the development of steamships, gave Europeans the desire to build a canal east of Cairo to connect the Mediterranean and Red Seas. In 1854, the French entrepreneur Ferdinand de Lesseps (lae-SEPS) signed a contract to begin building the Suez Canal. It was completed in 1869. The project brought little immediate benefit to Egypt, however. The costs of construction gave the Egyptian government a large debt and made the Egyptians more dependent on financial support from European states.

The British took an active interest in Egypt after the Suez (soo-EZ) Canal was opened in 1869. Believing that the canal was its "lifeline to India," Great Britain sought as much control as possible over the canal area. In 1875, Britain bought Egypt's share of stocks in the Suez Canal. When an Egyptian army revolt against foreign influence broke out in 1881, Britain stepped in and set up a protectorate over Egypt.

British interests in the Sudan, south of Egypt, soon brought a confrontation with the French. The British believed that they should control the Sudan in order to protect both Egypt and the Suez Canal. In 1881, the Muslim cleric Muhammad Ahmad, known as the

Mahdi (MAWD-ee) ("The Rightly Guided One," in Arabic), led a revolt that brought much of the Sudan under his control. Britain sent a military force under General Charles Gordon to restore Egyptian authority over the Sudan. However, Gordon's army was wiped out at Khartoum in 1885 by the Mahdi's troops thirty-six hours before a British rescue mission arrived. Gordon himself died in the battle.

It was not until 1898 that British troops were able to seize the Sudan. In the meantime, the French had been advancing eastward across the Sahara with the goal of controlling the regions around the upper Nile. French and British forces met unexpectedly at Fashoda, a small town on the Nile River in the Sudan. War between the two great European powers seemed inevitable. However, the French government was preoccupied with the Dreyfus affair, and it backed down. Britain retained control of most of the Sudan, leaving the French to rule in equatorial Africa.

The French were more successful elsewhere in North Africa. In 1879, after 150,000 French people had settled in the region of Algeria, the French government established control there. Two years later, France imposed a protectorate on neighboring Tunisia. In 1912, France established a protectorate over much of Morocco. The rest was left to Spain.

Italy joined in the scramble for North Africa, but it was defeated by Ethiopia in 1896. Italy now was the only European state to lose to an African state. This humiliating defeat led Italy to try again in 1911. Italy invaded and seized Turkish Tripoli, which it renamed Libya (LIB-ee-uh).

## Central Africa

Territories in central Africa were also added to the list of European colonies. Popular interest in the dense tropical jungles of central Africa was first aroused in

▲ *This drawing shows the historic meeting of Livingstone and Stanley. Which features in this artist's rendition do you believe are accurate? Which features do you think are inaccurate or imaginative?*

the 1860s and 1870s by explorers. David Livingstone, as we have seen, first arrived in Africa in 1841. For thirty years he trekked through unchartered regions. He spent much of his time exploring the interior of the continent. When Livingstone disappeared for a while, the *New York Herald* hired a young journalist, Henry Stanley, to find him. Stanley did, on the eastern shore of Lake Tanganyika (TAN-gun-YEE-kuh), and greeted the explorer with the now famous words "Dr. Livingstone, I presume."

After Livingstone's death in 1873, Stanley remained in Africa to carry on the great explorer's work. Unlike Livingstone, however, Stanley had a strong dislike of Africa. He once said, "I detest the land most heartily." In the 1870s, Stanley moved inland from the East African coast. He explored the Congo River and sailed down it to the Atlantic Ocean. Soon he was encouraging the British to send settlers to the Congo River basin. When Britain refused, he turned to King Leopold II of Belgium.

King Leopold II was the real driving force behind the colonization of central Africa. He rushed enthusiastically into the pursuit of an empire in Africa: "To open to civilization," he said, "the only part of our globe where it has not yet penetrated, to pierce the darkness which envelops whole populations, is a crusade, if I may say so, a crusade worthy of this century of progress." Profit, however, was more important to Leopold than progress. In 1876, he hired Henry Stanley to set up Belgian settlements in the Congo.

Leopold's claim to the vast territories of the Congo aroused widespread concern from other European states. France, in particular, rushed to plant its flag in the heart of Africa. Leopold ended up with the territories south of the Congo River, whereas France occupied the areas to the north.

## Arab Merchants and European Missionaries in East Africa

Events in East Africa followed their own pattern. The decline in the Atlantic slave trade led to an increase in slavery on the other side of the continent. A sudden growth in plantation agriculture in the region and on the islands off the coast led to a demand for slave labor.

## CONNECTIONS
### AROUND THE WORLD

**The Role of Quinine**    Before 1850, the fear of disease was a major factor in keeping many Europeans from moving into Africa. Especially frightening was malaria, an often fatal infection. Malaria is especially devastating in tropical and subtropical regions, which offer good conditions for breeding the mosquitoes that carry and spread the malaria parasites. When the mosquito bites a person, malaria parasites enter the victim's red blood cells. Intense attacks of chills, fevers, and sweats are often followed by death.

By 1850, European doctors had learned how to treat malaria with quinine, a drug that greatly reduced the death rate from malaria. Quinine is a bitter drug obtained from the bark of the cinchona tree, which is native to the slopes of the Andes Mountains in South America. The Indians of Peru were the first people to use the bark of the cinchona tree to treat malaria.

The Dutch, however, took the cinchona tree and began to grow it in the East Indies. The East Indies eventually became the chief source of quinine. With the use of quinine and other medicines, Europeans felt more secure about moving into Africa. By the beginning of the twentieth century, more than 90 percent of African lands were under the control of the European powers. A drug found in the bark of trees in Latin America and then Asia had been used by Europeans to make possible their conquest of Africa.

The French introduced the growing of sugar to the island of Réunion (ree-YOON-yun) early in the century. Clove plantations were set up on the island of Zanzibar. The Arab sultan of Oman established his capital at Zanzibar in 1840. From there, Arab merchants fanned out into Africa in search of slaves, ivory, and other local products. The slave trade in East Africa now made Zanzibar the largest slave market in Africa.

This slave traffic brought East Africa to the attention of the West and its Christian missionaries. David

◄ *This 1871 sketch shows slave traders murdering Africans during a slave raid on the Lualaba River, west of Lake Tanganyika. What effect might sketches such as these have had on slavery?*

Livingstone, for example, was passionately opposed to slavery. His protests created public outcries, especially in Britain, against the slave trade in East Africa. In 1873, the slave market at Zanzibar was finally closed as the result of pressure from Great Britain.

By that time, Britain and Germany had become the chief rivals in East Africa. Germany came late to the ranks of the imperialist powers. At first, the German chancellor Otto von Bismarck had downplayed the importance of colonies. As more and more Germans called for a German empire, however, Bismarck became a convert to colonialism. As he expressed it, "All this colonial business is a sham, but we need it for the elections." Germany controlled Togo, Cameroons, and Southwest Africa along the west coast of Africa. Germany also sought colonies in East Africa. Most of East Africa had not yet been claimed by any other power. However, the British were also interested, because control of East Africa would connect the British Empire in Africa from South Africa in the south to Egypt in the north. Portugal and Belgium also claimed parts of East Africa.

To settle the conflicting claims in East Africa, Bismarck held a conference in Berlin in 1884. The Berlin Conference, first of all, set basic rules for further annexations of African territory by European nations. Its goal was to avoid war and reduce tensions among European nations competing for the spoils of Africa. Second, the conference gave official recognition to both British and German claims for territory in East Africa. Portugal received a clear claim on Mozambique. No African delegates were present at this conference, which carved up their continent.

## Bantus, Boers, and British in South Africa

Nowhere in Africa did the European presence grow more rapidly than in the south. During the eighteenth century, European settlers gradually began to migrate eastward from the Cape Colony (see later in this section) into territory inhabited by Bantu-speaking people. Tribal warfare among the Bantus, however, had largely depopulated the area. This made it easier for

▲ *In 1879, the Zulu king Cetewayo met with British ambassadors who were representing Lord Chelmsford. Cetewayo, who was born c. 1825 and died in 1884, was the last king of independent Zululand. Cetewayo tried to ally himself with the British against the Afrikaners, but the British invaded Zululand and eventually defeated the Zulu forces.*

the Boers, or Afrikaners, as the descendants of the original Dutch settlers in the seventeenth century were called, to occupy the land.

In the early nineteenth century, however, another local people, the Zulus (zoo-LOOZ), under a talented ruler named Shaka, had carved out their own empire. A series of wars ensued between the Europeans and the Zulus. Eventually, Shaka was overthrown. The Boers continued their advance northeastward during the so-called Great Trek in the mid-1830s. By 1865, the total white population of the area had risen to nearly 200,000 people.

The Boers' eastward migration was motivated in part by the British. During the Napoleonic Wars, the British had seized Capetown from the Dutch. After the wars, the British encouraged settlers to come to what they called Cape Colony. The British government

seemed to care more about the rights of the local African population than did the Boers. Many Boers saw white superiority as ordained by God. Disgusted with British policies, the Boers fled northward on the Great Trek to the region between the Orange and Vaal (VAWL) Rivers and north of the Vaal River. In these areas, the Boers formed their own independent republics—called the Orange Free State and the Transvaal. The Boers put much of the native population in these areas on reservations.

Hostilities between the British and the Boers continued. In 1877, the British governor of Cape Colony seized the Transvaal. However, a Boer revolt led the British government to recognize the Transvaal as the independent South African Republic. In the 1880s, British policy in South Africa was largely set by Cecil Rhodes. Rhodes had founded both diamond and gold

**Map 6.2   The Struggle for South Africa**

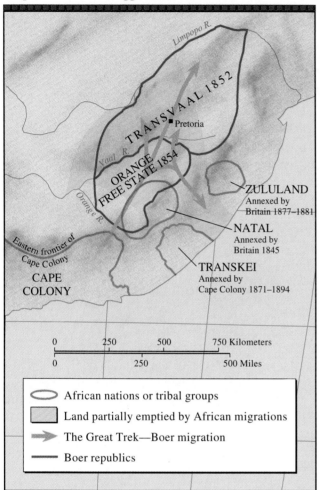

Limpopo R.

TRANSVAAL 1852

■ Pretoria

Vaal R.

ORANGE FREE STATE 1854

Orange R.

ZULULAND
Annexed by
Britain 1877–1881

NATAL
Annexed by
Britain 1845

Eastern frontier of
Cape Colony

CAPE
COLONY

TRANSKEI
Annexed by
Cape Colony 1871–1894

0   250   500   750 Kilometers

0   250   500 Miles

◯  African nations or tribal groups

▭  Land partially emptied by African migrations

➤  The Great Trek—Boer migration

―  Boer republics

companies that made him a fortune. He gained control of a territory north of the Transvaal, which he named Rhodesia after himself. He became its prime minister.

Rhodes was a great champion of British expansion. He said once, "If there be a God, I think what he would like me to do is to paint as much of Africa British red as possible." One of Rhodes's goals was to create a series of British colonies "from the Cape to Cairo"—all linked by a railroad. His ambitions, however, led to his downfall in 1896. The British government forced him to resign as prime minister of Rhodesia after he planned to overthrow the Boer government of the

South African Republic without British approval. Although the British government had hoped to avoid war with the Boers, it could not stop fanatics on both sides from starting a conflict that came to be known as the Boer War.

The Boer War dragged on from 1899 to 1902. Guerrilla resistance by the Boers was fierce. This angered the British. They responded by burning crops and herding more than 150,000 Boer women and children into detention camps, where lack of food caused 26,000 deaths. Eventually, the vastly larger British army won. British policy toward the defeated Boers was generous. In 1910, the British agreed to the creation of an independent Union of South Africa, which combined the old Cape Colony and the Boer republics. To appease the Boers, the British agreed that only whites would vote.

By 1914, Great Britain, France, Germany, Belgium, and Portugal had divided up Africa. Only Liberia and Ethiopia remained free states. Despite the talk about the "white man's burden," Africa had been conquered by European states determined to create colonial empires. Any native peoples who dared to resist (with the exception of the Ethiopians) were simply devastated by the superior military force of the Europeans (see "The Role of Science and Technology: The Machine Gun").

Furthermore, Europeans did not hesitate to deceive the natives in order to gain their way. One southern African king, Lo Bengula (LOE bun-GYOO-luh), informed Queen Victoria about how he had been cheated:

*Some time ago a party of men came to my country, the principal one appearing to be a man called Rudd. They asked me for a place to dig for gold, and said they would give me certain things for the right to do so. I told them to bring what they could give and I would show them what I would give. A document was written and presented to me for signature. I asked what it contained, and was told that in it were my words and the words of those men. I put my hand to it. About three months afterwards I heard from other sources that I had given by the document the right to all the minerals of my country.*[5]

**Map 6.3    Africa in 1914**

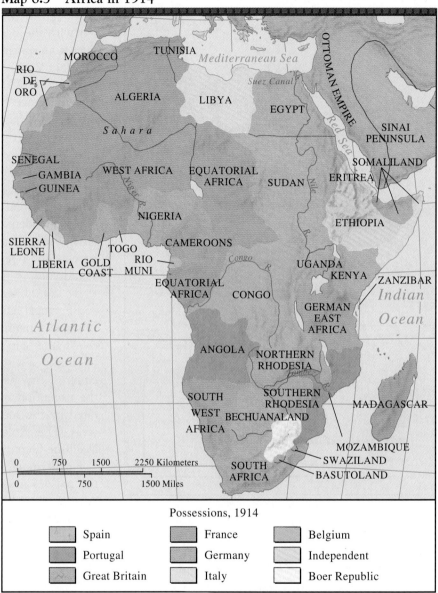

Possessions, 1914

- Spain
- Portugal
- Great Britain
- France
- Germany
- Italy
- Belgium
- Independent
- Boer Republic

## Colonialism in Africa

Except in isolated areas like the gold mines in the Transvaal and copper deposits in the Congo, European economic interests in Africa were limited. As a result, European interest in Africa declined once the continent had been conquered. Most European governments ruled their new territories with the least effort and expense possible. In many cases, this led to a form of indirect rule. The British especially followed this approach. Indirect rule meant relying on existing political elites and institutions. At first, in some areas the British simply asked a local ruler to accept British authority and to fly the British flag over official buildings.

The concept of indirect rule was introduced in the Islamic state of Sokoto, in northern Nigeria, in 1900.

# THE ROLE OF SCIENCE AND TECHNOLOGY
# The Machine Gun

The first effective quick-firing gun was invented in 1862 by an American, Richard Gatling. The Gatling gun was made with ten barrels and could fire six hundred shots a minute. This, and models like it, had to be operated by a hand crank.

In 1885, another American, Hiram Maxim, built a gun that used its own recoil energy to load and fire itself and to eject its own empty shells. This eliminated the need for a hand crank and created the first fully automatic machine gun. A soldier had only to hold the trigger, and the gun would keep firing until its ammunition was gone. The gun was supplied with ammunition by a mechanically fed canvas belt easily stored in a box. The belts could be changed rapidly. The gun weighed only forty pounds and could fire 650 rounds a minute.

▲ *Hiram Maxim invented this lightweight field gun that had a bulletproof shield. What features made this field gun preferable to field cannons?*

Of course, governments were quick to see the advantages of the Maxim machine gun. The British army was using it by 1891. From its beginning, the machine gun played an important role in the ability of Western armies to subdue peoples who were not yet armed with this weapon. At the Battle of Omdurman in 1898, when Sudanese tribespeople tried to stop a British expedition armed with the recently developed machine gun, the Sudanese were massacred. One observer noted: "It was not a battle but an execution. . . . The bodies were not in heaps—bodies hardly ever are; but they spread evenly over acres and acres. Some lay very composedly with their slippers placed under their heads for a last pillow; some knelt, cut short in the middle of a last prayer. Others were torn to pieces." The battle casualties at Omdurman tell the story: twenty-eight British deaths to eleven thousand Sudanese. The machine gun began a new era in deadly warfare.

1. What was revolutionary about the gun invented by Richard Gatling?

2. How did the machine gun affect the Western world's ability to dominate the non-Western world?

## CONNECTIONS
### TO OUR WORLD

**Boundaries and Tribal Rivalries in Africa**
Between 1870 and 1910, European states carved up the map of Africa. In drawing the boundaries that separated one colony from another (boundaries that often became the boundaries of the modern countries of Africa), Europeans paid no attention to the political divisions of the tribes of Africa. Europeans often divided a tribe between two colonies, or made two tribes that were hostile to each other, members of the same colony. Most colonies in Africa became collections of different tribes with little or no sense of national identity. This created a problem for many African states after they achieved independence. For example, Ibo tribespeople in the southeastern part of Nigeria became part of the new state of Nigeria. In 1967, they proclaimed a new state of Biafra, plunging Nigeria into civil war. In 1970, after the death of almost one million Ibos, Biafra capitulated. It remains part of Nigeria.

European powers also practiced policies of divide and conquer, as well as divide and rule. To conquer lands in Africa, European states often took advantage of tribal rivalries and allied with one tribe against another. To rule their African colonies, European states often set one tribe against another as a way of maintaining power. In Central Africa, the Belgians allowed the Tutsi to continue their domination of the Hutus as a way of controlling the area. In modern Rwanda, one of the states formed out of Belgian lands, the intense rivalry between Tutsis and Hutus has continued to this day. In 1994, a Hutu massacre of Tutsis in Rwanda led to the death of more than 500,000 Tutsis. Similar ethnic conflicts have occurred in Zimbabwe and Kenya.

At the central level, there was a British government under British officials. Local authority, however, was left in the hands of native chiefs. They were expected to maintain law and order and to collect taxes from the native population. Local customs were left as they had been. There was a dual legal system, with African laws for Africans and British laws for the British.

This system of indirect rule in Sokoto had one good feature: it did not disrupt local customs and institutions. However, it did have some unfortunate consequences. The system was basically a fraud, because British administrators made all major decisions. The native authorities served chiefly to enforce those decisions. Moreover, indirect rule kept the old African elite in power. Such a policy provided few opportunities for ambitious and talented young Africans from outside the old elite. Thus, British indirect rule sowed the seeds for class and tribal tensions, which erupted after independence came in the twentieth century.

The situation was somewhat different in East Africa, especially in Kenya. Kenya had a relatively large European population that had been attracted by the temperate climate in the central highlands. The local government had encouraged white settlers to come to the area as a way of promoting economic development. To attract Europeans, fertile farmlands in the central highlands were reserved for them. Less desirable lands were set aside for Africans. Soon, white settlers sought self-government. Unwilling to run the risk of provoking racial tensions with the African majority, the British agreed only to set up separate government offices for the European and African populations.

Most other European nations governed their African possessions through a form of direct rule. This was true in the French colonies. At the top was a French official, usually known as a governor-general. He was appointed from Paris and governed with the aid of a bureaucracy in the capital city of the colony. French commissioners were assigned to deal with local administrators. These administrators had to be able to speak French and could be sent to a new position to meet the needs of the central government.

Moreover, the French ideal was to assimilate the African subjects into French culture rather than preserve the native traditions. Africans were eligible to run for office and even serve in the French National Assembly in Paris. A few were appointed to high positions in the colonial administration.

## The Rise of Nationalism in Africa

As in Southeast Asia, in Africa a new class of leaders had emerged by the beginning of the twentieth century. Educated in colonial schools or even in the West, they were the first generation of Africans to know a great deal about the West. Some, like Kwame Nkrumah (KWAN-mee en KROO-muh) in the Gold Coast, even wrote in the language of their colonial masters.

On the one hand, the members of this "new class" admired Western culture and sometimes disliked the ways of their own countries. They were eager to introduce Western ideas and institutions into their own societies. On the other hand, many came to resent the foreigners and their arrogant contempt for colonial peoples. These intellectuals often resented the gap between theory and practice in colonial policy. Westerners had exalted democracy, equality, and political freedom but did not apply these values in the colonies. There were few democratic institutions. Colonial peoples could have only low-paying jobs in the colonial bureaucracy. Also feeding the resentment was the fact that the economic prosperity of the West was never brought to the colonies. To many Africans, colonialism meant the loss of their farmlands or terrible jobs on plantations or in sweatshops and factories run by foreigners.

Normally, middle-class Africans did not suffer as much as poor peasants or workers on plantations. However, members of the middle class also had complaints. They usually qualified only for menial jobs in the government or business. Even when employed, their salaries were lower than those of Europeans in similar jobs. The superiority of the Europeans over the natives was expressed in a variety of other ways. Segregated clubs, schools, and churches were set up as more European officials brought their wives and began to raise families. Europeans also had a habit of addressing natives by their first names or calling an adult male "boy."

Such conditions led many members of the new urban educated class to feel great confusion toward their colonial masters and the civilization the colonists represented. The educated Africans were willing to admit the superiority of many aspects of Western culture. However, these new intellectuals fiercely hated colonial rule and were determined to assert their own nationality and cultural destiny. Out of this mixture of hopes and resentments emerged the first stirrings of modern nationalism in Africa. During the first quarter of the twentieth century, in colonial societies across Africa, educated native peoples began to organize political parties and movements seeking the end of foreign rule.

## ❈ SECTION REVIEW ❈

1. **Locate:**
   (a) Algeria,   (b) Gold Coast,
   (c) South Africa,   (d) Sierra Leone,
   (e) Liberia,   (f) Nigeria,
   (g) Sudan,   (h) Sinai peninsula,
   (i) Sahara,
   (j) Tunisia,   (k) Morocco,
   (l) Libya,   (m) Congo River,
   (n) Zanzibar

2. **Identify:**
   (a) Muhammad Ali,   (b) Suez Canal,
   (c) Muhammad Ahmad,   (d) David Livingstone,
   (e) Henry Stanley,   (f) King Leopold II,
   (g) Zulus,   (h) Boers

3. **Recall:**
   (a) Why didn't the decline of the slave trade reduce the number of Europeans in West Africa?
   (b) What did Bismarck mean when he said, "All this colonial business is a sham, but we need it for the elections"?
   (c) What was the new class of Africans that developed in many African nations?
   (d) Why did many educated Africans come to hate colonial rule?

4. **Think Critically:** Why was the fact that no African delegates were invited to the Berlin Conference, which divided territories in Africa among European powers, important to the future of Africa?

## BRITISH RULE IN INDIA

In the course of the eighteenth century, British power in India had increased while that of the Mughal rulers had declined (see Chapter 2). The British East India Company, a trading company, was given the power by the British government to become actively involved in India's political and military affairs. The British were fortunate to have Sir Robert Clive as the chief representative of the East India Company in India. In 1757, a small British force put together by Clive defeated a much larger Mughal army. As a result, the British East India Company received from the Mughal emperor the right to collect taxes from lands around Calcutta. Less than ten years later, the British captured the Mughal emperor himself. During the next few decades, the British East India Company worked to consolidate its control over India, expanding from its base areas along the coast into the interior.

To rule India, the British East India Company had its own soldiers and forts. It had also hired Indian soldiers, known as **sepoys,** to protect the company's interests in the region. However, a growing Indian distrust of the British led to a revolt in 1857. The major immediate cause of the revolt was the spread of a rumor that

▼ *British punishment of the sepoys was quick and harsh. Why do you think so many troops have been called to witness this execution?*

**Map 6.4   India under British Rule, 1805–1937**

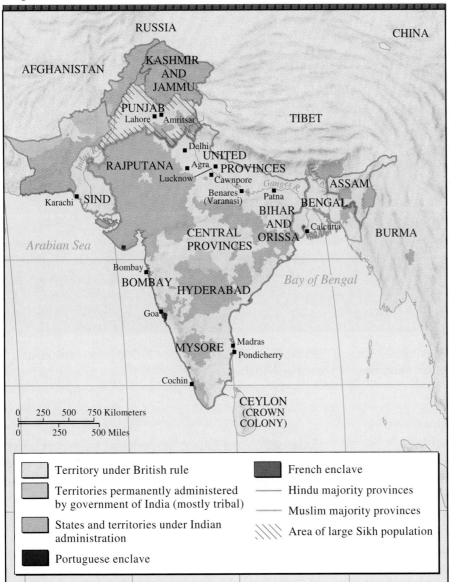

The revolt was known to the British as the Great Rebellion or the Sepoy Mutiny. (Indians call it the First War of Independence.) It quickly spread. Although Indian troops fought bravely and outnumbered the British by 240,000 to 40,000, they were poorly organized. Then, too, rivalries between Hindus and Muslims kept Indians from working together. Within a year, Indian troops loyal to the British and fresh British troops had crushed the revolt. Atrocities were terrible on both sides. At Cawnpore, Indian ruffians armed only with swords and knives massacred two hundred defenseless women and children in a building known as the House of the Ladies. When the British recaptured Cawnpore, they made their Indian captives lick the dried blood off the floor of the House of the Ladies before executing them.

As a result of the uprising, the British Parliament transferred the powers of the East India Company directly to the British government. In 1876, the title of Empress of India was bestowed upon Queen Victoria. The people of India were now her colonial subjects, and India became her "Jewel in the Crown." The British government ruled India directly. Parliament had overall supervision. Parliament's wishes were carried out by a British official known as a **viceroy,** who was assisted by a small British civil service. This civil service staff of about 3,500 officials ruled almost 300 million people, the largest colonial population in the world.

the British were issuing new bullets to their Indian troops that were greased with cow and pig fat. The cow was sacred to Hindus; the pig was taboo to Muslims. A group of sepoys at an army post near Delhi refused to load their rifles with the new bullets. When the British arrested them, the sepoys went on a rampage and killed fifty European men, women, and children.

▲ *The Victoria railway station in Bombay was designed to impress all who saw it. It also glorified the 25,000 miles of British railroads in India. Who do you think the railroads benefited more, the British or the Indians?*

## Colonial Rule in India

Not all the effects of British rule in India were bad. British rule brought order and stability to a society that had been badly divided by civil war. British control also led to a fairly honest and efficient government that in many ways operated to the benefit of the average Indian.

One of the benefits of the period was the new attention given to education. Through the efforts of the British administrator and historian Lord Macauley (muh-KAW-lee), a new school system was set up. Its goal was to train upper-class Indian children to serve as trained subordinates in the government and army. Macauley's attitude, however, was strongly pro-British. He argued that "all the historical information which has been collected from all the books written in the Sanskrit language is less valuable than what may be found in short textbooks used at preparatory schools in England." According to Macauley, it was better, then, to teach Indian elites about Western civilization "to form a class who may be interpreters between us and the millions whom we govern; a class of persons, Indian in blood and color, but English in taste, in opinions, in morals, and in intellect."[6] Classes were conducted in the rulers' English language. Moreover, the new system of education served only the elite, upper-class Indians. Ninety percent of the population remained illiterate.

Another benefit of British rule was that it brought an end to some of the more brutal aspects of Indian tradition. The practice of suttee (burning of widows) was outlawed, and widows were legally permitted to remarry. The British also tried to stamp out the religious fanatics (called *thugs*) who strangled their victims according to a ritual dedicated to their goddess Kali (KAW-lee). Railroads, the telegraph, and a postal service were introduced to India shortly after they appeared in Great Britain itself. The first rail network, from Calcutta to Delhi, was begun in 1839 and opened in 1853. By 1900, 25,000 miles of railroads crisscrossed India. Health and sanitation conditions also were improved.

The Indian people, however, paid a high price for the peace and stability brought by British rule. Perhaps the greatest cost was economic. British entrepreneurs and a small number of native Indians attached to the imperial system reaped financial benefits from British rule. However, imperialism brought hardship to millions of others in both the cities and the countryside. British manufactured goods destroyed native industries. Indian wealth was used to pay British officials and a large army. The introduction of British textiles put thousands of women out of work and severely damaged the Indian textile industry.

In rural areas, the British used the zamindar system (a zamindar was a local revenue collector). The British believed that this system would make it easier to collect taxes from the peasants. They also hoped that the zamindar system would create a new landed gentry that could become the foundation of imperial Indian rule, just as it had become the foundation of rule in Great Britain itself. However, the local gentry in India took advantage of their new authority. They increased taxes and forced the less fortunate peasants to become tenants or lose their land entirely. Peasant unrest grew. The British also encouraged many farmers to switch from growing food to growing cotton. As a consequence, food supplies could not keep up with the growing population. Between 1800 and 1900, thirty million Indians died of starvation.

The British also worked hard to keep modern industry out of India. Some limited industrialization took place, such as the manufacturing of textiles and jute (used in making rope). The first textile mill opened in 1856. Seventy years later, there were eighty mills in the city of Bombay alone. Nevertheless, by favoring British imports, the British government limited the development of new commercial and manufacturing operations in India itself.

Foreign rule also had a psychological effect on the Indian people. Many British colonial officials sincerely tried to improve the lot of the people in India. How-ever, British arrogance and contempt for native tradition cut deeply into the pride of many Indians. Those of high caste, who were used to a position of superior status in India, were especially disturbed. Educated Indians trained in the Anglo-Indian school system for a career in the civil service wondered where their true cultural loyalties lay. Even for the newly educated upper classes, who benefited the most from their Western-style educations, British rule was degrading. The best jobs and the best housing were reserved for Britons (see "Focus on Everyday Life: The British Official's Home in India"). Despite their education, the Indians were never considered equals of the British.

British racial attitudes were made quite clear by Lord Kitchener, one of Britain's foremost military commanders of India. He said, "It is this consciousness of the inherent superiority of the European which has won for us India. However well educated and clever a native may be, and however brave he may prove himself, I believe that no rank we can bestow on him would cause him to be considered an equal of the British officer."[7] The British also showed disrespect for India's cultural heritage. The Taj Mahal, for example, became a favorite site for English weddings and parties. Many partygoers even brought hammers to chip off souvenirs. British racial attitudes made it difficult for British rulers, no matter how well intentioned, ever to be ultimately accepted. These attitudes also led to the rise of an Indian nationalist movement.

## The Rise of an Indian Nationalist Movement

The first Indian nationalists were upper class and educated. Many of them were from urban areas, such as Bombay, Madras, and Calcutta. Some were trained in British law and were members of the civil service. At first, many preferred reform to revolution. They accepted the idea that India needed modernization before it could handle the problems of independence. Gopal Gokhale, an exponent of this view, was a moderate nationalist who hoped that he could convince the British to bring about needed reforms in Indian society. Gokhale and other like-minded reformers did have some

# FOCUS ON EVERYDAY LIFE
## The British Official's Home in India

During the time that India was a British colony, many British government officials spent a considerable amount of time there in fulfilling their administrative duties. Their families usually came with them during their tours of duty. British officials in India built comfortable bungalows, as they were called (the name comes from the Indian word *bangla*, meaning "Bengali"). Bungalows were elegant and spacious country houses. Many had colonnades (roofs supported by columns) that were open to breezes while protecting the inhabitants from the sun. Surrounding the bungalows were the cottages where dozens of Indian servants lived with their families.

The official's wife was the memsahib, or madam-sahib, queen of the bungalow. Her husband was the sahib—"the master." Wives of British officials generally brought their Victorian lifestyles and many of the furnishings that went with them to their new homes in India. The memsahib was expected to oversee the running of the household on a daily basis. At the beginning of each day, she assigned duties to all the servants. For example, she fixed the menu for the day with the cook. In the evening, the colonial official's wife was expected to entertain. Supper parties with other British families were the usual form of entertainment.

Many British officials had a high standard of living and were expected to have a large number of servants. One woman wrote in 1882, "It is one of the social duties of Indian life that you must keep three servants to do the work of one." A

▲ *This view of an English family enjoying an afternoon together accurately reflects the number of servants assigned to British families during colonial times. However, because children were schooled in England and husbands were often away on official business, family times such as these were infrequent.*

well-to-do family had at least twenty-five servants; even bachelors had at least a dozen. Indians served as cooks, maids, butlers, gardeners, tailors, and nursemaids for the children. All household servants wore uniforms—usually white with bands on their turbans—and went barefoot in the house.

1. What were the responsibilities of the wife of a British officer in India?

2. What do you learn about British-Indian social relations from this feature?

▲ *In spite of British attitudes toward India, it was not uncommon for the English to adopt some local customs. In this painting, an Englishman lives like an Indian prince with his harem, servants, and hookah, an Indian water pipe.*

effect. In the 1880s, the government launched a series of reforms introducing a measure of self-government for the first time. All too often, however, such efforts were sabotaged by local British officials.

The slow pace of reform convinced many Indian nationalists that relying on British goodwill was futile. In 1885, a small group of Indians met in Bombay to form the Indian National Congress (INC). They hoped to speak for all India, but most were high-caste English-trained Hindus. Members of the INC did not demand immediate independence. They accepted the need for reforms to end traditional abuses, such as child marriage. At the same time, they called for an Indian share in the governing process, as well as more spend-

ing on economic development and less on military campaigns along the frontier.

The British responded with a few concessions. However, change was slow. As members of the INC became frustrated, radical leaders, such as Balwantrao Tilak, openly criticized the British. Tilak's activities split the INC between moderates and radicals. He and his followers formed the New Party, which called for the use of terrorism and violence to achieve national independence. Eventually, the British jailed Tilak.

The INC also split over religious differences. The goal of the INC was to seek independence for all Indians, regardless of class or religious background. However, many of its leaders were Hindu and reflected

Hindu concerns. By the first decade of the twentieth century, Muslims began to call for the creation of a separate Muslim League to represent the interests of the millions of Muslims in Indian society.

In 1913, the return of a young Hindu lawyer from South Africa to become active in the INC brought new life to India's struggle for independence. Mohandas Gandhi (GAWN-dee) was born in 1869 in Gujarat (goo-ja-RAWT), in western India, the son of a government minister. In the late nineteenth century, he studied in London and became a lawyer. In 1893, he went to South Africa to work in a law firm serving Indian workers there. He soon became aware of the racial prejudice and exploitation experienced by Indians living in South Africa. He tried to organize them to protect their living conditions.

On his return home to India, Gandhi became active in the independence movement. Using his experience in South Africa, he set up a movement based on nonviolent resistance. Its aim was to force the British to improve the lot of the poor and grant independence to India. Gandhi had two goals: to convert the British to his own views and to strengthen the unity of all Indians. When the British tried to suppress Indian calls for independence, Gandhi called on his followers to refuse to obey British regulations. He began to manufacture his own clothes and dressed in a simple dhoti (DOTE-ee) (loincloth) made of coarse homespun cotton. He adopted the spinning wheel as a symbol of India's resistance to imports of British textiles. Ultimately, as we shall see in Chapter 9, Gandhi's movement would lead to Indian independence.

▲ Mohandas Gandhi practiced law in South Africa in the late 1800s. Then, at the age of forty-seven he made the decision to return to India, his native country, to champion the cause of the poor. Ultimately his leadership and dedication to the betterment of the Indian people were major factors in achieving independence from Great Britain.

## Culture and Nationalism in Colonial India

The love-hate tension that arose from British domination led to a cultural, as well as a political, awakening of India. The cultural revival began in the early nineteenth century with the creation of a British college in Calcutta. A local publishing house was opened. It issued textbooks on a variety of subjects, including the sciences, Sanskrit, and Western literature. The publisher also printed grammars and dictionaries in the various Indian languages. This revival soon spread to other regions of India. It led to a search for modern literary expression, as well as for a new national identity. Soon Indian novelists and poets were writing historical romances and epics. Some wrote in English, but most were uncomfortable with a borrowed colonial language. They preferred to use their own regional tongues.

The most illustrious Indian author was Rabindranath Tagore (ru-BIN-dru-NAWT tu GORE). A great poet, novelist, short-story writer, and dramatist, Tagore was also a social reformer, spiritual leader, educator, philosopher, singer, painter, and international spokesperson for the moral concerns of his age. He liked to invite the great thinkers of the time to his country estate where he set up a school that became an international university.

Tagore's life mission was to promote pride in a national Indian consciousness in the face of British domination. He wrote a widely read novel in which he portrayed the love-hate relationship of India toward its colonial mentor. The novel depicted a country that admired and imitated the British model while also ago-

# OUR LITERARY HERITAGE

## The Poetry of Tagore

*Rabindranath Tagore considered himself a poet above all. He wrote in Bengali (the language of the Indian state of Bengal) until the age of fifty and then translated some of his verse into English in 1912. Tagore won an international audience and was awarded the Nobel Prize for literature in 1913. The following lines were taken from Gitanjali: Song Offerings, which he wrote in Bengali but then translated into English.*

**Rabindranath Tagore,**
***Gitanjali: Song Offerings***

*Where the mind is without fear
    and the head is held high;
Where knowledge is free;
Where the world has not been
    broken up into fragments
    by narrow domestic walls;*

▲ *This photo of Rabindranath Tagore shows an inner intensity that is reflected in his poetry.*

*Where words come out from
    the depth of truth;
Where tireless striving stretches
    its arms toward perfection;
Where the clear stream of
    reason has not lost its ways
    into the dreary desert sand
    of dead habit;
Where the mind is led forward
    by thee into ever-widening
    thought and action—
Into that heaven of freedom,
    my Father, let my country
    awake.*

1. About what country did Tagore write? How do you know?

2. Put into your own words the line, "Where the clear stream of reason has not lost its ways into the dreary desert sand of dead habit."

nizing over how it could establish a modern identity separate from that of Great Britain.

Tagore, however, was more than an Indian nationalist. His life's work was one long prayer for human dignity, world peace, and the mutual understanding and union of East and West. As he once said, "It is my conviction that my countrymen will truly gain their India by fighting against the education that teaches them that a country is greater than the ideals of humanity." In his poetry as well, Tagore spoke of lofty ideals (see "Our Literary Heritage: The Poetry of Tagore").

## ❀ SECTION REVIEW ❀

1. **Locate:**
   (*a*) Delhi,   (*b*) Bombay,   (*c*) Madras,
   (*d*) Calcutta

2. **Define:**
   (*a*) sepoys,   (*b*) viceroy

3. **Identify:**
   (*a*) British East India Tea Company,

(*b*) Sepoy Mutiny,    (*c*) Gopal Gokhale,
(*d*) Balwantrao Tilak,    (*e*) Mohandas Gandhi,
(*f*) Rabindranath Tagore

4. **Recall:**
   (*a*) What positive effects may have resulted for the native population from the British rule of India?
   (*b*) What economic costs did the Indian people pay for the British occupation?
   (*c*) What objectives did the Indian National Congress (INC) have when it started to meet in Bombay in 1885?

5. **Think Critically:** Why do you think Gandhi chose to dress in a simple dhoti and adopt the spinning wheel as a symbol of resistance to British rule?

## NATION BUILDING AND IMPERIALISM IN LATIN AMERICA

The force of nationalism also affected the Americas. In both North America and Latin America, nation building became a prominent process. The Spanish and Portuguese colonial empires in Latin America had been part of the old monarchical structure of Europe for centuries. When that structure was challenged by the Napoleonic Wars, Latin America, too, experienced change.

### Nationalistic Revolts in Latin America

By the end of the eighteenth century, the new political ideals stemming from the successful revolution in North America against the British (see Chapter 3) were beginning to influence the **creole elites** (locally born descendants of the Europeans who became permanent inhabitants of Latin America). The principles of the equality of all people in the eyes of the law, free trade, and a free press proved very attractive. The Latin American elites, joined by a growing class of merchants, especially disliked the domination of their trade by Spain and Portugal.

The creole elites soon began to use their new ideas to denounce the rule of the Spanish and Portuguese monarchs and the **peninsulars** (Spanish and Portuguese officials who resided temporarily in Latin America for political and economic gain and then returned to their mother countries). The creole elites resented the peninsulars, who dominated Latin America and drained the Americas of their wealth.

At the beginning of the nineteenth century, Napoleon's wars provided the creoles an opportunity for change. When Napoleon overthrew the monarchies of Spain and Portugal, the authority of the Spaniards and Portuguese in their colonial empires was severely weakened. Between 1807 and 1825, a series of revolts enabled most of Latin America to become independent.

An unusual revolution came before the main independence movements. Saint-Domingue (san-doe-MAWNG)—the western third of the island of Hispaniola—was a French sugar colony. Led by François Dominique Toussaint L'Ouverture (too-SAN loo-vur-TOOR) (see "Biography: Toussaint L'Ouverture—Leader of a Slave Revolt"), more than 100,000 black slaves rose in revolt and seized control of all of Hispaniola. An army sent by Napoleon captured Toussaint L'Ouverture. However, the French soldiers, who were weakened by yellow fever, soon fell to the rebel forces. On January 1, 1804, the western part of Hispaniola, now called Haiti, announced its freedom and became the first independent state in Latin America.

Beginning in 1810, Mexico, too, experienced a revolt. It was fueled at first by the desire of the creole elites to overthrow the rule of the peninsulars. The first real hero of Mexican independence was Miguel Hidalgo y Costilla, a parish priest in a small village about 100 miles from Mexico City. Hidalgo had studied the French Revolution and roused the local Indians and mestizos (the offspring of Europeans and native American Indians) to free themselves from the Spanish: "My children, this day comes to us as a new dispensation. Are you ready to receive it? Will you be free? Will you make the effort to recover from the hated Spaniards the lands stolen from your forefathers 300 years ago?"[8] On September 16, 1810, a crowd of Indians and mestizos, armed with clubs, machetes, and a few guns, quickly formed a mob army to attack the Spaniards. Hidalgo was not a good organizer,

# BIOGRAPHY

## Toussaint L'Ouverture—Leader of a Slave Revolt

François Dominique Toussaint L'Ouverture, the grandson of an African king, was born a slave in Saint-Domingue in 1746. Educated by his godfather, Toussaint was able to amass a small private fortune through his own talents and the generosity of his French master. In 1791, black slaves in Saint-Domingue revolted, inspired by news of the French Revolution. Toussaint became their leader. For years, Toussaint and his ragtag army struck at the French. By 1801, after his army had come to control Saint-Domingue, Toussaint assumed the role of ruler and issued a constitution that freed all slaves.

Napoleon Bonaparte refused to accept Toussaint's control of France's richest colony, however. He sent a French army of 23,000 men under General Leclerc (leh-KLAIR), his brother-in-law, to crush the rebellion. Although yellow fever took its toll on the French army, that army's superior size and arms enabled it to gain the upper hand nevertheless. Toussaint was tricked into surrendering in 1802 because of the following promise by Leclerc: "You will not find a more sincere friend than myself." What a friend he was! Toussaint was arrested, put in chains, and shipped to France, where he died a year later in an obscure dungeon. Haiti, however, became free when Toussaint's lieutenants drove out the French forces in 1804. Toussaint L'Ouverture had been leader of the "only successful slave revolt in history." The romantic English poet William Wordsworth remembered him with a poem:

> Toussaint, the most unhappy man of men! . . .
> Though fallen thyself, never to rise again,

▲ *Toussaint L'Ouverture led this successful revolt against the better equipped French troops.*

> *Live, and take comfort. Thou hast left behind*
> *Powers that will work for thee; air, earth, and*
>     *skies;*
> *There's not a breathing of the common wind*
> *That will forget thee; thou hast great allies;*
> *Thy friends are exultations, agonies,*
> *And love, and man's unconquerable mind. (To*
>     *Toussaint L'Ouverture, 1802)*

1. For what is Toussaint L'Ouverture remembered?

2. Do you think L'Ouverture knew he was successful? Why or why not?

**Map 6.5    Latin America in the First Half of the Nineteenth Century**

however, and his forces were soon crushed. A military court sentenced Hidalgo to death, but his memory lived on. In fact, September 16, the first day of the uprising, is Mexico's Independence Day.

The participation of Indians and mestizos in Mexico's revolt against Spanish control frightened both creoles and peninsulars there. Afraid of the masses, they cooperated in defeating the popular revolutionary forces. The conservative elites—both creoles and peninsulars—then decided to overthrow Spanish rule as a way of preserving their own power. They selected a creole military leader, Augustín de Iturbide (ee-tur-BEE-they), as their leader and the first emperor of Mexico in 1821.

Elsewhere in Latin America, independence movements were the work of elites—primarily creoles—who

◄ *Théodore Géricault painted this heroic image of José de San Martín, one of the most famous of the Latin American liberators. Here San Martín leads his troops at the battle of Chacabuco, Chile.*

ter struggle for independence in Venezuela and then went on to liberate New Granada (Colombia) and Ecuador. In January 1817, San Martín led his forces over the high Andes Mountains, an amazing feat in itself. Two-thirds of the pack mules and horses died during the difficult journey. The soldiers suffered from lack of oxygen and severe cold while crossing mountain passes that were more than two miles above sea level. The arrival of San Martín's forces in Chile completely surprised the Spaniards, who were then badly defeated at the Battle of Chacabuco (CHAW-kaw-VOO-koe) on February 12, 1817. In 1821, San Martín moved on to Lima, Peru, the center of Spanish authority.

Convinced that he was unable to complete the liberation of Peru, San Martín welcomed the arrival of Bolívar and his forces. The "Liberator of Venezuela" took on the task of crushing the last significant Spanish army at Ayacucho on December 9, 1824. By then, Peru, Uruguay, Paraguay, Colombia, Venezuela, Argentina, Bolivia, and Chile had all become free states. In 1823, the Central American states had become independent and in 1838 and 1839 divided into five republics (Guatemala, El Salvador, Honduras, Costa Rica, and Nicaragua). Earlier, in 1822, the prince regent of Brazil had declared Brazil's independence from Portugal.

In the early 1820s, only one major threat remained to the newly won independence of the Latin American states. Members of the Concert of Europe favored the use of troops to restore Spanish control in Latin America. The British, who wished to trade with Latin America, disagreed and proposed joint action with the United States against any European moves in Latin America. Distrustful of British motives, U.S. president

overthrew Spanish rule and created new governments that they could dominate. The masses of people—Indians, blacks, mestizos, and mulattoes—gained little from the revolts.

José (hoe-ZAE) de San Martín of Argentina, a member of the creole elite, believed that the Spaniards must be removed from all of South America if any nation was to be free. San Martín and Simón Bolívar (see-MONE BAW-lee-VAR) (another member of the creole elite) were hailed as the "Liberators of South America."

By 1810, the forces of San Martín had freed Argentina from Spanish authority. Bolívar led the bit-

James Monroe acted alone in 1823. He guaranteed the independence of the new Latin American nations and warned against any European intervention in the New World in the famous Monroe Doctrine. Actually more important to Latin American independence than American words was Britain's navy. All of the continental powers were afraid of British naval power, which stood between Latin America and any European invasion force.

## The Difficulties of Nation Building in Latin America

The new Latin American nations, most of which began their existence as republics, faced a number of serious problems between 1830 and 1870. The wars for independence had resulted in a staggering loss of people, property, and livestock. The new nations, unsure of their precise boundaries, went to war with one another to settle border disputes. Poor roads, a lack of railroads, thick jungles, and mountains made communication, transportation, and national unity difficult.

Severe struggles between church and state were also common in the new nations. The Catholic Church had enormous landholdings in Latin America and exercised great power there. After independence, church officials often took positions in the new governments and wielded much influence. Throughout Latin America, a division arose between liberals, who wished to restrict the political powers of the church, and conservatives, who hoped to maintain all of the church's privileges. In Mexico, this division even led to civil war, the bloody War of Reform fought between 1858 and 1861.

The new nations of Latin America began with republican governments, but they had had no experience in ruling themselves. Soon after independence, strong leaders known as **caudillos** came into power. Caudillos ruled chiefly by military force and were usually supported by the landed elites. Many kept the new national states together. Sometimes they were also modernizers who built roads and canals, ports, and schools. Others, however, were destructive. Antonio

López y Santa Anna, for example, ruled Mexico from 1829 to 1855. He misused state funds, halted reforms, created chaos, and helped lose one-third of Mexico's territory to the United States. Other caudillos were supported by the masses, became extremely popular, and served as instruments for radical change. Juan Manuel de Rosas, for example, who led Argentina from 1829 to 1852, became very popular by favoring Argentine interests against foreigners. In general, the system of caudillos added to the instability in Latin America. The caudillo's authority depended on his personal power. When he died or lost power, civil wars for control of the country often erupted.

Political independence brought economic independence, but old patterns were quickly reestablished. Instead of Spain and Portugal, Great Britain now dominated the Latin American economy. British merchants moved into Latin America in large numbers, and British investors poured in funds. Old trade patterns soon reemerged. Latin America continued to serve as a source of raw materials and foodstuffs for the industrializing nations of Europe and the United States. Exports included wheat, tobacco, wool, sugar, coffee, and hides. At the same time, finished consumer goods, especially textiles, were imported and caused a decline in industrial production in Latin America. The emphasis on exporting raw materials and importing finished products ensured the ongoing domination of the Latin American economy by foreigners.

A fundamental, underlying problem for all of the new Latin American nations was the domination of society by the landed elites. Large estates remained a way of life in Latin America. By 1848, for example, the Sánchez Navarro family in Mexico possessed seventeen estates made up of sixteen million acres. Estates were often so large that they could not be farmed efficiently.

Land remained the basis of wealth, social prestige, and political power throughout the nineteenth century. Landed elites ran governments, controlled courts, and kept a system of inexpensive labor. These landowners made enormous profits growing single, specialized crops for export, such as coffee. The masses, unable to have land to grow basic food crops, experienced dire poverty.

## Change and Tradition in Latin America

After 1870, Latin America began an age of prosperity based to a large extent on the export of a few basic items, such as wheat and beef from Argentina, coffee from Brazil, coffee and bananas from Central America, and sugar and silver from Peru. These foodstuffs and raw materials were largely exchanged for finished goods—textiles, machines, and luxury items—from Europe and the United States. After 1900, Latin Americans also increased their own industrialization, especially by building textile, food-processing, and construction material factories.

Nevertheless, the growth of the Latin American economy came mostly from the export of raw materials. This simply added to the growing dependency of Latin America on the nations of the West. Old patterns still largely prevailed in society. Rural elites dominated their estates and their workers. Slavery had been abolished by 1888, but former slaves and their descendants were at the bottom of society. The Indians remained poverty stricken, and Latin America remained economically dependent on foreign investment. Despite its economic growth, Latin America was still an underdeveloped region of the world. Latin American countries remained economic colonies of Western nations.

One result of the prosperity that came from increased exports was growth in the middle sectors of Latin American society—lawyers, merchants, shopkeepers, businesspeople, schoolteachers, professors, bureaucrats, and military officers. These middle sectors made up only 5 to 10 percent of the population, hardly enough in numbers to make up a true middle class. Nevertheless, after 1900, the middle sectors of society continued to expand. Regardless of the country in which they lived, they shared some common characteristics. They lived in the cities; sought education and decent incomes; and saw the United States as a model, especially in regard to industrialization. The middle sectors in Latin America sought liberal reform, not revolution. Once they had the right to vote, they generally sided with the landholding elites.

As Latin American export economies boomed, the working class grew. So too did the labor unions, especially after 1914. Radical unions often advocated the use of the general strike as an instrument for change. By and large, the governing elites were able to stifle the political influence of the working class by limiting their right to vote.

As in Europe and the United States, in Latin America industrialization led to urbanization. Buenos Aires (called "the Paris of South America") had 750,000 inhabitants by 1900 and 2 million by 1914. By that time, 53 percent of Argentina's population lived in cities.

## Political Change in Latin America

After 1870, large landowners in Latin America began to take a more direct interest in national politics and even in governing. In Argentina and Chile, for example, landholding elites controlled the governments. They wrote constitutions similar to those of the United States and Europe, but they were careful to keep their power by limiting voting rights.

In some countries, large landowners supported dictators who looked out for the interests of the ruling elite. Porfirio Díaz (DEE-az), who ruled Mexico from 1876 to 1910, created a conservative, centralized government with the support of the army, foreign capitalists, large landowners, and the Catholic Church. All these groups benefited from their alliance. However, there were forces for change in Mexico that led to a revolution in 1910.

During Díaz's dictatorial reign, the real wages of workers had declined. Moreover, 95 percent of the rural population owned no land, whereas about 1,000 families owned almost all of Mexico. When a liberal landowner, Francesco Madero, forced Díaz from power, he opened the door to a wider revolution. Madero's ineffectiveness created a demand for agrarian reform led by Emiliano Zapata. He aroused the masses of landless peasants and began to seize the estates of the wealthy landholders.

Between 1910 and 1920, the revolution caused untold damage to the Mexican economy. Finally, a new constitution enacted in 1917 set up a strong presidency, created land-reform policies, established limits on foreign investors, and set an agenda to help the

▲ *Emiliano Zapata, who led a revolt against wealthy landowners in southern Mexico, is shown in this photograph.*

workers. The revolution also led to an outpouring of patriotism. Intellectuals and artists sought to capture what was unique about Mexico with special emphasis on its Indian past.

By this time, a new power had begun to exert influence over Latin America. By 1900, the United States, which had emerged as a world power, began to interfere in the affairs of its southern neighbors. As a result of the Spanish-American War (1898), Cuba became a U.S. protectorate, and Puerto Rico was annexed outright to the United States. In 1903, the United States supported a rebellion that enabled Panama to separate itself from Colombia and establish a new nation. In return, the United States was granted control of a ten-mile-wide canal zone. There the United States built the Panama Canal, which was opened in 1914.

American investments in Latin America soon followed, as did American resolve to protect those invest-

ments. Between 1898 and 1934, American military forces were sent to Cuba, Mexico, Guatemala, Honduras, Nicaragua, Panama, Colombia, Haiti, and the Dominican Republic to protect American interests. Some expeditions remained for many years. U.S. Marines were in Haiti from 1915 to 1934, and Nicaragua was occupied from 1909 to 1933. Increasing numbers of Latin Americans began to resent this interference from the "big bully" to the north.

## ❀ SECTION REVIEW ❀

1. **Locate:**
   (*a*) Haiti,   (*b*) Chile,   (*c*) Peru,
   (*d*) Uruguay,   (*e*) Paraguay,   (*f*) Colombia,
   (*g*) Venezuela,   (*h*) Argentina,   (*i*) Bolivia,
   (*j*) Brazil

2. **Define:**
   (*a*) creole elites,   (*b*) peninsulars,
   (*c*) caudillos

3. **Identify:**
   (*a*) Toussaint L'Ouverture,   (*b*) Miguel Hidalgo y Costilla,   (*c*) Augustín de Iturbide,   (*d*) José de San Martín,   (*e*) Monroe Doctrine,
   (*f*) Santa Anna

4. **Recall:**
   (*a*) How did the Napoleonic wars provide an opportunity for change in Latin America?
   (*b*) Why did the British oppose the return of European domination to Latin America?
   (*c*) What was the cause of the War of Reform in Mexico that was fought between 1858 and 1861?
   (*d*) Why didn't eliminating European domination from Latin America bring about significant economic or social change?

5. **Think Critically:**
   (*a*) Why did the ownership of large plots of land prevent economic development and social progress in Latin America?
   (*b*) How may the construction of the Panama Canal represent both positive and negative aspects of American involvement in Latin America?

## Conclusion

By 1914, virtually all of Africa and a good part of South and Southeast Asia were under some form of colonial rule. In Latin America, colonies of Spain and Portugal had won their independence at the beginning of the nineteenth century, only to become economic colonies of other Western nations during the course of the century. With the coming of the age of imperialism, a world economy was finally established. The domination of Western civilization over much of the world seemed to be complete.

Defenders of colonialism argue that the system was a necessary, if sometimes painful, stage in the evolution of human societies. They believe that Western imperialism was ultimately beneficial to colonial powers and subjects alike, because it created the conditions for world economic development and the spread of democratic institutions. Critics of colonialism, however, charge that the Western colonial powers were driven by a lust for profits. To them, the Western civilizing mission was simply an excuse to hide their greed. Critics of colonialism also reject the notion that imperialism played a helpful role in hastening the adjustment of traditional societies to the demands of industrial civilization. Two recent Western critics of imperialism have argued as follows: "Why is Africa (or for that matter Latin America and much of Asia) so poor? . . . The answer is very brief: we have made it poor."[9] Between these two extreme positions, where does the truth lie?

In one area of Asia, the spreading tide of imperialism did not result in formal Western colonial control. In East Asia, the societies of China and Japan were buffeted by the winds of Western expansionism during the nineteenth century but managed to resist foreign conquest. In the next chapter, we will see how these societies did this and how they fared in their encounter with the West.

## Notes

1. Quoted in G. H. Nadel and P. Curtis, eds., *Imperialism and Colonialism* (New York, 1964), p. 94.
2. Karl Pearson, *National Life from the Standpoint of Science* (London, 1905), p. 184.
3. Quoted in C. M. Turnbull, *A History of Singapore, 1819–1975* (Kuala Lumpur, Malaysia, 1977), p. 19.
4. Quoted in Ruth Bartlett, ed., *The Record of American Diplomacy: Documents and Readings in the History of American Foreign Relations* (New York, 1952), p. 385.
5. Quoted in Louis L. Snyder, ed., *The Imperialism Reader* (Princeton, N.J., 1962), p. 220.
6. Quoted in Stanley Wolpert, *A New History of India* (New York, 1977), p. 215.
7. Quoted in K. M. Panikkar, *Asia and Western Dominance* (London, 1959), p. 116.
8. Quoted in Hubert Herring, *A History of Latin America* (New York, 1961), p. 255.
9. Quoted in Tony Smith, *The Pattern of Imperialism: The United States, Great Britain, and the Late-Industrial World since 1815* (Cambridge, 1981), p. 81.

# CHAPTER 6 REVIEW

## USING KEY TERMS

1. The method of colonial government in which local rulers maintain their authority is called _____.

2. Indian soldiers in the service of the East India Company were called _____.

3. The establishment of overseas colonies is called _____.

4. Portuguese and Spanish officials who resided temporarily in Latin America and then returned home were called _____.

5. Control of a colony by the mother country is called _____.

6. A _____ is a political unit that depends on another state for its protection, such as Cambodia in its relationship with France in the 1880s.

7. After independence, strong leaders in Latin America, called _____, gained power and ruled by military force.

8. The _____ was the British representative of Parliament in India, charged with ruling nearly 300 million people.

9. _____ in Latin America denounced the rule of Spanish and Portuguese monarchs.

8. Which African state successfully defeated a European attempt to colonize it in the late nineteenth century?

9. Who came to dominate the East African slave trade? Where was this trade based? Who led the struggle to end this trade?

10. Why did the Boers go on the Great Trek?

11. By 1914, which countries had divided up Africa?

12. What event led to direct imperial control of India?

13. What benefits did British rule bring to India? What harm did British rule bring to India?

14. What were Mohandas Gandhi's goals?

15. Who was Toussaint L'Ouverture? Why was the Haitian Revolution unique?

16. What countries were liberated by Simón Bolívar?

17. What countries were liberated by José de San Martín?

18. What European nation provided important support for the new Latin American republics? Why did it do so?

19. Name two nineteenth-century caudillos and the nations they governed.

20. To what Latin American countries did the United States send troops to protect its interests?

## REVIEWING THE FACTS

1. Why did European states wish to establish colonies?

2. What colony was established by the British on the Malay Peninsula to act as a trading center?

3. Who was Emilio Aguinaldo?

4. What two African nations were founded as refuges for former slaves?

5. Who oversaw the digging of the Suez Canal?

6. Who was the Mahdi? Who was General Charles Gordon?

7. What happened at Fashoda?

## THINKING CRITICALLY

1. Why is the new imperialism called new?

2. What are the advantages and disadvantages of indirect rule of colonies? Use specific examples in your answer.

3. Were French and British education programs in their colonies consistent or inconsistent with moral idealism?

4. Why did the British come to regard control of the Suez Canal as vital to their national interest?

5. Why was David Livingstone significant for the European colonization of Africa?

6. What was Bismarck's purpose for the Berlin Conference of 1884, and how did he try to achieve

that purpose? How did the conference demonstrate European chauvinism?

7. What were Cecil Rhodes's goals in southern Africa? How did he go about achieving those goals? Do you regard him as successful or unsuccessful?

8. What can we infer about British rule in India from the major cause of the Sepoy Mutiny?

9. What led to the War of Reform in Mexico?

10. Explain the significance of Porfirio Díaz, Francisco Madero, and Emiliano Zapata.

## APPLYING SOCIAL STUDIES SKILLS

1. **Government:** What was the role and function of native elites given a European education in India, Africa, Asia, and Latin America?

2. **Government:** Why did Napoleon Bonaparte's victory over Spain lead to Wars of Liberation in South America?

3. **Government:** What is the weakness of caudillos as a system of government?

4. **Economics:** Compare the Latin American economy under Spanish rule with the Latin American economy as it evolved in the nineteenth century. Could the nineteenth century economy be accurately described as neocolonialism?

5. **Sociology:** Compare the role of landed elites in Latin America under Spanish rule with their role in the young republics of the nineteenth century? What has changed? What has remained the same?

## MAKING TIME AND PLACE CONNECTIONS

1. Watch either the movie *Khartoum* (starring Charleton Heston and Lawrence Olivier), or *Zulu* (starring Stanley Baker and Michael Caine). Do you think the film accurately portrays historical events? What is the most striking scene of the

movie? What message (if any) does the movie convey?

2. What do Kwame Nkrumah, Mohandas Gandhi, and Simón Bolivar have in common?

3. The Indian National Congress was composed mostly of high-caste, English-trained Hindus. Does this fact support or undermine the opinion of a French official in Indochina that educating the natives meant "one rebel more"?

4. Simón Bolivar is considered to be the George Washington of South America. Do you think this is a fair comparison? Why? Which man had a more difficult task? Which man was more successful?

5. Why are leaders of recent insurrections in southern Mexico called Zapatistas?

## BECOMING AN HISTORIAN

1. **Comparing and Contrasting:** Go back to Unit One and review European imperialism from 1492 to 1750. Construct a table comparing imperialism with the new imperialism of 1850–1914. Include the following comparisons: (1) Time period of the imperialism, (2) areas colonized and by whom, (3) purpose for colonies, (4) internal conditions permitting imperialist expansion, (5) role of technology in permitting expansion, (6) direct or indirect rule, and (7) reasons the imperialism came to an end.

2. **Primary and Secondary Sources:** Examine the speech by Albert J. Beveridge on p. 204. Where does he reveal moral idealism? Where does he reveal a desire for profit? Make a table classifying each sentence as "Fact," "Opinion," or "Uncertain." Remember that a fact is information that can be verified as true or untrue (even incorrect facts are still facts). An opinion is an evaluation, impression, or estimation that is open to dispute (an opinion may be true, it simply cannot be verified).

# BLACK GUNS IN THE PACIFIC:

**7**

Like the countries of South Asia, Southeast Asia, and Africa, the nations of East Asia faced a growing challenge from the power of the West in the nineteenth century. In East Asia, too, Westerners used their military superiority to pursue their goals. In 1860, for example, Great Britain and France decided to retaliate against Chinese efforts to restrict their activities. In July, an Anglo-French force arrived on the outskirts of Beijing, where it encountered the Summer Palace of the Chinese emperors. The soldiers were astounded by the riches they beheld and could not resist the desire to plunder. Beginning on October 6, British and French troops moved through the palace. They looted anything of value and smashed what they could not cart away. One British observer wrote, "You would see several officers and men of all ranks with their heads and hands brushing and knocking together in the same box." In another room, he said, "a scramble was going on over a collection of handsome state robes . . . others would be amusing themselves by taking shots at chandeliers." Lord Elgin, leader of the British forces in China, soon restored order. After the Chinese murdered twenty European hostages, however, Lord Elgin ordered the Summer Palace to be burned. Thoroughly intimidated, the Chinese government agreed to Western demands.

The events of 1860 were part of a regular pattern in East Asia in the nineteenth century. Backed by European guns, European merchants and missionaries pressed for the right to carry out their activities in China and Japan. The Chinese and Japanese resisted but were eventually forced to open their doors to the foreigners. Unlike other Asian societies, however, both Japan and China were able to maintain their national independence against the Western onslaught. Japan reacted quickly to the challenge of the West by adopting Western institutions and itself becoming an imperialist power. China, in contrast, fought the Western imperialist influence, which eventually destroyed the Manchu dynasty.

▲ *This detail from the roof of the Summer Palace in Beijing, China, shows the intricate carvings that adorn the palace walls. Why do you think the dragon head is predominant?*

# EAST ASIA IN AN AGE OF IMPERIALISM

## (1800 TO 1914)

### ERA OF EUROPEAN DOMINANCE

| 1800 | IMPERIALISM IN EAST ASIA | 1914 |
| 1800 | | 1914 |

## QUESTIONS TO GUIDE YOUR READING

1. Why did Manchu rule decline in nineteenth-century China?

2. In what ways did China become an economic colony of the West in the nineteenth century?

3. How did the Manchu dynasty finally collapse? What role did Sun Yat-sen play?

4. Why did China experience a civil war after the collapse of the Manchu dynasty?

5. What were the major political, economic, social, and military reforms launched by the Meiji rulers in Japan?

6. What steps did Japan take to become an imperialist power? Why did Japan take this route?

7. How did Japan move toward greater democracy during the first quarter of the twentieth century?

## OUTLINE

1. THE DECLINE OF THE MANCHUS IN CHINA

2. THE COLLAPSE OF THE OLD ORDER IN CHINA

3. A RICH COUNTRY AND A STRONG STATE: THE RISE OF MODERN JAPAN

4. IMPERIALISM AND THE MOVE TOWARD DEMOCRACY

### ① THE DECLINE OF THE MANCHUS IN CHINA

In 1800, the Manchu dynasty appeared to be at the height of its power. China had had a long period of peace and prosperity. Its borders were secure. A little over a century later, however, humiliated and harassed by the big ships and black guns of the Western powers, the Manchu dynasty collapsed in the dust.

No doubt, one important reason for the rapid decline and fall of the Manchu dynasty was the intense pressure applied to a proud but somewhat complacent society by the modern West. However, internal changes also played a role in the dynasty's collapse.

After an extended period of growth, the Manchu dynasty began to suffer from corruption, peasant unrest, and incompetence at court. These weaknesses were made worse by a rapid growth in the country's population. A long period of peace, the introduction of new crops from the Americas, and the cultivation of new, fast-growing strains of rice enabled the Chinese population to double by the end of the eighteenth century. It continued to grow during the nineteenth century. By 1900 it had reached the unheard-of level of 400 million and created a serious food shortage. One

▶ *Tea was a major export for China. This painting shows workers removing leaves from the bushes, packing the leaves into giant crates for shipment, and loading them onto ships bound for England.*

observer wrote in the 1850s, "Not a year passes in which a terrific number of persons do not perish of famine in some part or other of China." The ships, guns, and ideas of the foreigners simply highlighted the growing weakness of the Manchu dynasty and probably hastened its end. In doing so, Western imperialism made a real impact on the history of modern China.

## Opium and Rebellion

By 1800, Westerners had been in contact with China for more than 200 years, although Western merchants had been restricted to a small trading outlet at Canton (KAN-TAWN). This arrangement was not acceptable to the British, however. For years, the British had imported tea, silk, and porcelain from the Chinese and sent raw Indian cotton to China to pay for these imports. The raw cotton was not sufficient, however, and the British were forced to pay for their imports with silver. The British sent increasing quantities of silver to China, especially in exchange for tea, which was in great demand by the British.

At first, the British tried negotiations with the Chinese to improve their trade imbalance. When negotiations failed, the British solution was opium. Grown in northern India under the sponsorship of the British East India Company, opium was shipped directly to the Chinese market. Demand for opium—a highly addictive drug—in South China jumped dramatically. Soon, silver was flowing out of China into the pockets of the officials of the British East India Company.

The Chinese reacted strongly. They appealed to the British government on moral grounds to stop the traffic in opium. A government official wrote the following to Queen Victoria: "Suppose there were people from another country who carried opium for sale to England and seduced your people into buying and smoking it; certainly your honorable ruler would deeply hate it and be bitterly aroused." The British refused to halt their activity, however. This refusal led the Chinese government to blockade the foreign area in Canton in order to force traders to hand over their chests of opium. The British responded with force, thus starting the Opium War (1839 to 1842).

**Map 7.1   Canton and Hong Kong**

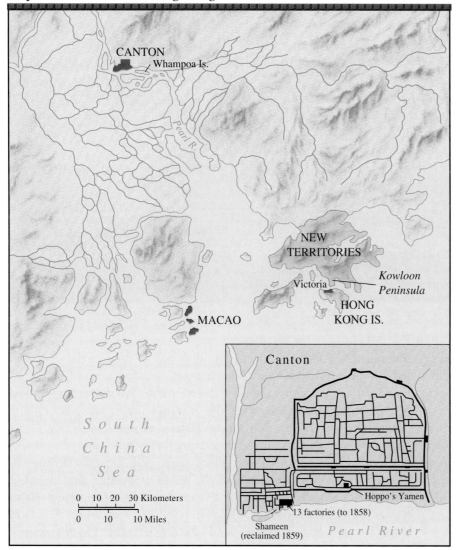

Hong Kong. Nothing was said in the treaty about the opium trade. Moreover, in the five ports, Europeans lived in their own sections and were subject not to Chinese laws but to their own, a practice known as **extraterritoriality**.

The Opium War was the first major stage in the Western penetration of China. For the time being, the Manchus tried to deal with the problem of foreigners by playing them off against one another. Concessions granted to the British were offered to other Western nations, including the United States. Soon thriving foreign areas were operating in the five treaty ports along the southern Chinese coast from Canton in the south to Shanghai, a bustling new port on a tributary of the Yangtze, in the center.

In the meantime, the failure of the Manchus to deal with pressing internal economic problems led to a major peasant revolt, known as the Taiping (TIE-PING) Rebellion (1850 to 1864). It was led by Hong Xiuquan (SHOO-GWAWN), a Christian convert who viewed himself as a younger brother of Jesus Christ. Hong was convinced that God had given him the mission of wiping out the Manchu dynasty. Joined by great crowds of peasants, Hong captured the town of Yongan and proclaimed a new dynasty—the Heavenly Kingdom of Great Peace (Taiping Tianguo in Chinese—hence the name Taiping Rebellion)—with himself as the Heavenly King. His divine mission, he announced, was "to kill all idolaters generally, and to possess the empire as its True Sovereign."

The Chinese were no match for the British. British warships destroyed Chinese coastal and river forts and seized the offshore island of Chusan. When a British fleet sailed virtually unopposed up the Yangtze River to Nanjing, the Manchu dynasty made peace. In the Treaty of Nanjing in 1842, the Chinese agreed to open five coastal ports to British trade, limit taxes on imported British goods, and pay for the costs of the war. China also agreed to give the British the island of

▶ *The Chinese navy was no match for its well-armed British opponent. This painting shows Chinese junks under attack from British steamships. Why do you think the Chinese, who invented gunpowder, had not modernized their military weapons?*

One of the strong appeals of Hong's regime was its call for social reforms. These reforms included a redistribution of land equally among all peasants and the treatment of women as equals of men. Women even served in their own units in the Taiping army. The regime also called for people to give up private possessions and hold all things in common. Hong outlawed alcohol and tobacco and eliminated the practice of foot binding of women. The Chinese Communist Revolution of the twentieth century (see Chapter 16) would have similar social goals.

In March 1853, the rebels seized Nanjing, the second largest city of the empire. They secured their victory by massacring 25,000 men, women, and children. The revolt continued for ten more years but gradually began to fall apart. Europeans came to the aid of the Manchu dynasty when they realized the destructive nature of the Taiping forces. As one British observer noted, there was no hope "of any good ever coming of the rebel movement. They do nothing but burn, murder, and destroy." In 1864, Chinese forces, with European aid, recaptured Nanjing and destroyed the remaining rebel force. The Taiping Rebellion proved to be one of the most devastating civil wars in history.

Probably twenty million people died in the course of the fourteen-year struggle.

One reason for the Manchu dynasty's failure to deal effectively with the internal unrest was its ongoing struggle with the Western powers. In 1856, Great Britain and France launched a new series of attacks against China. They seized the capital, Beijing, in 1860. In the ensuing Treaty of Tianjin, the Manchus agreed to legalize the opium trade, open new ports to foreign trade, and surrender the peninsula of Kowloon (opposite the island of Hong Kong) to Great Britain.

## The Climax of Imperialism in China

By the late 1870s, the old dynasty in China was well on the way to disintegrating. In fighting the Taiping Rebellion, the Manchus had been forced to rely for support on armed forces recruited by warlords in each region. The Manchus' own troops were unable by themselves to restore order. After crushing the revolt, many of these regional commanders or warlords refused to dismiss their units. With the support of the local gentry, they continued to collect local taxes for their

◄ *This picture shows French and British troops storming fortified barriers in Canton during the Taiping Rebellion. The rebels eventually occupied the Yangtze Valley before they were crushed.*

own use. The old pattern of imperial breakdown was appearing once again.

In its weakened state, the court finally began to listen to the appeals of reform-minded officials. They called for a new policy of **"self-strengthening."** By this they meant that China should adopt Western technology while keeping its Confucian values and institutions. This new policy guided Chinese foreign and domestic policy for the next twenty-five years.

Some reformers even called for changing China's traditional political institutions by introducing democracy. However, such ideas were too radical for most reformers. One of the leading court officials of the day, Zhang Zhidong (CHANG CHI-DONG), argued as follows:

*The doctrine of people's rights will bring us not a single benefit but a hundred evils. Are we going to establish a parliament? Among the Chinese scholars and people there are still many today who are content to be vulgar and rustic. They are ignorant of the general situation in the world, they do not understand the basic system of the state. They have not the most elementary idea about foreign countries—about the schools, the politi-cal systems, military training, and manufacture of armaments. Even supposing the confused and clamorous people are assembled in one house, for every one of them who is clear-sighted, there will be a hundred others whose vision is beclouded; they will converse at random and talk as if in a dream—what use will it be?[1]*

For the time being, Zhang Zhidong's arguments prevailed. During the last quarter of the nineteenth century, the Manchus tried to modernize China's military forces and build up an industrial base without touching the basic elements of traditional Chinese civilization. Railroads, weapons factories, and shipyards were built, but the Chinese value system remained unchanged.

In the end, however, the changes did not help. The European advance into China continued during the last two decades of the nineteenth century. In the north and northwest, Russia took advantage of the Manchu dynasty's weakness to force the concession of territories north of the Amur River in Siberia. In Tibet, a struggle between Russia and Great Britain kept either power from seizing the territory outright. This gave Tibetan authorities the chance to free themselves from Chinese influence.

## CONNECTIONS
### TO OUR WORLD

**The Return of Hong Kong to China**   In 1984, Great Britain and China signed a Joint Declaration in which Britain agreed to return its colony of Hong Kong to China on July 1, 1997. China promised that Hong Kong would keep its free market, capitalist economy and its way of life. The formula was: "one country, two systems." Many Hong Kong residents, although fearful of Chinese rule, were also delighted.

In 1841, Hong Kong was a small island with a few fishing villages on the southeastern coast of China. A British naval force seized the island and used it as a port for shipping opium into China. A year later, after a humiliating defeat in the Opium War, China agreed to give the island of Hong Kong to Britain. Later, the British took advantage of the declining power of China's Manchu dynasty to gain additional lands next to Hong Kong. In 1861, the Chinese government granted the Kowloon peninsula to Britain. In 1898, the Chinese granted the British a 99-year lease on the nearby New Territories, an area that provided much of the food for the colony of Hong Kong.

In the 1950s and 1960s, Hong Kong was filled with refugees from the new Communist regime in mainland China. The population of Hong Kong swelled to six million. Many of the refugees worked for starvation wages, and the economy of Hong Kong boomed. Today, Hong Kong is the eighth largest trading nation in the world.

Even more ominous changes were taking place in the Chinese heartland. European states began to create so-called **spheres of influence**. After the Taiping Rebellion, warlords in the provinces began to negotiate directly with foreign nations. In return for money, the warlords granted these nations exclusive trading rights or railroad-building and mining privileges. Britain, France, Germany, Russia, and Japan all established spheres of influence in China.

In 1894, one more blow led to further disintegration. The Manchus went to war with Japan over Japanese inroads into Korea, a land that the Chinese had controlled for a long time. The Chinese were roundly defeated. As a reward, Japan demanded and received the island of Taiwan (known to Europeans at the time as Formosa) and the Liaodong (li-OW-DOONG) (Liaotung) peninsula. Fearing Japan's growing power, the European powers forced Japan to give the Liaodong peninsula back to China.

European statesmen, however, were not concerned about the collapse of the Chinese Empire itself. New pressures for Chinese territory soon arose. The process began in 1897. Germany used the pretext of the murder of two German missionaries by Chinese rioters to demand the cession of territories in the Shandong (SHAWN-DOONG) peninsula. When the Chinese government approved the demand, other European nations made new claims on Chinese territory. Russia now demanded the Liaodong peninsula, with its ice-free port at Port Arthur. Great Britain asked for coaling stations in North China.

This latest scramble for territory had taken place at a time of internal crisis in China. In the spring of 1898, a reformer named Kang Youwei (YOE-WAE) had won the support of the young emperor Guangxu (GWAWN-shoo) for a massive reform program based on recent changes in Japan (see the discussion later in this chapter). During the next several weeks (known as the One Hundred Days of reform), the emperor issued edicts calling for major political, administrative, and educational reforms.

Kang's ideas for reform were opposed by many conservatives at court, however, who saw little advantage in copying the West. As one said, "An examination of the causes of success and failure in government reveals that . . . the adoption of foreignism leads to disorder."[2] What was needed, this conservative said, was to reform existing ways rather than give up the tried-and-true rules of the past.

Most important, the new reform program was opposed by the emperor's aunt, Empress Dowager Cixi (see "Biography: The Empress Dowager Cixi"). Cixi had become a dominant force at court and opposed Emperor Guangxu's reforms. With the aid of the impe-

# BIOGRAPHY

## The Empress Dowager Cixi

Born in 1835, Cixi was educated by her father, a civil servant. At a young age, she became a low-ranking concubine to Emperor Xian Feng (SHEE-AWN FUNG). Cixi proved ambitious. She used her learning and cleverness to rise to the rank of secretary to the emperor, a position that gave her experience in government affairs. Her position became even more influential in 1856, when she gave birth to the emperor's first and only son.

When the emperor died in 1861, Cixi's son, Tong Zhi, became the new emperor. Because he was only five years old, a council of regency under Cixi's direction ruled in his name. Although Tong Zhi came of age (seventeen) in 1873, his mother continued to rule from behind the scenes. Tong Zhi died two years later, a death for which some historians believe his mother was responsible. Cixi then chose her four-year-old nephew Guangxu as the new emperor and continued to rule in his name as regent.

When Guangxu came of age, he and a group of supporters tried to take charge and institute reforms. Cixi thought that Guangxu's reforms were an attempt to reduce her influence at court. With the aid of conservatives at court and the imperial army, she had the emperor jailed in the palace and several of his reformers executed. Guangxu's favorite concubine was also drowned. With Cixi's palace coup, the days of reform had come to an end. The empress continued to rule China until her death in 1908.

Empress Dowager Cixi ruled China for almost fifty years, during a crucial period in the nation's history. She was well aware of her own power. "I have often thought that I am the cleverest woman who ever lived. . . I have 400 million people all dependent on my judgement," she once said.

▲ *Empress Dowager Cixi held power in China until her death in 1908. This photograph, taken in her final years, shows her royal demeanor and dress. What do you think her long fingernails symbolize?*

Many Chinese regard her as the "most powerful woman in China's history." Her rule had some notable accomplishments, especially for women. Among other things, she ended the foot binding of women. However, in some ways her reign was disastrous. She allowed considerable corruption.

*(continued)*

# BIOGRAPHY

## The Empress Dowager Cixi, continued

Funds earmarked for the navy in the late 1880s, for example, were used instead to build a summer palace outside Beijing. Also, her unwillingness to make significant reforms no doubt weakened the Manchu dynasty and helped lead to its overthrow only three years after her death.

1. Explain how Cixi came to power in China.
2. During what dynasty did Cixi reign?

rial army, she imprisoned the emperor and ended the days of reform.

## Opening the Door to China

As foreign pressure on the Manchu dynasty grew stronger, both Great Britain and the United States came to fear the total collapse of the Manchu Empire. In 1899, U.S. secretary of state John Hay presented the other imperialist powers with a proposal to ensure equal economic access to the China market for all nations. Hay also suggested that all the powers join together to preserve the unity of the Chinese Empire. When none of the other governments flatly opposed the idea, Hay issued a second note. It stated that all major states with economic interests in China had agreed to an "Open Door" policy in China.

In part, the Open Door policy reflected the American concern for the survival of China. It also reflected, however, the interests of some trading companies in the United States. These companies wanted to operate in open markets and disliked the existing division of China into separate spheres of influence dominated by individual states. The Open Door policy did not end the system of spheres of influence. However, it did reduce the number of tariffs or quotas on foreign imports imposed by the dominating power within each sphere of influence.

The Open Door policy also had the practical effect of reducing imperialist hysteria over access to the

▼ *Following the Boxer Rebellion, many of the young rebels were rounded up and imprisoned.*

**Map 7.2   Foreign Possessions and Spheres of Influence about 1900**

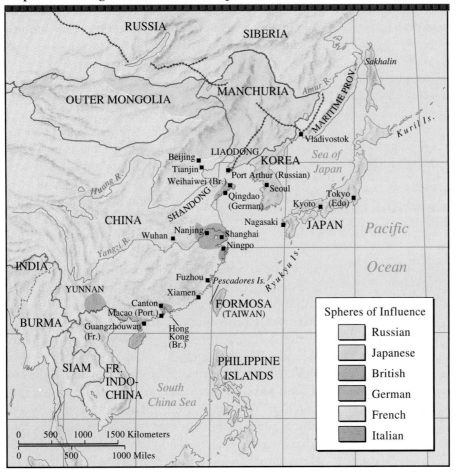

China market. The Open Door policy reduced fears in Britain, France, Germany, and Russia that other powers would take advantage of China's weakness to dominate the China market for themselves.

The Open Door policy came too late to stop the domestic explosion in China known as the Boxer Rebellion. *Boxers* was the popular name given to members of a secret organization called the Society of Harmonious Fists. Members practiced a system of exercise—a form of shadowboxing, or boxing with an imaginary opponent—that they thought would protect them from bullets. The Boxers were distressed by economic hardships and the foreign takeover of Chinese lands. They wanted to push foreigners out of China.

Their slogan was "destroy the foreigner." They especially disliked Christian missionaries and Chinese converts to Christianity. At the beginning of 1900, Boxer bands roamed the countryside and slaughtered foreign missionaries and Chinese Christians. They then expanded their victims to include railroad workers, foreign businessmen, and even the German envoy to Beijing.

Response to the killings was immediate and overwhelming. An allied army consisting of 20,000 British, French, German, Russian, American, and Japanese troops attacked Beijing in August 1900. The army restored order and demanded more concessions from the Chinese government. The Chinese government was forced to pay a heavy **indemnity** (large sum of money) to the powers that had crushed the uprising. The imperial government was now weaker than ever.

## ❁ SECTION REVIEW ❁

1. **Locate:**
   (*a*) Canton,   (*b*) Yangtze River,   (*c*) Hong Kong,
   (*d*) Siberia,   (*e*) Tibet,   (*f*) Korea,   (*g*) Taiwan

2. **Define:**
   (*a*) extraterritoriality,   (*b*) self-strengthening,
   (*c*) spheres of influence,   (*d*) indemnity

3. **Identify:**
   (*a*) opium,   (*b*) Hong Xiuquan,   (*c*) Treaty of
   Tianjin,   (*d*) One Hundred Days of reform,
   (*e*) Open Door policy,   (*f*) Boxer Rebellion

4. **Recall:**
   (*a*) What internal problems contributed to the decline and fall of the Manchu dynasty in China?
   (*b*) What problems did population growth cause in China during the nineteenth century?
   (*c*) Why did European powers come to the aid of the Manchu dynasty when it was attacked by the Taiping army in 1853?

5. **Think Critically:** Why would powerful European nations agree to the Open Door policy suggested by a weaker United States?

## THE COLLAPSE OF THE OLD ORDER IN CHINA

During the first few years after the Boxer Rebellion, the old dynasty in China tried desperately to reform itself. Empress Dowager Cixi, who had long resisted change, now embraced a number of reforms in education, administration, and the legal system. The old civil service examination system was dropped, and a new educational system based on the Western model was adopted. After 1905, legislative assemblies were set up at the provincial level. Even elections for a national assembly were held in 1910.

## The Fall of the Manchus

The reform moves won at least temporary support for the Manchu dynasty among progressive elements in the country. Many were soon disappointed, however. The emerging new provincial elite, composed of merchants, professionals, and reform-minded gentry, soon became impatient with the slow pace of political change. They were very angry when they found that the new assemblies were only asked for advice and not allowed to pass laws. In addition, the recent reforms had done nothing for the peasants, artisans, and miners, whose living conditions were getting worse as taxes increased. Rising unrest in the countryside was a sign of the deep-seated resentment to which the dynasty seemed unable to respond.

The first signs of revolution appeared during the last decade of the nineteenth century, when the young radical Sun Yat-sen (YAWT-SEN) formed the Revive China Society. Sun was born to a peasant family in a village south of Canton and was educated in Hawaii. He returned to China to practice medicine. Soon he turned his full attention to the ills of Chinese society.

Sun Yat-sen believed that the Manchu dynasty was in a state of decay and could no longer govern the country. Unless the Chinese were united under a strong government, they would be at the mercy of other countries. Sun believed that China should follow the pattern of the Western democracies, but he knew that the Chinese people were hardly ready for democracy. He called instead for a three-stage process: (1) a military takeover, (2) a transitional phase in which Sun's own revolutionary party would prepare the people for the final stage, and (3) a constitutional democracy.

Gathering support from radical students, merchants, and secret society members in South China, Sun launched a series of local rebellions to topple the Manchus. At first, his efforts went nowhere. In a convention in Tokyo in 1905, however, Sun united radical

**Map 7.3   The Manchu Empire in the Early Twentieth Century**

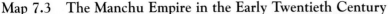

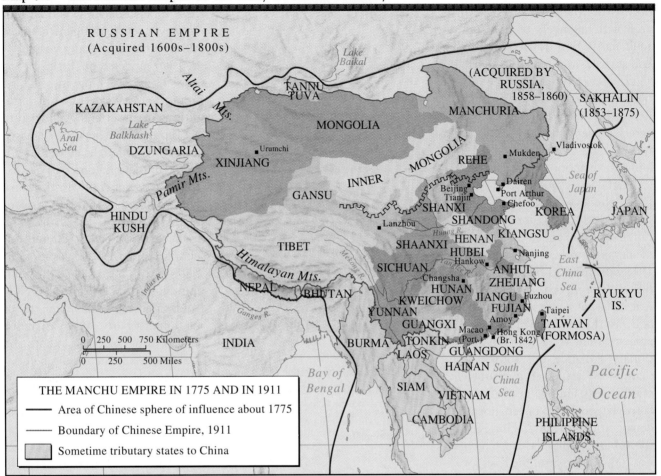

RUSSIAN EMPIRE
(Acquired 1600s–1800s)

*Lake Baikal*

KAZAKAHSTAN

*Aral Sea*

*Lake Balkhash*

*Altai Mts.*

TANNU TUVA

MONGOLIA

(ACQUIRED BY RUSSIA, 1858–1860)

MANCHURIA

SAKHALIN (1853–1875)

DZUNGARIA

XINJIANG

Urumchi

INNER MONGOLIA

REHE

Mukden

Vladivostok

*Sea of Japan*

*Pamir Mts.*

GANSU

Dairen
Beijing
Tianjin
Port Arthur
SHANXI
Chefoo
SHANDONG

KOREA

JAPAN

HINDU KUSH

Lanzhou

*Huang R.*

SHAANXI
HENAN
KIANGSU

TIBET

HUBEI

Nanjing

*East China Sea*

*Himalayan Mts.*

*Mekong R.*

SICHUAN

*Yangtze R.*

Hankow

ANHUI
ZHEJIANG

RYUKYU IS.

*Indus R.*

Changsha

HUNAN

KWEICHOW

JIANGU

Fuzhou

NEPAL

BHUTAN

YUNNAN

GUANGXI

FUJIAN
Amoy
Taipei

TAIWAN (FORMOSA)

*Ganges R.*

0   250   500   750 Kilometers

0   250   500 Miles

INDIA

BURMA

TONKIN

Macao (Port.)

Hong Kong (Br. 1842)

GUANGDONG

HAINAN

LAOS

*Bay of Bengal*

SIAM

VIETNAM

*South China Sea*

*Pacific Ocean*

CAMBODIA

PHILIPPINE ISLANDS

THE MANCHU EMPIRE IN 1775 AND IN 1911

—— Area of Chinese sphere of influence about 1775

—— Boundary of Chinese Empire, 1911

▨ Sometime tributary states to China

groups from across China in a Revolutionary Alliance (*Tongmenghui*). The program of the new organization was based on Sun's so-called Three People's Principles of Nationalism, Democracy, and People's Livelihood (see "You Are There: A Program for a New China"). The new organization was small and inexperienced. However, it benefited from rising discontent with the failure of Manchu reforms to improve conditions in China.

The Manchu dynasty was near its end. In 1908, Empress Dowager Cixi died. Her nephew Guangxu, a prisoner in the palace, died the day before his aunt. The throne was now occupied by China's "last emperor," the infant Henry Puyi (POO-YEE).

In October 1911, followers of Sun Yat-sen launched yet another uprising in the industrial center of Wuhan, on the Yangtze River in central China. At the time, Sun himself was traveling in the United States. Thus, the **insurrection** (act of revolting against an established government) had no leader, but the government was too weak to react. The dynasty collapsed, opening the way for new political forces.

Sun's party, however, had neither the military nor the political strength to form a new government. The party was forced to turn to a member of the old order, General Yuan Shikai (yoo-AWN SHIR-KIE). Yuan was a prominent figure in military circles, and he had been placed in charge of the imperial army sent to suppress the rebellion. He abandoned the Manchus and negotiated with members of Sun Yat-sen's party. Sun Yat-sen himself had arrived in China in January 1912, after reading about the revolution in a Denver, Colorado, newspaper. General Yuan Shikai agreed to serve as president of a new Chinese republic and to allow the election of a legislature.

In the eyes of Sun Yat-sen's party, the events of 1911 were nothing less than a glorious revolution that had ended 2,000 years of imperial rule. However, the 1911 uprising was hardly a revolution. It produced no new political or social order. Sun Yat-sen and his followers had not yet achieved much. Their Revolutionary Alliance was supported mainly by an emerging urban middle class, and its program was based largely on Western liberal democratic principles. However, the urban middle class in China was too small to form the basis for a new political order. Most of the Chinese people still lived on the land, and few peasants supported Sun Yat-sen's party. In effect, then, the events of 1911 were less a revolution than a collapse of the old order. The old dynasty, weakened by its own internal problems and by imperialism, had come to an abrupt end before new political and social forces were ready to take over.

▲ *Sun Yat-sen became the founder of the first Chinese republic. This photograph shows Sun in January 1912, shortly after he had returned from the United States. Why did General Yuan Shikai, rather than Sun Yat-sen, become president of the new republic?*

## The Era of Civil War

After the collapse of the Manchu dynasty, the military took over. As we have seen, Sun Yat-sen and his colleagues had accepted General Yuan Shikai as president of the new Chinese republic in 1911 because they lacked the military force to compete with his control over the army. Moreover, many feared that if the revolt lapsed into chaos, the Western powers would intervene. Then the last shreds of Chinese independence would be lost. However, even the general's new allies distrusted his motives.

Yuan understood little of the new ideas sweeping into China from the West. He ruled in a traditional manner and even tried to set up a new imperial dynasty. Yuan was hated by reformers for using murder and terror to destroy the new democratic institutions. He was hated by traditionalists for being disloyal to the dynasty he had served. Yuan's dictatorial efforts rapidly led to clashes with Sun's party, now renamed the Guomindang (GWOE-min TONG) (old spelling, *Kuomintang*), or Nationalist Party. When Yuan dissolved the new parliament, the Nationalists launched a rebellion. When the rebellion failed, Sun Yat-sen fled to Japan.

Yuan was strong enough to brush off the challenge from the revolutionary forces, but he could not turn back the clock of history. He died in 1916 and was succeeded by one of his military officers. For the next several years, China slipped into civil war as the power of the central government disintegrated and military warlords seized power in the provinces. Their soldiers caused massive destruction throughout China. One Chinese observer said, "In China today only cunning, vile, and ruthless people can flourish." Hunger spread throughout the land.

By 1920, central authority had almost ceased to exist in China. Two political forces began to emerge as competitors for the right to rule China. One was Sun Yat-sen's Nationalist Party, which had been driven from the political arena seven years earlier. The Nationalist Party reestablished itself on the mainland of China by making a military alliance with the warlord ruler of Guangdong (GWAWN-DUNG) province in South China. From Canton, Sun sought help from

# YOU ARE THERE
# A Program for a New China

◀ *Sun Yat-sen, third from left in the light-colored suit, was photographed in Hangzhou, China, with other members of the Revolutionary Alliance. Sun Yat-sen's wife, second from left, is attired in Western clothing. Why do you think both men and women are in the photograph?*

*In 1905, Sun Yat-sen united a number of groups into a single patriotic organization called the Revolutionary Alliance (Tongmenghui). The new organization eventually formed the basis of Sun's Nationalist Party. This excerpt is from the organization's program, published in 1905 in Tokyo.*

**Selection from the
Revolutionary Alliance Program**

Therefore we proclaim to the world in utmost sincerity the outline of the present revolution and the fundamental plan for the future administration of the nation.

1. Drive out the Tartars: The Manchus of today were originally the eastern barbarians beyond the Great Wall. They frequently caused border troubles during the Ming dynasty; then when China was in a disturbed state they conquered China and enslaved our Chinese people. The extreme cruelties and tyrannies of the Manchu government have now reached their limit. With the righteous army poised against them, we will overthrow that government, and restore our sovereign rights. . . .

*(continued)*

## YOU ARE THERE

# A Program for a New China, continued

2. Restore China: China is the China of the Chinese. The government of China should be in the hands of the Chinese. After driving out the Tartars we must restore our national state. . . .

3. Establish the Republic: Now our revolution is based on equality, in order to establish a republican government. All our people are equal and all enjoy political rights. The president will be publicly chosen by the people of the country. The parliament will be made up of members publicly chosen by the people of the country. A constitution of the Chinese Republic will be enacted, and every person must abide by it. . . .

4. Equalize land ownership: The good fortune of civilization is to be shared equally by all the people of the nation. We should improve our social and economic organization, and assess the value of all the land in the country. Its present price shall be received by the owner, but all increases in value resulting from reform and social improvements after the revolution shall belong to the state, to be shared by all the people, in order to create a socialist state, where each family within the empire can be well supported, each person satisfied, and no one fail to secure employment.

1. Why did Sun Yat-sen view the Manchus as foreigners?

2. Why did Sun Yat-sen want to end the Chinese monarchy?

3. Reread point number 4. How do you think these ideas would be received in the United States today?

abroad to carry out his national revolution. The other political force was the Chinese Communist Party, formed in Shanghai in the summer of 1921. We shall see the outcome of the rivalry between these political forces in Chapter 10.

## Chinese Society in Transition

When European traders began to move into China in greater numbers in the mid-nineteenth century, Chinese society was already in a state of transition. The growth of industry and trade was especially noticeable in the cities, where a national market for such commodities as oil, copper, salt, tea, and porcelain had appeared. The growth of faster and more reliable transportation and a better system of money and banking had begun to create the foundation for a money economy. New crops brought in from abroad increased food production and aided population growth. The Chinese economy had never been more productive.

The coming of westerners to China affected the Chinese economy in three ways. Westerners introduced modern means of production, transportation, and communications; they created an export market; and they integrated the Chinese market into the nineteenth-century world economy. To some, these changes were beneficial. The shaking of China out of its old ways quickened a process of change that had already begun in Chinese society (see "Young People in China: The New Youth"). This forced the Chinese to adopt new ways of thinking and acting. At the same time, however, China paid a heavy price for the new ways. Its local industry was largely destroyed. Also, many of the profits in the new economy flowed abroad.

## YOUNG PEOPLE IN CHINA

# The New Youth

In traditional China, children were thought of not as individuals but as members of a family. Indeed, children were valued because they—especially the sons—would help with the work in the fields, carry on the family name, and care for their parents in old age. However, these attitudes had changed by the beginning of the twentieth century.

Some of the changes were the result of the new educational system. After the government abolished the civil service examinations in 1905, a Confucian education was no longer the key to a successful career. New schools based on the Western model were set up. Especially in the cities, both public and private schools educated a new generation of Chinese who began to have less respect for the past.

By 1915, the attack on the old system and old values by educated youth was intense. The main focus of the attack was the Confucian concept of the family. Young people rejected the old family ideas of respect for elders, of supremacy of men over women, and of the sacrifice of individual needs to the demands of the family.

A spirit of individualism emerged out of the revolt of the youth. Young people now saw themselves as important in and for themselves. Sons no longer had to sacrifice their wishes for the concerns of the larger family. Young people demanded the right to choose their own mates and their own careers.

The new individualism and the revolt of the youth also affected the status of women. Young people now demanded that women have rights

◄ *The "new youth" in China adopted some Western customs, including dress. What might a peasant farmer think of this smiling young man?*

and opportunities equal to those enjoyed by men. They felt that women no longer should be subject to men.

This criticism by the youth had some beneficial results. During the early republic, the tyranny of the old family system began to decline, at least in the cities. Women sought education and jobs alongside men. Free choice in marriage became commonplace among affluent families in the cities. The teenage children of westernized elites copied the clothing and even the music of young people in Europe and America.

As a rule, these changes did not reach the villages, where traditional attitudes and customs persisted. Arranged marriages continued to be the rule rather than the exception. According to a survey taken in the 1930s, well over two-thirds of marriages, even among urban couples, had been arranged by the parents. In one rural area, only 3 villagers out of 170 had even heard of the idea of "modern marriage," or a marriage in which people freely choose their marriage partners.

1. Compare the old way of life for youths in China with the "new youth."

2. How do the "new youth" compare to the young people in the United States today?

During the first quarter of the twentieth century, the pace of change in China began to quicken. Spurred by World War I, which temporarily drew foreign investment out of the country, Chinese businesspeople began to develop new ventures. Shanghai, Wuhan, Tianjin, and Canton became major industrial and commercial centers with a growing middle class and an industrial working class.

## Daily Life

In 1800, daily life for most Chinese was not much different from what it had been for centuries. Most were farmers, living in millions of villages in rice fields and on hillsides throughout the countryside. A farmer's life was governed by the harvest cycle, village custom, and family ritual. Male children, at least the more fortunate ones, were educated in the Confucian classics. Females remained in the home or in the fields. All children were expected to obey their parents, and wives were expected to submit to their husbands.

A visitor to China 125 years later would have seen a different society, although it would have still been recognizably Chinese. The changes were most striking in the cities. Here the educated and wealthy had been visibly affected by the growing Western cultural presence. Confucian social ideals were declining rapidly in influence, and those of Europe and North America were on the rise.

## China's Changing Culture

Nowhere was the struggle between traditional and modern more visible than in the field of culture. Radical reformers condemned traditional culture as an instrument of oppression. By eliminating it entirely, they hoped to create a new China that could stand on its feet with dignity in the modern world.

The first changes in traditional culture had actually come in the late nineteenth century. Intellectuals began to introduce Western books, paintings, music, and ideas into China. By the first quarter of the twentieth century, Western culture flooded in as intellectuals called for a new culture based on that of the modern West. During the 1920s and 1930s, Western literature and art became popular in China, especially among the urban middle class. Traditional culture, however, remained popular with the more conservative elements of the population, especially in rural areas.

Literature in particular was influenced by foreign ideas. Western novels and short stories began to attract a larger audience. Although most Chinese novels written after World War I dealt with Chinese subjects, they reflected the Western tendency toward a realistic portrayal of society. Often, they dealt with the new Westernized middle class. Mao Dun's *Midnight*, for example, described the changing customs of Shanghai's urban elites. Ba Jin's famous novel *Family* described the disintegration of the traditional Confucian family (see "Our Literary Heritage: Ba Jin and the Chinese Novel"). Most of China's modern authors showed a clear contempt for the past.

## ❧ SECTION REVIEW ❧

1. **Identify:**
   (*a*) Sun Yat-sen,    (*b*) Revolutionary Alliance (*Tongmenghui*),    (*c*) Guomindang

2. **Define:**
   (*a*) insurrection

3. **Recall:**
   (*a*) Why didn't new legislative assemblies created in China in 1905 satisfy the need for reform?
   (*b*) What were the three stages that Sun Yat-sen believed were necessary for democracy in China?
   (*c*) Why was the 1911 Chinese revolution hardly a real revolution?
   (*d*) What happened to the government of China after the death of President Yuan Shikai in 1916?
   (*e*) What three ways did Western powers use to affect the Chinese economy during the nineteenth century?

4. **Think Critically:**
   (*a*) How may World War I have helped development of China's production and businesses?
   (*b*) What reasons may explain why many modern Chinese authors show a clear contempt for their country's past?

# OUR LITERARY HERITAGE

## Ba Jin and the Chinese Novel

◄ *Ba Jin was one of China's fore-most writers at the turn of the cen-tury. Shown with his four brothers and his stepmother, Ba Jin (far right) was well attuned to the rigors and expected obedience of Chinese family life. Do you think he was perceived as a radical by traditional-ists in China?*

*Ba Jin, who was born in 1904, wrote many novels and short stories. In his trilogy—Family, Spring, and Autumn—he described how the younger members of a large family tried to break away from their elders. This passage from Family shows how the old patterns still prevailed in the villages.*

### Ba Jin, *Family*

Brought up with loving care, after studying with a private tutor for a number of years, Chueh-hsin entered middle school. One of the school's best students, he graduated four years later at the top of his class. He was very interested in physics and chemistry and hoped to go on to a university in Shanghai or Peking, or perhaps study abroad, in

Germany. His mind was full of beautiful dreams. At the time he was the envy of his classmates.

In his fourth year at middle school, he lost his mother. His father later married again, this time to a younger woman who had been his mother's cousin. Chueh-hsin was aware of his loss, for he knew full well that nothing could replace the love of a mother. But . . . he was able to console him-self with rosy dreams of his future. Moreover, he had someone who understood him and could com-fort him—his pretty cousin Mei, "mei" for "plum blossom."

But then, one day, his dreams were shattered, cruelly and bitterly shattered. The evening he

*(continued)*

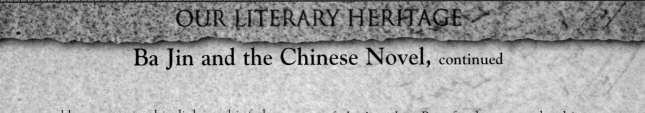

## OUR LITERARY HERITAGE

# Ba Jin and the Chinese Novel, continued

returned home carrying his diploma, his father called him into his room and said:

"Now that you've graduated, I want to arrange your marriage. Your grandfather is looking forward to having a great-grandson, and I, too, would like to be able to hold a grandson in my arms. You're old enough to be married; I won't feel easy until I fulfill my obligation to find you a wife. Although I didn't accumulate much money in my years away from home as an official, still I've put enough for us to get along on. My health isn't what it used to be; I'm thinking of spending my time at home and having you help me run the household affairs. All the more reason you'll be needing a wife. I've already arranged a match with the Li family. The thirteenth of next month is a good day. We'll announce the engagement then. You can be married within the year."

Chueh-hsin did not utter a word of protest, nor did such a thought ever occur to him. He merely nodded to indicate his compliance with his father's wishes. But after he returned to his own room, and shut the door, he threw himself down on his bed, covered his head with the quilt and wept. He wept for his broken dreams. . . . He did not fight back, he never thought of resisting. He only bemoaned his fate. But he accepted it. He complied with his father's will without a trace of resentment. But in his heart he wept for himself.

1. How do you explain the willingness of Chueh-hsin to follow his father's wishes?

2. Why is the father so unaware of his son's desires for the future?

3. Why is there so little communication between these two family members?

4. Are there any practices shown in this selection that are evident in American society?

## A RICH COUNTRY AND A STRONG STATE: THE RISE OF MODERN JAPAN

By the beginning of the nineteenth century, the Tokugawa shogunate had ruled the Japanese islands for 200 years (see Chapter 2). It had driven out foreign traders and missionaries and isolated the country from virtually all contacts with the outside world. The Tokugawa maintained formal relations only with Korea. Informal trading links with Dutch and Chinese merchants continued at Nagasaki.

Isolation, however, did not mean stagnation. Under Tokugawa rule, Japanese society had begun to undergo deep-seated changes. The changes were social and economic, as well as political. Under the centralized system of the Tokugawa, political power was largely concentrated in the hands of the shogunate in Edo. The *daimyo*, at least in theory, were directly subordinated to the shogunate. In the meantime, during the long period of peace and prosperity, both manufacturing and trade began to emerge and grow. Most Japanese were still farmers, but Japanese society was changing.

The Tokugawa system itself was beginning to come apart. There were signs that the shogunate was becoming less effective. Corruption plagued the central bureaucracy. Unrest, fueled by a series of bad harvests brought about by poor weather, swept the countryside. Farmers fled to the towns, where anger was already rising as a result of declining agricultural incomes for the samurai. Many of the samurai lashed out at the corruption in the government. In response, the shogunate government attacked its critics and tried to force fleeing peasants to return to their lands. In the meantime, the government intensified its efforts to keep the country isolated from the outside world. It drove away foreign ships that were beginning to prowl along the Japanese coast in increasing numbers.

## An End to Isolation

Japan, then, was ripe for change at the beginning of the nineteenth century. To the Western powers, the continued isolation of Japanese society was a challenge. Western nations were convinced that the expansion of trade on a global basis would benefit all nations. They now began to approach Japan in the hope of opening it up to foreign economic interests.

The first foreign power to succeed was the United States. American whalers and clipper ships followed a northern route across the Pacific, but they needed a fueling station before completing their long journey to China and other ports in the area. In the summer of 1853, an American fleet of four warships under Commodore Matthew C. Perry arrived in Edo Bay (now Tokyo Bay), seeking, as Perry said, "to bring a singular and isolated people into the family of civilized nations." Perry brought with him a letter from President Millard Fillmore, in which the president asked for better treatment of sailors shipwrecked on the Japanese islands and the opening of foreign relations between the United States and Japan (see "You Are There: A Letter to the Shogun"). Foreign sailors shipwrecked in Japan were treated as criminals and exhibited in public cages.

A few months later, Perry returned with an even larger fleet for an answer. While he was gone, shogunate officials had discussed the issue. Some argued that contacts with the West would hurt Japan. Others pointed to U.S. military superiority and recommended concessions. For the shogunate in Edo, the big black guns of Commodore Perry's ships proved decisive.

Under military pressure, Japan agreed to the Treaty of Kanagawa with the United States. This provided for the return of shipwrecked American sailors, the opening of two ports, and the establishment of a U.S. consulate in Japan. In 1858, U.S. consul Townsend Harris signed a more detailed treaty. It called for the opening of several new ports to U.S. trade and residence, as well as an exchange of ministers. Similar treaties were soon signed by Japan and several European nations.

The decision to open relations with the Western powers was highly unpopular in some quarters. Resistance was especially strong in two *daimyo* territories in the south, Satsuma and Choshu. Both had strong military traditions, and neither was at first exposed to heavy Western military pressure. In 1863, the Sat-Cho alliance (from Satsuma-Choshu) forced the shogun to promise to bring relations with the West to an end.

The rebellious groups soon showed their own weakness, however. When Choshu troops fired on Western ships in the Strait of Shimonoseki, which led into the Sea of Japan, the westerners fired back and destroyed the Choshu fortifications. The incident convinced the rebellious forces of the need to strengthen their military. They also became more determined not to give in to the West. As a result, Sat-Cho leaders continued to urge the shogun to take a stronger position against the foreigners. These leaders now took the initiative.

The Sat-Cho leaders demanded that the shogun resign and restore the power of the emperor. The reigning shogun agreed to resign in favor of a council composed of *daimyo* lords that would work under the emperor, with the shogun as prime minister. However, this arrangement did not please the leading members of the Sat-Cho faction. In January 1868, their armies attacked the shogun's palace in Kyoto and proclaimed that the authority of the emperor had been restored. After a few weeks, resistance collapsed. The shogunate system had come to an end.

## The Meiji Restoration

The Sat-Cho leaders had genuinely mistrusted the West, but they soon realized that Japan must change to survive. The new leaders embarked on a policy of

## YOU ARE THERE

# A Letter to the Shogun

*When U.S. commodore Matthew C. Perry arrived in Tokyo Bay on his first visit to Japan in July 1853, he carried a letter from Millard Fillmore, the president of the United States. This excerpt is from Fillmore's letter.*

**Letter of President Fillmore to the Emperor of Japan**

Millard Fillmore, President of the United States of America, To His Imperial Majesty, The Emperor of Japan. Great and Good Friend! . . .

I have directed Commodore Perry to assure your Imperial Majesty that I entertain the kindest feelings towards your Majesty's person and government; and that I have no other object in sending him to Japan, but to propose to your Imperial

▶ *This Japanese painting records Commodore Perry's arrival in Tokyo Bay in July 1853. Why do you think both Perry and his Japanese hosts are dressed in such formal attire?*

reform that transformed Japan into a modern industrial nation.

The symbol of the new era was the young emperor Mutsuhito (moo-TSOO-HEH-TOE). He called his reign the **Meiji** (Enlightened Rule) and began a remarkable transformation of Japan that has since been known as the Meiji Restoration. Of course, the Meiji ruler was controlled by the new leaders, just as earlier emperors had been controlled by the shogunate. In recognition of the real source of political power, the new capital was located at Edo (now renamed Tokyo, or "Eastern Capital"). The imperial court was moved to the shogun's palace in the center of the city.

### The Transformation of Japanese Politics

Once in power, the new leaders launched a comprehensive reform of Japanese political, social, economic, and cultural institutions. They moved first to abolish the old order and to strengthen executive power in their hands. To undercut the power of the *daimyo*, the great lords were stripped of the title to their lands in 1871. As compensation, they were given government bonds and were named governors of the territories formerly under their control (the territories were now called **prefectures**). The members of the *eta*, the traditional slave class, were granted legal equality. The

## YOU ARE THERE

# A Letter to the Shogun, continued

Majesty that the United States and Japan should live in friendship, and have commercial intercourse with each other. . . .

The United States of America reach from ocean to ocean, and our territory of Oregon and state of California lie directly opposite to the dominions of your Imperial Majesty. Our steamships can go from California to Japan in eighteen days.

Our great state of California produces about sixty millions of dollars in gold, every year, besides silver, quicksilver, precious stones, and many other valuable articles. Japan is also a rich and fertile country, and produces many very valuable articles. . . . I am desirous that our two countries should trade with each other, for the benefit both of Japan and the United States.

We know that the ancient laws of your Imperial Majesty's government do not allow of foreign trade except with the Dutch. But as the state of the world changes, and new governments are formed, it seems to be wise from time to time to make new

laws. . . . If your Imperial Majesty went so far to change the ancient laws, as to allow a free trade between the two countries, it would be extremely beneficial to both.

1. What did President Fillmore want from the Japanese?

2. Why can his letter be seen as a masterful combination of salesmanship, diplomacy, and firmness?

3. What do you think might have happened if the emperor had said "no" to the president's requests?

4. From the perspective of President Fillmore and others in the United States, the emperor's decision may have looked like an easy one. Explain why this would not have been a simple decision for the emperor.

---

samurai, which made up about 8 percent of the total population, received a lump-sum payment to replace their traditional payments. They were forbidden to wear the sword, the symbol of their special hereditary status.

The Meiji reformers now set out to create a modern political system based on the Western model. In 1868, the new leaders signed a Charter Oath, in which they promised to create a new legislative assembly within the framework of continued imperial rule. Although senior positions in the new government were given to the *daimyo*, the key posts were held by modernizing leaders from the Sat-Cho clique. The country

was divided into seventy-five prefectures. (The number was reduced to forty-five in 1889 and remains at that number today.)

During the next twenty years, the Meiji government undertook a careful study of Western political systems. A commission under Ito Hirobumi (EE-TOE hir-OH-BOO-MEE) traveled to Great Britain, France, Germany, and the United States to study their governments. As the process evolved, a number of factions appeared, each representing different political ideas within the ruling clique. Most prominent were the Liberals. They wanted political reform on the Western liberal democratic model, with supreme authority vested in the parliament as the representative of the people. The Progressives called for a sharing of power between the legislative and executive branches, although with more power for the executive branch. There was also an imperial party that wanted to keep supreme authority in the hands of the emperor.

During the 1870s and 1880s, these factions fought for control. In the end, the Progressives won. The Meiji Constitution, which was adopted in 1890, vested authority in the executive branch. In theory the emperor exercised all executive authority, but in practice he was a figurehead. Real executive authority rested in the hands of a prime minister and his cabinet of ministers, who were handpicked by the Meiji leaders. The upper house of the parliament was to be appointed and have equal legislative powers with the lower house, whose members were to be elected. An interesting feature of the new constitution was that although the **Diet** (the legislature) had the power to appropriate funds, if no agreement was reached, the budget would remain the same as in the previous year. This allowed the executive branch to remain in control.

The final result was a political system that was democratic in form but authoritarian in practice. Although modern in external appearance, it was still traditional, because power remained in the hands of a ruling oligarchy (the Sat-Cho leaders). Although a new set of institutions and values had emerged, the system allowed the traditional ruling class to keep its influence and economic power.

## Meiji Economics

With the end of the *daimyo* system, a new system of land ownership came to Japan. A land reform program made the traditional lands of the *daimyo* into the private property of the peasants. The *daimyo* were then compensated with government bonds. One reason for the new policy was that the government needed a regular source of income. To get it, the Meiji leaders levied a new land tax, which was set at an annual rate of 3 percent of the estimated value of the land.

The new tax was an excellent source of revenue for the government. However, it was quite burdensome for the farmers. Under the old system, farmers had paid a fixed percentage of their harvest to the landowners. In bad harvest years, they had owed little or nothing. Under the new system, the farmers had to pay the land tax every year, regardless of the quality of the harvest. As a result, in bad years, many peasants were unable to pay their taxes. This forced them to sell their lands to wealthy neighbors and become tenant farmers who paid rent to the new owners. By the end of the century, about 40 percent of all farmers were tenants.

With its budget needs met by the land tax, the government turned to the promotion of industry. The chief goal of the reformers was to create a "rich country and a strong state" in order to guarantee Japan's survival against the challenge of Western nations. In a broad sense, the reformers copied the process of industrial development followed by the nations of western Europe. They had an advantage, however, because a small but growing industrial economy already existed. By 1700, for example, manufacturing centers had already developed in Japan's growing cities, such as Tokyo, Kyoto, and Osaka.

Japan's industrial revolution received massive help from the Meiji Restoration. The government gave subsidies to needy industries, provided training and foreign advisors, improved transportation and communications, and started a new educational system that stressed applied science. In contrast to China, Japan was able to achieve results with little reliance on money from abroad. Although the first railroad—built in 1872—was financed by a loan from Great Britain, future projects were all paid for by local funds (primarily the land tax paid by peasants).

By 1900, Japan's industrial sector was beginning to grow. Besides tea and silk, other key industries were weapons, shipbuilding, and sake (SAWK-ee) (Japanese rice wine). From the start, the unique feature of the Meiji model was the close relationship between government and private business. The government encouraged the development of new industries by providing businesspeople with money and privileges. Once an individual enterprise or industry was on its feet, it was turned over entirely to private ownership. Even then, however, the government continued to play some role.

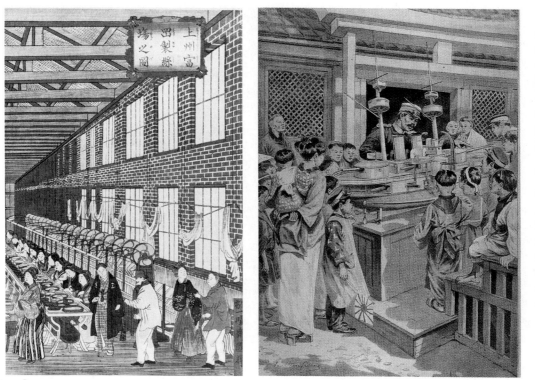

◄ *Workers at this silk mill at Tomioka (photo at left) were mostly women. What resemblance do you see between this mill and the cotton mills in England and the United States?*

*The Meiji leaders were determined to improve Japan's military equipment. In photo at right schoolchildren are watching while a naval officer discusses one of the country's new warships.*

The Meiji reforms had a negative impact on rural areas. The new land tax provided the government with funds to subsidize the industrial sector, but it imposed severe hardships on farmers. Many abandoned their farms and fled to the cities in search of jobs. This influx of people, in turn, benefited Japanese industry by providing an abundant source of cheap labor.

### Building a Modern Social Structure

The Meiji reformers also transformed other institutions. A key focus of their attention was the army. The Sat-Cho reformers were well aware of the need for a modern military force if they were to compete with the Western powers. Their motto was "Strengthen the Army." A new imperial army based on compulsory military service was formed in 1871. All Japanese men now served for three years. Before, only samurai could carry weapons and be warriors. The new army was well equipped with modern weapons.

Education also changed. The Meiji leaders realized the need for universal education, including instruction in modern technology. A new ministry of education, established in 1871, guided the changes. After a few years of experimentation, it adopted the American model of elementary schools, secondary schools, and universities. In the meantime, it sent bright students to study abroad and brought foreign specialists to Japan to teach in the new schools. Much of the content of the new system was Western in inspiration. However, a great deal of emphasis was still placed on the virtues of loyalty to the family and community. Loyalty to the emperor was especially valued. Both teachers and students were required to bow before a portrait of the emperor each day. In 1890, all students were told, "Should emergency arise, offer yourself courageously to the State; and thus guard and maintain the prosperity of our Imperial Throne."

### Daily Life and Women's Rights

Japanese society in the late Tokugawa Era, before the Meiji reforms, could be described by two words: *community* and *hierarchy*. The lives of all Japanese people

▲ *In addition to the Tokyo School of Fine Arts, a music school was begun. At this 1889 recital, the musicians wore Western cloth-ing and played Western music.*

were determined by their membership in a family, village, and social class. At the same time, Japanese society was highly hierarchical. Belonging to a particular social class determined a person's occupation and social relationships with others. Women were especially limited by the "three obediences": child to father, wife to husband, and widow to son. Whereas husbands could easily obtain a divorce, wives could not. Marriages were arranged, and the average marital age of females was sixteen years. Females did not share inheritance rights with males. Few received any education outside the family.

The Meiji Restoration had a marked effect on the traditional social system in Japan. Special privileges for the aristocracy were abolished. For the first time, women were allowed to get an education. As the economy shifted from an agricultural to an industrial base, thousands of Japanese began to get new jobs and establish new social relationships. Western fashions became ⌐age in elite circles. The ministers of the first Meiji ⌐ment were known as the "dancing cabinet"

because of their addiction to Western-style ballroom dancing. Young people were increasingly influenced by Western culture and values. A new generation of modern boys and girls began to imitate the clothing styles, eating habits, hairstyles, and social practices of European and American young people. Baseball was imported from the United States.

The social changes brought about by the Meiji Restoration also had a less attractive side. Many commoners were ruthlessly exploited in the coal mines and textile mills in the interest of building a "rich country and a strong state." One Japanese official of the time remarked that farmers "are the fertilizer of the nation." Workers labored up to twenty hours a day, often in conditions of incredible hardship. Coal miners who were employed on a small island in the harbor of Nagasaki worked naked in temperatures up to 130 degrees Fahrenheit. When they tried to escape, they were shot.

Popular resistance to such conditions was not unknown. In many areas, villagers were actively involved in the search for a new political culture. In some cases they demanded increased attention to human rights. Women took part in this process and formed a "Freedom and People's Rights Movement." This movement was demanding voting rights for women as early as 1876.

The transformation of Japan into a "modern society" did not detach the country entirely from its old values, however. Traditional values based on loyalty to the family and community was still an important subject in the new schools. Traditional values were also given a firm legal basis in the Constitution of 1890, which limited the right to vote to men. The Civil Code of 1898 played down individual rights and placed women within the context of their family role.

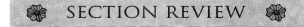

## ❀ SECTION REVIEW ❀

1. **Locate:**
   (*a*) Nagasaki,   (*b*) Edo,   (*c*) Kyoto

2. **Define:**
   (*a*) Meiji,   (*b*) prefectures,   (*c*) Diet

3. **Identify:**
   (*a*) Matthew C. Perry,   (*b*) Treaty of Kanagawa,
   (*c*) Sat-Cho alliance,   (*d*) Meiji Restoration,
   (*e*) Charter Oath,   (*f*) Meiji Constitution,
   (*g*) three obediences

4. **Recall:**
   (*a*) Why didn't isolation necessarily mean stagnation in Japan before 1858?
   (*b*) How did Japan plan its new government during the Meiji Restoration?
   (*c*) What differences were there between Liberals and Progressives in the Japanese political system of the 1880s?
   (*d*) How did the Meiji government obtain most of the money it needed?
   (*e*) What types of help did the Meiji government provide to the process of industrialization?

5. **Think Critically:** Why does the development of a nation's military power often increase the speed

and strength of that nation's industrial growth? Use Japan's experience as an example.

## IMPERIALISM AND THE MOVE TOWARD DEMOCRACY

The Japanese did not just imitate the domestic policies of their Western teachers. They also copied the Western approach to foreign affairs. This is perhaps not surprising. The Japanese saw themselves as vulnerable in the world economic arena. Their territory was small, lacking in resources, and densely populated. They had no natural room for expansion. To some Japanese, the lessons of history were clear. Western nations had amassed wealth and power not only because of their democratic and economic systems and high level of education but also because of their colonies. Colonies had provided the Western powers with sources of raw materials, inexpensive labor, and markets for their manufactured products.

### Joining the Imperialist Nations

Traditionally, Japan had not been an expansionist country. In other words, the Japanese had generally been satisfied to remain on their home islands. They had even deliberately isolated themselves from their neighbors during the Tokugawa Era.

The Japanese began their program of territorial expansion close to home. In 1874, Japan claimed control of the Ryukyu (ree-YOO-KYOO) Islands, which had long been subject to the Chinese Empire. Two years later, Japan's navy forced the Koreans to open their ports to Japanese trade. During the 1880s, Chinese-Japanese rivalry over Korea intensified. In 1894, the two nations went to war. Japanese ships destroyed the Chinese fleet and seized the Manchurian city of Port Arthur. In the Treaty of Shimonoseki (SHIM-uh-noe-SEK-ee), the Manchu rulers of China recognized the independence of Korea. They also ceded Taiwan and the Liaodong peninsula, with its strategic naval base at Port Arthur, to Japan.

Shortly thereafter, under pressure from the European powers, the Japanese returned the Liaodong peninsula to China. In the early twentieth century, however, the Japanese returned to the offensive. Rivalry with Russia over influence in Korea had led to increasingly strained relations between Japan and Russia. The Russians thought little of the Japanese and even welcomed the possibility of war. Tsar Nicholas II called Japanese diplomats "monkeys." One advisor to the tsar said, "We will only have to throw our caps at them and they will run away."

In 1904, Japan launched a surprise attack on the Russian naval base at Port Arthur, which Russia had taken from China in 1898. When Japanese forces moved into Manchuria and the Liaodong peninsula, Russian troops proved to be no match for them. The Russian commander in chief said, "It is impossible not to admire the bravery and activity of the Japanese. The attack of the Japanese is a continuous succession of waves, and they never relax their efforts by day or by night." In the meantime, Russia had sent its Baltic fleet halfway around the world to East Asia, only to be defeated by the new Japanese navy at Tsushima (tsoo-SHEE-muh) Strait, off the coast of Japan. After their defeat, the Russians agreed to a humiliating peace in 1905. They gave the Liaodong peninsula back to Japan, as well as southern Sakhalin (SACK-uh-LEEN) and the Kurile (CURE-EEL) Islands. Russia also agreed to abandon its political and economic influence in Korea and southern Manchuria, which now came increasingly under Japanese control. The Japanese victory stunned the world. Japan had become one of the Great Powers. The colonial peoples of Southeast Asia began to realize that the West was not unbeatable.

During the next few years, the Japanese consolidated their position in northeastern Asia, annexing Korea in 1908 as a part of Japan. When the Koreans protested, the harsh Japanese response caused thousands of deaths. The United States was the first nation to recognize Japan's annexation of Korea. In return, the United States asked for Japan's declaration of respect for American authority in the Philippines. In 1908, the two countries reached an agreement in which the United States recognized Japanese interests in the region in return for Japanese acceptance of the princi-

## Map 7.4  Japanese Overseas Expansion During the Meiji Era

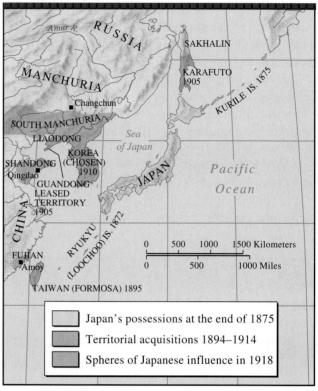

ples of the Open Door policy in China. However, mutual suspicion between the two countries was growing, sparked in part by U.S. efforts to restrict immigration from all Asian countries. President Theodore Roosevelt's "gentlemen's agreement" with Japan in 1905 resulted in a virtual halt in Japanese immigration to the United States. Moreover, the Japanese were still angry over the way Roosevelt had negotiated the Russo-Japanese peace in 1905. In turn, some Americans began to fear the rise of Japanese power in East Asia.

## Experiment in Democracy

During the first two decades of the twentieth century, Japan made remarkable progress toward the creation of an advanced society on the Western model. The economic and social reforms launched during the Meiji Era led to increasing prosperity and the development of a modern industrial and commercial sector. Many

▲ *The Japanese surprise attack on Port Arthur was a stunning defeat for the Russians, and it symbolized the growing power of the Japanese military forces.*

believed that Japan was on the road to becoming a full-fledged democracy.

Between 1900 and 1925, the Japanese political system appeared to be moving toward the Western democratic model. Political parties expanded their popular following and became increasingly competitive. Universal male suffrage was instituted in 1925. An independent press and a bill of rights also appeared.

The influence of the old ruling oligarchy, however, still remained strong. Moreover, social turmoil was increasing. Two opposing forces arose to challenge the growth toward democracy. On the left, a Marxist labor movement began to take shape in the early 1920s. It was a response to the increasing unrest among the urban and rural poor. On the right, ultranationalist groups called for a rejection of Western models of development and a more forceful approach to realizing national objectives. The radical nationalist Kita Ikki called for a military takeover and the establishment of

a new system similar to Nazism in Germany (see Chapter 9).

### A *Zaibatsu* Economy

Japan also continued to make impressive progress in economic development. Industrial production increased twelvefold between 1900 and 1930. Much of the increase went into the export market, which caused Western manufacturers to complain about the rising competition for markets from the Japanese.

One characteristic of the Meiji economic model was the concentration of various manufacturing processes within a single enterprise—the so-called **zaibatsu,** or large financial and industrial corporation. These firms gradually developed, often with government help, into vast companies that controlled a major segment of the Japanese industrial sector. By 1937, the four largest zaibatsu (Mitsui, Mitsubishi, Sumitomo, and Yasuda) controlled 21 percent of the banking industry, 26 percent of mining, 35 percent of shipbuilding, and over 60 percent of paper manufacturing and insurance.

The concentration of wealth led to growing economic inequalities. As we have seen, economic growth had been achieved at the expense of the peasants, many of whom fled to the cities to escape rural poverty. Those left on the farms continued to suffer. The labor surplus in the city benefited industry, but city workers were still poorly paid and housed. Rampant inflation in food prices led to food riots shortly after World War I. A rapid increase in population led to food shortages and the threat of rising unemployment. (The total population of the Japanese islands increased from an estimated 43 million in 1900 to 73 million in 1940.)

### Shidehara Diplomacy

In the early twentieth century, Japanese leaders began to have difficulty finding sources of raw materials and foreign markets for the nation's manufactured goods. Until World War I, Japan had dealt with the problem by seizing territories—such as Formosa, Korea, and southern Manchuria—and making them part of the growing Japanese Empire. That policy had succeeded brilliantly. However, it had also begun to arouse the concern of the Western nations. China was also becoming suspicious of Japanese intentions.

The United States was especially worried about Japanese aggressiveness. The United States had a strong interest in keeping Asia open for U.S. trading activities. In 1922, in Washington, D.C., the United States held a major conference of nations with interests in the Pacific. The major accomplishment of this Washington Conference was a nine-power treaty that recognized the territorial integrity of China and the maintenance of the Open Door policy. Japan accepted the provisions when the other nations recognized its special position in Manchuria.

During the remainder of the 1920s, the Japanese government tried to play by the rules laid down by the Washington Conference. Known as "Shidehara (SHEE-duh-HAW-rah) diplomacy" from the name of the foreign minister (and later prime minister) who tried to carry it out, this policy sought to use diplomatic and economic means to realize Japanese interests in Asia. However, this approach came under severe pressure. Japanese industrialists began to move into new areas, such as heavy industry, chemicals, mining, and the manufacturing of appliances and automobiles. These industries desperately needed resources not found in abundance in Japan. The Japanese government came under increasing pressure to find new sources of resources abroad. All too soon, the Japanese would begin to follow a more aggressive approach to solve this problem.

## Japanese Culture in an Era of Transition

The wave of Western technology and ideas that entered Japan in the last half of the nineteenth century greatly altered the shape of traditional Japanese culture. Literature was especially affected as European models became popular. Dazzled by this "new" literature, Japanese authors began translating and imitating the imported models.

The novel showed the greatest degree of change. One form that became popular was the naturalistic novel, patterned on the French tradition of Émile Zola. Naturalist Japanese authors tried to present society, the human condition, and the realities of war as objectively as possible.

Japanese victories over China and Russia sparked a great age of creativity in the early twentieth century. Japanese writers wrote novels filled with nostalgia for the old Japan. A well-known example is Junichiro Tanizaki's *Some Prefer Nettles*, published in 1928.

Other aspects of Japanese culture were also affected by the social upheaval that marked the Meiji Restoration. The Japanese invited technicians, engineers, architects, and artists from Europe and the United States to teach their "modern" skills to eager Japanese students. The Meiji Era was a time when the Japanese copied Western artistic techniques and styles. Huge buildings of steel and reinforced concrete, adorned with Greek columns, appeared in many Japanese cities.

A national reaction set in by the end of the nineteenth century, however. Many Japanese artists began to return to older techniques. In 1889, the Tokyo School of Fine Arts was set up to promote traditional

Japanese art. Japanese artists searched for a new but truly Japanese means of expression. Some artists tried to bring together native and foreign techniques. Others returned to past artistic traditions for inspiration.

Cultural exchange also went the other way. Japanese arts and crafts, porcelains, textiles, fans, folding screens, and woodblock prints became fashionable in Europe and North America. Japanese art influenced Western painters. Japanese gardens, with their close attention to the positioning of rocks and falling water, became especially popular in the United States.

## ❀ SECTION REVIEW ❀

1. **Locate:**
   (a) Manchuria,    (b) Port Arthur

2. **Define:**
   (a) zaibatsu

3. **Identify:**
   (a) Treaty of Shimonoseki,    (b) gentlemen's agreement,    (c) Shidehara diplomacy,
   (d) *Some Prefer Nettles*

4. **Recall:**
   (a) Why did many Japanese regard their nation as vulnerable in the world economic arena in the late nineteenth century?
   (b) What impact did Japan's defeat of Russia in 1905 have on other European powers in the Far East?
   (c) What situations led to social dissatisfaction and unrest in Japan during the period from 1900 to 1940?

5. **Think Critically:**
   (a) Why didn't the economic development of Japan in the early part of the twentieth century necessarily mean that country would have democracy and social stability?
   (b) Why may the Japanese have been particularly attracted to art forms that were purely Japanese?

## Conclusion

Few areas of the world resisted the Western advances as stubbornly and effectively as East Asia. Although military, political, and economic pressures by the European powers were intense during this era, both China and Japan were able to retain their independence. No doubt, one reason was that both had a long history as well-defined states with a strong sense of national community. Geography, too, was in their favor. As a continental nation, China was able to survive partly because of its sheer size. Japan possessed the advantage of an island location.

Even more striking, however, is the different way each state tried to deal with the challenge. The Japanese were practical. They borrowed foreign ideas and institutions that appeared to be of value and at the same time not in conflict with traditional attitudes and customs. China agonized over the issue for half a century. Conservative elements fought a desperate battle to keep intact most of China's traditional heritage.

No doubt the Japanese approach was more effective. Japan made an orderly transition from a traditional to an advanced society. In China, the old system collapsed in disorder. However, the Japanese experiment was by no means a complete success. Ambitious efforts by Japanese leaders to carve out a share in the spoils of the empire led to conflict with China and rival Western powers. Meanwhile in Europe, old rivalries were leading to a bitter conflict that eventually engulfed the entire world.

## Notes

1. Quoted in Ssu-yu Teng and John K. Fairbank, eds., *China's Response to the West: A Documentary Survey, 1839–1923* (New York, 1970), p. 140.
2. Quoted in William Theodore de Bary et al., eds., *Sources of Chinese Tradition* (New York, 1963), p. 472.

# CHAPTER 7 REVIEW

## USING KEY TERMS

1. A practice in which European colonial powers enforced their own laws for their subjects living in Chinese ports was called _____.
2. Emperor Mutsuhito of Japan used the term _____ to describe the time of his rule.
3. A _____ is a large financial and industrial business combination in Japan.
4. _____ were areas in China where a particular foreign nation was given exclusive trading rights.
5. The Chinese policy of adopting Western technology while keeping its Confucian values was called _____.
6. Territories given to Japan's lords to govern after 1871 were called _____.
7. The _____ of the Meiji government had the power to appropriate funds.
8. The act of revolting against an established government is an _____.
9. The Chinese government was forced to pay a heavy _____, or payment, to the powers that had crushed the Boxer Rebellion.

## REVIEWING THE FACTS

1. How did the British use opium to strengthen their economic and political position in China?
2. What was the Open Door policy?
3. What was the result of the Boxer Rebellion?
4. What was the purpose of the Revolutionary Alliance that was formed under the leadership of Sun Yat-sen?
5. What was the Guomindang?
6. Why did China experience a period of civil war after the death of President Yuan Shikai?
7. What did Matthew Perry achieve in Japan in 1858?
8. What was the goal of the Sat-Cho alliance?
9. What was the result of the Treaty of Shimonoseki?

10. Why did Japan feel it needed to gain foreign territories to become an economic success and a military power?

## THINKING CRITICALLY

1. Why did European powers choose to establish spheres of influence in China rather than just trading with the Chinese as they did with many other nations?
2. What reasons may explain why the Chinese were not able to successfully resist domination by foreign powers?
3. Why didn't European colonial powers fight each other in China for control over that country's trade?
4. Why do many people believe Sun Yat-sen's three stages for creating democracy were really just a way for him to gain and retain power?
5. What benefits may China have received as a result of its domination by European colonial powers?
6. Why can the influence of Western politics, economics, and technology be found in the changes that took place in Japan during the late nineteenth century?
7. Why were many Japanese farmers opposed to the tax policies of the Meiji government?
8. What social conventions caused men to dominate Japanese society?
9. Why was it necessary for Japan to emphasize the construction of a strong navy as it increased its military power?
10. Why didn't the growth of production lead to improved living conditions for most of Japan's people in the early twentieth century?

# CHAPTER 7 REVIEW

## APPLYING SOCIAL STUDIES SKILLS

1. **Government:** Explain why any political system that automatically passes power from one generation to the next within one family is almost certain to decline over time. Use the experience of China during the nineteenth century as an example.
2. **Economics:** Explain why the economic interests of European colonial powers would not have been served by fighting a war in the Far East.
3. **Geography:** Explain why control of the Malay peninsula and the archipelago of present-day Indonesia was vital to the success of European trade with China but of little importance to the United States.
4. **Geography:** Study Map 7.2 on page 247 that shows the spheres of influence that existed in the Far East. Explain why it would have been foolish for European powers to try to occupy and dominate all of China instead of only taking over areas surrounding major port cities.
5. **Sociology:** Describe social values and frustrations that probably led to the Boxer Rebellion in China and to the Sat-Cho alliance in Japan.
6. **Government:** Explain how Japanese loyalty to the emperor was apparently used by some people to serve their own interests and gain power.
7. **Economics:** Why was the tax on farm land in Japan really a tax on consumers in that nation as well?

## MAKING TIME AND PLACE CONNECTIONS

1. Compare the experiences of people who lived in Britain's American colonies during the 1700s with those of native peoples who lived in European spheres of influence in China in the late nineteenth century.
2. Identify and explain possible reasons why parts of China were occupied and exploited by European powers while Japan was not.
3. Explain why China's vast size and many different people may have made it easier for European powers to dominate its trade and economy.
4. Compare and contrast the economic problems faced by Britain in the 1700s and Japan in the 1800s.
5. Identify similarities between monopolies created by American "robber barons" in the late nineteenth century and the zaibatsus that dominated the Japanese economy at the same time.
6. Compare and contrast the economic, political, and social situations facing Japan after World War I with those of Germany.

## BECOMING AN HISTORIAN

1. **Comparing and Contrasting:** Reread the selection "Ba Jin and the Chinese Novel" on pages 255–256. In particular, consider the quotation at the bottom of the first column that begins, "Now that you've graduated, . . ." Write an essay in which you compare and contrast the social values you hold with those held by the young man in this story. Describe conclusions historians might reach about the role of the family in Chinese culture from this passage.
2. **Geography as a Key to History:** Reread the letter from President Fillmore to the Emperor of Japan that appears on page 258. Although the United States may have been sincere in its desire to trade with Japan, identify and explain other geographic objectives this country may have had for the Open Door policy. Remember that the United States had just taken the Philippine Islands and Guam from Spain at the time this policy was initiated.

# THE CRISIS OF THE

*Charles Cundall's painting* The Withdrawal from Dunkirk, 1940 *speaks of the true horror and suffering of war. British soldiers attempt to flee from Dunkirk and escape the heavy German shelling. British Royal aircraft provide some defense for the soldiers.*

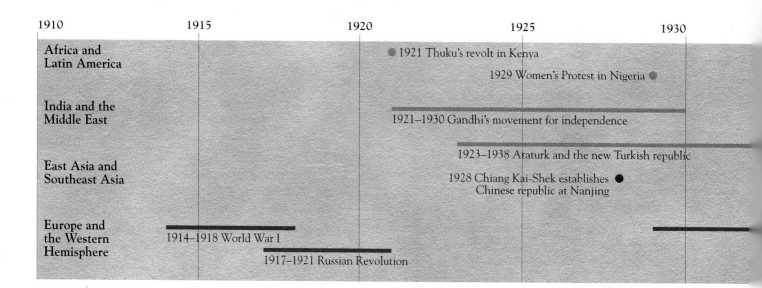

| | 1910 | 1915 | 1920 | 1925 | 1930 |
|---|---|---|---|---|---|
| **Africa and Latin America** | | | | ● 1921 Thuku's revolt in Kenya<br>1929 Women's Protest in Nigeria ● | |
| **India and the Middle East** | | | 1921–1930 Gandhi's movement for independence | | |
| **East Asia and Southeast Asia** | | | | 1923–1938 Ataturk and the new Turkish republic<br>1928 Chiang Kai-Shek establishes ●<br>Chinese republic at Nanjing | |
| **Europe and the Western Hemisphere** | 1914–1918 World War I<br>1917–1921 Russian Revolution | | | | |

# TWENTIETH CENTURY

## (1914–1945)

The period between 1914 and 1945 was one of the most destructive in the history of humankind. Probably sixty million people died as a result of World Wars I and II, the global conflicts that began and ended this era.

The two world wars transformed world history. By 1945, the era of European domination over world affairs was severely shaken. As World War I was followed by revolutions, the Great Depression, the mass-murder machines of totalitarian regimes, and the destructiveness of World War II, it appeared to many that European civilization had become a nightmare. Europeans, who had been accustomed to dominating the world at the beginning of the twentieth century, now watched helplessly at mid-century as the two new superpowers—the United States and the Soviet Union—created by two world wars took control of their destinies. Moreover, the power of the European states had been destroyed by the exhaustive struggles of World War II. The European colonial powers no longer had the energy or wealth to maintain their colonial empires after the war. With the decline of Western power, a new era of global relationships was about to begin.

## UNIT OUTLINE

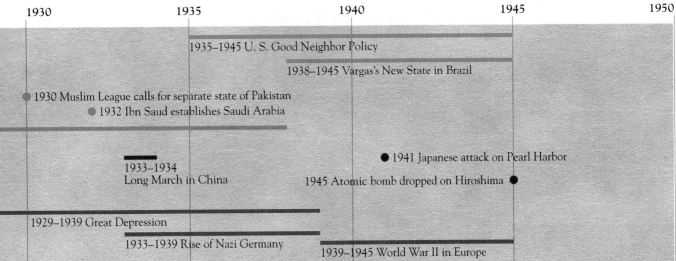

1930     1935     1940     1945     1950

1935–1945 U. S. Good Neighbor Policy

1938–1945 Vargas's New State in Brazil

1930 Muslim League calls for separate state of Pakistan

1932 Ibn Saud establishes Saudi Arabia

1933–1934 Long March in China

1941 Japanese attack on Pearl Harbor

1945 Atomic bomb dropped on Hiroshima

1929–1939 Great Depression

1933–1939 Rise of Nazi Germany

1939–1945 World War II in Europe

# THE BEGINNING OF
# THE TWENTIETH-CENTURY CRISIS:

8

On July 1, 1916, British and French infantry forces attacked German defensive lines along a twenty-five-mile front near the Somme River in France. Each soldier carried almost seventy pounds of equipment, which made it "impossible to move much quicker than a slow walk." German machine guns soon opened fire. "We were able to see our comrades move forward in an attempt to cross No-Man's-Land, only to be mown down like meadow grass," recalled one British soldier. "I felt sick at the sight of this carnage and remember weeping." In one day more than 21,000 British soldiers died. After six months of fighting, the British had advanced five miles. One million British, French, and German soldiers had died.

World War I (1914 to 1918) was the defining event of the twentieth century. It devastated the prewar economic, social, and political order of Europe. Its uncertain outcome prepared the way for an even more destructive war. People at the time, overwhelmed by the size of the war's battles and the number of casualties, simply called it the Great War.

The Great War was all the more disturbing to Europeans because it came after a period that many believed to have been an age of progress. There had

▶ *Poison gas, machine guns, and tanks made war more deadly than it had ever been before, particularly because military leaders did not understand the power of the weapons they possessed. This photo shows French soldiers assisting a wounded countryman.*

been international crises before 1914, but somehow Europeans had managed to avoid serious wars. Material prosperity and a strong belief in technological progress had convinced many people that human beings were on the verge of creating an "earthly paradise." The historian Arnold Toynbee expressed what the pre–World War I era had meant to his generation: "[It was expected] that life throughout the World would become more rational, more humane, and more democratic and that, slowly, but surely, political democracy would produce greater social justice. We had also expected that the progress of science and technology would make mankind richer, and that this increasing wealth would gradually spread from a minority to a majority. We had expected that all this would happen peacefully. In fact we thought that mankind's course was set for an earthly paradise."[1]

After 1918, when World War I ended, it was no longer possible to maintain naive illusions about the progress of Western civilization. World War I was followed by revolutions, the mass-murder machines of dictators, and the destructiveness of World War II. It became all too apparent that instead of a paradise, Western civilization had become a nightmare. World War I and the revolutions it spawned can properly be seen as the first stage in the crisis of the twentieth century.

# WAR AND REVOLUTION

## (1914 TO 1919)

CRISIS OF THE TWENTIETH CENTURY

WAR AND REVOLUTION
1914 | | 1919
1910                                    1945

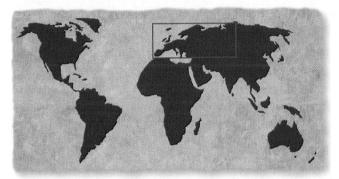

# QUESTIONS TO GUIDE YOUR READING

1. What were the long-range and immediate causes of World War I?

2. Why did World War I become a "war of attrition"?

3. What were the effects of World War I on political life, economic affairs, and women?

4. How did Lenin and the Bolsheviks manage to seize power in Russia despite their small numbers?

5. How did the Bolsheviks win the civil war in Russia?

6. Who were the participants in the 1919 Paris Peace Conference, and what were their objectives?

7. What were the most important results of the Paris Peace Conference?

# OUTLINE

1. THE ROAD TO WORLD WAR I

2. THE WAR

3. REVOLUTION AND THE END OF THE WAR

4. THE PEACE SETTLEMENTS

# THE ROAD TO WORLD WAR I

On June 28, 1914, the heir to the Austro-Hungarian throne, Archduke Francis Ferdinand, was assassinated in the Bosnian city of Sarajevo (SAWR-ee-YAE-VOE). This event was the immediate cause of World War I. However, long-range, underlying forces had been moving Europeans toward war for some time.

### Nationalism, the System of Alliances, and Internal Dissent

In the first half of the nineteenth century, liberals had believed that if European states were organized along national lines, these states would work together and create a peaceful Europe. The liberals had been very wrong. The system of nation-states that emerged in Europe in the last half of the nineteenth century led not to cooperation but to competition. Rivalries over colonies and trade intensified during an age of frenzied nationalism and imperialist expansion. At the same time, Europe's great powers had been divided into two loose alliances. Germany, Austria-Hungary, and Italy had formed the Triple Alliance in 1882. France, Great Britain, and Russia had created the Triple Entente (awn-TAWNT) in 1907 (see Chapter 5).

In the early years of the twentieth century, a series of crises had tested these alliances. Especially troublesome were the crises in the Balkans between 1908 and 1913, which taught the European states a dangerous lesson. Those governments that had exercised restraint in order to avoid war wound up being publicly humiliated. Those that went to the brink of war to maintain their national interests had often been praised for having preserved their national honor. By 1914, the major European states had come to believe that their allies were important. They now thought that their security depended on supporting their allies, even when the allies took foolish risks.

Diplomacy was often based on **brinkmanship** (the practice of threatening to go to war to achieve one's goals). This type of diplomacy was especially frightening in view of the nature of the European state system. Each nation-state regarded itself as subject to no higher interest or authority. Each state was guided by its own self-interest and success. Furthermore, most leaders thought that war was an acceptable way to preserve the power of their national states. These attitudes made war an ever-present possibility.

The growth of nationalism in the nineteenth century had yet another serious result. Not all ethnic groups had become nations. Slavic minorities in the Balkans and the Habsburg Empire, for example, still dreamed of creating their own national states. The Irish in the British Empire and the Poles in the Russian Empire had similar dreams.

National desires, however, were not the only source of internal strife at the beginning of the twentieth century. Socialist labor movements (see Chapter 5) had grown more powerful. They were increasingly inclined to use strikes, even

violent ones, to achieve their goals. Some conservative leaders, alarmed at the increase in labor strife and class division, even feared that European nations were on the verge of revolution. Some historians believe that the desire to suppress internal disorder may have encouraged some leaders to take the plunge into war in 1914.

## Militarism

The growth of mass armies after 1900 heightened the existing tensions in Europe. These armies also made it obvious that if war did come, it would be highly destructive. **Conscription** (a military draft) had been

**Map 8.1    Europe in 1914**

established as a regular practice in most Western countries before 1914. (The United States and Britain were exceptions.) European armies had doubled in size between 1890 and 1914. With its 1.3 million men, the Russian army had grown to be the largest. The French and German armies were not far behind, with 900,000 each. The British, Italian, and Austro-Hungarian armies numbered between 250,000 and 500,000 soldiers each.

Militarism, or aggressive preparation for war, was growing. As armies grew, so too did the influence of military leaders. They drew up vast and complex plans for quickly mobilizing millions of men and enormous quantities of supplies in the event of war. Military leaders feared that any changes in these plans would cause chaos in the armed forces. Thus, they insisted that their plans could not be altered. In the crises during the summer of 1914, this left European political leaders with little leeway. They were forced to make decisions for military instead of political reasons.

## The Outbreak of War: The Summer of 1914

Militarism, nationalism, the alliance system, and the desire to stifle internal dissent may all have played a role in the coming of World War I. However, it was the decisions made by European leaders in response to another crisis in the Balkans in the summer of 1914 that led directly to the conflict.

As we have seen, states in southeastern Europe had struggled to free themselves of Ottoman rule in the course of the nineteenth and early twentieth centuries. Furthermore, the rivalry between Austria-Hungary and Russia for domination of these new states created serious tensions in the region. By 1914, Serbia, supported

◀ *Russian troops greatly outnumbered the Germans, but the Germans were better trained and far better equipped. What do you think the American reaction would be if 2.5 million soldiers lost their lives in just one year?*

▲ *Hiram Maxim's invention, the machine gun, was used with deadly efficiency during World War I. The old war strategy of sending a mass of men against enemy lines quickly proved to be lethal to both sides.*

by Russia, was determined to create a large, independent Slavic state in the Balkans. Austria-Hungary, which had its own Slavic minorities to contend with, was equally determined to prevent that possibility. Many Europeans saw the potential danger in this explosive situation. The British ambassador to Vienna wrote in 1913:

> Serbia will some day set Europe by the ears, and bring about a universal war on the Continent. . . . I cannot tell you how exasperated people are getting here at the continual worry which that little country causes to Austria under encouragement from Russia. . . . It will be lucky if Europe succeeds in avoiding war as a result of the present crisis. The next time a Serbian crisis arises, . . . I feel sure that Austria-Hungary will refuse to admit of any Russian interference in the dispute and that she will proceed to settle her differences with her little neighbor by herself.[2]

It was against this backdrop of mutual distrust and hatred that the events of the summer of 1914 were played out.

On June 28, 1914, six young conspirators waited in the streets of Sarajevo during the visit of Archduke Francis Ferdinand of Austria-Hungary and his wife Sophia. The conspirators were members of the Black Hand, a Serbian terrorist organization that wanted Bosnia to be free of Austria-Hungary and part of a large Serbian kingdom. The plan was to kill the heir to the throne of Austria-Hungary, along with his wife. One of the six conspirators failed in the morning when the bomb he threw at the archduke's car glanced off and exploded against the car behind him. Later in the day, however, Gavrillo Princip, a nineteen-year-old Bosnian Serb, succeeded in shooting both the archduke and his wife.

The Austro-Hungarian government did not know whether or not the Serbian government had been directly involved in the archduke's assassination, but it did not care. It saw an opportunity to "render Serbia innocuous once and for all by a display of force," as the Austrian foreign minister put it. Austrian leaders, who feared Russian intervention on Serbia's behalf, sought the backing of their German allies. Emperor William II of Germany and his chancellor responded with a "blank check," saying that Austria-Hungary could rely on Germany's "full support," even if "matters went to the length of a war between Austria-Hungary and Russia."

Strengthened by German support, Austrian leaders sent an ultimatum to Serbia on July 23. In it, they made such extreme demands that Serbia had little choice but to reject some of them in order to preserve its sovereignty. Austria-Hungary then declared war on Serbia on July 28. Russia was determined to support Serbia's cause. On July 28, Tsar Nicholas II ordered partial mobilization of the Russian army against Austria-Hungary. (**Mobilization** is the process of assembling and making both troops and supplies ready for war. In 1914, it was considered an act of war.)

At this point, military war plans were at odds with diplomatic and political decisions. Leaders of the Russian army informed the tsar that their mobilization plans were based on a war against both Germany and Austria-Hungary at the same time. They could not par-

◄ *This photograph records the arrest of Gavrillo Princip shortly after the assassination of Archduke Francis Ferdinand and his wife.*

tially mobilize without creating chaos in the army. As a result, the Russian government ordered full mobilization of the Russian army on July 29, knowing that Germany would consider this an act of war against it. Indeed, Germany reacted quickly. It warned Russia that it must halt its mobilization within twelve hours. When Russia ignored this warning, Germany declared war on Russia on August 1.

At this stage of the conflict, German war plans determined whether or not France would become involved in the war. Under the guidance of General Alfred von Schlieffen (SHLEE-fun), chief of staff from 1891 to 1905, the German General Staff had drawn up a military plan. It was based on the assumption of a two-front war with France and Russia, because the two powers had formed a military alliance in 1894. The Schlieffen Plan called for a small holding action against Russia while most of the German army would make a rapid invasion of France before Russia could become effective in the east or before the British could cross the English Channel to help France. This meant invading France by moving quickly along the level coastal area through Belgium rather than through the rougher terrain to the southeast.

After the planned quick defeat of the French, most of the German army would then move to the east against Russia. Under the Schlieffen Plan, Germany could not mobilize its troops solely against Russia. Therefore, it declared war on France on August 3 after it had issued an ultimatum to Belgium on August 2 demanding the right of German troops to pass through Belgian territory. However, Belgium was a neutral nation. On August 4, Great Britain declared war on Germany, officially for violating Belgian neutrality. In fact, however, Britain was concerned about maintaining its world power. As one British diplomat put it, if Germany and Austria-Hungary would win the war, "what would be the position of a friendless England?" By August 4, all the great powers of Europe were at war.

### SECTION REVIEW

1. **Locate:**
   (*a*) Sarajevo,
   (*b*) English Channel

2. **Define:**
   (*a*) brinkmanship,    (*b*) conscription,
   (*c*) mobilization

3. **Identify:**
   (*a*) national honor,    (*b*) Black Hand,
   (*c*) General Alfred von Schlieffen

4. **Recall:**
   (*a*) Why was war an ever-present possibility in
   Europe at the beginning of the twentieth century?
   (*b*) How did the creation of military plans help
   lead the nations of Europe into World War I?
   (*c*) How did international alliances help to draw
   nations into World War I?

5. **Think Critically:** Why might the leaders of
   nations with internal problems be more willing to
   go to war than those that are economically, politically, and socially successful?

# THE WAR

Before 1914, many political leaders had become convinced that war involved so many political and economic risks that it was not worth fighting. Others had
believed that diplomats could easily control any situation and prevent the outbreak of war. At the beginning
of August 1914, both these prewar illusions were shattered. However, the new illusions that replaced them
soon proved to be equally foolish.

## 1914 to 1915: Illusions and Stalemate

Europeans went to war in 1914 with remarkable enthusiasm (see "You Are There: The Excitement of War").
Government propaganda had worked in stirring up
national hatreds before the war. Now, in August 1914,
the urgent pleas of governments for defense against
aggressors fell on receptive ears in every nation at war.
Most people seemed genuinely convinced that their
nation's cause was just.

A new set of illusions also fed the enthusiasm for
war. In August 1914, almost everyone believed that
the war would be over in a few weeks. People were
reminded that all European wars since 1815 had, in
fact, ended in a matter of weeks. Of course, they overlooked the U.S. Civil War (1861 to 1865), which was
the real model for World War I. Both the soldiers who
boarded the trains for the war front in August 1914 and
the jubilant citizens who showered them with flowers
when they left believed that the warriors would be
home by Christmas.

German hopes for a quick end to the war rested
upon a military gamble. The Schlieffen Plan had called
for the German army to make a vast encircling movement through Belgium into northern France. The army
would sweep around Paris and encircle most of the
French army. However, the German advance was
halted only twenty miles from Paris at the First Battle
of the Marne (MARN) (September 6 to 10). In their
desperate need to stop the Germans in this battle,
French military leaders took control of 2,000 Parisian
taxicabs, loaded them with fresh troops, and sent them
to the front line.

The war quickly turned into a stalemate, as neither
the Germans nor the French could dislodge each other
from the trenches they had begun to dig for shelter. Two
lines of trenches soon reached from the English Channel to the frontiers of Switzerland. The Western Front
had become bogged down in a **trench warfare** (fighting
from ditches, protected by barbed wire) that kept both
sides in virtually the same positions for four years.

In contrast to the Western Front, the war in the east
was marked by much more mobility. The cost in lives,
however, was equally enormous. At the beginning of
the war, the Russian army moved into eastern Germany but was decisively defeated at the Battle of Tannenberg on August 30 and the Battle of Masurian
Lakes on September 15. The Russians were no longer a
threat to German territory.

Austria-Hungary, Germany's ally, fared less well at
first. The Austrians had been defeated by the Russians
in Galicia (ga-LISH-ah) and thrown out of Serbia as
well. To make matters worse, the Italians betrayed the
Germans and Austrians and entered the war on the
Allied side by attacking Austria in May 1915. (France,

# YOU ARE THERE

## The Excitement of War

*The incredible outpouring of patriotic enthusiasm that greeted the declaration of war at the beginning of August 1914 demonstrated the power that nationalistic feeling had attained at the beginning of the twentieth century. This selection is taken from the autobiography of Stefan Zweig (ZWIGE [hard "g"]), an Austrian writer who captured well the celebration of war in Vienna in 1914.*

### Stefan Zweig, Selection from His Autobiography

The next morning I was in Austria. In every station placards had been put up announcing general mobilization. The trains were filled with fresh recruits, banners were flying, music sounded, and in Vienna I found the entire city in a tumult. . . . There were parades in the street, flags, ribbons, and music burst forth everywhere, young recruits were marching triumphantly, their faces lighting up at the cheering. . . .

As never before, thousands and hundreds of thousands felt what they should have felt in peace time, that they belonged together. A city of two million, a country of nearly fifty million, in that hour felt that they were participating in world history, in a moment which would never recur, and that each one was called upon to cast his small self into the glowing mass, there to be purified of all selfishness. All differences of class, rank, and language were flooded over at that moment by the rushing feeling of fraternity. Strangers spoke to one another in the streets, people who had avoided each other for years shook hands, everywhere one saw excited faces. Each individual was part of the people, and his person, his hitherto unnoticed person, had been given meaning. . . .

▲ *This photo captures the excitement of the troops as World War I was beginning. Compare and contrast this image with the picture that opens the chapter.*

What did the great mass know of war in 1914, after nearly half a century of peace? They did not know war, they had hardly given it a thought. They still saw it in the perspective of their school readers and of paintings in museums; brilliant cavalry attacks in glittering uniforms, the fatal shot always straight through the heart, the entire campaign a resounding march of victory—"We'll be home at Christmas," the recruits shouted laughingly to their mothers in August of 1914. . . . The young people were honestly afraid that they might

*(continued)*

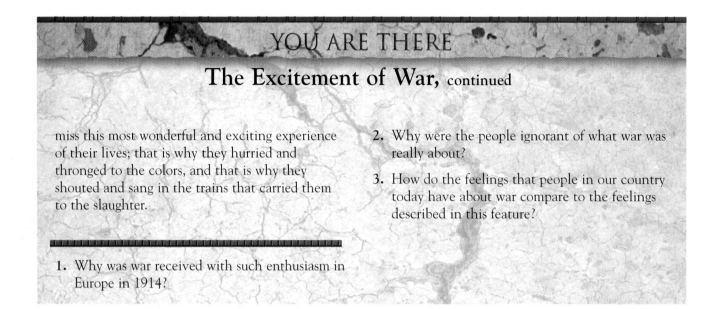

## YOU ARE THERE

# The Excitement of War, continued

miss this most wonderful and exciting experience of their lives; that is why they hurried and thronged to the colors, and that is why they shouted and sang in the trains that carried them to the slaughter.

1. Why was war received with such enthusiasm in Europe in 1914?

2. Why were the people ignorant of what war was really about?

3. How do the feelings that people in our country today have about war compare to the feelings described in this feature?

---

Great Britain, and Russia were called the Allied Powers, or Allies.) By this time, the Germans had come to the aid of the Austrians. A German-Austrian army defeated and routed the Russian army in Galicia and pushed the Russians back 300 miles into their own territory. Russian casualties stood at 2.5 million killed, captured, or wounded. The Russians had almost been knocked out of the war. Buoyed by their success, Germany and Austria-Hungary, joined by Bulgaria in September 1915, attacked and eliminated Serbia from the war.

## 1916 to 1917: The Great Slaughter

The successes in the east enabled the Germans to move back to the offensive in the west. The early trenches dug in 1914 had by now become elaborate systems of defense. The lines of trenches for both sides were protected by barbed wire entanglements three to five feet high and thirty yards wide, concrete machine-gun nests, and mortar batteries, supported further back by heavy artillery. Troops lived in holes in the ground, separated from each other by a no-man's-land.

The unexpected development of trench warfare baffled military leaders. They had been trained to fight wars of movement and maneuver. The only plan generals could devise was to attempt a breakthrough by throwing masses of men against enemy lines that had first been battered by artillery barrages. Once the decisive breakthrough had been achieved, they thought, they could then return to the war of movement that they knew best. At times, the high command on either side would order an offensive that would begin with an artillery barrage to flatten the enemy's barbed wire and leave the enemy in a state of shock (see "You Are There: The Reality of War—Trench Warfare"). After "softening up" the enemy in this fashion, a mass of soldiers would climb out of their trenches with fixed bayonets and hope to work their way toward the enemy trenches. The attacks rarely worked, however, because the mass of men advancing unprotected across open fields could be fired at by the enemy's machine guns. In 1916 and 1917, millions of young men died in the search for the elusive breakthrough. In ten months at Verdun in 1916, 700,000 men lost their lives over a few miles of land. World War I had turned into a **war of attrition,** or a war based on wearing the other side down by constant attacks and heavy losses.

Warfare in the trenches of the western front produced unimaginable horrors. Battlefields were hellish landscapes of barbed wire, shell holes, mud, and

**Map 8.2   The Western Front, 1914–1918**

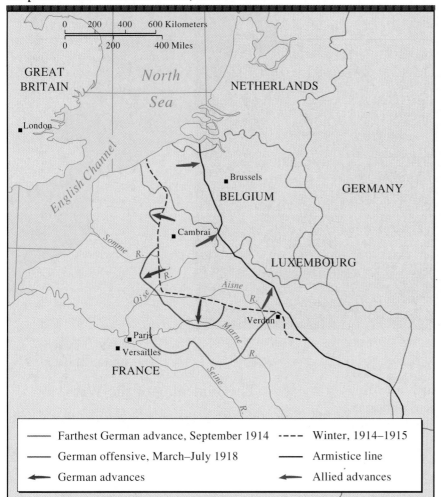

| | |
| --- | --- |
| —— Farthest German advance, September 1914 | ---- Winter, 1914–1915 |
| —— German offensive, March–July 1918 | —— Armistice line |
| ← German advances | ← Allied advances |

injured and dying men. The introduction of poison gas in 1915 produced new forms of injuries. One British writer described them:

> I wish those people who write so glibly about this being a holy war could see a case of mustard gas . . . could see the poor things burnt and blistered all over with great mustard-coloured suppurating [pus-forming] blisters with blind eyes all sticky . . . and stuck together, and always fighting for breath, with voices a mere whisper, saying that their throats are closing and they know they will choke.[3]

By the end of 1915, the airplane had also appeared on the battlefront for the first time in history. At first, planes were used to spot the enemy's position. However, planes soon began to support offensives by attacking ground targets, especially enemy communications. Fights for control of the air occurred and increased over time. At first, pilots fired shots at each other with handheld pistols. Next, machine guns were mounted on the noses of planes, which made the skies considerably more dangerous. The Germans also used their giant airships—the zeppelins (ZEP-uh-lunz)—to bomb

◄ *The city of Verdun, 125 miles east of Paris, was heavily damaged in a battle that took 700,000 lives and gained the German forces only a few miles of land. Why do you think both sides fought so bitterly over just one town?*

London and eastern England. This caused little damage but frightened many people. Germany's enemies, however, soon found that zeppelins, which were filled with hydrogen gas, quickly became raging infernos when hit by antiaircraft guns.

## The Widening of the War

Because of the stalemate on the Western Front, both sides sought to gain new allies who might provide a winning advantage. The Ottoman Empire had already

▲ *This French Breguet bomber plane brought a new kind of warfare to World War I. It was one of the first airplanes to have wing flaps.*

# YOU ARE THERE
# The Reality of War—Trench Warfare

*The romantic illusion about the adventure of war that filled the minds of so many young men who marched off to battle quickly fell apart after a short time in the trenches on the Western Front. This description of trench warfare is taken from the most famous novel that emerged from World War I, Erich Maria Remarque's (ruh-MARK['s]) All Quiet on the Western Front. Remarque had fought in the trenches in France.*

### Erich Maria Remarque, *All Quiet on the Western Front*

We wake up in the middle of the night. The earth booms. Heavy fire is falling on us. We crouch into corners. We distinguish shells of every calibre.

Each man lays hold of his things and looks again every minute to reassure himself that they are still there. The dug-out heaves, the night roars and flashes. We look at each other in the momentary flashes of light, and with pale faces and pressed lips shake our heads.

Every man is aware of the heavy shells tearing down the parapet [wall of earth], rooting up the embankment and demolishing the upper layers of concrete. . . . Already by morning a few of the recruits are green and vomiting. They are too inexperienced. . . .

The bombardment does not diminish. It is falling in the rear too. As far as one can see it spouts fountains of mud and iron. A wide belt is being raked.

The attack does not come, but the bombardment continues. Slowly we become mute. Hardly a man speaks. We cannot make ourselves understood.

Our trench is almost gone. At many places it is only eighteen inches high, it is broken by holes,

▲ *A British officer leads a raiding party out of a World War I trench and into the open field. How successful do you think these maneuvers were?*

and craters, and mountains of earth. A shell lands square in front of our post. At once it is dark. We are buried and must dig ourselves out. . . .

Towards morning, while it is still dark, there is some excitement. Through the entrance rushes in a swarm of fleeing rats that try to storm the walls. Torches light up the confusion. Everyone yells and curses and slaughters. The madness and despair of many hours unloads itself in this outburst. Faces are distorted, arms strike out, the beasts scream; we just stop in time to avoid attacking one another. . . .

Suddenly it howls and flashes terrifically, the dugout cracks in all its joints under a direct hit,

*(continued)*

## YOU ARE THERE

# The Reality of War—Trench Warfare, continued

fortunately only a light one that the concrete blocks are able to withstand. It rings metallically, the walls reel, rifles, helmets, earth, mud, and dust fly everywhere. Sulphur fumes poor in. . . . The recruit starts to rave again and two others follow suit. One jumps up and rushes out, we have trouble with the other two. I start after the one who escapes and wonder whether to shoot him in the leg—then it shrieks again. I fling myself down and when I stand up the wall of the trench is plastered with smoking splinters, lumps of flesh, and bits of uniform. I scramble back.

Suddenly the nearer explosions cease. The shelling continues but it has lifted and falls behind us, our trench is free. We seize the hand-grenades, pitch them out in front of the dug-out and jump after them. The bombardment has stopped and a heavy barrage now falls behind us. The attack has come.

No one would believe that in this howling waste there could still be men; but steel helmets now appear on all sides out of the trench, and fifty yards from us a machine-gun is already in position and barking.

The wire-entanglements are torn to pieces. Yet they offer some obstacle. We see the storm-troops coming. Our artillery opens fire. Machine-guns rattle, rifles crack. The charge works its way across. . . . We recognize the distorted faces, the smooth helmets: they are French. They have already suffered heavily when they reach the remnants of the barbed-wire entanglements. A whole line has gone down before our machine-guns; then we have a lot of stoppages and they come nearer.

I see one of them, his face upturned, fall into a wire cradle. His body collapses, his hands remain suspended as though he were praying. Then his body drops clean away and only his hands with the stumps of his arms, shot off, now hang in the wire.

1. At what time did the attack come?

2. Do you think an attack at night or one during the day would be more frightening? Why?

3. Why did the men "become mute"?

4. Why do you think the men attacked the rats so savagely?

come into the war on Germany's side in August 1914. Russia, Great Britain, and France declared war on the Ottoman Empire in November. The Allies tried to open a Balkan front by landing forces at Gallipoli (guh-LIP-uh-lee), southwest of Constantinople, in April 1915. However, Bulgaria entered into the war on the side of the Central Powers (as Germany, Austria-Hungary, and the Ottoman Empire were called), and a disastrous campaign at Gallipoli caused the Allies to withdraw. Italy, as we have seen, also entered the war on the Allied side. In return, France and Great Britain promised to let Italy have some Austrian territory. The Italian forces were completely ineffective, however, and the Allies had to come to their rescue.

By 1917, the war that had started in Europe had truly become a world conflict. In the Middle East, a British officer who came to be known as Lawrence of Arabia urged Arab princes to revolt in 1917 against their Ottoman overlords. In 1918, British forces from Egypt destroyed the Ottoman Empire in the Middle

**Map 8.3   The Eastern Front, 1914–1918**

0   200   400   600 Kilometers
0        200        400 Miles

SWEDEN

St. Petersburg

*Baltic Sea*

RUSSIA

Moscow

(EAST PRUSSIA)

Tannenberg

GERMAN EMPIRE

Masurian Lakes

Warsaw   Brest-Litovsk

Prague

Kiev   *Dnieper R.*   *Don R.*

AUSTRIA   GALICIA

Vienna   *Dniester R.*

CARPATHIAN MTS.   (UKRAINE)

HUNGARY

(CRIMEA)

ROMANIA

*Danube R.*   Belgrade

(BOSNIA)   *Black Sea*

SERBIA

BULGARIA

ITALY

Constantinople

ALBANIA   *Gallipoli*   *Bosphorus*

GREECE   *Dardanelles*   OTTOMAN EMPIRE

–·–   Russian advances: 1914 – 1916          ——   Brest-Litovsk boundary: 1918

·····   Deepest German penetration                 Battle site, 1914

---

East. For their Middle East campaigns, the British mobilized forces from India, Australia, and New Zealand. The Allies also took advantage of Germany's preoccupations in Europe and lack of naval strength to seize German colonies in the rest of the world. Japan seized a number of German-held islands in the Pacific. Australia seized German New Guinea.

Most important to the Allied cause was the entry of the United States into the war. At first, the United States tried to remain neutral in the Great War. As the war dragged on, however, it became more difficult to do so. The immediate cause of U.S. involvement grew out of the naval war between Germany and Great Britain.

Only once did the German and British naval forces actually engage in direct battle—at the Battle of Jutland on May 31, 1916, when the Germans won an inconclusive victory. Britain used its superior naval power to good effect, however, by throwing up a naval blockade of Germany. Germany retaliated by setting up its own blockade of Britain. It enforced its blockade with the use of unrestricted submarine warfare, which included the sinking of passenger liners. On May 7, 1915, the British ship *Lusitania* was sunk by German forces. There were 1,100 civilian casualties, including over 100 Americans. This brought strong U.S. protests. The German government suspended unrestricted submarine warfare in September 1915 to avoid further antagonizing the United States.

By January 1917, however, the Germans were eager to break the deadlock in the war. They decided on another military gamble by returning to unrestricted submarine warfare. German naval officers convinced Emperor William II that the use of unrestricted submarine warfare could starve the British into submission within five months. When the emperor expressed concern about the United States, he was told not to worry; the British would starve before the Americans could act. Even if the Americans did intervene, Admiral Holtzendorff assured the emperor, "I give your Majesty my word as an officer that not one American will land on the continent."

▶ *The two German military leaders of the war, Paul von Hindenburg (on the left) and Erich Ludendorff, are shown with Emperor William II. Why do you think the emperor gradually lost power during the war?*

The German naval officers were quite wrong, however. The British were not forced to surrender. Furthermore, the return to unrestricted submarine warfare brought the United States into the war on April 6, 1917. U.S. troops did not arrive in large numbers in Europe until 1918. However, the entry of the United States into the war in 1917 not only gave the Allied powers a psychological boost when they needed it but also brought them a major new source of money and war goods.

The year 1917 had not been a good one for the Allies. Allied offensives on the Western Front were badly defeated. The Italian armies were smashed in October. In November 1917, the Russian Revolution led to Russia's withdrawal from the war (see the discussion later in the chapter). Germany was now free to concentrate entirely on the Western Front. The cause of the Central Powers looked favorable, although war weariness in the Ottoman Empire, Bulgaria, Austria-Hungary, and Germany was beginning to take its toll. The home front was rapidly becoming a cause for as much concern as the war front.

## The Home Front: The Impact of Total War

As World War I dragged on, it became a **total war** (war involving a complete mobilization of resources and people) that affected the lives of all citizens in the warring countries, however remote they might be from the battlefields. Masses of men and matériel (equipment and supplies) had to be organized for years of combat. (Germany alone had 5.5 million men in uniform in 1916.) This need for organization led to three developments: an increased centralization of government powers, economic controls, and the manipulation of public opinion to keep the war effort going.

The war was expected to be short, so little thought had been given to long-term wartime needs. Governments had to respond quickly, however, when the war machines failed to achieve their knockout blows. More and more men and matériel were needed to continue the war. To meet these needs, governments expanded their powers. Most European countries had already set up some system of mass conscription, or military draft. It was now carried to unheard-of heights as countries

▲ *This patriotic poster was part of an active government campaign to recruit soldiers and create enthusiasm for the war effort. By 1916, even Britain, which had raised the largest volunteer army in modern times, was forced to adopt compulsory military service.*

mobilized tens of millions of young men for final victory. Even countries that continued to rely on volunteers were forced to resort to conscription. In 1916, compulsory military service was introduced in Great Britain. (Great Britain had the largest volunteer army in modern history—one million men—in 1914 and 1915.)

Throughout Europe, wartime governments also expanded their powers over their economies. Free-market capitalistic systems were temporarily put aside. Governments set up price, wage, and rent controls; rationed food supplies and materials; regulated imports and exports; and took over transportation systems and industries. In effect, in order to mobilize the entire

resources of their nations for the war effort, European nations set up **planned economies** (systems directed by government agencies). Under conditions of total war mobilization, the differences between soldiers at war and civilians at home were narrowed. In the view of political leaders, all citizens were part of a national army dedicated to victory. As U.S. president Woodrow Wilson said, the men and women "who remain to till the soil and man the factories are no less a part of the army than the men beneath the battle flags."

As the Great War dragged on and casualties grew worse, the patriotic enthusiasm that had marked the early stages of World War I waned. By 1916, there were numerous signs that civilian morale was beginning to crack under the pressure of total war. War governments, however, fought back against the growing opposition to the war. Of course, authoritarian regimes, such as those of Germany, Russia, and Austria-Hungary, had always relied on force to subdue their populations.

Under the pressures of the war, however, even democratic states expanded their police powers to stop internal dissent. The British Parliament passed a Defence of the Realm Act (DORA) at the very beginning of the war. It allowed the government to arrest protestors as traitors. Newspapers were censored, and sometimes their publication was even suspended. In France, government authorities had at first been lenient about public opposition to the war. By 1917, however, the authorities began to fear that open opposition to the war might weaken the French will to fight. When Georges Clemenceau (KLEM-un-SOE) became premier near the end of 1917, the lenient French policies came to an end. Basic civil liberties were suspended for the rest of the war. The editor of an antiwar newspaper was executed on a charge of helping the enemy. Journalists who wrote negative war reports were drafted.

Wartime governments made active use of propaganda to arouse enthusiasm for the war. At the beginning, public officials needed to do little to achieve this goal. The British and French, for example, exaggerated German atrocities in Belgium and found that their citizens were only too willing to believe these accounts. However, as the war progressed and morale sagged, governments were forced to devise new techniques for

▶ *During the war, women were employed in many kinds of jobs that had traditionally been held by men. Here German women work in a munitions factory. How do you think these women were viewed by women who stayed at home or by troops fighting on the front lines?*

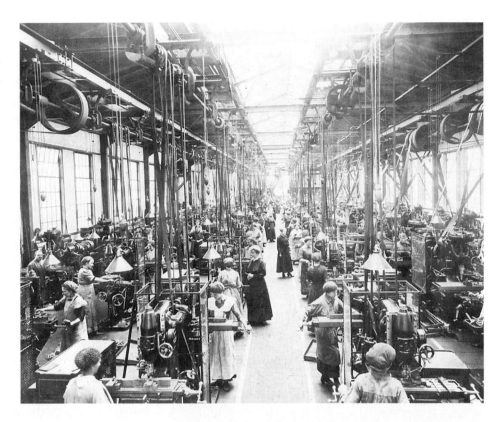

motivating the people. In one British recruiting poster, for example, a small daughter asked her father, "Daddy, what did YOU do in the Great War?" while her younger brother played with toy soldiers and cannons.

Total war made a significant impact on European society. For one thing, it brought an end to unemployment. Because millions of men were in the armed services, there were jobs available for everyone who was able to work. World War I also created new roles for women. Because so many men went off to fight at the front, women were called upon to take over jobs that had not been available to them before. The number of women employed in Great Britain who held new jobs or replaced men rose by 1,345,000. Women were also now employed in jobs that had been considered beyond the "capacity of women." These included such occupations as chimney sweeps, truck drivers, farm laborers, and above all, factory workers in heavy industry. Thirty-eight percent of the workers in the Krupp Armaments works in Germany in 1918 were women.

Women were employed at lower wages than men, but they now began to demand equal pay. The French government passed a law in July 1915 that provided a minimum wage for women who worked in the home textile industry. This industry had grown dramatically because of the need for military uniforms. In 1917, the government decreed that men and women should receive equal rates for piecework. Despite the noticeable increase in women's wages that resulted from government regulations, women's industrial wages still were not equal to men's wages by the end of the war.

Even worse, the place of women in the workforce was far from secure. Both men and women seemed to expect that many of the new jobs for women were only temporary. This was evident in the British poem "War Girls," written in 1916:

*There's the girl who clips your ticket for the train,*
*And the girl who speeds the lift from floor to floor,*
*There's the girl who does a milk-round in the rain,*
*And the girl who calls for orders at your door.*

*Strong, sensible, and fit,*
*They're out to show their grit,*
*And tackle jobs with energy and knack.*
*No longer caged and penned up,*
*They're going to keep their end up*
*Till the khaki soldier boys come marching back.*[4]

At the end of the war, governments quickly removed women from the jobs they had encouraged them to take earlier. By 1919, there were 650,000 unemployed women in Great Britain. Wages for the women who were still employed were lowered. The work benefits for women from World War I seemed to be short-lived as men returned to the job market.

Nevertheless, in some countries the role played by women in the wartime economies did have a positive impact on the women's movement for social and political emancipation. The most obvious gain was the right to vote that was given to women in Germany and Austria immediately after the war. (In Britain, women had obtained this right in January 1918.) Many upper- and middle-class women had also gained new freedoms. In ever-larger numbers, these young women took jobs; had their own apartments; and showed their new independence by smoking in public, wearing shorter dresses, and choosing new hairstyles.

## ❀ SECTION REVIEW ❀

1. **Locate:**
   (*a*) Verdun,   (*b*) Constantinople

2. **Define:**
   (*a*) trench warfare,   (*b*) war of attrition,
   (*c*) total war,   (*d*) planned economies

3. **Identify:**
   (*a*) First Battle of the Marne,   (*b*) mustard gas,
   (*c*) zeppelin,   (*d*) Lawrence of Arabia,
   (*e*) Woodrow Wilson,   (*f*) Defence of the Realm Act (DORA)

4. **Recall:**
   (*a*) What two beliefs were commonly held in Europe that convinced many people that World War I would not take place?

(*b*) Why was a "breakthrough" such an important military goal in World War I?
(*c*) How did unrestricted submarine warfare draw the United States into World War I?
(*d*) What three developments increased centralization of government power during World War I?

5. **Think Critically:** Why do times of war often speed the process of achieving greater rights for women?

# REVOLUTION AND THE END OF THE WAR

By 1917, total war was creating serious domestic problems in all of the warring European states. Only Russia, however, experienced a complete collapse in that year. Out of Russia's collapse came the Russian Revolution, the impact of which would be widely felt in Europe and the world for decades to come.

## Background to the Russian Revolution

Tsar Nicholas II of Russia was an autocratic ruler who relied on the army and bureaucracy to hold up his regime. However, World War I put the tsarist government to a test that it could not meet. Russia was unprepared both militarily and technologically for the total war of World War I. It had no competent military leaders. Even worse, the tsar—and of all European monarchs, only the tsar—insisted on taking personal charge of the armed forces despite his obvious lack of ability and training for such an awesome burden. Russian industry was unable to produce the weapons needed for the army. Many soldiers were trained with broomsticks. Others were sent to the front without rifles and told to pick one up from a dead comrade. Ill led and ill armed, the Russian army suffered incredible losses. Between 1914 and 1916, two million soldiers had been killed, and another four to six million had been wounded or captured. By 1917, the Russian will to fight had vanished.

## Map 8.4    The Russian Revolution and Civil War

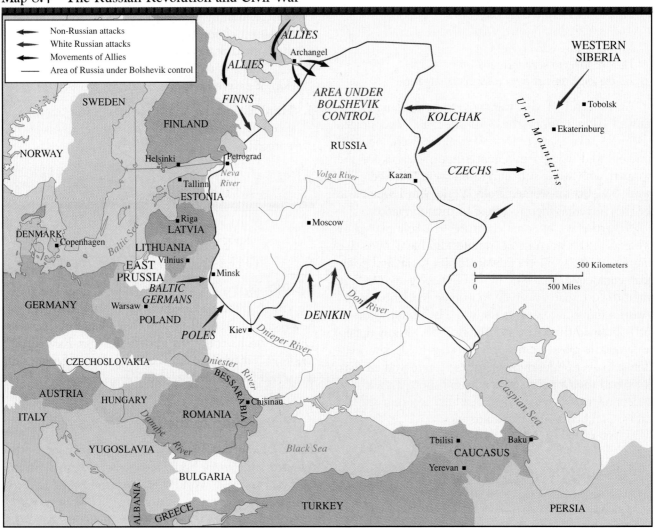

The tsarist government was totally unprepared for the tasks that it faced in 1914. Even conservative aristocrats were appalled by the incompetent and inefficient bureaucracy that controlled the political and military system. In the meantime, Tsar Nicholas II was increasingly cut off from events by his German-born wife, Alexandra. She was a willful and stubborn woman who had fallen under the influence of Rasputin (ra-SPYOOT-un), an uneducated Siberian peasant who claimed to be a holy man. Alexandra believed that Rasputin was holy, for he alone seemed able to stop the bleeding of her son Alexis. Alexis, the heir to the throne, had hemophilia (a deficiency in the ability of the blood to clot). With the tsar at the front, Alexandra made all important decisions. However, she insisted on first consulting Rasputin, the man she called "her beloved, never-to-be-forgotten teacher, savior, and mentor." Rasputin's influence made him an important power behind the throne. He did not hesitate to interfere in government affairs.

As the leadership at the top stumbled its way through a series of military and economic disasters, the

Russian middle class, aristocrats, peasants, soldiers, and workers grew more and more upset with the tsarist regime. Even conservative aristocrats who supported the monarchy felt the need to do something to save the situation. For a start, they assassinated Rasputin in December 1916. It was not easy to kill this man of incredible physical strength. They shot him three times and then tied him up and threw him into the Neva River. He drowned, but not before he had managed to untie the knots underwater. The assassination of Rasputin, however, proved to be too late to save the monarchy. Its fall came quickly.

At the beginning of March 1917, a series of strikes broke out in the capital city of Petrograd (formerly St. Petersburg). Here the actions of working-class women helped to change the course of Russian history. In February 1917, the government had introduced bread rationing in the capital city after the price of bread had skyrocketed. Many of the women who stood in the lines waiting for bread were also factory workers who worked twelve-hour days. The Russian government had become aware of the situation in the capital from a police report:

> Mothers of families, exhausted by endless standing in line at stores, distraught over their half-starving and sick children, are today perhaps closer to revolution than [the liberal opposition leaders] and of course they are a great deal more dangerous because they are the combustible material for which only a single spark is needed to burst into flame.[5]

On March 8, about 10,000 women marched through Petrograd demanding "Peace and Bread" and "Down with Autocracy." Soon the women were joined by other workers. Together they called for a general strike that was able to shut down all the factories in the city

▲ *Rasputin was an illiterate Siberian peasant. Why do you think people said that his eyes held hypnotic power?*

on March 10. Alexandra wrote Nicholas II at the battlefront, "This is a hooligan movement. If the weather were very cold they would all probably stay at home." Nicholas ordered the troops to break up the crowds by shooting them if necessary. Soon, however, large numbers of the soldiers joined the demonstrators. The Duma, or legislative body, which the tsar had tried to dissolve, met anyway. On March 12, it established a Provisional Government that urged the tsar to step down. Because he no longer had the support of the army or even the aristocrats, Nicholas II did step down, on March 15.

The Provisional Government headed by Alexander Kerensky decided to carry on the war to preserve Russia's honor. This was a major blunder. It satisfied neither the workers nor the peasants, who wanted above all an end to the war. The Provisional Government was also faced with another authority, the **soviets,** or councils composed of deputies from the workers and soldiers. The soviet of Petrograd had been formed in March 1917. At the same time, soviets sprang up in army units, factory towns, and rural areas. The soviets represented the more radical interests of the lower classes. They were largely made up of socialists of different kinds. One group—the Bolsheviks—came to play a crucial role.

## Lenin and the Bolshevik Seizure of Power

The Bolsheviks were a small faction of Russian Social Democrats (a Marxist party) who had come under the leadership of Vladimir Ulianov (ool-YAWN-uf), known to the world as V. I. Lenin. Born in 1870 to a middle-class family, Lenin received a legal education and became a lawyer. In 1887, he turned into a revolutionary—a dedicated enemy of tsarist Russia—when

▶ *Large crowds gathered in town squares throughout Russia to protest the tsarist governmental actions. Do you think Lenin would have gained power as quickly if the Provisional Government had withdrawn Russian troops from the war?*

his older brother was executed by the tsar's police for planning to assassinate the tsar. Lenin's search for a revolutionary faith led him to Marxism. In 1894, he moved to St. Petersburg, where he organized an illegal working-class group. Lenin was arrested for his revolutionary activity and was shipped to Siberia. After his release, he chose to go into exile in Switzerland. Eventually, he became the leader of the Bolshevik wing of the Russian Social Democratic Party.

Under Lenin's direction, the Bolsheviks became a party dedicated to violent revolution. He believed that only a violent revolution could destroy the capitalist system. A "vanguard" of activists, he said, must form a small party of well-disciplined professional revolutionaries to accomplish the task. Between 1900 and 1917, Lenin spent most of his time in Switzerland. When the Provisional Government was formed in March 1917, he believed that an opportunity for the Bolsheviks to seize power had come. In April 1917, the German military leaders, hoping to create disorder in Russia,

shipped Lenin to Russia in a "sealed train" by way of Finland.

Lenin's arrival in Russia opened a new stage of the Russian Revolution. Lenin maintained that the soviets of soldiers, workers, and peasants were ready-made instruments of power. He believed that the Bolsheviks needed to work toward gaining control of these groups and then use them to overthrow the Provisional Government. At the same time, the Bolsheviks would seek mass support through the use of propaganda by making promises to the people. These promises included an end to the war, the redistribution of all land to the peasants, the transfer of factories and industries from capitalists to committees of workers, and the transfer of government power from the Provisional Government to the soviets. Three simple slogans summed up the Bolshevik program: "Peace, Land, Bread," "Worker Control of Production," and "All Power to the Soviets."

By the end of October, the Bolsheviks had reached a slight majority in the Petrograd and Moscow soviets.

The number of party members had also grown from 50,000 to 240,000. With the close cooperation of Leon Trotsky, a dedicated revolutionary, Lenin organized a Military Revolutionary Committee within the Petrograd soviet. Its task was to plot the overthrow of the government. On the night of November 6, Bolshevik forces seized the Winter Palace, the seat of the Provisional Government. The Provisional Government quickly collapsed with little bloodshed.

This overthrow of the Provisional Government had been timed to coincide with a meeting in Petrograd of the all-Russian Congress of Soviets, which represented local soviets from all over the country. Outwardly, Lenin turned over the power of the Provisional Government to this Congress of Soviets. The real power, however, passed to a Council of People's Commissars, headed by Lenin (see "You Are There: Ten Days That Shook the World").

The Bolsheviks, soon renamed the Communists, still faced enormous obstacles. For one thing, Lenin had promised peace. Fulfilling that promise, he realized, would not be an easy task. It would mean the humiliating loss of much Russian territory. There was no real choice, however. On March 3, 1918, Lenin signed the Treaty of Brest-Litovsk with Germany and gave up eastern Poland, Ukraine, Finland, and the Baltic provinces. To his critics, Lenin argued that it made no difference. The spread of socialist revolution throughout Europe would make the treaty largely irrelevant. In any case, he had promised peace to the Russian people. Real peace did not come, however. The country soon sank into civil war.

## Civil War in Russia

Many people were opposed to the new Bolshevik, or Communist, regime. These people included not only groups loyal to the tsar but also liberals and anti-Leninist socialists. These groups were joined by thousands of Allied troops who were sent to different parts of Russia in the hope of bringing Russia back into the war.

Between 1918 and 1921, the Bolshevik (or Red) Army was forced to fight on many fronts. The first serious threat to the Bolsheviks came from Siberia. Here a

### CONNECTIONS
#### TO OUR WORLD

**The Mystery of Anastasia**   Soon after the murder of Tsar Nicholas II, his wife Alexandria, and their five children on the night of July 16, 1919, rumors began to circulate that some members of the family had survived. In 1921, a young woman in Dalldorf, Germany, claimed to be the Grand Duchess Anastasia, the youngest daughter of Nicholas II. Some surviving members of the Romanov family became convinced that she was Anastasia. Grand Duke Andrew, Nicholas II's first cousin, said after meeting with her, "For me there is definitely no doubt; it is Anastasia."

Later, the woman claiming to be Anastasia came to the United States. While in New York, she registered at a Long Island hotel as Anna Anderson and soon became known by that name. In 1932, she returned to Germany. During the next thirty years, she pursued a claim in German courts for part of the estate left to Empress Alexandra's German relatives. In the 1960s in the United States, Anna Anderson became even better known as a result of the popular play and film, *Anastasia*.

In 1968, Anna Anderson returned to the United States, where she died in 1984. In 1994, DNA testing of tissues from Anna Anderson revealed that she was not the Grand Duchess Anastasia. In all probability, Anna Anderson was Franziska Schanzkowska, a Polish farmer's daughter who had always dreamed of being an actress.

White (anti-Bolshevik) force attacked westward and advanced almost to the Volga River before being stopped. Attacks also came from the Ukrainians in the southeast and from the Baltic regions. In mid-1919, White forces swept through Ukraine and advanced almost to Moscow. However, they were pushed back. By 1920, the major White forces had been defeated and Ukraine retaken. The next year, the Communist regime regained control over the independent nation-

## YOU ARE THERE

# Ten Days That Shook the World

*John Reed was an American journalist who helped found the American Communist Labor party. Accused of treason, he fled the United States and went to Russia. In* Ten Days That Shook the World, *Reed left an eyewitness account of the Russian Revolution. He considered V. I. Lenin the great hero of the Bolshevik success.*

**John Reed, *Ten Days That Shook the World***

It was just 8:40 when a thundering wave of cheers announced the entrance of the presidium, with Lenin—great Lenin—among them. A short, stocky figure, with a big head set down in his shoulders, bald and bulging. Little eyes, a snubbish nose, wide, generous mouth, and heavy chin. Dressed in shabby clothes, his trousers much too long for him. Unimpressive, to be the idol of a mob, loved and revered as perhaps few leaders in history have been. . . .

Now Lenin, gripping the edge of the reading stand, letting his little winking eyes travel over the crowd as he stood there waiting, apparently oblivious to the long-rolling ovation, which lasted several minutes. When it finished, he said simply, "We shall now proceed to construct the Socialist order!" Again that overwhelming human roar.

"The first thing is the adoption of practical measures to realize peace. . . . We shall offer peace to the peoples of all the warring countries upon the basis of the Soviet terms—no annexations, no indemnities, and the right of self-determination of peoples. . . . This proposal of peace will meet with resistance on the part of the imperialist governments—we don't fool ourselves on that score. But we hope that revolution will soon break out in all the warring countries; that is why we address ourselves especially to the workers of France, England and Germany. . . .

"The revolution of November 6th and 7th," he ended, "has opened the era of the Social Revolution. . . . The labour movement, in the name of peace and Socialism, shall win, and fulfill its destiny. . . ."

---

alist governments in the Caucasus (KAW-ku-sus): Georgia, Russian Armenia, and Azerbaijan (AZ-ur-BIE-JAWN).

The royal family was yet another victim of the civil war. After the tsar had abdicated, he, his wife, and their five children had been taken into captivity. They were moved in August 1917 to Tobolsk, in Siberia. In April 1918, they were moved to Ekaterinburg, a mining town in the Urals. On the night of July 16, members of the local soviet murdered the tsar and his family and burned their bodies in a nearby mine shaft.

How had Lenin and the Communists triumphed in the civil war over what seemed to be overwhelming forces? For one thing, the Red Army was a well-disciplined fighting force. This was largely due to the organizational genius of Leon Trotsky. As commissar of war, Trotsky reinstated the draft and insisted on rigid discipline. Soldiers who deserted or refused to obey orders were executed on the spot.

Furthermore, the disunity of the anti-Communist forces weakened the efforts of the Whites. Political differences created distrust among the Whites and prevented them from cooperating effectively with one another. Some Whites insisted on restoring the tsarist regime. Others believed that only a more liberal and democratic program had any chance of success. These political differences made it virtually impossible for the Whites to achieve military cooperation.

## Ten Days That Shook the World, continued

There was something quiet and powerful in all this, which stirred the souls of men. It was understandable why people believed when Lenin spoke.

1. Did John Reed agree or disagree with Lenin?

2. How do you know that Reed's account of Lenin is biased?

▲ *Lenin may not have been a handsome man, but he was the driving force behind the Bolsheviks as they took control of Russia. In this 1917 photo, Lenin speaks to a crowd in Moscow.*

The Whites, then, had no common goal. The Communists, in contrast, had a single-minded sense of purpose. Inspired by their vision of a new socialist order, the Communists had the determination that comes from revolutionary fervor and convictions.

The Communists were also able to translate their revolutionary faith into practical instruments of power. A policy of **war communism,** for example, was used to ensure regular supplies for the Red Army. War communism meant government control of banks and most industries, the seizing of grain from peasants, and the centralization of state administration under Communist control. Another Communist instrument was rev-

olutionary terror. Although the old tsarist secret police had been abolished, a new Red secret police—known as the Cheka (CHAE-kaw)—replaced it. The Cheka began a Red Terror aimed at nothing less than the destruction of all those who opposed the new regime (much like the Reign of Terror in the French Revolution). The Red Terror added an element of fear to the Communist regime.

Finally, the presence of foreign armies on Russian soil enabled the Communists to appeal to the powerful force of Russian patriotism. The Allied powers had originally sent troops to Russia to encourage the Russians to remain in the war. With the end of the war on

▲ *Communists used agitational propaganda, such as this vibrant poster, very effectively during the civil war. Brief slogans coupled with stirring images, like the Red Army star, served to educate the Russian people about the Communists.*

November 11, 1918, however, the Allied troops were no longer needed. Nevertheless, they remained, and even more were sent. Allied countries did not hide their anti-Communist feelings. At one point, over 100,000 foreign troops—mostly Japanese, British, American, and French—were stationed on Russian soil. These forces rarely fought, however, nor did they pursue a common strategy. However, they did give material assistance to anti-Communist forces. The Allied troops also made it easy for the Communist government to appeal to patriotic Russians to fight the attempts of foreigners to control their country. Allied troops were never substantial enough to make a military difference in the civil war. They did serve indirectly, however, to help the Bolshevik cause.

By 1921, the Communists were in control of Russia. In the course of the civil war, the Communist regime had transformed Russia into a bureaucratically centralized state dominated by a single party. It was also a state that was largely hostile to the Allied powers that had sought to help the Communists' enemies in the civil war.

## The Last Year of the War

For Germany, the withdrawal of the Russians from the war in March 1918 offered new hope for a successful end to the war. The victory over Russia persuaded Erich von Ludendorff, who guided German military operations, to make one final military gamble—a grand offensive in the west to break the military stalemate.

The German attack was launched in March. By April, German troops were within fifty miles of Paris. However, the German advance was stopped at the Second Battle of the Marne, on July 18. French, Moroccan, and American troops (140,000 fresh American troops had just arrived), supported by hundreds of tanks, threw the Germans back over the Marne (see "The Role of Science and Technology: The Beginning of Tank Warfare"). Ludendorff's gamble had failed. With the arrival of two million more American troops, Allied forces began making a steady advance toward Germany.

On September 29, 1918, General Ludendorff informed German leaders that the war was lost. He demanded that the government sue for peace at once. German officials soon discovered, however, that the Allies were unwilling to make peace with the autocratic imperial government of Germany. Reforms were begun to create a liberal government. However, these constitutional reforms came too late for the exhausted and angry German people.

On November 3, sailors in Kiel (KEE-ul), in northern Germany, mutinied. Within days councils of workers and soldiers were forming throughout northern Germany and taking over civilian and military offices. William II gave in to public pressure and left the country on November 9. The Social Democrats under Friedrich Ebert then announced the creation of a democratic republic. Two days later, on November 11, 1918, the new German government agreed to an

# THE ROLE OF SCIENCE AND TECHNOLOGY
## The Beginning of Tank Warfare

▲ *This World War I photo shows British tanks on their way to the front lines. Why do you think the Allies did not use tanks more effectively during the war?*

Trench warfare on the Western Front made World War I a war of stalemate and a defensive slaughter. This state of affairs led some to seek a new way of moving to the offensive. The tank proved to be the answer.

The tank was an armored vehicle that could move across rough ground. A British army officer, Ernest Swinton, first conceived of the idea. The first tank—a British model—appeared in 1916. Its caterpillar tracks enabled it to cross rough terrain. Guns were mounted on its sides. "Male" tanks used two 57-millimeter guns to attack enemy machine gun positions. "Female" tanks carried four machine guns aimed chiefly at enemy infantry.

These first tanks, used in the Battle of the Somme in 1916, were not very effective. A new model, the Mark IV, had more success in November 1917 at the Battle of Cambrai (kam-BRAE).

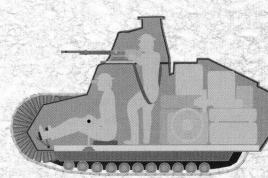

▲ *This diagram shows the working parts of a French Renault "mosquito" tank. This tank did not travel across rough terrain as well as British ones, but it could turn more quickly.*

Four hundred tanks spearheaded an advance that drove five miles into the enemy lines, and with relatively few casualties.

*(continued)*

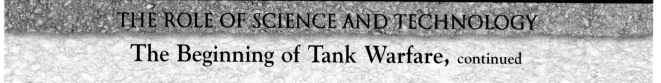

# THE ROLE OF SCIENCE AND TECHNOLOGY
## The Beginning of Tank Warfare, continued

The French soon followed with their own tanks. They were less effective, however. The Germans were contemptuous of the new tanks and considered them a sign of weakness. However, they, too, finally got around to producing their own tank—the A7V. It was unstable, required a crew of eighteen, and saw little action, however.

By 1918, the British had developed a Mark V model that had a more powerful engine and could be more easily maneuvered. Tanks, now used in large numbers and coordinated with infantry and artillery, became effective instruments in pushing back the retreating German army.

The tank came too late to have a great effect on the outcome of World War I. The lesson, however, was not lost on those who realized the tank's potential for creating a whole new kind of warfare. In World War II, lightning attacks that depended on tank columns and massive air power enabled armies to cut quickly across battle lines and encircle entire enemy armies. It was a far cry from the trench warfare of World War I.

1. Which country developed the first tank?

2. Why were the Germans contemptuous of the new tanks?

3. What impact did the development of tanks have on warfare?

armistice (a truce). The war was over, but the revolutionary forces set in motion by the war were not yet exhausted.

The Social Democrats had established a democratic republic in Germany on November 9, 1918. However, a group of radical socialists, unhappy with the moderate policies of the Social Democrats, formed the German Communist Party in December 1918. A month later, the Communists tried to seize power in Berlin. The new Social Democratic government, backed by regular army troops, crushed the rebels and brutally murdered Rosa Luxemburg and Karl Liebknecht (LEEP[kuh]NEKT), leaders of the German Communists. A similar attempt at Communist revolution in the city of Munich (MYOO-nik), in southern Germany, was also crushed. The new German republic had been saved from radical revolution. The attempt at revolution, however, left the German middle class with a deep fear of communism.

Austria-Hungary, too, experienced disintegration and revolution. As war weariness took hold of the empire, ethnic groups increasingly sought to achieve their independence. By the time the war ended, the Austro-Hungarian Empire was no more. It had been replaced by the independent republics of Austria, Hungary, and Czechoslovakia, along with the large monarchical state called Yugoslavia. Rivalries among the nations that succeeded Austria-Hungary would weaken eastern Europe for the next eighty years.

## ✿  SECTION REVIEW  ✿

1. **Locate:**
   (a) Petrograd,   (b) Volga River,   (c) Ukraine,
   (d) Caucasus,   (e) Ural Mountains

2. **Define:**
   (a) soviets,   (b) war communism

3. **Identify:**
   (a) Alexandra,   (b) Rasputin,   (c) Alexander Kerensky,   (d) Russian Social Democrats,

(*e*) Vladimir Ulanov,   (*f*) Leon Trotsky,
(*g*) Cheka,   (*h*) Second Battle of the Marne,
(*i*) Friedrich Ebert

4. **Recall:**
   (*a*) What factors limited Russia's ability to fight in World War I?
   (*b*) Why did Tsar Nicholas give up power in 1917?
   (*c*) What three promises did the Bolsheviks make to gain popular support in 1917?
   (*d*) What problem of the White Army forces probably kept them from defeating the Red Army?

5. **Think Critically:** Why is the presence of foreign soldiers in a nation likely to stir people to be more willing to fight?

## THE PEACE SETTLEMENTS

In January 1919, representatives of twenty-seven victorious Allied nations met in Paris. Their task was to make a final settlement of the Great War. Some delegates believed that this conference would avoid the mistakes made at Vienna in 1815. There, leaders had rearranged the map of Europe to meet the selfish desires of the great powers. Harold Nicolson, one of the British delegates in Paris, expressed what he believed this conference would achieve instead: "We were journeying to Paris not merely to liquidate the war, but to found a New Order in Europe. We were preparing not Peace only, but Eternal Peace. There was about us the halo of some divine mission. . . . For we were bent on doing great, permanent and noble things."[6]

### Background to Peacemaking

Nicolson's quest for "Eternal Peace" was a difficult one, however. Over a period of years, the reasons for fighting World War I had changed dramatically. European nations had gone to war in 1914 largely to achieve territorial gains. By the beginning of 1918, some leaders were using more idealistic reasons. No one expressed these reasons better than the U.S. president, Woodrow Wilson. Wilson outlined "Fourteen Points" to the U.S. Congress—his basis for a peace settlement that he believed justified the enormous military struggle then being waged. Later, Wilson spelled out additional steps for a truly just and lasting peace.

Wilson's proposals included "open covenants (binding agreements) of peace, openly arrived at" instead of secret diplomacy; the reduction of national armaments (military forces or weapons) to a "point consistent with domestic safety"; and the self-determination of people (each people could have its own state) so that "all well-defined national aspirations shall be accorded the utmost satisfaction." Wilson portrayed World War I as a people's war against "absolutism and militarism." These two enemies of liberty, he argued, could be eliminated only by creating democratic governments and a "general association of nations." The latter would guarantee the "political independence and territorial integrity to great and small states alike." Wilson became the spokesperson for a new world order based on democracy and international cooperation. When he arrived in Europe for the peace conference, he was enthusiastically cheered by many Europeans.

Wilson soon found, however, that more practical motives guided other states at the Paris Peace Conference. Secret treaties and agreements that had been made before the war had raised the hopes of European nations for territorial gains. These hopes could not be totally ignored, even if they did conflict with the principle of self-determination put forth by Wilson. National interests also complicated the deliberations of the Paris Peace Conference. For example, David Lloyd George, prime minister of Great Britain, had won a decisive victory in elections in December of 1918. His platform was simple: make the Germans pay for this dreadful war.

France's approach to peace, in contrast, was chiefly guided by its desire for national security. To Georges Clemenceau, the feisty premier of France who had led his country to victory, the French people had suffered the most from German aggression. They deserved revenge, but also security against future German aggression. Clemenceau wanted a Germany stripped of all weapons, vast German payments to cover the costs

▶ *The Big Four at the Paris Peace Conference were David Lloyd George, Britain; Vittorio Orlando, Italy; Georges Clemenceau, France; and Woodrow Wilson, United States. Which three countries made the major decisions during the conference?*

of the war, and a separate Rhineland as a buffer state between France and Germany. Wilson denounced these demands as contrary to the principle of national self-determination.

Twenty-seven nations met at the Paris Peace Conference, but the most important decisions were made by Wilson, Clemenceau, and Lloyd George. Italy, which was considered one of the so-called Big Four powers, played a much less important role than the other key powers—the United States, France, and Great Britain—called the Big Three. Germany, of course, was not invited to attend, and Russia could not be there because of its civil war.

In view of the many conflicting demands at the peace conference, it was no surprise that the Big Three quarreled. Wilson wanted to create a League of Nations to prevent future wars. Clemenceau and Lloyd George wanted to punish Germany. In the end, only compromise made it possible to achieve a peace settlement.

Wilson's wish that the creation of an international peacekeeping organization be the first order of business was granted. Already on January 25, 1919, the confer-

ence accepted the idea of a League of Nations. In return, Wilson agreed to make compromises on territorial arrangements. He did so because he believed that the League could later fix any unfair settlements. Clemenceau also compromised to get some guarantees for French security. He gave up France's wish for a separate Rhineland and instead accepted a defensive alliance with Great Britain and the United States. Both Great Britain and the United States pledged to help France if it were attacked by Germany.

## The Treaty of Versailles

The final peace settlement of Paris consisted of five separate treaties with the defeated nations—Germany, Austria, Hungary, Bulgaria, and Turkey. The Treaty of Versailles with Germany, signed at Versailles near Paris, on June 28, 1919, was by far the most important of the treaties. The Germans considered it a harsh peace. They were especially unhappy with Article 231, the so-called War Guilt Clause, which declared that

Germany (and Austria) were responsible for starting the war. Moreover, the treaty ordered Germany to pay **reparations** (financial compensation) for all the damage to which the Allied governments and their people had been subjected as a result of the war "imposed upon them by the aggression of Germany and her allies."

The military and territorial provisions of the Treaty of Versailles also angered the Germans. Germany had to reduce its army to 100,000 men, cut back its navy, and eliminate its air force. Alsace and Lorraine, taken by the Germans from France in 1871, were now returned. Sections of Prussia were awarded to a new Polish state. German land west and as far as thirty miles east of the Rhine was made a demilitarized zone and stripped of all weapons or fortifications. This, it was hoped, would serve as a barrier to any future German military moves westward against France. Outraged by the "dictated peace," the new German government vowed to resist rather than accept the treaty. However, it had no real alternative. Rejection of the treaty would mean a renewal of the war. That, as German army leaders pointed out, was no longer possible.

## The Other Peace Treaties

The separate peace treaties made with the other Central Powers (Austria, Hungary, Bulgaria, and Turkey) redrew the map of eastern Europe. Many of these changes had already taken place at the end of the war. Both the German and Russian Empires lost considerable territory in eastern Europe, and the Austro-Hungarian Empire disappeared altogether. New nation-states emerged from the lands of these three empires: Finland, Latvia, Estonia, Lithuania, Poland, Czechoslovakia, Austria, and Hungary. New territorial arrangements were also made in the Balkans. Romania acquired additional lands from Russia, Hungary, and Bulgaria. Serbia formed the nucleus of a new state, called Yugoslavia, which combined Serbs, Croats, and Slovenes.

The Paris Peace Conference was supposedly guided by the principle of self-determination. However, the mixtures of peoples in eastern Europe made it impossible to draw boundaries along neat ethnic lines. Compromises had to be made, sometimes to satisfy the national interests of the victors. France, for example, had lost Russia as its major ally on Germany's eastern border. Thus, France wanted to strengthen and expand Poland, Czechoslovakia, Yugoslavia, and Romania as much as possible. Those states could then serve as barriers against Germany and Communist Russia.

As a result of compromises, almost every eastern European state was left with a minorities problem that had the potential of leading to future conflicts. Germans in Poland; Hungarians, Poles, and Germans in Czechoslovakia; and the combination of Serbs, Croats, Slovenes, Macedonians, and Albanians in Yugoslavia all became sources of later conflict. Moreover, the new map of Eastern Europe was based upon the temporary collapse of power in both Germany and Russia. Neither country, however, accepted the new eastern frontiers. To many, it seemed only a matter of time before Germany or Russia would become strong again and make changes.

Yet another centuries-old empire—the Ottoman Empire—was broken up by the peace settlement after the war. To gain Arab support against the Ottoman Turks during the war, the Western Allies had promised to recognize the independence of Arab states in the Middle Eastern lands of the Ottoman Empire. Once the war was over, however, the Western nations changed their minds. France took control of Lebanon and Syria, whereas Britain received Iraq and Palestine. Both acquisitions were officially called mandates. Woodrow Wilson had opposed the outright annexation of colonial territories by the Allies. As a result, the peace settlement had set up a system of mandates whereby a nation officially governed but did not own a territory on behalf of the League of Nations.

The peace settlement reached at Paris soon came under attack, especially by the defeated Central Powers. There were others who also thought that the peacemakers had been shortsighted. The famous British economist John Maynard Keynes (KAYNZ), for example, condemned the concern with frontiers at the expense of economic issues. He thought that the economic provisions of the treaty would weaken the European economy.

**Map 8.5    Territorial Changes in Europe and the Middle East after World War I**

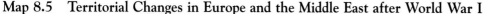

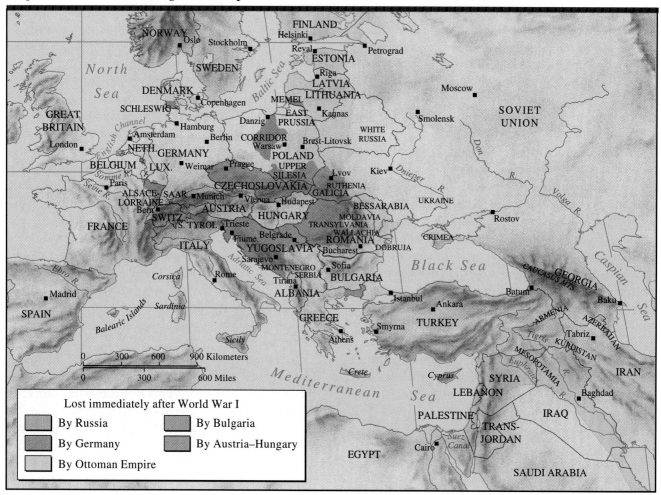

Others, however, thought the peace settlement was the best that could be achieved under the circumstances. Self-determination, they believed, had served reasonably well as a central organizing principle. The creation of the League of Nations, moreover, gave some hope that future conflicts could be resolved peacefully. However, within twenty years of the signing of the peace treaties, Europe was again engaged in war.

Some historians have suggested that perhaps the cause of the failure of the peace of 1919 was its lack of enforcement. To enforce the peace, the chief architects of the treaty needed to be actively involved. This was especially true in helping the new German state develop into a peaceful and democratic republic. The U.S. Senate was returning to a philosophy of isolationism, however, and thus failed to ratify the Treaty of Versailles. As a result, the United States never even joined the League of Nations. In addition, the U.S. Senate also rejected Wilson's defensive alliance with Great Britain and France. Already by the end of 1919, the United States was limiting its involvement in European affairs.

This retreat by the United States had dire consequences. American withdrawal from the defensive alliance with Britain and France led Britain to withdraw as well. Thus, by removing itself from European affairs, the United States forced France to stand alone in facing its old enemy. Frightened by this turn of events, France decided to take strong actions against Germany, and that only made the Germans more resentful. By the end of 1919, it appeared that the peace treaties of 1919 were not going to bring peace. As it turned out, they became the first steps toward World War II.

## ❀ SECTION REVIEW ❀

1. **Locate:**
   (*a*) Alsace-Lorraine,   (*b*) Lebanon,
   (*c*) Syria

2. **Define:**
   (*a*) reparations

3. **Identify:**
   (*a*) Fourteen Points,   (*b*) David Lloyd George,
   (*c*) Georges Clemenceau,   (*d*) League of Nations,
   (*e*) Article 231,   (*f*) mandates,   (*g*) John Maynard Keynes

4. **Recall:**
   (*a*) What French demands did the United States denounce as contrary to the principle of self-determination?
   (*b*) What did the creation of a League of Nations have to do with Woodrow Wilson's willingness to sign the Treaty of Versailles?
   (*c*) Why was it impossible to draw state boundaries along ethnic lines in Eastern Europe?
   (*d*) How did the United States leave France to stand alone against Germany after World War I?

5. **Think Critically:** Why may it have been a mistake for Woodrow Wilson to participate directly in the peace talks at the end of World War I?

## Conclusion

World War I shattered the liberal, rational society of late-nineteenth- and early-twentieth-century Europe. The incredible destruction and the death of almost ten million people undermined the whole idea of progress.

New propaganda techniques had been successful in leading entire populations to continue to participate in a devastating slaughter.

World War I was a total war—one that involved a complete mobilization of resources and people. The power of governments over the lives of their citizens increased. Civil liberties, such as freedom of the press and speech, were limited in the name of national security. World War I made the practice of strong central authority a way of life.

The turmoil created by World War I seemed to open the door to even greater insecurity. Revolutions broke up old empires and created new states, which led to new problems. The hope that Europe and the rest of the world would return to normalcy was soon dashed by the failure to achieve a lasting peace, economic depression, and the rise of dictatorial regimes that sought even greater control over the lives of their subjects (see Chapters 9 and 10).

Finally, World War I ended the age of European domination over world affairs. By destroying their own civilization on the battlefields of Europe in World War I, Europeans indirectly encouraged the subject peoples of their vast colonial empires to begin movements for national independence. World War II would complete the self-destructive process that Europeans had begun in 1914.

## Notes

1. Arnold Toynbee, *Surviving the Future* (New York, 1971), pp. 106–107.
2. Quoted in Joachim Remak, "1914—The Third Balkan War: Origins Reconsidered," *Journal of Modern History* 43 (1971): 364–365.
3. Quoted in J. M. Winter, *The Experience of World War I* (New York, 1989), p. 142.
4. Quoted in Catherine W. Reilly, ed., *Scars upon My Heart: Women's Poetry and Verse of the First World War* (London, 1981), p. 90.
5. Quoted in William M. Mandel, *Soviet Women* (Garden City, New York, 1975), p. 43.
6. Harold Nicolson, *Peacemaking, 1919* (Boston and New York, 1933), pp. 31–32.

# CHAPTER 8 REVIEW

## USING KEY TERMS

1. The practice of requiring young people to join the military, which was followed by many nations before World War I, was called _____.
2. World War I became a _____, or a war based on wearing the other side down by constant attacks and heavy losses.
3. _____ is the term used to describe the Soviet Union's centralization of control over its economy (for example, forcibly taking grain).
4. After World War I Germany was required by the Treaty of Versailles to make payments called _____ to the nations that won the war.
5. World War I involved a complete mobilization of resources and people that affected the lives of all citizens in the warring countries—a situation called _____.
6. Before World War I many European nations completed the _____ of their military by assembling troops and supplies for war.
7. After World War I communist leaders organized Russia by forming councils of workers and soldiers called _____.
8. The development of _____ baffled military leaders who had been trained to fight wars of movement.
9. Nations that have communist governments control their production and distribution of goods and services through _____.
10. The policy of threatening to go to war as a means to achieve national goals has been called _____.

## REVIEWING THE FACTS

1. What nations belonged to the Triple Alliance and the Triple Entente before the start of World War I?
2. A nationalist from what nation was accused of the assassination of Archduke Ferdinand?
3. What chemical agent was first used as a weapon in World War I?
4. How did the British government try to eliminate opposition from the people who were opposed to entering World War I?
5. Why were Alexandra and Rasputin able to almost control the Tsar's government during much of World War I?
6. What was the intended purpose of the League of Nations?
7. What territories did Germany give up to France at the end of World War I?

## THINKING CRITICALLY

1. How did the creation of the Triple Alliance and the Triple Entente contribute to the causes of World War I?
2. In what ways was the fighting in World War I different from the fighting that took place in earlier wars?
3. Why did the Germans use unrestricted submarine warfare in World War I, even though they realized the policy was likely to bring the United States into the war against them?
4. Why did Germany help Lenin return to Russia from Switzerland in 1917?
5. Why did the fact that Germany was fighting in the East and the West make it more difficult for them to win World War I?
6. What promise did Lenin make to gain the support of the Russian people in 1917?
7. Why do some people feel it is unlikely that a lasting peace could have been created at the end of World War I, no matter what was stated in the Treaty of Versailles?

# CHAPTER 8 REVIEW

## APPLYING SOCIAL STUDIES SKILLS

1. **Government:** Why were many people in Europe willing to allow their government leaders to draw them into a war without protest?
2. **Economics:** Why are raw materials of great importance in a war of attrition?
3. **Sociology:** What social values in the years prior to the war contributed to the willingness of many Europeans to go to war?
4. **Government:** What were the differences between the political processes in the United States and in that of many European nations that resulted in the United States being slower to enter World War I?
5. **Geography:** Draw a map of Europe that indicates geographic formations that influenced the course of World War I. Include mountains, rivers, seas, forests, etc. Provide a key that explains the importance of each feature.
6. **Government:** Why was it almost imperative that the leaders of the victorious nations in Europe place the responsibility for the war on Germany?

## MAKING TIME AND PLACE CONNECTIONS

1. How might a lack of systems for rapid mass communication (like radio and television) in the early twentieth century have made war more likely then than it is today?
2. Why might military and political leaders during World War I have been more willing than today's leaders to use the weapons of mass destruction?
3. When the United States and North Vietnam negotiated to end the war in Southeast Asia in the early 1970s, it took almost two years for them to agree on the shape of the negotiating table. The Treaty of Versailles that ended World War I,

a much larger war, was completed in only a few months. What made this speedy conclusion possible?
4. Why aren't geographic features like rivers, seas, or mountains likely to have as much importance in fighting a war today as they did in World War I?

## BECOMING AN HISTORIAN

1. **Cause and Effect:** What events resulted from each of the causes identified below?
   (*a*) the formation of alliances in Europe before World War I
   (*b*) the use of weapons of mass destruction in World War I
   (*c*) the decision of the Germans to use unrestricted submarine warfare
   (*d*) the decision of the victorious nations to impose unreasonable reparations on Germany
   (*e*) the decision of the United States Senate not to ratify the Treaty of Versailles
2. **Primary and Secondary Sources:** Although the United States Senate chose not to ratify the Treaty of Versailles, a number of U.S. senators stated that the Senate might reconsider its choice if changes were made in the treaty. Part of a specific change suggested by Senator Henry Cabot Lodge appears below. What insights does this primary source give you into the reasons and feelings of the Senate that you may not have found in a secondary source such as this textbook?

   *The United States assumes no obligation to preserve the territorial integrity or political independence of any other country or to interfere in controversies between nations. . . or to employ the military or naval forces of the United States under any article of the treaty for any purpose. . . .*

# DEPRESSION, DEMOCRACY, AND DICTATORSHIP: THE WESTERN

**9**

Only twenty years after the Treaty of Versailles, Europeans were again at war. In the 1920s, however, many people assumed that Europe and the world were about to enter a new era of international peace, economic growth, and political democracy. These hopes of the 1920s were never realized, however. After 1919, most people wanted peace but were unsure how to maintain it. Efforts to find new ways to resolve conflicts, especially through the new League of Nations, failed. Although everyone favored disarmament, few could agree on how to achieve it.

Europe was faced with severe economic problems after World War I. Most devastating of all was the Great Depression that began at the end of 1929. The Great Depression brought untold misery to millions of people. Begging for food on the streets became widespread, especially when soup kitchens were unable to keep up with the demand. Larger and larger numbers of people were homeless and moved from place to place looking for work and shelter. In the United States, the homeless set up

shantytowns they named "Hoovervilles" after the U.S. president, Herbert Hoover. In their misery, some people saw suicide as the only solution. One unemployed person said, "Today, when I am experiencing this for the first time, I think that I should prefer to do away with myself, to take gas, to jump into the river, or leap from some high place. . . . would I really come to such a decision? I do not know." Social unrest spread rapidly. Some of the unemployed staged hunger marches to get attention. In democratic countries, more and more people began to listen to, and vote for, radical voices calling for extreme measures.

According to Woodrow Wilson, World War I had been fought to make the world safe for democracy. For a while after 1919, political democracy did seem well established. The hopes for democracy soon faded, however, as dictatorial regimes spread into Italy and Germany and across eastern Europe.

▶ *Many middle-class families found themselves unexpectedly homeless during the Great Depression, and some people had to resort to desperate measures for finding food.*

# WORLD BETWEEN WORLD WARS

## (1919 TO 1939)

### CRISIS OF THE TWENTIETH CENTURY

| 1910 | 1919 | BETWEEN THE WORLD WARS | 1939 | 1945 |

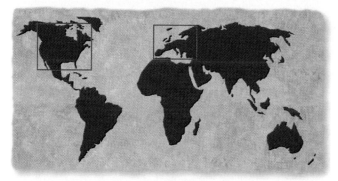

## QUESTIONS TO GUIDE YOUR READING

1. What were the causes of the Great Depression?

2. How did Great Britain, France, and the United States respond to the Great Depression?

3. To what extent was Fascist Italy a totalitarian state?

4. How did Joseph Stalin establish a totalitarian regime in the Soviet Union?

5. What were Adolf Hitler's basic ideas, and how did he rise to power?

6. What were the chief features of the Nazi total state?

7. What impact did the growth of mass culture and mass leisure have upon European society in the 1920s and 1930s?

## THE FUTILE SEARCH FOR A NEW STABILITY

The peace settlement at the end of World War I had tried to fulfill the nineteenth-century dream of nationalism by creating new boundaries and new states. From its beginning, however, this peace settlement had left nations unhappy. Conflicts over disputed border regions between Germany and Poland, Poland and Lithuania, Poland and Czechoslovakia, Austria and Hungary, and Italy and Yugoslavia poisoned mutual relations in eastern Europe for years. Many Germans viewed the Treaty of Versailles as a dictated peace and vowed to revise it.

### An Uncertain Peace: The Search for Security

The U.S. president Woodrow Wilson had realized that the peace treaties had unwise provisions that could serve as new causes for conflicts. He had placed many of his hopes for the future in the League of Nations.

307

The league, however, was not very effective in maintaining the peace. The failure of the United States to join the league had weakened its effectiveness from the beginning. Moreover, the league could use only economic sanctions to stop aggression. France wanted to make the league more effective by creating some kind of international army, but other nations feared France's suggestion. They did not want to give up any of their sovereignty to a larger international body.

After both the United States and Great Britain failed to honor their defensive military alliances with France, the French felt dangerously alone. Between 1919 and 1924, their desire for security led them to demand a strict enforcement of the Treaty of Versailles. This tough policy toward Germany began with the issue of reparations. These were the payments that the Germans were supposed to make for the damage they had done in the war.

In April 1921, the Allied Reparations Commission set a sum of 132 billion marks ($33 billion) for German reparations, payable in annual installments of 2.5 billion (gold) marks. Allied threats to occupy the Ruhr valley, Germany's chief industrial and mining center, led the new German republic to make its first payment in 1921. By the following year, however, the German government, faced with financial problems, announced that it was unable to pay any more. France was outraged and sent troops to occupy the Ruhr valley. Because Germany would not pay reparations, France would collect reparations in kind by operating and using the Ruhr mines and factories.

Both Germany and France suffered from the French occupation of the Ruhr. The German government adopted a policy of passive resistance to French occupation. German workers went out on strike, and the government paid their salaries, largely by printing more paper money. This only added to the inflation that had already begun in Germany by the end of the war. The German mark soon became worthless. In 1914, 4.2 marks equaled 1 dollar. By November 1, 1923, the ratio had reached 130 billion marks to 1 dollar. By the end of November, it had increased to an incredible 4.2 trillion to 1. Evidence of runaway inflation was everywhere. Workers used wheelbarrows to carry home their weekly pay. One woman left a basket

## CONNECTIONS
### AROUND THE WORLD

**The Great Flu Epidemic**   World War I, which cost the lives of ten million people, had a devastating effect on Europe. At the end of the war, a flu epidemic also proved disastrous to people all over the world. Some observers believe that it began among American soldiers in Kansas. When they were sent abroad to fight, they carried the virus to Europe. By the end of 1918, many soldiers in European armies had been stricken with the flu, which then spread quickly throughout Europe. The three chief statesmen at the Versailles peace conference—the American president Woodrow Wilson, the British prime minister David Lloyd George, and the French premier Georges Clemenceau—were all sick with the flu during the negotiations that led to the Treaty of Versailles.

The Spanish flu, as this strain of influenza was called, was known for its swift and deadly action. Many people died within a day of being infected. Complications also arose from bacterial infections in the lungs, causing a deadly form of pneumonia.

In 1918 and 1919, Spanish flu spread around the world with devastating results. Death tolls were enormous: in Russia, 450,000; in India, 5,000,000; in the United States, 550,000. It has been estimated that twenty-two million people, or more than twice the number of people killed in World War I, died from the great flu epidemic of 1918–1919.

of money outside while she went into a store. When she came out, the money was there, but the basket had been stolen.

Economic disaster led to political upheavals as Communists staged uprisings in October and Adolf Hitler's band of Nazis (NAWT-seez) tried to seize power in Munich in 1923 (see later in the chapter). Everyone began to seek a way out of the disaster. New governments in Great Britain and France decided to

**Map 9.1   Europe in 1919**

take a more conciliatory approach to Germany and the reparations problem. At the same time, a new German government led by Gustav Stresemann (shTRAE-zuh-MAWN) ended the policy of passive resistance. Germany also began to carry out the provisions of the Treaty of Versailles while seeking a new settlement of the reparations question.

In August 1924, an international commission produced a new plan for reparations. The Dawes (DAWZ) Plan, named after the American banker who chaired the commission, first reduced reparations. Then it tied

Germany's annual payments to its ability to pay. The Dawes Plan also granted an initial $200 million loan for German recovery, which soon opened the door to heavy American investments in Europe. A new era of European prosperity between 1924 and 1929 was the result.

With prosperity came a new age of European diplomacy. A spirit of cooperation was fostered by the foreign ministers of Germany and France, Gustav Stresemann and Aristide Briand (BREE-AW[n]). In 1925, they signed the Treaty of Locarno, which guaranteed

▲ *This German housewife is using her worthless paper money in 1923 to start a fire so that she can cook supper. Do you think the U.S. dollar could ever become this worthless? Why or why not?*

Germany's new western borders with France and Belgium. The Locarno pact was viewed by many as the beginning of a new era of European peace. On the day after the pact was concluded, the headlines in the *New York Times* read "France and Germany Ban War Forever." The *London Times* declared, "Peace at Last."[1]

The new spirit of cooperation grew even stronger when Germany joined the League of Nations in March 1926. Two years later, the Kellogg-Briand pact brought even more hope. Sixty-three nations signed this accord written by U.S. secretary of state Frank B. Kellogg and French foreign minister Aristide Briand. These nations pledged "to renounce war as an instrument of national

policy." Nothing was said, however, about what would be done if anyone violated the pact.

Unfortunately, the spirit of Locarno was based on little real substance. Germany did not have the military power to change its western borders even if it wanted to. Promises not to go to war without a way to enforce the promises were worthless. Furthermore, even the spirit of Locarno could not bring nations to cut back on their weapons. The League of Nations Covenant had suggested that nations reduce their military forces to make war less probable. Germany, of course, had been forced to reduce its military forces. At the time, it was thought that other states would later do the same. Numerous disarmament conferences failed to achieve anything, however. States were simply unwilling to trust their security to anyone but their own military forces. When a World Disarmament Conference met in Geneva in 1932, the issue of disarmament was already dead.

## The Great Depression

World War I had a devastating effect on the European economy. Recovery was slow. Thanks to U.S. loans, Europeans began to experience a new prosperity after 1924. Because of the Great Depression, however, the new prosperity was short-lived.

One important factor in the coming of the Great Depression was a series of economic problems in the second half of the 1920s. Already in the mid-1920s, prices for farm products, especially wheat, were falling rapidly because of overproduction. In 1925, states in central and eastern Europe began to impose tariffs to close their markets to other countries' goods, thus causing a decline in trade. An increase in the use of oil and hydroelectricity led to a slump in the coal industry even before 1929.

The other factor in the coming of the Great Depression was an international financial crisis created by the collapse of the U.S. stock market in 1929. Much of the European prosperity between 1924 and 1929 had been built upon U.S. bank loans to Germany. The U.S. loans to Germany were needed so that Germany could pay reparations to France and Great Britain. These nations, in turn, were then able to repay the United

◄ *France did not suffer from the Great Depression as quickly as some of its European neighbors, but by 1931, unemployed workers were lining up at free-food centers.*

States for war loans. Twenty-three billion marks had been invested in German municipal bonds and German industries since 1924. Already in 1928 and 1929, American investors had begun to pull money out of Germany in order to invest in the booming New York stock market. The crash of the U.S. stock market in October 1929 led panicky U.S. investors to withdraw even more of their funds from Germany and other European markets. The withdrawal of funds weakened the banks of Germany and other central European states. The Credit-Anstalt, Vienna's most famous bank, collapsed on May 31, 1931. By that time, trade was slowing down, industrial production was declining, and unemployment was rising.

Economic depression was by no means new to Europe. However, the extent of the economic downturn after 1929 truly made this the Great Depression. During 1932, the worst year of the depression, one British worker in every four was unemployed. Six million Germans, or 40 percent of the German labor force, were out of work at the same time. Between 1929 and 1932, industrial production fell almost 50 percent in the United States and over 40 percent in Germany. The unemployed and homeless filled the streets of the cities.

Governments did not know how to deal with the crisis. The classic liberal remedy for depression was a policy of balanced budgets. This included cutting costs by lowering wages and raising tariffs to exclude other countries' goods from home markets. These measures only made the economic crisis worse, however, and created even greater mass unrest.

One reaction to the Great Depression—even in countries that, like the United States, had a strong laissez-faire tradition, a belief that the government should not interfere in the economy—was the expansion of government activity in the economy. Another reaction was a renewed interest in Marxist doctrines. Hadn't Marx predicted that capitalism would destroy itself through overproduction? Communism thus became more popular, especially among workers and intellectuals. Finally, the Great Depression led masses of people to follow political leaders who offered simple solutions in return for dictatorial power. Everywhere, democracy seemed on the defensive in the 1930s.

## The Democratic States

Woodrow Wilson had claimed that World War I had been fought to make the world safe for democracy. In

1919, his claim seemed justified. Four major European states and a host of minor ones had democratic governments. Moreover, in a number of states, women could vote. Male political leaders had rewarded women for their contributions to World War I by granting them the right to vote (except in Italy, Switzerland, France, and Spain, where women had to wait until the end of World War II for the right). In the 1920s, Europe seemed to be returning to the political trends of the prewar era—parliamentary regimes and the growth of individual liberties. However, it was not an easy process. Four years of total war and four years of postwar turmoil made a "return to normalcy" difficult.

After World War I, Great Britain went through a period of serious economic difficulties. During the war, Britain had lost many of the markets for its industrial products, especially to the United States and Japan. The decline of such staple industries as coal, steel, and textiles, led to a rise in unemployment. In 1921, 2 million Britons were out of work. Britain soon rebounded, however, and experienced an age of prosperity from 1925 to 1929, although this prosperity was never very widespread. Even in these so-called prosperous years, unemployment remained at a startling level of 10 percent.

By 1929, Britain faced the growing effects of the Great Depression. The Labour Party, which had now become the largest party in Britain, failed to solve the nation's economic problems and fell from power in 1931. A new government, led by the Conservatives, claimed credit for bringing Britain out of the worst stages of the depression. It did so by using the old policies of balanced budgets and protective tariffs.

Political leaders in Britain had largely ignored the new ideas of a British economist, John Maynard Keynes, who published his *General Theory of Employment, Interest, and Money* in 1936. He condemned the traditional view that in a free economy, depressions should be left to work themselves out. Instead, Keynes argued that unemployment came not from overproduction but from a decline in demand. Demand, in turn, could be increased by putting people back to work by building highways and public buildings, even if the government had to go into debt to pay for these works, a concept known as **deficit spending.** These policies, of course, would require direct government intervention

in the economy, which was against the principles of laissez-faire. Britain's political leaders were unwilling to go that far in the 1930s.

After the defeat of Germany, France had become the strongest power on the European continent. Its greatest need was to rebuild the areas of northern and eastern France that had been devastated in World War I. However, no French government seemed capable of solving France's financial problems between 1921 and 1926. Like other European countries, though, France did experience a period of relative prosperity between 1926 and 1929.

Because it had a more balanced economy than other nations, France did not begin to feel the full effects of the Great Depression until 1932. Economic instability soon had political repercussions. During a nineteen-month period in 1932 and 1933, six different cabinets were formed as France faced political chaos. Finally, in June 1936, a coalition of leftist parties—Communists, Socialists, and Radicals—formed a Popular Front government.

The Popular Front was able to start a program for workers that some have called the French New Deal. This program was named after President Franklin Delano Roosevelt's New Deal in the United States. The French New Deal consisted of the right of **collective bargaining** (the right of unions to negotiate with employers over wages and hours), a forty-hour workweek, two-week paid vacations, and minimum wages. The Popular Front's policies, however, failed to solve the problems of the depression. By 1938, the French had little confidence in their political system. This lack of confidence left France unprepared to deal with the new—and aggressive—Nazi German state to the east.

The Imperial Germany of William II had come to an end in 1918, with Germany's defeat in World War I. A German democratic state known as the Weimar (VIE-mur) Republic was then set up. From its beginnings, the Weimar Republic was plagued by a series of problems. The republic had no truly outstanding political leaders. In 1925, Paul von Hindenburg, the World War I military hero, was elected president at the age of seventy-seven. Hindenburg was a traditional military man who at heart was not in favor of the republic he had been elected to serve.

◄ *The Works Progress Administration was one of the back-to-work programs funded by the Roosevelt administration during the Great Depression. This San Francisco mural is just one of the art projects sponsored by the WPA.*

The Weimar Republic also faced serious economic problems. Germany experienced runaway inflation in 1922 and 1923, along with serious social problems. Widows, orphans, retired older people, army officers, teachers, civil servants, and others who lived on fixed incomes all watched their monthly incomes become worthless or their lifetime savings disappear. Their economic losses increasingly pushed the middle class to the rightist parties that were hostile to the republic. To make matters worse, after a period of prosperity from 1924 to 1929, Germany faced the Great Depression. Unemployment increased to 3 million in March 1930 and to 4.38 million by December of the same year. The depression paved the way for social discontent, fear, and the rise of extremist parties. The political, economic, and social problems of the Weimar Republic explain in part why the extremist Adolf Hitler and the Nazis were able to rise to power.

After Germany, no Western nation was more affected by the Great Depression than the United States. By 1932, U.S. industrial production fell to 50 percent of what it had been in 1929. By 1933, there were 15 million unemployed. Under these circumstances, the Democrat Franklin Delano Roosevelt was able to win a landslide electoral victory in the 1932 presidential election. A believer in free enterprise, Roosevelt realized that capitalism would have to be reformed in order to "save it." He pursued a policy of active government intervention in the economy that came to be known as the New Deal.

At first, the New Deal tried to restore prosperity by creating the National Recovery Administration (NRA). The NRA required government, labor, and industrial leaders to work out regulations for each industry. However, the NRA was declared unconstitutional by the United States Supreme Court in 1935.

The NRA was soon replaced by other efforts, known as the Second New Deal. These included a stepped-up program of public works, such as the Works Progress Administration (WPA) established in 1935. The WPA was a government organization that employed between 2 and 3 million people who worked at building bridges, roads, post offices, and airports. The Roosevelt administration was also responsible for new social legislation that began the U.S. welfare system. In 1935, the Social Security Act created a system of old-age pensions and unemployment insurance.

No doubt, the New Deal provided social reform measures that perhaps avoided a social revolution in the United States. However, it did not solve the unemployment problems of the Great Depression. In 1938, American unemployment still stood at eleven million. Only World War II and the growth of weapons industries brought U.S. workers back to full employment.

## SECTION REVIEW

1. **Locate:**
   (a) Ruhr Valley

2. **Define:**
   (a) deficit spending,
   (b) collective bargaining

3. **Identify:**
   (a) Gustav Stresemann,   (b) Dawes Plan,
   (c) Treaty of Locarno,   (d) Kellogg-Briand Pact,
   (e) return to normalcy,   (f) New Deal,
   (g) Weimar Republic,   (h) National Recovery Administration (NRA)

4. **Recall:**
   (a) What was the only sanction that could be used by the League of Nations against nations that broke international agreements?
   (b) What did Germany do to cause high rates of inflation after World War I?
   (c) How did the collapse of the American stock market in 1929 harm the German economy?
   (d) How did the Great Depression pave the way for social discontent, fear, and extremist political parties throughout the world?

5. **Think Critically:** Why is the following quotation almost certainly true? "Promises not to go to war without a way to enforce them were rather worthless."

## ② THE RETREAT FROM DEMOCRACY: DICTATORIAL REGIMES

The triumph of democracy in Europe in 1919 was extremely short-lived. By 1939, only two major states (France and Great Britain) and a number of minor ones remained democratic. Italy, Germany, the Soviet Union under Joseph Stalin, and many other European states adopted dictatorial regimes that took on both old and new forms.

Dictatorship was by no means new, of course, but the modern **totalitarian state** was. The totalitarian regimes, the best examples of which can be found in Stalinist Russia and Nazi Germany, pushed the power of the central state far beyond what it had been in the past. A totalitarian state was a government that aimed to control not only the political side of life but the economic, social, intellectual, and cultural lives of its citizens as well. The immediate origins of the totalitarian state can be found in the total warfare of World War I, when governments used controls over economic, political, and personal freedom in order to achieve victory.

Totalitarian states wanted more than the passive obedience of their subjects. They wanted to conquer the minds and hearts of their subjects, which they did through mass propaganda techniques and high-speed modern communication. Totalitarian states expected the active involvement of the masses in the achievement of the regime's goals, whether they be war, a socialist state, or a thousand-year empire, as Adolf Hitler wanted to establish.

The modern totalitarian state was led by a single leader and a single party. It rejected the liberal ideal of limited government power and guarantees of individual freedoms. Indeed, individual freedom was to be subordinated to the collective will of the masses, which was organized and determined for them by a leader or leaders. Modern technology also gave totalitarian states unheard-of police controls to enforce their wishes on their subjects.

### The Birth of Fascism in Italy

In the early 1920s, Benito Mussolini (MOO-suh-LEE-nee) burst upon the Italian scene with the first Fascist movement in Europe. Mussolini began his political career as a socialist. However, he was kicked out of the Socialist Party after supporting Italy's entry into World War I, a position contrary to the socialist position of

◄ *Mussolini wanted to be known as a dynamic, strong leader. In this photo, he wears full dress uniform as he jogs with his officers. Do you think this photo was staged, or do you think these exercises were part of Mussolini's daily routine?*

strict neutrality. In 1919, Mussolini created a new political group, the Fascio di Combattimento (FAW-SHO-de-kom-BATT-e-MEN-toe), or League of Combat (hence the name Fascists (FASH-ists). The group received few votes in the elections of 1919, and Mussolini said bitterly that Fascism had "come to a dead end."

Political stalemate in Italy's government, however, soon came to the rescue of Mussolini and the Fascists. The new parliament elected in November 1919 was unable to govern Italy. The three major parties could not form an effective governmental coalition. At the same time, the Socialists, who had now become the largest party, spoke in theory of the need for revolution. This alarmed conservatives, who quickly associated socialists with Bolsheviks or Communists. Thousands of industrial and agricultural strikes in 1919 and 1920 created a climate of class warfare and continual violence.

In 1920 and 1921, Mussolini formed bands of black-shirted, armed Fascists called **squadristi.** These bands were turned loose in attacks on socialist offices and newspapers. They also used violence to break up strikes by trade unionists and socialist workers. A favorite tactic of the squadristi, also known as Blackshirts, was to pour a bottle of castor oil down the throats of their victims. Middle-class industrialists who feared working-class strikes, as well as large landowners who objected to the agricultural strikes, began to support Mussolini's Fascist movement.

Mussolini realized that the Italian people were angry over the failure of Italy to receive more land after World War I. He understood that nationalism was a powerful force. Thus, Mussolini demanded more land for Italy and began to win thousands of converts to Fascism with his patriotic appeals. By 1922, Mussolini's movement began to mushroom. His nationalist rhetoric and the middle-class fear of socialism, Communist revolution, and disorder made the Fascists more and more attractive. On October 29, 1922, Mussolini and the Fascists threatened to march on Rome if they were not given power. Mussolini exclaimed, "Either we are allowed to govern, or we will seize power by marching on Rome." King Victor Emmanuel III gave in and made Mussolini prime minister of Italy.

▶ *Young Fascists, dressed in military uniforms and bearing rifles, helped celebrate Rome's birthday in 1933. How does this compare to patriotic parades that you have seen?*

Within four years, Mussolini had used his position as prime minister to create a Fascist dictatorship. Press laws gave the government the right to suspend any publications that showed a lack of respect for the Catholic Church, the monarchy, or the state. The prime minister was made "Head of Government" with the power to make laws by decree. The police were given the power to arrest and jail anybody for both nonpolitical and political crimes without a trial. In 1926, all other political parties were outlawed. A secret police, known as the OVRA, was also set up. By the end of 1926, Mussolini ruled Italy as *Il Duce* (DOO-chae), "the leader."

Mussolini conceived of the Fascist state as totalitarian: "Fascism is totalitarian, and the Fascist State, the synthesis and unity of all values, interprets, develops and gives strength to the whole life of the people."[2] Mussolini did try to create a police state, but it was not very effective. Police activities in Italy were never as repressive, efficient, or savage as those of Nazi Germany. The Italian Fascists also tried to exercise control over all forms of mass media, including newspapers, radio, and cinema. In this way, propaganda could serve to integrate the masses into the state. Here, too, Mussolini failed to reach his major goals. Fascist propaganda came to consist chiefly of simple slogans, such as

"Mussolini Is Always Right," plastered on walls all over Italy.

Mussolini and the Fascists also tried to mold Italians into a single-minded community by creating Fascist organizations. Fascist youth groups, known as the Young Fascists, were used to teach Fascist ideals to the young people of the nation. By 1939, about 6.8 million children, teenagers, and young adults of both sexes—or 66 percent of the population between the ages of eight and eighteen—were enrolled in some kind of Fascist youth group. Activities for these groups included Saturday afternoon marching drills, mountain summer camps, and youth contests. Underlying all of these activities was the Fascist insistence on military values. The Fascists worshiped war. Beginning in the 1930s, all male youth groups were given premilitary exercises to develop discipline and provide training for war. Results were mixed. Italian teenagers, who liked neither military training nor routine discipline of any kind, simply refused to attend Fascist youth group meetings on a regular basis.

The Fascist organizations hoped to create a new Italian, who would be hardworking, physically fit, disciplined, intellectually sharp, and war loving. In practice, the Fascists largely maintained traditional social attitudes in Italy. This is especially evident in their policies regarding women. The Fascists portrayed the family as the pillar of the state and women as the basic foundation of the family. "Woman into the Home" became the Fascist slogan. Women were to be homemakers and baby producers, which was "their natural and fundamental mission in life," according to Mussolini.

The Fascists viewed population growth as a sign of national strength. Employment outside the home kept women from having babies. Mussolini said the following about such employment: "It forms an independence and consequent physical and moral habits contrary to child bearing."[3] There was another reason for the Fascist attitude toward working women: they would compete with males for jobs. Eliminating women from the market lowered unemployment figures for men in the depression economy of the 1930s.

Despite the instruments of repression, the use of propaganda, and the creation of numerous Fascist organizations, Mussolini did not achieve the degree of totalitarian control accomplished in Hitler's Germany or Stalin's Soviet Union. Mussolini and the Fascist Party never really destroyed the old power structure. Some institutions, including the armed forces and the monarchy, were never absorbed into the Fascist state. They managed to keep most of their independence. Mussolini had boasted that he would help workers and peasants. Instead, he allied himself with the interests of industrialists and large landowners at the expense of the lower classes.

Mussolini's compromise with the traditional institutions of Italy was especially evident in his attempt to gain the support of the Catholic Church. In the Lateran Accords of February 1929, Mussolini's regime recognized the sovereign independence of a small area of 109 acres within Rome, known as Vatican City. This territory had remained in the Catholic Church's hands since Italian unification in 1870. In return, the papacy recognized the Italian state. The Lateran Accords also gave the church a large grant of money and recognized Catholicism as the "sole religion of the state." In return, the Catholic Church urged Italians to support the Fascist regime.

In all areas of Italian life under Mussolini and the Fascists, there was a large gap between Fascist ideals and practice. The Italian Fascists promised much but delivered considerably less. They were soon overshadowed by a much more powerful Fascist movement to the north. Adolf Hitler was a student and great admirer of Mussolini. However, the German pupil soon proved to be far more adept in the use of power than was his Italian teacher.

## A New Era in the Soviet Union

The civil war in Russia had taken an enormous number of lives. As we have seen, during the civil war, Lenin had followed a policy of war communism. Once the war was over, however, peasants began to sabotage the program by hoarding food. Added to this problem was the problem of drought, which caused a great famine between 1920 and 1922 that claimed as many as five million lives. With agricultural disaster came industrial collapse. By 1921, industrial output was only 20 percent of its 1913 levels. Russia was exhausted. A peasant banner proclaimed, "Down with Lenin and horseflesh, Bring back the Tsar and pork." As Leon Trotsky said, "The country, and the government with it, were at the very edge of the abyss."

### Lenin and the New Communist Order

In March 1921, Lenin pulled Russia back from the abyss. He abandoned war communism in favor of his **New Economic Policy** (NEP). The NEP was a modified version of the old capitalist system. Peasants were now allowed to sell their produce openly. Retail stores, as well as small industries that employed fewer than twenty workers, could be privately owned and operated. Heavy industry, banking, and mines, however, remained in the hands of the government.

In 1922, Lenin and the Communists formally created a new state called the Union of Soviet Socialist Republics, known as the U.S.S.R. by its initials or the Soviet Union by its shortened form. Already by that year, a revived market and a good harvest had brought an end to famine. Soviet agricultural production climbed to 75 percent of its prewar level. Industry, especially state-owned heavy industry, fared less well and continued to stagnate. Only coal production had reached prewar levels by 1926. Overall, the NEP had

▶ *In this 1933 photograph, Stalin is shown signing what is supposedly a death warrant. Terror was one strategy Stalin used to maintain an authoritarian system in the U.S.S.R.*

saved the Soviet Union from complete economic disaster. Lenin and other leading Communists, however, intended the NEP to be only a temporary retreat from the goals of communism.

### The Rise of Stalin

Lenin died in 1924. A struggle for power among the seven members of the **Politburo** (paw-LIT-byoo-roe), the committee that had become the leading policymaker of the Communist Party, began at once. The Politburo was severely divided over the future direction of the Soviet Union. The Left, led by Leon Trotsky, wanted to end the NEP and launch Russia on a path of rapid industrialization, chiefly at the expense of the peasants. The same group wanted to spread communism abroad and believed that the revolution in Russia would not survive without other Communist states.

Another group in the Politburo, called the Right, rejected the idea of worldwide Communist revolution. It wanted instead to focus on building a socialist state in Russia and to continue Lenin's NEP. Rapid industrialization, it believed, would harm the living standards of the Soviet peasants.

These divisions were underscored by an intense personal rivalry between Leon Trotsky and Joseph Stalin (STAW-lin). In 1924, Trotsky held the post of commissar of war and was the leading spokesperson for the Left in the Politburo. Stalin had joined the Bolsheviks in 1903 and had come to Lenin's attention after staging a daring bank robbery to get funds for the Bolshevik cause. Stalin was neither a dynamic speaker nor a forceful writer. He was a good organizer, however (his fellow Bolsheviks called him "Comrade Card-Index"). He was content to hold the dull bureaucratic job of party general secretary while other Politburo members held party positions that enabled them to display their brilliant oratorical abilities. The other members of the Politburo soon found, however, that the position of general secretary was really the most important in the party. The general secretary appointed the regional, district, city, and town party secretaries. In 1922, for example, Stalin had appointed some ten thousand people, who proved valuable later in his struggle for power.

Stalin used his post as party general secretary to gain complete control of the Communist Party. Expelled from the party in 1927, Trotsky made his way to Mexico. There he was murdered (with a pickax in the head) in 1940, no doubt on Stalin's orders. By 1929, Stalin had eliminated from the Politburo the Old Bolsheviks of the revolutionary era and had established a powerful dictatorship.

### Stalinist Russia

The Stalinist Era marked the beginning of an economic, social, and political revolution that was more sweeping in its results than were the revolutions of 1917. Stalin made a significant shift in economic policy in 1928. He launched his first five-year plan. Its real goal was nothing less than the virtually overnight transformation of Russia from an agricultural into an industrial country.

Instead of stressing the production of consumer goods, the first five-year plan emphasized maximum production of capital goods (goods devoted to the production of other goods, such as heavy machines) and armaments. The plan quadrupled the production of heavy machinery and doubled oil production. Between 1928 and 1937, during the first two five-year plans, steel production increased from 4 million to 18 million tons per year. Hard coal output went from 36 million to 128 million tons. At the same time, new industrial cities, located near iron ore and coal deposits, sprang up overnight in the Urals and Siberia.

The social and political costs of industrialization were enormous. Little provision was made for caring for the expanded labor force in the cities. The number of workers increased by millions between 1932 and 1940, but total investment in housing actually declined after 1929. The result was that millions of workers and their families lived in pitiful conditions. Real wages in industry also declined by 43 percent between 1928 and 1940. Strict laws even limited where workers could move. To keep workers content, government propaganda stressed the need for sacrifice to create the new socialist state.

With rapid industrialization came an equally rapid **collectivization** of agriculture. Its goal was to eliminate private farms and push people into collective farms (see "You Are There: The Formation of Collective Farms"). Strong resistance to Stalin's plans came from peasants, who responded by hoarding crops and killing livestock. However, these actions only led Stalin to step up the program. By 1930, 10 million peasant households had been collectivized. By 1934, Russia's 26 million family farms had been collectivized into 250,000 units.

The collectivization of agriculture was done at tremendous cost. The hoarding of food and the slaughter of livestock produced widespread famine. Stalin himself is supposed to have told Winston Churchill during World War II that ten million peasants died in the famines of 1932 and 1933. The only concession Stalin made to the peasants was that each collective farm worker was allowed to have one tiny, privately owned garden plot.

There were other costs to Stalin's program of rapid industrialization as well. To achieve his goals, Stalin strengthened the party bureaucracy under his control. Those who resisted were sent into forced labor camps in Siberia. Stalin's desire for sole control of decision making also led to purges of the Old Bolsheviks. Between 1936 and 1938, the most prominent Old Bolsheviks were put on trial and condemned to death. During this same time, Stalin undertook a purge of army officers, diplomats, union officials, party members, intellectuals, and numerous ordinary citizens. An estimated eight million Russians were arrested. Millions were sent to forced labor camps in Siberia, from which they never returned.

The Stalin Era also undid much of the permissive social legislation of the early 1920s. Believing in complete equality of rights for women, the Communists had made divorce and abortion easy to get. They had also encouraged women to work outside the home and to liberate themselves sexually. After Stalin came to power, the family was praised as a small collective in which parents were responsible for teaching the values of hard work, duty, and discipline. Abortion was outlawed. Divorced fathers who did not support their children were heavily fined.

## Authoritarian States in the West

There were a number of states in the Western world that were not totalitarian but that did possess conservative authoritarian governments. These states adopted

## YOU ARE THERE

# The Formation of Collective Farms

*The collectivization of agriculture transformed Russia's 26 million family farms into 250,000 collective farms (kolkhozes) (kawl-KAWZ-uz). In this firsthand account, we see how the process worked.*

**Max Belov, *The History of a Collective Farm***

General collectivization in our village was brought about in the following manner: Two representatives of the [Communist] Party arrived in the village. All the inhabitants were summoned by the ringing of the church bell to a meeting at which the policy of general collectivization was announced. . . . The upshot was that although the meeting lasted two days, from the viewpoint of the Party representatives nothing was accomplished.

After this setback the Party representatives divided the village into two sections and worked each one separately. Two more officials were sent to reinforce the first two. A meeting of our section of the village was held in a stable which had previously belonged to a kulak [wealthy peasant]. The meeting dragged on until dark. Suddenly someone threw a brick at the lamp, and in the dark the

*These Russian peasants use scythes to harvest their grain crops. How does their work compare to harvesting practices in Western Europe or the United States in the 1930s?*

some of the features of totalitarian states, especially their wide police powers. However, their greatest concern was not to create a new kind of mass society but only to preserve the existing social order. As a result, the authoritarian states were content with passive obedience rather than active involvement in the goals of the regime.

Nowhere had the map of Europe been more drastically altered by World War I than in eastern Europe. The new states of Austria, Poland, Czechoslovakia, and Yugoslavia (known as the kingdom of the Serbs,

Croats, and Slovenes until 1929) adopted parliamentary systems. The kingdoms of Romania and Bulgaria had already gained new parliamentary constitutions in 1920. Greece became a republic in 1924. Hungary's government was parliamentary in form, but it was controlled by its landed aristocrats. At the beginning of the 1920s, political democracy seemed well established in eastern Europe. That situation did not last very long, however.

Several problems threatened political democracy. The eastern European states had little tradition of par-

# YOU ARE THERE

## The Formation of Collective Farms, continued

peasants began to beat the Party representatives who jumped out the window and escaped from the village barely alive. The following day seven people were arrested. The militia was called in and stayed in the village until the peasants, realizing their helplessness, calmed down. . . .

By the end of 1930 there were two kolkhozes in our village. Though at first these collectives embraced at most only 70 percent of the peasant households, in the months that followed they gradually absorbed more and more of them.

In these kolkhozes the great bulk of the land was held and worked communally, but each peasant household owned a house of some sort, a small plot of ground and perhaps some livestock. All the members of the kolkhoz were required to work on the kolkhoz a certain number of days each month; the rest of the time they were allowed to work on their own holdings. They derived their income partly from what they grew on their garden strips and partly from their work in the kolkhoz.

When the harvest was over, and after the farm had met its obligations to the state and to various special funds and had sold on the market whatever undesignated produce was left, the remaining produce and the farm's monetary income were divided among the kolkhoz members according to the number of "labor days" each one had contributed to the farm's work. . . . After they had received their earnings, one of them remarked, "You will live, but you will be very, very thin. . . ."

By late 1932 more than 80 percent of the peasant households . . . had been collectivized. . . . That year the peasants harvested a good crop and had hopes that the calculations would work out to their advantage and would help strengthen them economically. These hopes were in vain. The kolkhoz workers received only 200 grams of flour per labor day for the first half of the year; the remaining grain, including the seed fund, was taken by the government. The peasants were told that industrialization of the country, then in full swing, demanded grain and sacrifices from them.

1. What is a collective farm?

2. Why did the peasants resist the collective farms?

liamentary politics and no real middle class to support that tradition. Then, too, these states were mostly rural and agrarian. Many of the peasants were illiterate, and much of the land was still dominated by large landowners who feared the peasants. Ethnic conflicts also threatened to tear these countries apart. Powerful landowners, the churches, and even some members of the small middle class feared land reform, Communist upheaval, and ethnic conflict. Thus, they looked to authoritarian governments to maintain the old system. Only Czechoslovakia, with its large middle class, liberal tradition, and strong industrial base, maintained its political democracy.

In Spain, political democracy failed to survive. Led by General Francisco Franco (FRAWNG-KOE), Spanish military forces revolted against the democratic government in 1936. A brutal and bloody civil war began. Foreign intervention complicated the Spanish Civil War. The fascist regimes of Italy and Germany aided Franco's forces with arms, money, and men. Hitler used the Spanish Civil War as an opportunity to test the new weapons of his revived air force. The horrible destruction of Guernica (gair-NEE-kaw) by German bombers in April 1937 was immortalized in a painting by the Spanish artist Pablo Picasso.

The Spanish republican government was aided by forty-thousand foreign volunteers and trucks, planes, tanks, and military advisors from the Soviet Union. After Franco's forces captured Madrid on March 28, 1939, the Spanish Civil War finally came to an end. Franco then set up a dictatorship that favored large landowners, businesspeople, and the Catholic clergy. It was yet another example of a traditional, conservative, authoritarian regime.

## ❀ SECTION REVIEW ❀

1. **Locate:**
    (a) Madrid,    (b) Russia,    (c) Czechoslovakia

2. **Define:**
    (a) totalitarian state,
    (b) squadristi,
    (c) New Economic Policy,
    (d) Politburo,
    (e) collectivization

3. **Identify:**
    (a) Fascio di Combattimento,
    (b) Il Duce,
    (c) Lateran Accords,
    (d) Joseph Stalin,
    (e) Five-Year Plan,
    (f) General Francisco Franco

4. **Recall:**
    (a) Why couldn't the parliament of Italy form a stable government in 1919?
    (b) Why did Trotsky's followers want to spread communism to other nations?
    (c) What ability did Stalin possess that helped him gain power?
    (d) Why did the Soviet Union and Germany choose to become involved in the Spanish Civil War?

5. **Think Critically:** Why did German and Italian policies of keeping women at home rather than working in factories weaken these countries' ability to prepare for and fight the war?

## HITLER AND NAZI GERMANY

In 1923, a small, south German rightist party, known as the Nazis, led by an obscure Austrian rabble-rouser named Adolf Hitler, created a stir when it tried to seize power in southern Germany. Although the attempted takeover failed, it brought Hitler and the Nazis national attention. Within ten years, Hitler and the Nazis had taken over complete power and established another fascist state.

### The Rise of Hitler

Born on April 20, 1889, Adolf Hitler was the son of an Austrian customs official. He was a total failure in secondary school and eventually made his way to Vienna to become an artist. He was rejected by the Vienna Academy of Fine Arts and was supported by an inheritance and orphan's pension. Hitler stayed on in Vienna to live the carefree lifestyle of an artist. While there, he established the basic ideas of an ideology from which he never deviated for the rest of his life. At the core of Hitler's ideas was racism, especially his **anti-Semitism** (hostility toward Jews). His hatred of the Jews lasted to the end of his life. Hitler had also become an extreme German nationalist and had learned from the mass politics of Vienna how political parties could effectively use propaganda and terror. Finally, in his Viennese (VEE-uh-NEEZ) years, Hitler came to a firm belief in the need for struggle, which he saw as the "granite foundation of the world."

In 1913, Hitler moved to Munich, still with no real future in sight. He described how World War I then saved him: "Overpowered by stormy enthusiasm, I fell down on my knees and thanked Heaven . . . for granting me the good fortune of being permitted to live at this time."[4] At the end of World War I, after four years of service as a dispatch runner on the Western Front, Hitler went to Munich and decided to enter politics.

In 1919, Hitler joined the little-known German Worker's Party, one of a number of right-wing extreme nationalist parties in Munich. By the summer of 1921, Hitler had taken over total control of the party, which he renamed the National Socialist German Workers' Party (NSDAP), or Nazi for short. His idea was that the party's name would distinguish the Nazis from the socialist parties. At the same time, it would gain support from both workers and German nationalists.

Hitler worked hard to develop the party into a mass political movement with flags, party badges, uniforms, and its own newspaper. It also had its own police force, or party militia, known as the SA, the Sturmabteilung, or the Storm Troops (also known as the Brownshirts, after the color of their uniforms). The Storm Troops were used to defend the party in meeting halls and to break up the meetings of other parties. Their existence added an element of force and terror to the growing Nazi movement. Hitler's own oratorical skills were largely responsible for attracting an increasing number of followers. By 1923, the party had grown from its early hundreds into a membership of 55,000, with 15,000 SA members.

Overconfident, Hitler staged an armed uprising against the government in Munich in November 1923. The Beer Hall Putsch was quickly crushed, and Hitler was sentenced to prison. During his brief stay in jail, Hitler wrote *Mein Kampf* (MINE KAWMPF) (*My Struggle*), an autobiographical account of his movement and its basic ideas. Extreme German nationalism, a strong anti-Semitism, and anticommunism were linked together by a Social Darwinian theory of struggle. This theory stressed the right of superior nations to *Lebensraum* (LAY-bunz-ROWM)—living space—through expansion, as well as the right of superior individuals to secure authoritarian leadership over the masses. *Mein Kampf* is remarkable. It spelled out a series of ideas that directed Hitler's actions once he took power. That others refused to take Hitler and his extreme ideas seriously was one of his greatest advantages.

## The Victory of Nazism

While he was in prison, Hitler came to an important conclusion. He realized that the Nazis would have to come to power by constitutional means, not by a violent overthrow of the Weimar Republic. This meant that the Nazi Party would have to be a mass political party that would compete for votes with the other political parties. After his release from prison, Hitler worked to build such a party. He expanded the Nazi Party to all parts of Germany. By 1929, it had a national party organization. It also grew from 27,000 members in 1925 (it had lost members while Hitler was in jail) to 178,000 by the end of 1929.

Especially noticeable was the youthfulness of the regional, district, and branch leaders of the Nazi organization. Many were between the ages of twenty-five and thirty. They were fiercely committed to Hitler, because he gave them the kind of active politics they sought. Rather than debate, they wanted brawls in beer halls, fiery speeches, and comradeship in the building of a new Germany. One new, young Nazi member expressed his excitement about the party:

*For me this was the start of a completely new life. There was only one thing in the world for me and that was service in the movement. All my thoughts were centred on the movement. I could talk only politics. I was no longer aware of anything else. At the time I was a promising athlete; I was very keen on sport, and it was going to be my career. But I had to give this up too. My only interest was agitation and propaganda.*[5]

Such youthful enthusiasm gave the Nazi movement the air of a "young man's movement." The other parties could not match its sense of dynamism.

By 1932, the Nazi Party had 800,000 members and had become the largest party in the **Reichstag** (RYKS-tahg) (the German parliament). No doubt, Germany's economic difficulties were a crucial factor in the Nazi rise to power. Unemployment had risen dramatically, from 4.35 million in 1931 to 6 million by the winter of 1932. The economic and psychological impact of the Great Depression made extremist parties more attractive.

The Nazi rise was also due to the fact that the Nazis developed especially effective modern electioneering

▶ *Hitler used a variety of cere-monial actions to strengthen the ties between party members and himself. Here Hitler touches a flag that was supposedly stained with Nazi blood during the Beer Hall Putsch. The man holding the banner makes a "blood oath" of allegiance to Hitler.*

techniques. In their election campaigns, party members pitched their themes to the needs and fears of different social groups. In working-class districts, for example, the Nazis attacked international high finance. In middle-class neighborhoods, they exploited fears of a Communist revolution and its threat to private property. At the same time that the Nazis made blatant appeals to class interests, they were denouncing conflicts of interest. They stood above classes and parties, they proclaimed. Hitler, in particular, claimed to stand above all differences and promised to create a new Germany free of class differences and party infighting. His appeal to national pride, national honor, and traditional militarism struck chords of emotion in his listeners. A schoolteacher in Hamburg said after attending one of Hitler's rallies, "When the speech was over, there was roaring enthusiasm and applause. . . . Then he went.—How many look up to him with touching faith as their helper, their saviour, their deliverer from unbearable distress."[6]

Elections proved to have their limits. In the elections of July 1932, the Nazis won 230 seats, making them the largest party in the Reichstag. Four months later, however, in November, they declined to 196 seats. It became apparent to many Nazis that they would not gain power simply by the ballot box. Hitler saw clearly, however, that the Reichstag after 1930 was not all that important, because the government ruled by decree with the support of President Hindenburg.

More and more, the right-wing elites of Germany—the industrial leaders, landed aristocrats, military officers, and higher bureaucrats—came to see Hitler as the man of the hour. He had the mass support to set up a right-wing, authoritarian regime that would save Germany and people in privileged positions from a Communist takeover. Under pressure, Hindenburg agreed to allow Hitler to become chancellor (on January 30, 1933) and create a new government.

Within two months, Hitler had laid the foundation for the Nazis' complete control over Germany. On February 27, a fire, supposedly caused by the Communists, broke out in the Reichstag building. The next day, Hitler convinced Hindenburg to issue a decree that gave the government emergency powers. The decree suspended all basic rights of the citizens for the full duration of the emergency. The Nazis could now arrest and jail anyone. The crowning step of Hitler's "legal seizure" of power came on March 23, when a two-thirds vote of the Reichstag passed the Enabling Act. This gave the government the power to ignore the constitution for four years while it issued laws that dealt with the country's problems. The Enabling Act gave Hitler's later acts a legal basis. He no longer needed the Reichstag or President Hindenburg. In effect, Hitler became a dictator appointed by the parliamentary body itself.

With their new source of power, the Nazis acted quickly to bring all institutions under Nazi control. The civil service was purged of Jews and democratic elements. Concentration camps were set up for opponents of the new regime. Trade unions were dissolved. All political parties except the Nazis were abolished. By the end of the summer of 1933, within seven months of being appointed chancellor, Hitler and the Nazis had established the basis for a totalitarian state. When Hindenburg died on August 2, 1934, the office of president was abolished. Hitler became sole ruler of Germany. Public officials and soldiers were all required to take a personal oath of loyalty to Hitler as the "Führer (Leader) of the German Reich and people."

## The Nazi State, 1933 to 1939

Hitler now felt the real task was at hand: to develop the "total state." Hitler's aims had not been simply power for power's sake. Hitler had a larger goal—the development of an Aryan racial state that would dominate Europe and possibly the world for generations to come.* To achieve this goal, the German people must be actively involved, not passively cowed by force.

---

*Aryan* was a term borrowed from linguists, who used it to identify people speaking a common set of languages known as Indo-European (see Chapter 1). The Nazis misused the term and identified the Aryans with the Greeks and Romans of the past and the Germans and Scandinavians of the present. The Germans were seen by the Nazis as the true descendants and chief leaders of the Aryans.

Hitler stated:

> *We must develop organizations in which an individual's entire life can take place. Then every activity and every need of every individual will be regulated by the collectivity represented by the party. There is no longer any arbitrary will, there are no longer any free realms in which the individual belongs to himself. . . . The time of personal happiness is over.*[7]

The Nazis pursued the creation of this totalitarian state in a variety of ways. Mass demonstrations and spectacles were used to make the German people an instrument for Hitler's policies (see "You Are There: Mass Meetings in Nazi Germany"). These meetings, especially the Nuremberg party rallies that were held every September, had great appeal. They usually evoked mass enthusiasm and excitement.

The state apparatus of Hitler's "total state" offers some confusing features. One usually thinks of Nazi Germany as having an all-powerful government that maintained absolute control and order. In truth, Nazi Germany was the scene of almost constant personal and institutional conflict. This resulted in administrative chaos. Struggle was a basic feature of relationships within the party, within the state, and between party and state. Hitler, of course, was the ultimate decision maker and absolute ruler.

Hitler and the Nazis also established control in the economic sphere. Hitler made use of public works projects and grants to private construction firms to put people back to work and end the depression. A massive rearmament program, however, provided far more help in solving the unemployment problem. Unemployment, which had stood at 6 million in 1932, dropped to 2.6 million in 1934 and less than 500,000 in 1937. The regime claimed full credit for solving Germany's economic woes. No doubt, the new regime's part in bringing an end to the depression was an important factor in leading many Germans to accept Hitler and the Nazis.

For those who needed coercion, the Nazi total state had its instruments of terror and repression. Especially important were the Schutzstaffeln (guard squadrons), known simply as the SS. The SS was originally created as Hitler's personal bodyguard. Under the direction of

## YOU ARE THERE

# Mass Meetings in Nazi Germany

*Propaganda and mass rallies were two of the chief instruments that Adolf Hitler used to prepare the German people for the tasks he set before them. In the first excerpt that follows, which is taken from Hitler's book Mein Kampf, Hitler explains the psychological importance of mass meetings. In the second excerpt, which is taken from Hitler's speech to a crowd at Nuremberg, he describes the mystical bond he hoped to create through his mass rallies.*

### Adolf Hitler, *Mein Kampf*

The mass meeting is also necessary for the reason that in it the individual . . . for the first time gets the picture of a larger community. . . . When from his little workshop or big factory, in which he feels very small, he steps for the first time into a mass meeting and has thousands and thousands of people of the same opinions around him, when, as a seeker, he is swept away by three or four thousand others into the mighty effect of suggestive intoxication, when the visible success and agreement of thousands confirm to him the rightness of the new doctrine and for the first time arouse doubt in the truth of his previous conviction—then he himself has succumbed to the magic influence of what we designate as "mass suggestion." The will, the longing, and also the power of thousands are accumulated in every individual. The man who enters such a meeting doubting and wavering leaves it inwardly reinforced: he has become a link in the community.

### Hitler's Speech at Nuremberg

Do we not feel once again in this hour the miracle that brought us together? Once you heard the voice of a man, and it struck deep into your hearts; it awakened you, and you followed this voice. Year after year you went after it, though him who had spoken you never even saw. You heard only a voice, and you followed it. When we meet each other here, the wonder of our coming together fills us all. Not everyone of you sees me, and I do not see everyone of you. But I feel you, and you feel me. It is the belief in our people that has made us small men great, that has made us poor men rich, that has made brave and coura-

Heinrich Himmler (see "Biography: Heinrich Himmler—Leader of Terror"), the SS came to control all of the regular and secret police forces. The SS was based on two principles: terror and ideology. Terror included the instruments of repression and murder: the secret police, criminal police, concentration camps, and later the execution squads and death camps for the extermination of the Jews. For Himmler, the SS was a crusading order whose chief goal was to further the Aryan master race.

Other institutions, such as the Catholic and Protestant Churches, primary and secondary schools, and universities, were also brought under the control of the Nazi totalitarian state. Nazi professional organizations and leagues were formed for civil servants, teachers, women, farmers, doctors, and lawyers. Youth organizations, too, were set up to teach young people the Nazi ideals (see "Young People in Nazi Germany: The Hitler Youth").

The creation of the Nazi total state also had an impact on women. Women played a crucial role in the Aryan racial state as bearers of the children who, it was believed, would bring about the triumph of the Aryan race. The Nazis believed there were natural differences

# YOU ARE THERE
## Mass Meetings in Nazi Germany, continued

◄ *Hitler and the Nazi Party used mass rallies to create enthusiastic support for their policies. Almost one million people attended this 1937 Harvest Festival near Hamelin. How do you think it would feel to be part of this cheering crowd?*

geous men out of us wavering, spiritless, timid folk; this belief made us see our road when we were astray; it joined us together into one whole! . . . You come, that . . . you may, once in a while, gain the feeling that now we are together; we are with him and he with us, and we are now Germany!

1. Why did Hitler say the mass meetings were necessary?

2. How did Hitler try to maximize the effects of the meetings?

between men and women. Men were warriors and political leaders. Women were destined to be wives and mothers. By maintaining this clear distinction, each could best serve to "maintain the whole community."

Nazi ideas determined employment opportunities for women. The Nazis hoped to drive women out of certain areas of the labor market. These included jobs in heavy industry or other jobs that might hinder women from bearing healthy children. Certain professions, including university teaching, medicine, and law, also were considered unsuitable for women, especially married women. The Nazis encouraged women to pursue professional occupations that had direct practical application, such as social work and nursing. The Nazi regime pushed its campaign against working women with poster slogans such as "Get ahold of pots and pans and broom and you'll sooner find a groom!"

The Nazi total state was intended to be an Aryan racial state. From its beginning, the Nazi Party reflected the strong anti-Semitic beliefs of Adolf Hitler. Once in power, the Nazis translated anti-Semitic ideas into anti-Semitic policies. In September 1935, the Nazis announced new racial laws at the annual party rally in Nuremberg. These "Nuremberg laws" excluded

# BIOGRAPHY

## Heinrich Himmler—Leader of Terror

Born in 1900, Heinrich Himmler was the son of a middle-class schoolteacher. While a student in agriculture at a technical institute in Munich, he joined the Nazi Party. For a while, he worked as a fertilizer salesperson. He then tried, unsuccessfully, to make a living raising chickens. All the while, he remained in the Nazi Party. In 1929, Adolf Hitler made him leader of the SS.

The SS had been formed in 1925 as Hitler's elite bodyguard. To Hitler, Himmler was an ideal leader, because he was totally obedient to the Führer. Like Hitler, Himmler believed that the racial struggle between Aryans and Jews was the key to world history. To Himmler, the SS should become the elite group of Nazism that would fulfill the dream of Aryan supremacy.

Himmler was a cold, calculating, efficient bureaucrat whose ruthlessness made him an ideal head of the SS. Beginning in 1929, Himmler began to recruit new members for the SS on the basis of his ideas of racial purity. Recruits were pure German types with blond hair, blue eyes, and good physiques. To maintain his racial elite, Himmler insisted that SS men marry only racially pure Aryan women.

As the SS continued to grow, Himmler sought new sources of power through his control of the police. By 1936, he had become chief of the regular police. He then set up new divisions in the SS. The Gestapo was a secret police force that rounded up the regime's enemies. The Security

▲ *Heinrich Himmler quickly rose through the Nazi ranks to lead the Schutzstaffeln.*

Service was a network of spies. The Death's Head Formations were responsible for running the concentration camps. The Waffen (VAWF-un)-SS was a group of combat soldiers—the SS's own army. The Einsatzgruppen were responsible in conquered countries for rounding up and shooting Jews and other "racial undesirables." Himmler had become leader of a total system of terror.

During the war, Hitler made Himmler overseer of Nazi plans for reorganizing Europe along racial lines. Himmler acted ruthlessly. He said: "What happens to the Russians, what happens to the Czechs, is a matter of utter indifference to me. . . . Whether or not 10,000 Russian women collapse from exhaustion while digging a tank ditch interests me only in so far as the tank ditch is completed for Germany."

At the end of the war, with the Nazi Empire in collapse, Himmler sought to escape by taking on a false identity. He was captured by the British and ended his life by swallowing a poison vial he had hidden in his mouth.

1. Why did Hitler consider Himmler to be the ideal leader?

2. Name and explain four of the SS divisions developed by Himmler.

3. What is meant by the term "Aryan supremacy"?

## YOUNG PEOPLE IN NAZI GERMANY

# The Hitler Youth

In setting up a total state, the Nazis recognized the importance of winning the youth over to their ideas. The Hitler Youth, an organization for young people between the ages of ten and eighteen, was formed in 1926. By 1939, all German young people were expected to join the Hitler Youth. Upon entering, each took an oath: "In the presence of this blood banner, which represents our Führer, I swear to devote all my energies and my strength to the savior of our country, Adolf Hitler. I am willing and ready to give up my life for him, so help me God."

Members of the Hitler Youth had their own uniforms and took part in a number of activities. For males, these included camping and hiking trips, sports activities, and evenings together in special youth "homes." Almost all activities were competitive and meant to encourage fighting and heroic deeds.

Above all, the Hitler Youth organization worked to foster military values and virtues, such as duty, obedience, strength, and ruthlessness. Uniforms and drilling became a way of life. By 1938, training in the military arts also became part of the routine. Even boys ten to fourteen years old were given small-arms drill and practice with dummy hand grenades. Those who were fourteen to eighteen years old bore army packs and rifles while on camping trips in the countryside.

The Hitler Youth had a female division, known as the League of German Girls, for girls aged ten to eighteen. They, too, had uniforms: white blouses, blue ankle-length skirts, and sturdy hiking shoes. Camping and hiking were also part of the girls' activities. More important, however, girls were taught domestic skills—how to cook, clean houses, and take care of children. In Nazi Ger-

▲ Many young children were drawn to the Hitler Youth. The children shown here wave their flags, obviously proud to be part of the movement. Do you think youth groups receive strong support in the United States? Why or why not?

many, women were expected to be faithful wives and dutiful mothers.

1. Explain the ideals and values that Nazi leaders tried to instill in the young people of Germany through the Hitler Youth organization.

2. Use your own perspective to evaluate these virtues and ideals.

German Jews from German citizenship and forbade marriages between Jews and German citizens. The "Nuremberg laws" basically separated Jews from the Germans politically, socially, and legally.

A more violent phase of anti-Jewish activity took place in 1938 and 1939. It began on November 9–10, 1938—the Kristallnacht (KRIS-tul-NAWKT), or "night of shattered glass." The assassination of a third secretary in the German embassy in Paris gave Nazis an excuse for a destructive rampage against the Jews. Synagogues were burned, and 7,000 Jewish businesses were destroyed. At least 100 Jews were killed. Moreover, 30,000 Jewish males were rounded up and sent to concentration camps. Kristallnacht also led to further drastic steps. Jews were barred from all public buildings and prohibited from owning, managing, or working in any retail store. Finally, under the direction of the SS, Jews were encouraged to "emigrate from Germany." After the outbreak of World War II, the policy of emigration was replaced by a more gruesome one (see Chapter 11).

## ❀ SECTION REVIEW ❀

1. **Locate:**
   (a) Nuremberg

2. **Define:**
   (a) anti-Semitism,    (b) Reichstag

3. **Identify:**
   (a) National Socialist German Workers' Party,
   (b) *Mein Kampf,*    (c) Lebensraum,
   (d) Enabling Act,    (e) Aryan race,
   (f) Nuremberg rallies,    (g) Nuremberg laws,
   (h) Kristallnacht

4. **Recall:**
   (a) Why did Hitler feel struggle was important to the growth of nations?
   (b) What did Hitler accomplish while he was in prison during the 1920s?
   (c) What three appeals did Hitler make to gain popularity in Germany during the 1930s?

(d) How did Hitler solve the German unemployment problem during the 1930s?

5. **Think Critically:** Why was it important that Hitler made German soldiers swear allegiance to him personally rather than to the German nation?

## SOCIAL, CULTURAL, AND INTELLECTUAL TRENDS IN THE INTERWAR YEARS

Technology continued to have profound effects upon European society. Nowhere is this more evident than in the expansion of mass culture and mass leisure after World War I. Because of technology, popular forms of entertainment could now reach millions of people. No doubt, the new obsession with entertainment and games such as movies, radio, and sporting events was also part of the desire to forget the horrors of the Great War—a "live for today, for tomorrow we may die" mentality.

### Mass Culture: Radio and Movies

A series of inventions in the late nineteenth century had led the way for a revolution in mass communications. Especially important was Marconi's discovery of "wireless" radio waves (see Chapter 5). It was not until June 16, 1920, however, that a radio broadcast for a mass audience was tried. The broadcast was a concert by soprano Nellie Melba from London. Broadcasting facilities were then built in the United States, Europe, and Japan during 1921 and 1922. At the same time, the mass production of radios began. In 1926, there were 2.2 million radios in Great Britain. By the end of the 1930s, there were 9 million. Broadcasting networks in the United States were privately owned and financed by advertising. Those in Europe were usually controlled by the government.

Motion pictures had first emerged in the 1890s. However, it was not until shortly before World War I that full-length features appeared. The Italian film *Quo Vadis* (KWOE VAE-dis) and the American film *Birth of*

◄ *The classic movie* Quo Vadis *starred Robert Taylor, Deborah Kerr, and Peter Ustinov in a story of a Roman commander who falls in love with a Christian girl. Does this plot remind you of any movies you have seen in the past year?*

*a Nation* made it apparent that cinema was a new form of mass entertainment. By 1939, about 40 percent of adults in the more advanced industrial countries were attending a movie once a week. That figure increased to 60 percent by the end of World War II.

Of course, radio and the movies could be used for political purposes. Hitler had said, "Without motorcars, sound films, and wireless, no victory of National Socialism." Radio offered great opportunities for reaching the masses. This became obvious when it was discovered that the fiery speeches of Adolf Hitler made just as great an impact on people when heard on radio as in person. The Nazi regime encouraged radio listening by urging manufacturers to produce inexpensive radios that could be bought on an installment plan.

Film, too, had propaganda potential, a possibility not lost on Joseph Goebbels (GU[r]B-ulz), the propaganda minister of Nazi Germany. Believing that film was one of the "most modern and scientific means of influencing the masses," Goebbels created a special film section in his Propaganda Ministry. He aided the making of both documentaries and popular feature films that carried the Nazi message. *The Triumph of the Will,* for example, was a documentary of the 1934 Nuremberg party rally. This movie was filmed by Leni Riefenstahl, an actress turned director. It forcefully conveyed to viewers the power of National Socialism.

## Mass Leisure

Mass leisure activities had developed at the turn of the century (see Chapter 5), but new work patterns after World War I provided people with more free time to take advantage of these activities. By 1920, the eight-hour day had become the norm for many office and factory workers in northern and western Europe.

Professional sporting events for mass audiences were an important aspect of mass leisure (see "Sports and Contests: The Growth of Professional Sports"). Travel opportunities also added new dimensions to mass leisure activities. The military use of aircraft during World War I helped to improve planes and make civilian air travel a reality. The first regular international mail service began in 1919. Regular passenger service

# SPORTS AND CONTESTS

## The Growth of Professional Sports

After World War I, sports became an important part of the expansion of mass leisure. Live radio broadcasts of sporting events, especially in the United States, converted sports into a form of mass entertainment. Until the 1920s, sports had been regarded as a pastime of amateurs (people who were not paid). In the 1920s, players began to be paid to play on a regular basis, making them professional athletes. Businesses began to use sports and sports figures as tools to advertise and sell their goods. As the popularity of mass spectator sports grew, so did the amount of money spent on betting.

In Europe, attendance at soccer games grew dramatically. The creation of the World Cup contest in 1930 added to the nationalistic rivalries that had begun to surround soccer and other mass sporting events. Increased attendance at sports events also made the 1920s and 1930s a great era of stadium building. For the 1936 Olympics, Germany built a stadium in Berlin that seated 140,000 people. Strahav Stadium in Prague held 240,000 spectators for gymnastics and track meets, even though these sports remained games chiefly for amateurs.

In the 1930s, sports and politics grew closer together. Benito Mussolini poured lavish sums of money into Italy's soccer team, which enabled it to win the World Cup twice in the 1930s. Even the Olympic Games, played every four years since their initiation in 1896 and intended to bolster the achievements of amateurs, were used for politi-

▲ *This soccer final between Italy and Austria took place at the 1936 Olympics in Berlin. Which country do you think was victorious?*

cal purposes. Adolf Hitler used the Eleventh Olympic Games, held in Berlin in 1936, to show to the world Germany's physical strength and newfound prestige. The victories of Jesse Owens, an African American, were especially devastating to the Nazi regime, which believed in the superiority of whites over blacks and other races.

1. According to this feature, what "converted sports into a form of mass entertainment"?

2. Why were the Nazis disturbed by Jesse Owens' victories during the 1936 Olympics?

soon followed. Of course, it was mostly the wealthy who used air travel. However, trains, buses, and cars made trips to beaches or holiday resorts more and more popular and affordable. Beaches, such as the one at Brighton in Great Britain, were mobbed by crowds of people from all social classes.

Mass leisure gave totalitarian states new ways to control the people. Mussolini's Italy created the

Dopolavoro (Afterwork) as a vast national recreation agency. The Dopolavoro set up clubhouses in almost every town and village. They contained libraries, radios, and athletic facilities. In some places, they included travel agencies that arranged tours, cruises, and resort vacations on the Adriatic at reduced rates. Dopolavoro groups gave many Italians their first experience of mass culture and mass leisure with activities such as band concerts, movies, and ballroom dancing. With the Dopolavoro, the Italian government not only provided, but also supervised, recreational activities.

The Nazi regime adopted a program similar to the Dopolavoro in its Kraft durch Freude (Strength through Joy). Strength through Joy offered a variety of leisure activities to fill the free time of the working class. These activities included concerts, operas, films, guided tours, and sporting events. Especially popular were the inexpensive vacations, which were basically modern package tours. A vacation could be a cruise to Scandinavia or the Mediterranean. More likely for workers, it was a shorter trip to different sites in Germany. Only 130,000 workers took cruises in 1938, compared with the 7 million who took short trips.

More and more, mass culture and mass leisure had the effect of giving all the people in a nation similar ideas and similar experiences. Local popular culture was being replaced by a national, and even international, mass culture that brought similar ideas and similar clothing and fashion styles to people throughout Europe.

## Artistic and Intellectual Trends

Before World War I, new artistic and intellectual trends had emerged that shocked many Europeans (see Chapter 5). Only a small group of avant-garde artists and intellectuals had been responsible for these new developments. After 1918, however, the new trends became more widespread. In the 1920s and 1930s, artists and intellectuals continued to work out the implications of the ideas developed before 1914. What made the prewar avant-garde culture acceptable in the 1920s and 1930s? Perhaps the most important factor was the impact of World War I.

Four years of devastating war left many Europeans with a profound sense of despair. To many people, World War I could mean only that something was dreadfully wrong with Western values. The experiences of World War I seemed to confirm the prewar avant-garde belief that human beings were really violent animals who were incapable of creating a sane and rational world. The Great Depression, as well as the growth of fascist movements based on violence, only added to the despair created by World War I.

The crisis of confidence in Western civilization indeed ran deep. It was well captured in the words of the French poet Paul Valéry (VAL-uh-REE) in the early 1920s:

> The storm has died away, and still we are restless, uneasy, as if the storm were about to break. Almost all the affairs of men remain in a terrible uncertainty. We think of what has disappeared, and we are almost destroyed by what has been destroyed; we do not know what will be born, and we fear the future,...Doubt and disorder are in us and with us. There is no thinking man, however shrewd or learned he may be, who can hope to dominate this anxiety, to escape from this impression of darkness.[8]

With political, economic, and social uncertainties came intellectual uncertainties. These were evident in the artistic and intellectual achievements of the interwar years.

### Nightmares and New Visions: Art and Music

After 1918, artistic trends were largely a working out of the implications of developments before the war. Abstract expressionism, for example, became ever more popular. In addition, the prewar fascination with the absurd and the unconscious content of the mind seemed even more appropriate in light of the nightmare landscapes of World War I battlefronts. "The world does not make sense, so why should art?" was a common response. This gave rise to both the Dada movement and surrealism (see "Our Artistic Heritage: Dadaism and Surrealism").

The move to **functionalism** (a theory of design that places great emphasis on how an object will be used) in

# OUR ARTISTIC HERITAGE

## Dadaism and Surrealism

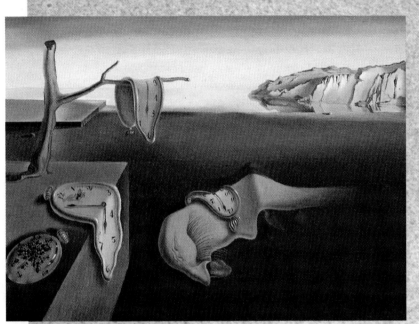

*Surrealistic paintings often suggest a dream world, the world of the unconscious. In* The Persistence of Memory, *1931, Dalí painted recognizable objects in contexts that seem out of place. What does this painting suggest to you?*

The Dadaists were artists who were obsessed with the idea that life had no purpose. Tristan Tzara, one of the founders of Dadaism, wrote: "Dada is a state of mind. . . . Dada applies itself to everything, and yet it is nothing. Like everything in life, Dada is useless. Dada is without pretension, as life should be." The Dadaists were revolted by the insanity of life and tried to express that feeling by creating antiart. The 1918 Berlin Dada Manifesto stated, "Dada is the international expression of our times, the great rebellion of artistic movements."

In the hands of Hannah Höch, Dada became an instrument to comment on women's roles in the new mass culture. Höch was the only female member of the Berlin Dada Club, a group of people working in the medium of photomontage. Her work was part of the first Dada show in Berlin in 1920. In her works, Höch created positive images of the modern woman and expressed a keen interest in new freedoms for women.

Perhaps more important than Dada as an artistic movement was surrealism. It sought a reality beyond the material world and found it in the world of the unconscious. By portraying fantasies, dreams, and even nightmares, the surrealists sought to show the "greater reality" that existed beyond the world of physical appearances. The surrealists employed logic to show the illogical and thus created disturbing images.

The Spaniard Salvador Dalí (DAW-lee) was the high priest of surrealism. In *The Persistence of Memory*, as in many of his artistic works, Dalí painted objects that were easily recognizable yet separated from their normal contexts. By placing recognizable objects in unrecognizable relationships, Dalí created a strange world in which the irrational became visible.

1. Explain the philosophy behind Dadaism.

2. Explain the philosophy behind surrealism.

3. What does the author mean when he calls Salvador Dalí the "high priest" of surrealism?

modern architecture also became more widespread in the 1920s and 1930s. Especially important in the spread of functionalism was the Bauhaus school of art, architecture, and design, founded in 1919 at Weimar, Germany, by the Berlin architect Walter Gropius. The Bauhaus teaching staff was made up of architects, artists, and designers. They worked together to combine the study of fine arts (painting and sculpture) with the applied arts (printing, weaving, and furniture making). Gropius urged his followers to foster a new union of arts and crafts in order to create the buildings and objects of the future.

Not everybody accepted modern art forms, however. Many people denounced what they saw as decay in the arts. Nowhere was this more evident than in the totalitarian states of Nazi Germany and the Soviet Union.

In the 1920s, Weimar Germany was one of the chief European centers for modern arts and sciences. Hitler and the Nazis rejected modern art as "degenerate" art. In a speech in July 1937, Hitler proclaimed:

> The people regarded this art [modern art] as the outcome of an impudent and shameless arrogance or of a simply shocking lack of skill; it felt that . . . these achievements which might have been produced by untalented children of from eight to ten years old—could never be valued as an expression of our own times or of the German future.[9]

Hitler and the Nazis believed that they were creating a new and genuine German art. It would glorify the strong, the healthy, and the heroic—all of which were supposedly qualities of the Aryan race. The new German art was actually the old nineteenth-century folk art with its emphasis on realistic scenes of everyday life.

Soviet painting, like German painting, was expected to focus on a nineteenth-century realistic style. Both the new German art and the "socialist realism" art of the Soviet Union were meant to instill social values useful to the ruling regimes.

At the beginning of the twentieth century, a revolution had come to music with the work of Igor Stravinsky (see Chapter 5). However, Stravinksy still wrote music in a definite key. In 1924, the Viennese composer Arnold Schönberg (SHU[r]N-BURG) wrote a piano suite in which he used a scale composed of

twelve notes free of any tonal key. His atonal music was similar to abstract painting. Abstract painting arranged colors and lines without concrete images. Atonal music organized sounds without any recognizable harmonies. Unlike modern art, however, modern music found little favor until after World War II.

### Literature: The Search for the Unconscious

The interest in the unconscious that was evident in art was also a part of new literary techniques. One example was a "stream of consciousness" technique, by which the writer gave a report of the innermost thoughts of each character. The most famous example of this approach was written by the Irish exile James Joyce. His *Ulysses* (yoo-LISS-eez), published in 1922, told the story of one day in the life of ordinary people in Dublin by following the flow of their inner thoughts.

The German writer Hermann Hesse dealt with the unconscious in a quite different fashion. His novels reflected the influence of both Freud's psychology and Eastern religions. The works focused on, among other things, the spiritual loneliness of modern human beings in a mechanized urban society. In both *Siddhartha* (si-DAWR-ta) and *Steppenwolf*, Hesse used Buddhist ideas to show the psychological confusion of modern existence (see "Our Literary Heritage: The Novels of Hermann Hesse"). Hesse's novels had a large impact on German youth in the 1920s. He won the Nobel Prize for literature in 1946.

### The "Heroic Age of Physics"

The prewar revolution in physics begun by Albert Einstein continued in the years between the wars. In fact, Ernest Rutherford, one of the physicists who showed that the atom could be split, dubbed the 1920s the "heroic age of physics." By the early 1940s, seven subatomic particles had been identified.

The new picture of the universe that was unfolding from physicists undermined the old certainties of classical physics. A basic belief in physics had been that all phenomena could be completely defined and subject to predictability. Thus, the weather could be predicted if we only knew everything about the wind, sun, and

## OUR LITERARY HERITAGE

# The Novels of Hermann Hesse

*The novels of Hermann Hesse made a strong impact on young people, first in Germany in the 1920s and then in the United States in the 1960s (after the novels' translation into English). Many of these young people shared Hesse's fascination with the unconscious and his dislike of modern industrial civilization. This excerpt from Demian spoke directly to many young people.*

### Hermann Hesse, *Demian*

The following spring I was to leave the preparatory school and enter a university. I was still undecided, however, as to where and what I was to study. I had grown a thin mustache, I was a full-grown man, and yet I was completely helpless and without a goal in life. Only one thing was certain: the voice within me, the dream image. I felt the duty to follow this voice blindly wherever it might lead me. But it was difficult and each day I rebelled against it anew. Perhaps I was mad, as I thought at moments; perhaps I was not like other men? But I was able to do the same things the others did; with a little effort and industry I could read Plato, was able to solve problems in trigonometry or follow a chemical analysis. There was only one thing I could not do: wrest the

▲ *Herman Hesse, pictured here, was one of the most influential authors in Europe in the 1920s and early 1930s. His works were especially appealing to young people.*

dark secret goal from myself and keep it before me as others did who knew exactly what they wanted to be—professors, lawyers, doctors, artists, however long this would take them and whatever difficulties and advantages this decision would bear in its wake. This I could not do. Perhaps I would become something similar, but how was I to know? Perhaps I would have to continue my search for years on end and would not become anything, and would not reach a goal. Perhaps I would reach this goal but it would turn out to be an evil, dangerous, horrible one?

I wanted only to try to live in accord with the promptings which came from my true self. Why was that so very difficult?

1. Who were most strongly impacted by Hermann Hesse's writings?

2. Why do you think his writings appealed more to a certain age group?

3. Does this passage from *Demian* have any impact on you? Why or why not?

water. In 1927, the German physicist Werner Heisenberg (HIZE-un-BURG) explained the **Uncertainty Principle.** According to this principle, no one could determine the path of an electron, because the act of observing with light affects the electron's location. The Uncertainty Principle was more than an explanation of the path of an electron, however. It was a new worldview. Heisenberg dared to suggest that at the bottom of all the physical laws was uncertainty. Few nonscientists probably understood the implications of Heisenberg's work, but the principle of uncertainty fit in well with the other uncertainties of the interwar years.

## SECTION REVIEW

1. **Define:**
   (a) functionalism,    (b) Uncertainty Principle

2. **Identify:**
   (a) *The Triumph of the Will,*    (b) Dopolavoro,
   (c) surrealism,    (d) Bauhaus,    (e) socialist realism,    (f) Arnold Schönberg,    (g) James Joyce,    (h) Herman Hesse

3. **Recall:**
   (a) What factors led many people to have similar experiences and ideas during the 1930s?
   (b) Why did many more people come to accept the point of view of avant-garde artists after World War I?
   (c) Why did Hitler label modern art as "degenerate"?

4. **Think Critically:** Why is the fact that radio stations were owned by governments rather than by private citizens in most of Europe important to bringing about conditions that would lead to World War II?

## Conclusion

The devastation wrought by World War I destroyed the liberal optimism of the prewar era. However, many people in the 1920s still hoped that the progress of Western civilization, so evident before 1914, could be restored. These hopes proved largely unfounded as plans for economic revival gave way to inflation and to an even more devastating Great Depression at the end of the 1920s. Likewise, confidence in political democracy was soon shattered by the rise of dictatorial governments. These governments not only restricted individual freedoms but also, in the case of Italy, Germany, and the Soviet Union, sought even greater control over the lives of their subjects in order to guide them to achieve the goals of the totalitarian regimes. To many people, these mass movements, even if they meant the loss of personal freedom, at least offered some sense of security in a world that seemed filled with uncertainties.

When Europeans devastated their civilizations in World War I, they also unexpectedly opened the door to movements for national independence in their colonies around the world. Although those movements would not be successful until after World War II, the next chapter will examine their beginnings.

## Notes

1. Quoted in Robert Paxton, *Europe in the Twentieth Century,* 2d ed. (San Diego, 1985), p. 237.
2. Benito Mussolini, "The Doctrine of Fascism," *Italian Fascisms,* ed. Adrian Lyttleton (London, 1973), p. 42.
3. Quoted in Alexander De Grand, "Women under Italian Fascism," *Historical Journal* 19 (1976): 958–959.
4. Adolf Hitler, *Mein Kampf,* trans. Ralph Manheim (Boston, 1943), p. 161.
5. Quoted in Jeremy Noakes and Geoffrey Pridham, eds., *Nazism 1919–1945,* vol. 1 (Exeter, England, 1983), pp. 50–51.
6. Quoted in Jackson Spielvogel, *Hitler and Nazi Germany: A History,* 3rd ed. (Englewood Cliffs, N.J., 1996), p. 58.
7. Quoted in Joachim Fest, *Hitler,* trans. Richard Winston and Clara Winston (New York, 1974), p. 418.
8. Paul Valéry, *Variety,* trans. Malcolm Cowley (New York, 1927), pp. 27–28.
9. Norman H. Baynes, ed., *The Speeches of Adolf Hitler, 1922–1939,* vol. 1 (Oxford, 1942), p. 591.

# CHAPTER 9 REVIEW

## USING KEY TERMS

1. The _____ was a name given to Fascists who attacked socialist offices and newspapers in Italy after World War I.
2. _____ is a sense of prejudice against Jewish people.
3. The Soviet government followed a policy of _____ when it took private property after World War I without payments to the former owners.
4. A _____ exists when almost all power in a nation is held by the central government.
5. Lenin abandoned war communism in 1921 in favor of his _____, a modified version of the old capitalist system.
6. The government policy of going into debt to pay for public works projects, such as building highways, is called _____.
7. According to the _____ no one could determine the path of an electron, meaning all physical laws had elements of unpredictability.
8. The Bauhaus school spread the theory of design called _____.
9. The German parliament is known as the _____.
10. The _____ was the leading policymaker of the Communist Party.
11. _____ is the right of unions to negotiate with employers.

## REVIEWING THE FACTS

1. What 1925 treaty tried to reduce fears of a new war by guaranteeing national borders between Germany, France, and Belgium?
2. What was promised by the nations that signed the Kellogg-Briand Pact in 1928?
3. What did President Roosevelt call the laws designed to fight the depression in the United States?
4. Who took over the government of Italy in 1922 and created a fascist totalitarian state?
5. What leader ended the New Economic Policy in the Soviet Union and collectivized farms in that nation?
6. What was the purpose of the five-year plans during the 1930s in the Soviet Union?
7. What was the official name of the Nazi party in Germany?
8. Why was the Enabling Act of 1933 important to Hitler's success in controlling Germany?
9. What was the basic purpose of the Nuremberg Laws?
10. How did avant-guarde artistic styles find support in the political and social atmosphere after World War I?

## THINKING CRITICALLY

1. Why wasn't the League of Nations an effective organization for enforcing international agreements?
2. Why might the government of Germany have deliberately caused rapid inflation in that country after World War I?
3. How might the depression have helped extremist leaders to gain power in many nations during the 1930s?
4. What abilities, in addition to being a forceful speaker, can help a person gain political power?
5. Why do totalitarian leaders often involve their nations in relatively small wars?
6. What economic problems were resolved in Germany by the military buildup undertaken by Hitler's government?
7. Why did totalitarian leaders like Hitler, Stalin, and Mussolini encourage popular involvement in particular artistic styles?

# CHAPTER 9 REVIEW

## APPLYING SOCIAL STUDIES SKILLS

1. **Economics:** In 1932 the unemployment rate in the United States was 33 percent, 31 percent in Great Britain, and 37 percent in Germany. Compare and contrast the ways in which leaders of these nations attempted to deal with their unemployment problem and how their policies contributed to the causes of World War II.

2. **Economics:** The total value of reparations assessed on Germany by the Treaty of Versailles has been estimated to have exceeded $30 billion. In 1928 the total value of all income earned in Germany was measured at a value of $12 billion. Use this information to write a paragraph that explains why it was unrealistic to expect Germany to pay all of its reparations.

3. **Government:** During the 1930s the governments of Great Britain, France, and the United States did almost nothing to discourage Hitler's Germany from rearming and taking over many lands in Europe. Write an essay that discusses why it is difficult for democratic nations to take action quickly when faced by aggression from totalitarian states.

4. **Sociology:** What events and conditions caused a large part of American society to have an isolationist point of view after World War I?

## MAKING TIME AND PLACE CONNECTIONS

1. Compare recent military actions of the United Nations in wars in Africa, Eastern Europe, and the Middle East with the inaction of the League of Nations. Why do you believe there has been an apparent difference in the ability of these two organizations to settle international disputes?

2. A reaction of many nations to the start of the depression was to impose high taxes on imported goods. This policy caused a rapid decline in international trade in the 1930s. In recent years most nations have lowered tariffs on imported goods. How might these different policies have affected international relations and the likelihood of war in the 1930s and at the present?

3. Compare the reaction of world powers to Hitler's aggression in the 1930s with actions taken when Iraq invaded Kuwait in 1990.

4. A good deal of American popular art, literature, and music during the 1960s and 1970s focused on anti-establishment ideas and themes. In what way was the art of the 1920s and 1930s in Europe similar?

5. Compare your personal rights and freedoms as an American citizen with those of people who lived in post World War I Germany.

## BECOMING AN HISTORIAN

1. **Fact versus Opinion:** The final sentence in Hitler's book, *Mein Kampf* reads, "A state which, in an epoch of race poisoning, dedicates itself to the cherishing of its best racial elements, must some day be master of the world." Discuss how confusion between facts and opinions may have helped Hitler gain power in Germany.

2. **Making Hypotheses and Predicting Outcomes:** The following is a partial contents of the Treaty of Versailles. Pretend you are an historian in 1920 and use this list to form and explain a hypothesis about the likelihood of the treaty's success.
   (*a*) Germany was required to give up almost 25 percent of its land and all of its colonies.
   (*b*) Germany's military forces were limited to 100,000 people.
   (*c*) France was given the right to control and use coal from Germany's Saar river basin for 15 years.
   (*d*) France was given the provinces of Alsace and Lorraine.
   (*e*) Germany was accused of causing the war and was required to pay reparations.

3. **Map Interpretation:** Study Map 9.1 on page 309. Use it to evaluate the geographic problems Germany faced after World War I.

# NATIONALISM, REVOLUTION, AND DICTATORSHIP: THE MIDDLE EAST,

**10**

In 1930, Mohandas Gandhi, the sixty-one-year-old leader of the Indian nonviolent movement for independence from British rule, began a march to the sea with seventy-eight followers. Their destination was Dandi, a little coastal town some 240 miles away. The group covered about 12 miles a day. As they went, Gandhi preached his doctrine of nonviolent resistance to British rule in every village through which he passed: "Civil disobedience is the inherent right of a citizen. He dare not give it up without ceasing to be a man." By the time Gandhi reached Dandi, twenty-four days later, his small group had become a nonviolent army of thousands.

When Gandhi and his followers arrived at Dandi, Gandhi picked up a pinch of crystallized seasalt from the sand. Thousands of people all along the coast did likewise. In so doing, they were openly breaking British laws that prohibited Indians from making their own salt. The British had long profited from their monopoly on the making and sale of salt, an item much in demand in a tropical country. By their simple acts of disobedience, Gandhi and the Indian people had taken yet another step on their long march to independence from the British. The Salt March was but one of many nonviolent activities that Gandhi undertook to win India's goal of national independence from

British rule between World War I and World War II.

World War I not only deeply affected the lives of Europeans but also ended the age of European domination over world affairs. After the Europeans had devastated their own civilization on the battlegrounds of Europe, the people living in the colonies controlled by the European countries began to hope that they might now gain their independence. In Africa and Asia, movements for national independence began to take shape. Some were inspired by the nationalist and liberal movements of the West. Others began to look toward the new Marxist model provided by the victory of the Communists in the Soviet Union, who soon worked to spread their revolutionary vision to African and Asian societies. In the Middle East, World War I ended the rule of the Ottoman Empire and created new states, some of whom adopted Western features in order to modernize their countries. For some Latin American countries, the fascist dictatorships of Italy and Germany provided models for change.

◄ *Mohandas Gandhi's concern for and involvement with the poorer classes in India never ceased. Here he is joined by his followers on the Salt March in 1930. Why do you think Gandhi's nonviolent demonstrations were so successful against the British?*

# AFRICA, ASIA, AND LATIN AMERICA

## (1919 TO 1939)

CRISIS OF THE TWENTIETH CENTURY

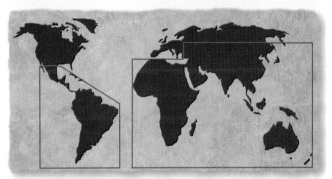

| | NATIONALISM, REVOLUTION | |
|---|---|---|
| 1919 | AND DICTATORSHIP | 1939 |

1910                                             1945

## QUESTIONS TO GUIDE YOUR READING

1. What actions did Kemal Ataturk take to modernize Turkey?

2. What forms did modernization take in Iran?

3. In what ways were the independence movements in the Middle East, Africa, and India similar? In what ways were they different?

4. What role did Mohandas Gandhi play in the Indian movement for independence?

5. What were the major successes and failures of the Nationalists and the Communists in China from 1919 to 1939?

6. What economic and political problems did Latin American countries have in the 1920s and 1930s?

## OUTLINE

1. THE NATIONALIST REVOLT IN THE MIDDLE EAST

2. NATIONALISM AND REVOLUTION IN AFRICA AND ASIA

3. REVOLUTIONARY CHAOS IN CHINA

4. NATIONALISM AND DICTATORSHIP IN LATIN AMERICA

## 1

## THE NATIONALIST REVOLT IN THE MIDDLE EAST

In the Middle East, as in Europe, World War I brought the collapse of old empires. The Ottoman Empire had been growing steadily weaker since the end of the eighteenth century, which led European nations to call it the "sick man of Europe." Government corruption, a decline in the power of the sultans, and the loss of much territory in the Balkans were all visible signs of this decline. In North Africa, Ottoman rule had ended in the nineteenth century when France seized Algeria and Tunisia (too-NEE-zhee-uh) and when Great Britain took control of Egypt.

### Decline and Fall of the Ottoman Empire

Reformers in Constantinople had tried to stop the Ottoman Empire's decline. In the eighteenth century, westernizing forces concerned about the shrinking of the empire had tried to modernize the army. However, a modern army could not make up for decaying political and social institutions. One energetic sultan, Selim III, tried at the end of the eighteenth century to establish a "new order" that would update the civilian, as well as the military, bureaucracy. However, the Janissaries (the sultan's special military forces), alarmed at the possible loss of their power, revolted and brought the experiment to an end.

Further efforts at reform during the first half of the nineteenth century were somewhat more successful. The government removed the Janissaries from power and began a series of bureaucratic, military, and educational reforms. New roads were built, and the power of local landlords was reduced. An imperial decree issued in 1856 granted equal rights to all subjects of the empire, whatever their religion.

Reforms failed to halt the decline of the empire. Greece declared its independence, and Ottoman power declined steadily in the Middle East. A rising sense of nationality among Serbs, Armenians, and other minority peoples threatened the stability and cohesion of the empire. In the 1870s, a new generation of Ottoman reformers seized power in Constantinople. In 1876 they pushed through a constitution aimed at forming a legislative assembly that would represent all the peoples in the state. However, the sultan they placed on the throne, Sultan Abdulhamid, suspended the new constitution and tried to rule by traditional authoritarian means. Abdulhamid paid a high price for his actions—he lived in constant fear of assassination. He kept a thousand loaded revolvers hidden throughout his guarded estate and insisted that his pets taste his food before he ate it.

By the end of the nineteenth century, the suspended 1876 constitution had become a symbol of change for reformers who now established a group known as the "Young Turks." Leading members of the group set up a Committee of Union and Progress (CUP). It gained support within the Ottoman army and administration, as well as among Turks living in exile. In 1908, Young Turk elements forced the sultan to restore the 1876 constitution and then removed him from power the following year.

The Young Turks had come at a difficult moment for the empire, however. Internal rebellions, combined with new losses of Ottoman territories in the Balkans, undermined the support for the new government and led the army to step in. By this time, most minorities

▲ *The campaigns and adventures of T. E. Lawrence gained him fame throughout the world. Several movies have been made showing him as a dashing, romantic figure.*

from the old empire were no longer under Ottoman authority. Many ethnic Turks began to embrace a new concept of a Turkish state that would encompass all people of Turkish nationality.

The final blow to the old empire came in World War I. The Ottoman government decided to ally with Germany in the hope of driving the British from Egypt and restoring Ottoman rule there. The new sultan called for a holy war by Muslim subjects in Russia and in territories in the Middle East ruled by Britain and France. In response, Great Britain declared an official protectorate over Egypt. To undermine Ottoman rule in the Arabian peninsula, Britain supported Arab Nationalist activities there. The Nationalists were aided by the efforts of the dashing British adventurer T. E. Lawrence, popularly known as "Lawrence of Ara-

## Map 10.1   The Middle East, 1919–1939

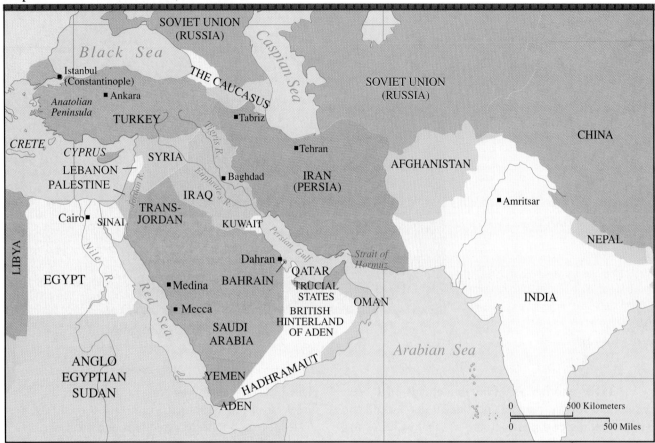

bia." In 1916, the local governor of Mecca, encouraged by Great Britain, declared Arabia independent from Ottoman rule. British troops, advancing from Egypt, seized Palestine. In October 1918, having suffered more than 300,000 dead during the war, the Ottoman Empire made peace with the Allied Powers.

During the war, the Turks had further alienated the Allies with Turkish policies toward their minority subjects, especially the Armenians. The Christian Armenian minority had pressed the Ottoman government for its independence for some time. In 1915, after an Armenian uprising, the government retaliated with fury by killing Armenian men and expelling women and children. Within seven months, 600,000 Armenians had been killed, and 500,000 had been deported (sent out of the country). Of the latter, 400,000 died

while marching through the deserts and swamps of Syria and Mesopotamia. By September 1915, an estimated 1 million Armenians were dead. They were victims of **genocide,** the deliberate mass murder of a group of people. (The practice was called **ethnic cleansing** in the Bosnian War of 1993 to 1996.) One eyewitness described the 1915 Armenian deportation:

*She saw vultures hovering over children who had fallen dead by the roadside. She saw beings crawling along, maimed, starving and begging for bread. From time to time she passed soldiers driving before them with whips and rifle-butts whole families, men, women and children, shrieking, pleading, wailing. These were the Armenian people setting out for exile into the desert from which there was no return.*[1]

▶ *Kemal Ataturk worked hard to bring modern traditions and reform to Turkey. In this photo taken during the Turko-Greek War, he chats with camel drivers.*

By 1918, another 400,000 Armenians had been massacred. Russia, France, and Britain denounced the Turkish killing of the Armenians as "against humanity and civilization." Because of the war, however, the killings went on.

At the end of World War I, the tottering Ottoman Empire began to fall apart. Great Britain and France made plans to divide up Ottoman territories in the Middle East. At the same time, Greece won Allied approval to seize the western parts of the Anatolian peninsula. Greece dreamed of recreating much of the old Byzantine Empire.

The approaching collapse alarmed key elements in Turkey under the leadership of a war hero, Colonel Mustapha Kemal (moo-staw-FAW kuh-MAWL). Kemal had commanded Turkish forces in their heroic defense of the Dardanelles (the Battle of Gallipoli) against a British invasion during World War I. Now Kemal resigned from the army and summoned a National Congress that called for the creation of an elected government and the preservation of the remaining territories of the old empire in a new Republic of Turkey. Kemal

placed his new capital at Ankara. His forces drove the Greeks from the Anatolian peninsula. Kemal then persuaded Great Britain to agree to a new treaty. In 1923, the last of the Ottoman sultans fled the country, which was now declared to be the Turkish Republic. The Ottoman Empire had finally come to an end.

## Mustapha Kemal and the Modernization of Turkey

During the next few years, President Kemal (now popularly known as Ataturk [aw-taw-TURK], or "father Turk,") tried to transform Turkey into a modern state. The trappings of a democratic system were put in place with an elected Grand National Assembly. However, the president did not tolerate opposition and harshly suppressed his critics. Turkish nationalism was stressed. The Turkish language, now written in the Roman alphabet, was shorn of many of its Arabic elements. Popular education was introduced, and old aristocratic titles were abolished. All Turkish citizens were forced to adopt family names, in the European style.

Ataturk also took steps to modernize Turkey's economy. Factories to produce textiles, glass, paper, and cement were established. A five-year plan on the Soviet model was drawn up to provide for state direction over the economy. Ataturk was no fan of Soviet communism, however. The Turkish economy could be better described as a form of state capitalism. Ataturk also tried to modernize farming, but he had little effect on the nation's mostly conservative peasants.

Perhaps the most significant aspect of Ataturk's reform program was his attempt to break the power of the Islamic religion and transform Turkey into a **secular state** (a state that rejects any church influence on its policies). The caliphate was formally abolished in 1924. Ataturk said, "Religion is like a heavy blanket that keeps the people of Turkey asleep." Wearing the **fez** (the brimless cap worn by Turkish Muslims) was forbidden. When Ataturk began wearing a Western panama hat, one of his critics remarked, "You cannot make a Turk into a Westerner by giving him a hat." Women were forbidden to wear the veil, a traditional Islamic custom. New laws gave women equal rights with men in all aspects of marriage and inheritance. In 1934, women received the right to vote. Education and the professions were now open to citizens of both sexes. Some women even began to take part in politics. All citizens were now given the right to convert to another religion at will.

The legacy of Mustapha Kemal Ataturk was enormous. Not all of his reforms were widely accepted in practice, especially by devout Muslims. However, most of the changes that he introduced were kept after his death in 1938. By and large, the Turkish Republic was the product of Ataturk's determined efforts to create a modern Turkish nation.

## Modernization in Persia: The Beginnings of Modern Iran

In the meantime, a similar process of modernization was under way in Persia. Under the Qajar dynasty (1794 to 1925), the country had not been very successful in resisting Russian advances in the Caucasus or in resolving its domestic problems. To secure themselves from foreign influence, the shahs moved the capital from Tabriz (tuh-BREEZ) to Tehran (TAE-RAN), in a mountainous area just south of the Caspian

◄ Oil discoveries early in the century began to bring wealth to Persia. These workers are developing the fields at Petroleum Springs, Dalaki, in Persia. How do you think Persia used these early revenues?

Sea. During the mid-nineteenth century, one modernizing shah tried to introduce political and economic reforms, but he was stopped by resistance from tribal and religious forces. Increasingly, the dynasty turned to Russia and Great Britain to protect itself from its own people.

The growing foreign presence, however, led to the rise of a native Persian nationalist movement. Much of it was directed at Russian advances in the northwest. However, the nationalists also condemned the growing European influence within the small, modern industrial sector. The profits from these industries went to foreign investors or found their way into the pockets of the dynasty's ruling elite. Opposition to the regime was supported actively by Islamic religious leaders and rose steadily among both peasants and merchants in the cities. In 1906, popular pressure forced the reigning shah to grant a constitution on the Western model.

The modernizers had moved too soon, however. Their power base was not yet secure. With the support of Russia and Great Britain, the shah was able to retain control. The two foreign powers, however, began to divide the country into separate spheres of influence. One reason for the growing foreign presence in Persia was the discovery of oil in the southern part of the country in 1908. Within a few years, oil exports increased rapidly. Most of the profits went into the pockets of British investors.

In 1921, Reza Khan, an officer in the Persian army, led a military mutiny that seized power in Tehran. The new ruler's original aim had been to declare the establishment of a republic, but resistance from traditional forces stopped his efforts. In 1925, a new Pahlavi (PAL-uh-VEE) dynasty, with Reza Khan as shah, replaced the old dynasty. During the next few years, Reza Khan tried to follow the example of Mustapha Kemal Ataturk in Turkey. He introduced a number of reforms to strengthen the central government, modernize the civilian and military bureaucracy, and establish a modern economic system. Persia had become the modern state of Iran.

Unlike Mustapha Kemal Ataturk, Reza Khan did not try to destroy the power of Islamic beliefs. However, he did encourage the creation of a Western-style educational system and forbade women to wear the veil in public. Foreign powers, however, continued to harass Iran. To free himself from Great Britain and the Soviet Union, Reza Khan drew closer to Nazi Germany. During World War II, when the shah rejected the demands of Great Britain and the Soviet Union to expel a large number of Germans from Iran, the Soviet Union and Great Britain sent troops into the country. Reza Khan resigned in protest and was replaced by his son, Mohammad Reza Shah.

## The Rise of Arab Nationalism and the Problem of Palestine

We have already mentioned the Arab uprising against Ottoman rule during World War I. Unrest against Ottoman rule had existed in the Arabian peninsula since the eighteenth century. At that time, a group of reformers known as the Wahhabis (wuh-HAWB-eez) revolted. They tried to drive out foreigners and cleanse Islam of the outside influences and corrupt practices that had developed in past centuries. The revolt was eventually suppressed, but the influence of the Wahhabi movement continued.

World War I offered an opportunity for Arabs to throw off the shackles of Ottoman rule. However, what would replace that rule? The Arabs were not a nation but an idea, a loose collection of peoples. They often did not see eye to eye on what made up their common sense of community. In fact, disagreement over what makes an Arab has plagued the efforts of generations of political leaders who have sought unsuccessfully to knit together the different peoples of the region into a single Arab nation.

As was noted, in 1916 the local governor of Mecca declared Arabia's independence from Ottoman rule and hoped for British support in the efforts of the Arab nationalists. These nationalists were sorely disappointed, however. At the close of the war, Britain agreed to share with France in the creation of a number of mandates in the area to be placed under the general supervision of the new League of Nations. Iraq and Jordan were assigned to Great Britain. Syria and Lebanon were given to France. (The two areas were separated so that Christian peoples in Lebanon could be placed

▸ *European Jewish refugees emigrated to Palestine both before and after World War II, but with one goal, to build a new life in a Jewish homeland. Like refugees aboard this ship, they all celebrated as they reached the safety of Palestine. The sign reads "Keep the gates open."*

under Christian administration.) These Middle Eastern states were, for the most part, the creation of Europeans. The Europeans arranged the borders and divided the peoples, but there was no strong identification on the part of most people with their designated countries. There was, however, a sense of Arab nationalism.

In the early 1920s, a leader of the Wahhabi movement, Ibn Saud, united Arab tribes in the northern part of the Arabian peninsula and drove out the remnants of Ottoman rule. Ibn Saud (from whom came the name Saudi Arabia) was a descendant of the family that had led the Wahhabi revolt in the eighteenth century. Devout and gifted, he won broad support among Arab tribal peoples and established the kingdom of Saudi Arabia throughout much of the peninsula in 1932.

At first the new kingdom, consisting mostly of the vast wastes of central Arabia, was desperately poor. Its financial resources were limited to the income from Muslim pilgrims visiting the holy spots in Mecca and Medina. During the 1930s, however, U.S. prospectors began to explore for oil. Standard Oil made a successful strike at Dahran, on the Persian Gulf, in 1938. Soon an Arabian-American oil company, popularly

called Aramco, was set up. The isolated kingdom was suddenly flooded by people in the Western oil industry, along with untold wealth.

Complicating matters in the Middle East was the land of Palestine. In antiquity it had been the home of the Jews. Now under British control, Palestine was inhabited primarily by Muslim Palestinians. According to the Balfour Declaration, issued by British foreign secretary Lord Balfour in November 1917, Palestine was to become a national home for the Jews. It stated: "His Majesty's Government views with favor the establishment in Palestine of a national home for the Jewish people." The declaration promised that the decision would not undermine the rights of the existing non-Jewish peoples currently living in the area. However, Arab nationalists were angered. They questioned how a national home for the Jewish people could be established in a territory in which 98 percent of the population was Muslim.

In the meantime, Jewish settlers began to arrive in Palestine in response to the promises made in the Balfour Declaration. The Zionist movement (see Chapter 5) had long advocated the return of Jews to Palestine as their homeland. Tensions between the new arrivals and existing Muslim residents began to escalate, especially during the 1930s. At the same time, the increased persecution of Jews with the rise of Nazi Germany led increasing numbers of European Jews to flee to Palestine. By 1939, there were about 450,000 Jews in Palestine. The British, fearing the effect of aroused Arab nationalism, then moved to restrict Jewish immigration into the territory. In 1939, the British government declared that only 75,000 Jewish immigrants would be allowed into Palestine over the next five years. After that, no more Jews could enter Palestine. The stage was set for the conflicts that would take place in the region after World War II.

## SECTION REVIEW

1. **Locate:**
   (*a*) Tunisia,  (*b*) Mecca,
   (*c*) Ankara,  (*d*) Anatolian peninsula,
   (*e*) Persia,  (*f*) Tehran

2. **Define:**
   (*a*) genocide,  (*b*) ethnic cleansing,
   (*c*) secular state,  (*d*) fez

3. **Identify:**
   (*a*) "sick man of Europe,"  (*b*) Janissaries,
   (*c*) Young Turks,  (*d*) Colonel Mustapha Kemal,
   (*e*) Wahhabi movement,  (*f*) Balfour Declaration

4. **Recall:**
   (*a*) How did the Ottoman Empire react to the Armenian uprising in 1915?
   (*b*) Why didn't Turkish efforts to create a democratic government in 1920 succeed?
   (*c*) What happened in 1908 that increased foreign interest in Persia?
   (*d*) Why was it difficult for Arab people to form a nation?

5. **Think Critically:**
   (*a*) What is the meaning of the following quotation, and why is it true?

"You cannot make a Turk into a Westerner by giving him a hat."

(*b*) Why did harsh treatment of Jewish people in Europe create problems for Arab people in the Middle East?

# NATIONALISM AND REVOLUTION IN AFRICA AND ASIA

Between 1919 and 1939, leaders emerged in Africa and Asia who sought to free their people from the power of the Western imperialists. None of these nationalist movements were successful before World War II, but they were a beginning.

## Independence Movements in Africa

Black Africans who fought in World War I in the armies of the British and French hoped for independence after the war. As one newspaper in the Gold Coast put it, if African volunteers who fought on European battlefields were "good enough to fight and die in the Empire's cause, they were good enough to have a share in the government of their countries." This feeling was shared by many. The peace settlement after World War I, then, turned out to be a great disappointment. Germany was stripped of its African colonies, but these colonies were awarded to Great Britain and France to be administered as mandates for the League of Nations. Britain and France now had so much territory in Africa that even they did not know what to do with it all.

After World War I, Africans became more active politically. Those Africans who had fought in World War I had learned new ideas in the West about freedom and nationalism. In Africa itself, missionary schools had often taught their African pupils ideas about liberty and equality. As more Africans became aware of the enormous gulf between Western ideals and practices, they decided to seek reform. Independence, however, remained but a dream.

## Map 10.2   Africa, 1919–1939

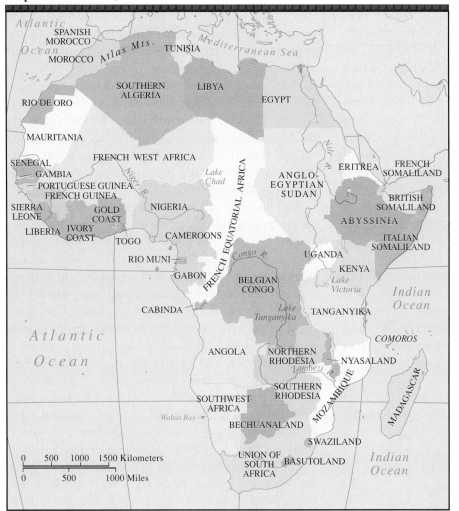

Thuku, a telephone operator, especially protested the high taxes levied by the British rulers. His message was simple: "Hearken, every day you pay hut tax to the Europeans of Government. Where is it sent? It is their task to steal the property of the Kikuyu people." Thuku was arrested. When an angry crowd stormed the jail and demanded his release, government authorities fired into the crowd and killed fifty people. Thuku was sent into exile.

In North Africa, there were also violent attempts at independence. Tribes in the Moroccan mountains, led by Muhammad Abd al-Krim, rebelled against Spanish control in 1921. This led to a lengthy struggle. France, which held the rest of Morocco, then intervened and crushed the revolt. Krim was exiled in 1926.

A struggle against Italian rule in Libya also broke out in the 1920s. Forces led by Omar Mukhtar used guerrilla warfare against the Italians and defeated them a number of times. The Italians reacted ferociously. They established concentration camps and used planes and all available modern weapons to crush the revolt. The death of Mukhtar ended the movement.

Colonial powers responded to these movements with force. However, they also began to make some reforms in the hope of satisfying native peoples. Reforms, however, were too few and too late. By the 1930s, an increasing number of African leaders were calling for independence, not reform.

The clearest calls came from a new generation of young African leaders who had been educated abroad, in Europe and the United States. Those who went to

Protest took different forms. In Nigeria and South Africa, workers created trade unions that tried to gain benefits for themselves. There were also cases of violent protest. In British Nigeria in 1929, a group of women protested the high taxes that were levied on the goods they were selling in the markets. During the riot that ensued, women cried for all white men to leave their country. The British killed fifty women and ended the riot.

In 1921, Kenya also witnessed a protest movement. The Young Kikuyu Association, organized by Harry

the United States were especially influenced by the ideas of W. E. B. Du Bois and Marcus Garvey. Du Bois, an African American educated at Harvard University, was the leader of a movement that tried to make all Africans aware of their own cultural heritage. Garvey, a Jamaican who lived in Harlem in New York City, also stressed the need for the unity of all Africans, a movement known as **Pan-Africanism.** His Declaration of the Rights of the Negro Peoples of the World, issued in 1920, had a strong impact on later African leaders.

Leaders and movements in individual African nations also appeared. Jomo Kenyatta (kun-YAH-tuh) of Kenya had been educated in Great Britain. In his book *Facing Mount Kenya,* he argued that British rule was destroying the traditional culture of the peoples of black Africa (see "You Are There: If Africans Were Left in Peace"). Léopold Senghor, who had studied in France and written poetry about African culture, organized an independence movement in Senegal. Nnamdi Azikiwe, of Nigeria, began a newspaper, *The West African Pilot,* in 1937 and advocated nonviolence as a method to gain independence. These are but three of the leaders who organized demonstrations and borrowed methods of political organization from the West to gain more followers. All of them were part of a growing movement to end colonial rule in Africa. Success would not come until after World War II, however.

## Gandhi and the Movement for Indian Independence

By the time of World War I, the Indian people had already begun to refer to Mohandas Gandhi as India's "Great Soul," or **Mahatma.** He now organized mass protests to achieve his aims. In 1919, the protests got out of hand and led to violence and a strong British reaction. British troops killed hundreds of unarmed protesters in the enclosed square in the city of Amritsar, in northwestern India. Horrified at the violence, Gandhi briefly retreated from active politics. Nevertheless, he was arrested for his role in the protests, and he spent several years in prison.

While Gandhi was in prison, Great Britain passed the Government of India Act. This act expanded the role of Indians in the governing process. What had been the Legislative Council that only gave advice was changed into a two-house parliament. Two-thirds of its members would be elected. Similar bodies were created at the provincial level. In one stroke, five million Indians had been given the right to vote.

Reforms, however, were no longer enough for many members of the Indian National Congress (INC; see Chapter 6). Under its new leader, Motilal Nehru, the INC wanted to push aggressively for full independence. Britain made the situation worse by increasing the salt tax and prohibiting the Indian people from manufacturing or harvesting their own salt.

Gandhi, now released from prison, returned to his earlier policy of civil disobedience (see "You Are There: Gandhi Takes the Path of Civil Disobedience"). He worked hard to inform ordinary Indians everywhere of his beliefs and methods. He believed that it was wrong to harm any living being. Hate could only be overcome by love, and love, rather than force, could win people over to one's position. Nonviolence, then, was crucial. It could be used in a campaign of noncooperation and civil disobedience. Gandhi said, "Don't pay your taxes or send your children to an English-supported school. . . . Make your own cotton cloth by spinning the thread at home, and don't buy English-made goods. Provide yourselves with home-made salt, and do not buy government-made salt."

In 1930, Gandhi used the British measures on salt as the basis for civil disobedience. He openly joined seventy-eight supporters and walked some 240 miles to the sea. Along the way, thousands of new supporters joined him. When they reached the sea, Gandhi picked up a pinch of salt and urged Indians to do the same and ignore the law. (The British used saltflats along the seashore to collect crystallized seasalt.) When thousands of Indians followed Gandhi's policy of civil disobedience, he and many other members of the INC were arrested.

In the 1930s, a new figure entered the movement. Jawaharlal Nehru, the son of the INC leader Motilal Nehru, was educated in law in Great Britain. The younger Nehru was a good example of the new Anglo-Indian politician. He was secular, rational, upper class, and an intellectual. In fact, he appeared to be everything that Gandhi was not.

# YOU ARE THERE

## If Africans Were Left in Peace

*Jomo Kenyatta was an eloquent spokesperson for independence for Kenya from British rule. His book* Facing Mount Kenya *was a detailed description of the ways of life of his native Kikuyu people. He ended the book with a plea for African independence.*

### Jomo Kenyatta, *Facing Mount Kenya*

If Africans were left in peace on their own lands, Europeans would have to offer them the benefits of white civilization in real earnest before they could obtain the African labor which they want so much. They would have to offer the African a way of life which was really superior to the one his fathers lived before him, and a share in the prosperity given them by their command of science. They would have to let the African choose what parts of European culture could be beneficially transplanted, and how they could be adapted. He would probably not choose the gas bomb or the armed police force, but he might ask for some other things of which he does not get so much today. As it is, by driving him off his ancestral lands, the Europeans

◀ *Jomo Kenyatta, founder of the Kikuyu Central Association, was initially interested in improving living conditions for Africans. He became president of Kenya in 1964.*

have robbed him of the material foundations of his culture, and reduced him to a state of serfdom incompatible with human happiness. The African is conditioned, by the cultural and social institutions of centuries, to a freedom of which Europe has little conception, and it is not in his nature to accept serfdom forever. He realizes that he must fight unceasingly for his own complete emancipation; for without this he is doomed to remain the prey of rival imperialisms, which in every successive year will drive their fangs more deeply into his vitality and strength.

1. In your own words, describe the appeal that Jomo Kenyatta is making in regard to Africa.

2. How would you, as a westerner, respond to Kenyatta's appeal?

With the emergence of Nehru, the independence movement split into two paths. The one identified with Gandhi was religious, native, and traditional. The other, identified with Nehru, was secular, Western, and modern. Both Gandhi and Nehru were leaders in the INC. Thus, the INC leadership had a duality that probably made the independence movement stronger. After all, the two main impulses behind the desire for independence—nationalism and the primal force of Indian traditionalism—were brought together. However, the existence of two approaches made people uncertain how to define India's future path in the contemporary world.

In the meantime, another problem arose in the independence movement. Hostility between Hindus and Muslims had existed for centuries. Muslims now

## YOU ARE THERE

# Gandhi Takes the Path of Civil Disobedience

*Mohandas Gandhi became convinced that only a policy of civil disobedience could free India from British rule. In this letter to a British official, he explains why British rule must end.*

### Mohandas Gandhi, Letter to a British Official

Before embarking on civil disobedience and taking the risk I have dreaded to take all these years, I would fain approach you and find a way out.

My personal faith is absolutely clear. I cannot intentionally hurt anything that lives, much less fellow human beings, even though they may do the greatest wrong to me and mine. Whilst, therefore, I hold the British rule to be a curse, I do not intend harm to a single Englishman or to any legitimate interest he may have in India.

I must not be misunderstood. Though I hold the British rule in India to be a curse, I do not, therefore, consider Englishmen in general to be worse than any other people on earth. I have the privilege of claiming many Englishmen as dearest friends. Indeed much that I have learned of the evil of British rule is due to the writings of frank and courageous Englishmen who have not hesitated to tell the truth about that rule.

And why do I regard British rule as a curse? It has impoverished the ignorant millions by a system of progressive exploitation and by a ruinously expensive military and civil administration which the country can never afford.

It has reduced us politically to serfdom. It has sapped the foundations of our culture. And, by the policy of cruel disarmament, it has degraded us spiritually. Lacking the inward strength, we have been reduced, by all but universal disarmament, to a state bordering on cowardly helplessness. . . .

▲ *Throughout his life, Gandhi crusaded for rights for both men and women of all classes, from educated professionals to the Untouchables.*

I know that in embarking on non-violence I shall be running what might fairly be termed a mad risk. But the victories of truth have never been won without risks, often of the gravest character. Conversion of a nation that has consciously or unconsciously preyed upon another, far more numerous, far more ancient and no less cultured than itself, is worth any amount of risk.

1. According to Gandhi, what had British rule done to India?

2. What is civil disobedience?

3. Why do you think Gandhi believed that non-violent civil disobedience would encourage the British to free India?

◄ *By 1932, Japanese forces had occupied a number of walled cities in Manchuria. Why do you think the Chinese were unable to stop the Japanese forces from invading?*

became unhappy with the Hindu dominance of the INC and raised the cry that "Islam is in danger." In 1930, the Muslim League, under the leadership of Muhammad Ali Jinnah, called for the creation of a separate Muslim state of Pakistan (meaning "the land of the pure") in the northwest. Conflict between Muslims and Hindus now began to grow. As it did, many Indians came to realize with sorrow that British rule was all that stood between peace and civil war.

## The Rise of a Militarist Japan

As we saw in Chapter 7, during the first two decades of the twentieth century, Japan seemed to be moving toward a more democratic government. The parliament and political parties had grown stronger. Civilian political leaders had been able to control the military. However, appearances were deceiving. The influence of the old ruling oligarchy remained strong. Furthermore, at the end of the 1920s, new problems led to the emergence of militant (aggressive) forces that moved Japan toward an authoritarian and militaristic state.

No doubt, economic crises added to the problem. Japan's economy had already begun to experience problems in the 1920s. The Great Depression made the situation worse. Workers, and especially farmers, suffered the most. With hardships came cries against the West and calls for a return to traditional Japanese values. At the same time, many citizens denounced Japan's attempt to find security through cooperation with the Western powers. Instead, they called upon Japan to use its own strength to dominate Asia in order to meet its needs. Extreme patriotism and a strong militarism marked the Japan of the 1930s.

The rise of militant forces in Japan was not the result of the takeover of power by a new political party, as it was in Fascist Italy and Nazi Germany. The Japanese constitution of 1889 was not abolished. Instead, a new group of militant people was able to control the political system. Some, like the publicist Kita Ikki, were civilians convinced that the parliamentary system had been corrupted by Western values. Others were members of the military who were angered at budget cuts in military expenditures and at the pacifist policies followed by the government during the early 1920s.

## CONNECTIONS
### AROUND THE WORLD

**Paths to Modernization**    After World War I, new states in the Middle East and Asia sought to modernize their countries. To many people, modernization meant westernization, or the adoption of both political and economic reforms based on Western models. These included the adoption of democratic principles and a free-market, or capitalist, economic system based on industrialization.

After the success of the Communist revolution in Russia, however, a second model for modernization appeared. To some people, a Marxist system seemed to offer a better and quicker way to transform a backward agricultural state into a modern industrial state. The new system would be a socialist model in which an authoritarian state, not private industry, would own and control the economy.

Between World War I and World War II, new republics in Turkey and China tended to combine features of both systems. In Turkey, Kemal Ataturk, creator of the new Turkish republic, set up a National Assembly but ruled with an iron fist. His economic modernization combined private industries with state direction of the economy.

In China, the Nanjing Republic under Jiang Jieshi supported the idea of democracy but maintained the need for dictatorial government as a first stage to prepare the Chinese people for democracy. Economic modernization in the new Chinese republic combined a modern industrial state with the traditional Chinese values of hard work and obedience.

During the early 1930s, extremist patriotic organizations, such as the Black Dragon Society, were formed by civilians, but even more so within the army and the navy. One of these groups, consisting of middle-level officers in the army, waged the takeover of Manchuria in the autumn of 1931. The government opposed the action. The Japanese people received it with great enthusiasm, however, and the government could do nothing to undo the takeover.

Other patriotic military groups terrorized Japanese society by assassinating businessmen and government officials. Moderate elements were forced into silence. Those who were put on trial for their part in assassination attempts were given light sentences while being allowed to portray themselves as selfless patriots. National elections continued to take place, but government cabinets were dominated by the military and other supporters of Japanese expansionism.

In the 1930s, Japanese society was put on a wartime status. A military draft law was passed in 1938. Economic resources were placed under strict government control. All political parties were merged into an Imperial Rule Assistance Association, which served as a mouthpiece for expansionist elements within the government and the military. Labor unions were broken up. Education and culture were purged of all corrupt Western ideas. Militant leaders insisted on the need for stressing traditional Japanese values instead.

## Nationalism
## and Revolution in Asia

Until the outbreak of World War I in 1914, the term **westernization,** to most intellectuals in Asia, had one meaning. It was identified with the capitalist democratic civilization in western Europe and the United States. The intellectuals had little interest in the doctrine of social revolution known as Marxism. That fact is not surprising. Until the Russian Revolution in 1917, Marxism was merely an idea rather than a concrete system of government. To many intellectuals, Marxism had little value for conditions in Asia anyway. Marxist doctrine, after all, declared that a Communist society would arise only with the collapse of an advanced capitalism. Most societies in Asia were still agricultural and were hardly ready for a socialist revolution.

Many patriotic intellectuals in Asia, then, at first found Marxism to have little appeal. That situation began to change after the revolution in Russia in 1917.

The rise to power of the Bolsheviks led by Lenin showed that a revolutionary Marxist party could overturn a not fully industrialized, corrupt system and begin a new one. Then, in 1920, Lenin adopted a new revolutionary strategy aimed at the societies outside the Western world.

One of Lenin's reasons for doing so was quite simple. Soviet Russia, surrounded by capitalist powers, desperately needed allies in its struggle to survive in a hostile world. To Lenin, the anticolonial movements now arising in North Africa, Asia, and the Middle East seemed to be the natural allies of the new regime in Moscow. However, there were problems in creating such an alliance. Most nationalist leaders in colonial countries belonged to the urban middle class. Many detested the idea of a Communist revolution.

Lenin sought a compromise. He forged a strategy by which Communist parties could be created among the working class, small as it was in the agricultural societies of Asia and Africa. Such parties would then propose informal alliances with existing middle-class parties to struggle against their Western rulers. Such alliances, of course, would not be permanent. Once the Western imperialists had been overthrown, Communist parties would turn against their nationalist partners and seize power on their own, thus creating the socialist revolution.

Lenin's proposal was adopted as a part of Soviet foreign policy in 1920. Beginning in 1921, Soviet agents fanned out throughout the world to carry the word of Karl Marx beyond the boundaries of Europe. The chief instrument of this effort was the Communist International, or Comintern for short. Formed in 1919 at Lenin's prodding, the Comintern was a worldwide organization of Communist parties dedicated to the advancement of world revolution. At the Comintern's headquarters in Moscow, agents from around the world were trained in the ideas of world communism and then returned to their own countries to form Marxist parties and promote the cause of social revolution. By the end of the 1920s, practically every colonial society in Asia had a Communist party. Moscow had less success in the Middle East or in Africa.

Who joined these early revolutionary parties, and why? According to Marxist doctrine, the members of

Communist parties should be urban workers angered by inhuman working conditions in the factories. In practice, most early Marxists were intellectuals. Some were probably drawn into the movement for reasons of patriotism. They saw Marxism as a new means of modernizing their societies and removing the colonial powers (see "You Are There: The Path to Liberation"). Others were attracted by the basic message of communism and its utopian dream of a classless society. The movement gave all who joined a practical strategy for the liberation of their societies from colonial rule.

There were, of course, wide variations in the degree of appeal of the new doctrine in Asian societies. In China and Vietnam, traditional Confucian belief systems had lost favor to a large degree because of their failure to counter the Western challenge. Communism had an almost immediate appeal in these countries and rapidly became a major factor in the anticolonial movement. The situation was different in Malaya, however, where the sense of nationhood was weak. It also differed in Thailand, which, alone in Southeast Asia, had not fallen under colonial rule. In these two countries, the base of the support for the local Communist Party came from minority groups such as the Chinese who lived in the cities.

How successful were these new parties in establishing alliances with existing nationalist parties and in building a solid base of support among the mass of the population? Here again, the answer varied from one society to another. In some instances, the local Communists were briefly able to establish a cooperative relationship with middle-class Nationalist parties in a common struggle against Western imperialism. As we shall see in the next section, this was true in China.

Similar patterns took shape elsewhere. In the Dutch East Indies, the Indonesian Communist Party (known as the PKI) set up an alliance with the middle-class nationalist group Sarekat Islam. Later, the PKI broke loose in an effort to organize its own mass movement among poor peasants. Similar problems occurred in French Indochina. Vietnamese Communists, organized by the Moscow-trained revolutionary Ho Chi Minh (HOE CHEE MIN), sought to cooperate with middle-class nationalist parties against the colonial regime. In 1928, such efforts were abandoned. The Comintern

## YOU ARE THERE

# The Path to Liberation

*The Vietnamese revolutionary Ho Chi Minh first became acquainted with the revolution in Bolshevik Russia in 1919 while living in France. He became a dedicated follower of V. I. Lenin and eventually became a leader of the Vietnamese Communist movement. In the following passage, Ho Chi Minh talks about his reasons for becoming a Communist.*

### Ho Chi Minh, On Becoming a Communist

After World War I, I made my living in Paris, now as a retoucher at a photographer's, now as a painter of "Chinese antiquities" (made in France!). I would distribute leaflets denouncing the crimes committed by the French colonialists in Vietnam.

At that time, I supported the Russian Revolution only instinctively, not yet grasping all its historic importance. I loved and admired Lenin because he was a great patriot who liberated his compatriots; until then, I had read none of his books.

The reason for my joining the French Socialist Party was that these "ladies and gentlemen"—as I called my comrades at that moment—had shown their sympathy toward me, toward the struggle of the oppressed peoples. But I understood neither what was a party, a trade-union, nor what was

*This photo of Ho Chi Minh was taken in 1957. Do you think it was difficult for him to return to Vietnam after living in Paris? Why or why not?*

Socialism nor Communism. . . . A comrade gave me Lenin's "Thesis on the National and Colonial Questions" to read.

There were political terms difficult to understand in this thesis. But by dint of reading it again and again, finally I could grasp the main part of it. What emotion, enthusiasm, clear-sightedness, and confidence it instilled in me! I was overjoyed to tears. Though sitting alone in my room, I shouted aloud as if addressing large crowds. "Dear martyrs, compatriots! This is what we need, this is the path to our liberation!"

After that, I had entire confidence in Lenin.

1. Why was Ho Chi Minh living in France?

2. What were Ho Chi Minh's feelings toward Lenin?

3. Why did he join the French Socialist Party?

4. If American foreign policy makers had known of this document after World War II, how might things have gone differently in Vietnam?

declared that Communist parties should recruit only the most revolutionary elements in society; namely, those among urban intellectuals and the working class.

Harassed by colonial authorities, and saddled with directions from Moscow that often had little relevance to local conditions, Communist parties in most colonial societies had little success in the 1930s. They failed to build a secure base of support among the mass of the population. However, this was not entirely the case in China.

## ❀ SECTION REVIEW ❀

1. **Locate:**
   (*a*) Nigeria,   (*b*) South Africa,
   (*c*) Amritsar,   (*d*) Kenya

2. **Define:**
   (*a*) Pan-Africanism,   (*b*) Mahatma,
   (*c*) westernization

3. **Identify:**
   (*a*) Young Kikuyu Association,   (*b*) *Facing Mount Kenya*,   (*c*) Government of India Act,
   (*d*) Jawaharlal Nehru,   (*e*) Kita Ikki,
   (*f*) Comintern,   (*g*) Ho Chi Minh

4. **Recall:**
   (*a*) Why did many Africans expect to gain independence for their countries after World War I?
   (*b*) How did Mohandas Gandhi encourage his followers to work against colonial rule?
   (*c*) What was the function of the Imperial Rule Assistance Association in Japan?
   (*d*) Why were communists more successful in China than in Siam during the 1920s and 1930s?

5. **Think Critically:**
   (*a*) Why would an act as harmless as picking up a pinch of salt from the sand be seen as worthy of putting a person in jail in India?
   (*b*) What did the Japanese army's invasion of Manchuria in 1931 show about the political situation in Japan at that time?

# 3

# REVOLUTIONARY CHAOS IN CHINA

It was in China that revolutionary Marxism had its greatest impact. In 1919, a group of young radicals, including several faculty and staff members from Beijing University, founded the Chinese Communist Party (CCP) in the commercial and industrial city of Shanghai. The new party was soon advised by Com-

intern agents to link up with the more experienced Nationalists.

## Nationalists and Communists: Cooperation and Tensions

Sun Yat-sen, leader of the Nationalists (see Chapter 7), welcomed the cooperation. He needed the expertise and the diplomatic support that the Soviet Union could provide. His anti-imperialist words had alienated many Western powers. One English-language newspaper in Shanghai wrote, "All his life, all his influence, are devoted to ideas that keep China in turmoil, and it is utterly undesirable that he should be allowed to prosecute those aims here."[2] In 1923, the two parties—Nationalists and Communists—formed an alliance to oppose the warlords and drive the imperialist powers out of China.

For three years, with the help of a Comintern office set up in Canton, the two parties overlooked their mutual suspicions and worked together. They mobilized and trained a revolutionary army to march north and seize control over China. The so-called Northern Expedition began in the summer of 1926. By the following spring, revolutionary forces had seized control over all of China south of the Yangtze River, including the major river ports of Wuhan and Shanghai.

Internal tensions between the two parties now rose to the surface. Sun Yat-sen had died of cancer in 1925. He was succeeded as head of the Nationalist Party by his military subordinate Jiang Jieshi (jee-ONG jee-AE-SHEE) (Chiang Kai-shek [jee-ONG-KIE-shek]). Jiang pretended to support the alliance with the Communists but actually planned to destroy them. In April 1927, he struck against the Communists and their supporters in Shanghai, killing thousands. The Communists reacted by raising the flag of revolt in central China and Canton. The uprisings were defeated, however, and their leaders were killed or forced into hiding.

## The Nanjing Republic

In 1928, Jiang Jieshi founded a new Chinese republic at Nanjing. During the next three years he worked to reunify China. He combined military operations with

**Map 10.3    China, 1919–1939**

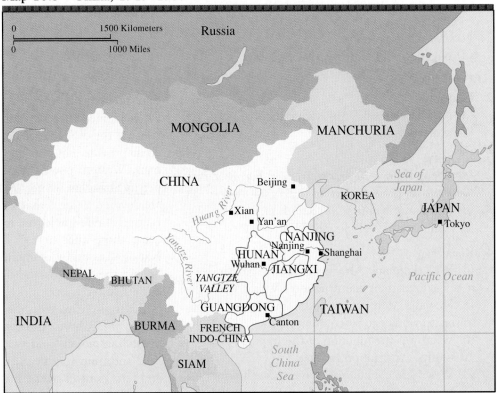

inducements to various northern warlords to join his movement. One of his key targets was the warlord Zhang Zuolin, who controlled Manchuria under the control of Japan. When Zhang agreed to throw in his lot with the Nationalists, the Japanese had him assassinated by placing a bomb under his train as he was returning to Manchuria. The Japanese hoped that Zhang Zuolin's son and successor, Zhang Xueliang, would be more cooperative. However, they had miscalculated. Zhang had been promised a major role in Jiang Jieshi's government, Thus, he began to integrate Manchuria politically and economically into the Nanjing Republic.

Jiang Jieshi saw Japan as a serious threat to the Chinese nation. However, in his mind, Japan was less dangerous than his other enemy, the Communists. He once remarked to an American reporter that "the Japanese are a disease of the skin, but the Communists are a disease of the heart."

### The Communist Movement

After the Shanghai Massacre of April 1927, most of the Communist leaders had gone into hiding in the city. There they tried to revive the Communist movement in its traditional urban base among the working class. Shanghai was a rich recruiting ground for the party. It was a city of millionaires, paupers, prostitutes, gamblers, and adventurers. Some party members, however, fled to the hilly areas south of the Yangtze River. They were led by the young Communist organizer Mao Zedong (MOU zuh-DUNG) (Mao Tse-Tung).

Unlike most other leading members of the Communist Party, Mao was convinced that a Chinese revolution must be based on the poverty-stricken peasants in the countryside rather than the urban working class. Mao, the son of a prosperous peasant, had helped to organize a peasant movement in South China during the early 1920s. He had then served as an agitator in

▲ *Jiang Jieshi was active in the 1911 revolution that ousted the Manchu dynasty. He served as president of China twice, from 1928 to 1931 and from 1943 to 1949.*

rural villages in his native province of Hunan during the Northern Expedition in the fall of 1926. At that time he wrote a famous report to party leaders suggesting that the Communist Party support peasant demands for a land revolution (see "You Are There: A Call for Revolt"). Mao's superiors refused. They feared that adopting such radical policies would destroy the alliance with the Nationalists.

After the spring of 1927, the Communist-Nationalist alliance ceased to exist. Jiang Jieshi tried to root the Communists out of their urban base in Shanghai and their rural base in Jiangxi province. He succeeded in the first task in 1931. Most party leaders were forced to flee Shanghai for Mao's base in South China.

Jiang Jieshi then turned his forces against Mao's stronghold in Jiangxi province. Jiang's forces far outnumbered Mao's, but the latter made effective use of guerrilla tactics. Four slogans by Mao explain his methods:

*When the enemy advances, we retreat!*
*When the enemy halts and camps, we trouble them!*
*When the enemy tries to avoid battle, we attack!*
*When the enemy retreats, we pursue!*

In 1933, Jiang's troops, using their superior military strength, surrounded the Communist base in Jiangxi. Mao's young People's Liberation Army (PLA), how-

▲ *Mao Zedong, on the left, led his weary troops on the Long March to their new headquarters at Yan'an, just south of the Gobi Desert. Why do you think the men wear padded jackets?*

ever, was able to break through the Nationalist lines. It then began its famous "Long March." Moving on foot through mountains, marshes, and deserts, Mao's army traveled almost six thousand miles to reach the last-surviving Communist base in the northwest of China. His troops had to fight all the way. Many froze or starved. One survivor remembered, "As the days went by, there was less and less to eat. After our grain was finished, we ate the horses, and then we lived on wild vegetables. When even the wild vegetables were finished, we ate our leather belts. After that we had to march on empty stomachs."

One year later, Mao's troops reached safety in the small provincial town of Yan'an (YAWN-an), two hun-

## YOU ARE THERE
## A Call for Revolt

*In the fall of 1926, the young Communist Mao Zedong submitted a report to the Chinese Communist Party Central Committee calling for a massive peasant revolt against the ruling order. The report shows his confidence that peasants could play an active role in a Chinese revolution.*

### Mao Zedong, Report to the Chinese Communist Party Central Committee

During my recent visit to Hunan I made a firsthand investigation of conditions in five countries. In a very short time, in China's Central, Southern, and Northern provinces, several hundred million peasants will rise like a mighty storm, like a hurricane, a force so swift and violent that no power, however great, will be able to hold it back. They will smash all the trammels [restraints] that bind them and rush forward along the road to liberation. They will sweep all the imperialists, warlords, corrupt officials, local tyrants, and evil gentry into their graves. Every revolutionary party and every revolutionary comrade will be put to the test, to be accepted or rejected as they decide. . . .

The main targets of attack by the peasants are the local tyrants, the evil gentry and the lawless landlords, but in passing they also hit out against patriarchal ideas and institutions, against the corrupt officials in the cities and against bad practices and customs in the rural areas. In force and momentum the attack is tempestuous; those who bow before it survive and those who resist perish. As a result, the privileges which the feudal landlords enjoyed for thousands of years are being shattered to pieces. Every bit of the dignity and prestige built up by the landlords is being swept into the dust. . . .

Every revolutionary comrade should know that the national revolution requires a great change in the countryside. The Revolution of 1911 did not bring about this change, hence its failure. This change is now taking place, and it is an important factor for the completion of the revolution. Every revolutionary comrade must support it.

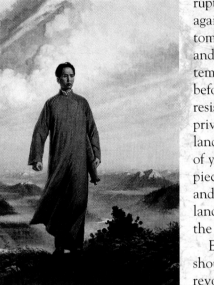

▲ *This cultural revolution poster shows Mao Zedong as a young man standing high above the world. What do you think the mountaintop setting symbolizes? What caption would you write to accompany this poster?*

1. What did Mao Zedong report to the Chinese Communist Party Central Committee?

2. According to Mao, why should the central committee support the peasant revolt?

3. Why would the committee be opposed to supporting the revolt?

dred miles north of the modern-day city of Xian in the dusty hills of North China. In the course of the Long March, Mao Zedong had become the sole leader of the Chinese Communist Party. Of the ninety thousand troops who had embarked on the journey in October 1933, only nine thousand arrived in Yan'an a year later. To people who lived at the time, it must have seemed that the Communist threat to the Nanjing regime was over. To the Communists, however, there remained hope for the future.

### The New China of Jiang Jieshi

In the meantime, Jiang Jieshi had also been trying to build a new nation. When the Nanjing Republic was set up in 1928, Jiang had publicly declared his commitment to Sun Yat-sen's Three Principles of the People (see Chapter 7). In a program announced in 1918, Sun had written about the all-important second stage of "political tutelage":

> *China . . . needs a republican government just as a boy needs school. As a schoolboy must have good teachers and helpful friends, so the Chinese people, being for the first time under republican rule, must have a farsighted revolutionary government for their training. This calls for the period of political tutelage, which is a necessary transitional stage from monarchy to republicanism. Without this, disorder will be unavoidable.*[3]

In keeping with Sun's program, Jiang announced a period of political tutelage to prepare the Chinese people for a final stage of constitutional government. In the meantime, the Nationalists would use their dictatorial power to carry out a land-reform program and the modernization of the urban industrial sector.

It would take more than plans on paper to create a new China, however. Years of neglect and civil war had severely weakened the political, economic, and social fabric of the nation. There were faint signs of an impending industrial revolution in the major urban centers. However, most of the people in the countryside were drained by warfare and civil strife. They were still very poor and overwhelmingly illiterate, and they made up 80 percent of China's population.

A westernized middle class had begun to form in the cities. It was there that the new Nanjing government found much of its support. However, the new westernized elite was concerned with the middle-class values of individual advancement and material accumulation. They had few links with the peasants in the countryside or with the **ricksha** (a small two-wheeled cart pulled by a person that carries usually one passenger) driver, "running in this world of suffering," in the words of a Chinese poet. Some critics dismissed Jiang Jieshi and his chief followers as "banana Chinese"—yellow (Chinese) on the outside but white (Western) on the inside.

Jiang Jieshi was aware of the problem of introducing foreign ideas into a population that was still culturally conservative. Thus, while building a modern industrial state, he tried to bring together modern Western ideas with traditional Confucian values of hard work, obedience, and integrity. Jiang and his U.S.–educated wife Mei (MAY)-ling Soong, set up a "New Life Movement." Its goal was to promote traditional Confucian social ethics, such as integrity, propriety, and righteousness. At the same time, it rejected the excessive individualism and material greed of Western capitalist values.

Unfortunately for Jiang Jieshi, Confucian ideas had been widely discredited when the traditional system had failed to provide answers to China's decline. Moreover, Jiang faced a host of other problems. The Nanjing government had total control over only a handful of provinces in the Yangtze valley. As we shall see in the next chapter, the Japanese also threatened to gain control of North China. The Great Depression was also having an ill effect on China's economy. With all of these problems, it was difficult for Jiang to make much progress with his program. He did have some success, however. He undertook a massive road-building project and repaired and extended much of the country's railroad system as well. He also established a national bank and improved the education system.

Fearing Communist influence, Jiang repressed all opposition and censored free expression. In so doing, he alienated many intellectuals and political moderates. Because his support came from the urban middle class and the rural landed gentry, he avoided programs leading to a redistribution of wealth. A land-reform program was enacted in 1930, but it had little effect.

Jiang Jieshi's government had little more success in promoting industrial development. Between 1927 and 1937, industrial growth averaged only about 1 percent per year. Much of the national wealth was in the hands of the so-called four families, a group of senior officials and close subordinates of the ruling elite. Military expenses took up half the budget. Little was left for social or economic development.

The new government, then, had little success in dealing with the deep-seated economic and social problems that affected China during the interwar years. This was especially true during the Great Depression. China experienced internal disintegration and foreign pressure during this virtual collapse of the global economic order. In addition, militant political forces in Tokyo were determined to extend Japanese influence and power in an unstable China. These forces and the turmoil they unleashed will be examined in the next chapter.

### ❀ SECTION REVIEW ❀

1. **Locate:**
    (a) Wuhan,    (b) Shanghai,    (c) Hunan province

2. **Define:**
    (a) ricksha

3. **Identify:**
    (a) Jiang Jieshi,    (b) Zhang Xueliang,
    (c) Shanghai Massacre,    (d) Mao Zedong,
    (e) Long March,    (f) New Life Movement

4. **Recall:**
    (a) Why did the Nationalist and Communist Chinese form an alliance in 1923?
    (b) What was Mao able to accomplish during the Long March?
    (c) What impact did years of neglect and civil war have on China's economy during the 1920s and 1930s?
    (d) What actions did Jiang's fear of communism eventually cause him to take?

5. **Think Critically:**
    (a) What did Jiang Jieshi mean when he said,

"The Japanese are a disease of the skin but the Communists are a disease of the heart"?
    (b) Why didn't the nations of Europe take stronger actions to protect their interests in China during the 1920s and 1930s?

# NATIONALISM AND DICTATORSHIP IN LATIN AMERICA

The nations of Latin America played little role in World War I. However, that conflict did have an impact on Latin America, especially on its economy. The Great Depression also had a profound effect on both the economic and political life of the nations of Latin America.

## The Latin American Economy and the United States

By the beginning of the twentieth century, the Latin American economy was based largely on the export of foodstuffs and raw materials. Many countries had only one or two products that they relied on for sale abroad. Argentina sent beef and wheat; Chile, nitrates and copper; Brazil, sugar; Central America, bananas; and Cuba and the Caribbean nations, sugar. At the end of the nineteenth and beginning of the twentieth centuries, these exports brought a certain level of prosperity, which varied from country to country. Large landowners in Argentina, for example, grew rich from the sale of beef and wheat abroad.

World War I brought an increased demand from the European states for Latin America's raw materials. For example, the export of Chilean nitrates, a mineral used to make explosives, tripled during the war. However, the war years also saw the beginning of a process in which European nations invested less and the U.S. invested more in Latin America.

Beginning in the 1920s, the United States began to replace Great Britain as the foremost investor in Latin

**Map 10.4   Latin America, 1919–1939**

America. Unlike the British investors, however, U.S. investors put funds directly into production enterprises. In this way, large segments of Latin America's export industries fell into U.S. hands. The U.S.–owned United Fruit Company, for example, turned a number of Central American states into **banana republics** (small countries dependent on large, wealthy nations)

by owning land, packing plants, and railroads there. U.S. companies also gained control of the copper-mining industry in Chile and Peru, as well as of the oil industry in Mexico, Peru, and Bolivia.

The United States has always cast a large shadow over Latin America. It had intervened militarily in Latin American affairs for years. This was especially true in Central America and the Caribbean. Many Americans considered both regions their backyard and thus felt they were vital to U.S. security.

The control of many Latin American industries by U.S. investors fueled Latin American hostility toward the United States. A growing nationalist consciousness led many Latin Americans to view the United States as an imperialist power. It was not difficult for Latin American nationalists to show that profits from U.S. businesses were often used to keep ruthless dictators in power. In Venezuela, for example, there was no doubt that U.S. oil companies had a close relationship with the dictator Juan Vicente Gómez.

▲ *Chuquicatama, the world's largest copper mine, is now government owned. It is located near the Calama Desert in Chile. Why was the copper-mining industry so important to both U.S. investors and the Chilean government?*

The United States, however, also tried to change its relationship with Latin America. In 1933, Franklin Delano Roosevelt became president of the United States. Two years later, in 1935, the Roosevelt administration announced the Good Neighbor policy. This policy rejected the use of U.S. military force in Latin America. Adhering to his word, the president withdrew the last U.S. Marines from Haiti in 1936. For the first time in thirty years, there were no U.S. troops in Latin American countries.

In the 1930s, the Great Depression underscored a basic weakness in the Latin American economy. As we have seen, Latin Americans exported raw materials while importing the manufactured goods of Europe and the United States. At the beginning of the 1930s, Latin America was still dependent on this **export-import economy.**

The Great Depression, however, was a disaster for this kind of economy. The weakening of U.S. and European economies led to a decreased demand for Latin American foodstuffs and raw materials, especially coffee, sugar, metals, and meat. The total value of Latin American exports in 1930 was almost 50 percent below the figures for the years between 1925 and 1929. The countries that depended on the export of only one product, rather than multiple products, especially faced economic disaster.

The Great Depression had one positive effect on the Latin American economy, however. With a decline in exports, Latin American countries no longer had the revenues to buy manufactured goods. This led many Latin American countries to encourage the development of new industries that would produce the goods that were formerly imported. This process of industrial development was supposed to achieve greater economic independence for Latin America. Because of a shortage of capital in the private sector, governments often invested in the new industries. This led to government-run steel industries in Chile and Brazil, along with government-run oil industries in Argentina and Mexico.

# The Move to Authoritarianism

Most Latin American countries had begun in the nineteenth century with republican forms of government. In reality, a relatively small group of church officials, military leaders, and large landowners dominated each country. This elite group controlled the masses of people, who were mostly poverty-stricken peasants. Military forces were often crucial in keeping these special-interest groups in power. Indeed, military leaders often took control of the government. Foreign investors, either British or U.S., also supported these oligarchies so that they could maintain order.

The trend toward authoritarianism was increased in the 1930s, largely because of the impact of the Great Depression. Domestic instability from economic crises led to military coups and the creation of military dictatorships at the beginning of the 1930s in Argentina, Brazil, Chile, Peru, Guatemala, El Salvador, and Honduras. These were not totalitarian states but traditional authoritarian regimes. We can examine this trend by looking at three countries: Argentina, Brazil, and Mexico. Together, they possessed over half of the land and wealth of Latin America.

## Argentina

Argentina had grown wealthy from the export of beef and wheat. A conservative oligarchy of large landowners basically controlled the country. Their chief emphasis was on continuing Argentina's export economy, which, of course, was the source of their wealth.

The oligarchy, however, failed to realize the growing importance of industry and the cities. This group ignored the growing middle class, which reacted by forming the Radical Party in 1890. In 1916, its leader, Hipólito Irigoyen (ee-PAW-lee-TOE IR-i-GOE-YEN), was chosen to be president of Argentina. The Radical Party achieved little, however. It feared the industrial workers, who were using strikes to improve their conditions, and thus was drawn even closer to the large landowners. The Radical Party also grew more corrupt. By the end of the 1920s, it was no longer able to lead.

In 1930, the Argentine military stepped in. It overthrew President Irigoyen and reestablished the power of the large landowners. By this action, the military hoped to continue the old export economy and thus avoid the growth of working-class power that would come with more industrialization. During World War II, restless military officers formed a new organization, known as the Group of United Officers (GOU). They were unhappy with the civilian oligarchy and overthrew it in June 1943. Three years later, one GOU member, Juan Perón (pae-RONE), established sole power (see Chapter 14).

## Brazil

Brazil also followed an authoritarian path. In 1889, the army overthrew the Brazilian monarchy and established a republic. The republic lasted until 1930. It was controlled chiefly by the landed elites, especially those who dominated the growing of coffee. By 1900, three-quarters of the world's coffee was grown in Brazil. As long as coffee prices remained high, the republican oligarchy was able to maintain its power. The oligarchy largely ignored the growth of urban industry and the working class that came with it.

The Great Depression devastated the coffee industry. Already by the end of 1929, coffee prices had hit a record low. In 1930, a military coup made Getúlio Vargas, a wealthy rancher, president of Brazil. Vargas ruled Brazil from 1930 to 1945. Early in his rule, Vargas appeased workers with an eight-hour day and a minimum wage. However, faced with strong opposition in 1937, Vargas established himself as a dictator.

Between 1938 and 1945, Vargas established his New State. This was basically an authoritarian, fascist-like state. It outlawed political parties and restricted civil rights. A secret police that used torture silenced Vargas's opponents. Vargas also pursued a policy of stimulating new industries. The government established the Brazilian steel industry and set up a company to explore for oil. By the end of World War II, Brazil was becoming Latin America's chief industrial power. In 1945, the army, fearing that Vargas might prolong his power illegally after calling for new elections, forced him to resign.

## Mexico

Mexico was not an authoritarian state, but neither was it democratic. The Mexican Revolution at the beginning of the twentieth century had been the first significant effort in Latin America to overturn the system of large landed estates and increase the living standards of the masses (see Chapter 6). Out of the political revolution in Mexico emerged a relatively stable political order. It was democratic in form. However, the official political party of the Mexican Revolution, known as the Institutional Revolutionary Party, or PRI, controlled the major groups within Mexican society. Every six years, party bosses of the PRI chose the party's presidential candidate. That candidate was then dutifully elected by the people.

▲ Getúlio Vargas was a rancher and a lawyer before he turned to politics. How does his background resemble that of recent U.S. presidents?

A new wave of change began with Lázaro Cárdenas (CARD-un-AWS), who was president of Mexico from 1934 to 1940. He moved to fulfill some of the original goals of the revolution. His major step was to distribute forty-four million acres of land to landless Mexican peasants, an action that made Cárdenas enormously popular with the peasants.

Cárdenas also took a strong stand with the United States, especially over oil. By 1900, it became known that Mexico had enormous oil reserves. Over the next thirty years, foreign oil companies—some British but mostly U.S.—made large investments in Mexico. After a dispute with the foreign-owned oil companies over workers' wages, the Cárdenas government nationalized, or seized control of, the oil fields and property of the oil companies.

The U.S. oil companies were furious and asked President Roosevelt to intervene. He refused, reminding them of his promise in the Good Neighbor policy not to send U.S. troops into Latin America. Mexicans were delighted with Cárdenas, who was cheered as the president who had stood up to the United States. Eventually, the Mexican government did pay the owners for the property it had taken. It then set up PEMEX, a national oil company, to run the oil industry.

## Culture in Latin America

Two major factors influenced cultural development in Latin America in the early twentieth century: (1) the influence of the modern artistic and literary movements in Europe that we examined in Chapters 5 and 9 and (2) the growth of nationalism. Symbolism and surrealism were very important in setting new directions in both art and literature. Especially in the cities, such as Buenos Aires in Argentina and Sao Paulo in Brazil, wealthy elites expressed great interest in the work of avant-garde artists. Others became interested in following European models. Latin American artists

# OUR ARTISTIC HERITAGE
## The Mural Art of Mexico

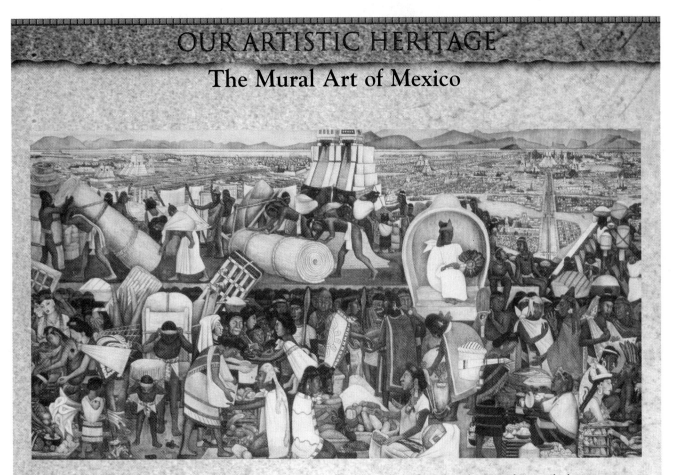

▲ *Diego Rivera's mural conveys the complexity and variety of Aztec civilization. When the Spanish arrived, they were amazed at the variety of foods and merchandise for sale in the marketplace in Tenochtitlán. What do you think is symbolized by the figure sitting in the covered chair?*

The national art that was created in Mexico in the 1920s and 1930s was also a public art. The Mexican government provided funds for the painting of murals on the walls of public buildings, including schools and government offices. Two artists were especially prominent in the development of Mexico's mural art: Diego Rivera and José Clemente Orozco.

Diego Rivera had studied in Europe, where he was especially influenced by fresco painting in Italy. Upon his return to Mexico, he developed a monumental style that filled wall after wall with murals. Rivera sought to create a national art that would serve two purposes. One was to portray Mexico's past and native traditions. He portrayed Aztec legends, as well as Mexican festivals and folk customs.

Rivera also had a political and social message in his national art. His second purpose was to make the masses aware of the new Mexican political order. Rivera did not want people to forget the Mexican Revolution that had overthrown the large landowners and the foreign interests that supported them. Indeed, his works were not for a

*(continued)*

# OUR ARTISTIC HERITAGE

## The Mural Art of Mexico, continued

Orozco's mural of Miguel Hidalgo at the Government Palace in Guadalajara, Mexico, pays homage to the priest who led the 1810 Mexican uprising against the Spanish. What do you think the lighted torch represents?

cultivated audience but for the masses of people, many of whom could not even read. His wall paintings can be found in such diverse places as the Ministry of Education, the Chapel of the Agri-culture School at Chapingo, and the Social Security Hospital.

Another leader in the development of Mexican mural art was José Clemente Orozco. Orozco was especially concerned with the cruelty of human beings, as well as their suffering as individuals. His early works showed the brutality imposed on the common people, especially the Indians, by their Spanish masters. In his later work, he became more intrigued with Mexico's native past, especially Aztec religious practices and legends. His murals, like those of Rivera, appeared in diverse places, including the Industrial School at Orizaba, the National Preparatory School, and the Orphanage at Guadalajara.

1. Why would Mexican mural art of the 1920s and 1930s be considered a national art and a public art?

2. Can you think of any examples of art in the United States that might be considered national and public?

who went abroad brought back modern techniques, which they often adapted to their own native roots.

In the 1900s, people in the various countries of Latin America began to seek their national essence. By the 1920s, this trend had led intellectuals to a discovery of popular traditions and ethnic lore. For the rest of the twentieth century, the quest for national identity would dominate cultural life in Latin America. Writers and artists took on new importance in this quest. They became the people who helped to define the new national culture that was in the making. The attempt

to create a national art that would combine both new techniques and old traditions was especially evident in the mural art of Mexico (see "Our Artistic Heritage: The Mural Art of Mexico").

## ❀ SECTION REVIEW ❀

1. **Locate:**
   (a) Central America,   (b) Cuba

2. **Define:**
   (*a*) banana republics,    (*b*) export-import economy

3. **Identify:**
   (*a*) Good Neighbor policy,    (*b*) Hipólito Irigoyen,
   (*c*) Juan Perón,    (*d*) Getúlio Vargas,    (*e*) Lázaro
   Cárdenas,    (*f*) PEMEX

4. **Recall:**
   (*a*) Why is having only a few types of products for
   export a danger to a nation's economy?
   (*b*) Why did Americans come to own many Latin
   American businesses?
   (*c*) How did the Great Depression help some Latin
   American businesses?
   (*d*) How did Brazil encourage its industrial growth
   in the 1920s and 1930s?
   (*e*) What quest dominated Latin American intellectual and artistic movements after 1920?

5. **Think Critically:** Why is it unlikely that there
   will be rapid progress toward a representative form
   of government in nations that have only one
   strong political party? Use the Mexican experience
   as an example.

## Conclusion

The turmoil brought by World War I seemed to open
the door to upheaval throughout the world. In the Middle East, the decline and fall of the Ottoman Empire
led, first of all, to the creation of a new, secular Turkish
Republic. Arab states, too, emerged with the collapse of
Ottoman power, but they were only given mandate status under Great Britain and France. A new state, Saudi
Arabia, emerged in the Arabian peninsula. Palestine
became a source of tension between newly-arrived Jewish settlers and long-time Muslim Palestinians.

Africa and Asia also witnessed movements for
national independence. In Africa these movements
were led by native Africans who were educated in
Europe and the United States. Mohandas Gandhi and
his campaign of civil disobedience played a crucial role
in India's bid to be free of British rule. Communist
movements also began to emerge in Asian societies as
instruments for the overthrow of Western imperialism.
Japan followed its own path to an authoritarian and
militaristic system.

Between 1919 and 1939, China experienced a dramatic struggle to establish a modern nation. Two
forces—the Nationalists and the Communists—first
cooperated and then fought for control of China. The
Nationalists emerged supreme but found it difficult to
control all of China and bring about the kind of modernization they wanted. Japanese interference in Chinese affairs complicated these events.

During the interwar years, the nations of Latin
America faced economic problems because of their
dependence on the export of foodstuffs and raw materials. U.S. investments in Latin America especially led
to hostility against the powerful neighbor to the north.
The Great Depression had two important effects on
Latin Americans. First, it forced them to begin the
development of new industries. Second, it led to military dictatorships and authoritarian governments.

By weakening their own civilization on the battlegrounds of Europe in World War I, Europeans had indirectly helped the subject peoples of the vast colonial
empires to begin their movements for national independence. Once Europeans had again weakened themselves in the even more destructive conflict of the Second World War, the hopes for national freedom could
at last be realized. It is to that devastating world conflict that we now turn.

## Notes

1. Quoted in Martin Gilbert, *The First World War* (New
   York, 1994), p. 213.
2. Quoted in Nicholas Rowland Clifford, *Spoilt Children of
   Empire: Westerners in Shanghai and the Chinese Revolution
   of the 1920s* (Hanover, N.H., 1991), p. 93.
3. Quoted in William Theodore de Bary et al., eds., *Sources
   of Chinese Tradition* (New York, 1963), p. 783.

# CHAPTER 10 REVIEW

## USING KEY TERMS

1. A name meaning "great soul," given by his followers to Mohandas Gandhi, was _____.
2. A _____ driver pulls a small two-wheel cart.
3. _____ was a movement stressing unity of all Africans.
4. A policy of killing people of a particular ethnic or racial group is called _____.
5. Asian intellectuals identified _____ with the capitalist democratic civilization in western Europe and the United States.
6. Serbian forces in the recent war in Bosnia followed a policy called _____ when they tried to eliminate Muslims from the land.
7. Latin Americans depended on an _____, exporting raw materials while importing manufactured goods.
8. The goal of Ataturk was to break the power of Islamic religion and turn Turkey into a _____.
9. Many Central American states became _____ when U.S. companies gained control of export industries.
10. A _____ is a brimless cap worn by Turkish Muslims.

## REVIEWING THE FACTS

1. Why was the Ottoman Empire called the "sick man of Europe"?
2. What was the objective of the Wahhabi Movement?
3. Why were many Arabs opposed to the intent of the Balfour Declaration?
4. What message did Jomo Kenyatta use as the basic theme for his book, *Facing Mount Kenya*?
5. What did the British do to try to make Indian people less opposed to their colonial government in 1919?
6. What was the purpose of the Comintern?
7. What happened to cause the Chinese communists to undertake the Long March in 1933?
8. What actions by Jiang Jieshi cost him the support of many intellectuals and political moderates during the 1920s?
9. What did the United States hope to accomplish through its Good Neighbor Policy toward Latin America?
10. Why do people in some apparently democratic Latin American nations have little voice in their country's government?
11. What action has been taken by several Latin American nations to try to eliminate foreign influence from their economies?

## THINKING CRITICALLY

1. Why is any government that is dominated by only one person likely to experience decline over time?
2. Why did technological changes tend to also change the relative importance of lands in the Middle East?
3. What events increased opposition to colonial rule in Africa and India after World War I?
4. Why was non-violent opposition to colonial rule often an effective tool for colonies attempting to gain their independence?
5. How was opposition to the military's policy of foreign expansion put down in Japan in the 1930s?
6. What is likely to happen to any government that chooses leaders based on political or family relationships instead of according to their qualifications to do a job? What does this have to do with problems experienced by the Nationalist Chinese government of Jiang Jieshi?
7. Why would some Latin American people be more upset by American firms buying their land and businesses than they were by European colonial domination of their governments?
8. Why did the Great Depression cause many Latin American countries to take steps to improve their

economic systems and gain more freedom from foreign economic dominance?

## APPLYING SOCIAL STUDIES SKILLS

1. **Geography:** Identify important trade routes in the 1920s and 1930s by drawing them on a map of the world. On the same map circle nations that worked to gain their independence from colonial powers during this time. Does there appear to be any relationship between location on an important trade route and working to gain national independence?
2. **Government:** Although many national groups have been willing to work together to end colonial rule they were less willing to work together to create new governments. What reasons have contributed to this problem?
3. **Sociology:** What social forces may have caused colonial powers to try to maintain their colonies even after they clearly cost more than they were worth?
4. **Economics:** Why were native boycotts of products produced by colonial powers effective tools in many nations' efforts to gain independence?
5. **Geography:** Consider a map of North and South America. Identify geographic reasons for the desire of the United States to dominate Latin America's economic, political, and military conditions.

## MAKING TIME AND PLACE CONNECTIONS

1. What relationships can you see between the desire of African nations to gain their independence from colonial powers and the desire of African Americans to achieve equality in the United States?

2. Why are policies of genocide like that of the Turks against the Armenians or the Nazis against the Jews not likely to achieve a government's objectives in the long run?
3. Compare and contrast the Black Dragon Society in Japan with neo-Nazi right wing militia groups in the United States or skinheads in Germany.
4. Why do leaders who seek great personal power, like Jiang Jieshi, Mao Zedong, Stalin, Hitler, or even Richard Nixon, often become paranoid?
5. What similarities and differences can you see between the efforts of the American colonies to gain independence from England in 1776 and India's desire for independence in the 1930s?

## BECOMING AN HISTORIAN

1. **Economics as a Key to History:** Use a map of the world to identify important raw material sources that existed in the Middle East, Africa, India, and the Far East over which European colonial powers wanted to maintain their control.
2. **Recognizing and Understanding Bias:** Reread and evaluate the quotation from Sun Yat-sen's writings on page 361. What does the quotation apparently say and what does it really mean? How is there a self-serving bias in the statement from Sun Yat-sen's point of view?
3. **Fact versus Opinion:** When Mao Zedong called for a revolt against the ruling order in China in 1926 he stated,

*The main targets of attack by the peasants are the local tyrants, the evil gentry and the lawless landlords, but in passing they also hit out against patriarchal ideas and institutions, against the corrupt officials in the cities and against bad practices and customs in the rural areas.*

Identify each word in this quotation that is based on opinion rather than fact. What does this tell you about much of political propaganda?

# THE CRISIS DEEPENS:

On February 3, 1933, only four days after he had been appointed chancellor of Germany, Adolf Hitler met secretly with Germany's leading generals. He revealed to them his desire to remove the "cancer of democracy," create a new authoritarian leadership, and forge a new domestic unity. All Germans would need to realize that "only a struggle can save us and that everything else must be subordinated to this idea." The youth especially would have to be trained and their wills strengthened "to fight with all means." Because Germany's living space was too small for its people, above all, Hitler said, Germany must rearm and prepare for "the conquest of new living space in the east and its ruthless Germanization."

Even before he had consolidated his power, Hitler had a clear vision of his goals. Reaching these goals meant another European war. World War II was clearly Hitler's war. Although other countries may have helped to make the war possible by not resisting Hitler's Germany earlier, when it was not so strong, it was Nazi Germany's actions that made World War II inevitable.

World War II was more than just Hitler's war, however. World War II consisted of two conflicts. One arose from the ambitions of Germany in Europe. The other arose from the ambitions of Japan in Asia. By 1941, with the involvement of the United States in both conflicts, the two had merged into one global war.

Although World War I has been described as a total war, World War II was even more so. It was fought on a scale unprecedented in history. The entire populations of warring countries were involved. Some were soldiers. Some were workers in wartime industries. Some were innocent civilians who suffered invasion, occupation, and aerial bombing. Some were victims of persecution and mass extermination. The world had never seen such widespread human-made death and destruction.

GIVE 'EM BOTH BARRELS

▲ *High-impact posters such as this helped to glorify the determination and courage needed to fight World War II.*

# WORLD WAR II

## (1939 TO 1945)

CRISIS OF THE TWENTIETH CENTURY

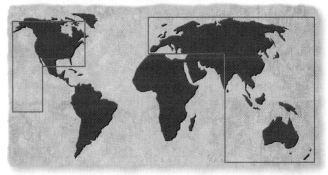

## QUESTIONS TO GUIDE YOUR READING

1. What were the steps taken by Nazi Germany from 1933 to 1939 that led to war?

2. What were the steps taken by Japan from 1931 to 1939 that led to war?

3. What were the early successes of the Germans and the Japanese, from 1939 to 1941? How do you account for these successes?

4. What were the major events in the last years of World War II?

5. What kinds of New Order did Germany and Japan try to establish in Europe and Asia?

6. What was the Final Solution, and how did the Nazis attempt to carry it out?

7. How did the attempt to arrive at a peace settlement after World War II lead to the beginnings of a new conflict, known as the Cold War?

## OUTLINE

1. THE PATH TO WAR
2. THE COURSE OF WORLD WAR II
3. THE NEW ORDER
4. THE HOME FRONT AND THE AFTERMATH OF THE WAR

## THE PATH TO WAR

Only twenty years after the war to end all wars, the world plunged back into the nightmare of total war. The efforts to end war in the 1920s—the League of Nations, the attempts at disarmament, the pacts and treaties—all proved meaningless in view of the growth of Nazi Germany and the rise of Japan.

### The German Path to War

World War II in Europe had its beginnings in the ideas of Adolf Hitler. He believed that only the Aryans were capable of building a great civilization. Hitler also believed that the Germans (the supreme group of Aryans) were threatened from the east by a large mass of inferior peoples, the Slavs, who had learned to use German weapons and technology. Germany needed more land to support a larger population and be a great power. Already in the 1920s, in the second volume of *Mein Kampf*, Hitler had stated where a Nazi regime would find this land: "And so we National Socialists . . . take up where we broke off six hundred years ago. We stop the endless German movement to the south and west, and turn our gaze toward the land in the east.

. . . If we speak of soil in Europe today, we can primarily have in mind only Russia and her vassal border states."[1]

Once Russia had been conquered, according to Hitler, its land could be resettled by German peasants. The Slavic peoples could be used as slave labor to build the **Aryan racial state** that would dominate Europe for a thousand years. Hitler's conclusion was clear. Germany must prepare for its inevitable war with the Soviet Union. Hitler's ideas were by no means secret. He had spelled them out in *Mein Kampf,* a book readily available to anyone who wished to read it.

When Hitler became chancellor of Germany on January 30, 1933, Germany's situation in Europe seemed weak. The Treaty of Versailles had created a demilitarized zone on Germany's western border that would allow the French to move into the heavily industrialized parts of Germany in the event of war. To Germany's east, the smaller states, such as Poland and Czechoslovakia, had defensive treaties with France. The Treaty of Versailles had also limited Germany's army to 100,000 troops, with no air force and only a small navy.

Hitler posed as a man of peace in his public speeches. He stressed that Germany wished only to revise the unfair provisions of the Treaty of Versailles by peaceful means. Germany, he said, only wanted its rightful place among the European states. On March 9, 1935, Hitler announced the creation of a new air force. One week later, he began a military draft that would expand Germany's army from 100,000 to 550,000 troops. These steps were a direct violation of the Treaty of Versailles. France, Great Britain, and Italy condemned Germany's action and warned against future aggressive steps. Distracted by their own internal problems caused by the Great Depression, however, they did nothing further.

Hitler by now was convinced that the Western states had no intention of using force to maintain the Treaty of Versailles. Hence, on March 7, 1936, Hitler sent German troops into the demilitarized Rhineland. According to the Treaty of Versailles, France had the right to use force against any violation of the demilitarized Rhineland. However, France would not act without British support. Great Britain viewed the occupa-

tion of German territory by German troops as another reasonable action by a dissatisfied power. The *London Times* noted that the Germans were only "going into their own back garden." Great Britain was starting a policy of **appeasement.** This policy was based on the belief that if European states satisfied the reasonable demands of dissatisfied powers, the latter would be content, and stability and peace would be achieved in Europe. The British appeasement policy was grounded in large part upon Britain's desire to avoid another war.

Meanwhile, Hitler gained new allies. Benito Mussolini had long dreamed of creating a new Roman Empire in the Mediterranean, and in October 1935, Fascist Italy invaded Ethiopia. Angered by French and British opposition to his invasion, Mussolini welcomed Hitler's support. He began to draw closer to the German dictator he had once called a buffoon. In 1936 both Germany and Italy sent troops to Spain to help General Francisco Franco in the Spanish Civil War. This action brought Italy and Germany closer together. In October 1936, Mussolini and Hitler made an agreement that recognized their common political and economic interests. Only one month later, Mussolini spoke publicly of the new alliance between Italy and Germany, known as the Rome-Berlin Axis. Also in November, Germany and Japan (the rising military power in the Far East) signed the Anti-Comintern Pact, promising to maintain a common front against communism.

By the end of 1936, Hitler and Nazi Germany had achieved a diplomatic revolution in Europe. The Treaty of Versailles had been virtually scrapped. Germany was once more a "World Power," as Hitler proclaimed. Hitler was convinced that neither France nor Great Britain would provide much opposition to his plans. In 1938, he decided to move to achieve one of his longtime goals: **Anschluss** (union) with Austria, his native land.

By threatening Austria with invasion, Hitler forced the Austrian chancellor to put Austrian Nazis in charge of the government. The new government promptly invited German troops to enter Austria and "help" in maintaining law and order. One day later, on March 13, 1938, after his triumphal return to his native land, Hitler annexed Austria to Germany.

**Map 11.1   Changes in Central Europe, 1936–1939**

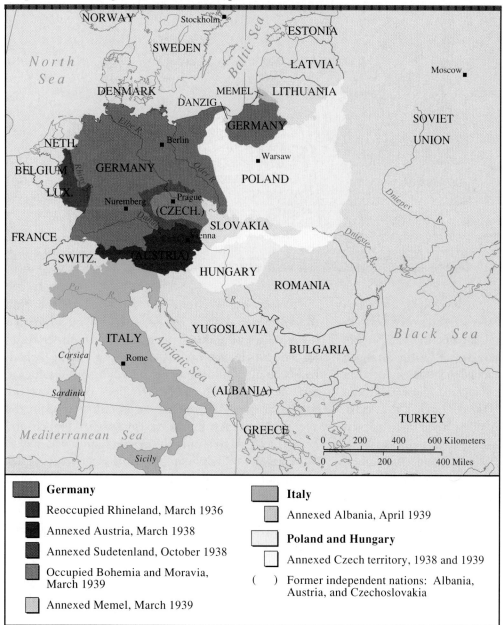

**Germany**

Reoccupied Rhineland, March 1936

Annexed Austria, March 1938

Annexed Sudetenland, October 1938

Occupied Bohemia and Moravia, March 1939

Annexed Memel, March 1939

**Italy**

Annexed Albania, April 1939

**Poland and Hungary**

Annexed Czech territory, 1938 and 1939

(    )   Former independent nations:  Albania, Austria, and Czechoslovakia

The annexation of Austria improved Germany's strategic position in central Europe and put Germany in position for Hitler's next objective—the destruction of Czechoslovakia. This goal might have seemed unrealistic. Democratic Czechoslovakia, after all, was quite prepared to defend itself. Furthermore, it was well supported by pacts with France and Soviet Russia. Hitler believed, however, that France and Britain would not use force to defend Czechoslovakia.

Hitler was right again. On September 15, 1938, he demanded the cession to Germany of the Sudetenland (soo-DATE-un-LAND), an area in northwestern

▶ *In October 1938, Hitler entered Eger (now Cheb) in the Sudetenland, an area of Czechoslovakia with a German population of 3.5 million. The crowds who came out to meet Hitler and his entourage cheered him enthusiastically. How do you think Americans would react if their state or area were suddenly annexed to another country?*

Czechoslovakia that was inhabited largely by Germans. He expressed his willingness to risk "world war" to achieve his objective. Instead of objecting, the British, French, Germans, and Italians—at a hastily arranged conference in Munich—reached an agreement that met virtually all of Hitler's demands. German troops were allowed to occupy the Sudetenland. The Czechs, abandoned by their Western allies, stood by helplessly. The Munich Conference was the high point of Western appeasement of Hitler. When Neville Chamberlain, the British prime minister, returned to England from Munich, he boasted that the Munich agreement meant "peace for our time." Hitler had promised Chamberlain that he had made his last demand. Like scores of politicians before him, Chamberlain believed Hitler's promises.

In fact, Hitler believed more than ever that the Western democracies were weak and would not fight. Increasingly, Hitler was convinced that he could not make a mistake, and he had by no means been satisfied at Munich. In March 1939, Hitler occupied the Czech lands (Bohemia and Moravia). The Slovaks, with Hitler's encouragement, declared their independence of the Czechs and became a puppet state (Slovakia) of Nazi Germany. On the evening of March 15, 1939, Hitler triumphantly declared in Prague that he would be known as the greatest German of them all.

At last, the Western states reacted to the Nazi threat. Hitler's naked aggression had made clear that his promises were utterly worthless. Now Hitler began to demand the return to Germany of Danzig (which had been made a free city by the Treaty of Versailles to serve as a seaport for Poland). Great Britain saw the danger at once and offered to protect Poland in the event of war. At the same time, both France and Britain realized that only the Soviet Union was powerful enough to help contain Nazi aggression. They began political and military negotiations with Joseph Stalin and the Soviets. Their distrust of Soviet communism, however, made an alliance unlikely.

Meanwhile, Hitler pressed on in the belief that the West would not really fight over Poland. Hitler now feared, however, that the West and the Soviet Union might make an alliance. To prevent this possibility, which would create the danger of a two-front war, Hitler made his own nonaggression pact with Stalin, the Soviet dictator. Stalin had come to believe that Britain and France were not serious about fighting. He feared they were trying to involve him in a war with Hitler. To get the nonaggression pact, Hitler offered Stalin control of eastern Poland and the Baltic states. Because he expected to fight the Soviet Union anyway, it did not matter to Hitler what he promised—he was accustomed to breaking promises.

Hitler shocked the world with the announcement of the nonaggression pact on August 23, 1939. The treaty with the Soviet Union gave Hitler the freedom to attack Poland. He told his generals, "Now Poland is in the position in which I wanted her . . . I am only afraid that at the last moment some swine or other will yet submit to me a plan for mediation."[2] Hitler need not have worried. On September 1, German forces invaded Poland. Two days later, Britain and France declared war on Germany. Europe was again at war.

## The Japanese Path to War

In September 1931, Japanese soldiers seized Manchuria, an area of northeastern China that had natural resources Japan needed. Japan used as an excuse the Chinese attack on a Japanese railway near Mukden. (The "Mukden incident" had actually been carried out by Japanese soldiers disguised as Chinese forces.) Japanese officials in Tokyo were divided over the Manchurian issue. The moderates, however, were unable to control the army. Eventually, worldwide protests against the Japanese action led the League of Nations to send investigators to Manchuria. When the investigators issued a report condemning the seizure, Japan withdrew from the league. Over the next several years, Japan strengthened its hold on Manchuria. Japan renamed it Manchukuo (MAN-CHOO-KWOE) and placed it under the authority of the former Chinese emperor and now Japanese puppet Henry Pu Yi. Japan now began to expand into North China.

Not all political leaders in Tokyo agreed with the aggressive policy. However, right-wing terrorists assassinated some of the key critics and intimidated others into silence. By the mid-1930s, militants connected with the government and the armed forces were effectively in control of Japanese politics.

▲ *On September 1, 1939, Hitler announced the beginning of war to the German Reichstag. Do you think German people were surprised at Hitler's proclamation? Why or why not?*

The United States refused to recognize the Japanese takeover of Manchuria but was unwilling to threaten the use of force. Instead, the United States tried to appease Japan in the hope of encouraging moderate forces in Japanese society. A senior U.S. diplomat warned the president: "Utter defeat of Japan would be no blessing to the Far East or to the world. It would merely create a new set of stresses, and substitute for

**Map 11.2    Japanese Expansion, 1933–1942**

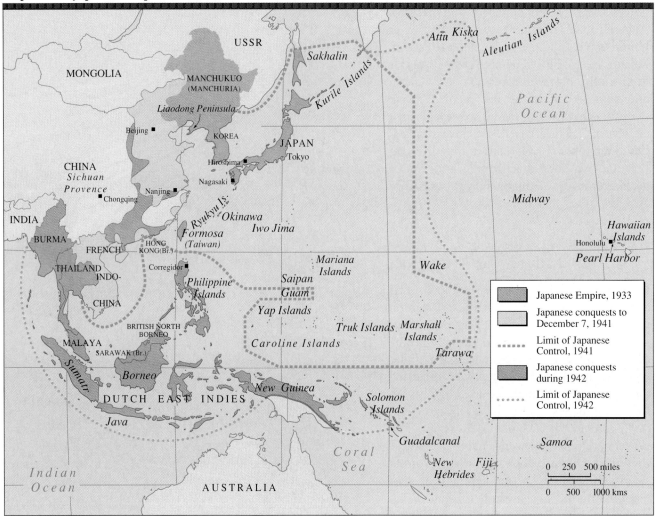

Japan the USSR as the successor to Imperial Russia—as a contestant (and at least an equally unscrupulous and dangerous one) for the mastery of the East. Nobody except perhaps Russia would gain from our victory in such a war."[3]

For the moment, the chief victim of Japanese aggression was China. Jiang Jieshi tried to avoid a conflict with Japan so that he could deal with what he considered the greater threat from the Communists. When

clashes between Chinese and Japanese troops broke out, he sought to appease Japan by allowing it to govern areas in North China. However, as Japan moved steadily southward, popular protests in Chinese cities against Japanese aggression grew stronger. In December 1936, Jiang was briefly kidnapped by military forces led by General Shang Xueliang. He forced Jiang to end his military efforts against the Communists in Yan'an and to form a new united front against the Japanese. In July

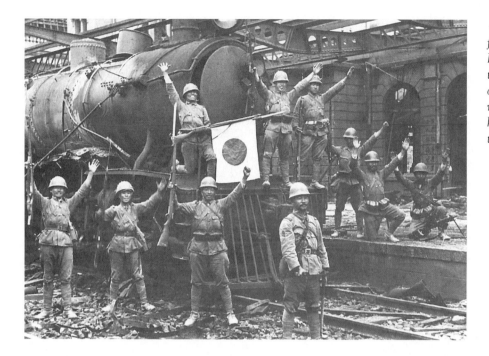

◄ *After seizing Manchuria, Japanese forces moved further into North and East China. By 1939, Japan had taken most of eastern China. Victorious Japanese soldiers celebrated in the ruins of the railway station in Hankow, China's temporary capital after the fall of Nanjing.*

1937, Chinese and Japanese forces clashed at Marco Polo Bridge, south of Beijing. China refused to apologize, and hostilities spread.

Japan had not planned to declare war on China. However, neither side would compromise, and the 1937 incident eventually turned into a major conflict. The Japanese advanced up the Yangtze valley and seized the Chinese capital of Nanjing in December. Jiang Jieshi refused to surrender, however, and moved his government upriver to Hankow. When the Japanese seized that city, Jiang moved on to Chongqing, in remote Sichuan Province.

Japanese military leaders had hoped to force Jiang to agree to join a new Japanese-dominated New Order in East Asia, comprising Japan, Manchuria, and China. This was part of a larger plan to seize Soviet Siberia, with its rich resources, and create a new order in Asia. Japan, it was thought, would guide its Asian neighbors on the path to development and prosperity. After all, who could better teach Asian societies how to modernize than the one Asian country that had already achieved modernization?

During the late 1930s, Japan began to cooperate with Nazi Germany. Japan assumed that the two countries would ultimately launch a joint attack on the Soviet Union and divide up its resources between themselves. When Germany signed a nonaggression pact with the Soviets in August 1939, however, Japanese leaders thought again about their long-term objectives. Japan was not strong enough to defeat the Soviet Union alone. Thus, the Japanese began to shift their eyes south to the vast resources of Southeast Asia—the oil of the Dutch East Indies, the rubber and tin of Malaya, and the rice of Burma and Indochina.

A move southward, of course, would risk war with the European colonial powers and the United States. Japan's attack on China in the summer of 1937 had already aroused strong criticism abroad, especially from the United States. President Franklin Delano Roosevelt threatened to use economic sanctions against the aggressors after Japanese military units bombed a U.S. naval ship operating in China. Public fear of involvement, however, forced the president to draw back. Then, when Japan suddenly demanded the right to exploit economic resources in French Indochina in the summer of 1940, the United States objected. It warned Japan that it would apply economic sanctions unless Japan withdrew from the area and returned to its borders of 1931.

Japan viewed the U.S. threat of retaliation as a threat to its long-term objectives. Japan badly needed oil and scrap iron from the United States. Should these resources be cut off, Japan would have to find them elsewhere. Japan was thus caught in a dilemma. To guarantee its access to raw materials in Southeast Asia, which would be necessary to fuel the Japanese military machine, Japan must risk a cutoff of its current source of raw materials (the United States), which would still be needed in case of a conflict. After much debate, Japan decided to launch a surprise attack on U.S. and European colonies in Southeast Asia. It hoped for a quick victory that would push the United States from the region.

## SECTION REVIEW

1. **Locate:**
   (*a*) Austria,   (*b*) Prague,
   (*c*) Slovakia,   (*d*) Danzig

2. **Define:**
   (*a*) Aryan racial state,
   (*b*) appeasement,
   (*c*) Anschluss

3. **Identify:**
   (*a*) Munich Conference

4. **Recall:**
   (*a*) Why did Germany say it needed more land?
   (*b*) How did Germany break the Treaty of Versailles during the 1930s?
   (*c*) Why did Hitler and Stalin sign a non-aggression pact in 1939?
   (*d*) Why did Japan withdraw from the League of Nations in 1931?
   (*e*) Why did Japan shift its expansionary interest to South Asia in 1939?

5. **Think Critically:** Why isn't a policy of appeasement with an aggressive nation likely to result in a lasting peace? Use events that took place in the 1930s as examples in your answer.

# THE COURSE OF WORLD WAR II

Hitler stunned Europe with the speed and efficiency of the German attack on Poland. His **Blitzkrieg,** or "lightning war," used armored columns or panzer divisions (a panzer division was a strike force of about three hundred tanks and accompanying forces and supplies) supported by airplanes. These forces were used to break quickly through Polish lines and encircle the bewildered Polish troops. Regular infantry units then moved in to hold the newly conquered territory. Within four weeks, Poland had surrendered. On September 28, 1939, Germany and the Soviet Union divided Poland between themselves.

## Europe at War

Hitler's hopes to avoid a war with the West were dashed when France and Britain declared war on September 3, 1939. Nevertheless, Hitler was confident that he could still control the situation. After a winter of waiting (called the "phony war"), Hitler resumed the attack on April 9, 1940, with another Blitzkrieg against Denmark and Norway. One month later, on May 10, Germany launched its attack on the Netherlands, Belgium, and France. The main assault through Luxembourg and the Ardennes (awr-DEN) forest was completely unexpected by the French and British forces. German panzer divisions broke through the weak French defensive positions there and raced across northern France, splitting the Allied armies and trapping French troops and the entire British army on the beaches of Dunkirk. Only by heroic efforts did the British manage to evacuate 338,000 Allied (mostly British) troops.

The French surrendered on June 22. German armies occupied about three-fifths of France. An authoritarian regime known as Vichy (VISH-ee) France, led by the aged French hero of World War I, Marshal Henri Pétain (PAE-ta[n]), was set up over the remainder of the country. Germany was now in control of western

## Map 11.3   World War II in Europe and North Africa

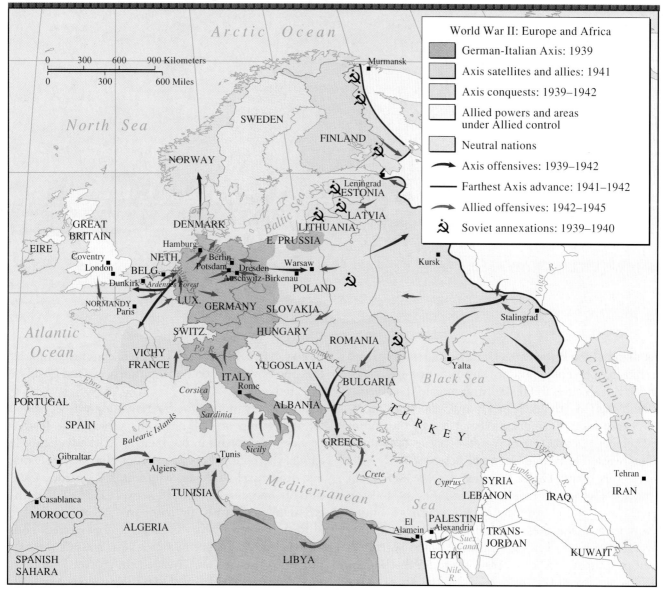

World War II: Europe and Africa

German-Italian Axis: 1939

Axis satellites and allies: 1941

Axis conquests: 1939–1942

Allied powers and areas under Allied control

Neutral nations

→ Axis offensives: 1939–1942

— Farthest Axis advance: 1941–1942

→ Allied offensives: 1942–1945

☭ Soviet annexations: 1939–1940

and central Europe, but Britain had still not been defeated.

As Hitler realized, an amphibious (land-sea) invasion of Britain would be possible only if Germany gained control of the air. At the beginning of August 1940, the **Luftwaffe** (LOOFT-vah-fuh) (the German air force) launched a major offensive against British air

and naval bases, harbors, communication centers, and war industries. The British fought back with determination. They were supported by an effective radar system that gave them early warning of German attacks.

Nevertheless, by the end of August, the British air force had suffered critical losses. A change of strategy by Hitler, however, came to its rescue. In September, in

▶ *The bombing of London dev-astated entire sections of that city. This photograph, taken after the first daylight raid on the English capital on July 1, 1940, shows how far reaching the German attack was. Do you think an enemy attack on Washington D.C. would strengthen or weaken American resolve to fight a war?*

retaliation for a British attack on Berlin, Hitler ordered a shift from bombing military targets to massive bombing of British cities to break British morale. The British rebuilt their air strength quickly and were soon inflicting major losses on Luftwaffe bombers. By the end of September, Germany had lost the Battle of Britain. The invasion of Britain had to be postponed.

At this point, Hitler considered a Mediterranean strategy. This would involve capturing Egypt and the Suez Canal and closing the Mediterranean to British ships, thereby shutting off Britain's supply of oil. However, Hitler was never fully committed to the Mediterranean strategy. His initial plan was to let the Italians decisively defeat the British in North Africa. This strategy failed, however, when the British routed the Italian army. Hitler then sent German troops to the North African theater of war. His chief concern, however, lay elsewhere. He had already reached the decision to fulfill his lifetime obsession with the acquisition of territory to the east of Germany.

Although he had no desire for a two-front war, Hitler became convinced that Britain was remaining in the war only because it expected Soviet support. If the Soviet Union were smashed, Britain's last hope would

be eliminated. Moreover, Hitler had convinced himself that the Soviet Union had a pitiful army and could be defeated quickly.

Hitler's invasion of the Soviet Union was scheduled for the spring of 1941, but the attack was delayed because of problems in the Balkans. Hitler had already gained the political cooperation of Hungary, Bulgaria, and Romania. However, Mussolini's disastrous invasion of Greece in October 1940 exposed Hitler's southern flank to British air bases in Greece. To secure Hitler's Balkan flank, German troops seized both Yugoslavia and Greece in April. Now reassured, Hitler turned to the east and invaded the Soviet Union on June 22, 1941. He believed that the Russians could still be decisively defeated before winter set in.

The massive attack stretched out along an 1,800-mile front. German troops advanced rapidly, capturing two million Russian soldiers. By November, one German army group had swept through Ukraine. A second was besieging Leningrad, while a third approached within twenty-five miles of Moscow, the Russian capital. An early Russian winter and unexpected fierce Russian resistance, however, halted the German advance. Because of their planned spring date for the

◄ *German panzer troops leave their armored tanks to flush out Russian soldiers who have taken refuge in the farmhouse. The initial success of the German Army in Russia led many to believe that Russia would fall within two weeks or a month. What other European army met defeat in the cruel Russian winter?*

invasion, the Germans had no winter uniforms. For the first time in the war, German armies had been stopped. A counterattack in December 1941 by a Soviet army supposedly exhausted by Nazi victories came as an ominous ending to the year for the Germans.

By that time, Hitler had made another fatal decision. When Japan attacked Pearl Harbor, Hitler fulfilled his promises to Japan and declared war on the United States. In doing so, Hitler's eventual defeat appeared more likely. At the same time, another European conflict had been turned into a global war.

## Japan at War

On December 7, 1941, Japanese aircraft attacked the U.S. naval base at Pearl Harbor in the Hawaiian Islands. The same day, other Japanese units launched additional assaults on the Philippines and began advancing toward the British colony of Malaya. Soon after, Japanese forces invaded the Dutch East Indies and occupied a number of islands in the Pacific Ocean. In some cases, as on the Bataan peninsula and the island of Corregidor in the Philippines, resistance was fierce. By the spring of 1942, however, almost all of Southeast Asia and much of the western Pacific had fallen into Japanese hands.

A triumphant Japan now declared the creation of a Great East-Asia Co-prosperity Sphere in the entire region under Japanese direction. Japan also announced its intention to liberate the colonial areas of Southeast Asia from Western colonial rule. For the moment, however, Japan needed the resources of the region for its war machine, and it treated the countries under its rule as conquered lands.

Japanese leaders had hoped that their lightning strike at American bases would destroy the U.S. Pacific Fleet. The Roosevelt administration, they thought, would now accept Japanese domination of the Pacific. The American people, in the eyes of Japanese leaders, had been made soft by material indulgence. The Japanese had miscalculated, however. The attack on Pearl Harbor galvanized American opinion and won broad support for Roosevelt's war policy. The United States now joined with European nations and Nationalist China in a combined effort to defeat Japan. Believing the American involvement in the Pacific would make the United States ineffective in the European theater

▲ *The surprise Japanese attack on Pearl Harbor on December 7, 1941, killed nearly 2,400 Americans and wounded 1,200 others. Nineteen American ships were either sunk or disabled, and over 120 U.S. airplanes were destroyed.*

of war, Hitler declared war on the United States four days after Pearl Harbor.

## The Turning Point of the War, 1942–1943

The entry of the United States into the war created a coalition (the Grand Alliance) that ultimately defeated the Axis powers (Germany, Italy, and Japan). Nevertheless, the three major Allies—Great Britain, the United States, and the Soviet Union—had to overcome mutual suspicions before they could operate as an effective alliance. Two factors aided that process. First, Hitler's declaration of war on the United States made it easier for the United States to accept the British and Russian argument that the defeat of Ger-

## CONNECTIONS
### AROUND THE WORLD

**Female Spies in World War II**   For thousands of years, governments have relied on spies to gather information about their enemies. Until the twentieth century, most spies were men. During World War II, however, many women became active in the world of espionage.

Yoshiko Kawashima was born in China but raised in Japan. In 1932, she was sent to China by Japanese authorities to gather information for the Japanese invasion of China. Disguised as a young man, Kawashima was an active and effective spy until her arrest by the Chinese in 1945. The Chinese news agency announced that "a long-sought-for beauty in male costume was arrested today in Beijing." She was executed soon after her arrest.

Hekmath Fathmy was an Egyptian dancer. Her hatred of the British, who had occupied Egypt, caused her to become a spy for the Germans. Fathmy sang and danced for British troops in the Kit Kat Club, a nightclub in Cairo. After shows, she took British officers to her houseboat on the banks of the Nile. Any information she was able to obtain from her guests was passed on to John Eppler, a German spy in Cairo. Eventually, she was caught but served only a year in prison for her spying activities.

Violette Szabo became a spy after her husband died fighting the Germans in North Africa. She joined Special Operations Executive, an arm of British Intelligence. In August 1944, she parachuted into France to spy on the Germans. Caught by Gestapo forces at Salon La Tour, she was questioned under torture and then shipped to Ravensbruck, a women's concentration camp near Berlin. She was executed there in April 1945.

many was more important than these countries' differences. For that reason, the United States, under its Lend-Lease program, sent large amounts of military

**Map 11.4    World War II in Asia and the Pacific**

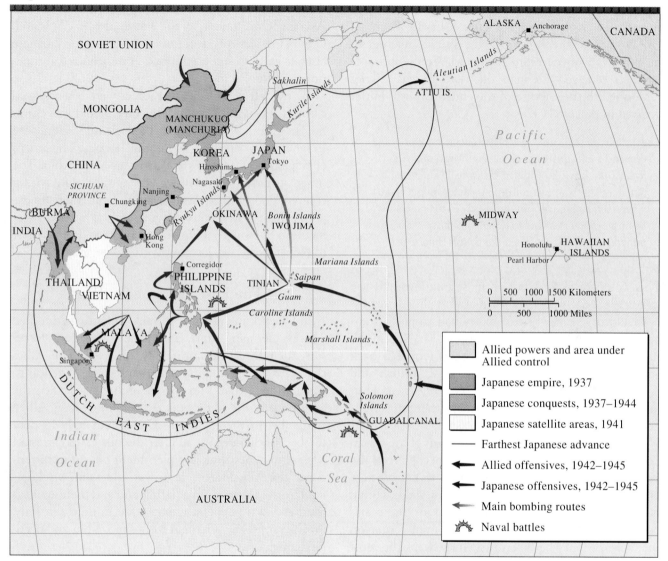

aid—including $50 billion worth of trucks, planes, and other arms—to Great Britain and the Soviet Union.

The alliance was also strengthened when the three chief Allies agreed to stress military operations while ignoring political differences. At the beginning of 1943, the Allies agreed to fight until the Axis powers surrendered unconditionally. Some people think that this principle of **unconditional surrender** might have discouraged dissident Germans and Japanese from over-

throwing their governments in order to arrange a negotiated peace. In any case, the unconditional surrender principle did cement the Grand Alliance by making it nearly impossible for Hitler to divide his foes.

Defeat, however, was far from Hitler's mind at the beginning of 1942. As Japanese forces advanced into Southeast Asia and the Pacific, Hitler and his European allies continued the war in Europe against Britain and the Soviet Union. Until the fall of 1942, it appeared that the Germans might still prevail on the battlefield. Reinforcements in North Africa enabled the Afrika Korps under General Erwin Rommel (RAW-mul) to break through the British defenses in Egypt and advance toward Alexandria. In the spring of 1942, a renewed German offensive in the Soviet Union led to the capture of the entire Crimea. Hitler boasted in August 1942:

> As the next step, we are going to advance south of the Caucasus and then help the rebels in Iran and Iraq against the English. Another thrust will be directed along the Caspian Sea toward Afghanistan and India. Then the English will run out of oil. In two years we'll be on the borders of India. Twenty to thirty elite German divisions will do. Then the British Empire will collapse.[4]

This would be Hitler's last optimistic outburst. By the fall of 1942, the war had turned against the Germans.

In North Africa, British forces had stopped Rommel's troops at El Alamein (EL-AL-uh-MANE) in the summer of 1942. The Germans then retreated back across the desert. In November 1942, British and American forces invaded French North Africa. They forced the German and Italian troops there to surrender in May 1943.

On the eastern front, the turning point of the war in Europe occurred at Stalingrad. After the capture of the Crimea, Hitler's generals wanted him to concentrate on the capture of the Caucasus and its oil fields. Hitler, however, was obsessed by a city named for Stalin and decided that Stalingrad, a major industrial center on the Volga, should be taken first. In perhaps the most terrible battle of the war, between November 1942 and February 2, 1943, German troops were stopped, then encircled, and finally forced to surrender (see "You Are There: A German Soldier at Stalingrad"). The entire German Sixth Army of 300,000 men was lost. By February 1943, German forces in Russia were back to their positions of June 1942. By the spring of 1943, even Hitler knew that the Germans would not defeat the Soviet Union.

In 1942, the tide of battle in the Far East also changed dramatically. In the Battle of the Coral Sea on May 7 and 8, 1942, American naval forces stopped the Japanese advance and temporarily relieved Australia of the threat of invasion. The turning point of the war in Asia came on June 4, at the Battle of Midway Island. U.S. planes destroyed all four of the attacking Japanese aircraft carriers and established American naval superiority in the Pacific.

By the fall of 1942, Allied forces were beginning to gather for two chief operations. One would move into South China from Burma through the islands of Indonesia by a process of "island hopping" by troops commanded by U.S. general Douglas MacArthur. The other operation would move across the Pacific with a combination of U.S. Army, Marine, and Navy attacks on Japanese-held islands. After a series of bitter engagements in the waters of the Solomon Islands from August to November 1942, Japanese fortunes began to fade.

## The Last Years of the War

By the beginning of 1943, the tide of battle had turned against Germany, Italy, and Japan. The Axis forces surrendered in Tunisia on May 13, 1943. The Allies then crossed the Mediterranean and carried the war to Italy, an area that Winston Churchill had called the "soft underbelly" of Europe. After taking Sicily, Allied troops began the invasion of mainland Italy in September. In the meantime, after the ouster and arrest of Mussolini, a new Italian government offered to surrender to the Allied forces. However, Mussolini was liberated by the Germans in a daring raid and then set up as the head of a puppet German state in northern Italy. At the same time, German troops moved in and occupied much of Italy.

The new defensive lines set up by the Germans in the hills south of Rome were very effective. The Allied advance up the Italian peninsula turned into a painstaking affair with very heavy casualties. Rome did not fall to the Allies until June 4, 1944. By that time, the Italian war had assumed a secondary role as the Allies opened their long-awaited "second front" in western Europe. Stalin had been pushing for this invasion to relieve the Nazi pressure against the Soviet Union.

Since the autumn of 1943, the Allies had been planning a cross-channel invasion of France from Great

# YOU ARE THERE
# A German Soldier at Stalingrad

*The Russian victory at Stalingrad was a major turning point in World War II. These words come from the diary of a German soldier who fought and died in the Battle of Stalingrad.*

### A German Soldier on the Battle of Stalingrad

Today, after we'd had a bath, the company commander told us that if our future operations are as successful, we'll soon reach the Volga, take Stalingrad and then the war will inevitably soon be over. Perhaps we'll be home by Christmas.

*July 29.* The company commander says the Russian troops are completely broken, and cannot hold out any longer. To reach the Volga and take Stalingrad is not so difficult for us. The Führer knows where the Russians' weak point is. Victory is not far away. . . .

*August 10.* The Führer's orders were read out to us. He expects victory of us. We are all convinced that they can't stop us. . . .

*September 4.* We are being sent northward along the front towards Stalingrad. We marched all night and by dawn had reached Voroponovo Station. We can already see the smoking town. It's a happy thought that the end of the war is getting nearer.

*September 8.* Two days of non-stop fighting. The Russians are defending themselves with insane stubbornness. Our regiment has lost many men. . . .

*September 16.* Our battalion, plus tanks, is attacking the [grain storage] elevator, from which smoke is pouring—the grain in it is burning, the Russians seem to have set light to it themselves. Barbarism. The battalion is suffering heavy losses. . . .

*October 10.* The Russians are so close to us that our planes cannot bomb them. We are preparing

▲ *As the war dragged on in Russia, it became more difficult for Nazi troops to conquer their opponents. Here a German soldier is trapped and trying to escape from a dugout in Stalingrad.*

for a decisive attack. The Führer has ordered the whole of Stalingrad to be taken as rapidly as possible. . . .

*October 22.* Our regiment has failed to break into the factory. We have lost many men; every time you move you have to jump over bodies. . . .

*(continued)*

# YOU ARE THERE

## A German Soldier at Stalingrad, continued

*November 10*. A letter from Elsa today. Everyone expects us home for Christmas. In Germany everyone believes we already hold Stalingrad. How wrong they are. If they could only see what Stalingrad has done to our army. . . .

*November 21*. The Russians have gone over to the offensive along the whole front. Fierce fighting is going on. So, there it is—the Volga, victory and soon home to our families! We shall obviously be seeing them next in the other world.

*November 29*. We are encircled. It was announced this morning that the Führer has said: "The army can trust me to do everything necessary to ensure supplies and rapidly break the encirclement."

*December 3*. We are on hunger rations and waiting for the rescue that the Führer promised. . . .

*December 26*. The horses have already been eaten. I would eat a cat; they say its meat is also tasty. The soldiers look like corpses or lunatics, looking for something to put in their mouths.

They no longer take cover from Russian shells; they haven't the strength to walk, run away and hide. A curse on this war!

1. What city was the German army trying to take?

2. Why was it important for them to take this city?

3. How accurate was the information received by the German soldiers prior to the attack?

4. At what point in the diary does it become obvious that the German soldier knew he would not return home alive?

5. Do you think the German soldiers still trusted the Führer when they knew they would be defeated? Why or why not?

---

Britain. A series of Allied deceptions caused the Germans to believe that the invasion would come on the flat plains of northern France. Instead, the Allies, under the direction of the U.S. general Dwight D. Eisenhower, landed five assault divisions on the Normandy beaches on June 6 in history's greatest naval invasion. The Germans were not sure this was the real invasion, and their slow response enabled the Allied forces to set up a beachhead. Within three months, the Allies had landed two million men and a half-million vehicles, which pushed inland and broke through German defensive lines.

After the breakout, Allied troops moved south and east. They liberated Paris by the end of August. By March 1945, they had crossed the Rhine River and advanced into Germany. At the end of April 1945, Allied armies in northern Germany moved toward the Elbe (EL-buh) River, where they finally linked up with the Soviets.

The Soviets had come a long way since the Battle of Stalingrad in 1943. In the summer of 1943, Hitler gambled on taking the offensive by making use of newly developed heavy tanks. German forces were soundly defeated by the Soviets at the Battle of Kursk (July 5 to 12), the greatest tank battle of World War II. Soviet forces now began a steady advance westward. They had reoccupied Ukraine by the end of 1943. They had lifted the siege of Leningrad and moved into the Baltic states by the beginning of 1944. Advancing along a northern front, Soviet troops occupied Warsaw in Jan-

◄ *Following the Normandy invasion and the liberation of France, Allied forces began their move toward Germany. Pontoon bridges like this one across the Rhine River made it possible for the Allies to advance into Germany. These troops are part of the 7th United States Army under American General Alexander Patch.*

uary 1945 and entered Berlin in April. Meanwhile, Soviet troops along a southern front swept through Hungary, Romania, and Bulgaria.

In January 1945, Adolf Hitler had moved into a bunker fifty-five feet under Berlin to direct the final stages of the war. In his final political testament, Hitler, consistent to the end in his rabid anti-Semitism, blamed the Jews for the war. He wrote, "Above all I charge the leaders of the nation and those under them to scrupulous observance of the laws of race and to merciless opposition to the universal poisoner of all peoples, international Jewry."[5] Hitler committed suicide on April 30, two days after Mussolini had been shot by partisan Italian forces. On May 7, German commanders surrendered. The war in Europe was over.

The war in Asia continued. Beginning in 1943, U.S. forces had gone on the offensive and advanced their way, slowly at times, across the Pacific. U.S. forces took an increasing toll of enemy resources, especially at sea and in the air. As Allied military power drew closer to

the main Japanese islands in the first months of 1945, President Harry S Truman, who had become president on the death of Roosevelt in April, had a difficult decision to make. Should he use the newly developed atomic weapons to bring the war to an end, thus avoiding an Allied invasion of the Japanese homeland? The Japanese had made extensive preparations to defend their homeland. Truman and his advisors had become convinced that American troops would suffer heavy casualties in an invasion of Japan. At the time, however, only two bombs were available, and no one knew how effective they would be.

As the world knows, Truman decided to use the bombs. The first bomb was dropped on the Japanese city of Hiroshima (HIR-uh-SHEE-muh) on August 6. Three days later, a second bomb was dropped on Nagasaki. Japan surrendered unconditionally on August 14. World War II was finally over. Seventeen million had died in battle. Perhaps twenty million civilians had perished as well (some estimate total losses at fifty million).

## ❈ SECTION REVIEW ❈

1. **Locate:**
   (a) Ardennes forest,    (b) Dunkirk,
   (c) Corregidor,    (d) Alexandria,    (e) El Alamein,
   (f) Volga River,    (g) Normandy,    (h) Stalingrad,
   (i) Hiroshima,    (j) Nagasaki

2. **Define:**
   (a) Blitzkrieg,    (b) Luftwaffe,    (c) unconditional surrender

3. **Identify:**
   (a) Vichy France,    (b) Erwin Rommel,
   (c) Battle of the Coral Sea,    (d) Battle of Midway,
   (e) General Douglas MacArthur,    (f) Winston Churchill,    (g) Dwight D. Eisenhower

4. **Recall:**
   (a) Why did Hitler shift his air attacks to British cities in 1940?
   (b) Why did German soldiers lack winter uniforms during the winter of 1940 in the Soviet Union?
   (c) Why did the Japanese military leadership feel they could attack United States forces without fear of reprisal in 1941?
   (d) Why were the Allied forces able to land at Normandy in 1944 with relatively little German opposition?

5. **Think Critically:** In what ways may the Allied forces' demand for unconditional surrender by Germany and Japan have helped and harmed their efforts to win the war?

# THE NEW ORDER

The early victories of Germany and Japan had given these nations the opportunity to create new orders (political systems) in Europe and Asia. Both countries painted positive images of these new orders for public-ity purposes. In truth, however, both followed policies of ruthless domination of their subject peoples.

## The New Order in Europe

After the German victories in Europe, Nazi propagandists created glowing images of a new European order based on "equal chances" for all nations. However, this was not Hitler's conception of a new Europe. He saw the Europe he had conquered simply as being subject to German domination. Only the Germans, he once said, "can really organize Europe."

In 1942, the Nazi Empire stretched across continental Europe from the English Channel in the west to the outskirts of Moscow in the east. In no way was this empire organized in an orderly fashion or governed efficiently. Nazi-occupied Europe was largely organized in one of two ways. Some areas, such as western Poland, were directly annexed by Nazi Germany and made into German provinces. Most of occupied Europe, however, was run by German military or civilian officials with help from local people who were willing to collaborate with the Nazis.

Race played an important role in how conquered peoples were treated. Governments run by German civil officials were set up in Norway, Denmark, and the Netherlands, because the Nazis believed the peoples in these areas to be Aryan, or racially akin to the Germans. These conquered peoples, according to the Nazis, were thus worthy of more lenient treatment. "Inferior" Latin peoples, such as the occupied French, were given military administrations. By 1943, however, as Nazi losses continued to multiply, all the occupied territories of northern and western Europe were ruthlessly exploited to provide the material goods and labor that Germany needed.

Nazi administration in the conquered lands to the east was even more ruthless. These lands were seen as the living space for German expansion. They were populated, in Nazi eyes, by racially inferior Slavic peoples. Hitler's plans for an Aryan racial empire were so important to him that he and the Nazis began to put their racial program into effect soon after the conquest of Poland.

Heinrich Himmler, a fanatic believer in Nazi racial ideas and the leader of the SS, was put in charge of German resettlement plans in the east. Himmler's task was to move the inferior Slavic peoples out and replace them with Germans. This policy was first applied to the new German provinces created from the lands of western Poland. One million Poles were uprooted and dumped in southern Poland. Hundreds of thousands of ethnic Germans (descendants of Germans who had migrated years ago from Germany to different parts of southern and eastern Europe) were brought in to colonize the German provinces in Poland. By 1942, two million ethnic Germans had been settled in Poland.

The invasion of the Soviet Union made the Nazis even more excited about German colonization in the east. Hitler spoke to his intimate circle of a colossal project of social engineering after the war. Poles, Ukrainians, and Russians would be removed from their lands and become slave labor while German peasants settled on the abandoned lands and germanized them. The Nazis involved in this kind of planning were well aware of the human costs. Himmler told a gathering of SS officers that thirty million Slavs might die in order to achieve German plans in the east. He continued, "Whether nations live in prosperity or starve to death interests me only insofar as we need them as slaves for our culture. Otherwise it is of no interest."[6]

Labor shortages in Germany led to a policy of rounding up foreign workers for Germany. After the invasion of Russia, the four million Russian prisoners of war captured by the Germans became a chief source of heavy labor, although three million of them died because of neglect by their captors.

In 1942, a special office was set up to recruit labor for German farms and industries. By the summer of 1944, seven million foreign workers were laboring in Germany. They made up 20 percent of Germany's labor force. At the same time, another seven million workers were forced to labor for the Nazis in their own countries on farms, in industries, and even in military camps. Forced labor was often counterproductive, however. Sending so many workers to Germany disrupted industrial production in the occupied countries that could have helped Germany. Then, too, the brutal way in which Germany recruited foreign workers

often led more and more people to resist the Nazi occupation forces.

## The Holocaust

There was no more terrifying aspect of the Nazi New Order than the deliberate attempt to exterminate the Jewish people of Europe. Racial struggle was a key element in Hitler's world of ideas. To him, racial struggle was a clearly defined conflict of opposites. On one side were the Aryans, creators of human cultural development. On the other side were the Jews, parasites who were trying to destroy the Aryans. By the beginning of 1939, Nazi policy focused on encouraging German Jews to leave Germany. Once the war began in September 1939, the so-called Jewish problem took on new dimensions. For a while there was discussion of the Madagascar Plan, under which Jews would be shipped in large numbers to the African island of Madagascar. When the war made this plan impractical, an even more drastic policy was conceived.

Himmler and the SS closely shared Hitler's racial ideas. The SS was given responsibility for what the Nazis called their Final Solution to the Jewish problem. The **Final Solution** was the physical extermination of the Jewish people. Reinhard Heydrich, head of the SS's Security Service, was given the task of administering the Final Solution. Heydrich created special strike forces (Einsatzgruppen) to carry out Nazi plans. After the defeat of Poland, he ordered these forces to round up all Polish Jews and put them in ghettos set up in a number of Polish cities.

In June 1941, the Einsatzgruppen were given the new job of acting as mobile killing units. These SS death squads followed the regular army's advance into the Soviet Union. Their job was to round up Jews in their villages, execute them, and bury them in mass graves. The graves were often giant pits dug by the victims themselves before they were shot. The leader of one of these death squads described the mode of operation:

*The unit selected for this task would enter a village or city and order the prominent Jewish citizens to call together all Jews for the purpose of resettlement. They*

# BIOGRAPHY

## Anne Frank: A Holocaust Victim

In 1933, after the Nazis had come to power in Germany, Otto Frank and his family moved to the Netherlands. He established a business in Amsterdam. His two daughters, Margot and Anne, soon learned Dutch and became used to their routine in their adopted city. The Franks, a Jewish family, had not really escaped the Nazis, however. The Nazis seized the Netherlands in May 1940. When it became apparent to Hans Frank that the Nazis were beginning to round up Jews, he decided to hide his family. With the help of friends, the Frank family, along with one other family, moved into a secret annex above the family business's warehouse on a street called Prinsengracht. Employees of the Frank family provided food and became their lifeline to the outside world.

Anne and the other refugees established a daily routine for the sake of their survival. During the day, while people were working in the warehouse, they remained very quiet. At night, they had more freedom to move about, but they were still confined to the house itself. Anne's father insisted that his daughters be educated, and he became their teacher. Aspiring to be a writer, Anne was glad to spend much of her time with her studies.

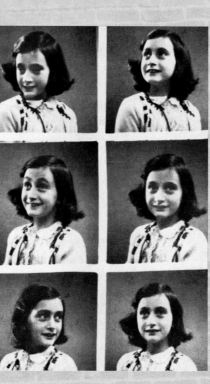

▲ *Anne Frank led a normal schoolgirl life until she was forced into hiding. How difficult do you think it might have been for you to spend your teenage years concealed in an attic?*

She also began writing in a diary. She recorded her daily routine, as well as her dreams for the future.

At times life in hiding was extremely challenging for the thirteen-year-old girl. Anne wrote this once about her daily routine and the fear of being caught: "My nerves often get the better of me; it is especially on Sundays that I feel rotten. . . . I go and lie on the divan and sleep, to make the time pass more quickly, and the stillness and the terrible fear, because there is no way of killing them." Nevertheless, Anne remained hopeful. In the second-to-last entry in her diary, dated July 15, 1944, she wrote, "It's really a wonder that I haven't dropped all my ideals, because they seem so absurd and impossible to carry out. Yet I keep them, because in spite of everything I still believe that people are really good at heart. I simply can't build up my hopes on a foundation consisting of confusion, misery, and death."

On August 4, 1944, after the Franks had spent two years in hiding, an informant, who was paid five gulden (GOOL-dun) ($1.40) per person, told the Nazis about the secret annex. The Franks were

*(continued)*

# BIOGRAPHY

## Anne Frank: A Holocaust Victim, continued

sent to Auschwitz. Because of the advance of the Allies, theirs was the last train shipped to Auschwitz from the Netherlands. Only Otto Frank survived. Both Anne and her sister had been sent from Auschwitz to Bergen-Belsen in Germany, where they died of typhus shortly before that concentration camp was liberated. Otto Frank later found his daughter's diary and had it published in 1947. *The Diary of Anne Frank* became an international best-seller. For Anne, who wanted to be a writer, it was a fitting tribute.

1. Why did Anne Frank and her family go into hiding?

2. What would you say was Anne's greatest "enemy" while she was in hiding?

3. What do you think would cause someone to "sell" Jews to the Germans for $1.40 per person?

---

*were requested to hand over their valuables to the leaders of the unit, and shortly before the execution to surrender their outer clothing. The men, women, and children were led to a place of execution which in most cases was located next to a more deeply excavated anti-tank ditch. Then they were shot, kneeling or standing, and the corpses thrown into the ditch.*[7]

Such constant killing produced morale problems among the SS executioners. During a visit to Minsk in the Soviet Union, SS leader Himmler tried to build morale by pointing out, "I would not like it if Germans did such a thing gladly. But their conscience was in no way impaired, for they were soldiers who had to carry out every order unconditionally. I alone had responsibility before God and Hitler for everything that was happening, . . . and I was acting from a deep understanding of the necessity for this operation."[8]

Probably one million Jews were killed by the Einsatzgruppen. This approach to solving the Jewish problem was soon seen as too slow, however. Instead, the Nazis decided to kill the European Jewish population in specially built death camps. The plan was simple. Jews from countries occupied by Germany (or sympathetic to Germany) would be rounded up, packed like cattle into freight trains, and shipped to Poland. Six extermination centers were built in Poland for this purpose. The largest and most famous was Auschwitz (OWSH-vits)-Birkenau. Medical technicians chose Zyklon B (the commercial name for hydrogen cyanide) as the most effective gas for quickly killing large numbers of people in gas chambers designed to look like shower rooms. After gassing, the corpses were burned in specially built crematoriums (ovens).

By the spring of 1942, the death camps were in full operation. First priority was given to the elimination of the ghettos in Poland. By the summer of 1942, however, Jews were also being shipped from France, Belgium, and Holland (see "Biography: Anne Frank—A Holocaust Victim"). Even as the Allies were winning the war in 1944, Jews were being shipped from Greece and Hungary. These shipments depended on the cooperation of Germany's Transport Ministry. Indeed, despite desperate military needs, even late in the war when Germany faced utter defeat, the Final Solution had priority in using railroad cars for the shipment of Jews to death camps.

A horrifying experience awaited the Jews when they arrived at one of the six death camps. Rudolf

Höss (HAWSS), commanding officer at Auschwitz-Birkenau, described the experience:

*We had two SS doctors on duty at Auschwitz to examine the incoming transports of prisoners. The prisoners would be marched by one of the doctors who would make spot decisions as they walked by. Those who were fit for work were sent into the camp. Others were sent immediately to the extermination plants. Children of tender years were invariably exterminated since by reason of their youth they were unable to work. . . . at Auschwitz we endeavored to fool the victims into thinking that they were to go through a delousing process. Of course, frequently they realized our true intentions and we sometimes had riots and difficulties due to that fact.*[9]

About 30 percent of the arrivals at Auschwitz were sent to a labor camp. The remainder went to the gas chambers (see "You Are There: The Holocaust—The Camp Commandant and the Camp Victims"). After they had been gassed, the bodies were burned in the crematoriums. The victims' goods, and even their bodies, were used for economic gain. Female hair was cut off, collected, and turned into mattresses or cloth. Some inmates were subjected to cruel and painful "medical" experiments. The Germans killed between five and six million Jews, over three million of them in the death camps. Virtually 90 percent of the Jewish populations of Poland, the Baltic countries, and Germany were killed. Overall, the Holocaust was responsible for the death of nearly two out of every three European Jews.

The Nazis were also responsible for the deliberate death by shooting, starvation, or overwork of at least another nine to ten million people. The Nazis considered the Gypsies of Europe, like the Jews, to be a race containing alien blood. The Gypsies, too, were rounded up for mass killing. About 40 percent of Europe's one million Gypsies were killed in the death camps. The leading elements of the "subhuman" Slavic peoples—the clergy, intellectuals, civil leaders, judges, and lawyers—were arrested and killed. Probably an additional four million Poles, Ukrainians, and Belorussians lost their lives as slave laborers for Nazi Germany.

Finally, probably at least three million to four million Soviet prisoners of war were killed in captivity.

## The New Order in Asia

Japanese war policy in the areas in Asia occupied by Japan was basically defensive. Japan hoped to use its new possessions to meet its growing needs for raw materials, such as tin, oil, and rubber. The new possessions also would be an outlet for Japanese manufactured goods. To organize Japan's possessions, Japanese leaders set up a so-called Great East-Asia Co-prosperity Sphere. This was an economic community designed to provide mutual benefits to the occupied areas and the home country. A Ministry for Great East Asia, staffed by civilians, was established in Tokyo in October 1942 to handle arrangements between Japan and the conquered territories.

The Japanese conquest of Southeast Asia had been done under the slogan "Asia for the Asiatics." Many Japanese probably sincerely believed that their government was bringing about the liberation of the Southeast Asian peoples from European colonial rule. Local Japanese officials in occupied territories quickly made contact with anticolonialist elements. They promised the people that independent governments would be established under Japanese control. Such governments were eventually set up in Burma, the Dutch East Indies, Vietnam, and the Philippines.

In fact, however, real power rested with Japanese military authorities in each territory. In turn, the local Japanese military command was directly subordinated to the Army General Staff in Tokyo. The economic resources of the colonies were used for the benefit of the Japanese war machine. The native peoples in occupied lands were recruited to serve in local military units or were forced to work on public works projects. In some cases, these policies brought severe hardships to peoples living in the occupied areas. In Indochina, for example, local Japanese authorities forcibly took rice and shipped it abroad. This led directly to a food shortage that caused over a million Vietnamese to starve to death in 1944 and 1945.

Japanese authorities worked to instill a new moral and social, as well as a new political and economic,

# YOU ARE THERE

## The Holocaust—The Camp Commandant and the Camp Victims

▲ *Polish children whose appearance fit the Nazi idea of a "master race" were often taken from their parents and sent to Germany where they were adopted by German parents. These children, just a few of the 50,000 taken, are being held at Auschwitz en route to new German homes.*

*The Holocaust is one of the most horrifying events in history. The first paragraph that follows is taken from an account by Rudolf Höss, commandant of the extermination camp at Auschwitz-Birkenau. The second paragraph contains the words of a French doctor who explains what happened at one of the crematoriums described by Höss.*

### Rudolf Höss, Describing the Crematoriums at Auschwitz-Birkenau

The two large crematoria, Nos. I and II, were built during the winter of 1942–43. . . . They each could cremate c. 2,000 corpses within twenty-four hours. . . . Crematoria I and II both had underground undressing and gassing rooms which could be completely ventilated. The corpses were brought up to the ovens on the floor above by lift. The gas chambers could hold c. 3,000 people. The firm of Topf had calculated that the two smaller crematoria, III and IV, would each be able to cremate 1,500 corpses within twenty-four hours. However, owing to the wartime shortage of materials, the builders were obliged to economise and so the undressing rooms and gassing rooms were built above ground and the ovens were of a less solid construction. But it soon became apparent

*(continued)*

# The Holocaust—The Camp Commandant and the Camp Victims, continued

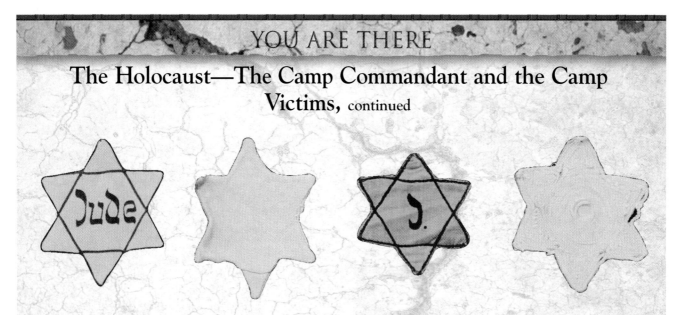

▲ *In Nazi-controlled territories, Jews were forced to wear identifying star badges like these whenever they went out in public. How do you think others, such as shopkeepers, reacted when they saw the yellow stars?*

that the flimsy construction of these two four-retort ovens was not up to the demands made on it. No. III ceased operating altogether after a short time and later was no longer used. No. IV had to be repeatedly shut down since after a short period in operation of 4–6 weeks, the ovens and chimneys had burnt out. The victims of the gassing were mainly burnt in pits behind crematorium IV.

## A French Doctor, Describing the Victims of One of the Crematoriums

It is mid-day, when a long line of women, children, and old people enter the yard. The senior official in charge . . . climbs on a bench to tell them that they are going to have a bath and that afterwards they will get a drink of hot coffee. They all undress in the yard. . . . The doors are opened and an indescribable jostling begins. The first people to enter the gas chamber begin to draw back. They sense the death which awaits them. The SS men put an end to the pushing and shoving with blows from their rifle butts beating the heads of the horrified women who are desperately hugging

their children. The massive oak double doors are shut. For two endless minutes one can hear banging on the walls and screams which are no longer human. And then—not a sound. Five minutes later the doors are opened. The corpses, squashed together and distorted, fall out like a waterfall. The bodies which are still warm pass through the hands of the hairdresser who cuts their hair and the dentist who pulls out their gold teeth . . . One more transport has just been processed through No. IV crematorium.

1. What death camp procedures did the Nazis follow to exterminate the Jews and other so-called undesirables?

2. Why do you think the Nazis were so careful in these procedures?

3. What was your reaction to these two accounts?

order in occupied areas. Occupation policy stressed such traditional values as obedience, community spirit, respect for parents, and discipline. These, of course, were the traditional values of Japanese society. At the same time, the Japanese denounced the Western values of liberalism and individualism. To promote the creation of this New Order, as it was called, occupation authorities gave strong support to local religious groups.

At first, many Southeast Asian nationalists took Japanese promises at face value and agreed to cooperate with their new masters. In Burma, for example, an independent government was set up in 1943 and declared war on the Allies. Eventually, the nature of Japanese occupation policies became clear, and sentiment turned against the New Order. Japanese officials sometimes provoked such attitudes by their arrogance and contempt for local customs. In the Dutch East Indies, for example, Indonesians were required to bow in the direction of Tokyo and to recognize the divinity of the Japanese emperor. Such practices, of course, were extremely distasteful to Muslims. In Burma, Buddhist pagodas were sometimes used as military latrines.

Japanese military forces often had little respect for even the lives of their subject peoples. In their conquest of Nanjing, China, in 1937, Japanese soldiers spent several days killing, raping, and looting. After the conquest of Korea, almost 800,000 Koreans were sent to Japan, most of them as forced laborers. Tens of thousands of Korean women were forced to be "comfort women" (prostitutes) for Japanese troops. In construction projects to help their war effort, the Japanese made extensive use of labor forces composed of both prisoners of war and local peoples. In building the Burma-Thailand railway in 1943, for example, the Japanese used 61,000 Australian, British, and Dutch prisoners of war and almost 300,000 workers from Burma, Malaya, Thailand, and the Dutch East Indies. An inadequate diet and appalling work conditions in an unhealthy climate led to the death of 12,000 Allied prisoners of war and 90,000 native workers by the time the railway was completed.

Such Japanese behavior created a dilemma for many nationalists in the occupied lands. They had no desire to see the return of the colonial powers, but they did

not like what the Japanese were doing. Some turned against the Japanese. Others simply did nothing. Indonesian patriots tried to have it both ways. They pretended to support Japan while actually sabotaging the Japanese administration. In French Indochina, Ho Chi Minh's Communist Party made contact with U.S. military units in South China. The Communists agreed to provide information on Japanese troop movements and to rescue downed American fliers in the area. In Malaya, where Japanese treatment of ethnic Chinese residents was especially harsh, many joined a guerrilla movement against the occupying forces. By the end of the war, little support remained in the region for the Japanese "liberators."

## ❀ SECTION REVIEW ❀

1. **Locate:**
   (a) Auschwitz-Birkenau

2. **Define:**
   (a) Final Solution

3. **Identify:**
   (a) Heinrich Himmler,
   (b) the Holocaust,
   (c) the Madagascar Plan,
   (d) Reinhard Heydrich,
   (e) Einsatzgruppen,
   (f) Rudolf Höss,
   (g) Asia for the Asiatics

4. **Recall:**
   (a) In what two ways was German occupation of foreign lands organized?
   (b) Why did Germans make particular efforts to eliminate leaders of Slavic peoples?
   (c) What traditional values did Japan's occupation stress?
   (d) Why did Japanese brutality create a dilemma for nationalists in lands they occupied?

5. **Think Critically:** Why was Germany's attempt to solve labor shortages by forcing people from occupied lands to work against their will probably counterproductive?

# THE HOME FRONT AND THE AFTERMATH OF THE WAR

World War II was even more of a total war than was World War I. Fighting was much more widespread and covered most of the world. Economic mobilization was more extensive; so, too, was the mobilization of women. The number of civilians killed—almost twenty million—was far higher. Many of these victims were children (see "Young People in World War II: The Other Victims").

## The Mobilization of Peoples: Four Examples

The home fronts of the major warring states varied a great deal. World War II had an enormous impact on the Soviet Union, the United States, Germany, and Japan.

### The Soviet Union

Known to the Soviets as the Great Patriotic War, the German-Soviet war witnessed the greatest land battles in history, as well as incredible ruthlessness. To Nazi Germany, the war against Russia was a war of oppression and annihilation that called for drastic measures. Two out of every five persons killed in World War II were Soviet citizens.

The initial defeats of the Soviet Union led to drastic emergency measures that affected the lives of the civilian population there. Leningrad, for example, experienced nine hundred days of siege, during which its inhabitants became so desperate for food that they ate dogs, cats, and mice. Probably 1.5 million people died in the city. As the German army made its rapid advance into Soviet territory, Soviet workers dismantled and shipped the factories in the western part of the Soviet Union to the interior—to the Urals, western Siberia, and the Volga regions. Machines were placed on the bare ground. As laborers began their work, walls went up around them.

Stalin called the widespread military and industrial mobilization of the nation a "battle of machines." The Soviets won, producing 78,000 tanks and 98,000 artillery pieces. In 1943, fifty-five percent of the Soviet national income went for war materials, compared with 15 percent in 1940. As a result of the emphasis on military goods, Soviet citizens experienced severe shortages of both food and housing.

Soviet women played a major role in the war effort. Women and girls worked in industries, mines, and railroads. Overall, the number of women working in industry increased almost 60 percent. Soviet women were also expected to dig antitank ditches and work as air raid wardens. In addition, the Soviet Union was the only country in World War II to use women in battle. Soviet women served as snipers and also in aircrews of bomber squadrons. The female pilots who helped to defeat the Germans at Stalingrad were known as the "Night Witches."

### The United States

The home front in the United States was quite different from that of the other major powers. The United States faced no threat of war in its own territory. Eventually the United States became the arsenal of the Allied powers; it produced the military equipment the Allies needed. At the height of war production in November 1943, the country was building six ships a day, $6 billion worth of war-related goods a month, and ninety-six thousand planes per year.

The mobilization of the American economy created social problems. The construction of new factories created boom towns where thousands came to work but then faced a shortage of houses and schools. Economic mobilization also led to a widespread movement of people. Sixteen million men and women were enrolled in the military. Another sixteen million, mostly wives and girlfriends of servicemen or workers looking for jobs, also moved around the country. Over one million African Americans moved from the rural South to the cities of the North and West, looking for jobs in industry. The presence of African Americans in areas where they had not lived before led to racial tensions and sometimes even racial riots. In Detroit in June 1943,

# YOUNG PEOPLE IN WORLD WAR II

## The Other Victims

Young people of all ages were also the victims of World War II. They, too, were subject to the same dangers as adults. Jewish children, along with their mothers, were the first ones selected for gas chambers upon their arrival in the death camps of Poland. As Rudolf Höss, commandant at Auschwitz, explained, "Children of tender years were invariably exterminated, since by reason of their youth they were unable to work." Young Jewish males soon learned to look as adult as possible in order to survive. Altogether, 1.2 million Jewish children died in the Holocaust.

Many children on both sides were evacuated from the cities during the war in order to avoid the bombing. The Germans had a program that created about 9,000 camps for children in the countryside. In Japan, 15,000 children were evacuated from Hiroshima before its destruction. The British moved about 6 million children and their mothers in 1939. Some British parents even sent their children to Canada and the United States, although this, too, could be dangerous. When the ocean liner *Arandora Star* was hit by a German torpedo, it had seventy-seven British children on board. They never made it to Canada.

Children evacuated to the countryside did not always see their parents again. Many other children also became orphaned when their parents were killed. In 1945, there were possibly thirteen million orphaned children in Europe. Poland alone had one million orphans.

In eastern Europe, children especially suffered under harsh German occupation policies. All secondary schools in German-occupied eastern

*The war left millions of orphans who had neither homes nor any remaining family to help them. These two German-Jewish children on the St. Louis were refused entrance in Cuba and Miami, Florida, and were then returned to Antwerp. Do you think the world reaction to war orphans has changed since World War II? Why or why not?*

Europe were closed. Their facilities and equipment were destroyed.

Heinrich Himmler, head of the SS, said of these Slavic children that their education should consist only "in teaching simple arithmetic up to 500, the writing of one's name, and that God has ordered obedience to the Germans, honesty, diligence, and politeness. I do not consider an ability to read as necessary."

At times, young people were expected to carry the burden of fighting the war. In the last year of the war, fanatical Hitler Youth members, often only fourteen or fifteen years old, could be found in the front lines. In the Soviet Union, children as young as thirteen or fourteen spied on German positions and worked with the resistance movement. Some were even given decorations for killing the enemy.

1. In what ways were young people "the other victims" in World War II?

2. What is your reaction to Heinrich Himmler's statement about the education of Slavic children?

3. How would living through a war make a child grow up more quickly?

▶ *Soviet women were expected to contribute as much to the war effort as Soviet men. Here a group working at a munitions factory put the final touch—grease—on shells.*

for example, white mobs roamed the streets attacking blacks. One million blacks enrolled in the military. There they were segregated in their own battle units. Angered by the way they were treated, some became militant and prepared to fight for their civil rights.

Japanese Americans were treated even worse. On the West Coast, 110,000 Japanese Americans, 65 percent of whom had been born in the United States, were removed to camps surrounded by barbed wire and required to take loyalty oaths. Public officials claimed this policy was necessary for security reasons. However, no similar treatment of German Americans or Italian Americans ever took place. The racism in this treatment of Japanese Americans was evident when the California governor, Culbert Olson, said, "You know, when I look out at a group of Americans of German or Italian descent, I can tell whether they're loyal or not. I can tell how they think and even perhaps what they are thinking. But it is impossible for me to do this with inscrutable orientals, and particularly the Japanese."[10]

### Germany

In August 1914, Germans had enthusiastically cheered their soldiers marching off to war. In September 1939,

the streets were quiet. Many Germans did not care or, even worse for the Nazi regime, feared disaster. Hitler was well aware of the importance of the home front. He believed that the collapse of the home front in World War I had caused Germany's defeat. In his determination to avoid a repetition of that experience, he adopted economic policies that may indeed have cost Germany the war.

To maintain the morale of the home front during the first two years of the war, Hitler refused to cut consumer goods production or to increase the production of armaments. Blitzkrieg gave the Germans quick victories and enabled them to plunder the food and raw materials of conquered countries. In this way, they could avoid taking resources away from the civilian economy.

After German defeats on the Russian front and the American entry into the war, however, the economic situation in Germany changed. Early in 1942, Hitler finally ordered a massive increase in armaments production and in the size of the army. Hitler's architect, Albert Speer, was made minister for armaments and munitions in 1942. By careful management, Speer was able to triple the production of armaments between 1942 and 1943, despite the intense Allied air raids.

Speer's urgent plea for a total mobilization of resources for the war effort went unheeded, however. Hitler, afraid of civilian morale problems that would undermine the home front, refused to make any dramatic cuts in the production of consumer goods. A total mobilization of the economy was not put into effect until July 1944. Schools, theaters, and cafes then were closed. Speer was finally permitted to use all remaining resources for the production of a few basic military items. By that time, it was in vain. Total war mobilization was too little and too late to save Germany from defeat.

Nazi attitudes toward women changed in the course of the war. Before the war, the Nazis had worked to keep women out of the job market. As the war progressed and more and more men were called up for military service, this position no longer made sense. Nazi magazines now proclaimed, "We see the woman as the eternal mother of our people, but also as the working and fighting comrade of the man."[11] However, the number of women working in industry, agriculture, commerce, and domestic service increased only slightly. The total number of employed women in September 1944 was 14.9 million, compared with 14.6 million in May 1939. Many women, especially those of the middle class, did not want jobs, especially in factories.

### Japan

Wartime Japan was a highly mobilized society. To guarantee its control over all national resources, the government created a planning board to control prices, wages, labor, and resources. Traditional habits of obedience and hierarchy were used to encourage citizens to sacrifice their resources, and sometimes their lives, for the national cause. The calls for sacrifice reached a high point in the final years of the war. Young Japanese were encouraged to volunteer to serve as pilots (known as **kamikaze,** or "divine wind") in the suicide missions against U.S. fighting ships at sea.

Japan was extremely reluctant to mobilize women on behalf of Japan's war effort. General Hideki Tojo (TOE-JOE), prime minister from 1941 to 1944, opposed female employment. He argued that "the weakening of the family system would be the weakening of the nation . . . we are able to do our duties only because we have wives and mothers at home."[12] In other words, women should remain at home and fulfill their responsibilities by bearing more children. Female employment increased during the war, but only in such areas as the textile industry and farming, where women had traditionally worked. Instead of using women to meet labor shortages, the Japanese government brought in Korean and Chinese laborers.

## The Frontline Civilians: The Bombing of Cities

Bombing was used in World War II against a variety of targets, including military targets, enemy troops, and civilian populations. The bombing of civilians made World War II as dangerous on the home front as it was on the battlefield. There had been a small number of bombing raids in the last year of World War I. These bombings had given rise to the argument that the public outcry created by the bombing of civilian populations would be an effective way to force governments into making peace. As a result, European air forces began to develop long-range bombers in the 1930s.

The first sustained use of civilian bombing proved wrong the theory that such bombing would force peace. Beginning in early September 1940, the German air force bombed London and many other British cities and towns nightly. The Blitz, as the British called the German air raids, became a national experience. Londoners took the first heavy blows. Their ability to maintain their morale set the standard for the rest of the British population.

London morale, however, was helped by the fact that the German raids were widely scattered over a very large city. Smaller towns were more directly affected by the air raids. On November 14, 1940, for example, the German air force destroyed hundreds of shops and one hundred acres of the city center of Coventry. The bombings produced morale problems as wild rumors of casualties spread quickly in these smaller communities. Nevertheless, morale was soon restored. War production in these areas, in any case, seems to have been little affected by the raids.

▲ *Clydebank, a city near Glasgow, Scotland, was heavily bombed in March 1941. Only seven homes remained without damage, and 35,000 of the city's 47,000 residents became homeless in just one night. Where would you and your family live if your home and town were suddenly destroyed?*

The British failed to learn from their own experience, however. They soon began to bomb Germany. Churchill and his advisors believed that destroying German communities would break civilian morale and bring victory. Major bombing raids began in 1942 under the direction of Arthur Harris, the wartime leader of the British Air Force's Bomber Command. Britain's four-engine heavy bombers were capable of taking the war into the center of occupied Europe. On May 31, 1942, Cologne became the first German city to be attacked by a thousand bombers.

The entry of the United States into the war produced a new bombing strategy. American planes flew daytime missions aimed at the precise bombing of transportation facilities and wartime industries. The British Bomber Command continued nighttime saturation bombing of all German cities with populations over 100,000.

Bombing raids added an element of terror to circumstances already made difficult by growing shortages of food, clothing, and fuel. Germans especially feared the incendiary bombs, which created firestorms that swept destructive paths through the cities. Four raids on Hamburg in August 1943 produced temperatures of 1,800 degrees Fahrenheit, obliterated half the city's buildings, and killed 50,000 civilians. The ferocious bombing of Dresden from February 13 to 15, 1945, created a firestorm that may have killed as many as 100,000 inhabitants and refugees. Even some Allied leaders began to criticize what they saw as the unnecessary terror bombing of German cities.

Germany suffered enormously from the Allied bombing raids. Millions of buildings were destroyed, and possibly half a million civilians died from the raids (see "Focus on Everyday Life: Homelessness on the Home Front"). Nevertheless, it is highly unlikely that Allied bombing sapped the morale of the German people. Instead, Germans, whether pro-Nazi or anti-Nazi, fought on stubbornly, often driven simply by a desire to live. Nor did the bombing destroy Germany's industrial capacity. The Allied Strategic Bombing Survey revealed that the production of war materials actually increased between 1942 and 1944. Even in 1944 and 1945, Allied raids cut German production of armaments by only 7 percent. Nevertheless, the widespread destruction of transportation systems and fuel supplies made it extremely difficult for the new materials to reach the German military.

In Japan, the bombing of civilians reached a new level with the use of the first atomic bomb. Japan was especially open to air raids, because its air force had been almost destroyed in the course of the war. Moreover, its crowded cities were built of flimsy materials that were especially vulnerable to fire bombing. Attacks on Japanese cities by the new U.S. B-29 Superfortresses, the biggest bombers of the war, had begun on November 24, 1944. By the summer of 1945, many of Japan's industries had been destroyed, along with one-fourth of its dwellings. After the Japanese government decreed the mobilization of all people between the ages of thirteen and sixty into a People's Volunteer Corps, President Truman and his advisors decided that Japanese fanaticism might mean a million U.S. casualties. As we have seen, Truman then decided to drop the atomic bomb on Hiroshima and Nagasaki (see "The Role of Science and Technology: The Atomic Bomb").

# FOCUS ON EVERYDAY LIFE
## Homelessness on the Home Front in Europe

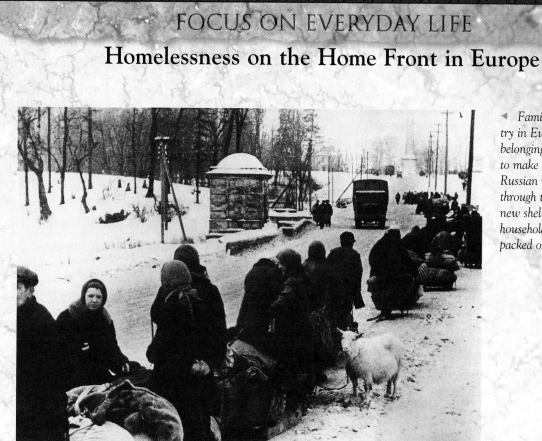

◄ *Families in every country in Europe lost homes, belongings, and the means to make a living. These Russian refugees trudge through the snow to find new shelters, all their household belongings packed onto small carts.*

World War II was the most destructive conflict in history. One of its results was homelessness on a scale never before imagined in history. Air raids virtually turned the home front into another fighting front. Air raids killed people, but they also destroyed dwellings. This created a mass of homeless people who became refugees in search of a safer area. In Germany alone, by 1945 almost twelve million people had become homeless. Many had lost all of their possessions. Even the threat of severe penalties did not keep many from stealing. One historian observed, "Thus on 31 May 1942 Paula W., a seamstress from Cologne, took some clothes, coffee and a suitcase which did not belong to her out of the burning apartment house in which she lived. She was denounced by a neighbor, promptly arrested, hauled in front of a special Court and guillotined on June 3."

Homeless refugees were a major feature of World War II. They were evident from the very beginning of the war. Millions of Polish, Belgian, French, and Soviet citizens fled in all directions when German bombs or gunfire destroyed their homes. In the last year of the war, millions of Germans also became refugees. Most fled westward to escape the advancing Soviet forces.

*(continued)*

## FOCUS ON EVERYDAY LIFE
# Homelessness on the Home Front in Europe, continued

By the end of the war, 30 million homeless refugees clogged the roads of Europe. The newly founded United Nations set up a special organization to deal with them. The United Nations Relief and Rehabilitation Administration (UNRRA) set up camps for displaced persons on the edges of cities all over Western and Central Europe. UNRRA passed out some 25 million tons of food in seventeen countries between 1945 and 1947.

1. Why was there more homelessness as a result of World War II than any other war fought before?

2. What organization was set up to help the homeless in Europe after World War II?

3. In addition to being homeless, what did the refugees also have to face?

## The Emergence of the Cold War

The total victory of the Allies in World War II was followed not by a real peace but rather by the beginnings of a new conflict, known as the Cold War. This conflict was to dominate world politics until the end of the 1980s. The Cold War stemmed from the differences between the Soviet Union and the United States. These differences became apparent at the Allied war conferences held in the last years of the war. Allied leaders had different visions of what the world should be like after the war.

Stalin, Roosevelt, and Churchill, the leaders of the Big Three of the Grand Alliance, met at Tehran (the capital of Iran) in November 1943 to decide the future course of the war. Their major tactical decision concerned the final assault on Germany. Stalin and Roosevelt argued successfully for an American-British invasion of the Continent through France. This was scheduled for the spring of 1944. The acceptance of this plan had important consequences. It meant that Soviet and British-American forces would meet in defeated Germany along a north-south dividing line. Most likely, Eastern Europe would be liberated by Soviet forces. The Allies also agreed to a partition of postwar Germany.

By the time of the conference at Yalta in southern Russia in February 1945, the defeat of Germany was obvious. The Western powers, which had earlier believed that the Soviets were in a weak position, were now faced with the reality of eleven million Red Army soldiers taking possession of Eastern and much of Central Europe.

Stalin was deeply suspicious of the Western powers. He wanted a buffer to protect the Soviet Union from possible future Western aggression. At the same time, however, Stalin was eager to gain important resources. Roosevelt, by this time, was moving toward the idea of self-determination for Europe. In other words, the Grand Alliance pledged to help liberated Europe in the creation of "democratic institutions of their own choice." Liberated countries were to hold free elections to determine their political systems.

At Yalta, Roosevelt sought Russian military help against Japan. At that time, the atomic bomb was not yet a certainty. Then, too, American military planners feared the possible loss of as many as one million men in the attacks on the Japanese home islands. Roosevelt therefore agreed to Stalin's price for military aid against Japan: possession of Sakhalin (SACK-uh-LEEN) and the Kurile Islands, as well as two warm-water ports and railroad rights in Manchuria.

## THE ROLE OF SCIENCE AND TECHNOLOGY

# The Atomic Bomb

▲ *Until August 6, 1945, the world had never experienced the total, mass destruction produced by an atomic bomb. This view of Hiroshima is a commanding visual record of the power of this new weapon.*

The discovery at the beginning of the twentieth century that atoms contained enormous amounts of energy first gave rise to the idea that splitting the atom might be the basis of a devastating weapon. However, it was some time before the idea was taken seriously. In fact, it took the demands of World War II and the fear that the Germans might make an atomic bomb first to convince the U.S. government to try to build an atomic bomb. In 1942, the United States set in motion the Manhattan Project.

The Manhattan Project was a code name for the enormous industrial and technical enterprise that produced the first atomic bomb. The making of the atomic bomb was both complicated and expensive. It cost 2 billion dollars and employed the efforts of 600,000 people. Colonel Leslie Groves had overall supervision. The physicist J. Robert Oppenheimer (AWP-un-HIE-mur) was director of the Los Alamos, New Mexico, center where the bomb was actually built. A successful test explosion on July 16, 1945, near Alamogordo, New Mexico, meant that the bomb could now be used. The war in Europe had already ended, but there was no doubt that the bomb would be used against the Japanese. A committee had already chosen the city of Hiroshima as the first target.

The bomb was dropped on August 6, 1945, by a U.S. B-29 bomber nicknamed "Enola Gay." The destruction was incredible. An area of five square miles was turned to ashes. Of the 76,000 buildings in Hiroshima, 70,000 were flattened. Of the city's 350,000 inhabitants, 140,000 had died by the end of 1945. By the end of 1950, another 50,000 had died from the effects of radiation. A second bomb was dropped on Nagasaki on August 9. The dropping of the first atomic bomb on Hiroshima had introduced the world to the Nuclear Age.

1. Why was the first atomic bomb developed?

2. Why was the atomic bomb dropped on Japan?

3. Imagine yourself in the "Enola Gay" when the first atomic bomb was dropped on Hiroshima. Describe your feelings.

**Map 11.5    Territorial Changes in Europe after World War II**

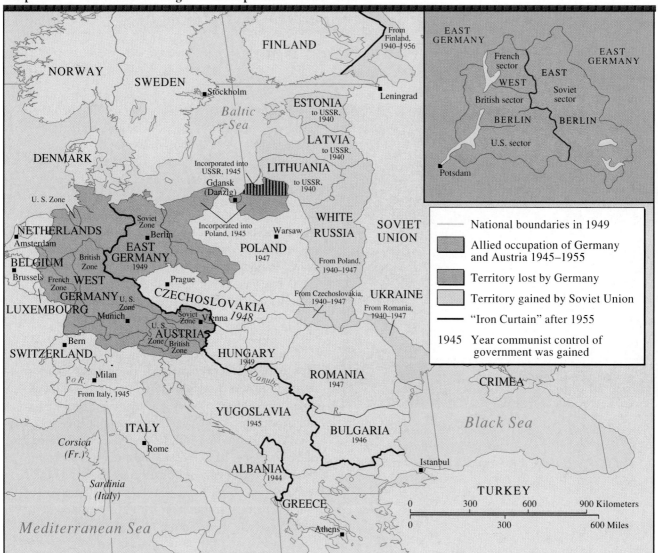

The creation of the United Nations was a major American concern at Yalta. Roosevelt wanted the Big Three powers to be part of such a postwar international organization before difficult issues divided them into hostile camps. Both Churchill and Stalin accepted Roosevelt's plans for the establishment of a United Nations organization and set the first meeting for San Francisco in April 1945.

The issues of Germany and eastern Europe were treated less decisively. The Big Three reaffirmed that Germany must surrender unconditionally and be divided into four zones, which would be occupied and governed by the military forces of the United States, Great Britain, France, and the Soviet Union. German reparations were set at $20 billion. A compromise was also worked out in regard to Poland. Stalin agreed to free elections in the future to determine a new government in that country.

**Map 11.6 Territorial Changes in Asia after World War II**

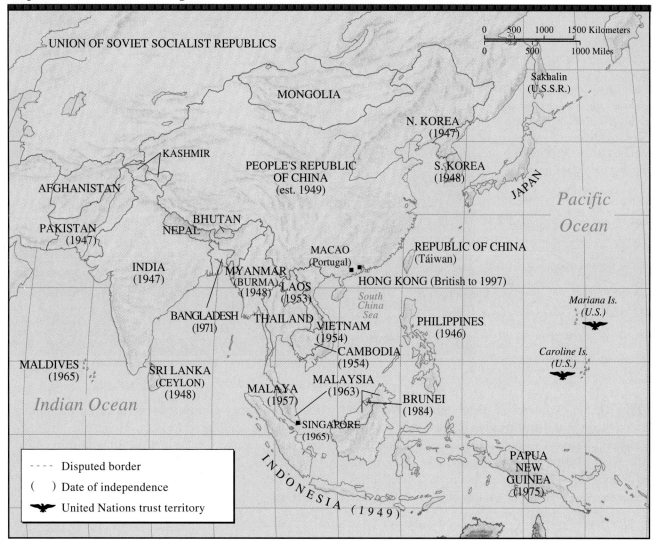

The issue of free elections in Eastern Europe caused a serious split between the Soviets and the Americans, however. The principle was that Eastern European governments would be freely elected, but they were also supposed to be pro-Russian. As Churchill expressed it, "The Poles will have their future in their own hands, with the single limitation that they must honestly follow in harmony with their allies, a policy friendly to Russia."[13] This attempt to reconcile two irreconcilable goals was doomed to failure, as soon became evident at the next conference of the Big Three powers at Potsdam.

Even before the conference at Potsdam took place in July 1945, Western relations with the Soviets were deteriorating rapidly. During the war, the Grand Alliance had been based on the needs of the war. The Allied powers' only common aim was the defeat of Nazism. Once this aim had all but been accomplished, the many differences between the Soviets and the West came to the surface.

▶ *During the Yalta conference, February 5–11, 1945, Winston Churchill, Franklin D. Roosevelt, and Joseph Stalin hammered out agreements for postwar Europe and Asia. Roosevelt died two months later. Why do you think each of the Big Three in this photo look so determined and unsmiling? How does this photo compare to current photos of world leaders taken at international meetings?*

The Potsdam conference of July 1945 thus began under a cloud of mistrust. Roosevelt had died on April 12 and had been succeeded as president by Harry Truman. At Potsdam, Truman demanded free elections throughout Eastern Europe. Stalin responded, "A freely elected government in any of these East European countries would be anti-Soviet, and that we cannot allow."[14] After a bitterly fought and devastating war in which the Soviets lost more people than any other country, Stalin sought absolute military security. To him, this security could be gained only by the presence of Communist states in Eastern Europe. Free elections might result in governments hostile to the Soviets. By the middle of 1945, only an invasion by Western forces could undo the developments in eastern Europe. After the world's most destructive conflict had just ended, few people favored such a policy.

As the war slowly receded into the past, a new struggle was already beginning. Many in the West thought Soviet policy was part of a worldwide Communist conspiracy. The Soviets viewed Western, and especially American, policy as nothing less than global capitalist expansionism. In March 1946, in a speech to an American audience, the former British prime minister Winston Churchill declared that "an iron curtain" had "descended across the continent," dividing Germany and Europe into two hostile camps. Stalin branded Churchill's speech a "call to war with the Soviet Union." Only months after the world's most devastating conflict had ended, the world seemed to be bitterly divided once again.

## ❋ SECTION REVIEW ❋

1. **Locate:**
   (*a*) Leningrad,   (*b*) Coventry,   (*c*) Tehran,
   (*d*) Yalta,   (*e*) Potsdam

2. **Define:**
   (*a*) kamikaze

3. **Identify:**
   (a) Night Witches,   (b) Albert Speer,
   (c) General Hideki Tojo,   (d) the Blitz,
   (e) Arthur Harris,   (f) the Cold War,
   (g) the Iron Curtain

4. **Recall:**
   (a) Why didn't increased war production do much to improve Germany's ability to fight the war?
   (b) What important decision was made at the 1943 Tehran conference?
   (c) What important decision was made at the 1945 Yalta conference?
   (d) What events took place at the 1945 Potsdam conference that showed the Cold War had already begun?

5. **Think Critically:** Why were the United States and other Allied powers willing to allow the Soviet Union to place Communist governments in Eastern Europe after World War II?

## Conclusion

World War II was the most devastating total war in human history. Germany, Italy, and Japan had been utterly defeated. Perhaps as many as fifty million people—both soldiers and civilians—had been killed in only six years. In Asia and Europe, cities had been reduced to rubble. Millions of people faced starvation as once-fertile lands stood neglected or wasted. Untold millions of people had become refugees.

The Germans, Italians, and Japanese had lost, but only after tremendous sacrifices and costs. Europeans, who had been accustomed to dominating the world at the beginning of the twentieth century, now watched helplessly at mid-century as the two new superpowers created by the two world wars—the United States and the Soviet Union—took control of their destinies. Even before the last battles had been fought, the United States and the Soviet Union had arrived at different visions of the postwar world. No sooner had the war ended than their differences created a new and potentially even more devastating conflict, known as the Cold War. Even though the Europeans seemed merely pawns in the struggle between the two superpowers, they managed to stage a remarkable recovery of their own civilization. In Asia, a defeated Japan made a miraculous economic recovery, and an era of European domination finally came to an end.

## Notes

1. Adolf Hitler, *Mein Kampf,* trans. Ralph Manheim (Boston, 1971), p. 654.
2. *Documents on German Foreign Policy,* Series D, vol. 7 (London, 1956), p. 204.
3. Memorandum by John Van Antwerp MacMurray, cited in Arthur Waldron, *How the Peace Was Lost: The 1935 Memorandum* (Stanford, 1992), p. 5.
4. Albert Speer, *Spandau,* trans. Richard Winston and Clara Winston (New York, 1976), p. 50.
5. *Nazi Conspiracy and Aggression,* vol. 6 (Washington, D.C., 1946), p. 262.
6. International Military Tribunal, *Trial of the Major War Criminals,* vol. 22 (Nuremberg, 1947–1949), p. 480.
7. *Nazi Conspiracy and Aggression,* vol. 5 (Washington, D.C., 1946), pp. 341–342.
8. Quoted in Raul Hilberg, *The Destruction of the European Jews,* vol. 1, rev. ed. (New York, 1985), pp. 332–333.
9. *Nazi Conspiracy and Aggression,* vol. 6, p. 789.
10. Quoted in John Campbell, *The Experience of World War II* (New York, 1989), p. 170.
11. Quoted in Claudia Koonz, "Mothers in the Fatherland: Women in Nazi Germany," in *Becoming Visible: Women in European History,* ed. Renate Bridenthal and Claudia Koonz (Boston, 1977), p. 466.
12. Quoted in Campbell, *The Experience of World War II,* p. 143.
13. Quoted in Norman Graebner, *Cold War Diplomacy, 1945–1960* (Princeton, N.J., 1962), p. 117.
14. Quoted in *ibid.*

# CHAPTER 11 REVIEW

## USING KEY TERMS

1. The policy of giving in to Hitler's demands before World War II has been called _____.
2. Union with Austria, or _____, was one of Hitler's longtime goals.
3. Toward the end of World War II Japanese _____ pilots crashed their planes into American ships.
4. The German style of attack that called for rapidly overrunning the positions of opposing forces was called a _____.
5. The principle of _____ cemented the Grand Alliance by making it nearly impossible for Hitler to divide his enemies.
6. Hitler wanted to create an _____ in Russia, settled by German peasants and built by slavic slave labor.
7. The German airforce, or _____, inflicted heavy losses on British military targets in 1940.
8. The _____ was the physical extermination of the Jewish people.

## REVIEWING THE FACTS

1. What agreement was reached at the Munich Conference?
2. What agreement was reached between Germany and the Soviet Union in 1939?
3. Why did Japan feel a great need to control nations that had significant supplies of natural resources?
4. What was the American Lend Lease policy?
5. What decision by Hitler contributed to Germany's loss of the Battle of Britain in 1940?
6. What hope encouraged Japan to attack United States possessions in the Pacific?
7. To what Nazi policy does the term *Holocaust* refer?
8. Why did Japan's policy of Asia for the Asiatics create a problem for leaders of nationalist forces in the rest of Asia?
9. Germany's ability to produce many weapons failed to provide the German military with a great advantage in the war? Why?
10. What decisions were made at the Yalta conference in 1945?

## THINKING CRITICALLY

1. Restate in your own words what you believe Hitler's attitude was toward nations that were reluctant to go to war.
2. What technological advancements made Hitler's Blitzkrieg possible?
3. What common interest caused Japan and Germany to form an alliance although they were located thousands of miles from each other?
4. Why did Hitler try to defeat the Soviet Union before the Allied powers could open a second front in Western Europe?
5. How might the Allied demand for unconditional surrender have helped Hitler maintain his control over Germany?
6. How did Hitler's effort to eliminate Jewish people from occupied lands harm his ability to win the war?
7. Why was the U.S. policy of island hopping particularly effective in its effort to defeat Japan?
8. What fear may have caused President Truman to order the dropping of atomic weapons on Japan?
9. What were several possible reasons for Stalin's desire to control Eastern European nations after World War II?
10. In what way was Stalin the most secure leader at the Yalta conference? How did this affect his bargaining position?

# CHAPTER 11 REVIEW

## APPLYING SOCIAL STUDIES SKILLS

1. **Government:** What effect did the bombing of Pearl Harbor have on United States foreign policy? How did Great Britain benefit from the change in American policy?
2. **Economics:** Make a list and explain the ways that the United States benefitted economically from World War II.
3. **Sociology:** What social values were typically held by Japanese people that made them effective soldiers?
4. **Geography:** Although the Soviet Union dominated Eastern Europe after World War II, many historians believe the Soviets would have been a much more serious threat to the rest of Europe and the United States had they succeeded in taking all of Germany or other nations that were further to the West. Explain the probable logic behind this belief.
5. **Government:** Explain why the United States was concerned about whether or not Communist totalitarian governments were created in Eastern Europe by the Soviet Union.

## MAKING TIME AND PLACE CONNECTIONS

1. In what ways was the domination of much of Asia by Japanese forces in World War II different from the European colonial domination that came before?
2. How was the decision of the United States to enter World War I different from its decision to enter World War II?
3. During the 1930s the Soviet Union achieved rapid military and industrial growth under a series of five-year plans. Why should the United States, Great Britain, France, and other western nations be pleased Stalin achieved this growth?

4. Why was air power able to destroy Germany's transportation system in World War II but unable to allow the United States to win the war in Vietnam in the 1960s and 1970s?
5. Compare and contrast the leadership styles and military careers of Adolf Hitler and Napoleon Bonaparte.

## BECOMING AN HISTORIAN

1. **Fact versus Opinion:** An excerpt from a 1941 speech* given by American aviator Charles A. Lindbergh appears below. Outspoken opposition by many popular Americans may have slowed this nation's entry into the war. How much of what Lindbergh said was fact and what part was opinion?

   *It is not only our right but it is our obligation as American citizens to look at this war objectively and to weigh our chances for success if we should enter it. I have attempted to do this, especially from the standpoint of aviation; and I have been forced to the conclusion that we cannot win this war for England, regardless of how much assistance we extend.*

2. **Making Hypotheses and Predicting Outcomes:** Some historians believe that President Truman chose to drop atomic weapons on Japan not to end the war in the Pacific but to impress the Soviet Union with United States military power. They believe Truman hoped to prevent further attempts by Stalin to gain territory in other parts of the world. Evaluate this hypothesis in light of what you have learned about Stalin and the United States. In what ways might the history of the last half of the twentieth century have been different if Truman had chosen not to drop the bomb?

*Quoted in *Selected Readings on Great Issues in American History*, Encyclopedia Britannica Educational Corporation, 1969, p. J4. From the Congressional Record of the 77th Congress.

# TOWARD A GLOBAL CIVILIZATION:

▶ *This wall mural entitled Crosswinds was painted on a wall near Central Square in Cambridge, Massachusetts, in 1992. The first documented example of street art was done in Chicago in 1967, but the style quickly spread to other major cities throughout the United States. A recurring theme is the aspirations, and sometimes the difficulties, faced by ethnic groups that reside within the city.*

| 1940 | 1945 | 1950 | 1955 | 1960 | 1965 | 1970 |
|------|------|------|------|------|------|------|

**Africa and the Middle East**
● 1948 Formation of state of Israel
1957–1975 Independence for African states
1963 Formation of Organization for African Unity ●

**India and Southeast Asia**
● 1947 India and Pakistan become independent
1963–1975 War in Vietnam
1965 Military seizes power in Indonesia ●

**East Asia**
● 1950 End of U.S. occupation of Japan
1950–1953 Korean War

**Europe and the Western Hemisphere**
● 1949 Cold War in Europe: Formation of NATO
1962 Cuban Missile Crisis ●

# THE WORLD SINCE 1945

## (1945 TO PRESENT)

World War II can be seen as the end of an era of European domination of the world. At the end of the war, Europe quickly divided into hostile camps as the Cold War rivalry between the United States and the Soviet Union forced the European nations to become dependent on one or the other of the superpowers. In the late 1980s, however, the Soviet Empire began to come apart, and the Cold War quickly came to an end.

In the meantime, the peoples of Africa and Asia had their own reasons for optimism as World War II came to a close. World War II had severely undermined the stability of the colonial order in these lands. By the end of the 1940s, most colonies in Asia had received their independence. Africa followed a decade or two later. In a few instances, such as in Algeria, Indonesia, and Vietnam, the transition to independence was a violent one. For the most part, independence was realized by peaceful means.

## UNIT OUTLINE

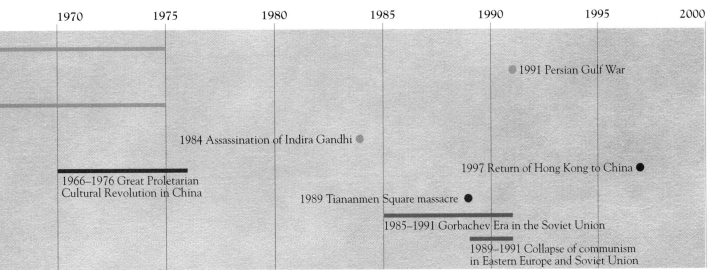

1970    1975    1980    1985    1990    1995    2000

1991 Persian Gulf War

1984 Assassination of Indira Gandhi

1966–1976 Great Proletarian Cultural Revolution in China

1997 Return of Hong Kong to China

1989 Tiananmen Square massacre

1985–1991 Gorbachev Era in the Soviet Union

1989–1991 Collapse of communism in Eastern Europe and Soviet Union

# COLD WAR AND

The end of World War II in Europe had been met with great joy. One visitor in Moscow reported, "I looked out of the window [at 2 A.M.], almost everywhere there were lights in the window—people were staying awake. Everyone embraced everyone else, someone sobbed aloud."

After the victory parades and celebrations, however, Europeans awoke to a devastating realization: their civilization was in ruins. Almost forty million people (both soldiers and civilians) had been killed over the last six years. Massive air raids had reduced many of the great cities of Europe to heaps of rubble. An American general described Berlin: "Wherever we looked we saw desolation. It was like a city of the dead. Suffering and shock were visible in every face. Dead bodies still remained in canals and lakes and were being dug out from under bomb debris."

Millions of Europeans faced starvation, because grain harvests were only half of what they had been in 1939. Millions were also homeless. In the parts of the Soviet Union that had been occupied by the Germans, almost twenty-five million people were without

homes. The destruction of bridges, roads, and railroads left transportation systems paralyzed. Untold millions of people had been uprooted by the war and became the "displaced persons" who tried to find food and then their way home. Eleven million prisoners of war had to be returned to their native countries. Fifteen million Germans and East Europeans were driven out of countries where they were no longer wanted. Despite the chaos, however, Europe was soon on the road to a remarkable recovery.

World War II had also destroyed European supremacy in world affairs, and from this, Europe did not recover. As the Cold War conflict between the world's two superpowers—the United States and the Soviet Union—grew stronger, the European nations were divided into two armed camps dependent upon one or the other of these two major powers. The United States and the Soviet Union, whose rivalry brought the world to the brink of nuclear war, seemed to hold the survival of Europe and the world in their hands.

▲ *In May 1945, joyous crowds took to the streets to celebrate VE Day not only in London, pictured here, but throughout the world.*

# A NEW ORDER IN THE WEST

## (1945 TO 1970)

THE WORLD SINCE 1945

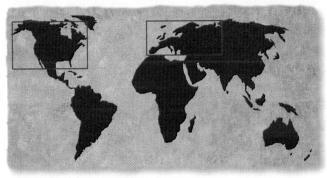

| 1945 | THE COLD WAR | 1970 |
|------|--------------|------|
| 1945 | | 2000 |

## QUESTIONS TO GUIDE YOUR READING

1. What were the major turning points in the development of the Cold War from 1945 to 1970?

2. What were the major developments in the Soviet Union between 1945 and 1970?

3. How did Soviet policies affect the political and economic history of Eastern Europe from 1945 to 1970?

4. What were the major developments in domestic politics in France, West Germany, and Great Britain between 1945 and 1970?

5. What were the major developments in U.S. and Canadian domestic politics between 1945 and 1970?

6. What were the major social changes in Western society between 1945 and 1970?

## THE DEVELOPMENT OF THE COLD WAR (1945 TO 1970)

During World War II, the two major Allied powers—the United States and the Soviet Union—had worked together because of the urgent need to defeat the Axis powers. Once the Axis powers were defeated, however, the differences between the two states came to the front. Stalin had never overcome his fear of the capitalist West, whereas Western leaders still had great fear of communism.

### The Confrontation of the Superpowers

There has been much debate about who was more responsible for the beginning of the Cold War. No doubt, both the United States and the Soviet Union took steps at the end of the war that were unwise and that might have been avoided. Both nations, however, were the heirs to the European tradition of power politics. It should not surprise us that two such different

415

systems would become rivals. Because of its need to feel secure on its western border, the Soviet Union was not prepared to give up its control of Eastern Europe after Germany's defeat. American leaders were not willing to give up the power and prestige the United States had gained throughout the world. Suspicious of each other's motives, the United States and the Soviet Union soon became rivals. Between 1945 and 1949, a number of events led the two countries to oppose each other.

### Confrontation in Europe

Eastern Europe was the first area of disagreement. The United States and Great Britain believed that the liberated nations of Eastern Europe should freely determine their own governments. Stalin, however, fearful that the Eastern European nations would be anti-Soviet if they were permitted free elections, opposed the West's plans. Having freed Eastern Europe from the Nazis, the Red Army stayed in the conquered areas and set up pro-Soviet regimes in Poland, Romania, Bulgaria, and Hungary. These pro-Soviet governments satisfied Stalin's desire for a buffer zone against the West, but the local populations and the West saw these regimes as an expansion of Stalin's empire. Only another war could change this situation, and few people wanted another armed conflict.

A civil war in Greece created another area of conflict between the superpowers. The Communist People's Liberation Army and the anticommunist forces supported by Great Britain were fighting each other for control of Greece in 1946. However, Britain had its own economic problems, which caused it to withdraw from the active role it had been playing in both Greece and Turkey.

President Harry S Truman of the United States, alarmed by the British weakness and the possibility of Soviet expansion into the eastern Mediterranean,

*On March 12, 1947, President Truman addressed a joint session of Congress asking for money and military assistance for Greece and Turkey. What U.S. policy was enacted as a result of the president's actions?*

responded with the Truman Doctrine. The Truman Doctrine said that the United States would provide money to countries (in this case, Greece and Turkey) that were threatened by Communist expansion. If the Soviets were not stopped in Greece, the Truman argument ran, then the United States would have to face the spread of communism throughout the free world. As Dean Acheson (ATCH-uh-sun), the U.S. secretary of state, explained, "Like apples in a barrel infected by disease, the corruption of Greece would infect Iran and all the East . . . likewise Africa, Italy, France. . . . Not since Rome and Carthage had there been such a polarization of power on this earth."[1]

The Truman Doctrine was soon followed, in June 1947, by the European Recovery Program, better known as the Marshall Plan. This program was intended to rebuild prosperity and stability. It included $13 billion in U.S. loans for the economic recovery of war-torn Europe. Underlying it was the belief that Communist aggression fed off economic turmoil. General George C. Marshall, U.S. secretary of state, noted in a speech at Harvard, "Our policy is not directed against any country or doctrine but against hunger, poverty, desperation and chaos."[2]

From the Soviet perspective, the Marshall Plan was nothing less than a thinly veiled attempt to buy the support of the smaller European countries. In return, these countries would be exploited economically by the United States. The Marshall Plan did not intend to shut out either the Soviet Union or its Eastern European satellite states, but they refused to participate. According to the Soviet view, the Marshall Plan guaranteed "the American loans in return for the relinquishing by the European states of their economic and later also their political independence."[3] The Soviet Union, however, was in no position to compete financially with the United States. In 1949, it founded a

Council for Mutual Assistance (COMECON) for the economic cooperation of the Eastern European states. COMECON was intended as a Soviet version of the Marshall Plan, but it largely failed because of the inability of the Soviet Union to provide large amounts of financial aid.

By 1947, the split in Europe between the United States and the Soviet Union had become a fact of life. At the end of World War II, the United States had favored a quick end to its commitments in Europe. American fears of Soviet aims, however, caused the United States to play an increasingly important role in European affairs. In an article in *Foreign Affairs* in July 1947, George Kennan, a well-known U.S. diplomat with much knowledge of Soviet affairs, argued for a **policy of containment** to keep communism within its existing geographical boundaries and prevent further aggressive Soviet moves. After the Soviet blockade of Berlin in 1948 (to be discussed later), containment of the Soviet Union became formal U.S. policy.

### The Division of Germany

The fate of Germany also became a source of heated contention between East and West. At the end of the war, the Allied powers had divided Germany (and Berlin) into four zones, each one occupied by one of the Allies. The city of Berlin itself was located deep inside the Soviet zone. Besides dividing Germany (and Berlin) into four occupied zones, the Allied powers had agreed on little else with regard to the conquered nation. The Soviets, hardest hit by the war, took reparations from Germany in the form of industrial materials. The Soviets took apart and removed to the Soviet Union 380 factories from the western zones of Berlin before turning their control over to the Western powers. By the summer of 1946, two hundred chemical, paper, and textile factories in the Soviets' East German zone had likewise been shipped to the Soviet Union. At the same time, the German Communist Party was reestablished and was soon in charge politically of the Soviet zone in eastern Germany.

The foreign ministers of the four occupying powers (the United States, the Soviet Union, Great Britain, and France) met repeatedly in an attempt to arrive at a

▲ *The devastation in Europe led to widespread hunger, and in some cases, famine. Through the Marshall Plan, the U.S. supplied economic aid that made it possible for countries to recover financially and for people to improve their war-torn lives. This photograph, taken in France in 1947, shows new American tractors working together with horses to plow a field. How does this labor combination compare to American agricultural practices in the late 1940s?*

final peace treaty with Germany. However, they only moved further and further apart. At the same time, Great Britain, France, and the United States gradually began to merge their zones economically. By February 1948, they were making plans to unify these three Western sections of Germany and create a West German government. The Soviets reacted with a blockade of West Berlin, which allowed neither trucks, trains, nor barges to enter the three Western zones of Berlin. The Russians hoped to secure economic control of all Berlin and force the Western powers to halt the creation of a separate West German state.

The Western powers were faced with a dilemma. No one wanted to risk World War III. Therefore, an attempt to break through the Soviet blockade with

▶ *Residents of Berlin watch as a U.S. plane arrives loaded with supplies for the city. The fifteen-month-long airlift was directed by the American General Lucius Clay, military governor of Germany.*

tanks and trucks was ruled out. However, how could the 2.5 million people in the three Western zones of Berlin be kept alive, when the whole city was inside the Soviet zone? The solution was the Berlin Air Lift. Berlin would get its supplies by air; they would be flown in by American and British airplanes. For more than fifteen months, over 200,000 flights that carried 1.5 million tons of supplies were made. At the height of the Berlin Air Lift, 13,000 tons of supplies were flown daily to Berlin. The Soviets, also not wanting war, gave in and finally lifted the blockade in May 1949.

The blockade of Berlin increased tensions between the United States and the Soviet Union. It also brought the separation of Germany into two states. West Germany, or the Federal Republic of Germany, was formally created in September 1949. A month later, a separate German Democratic Republic, or East Germany, was set up. Berlin remained a divided city, a vivid reminder of the division of West and East.

### The Spread of the Cold War

In that same year, the Cold War spread from Europe to the rest of the world. The victory of the Chinese Com-

munists in 1949 in the Chinese civil war (see Chapter 16) created a new Communist regime and strengthened U.S. fears about the spread of communism. The Soviet Union also exploded its first atomic bomb in 1949. All too soon, both the United States and the Soviet Union were involved in a growing arms race that led to the building of ever more destructive nuclear weapons. In 1952, both nations developed the far more destructive hydrogen bomb. Moreover, by the mid-1950s, both powers had built intercontinental ballistic missiles (ICBMs), which enabled the United States and the Soviet Union to send their destructive nuclear warheads to any part of the world.

Soon the search for security took the form of **mutual deterrence.** This was a policy based on the belief that an arsenal of nuclear weapons prevented war by ensuring that even if one nation launched its nuclear weapons in a first strike, the other nation would still be able to respond and devastate the attacker. Mutually assured destruction (MAD), it was believed, would keep either side from risking the use of the massive supply of weapons that had been built up.

The search for security in the new world of the Cold War also led to the formation of military alliances. The North Atlantic Treaty Organization (NATO) was

◀ *This ominous cloud is the result of a hydrogen bomb explosion from a testing done in 1952. Although the clouds from hydrogen bombs and atomic bombs are very similar, a hydrogen bomb is the fusion of light nuclei.*

formed in April 1949 when Belgium, Luxembourg, the Netherlands, France, Great Britain, Italy, Denmark, Norway, Portugal, and Iceland signed a treaty with the United States and Canada. All the powers agreed to provide mutual help if any one of them was attacked. A few years later, West Germany and Turkey joined NATO.

The Eastern European states soon followed suit with their own military alliance. In 1955, the Soviet Union joined with Albania, Bulgaria, Czechoslovakia, East Germany, Hungary, Poland, and Romania in a formal military alliance, known as the Warsaw Pact. As a result of this agreement Europe was once again divided into hostile alliance systems, just as it had been before World War I.

A system of military alliances also spread to the rest of the world after the United States became involved in the Korean War (see Chapter 16). On June 25, 1950, with the apparent approval of Joseph Stalin, Communist North Korean forces invaded South Korea. The United States, seeing this as yet another example of Communist aggression and expansion, gained the approval of the United Nations (UN) and

sent U.S. troops to turn back the invasion. Several other countries sent troops as well. By September, UN forces had marched northward into North Korea with the aim of unifying Korea. However, Chinese forces then came into the war on the side of North Korea and forced the U.S. and South Korean troops to retreat back to South Korea. In 1953, after two more years of fighting, an uneasy truce was reached. The division of Korea was reaffirmed. To many Americans, the policy of containing communism had succeeded in Asia, just as it had earlier in Europe.

The Korean War confirmed American fears of Communist expansion. The United States was now more determined than ever to contain Soviet power. In the mid-1950s, the administration of President Dwight D. Eisenhower adopted a policy of massive retaliation. Any Soviet advance, even a ground attack in Europe, would be met with the full use of U.S. nuclear bombs. Moreover, U.S. military alliances were extended around the world. As Eisenhower explained, "The freedom we cherish and defend in Europe and in the Americas is no different from the freedom that is imperiled in Asia."

**Map 12.1   The New European Alliance Systems in the 1950s and 1960s**

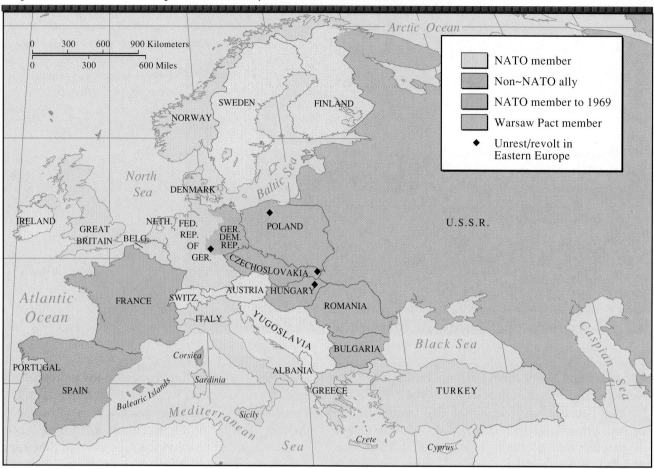

The Central Treaty Organization (CENTO) of Turkey, Iraq, Iran, Pakistan, Great Britain, and the United States was intended to prevent the Soviet Union from expanding at the expense of its southern neighbors. To stem Soviet aggression in the Far East, the United States, Great Britain, France, Pakistan, Thailand, the Philippines, Australia, and New Zealand formed the Southeast Asia Treaty Organization (SEATO). By the mid-1950s, the United States found itself allied militarily with forty-two states around the world.

A crisis over Berlin added to the tension in the late 1950s. In August 1957, the Soviet Union had launched its first intercontinental ballistic missile (ICBM), capable of reaching the United States from its bases in the U.S.S.R. (The United States had already launched its first.) Shortly afterward, the Soviets sent *Sputnik* I, the first man-made space satellite, to orbit the Earth. New fears seized the American public. Did the Soviet Union have a massive lead in building missiles that was creating a "missile gap" between the United States and the Soviet Union? Could the Soviet Union build a military base in outer space by which it could dominate the world? One American senator said, "It was time for Americans to be prepared to shed blood, sweat and tears if this country and the free world are to survive."

Nikita Khrushchev (nuh-KEET-uh KROOSH-chawf), the new leader of the Soviet Union, tried to take advantage of the American concern over missiles

◄ *During the Cuban Missile Crisis, President Kennedy met frequently with his cabinet. In this October 1962 photograph, Robert McNamara, secretary of defense, sits to the left of the president, and on Kennedy's right is Dean Rusk, secretary of state. What were the international consequences of this crisis?*

to solve the problem of West Berlin. West Berlin had remained a "Western island" of prosperity in the midst of the relatively poverty-stricken East Germany. Many East Germans, tired of Communist repression, managed to escape East Germany by fleeing through West Berlin. In November 1958, Khrushchev announced a new policy. Unless the West removed its forces from West Berlin within six months, he said, he would turn over control of the access routes into Berlin to the East Germans. Unwilling to abandon West Berlin to the Communists, President Eisenhower beefed up American military forces in Europe and stood firm. Khrushchev eventually backed down.

A brief thaw in the Cold War then set in. Eisenhower was invited to visit the Soviet Union. A summit conference on Berlin was arranged. On May 1, 1960, however, Soviet missiles shot down an American U-2 plane over the Soviet Union. Gary Powers, the downed pilot, admitted that the United States had been using U-2 planes to spy on the Soviet Union. An outraged Khrushchev denounced American aggression and cancelled Eisenhower's visit. The summit conference on Berlin also came to an end. American-Soviet relations took a turn for the worse.

## The Cuban Missile Crisis and Its Effect

During the administration of John F. Kennedy, the Cold War confrontation between the United States and the Soviet Union reached frightening levels. Kennedy began his presidency with a foreign policy disaster—the Bay of Pigs invasion. In 1959, a left-wing revolutionary named Fidel Castro had overthrown the Cuban dictator Fulgencio Batista (buh-TEE-stuh) and set up a Soviet-supported totalitarian regime in Cuba (see Chapter 14). Kennedy approved a secret plan, first devised by the Eisenhower administration, for an invasion of Cuba by Cuban exiles in the hope of causing a revolt against Castro. The invasion, however, was a disaster. Many of the exiles were killed or captured when they attempted a landing at the Bay of Pigs. The new American president was shaken by the utter failure of the U.S.–supported operation to overthrow Castro.

At a summit meeting in Vienna in 1961, Khrushchev took advantage of the American failure by threatening Kennedy with another six-month ultimatum over West Berlin. Kennedy left Vienna convinced of the need to deal firmly with the Soviet Union. He announced the call-up of U.S. reserve forces and pointed out the U.S. superiority in missiles. Khrushchev was forced once again to lift his six-month ultimatum. He realized, however, the need to stop the flow of refugees from East Germany through West Berlin. In August 1961, the East German government began to build a wall separating West Berlin from East Berlin. Eventually, it became a massive barrier guarded by barbed wire, floodlights, machine-gun towers, minefields, and vicious dog patrols. The Berlin Wall became a striking symbol of the division between the two superpowers.

Stung by reverses and determined to achieve some foreign policy success, Khrushchev soon embarked on a very dangerous adventure in Cuba. Ever since the Bay of Pigs, the Soviet Union had sent arms and military advisors to Cuba. In 1962, Khrushchev began to place medium-range nuclear missiles in Cuba. The United States was not willing to allow nuclear weapons within such close striking distance of the U.S. mainland, despite the fact that the United States had placed nuclear weapons in Turkey within easy range of the Soviet Union. Khrushchev was quick to point out that "your rockets are in Turkey. You are worried by Cuba . . . because it is 90 miles from the American coast. But Turkey is next to us."[4]

In October 1962, the United States found out that Soviet ships carrying missiles were heading to Cuba. Kennedy decided to blockade Cuba and prevent the fleet from reaching its destination. This approach to the problem gave each side time to find a peaceful solution. Khrushchev agreed to turn back the fleet and remove Soviet missiles from Cuba if Kennedy pledged not to invade Cuba. Kennedy quickly agreed.

The Cuban Missile Crisis brought the world frighteningly close to nuclear war. Indeed, in 1992 a high-ranking Soviet officer revealed that short-range rockets armed with nuclear devices would have been used against U.S. troops if the United States had invaded Cuba, an option that Kennedy fortunately had rejected. The realization that the world might have been destroyed in a few days had a profound influence on both sides. A hotline communications system between Moscow and Washington, D.C., was installed in 1963. The two superpowers could now communicate quickly in a time of crisis. In the same year, the two

powers agreed to ban nuclear tests in the atmosphere. This step at least served to lessen the tensions between the two nations and keep the Earth's atmosphere free of nuclear pollution.

## Vietnam and the Domino Theory

By that time, the United States had also been drawn into a new struggle that had an important impact on the Cold War—the Vietnam War (see Chapter 16). In 1964, under President Lyndon B. Johnson, increasing numbers of U.S. troops were sent to Vietnam. Their purpose was to keep the Communist regime of North Vietnam from gaining control of South Vietnam. U.S. policy makers saw the conflict in terms of a **domino theory** concerning the spread of communism. If the Communists succeeded in South Vietnam, the argument went, all the other countries in the Far East that were freeing themselves from colonial domination would likewise fall (like dominoes) to communism.

Despite the massive superiority in equipment and firepower of the American forces, the United States failed to defeat the determined North Vietnamese, and especially the Vietcong—the South Vietnamese Communist guerrillas who were being supported by North Vietnam. The growing number of American troops sent to Vietnam soon produced a persistent antiwar movement in the United States, especially among college students of draft age. The mounting destruction of the conflict, brought into American homes every evening on television, also turned American public opinion against the war. Finally, President Richard M. Nixon reached an agreement with North Vietnam in 1973 that allowed the United States to withdraw its forces. Within two years after the American withdrawal, Vietnam had been forcibly reunited by Communist armies from the North.

Despite the success of the North Vietnamese Communists, the domino theory proved unfounded. A noisy split between Communist China and the Soviet Union put an end to the theory of a single communism directed by Moscow. Under President Nixon, American relations with China were resumed. New nations in Southeast Asia also managed to avoid Communist governments. Above all, Vietnam helped to show the limitations of American power. By the end of the Vietnam War, a new era in American-Soviet relations had begun to emerge.

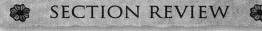

## SECTION REVIEW

1. **Locate:**
   (a) Greece,   (b) Turkey

2. **Define:**
   (a) policy of containment,   (b) mutual deterrence,   (c) domino theory

3. **Identify:**
   (a) Truman Doctrine,   (b) Dean Acheson,
   (c) Marshall Plan,   (d) COMECON,
   (e) NATO,   (f) Warsaw Pact,   (g) CENTO,
   (h) SEATO,   (i) Nikita Khrushchev,
   (j) Vietcong

4. **Recall:**
   (a)  What happened to relations between the United States and the Soviet Union after the Axis powers were defeated in World War II?
   (b)  How did the Soviets react when the United States, Great Britain, and France made plans to create West Germany in 1948?
   (c)  What did the United States believe the invasion of South Korea by North Korea proved about Communist intentions?
   (d)  How was the Cuban Missile Crisis resolved?

5. **Think Critically:** Why was it unrealistic for people to think that there was just one united Communist movement in the world after World War II?

## THE SOVIET UNION AND ITS EASTERN EUROPEAN SATELLITES (1945 TO 1970)

World War II had left the Soviet Union one of the world's two superpowers. Its leader, Joseph Stalin, was at the height of his power. As a result of the war, Stalin

and the Soviet forces were now in control of a vast empire that included Eastern Europe, much of the Balkans, and new territory gained from Japan in the Far East.

## The Reign of Stalin

World War II devastated the Soviet Union. Over twenty million citizens had lost their lives. Cities like Kiev and Leningrad lay in ruins. The Soviet people faced incredibly difficult conditions. They worked long hours and ate little. They were badly housed and poorly clothed.

In the immediate postwar years, the Soviet Union removed goods and materials from occupied Germany and took valuable raw materials from its satellite states in Eastern Europe. To create a new industrial base, Stalin returned to the method that he had used in the 1930s. Working hard for little pay, poor housing, and few consumer goods, Soviet workers were expected to produce goods for export with little in return for themselves. The incoming capital from abroad could then be used to buy machinery and Western technology. The loss of millions of men in the war, however, meant that much of this tremendous workload fell upon Soviet women. Almost 40 percent of heavy labor in factories was done by women.

The old methods brought about a spectacular economic recovery in the Soviet Union. By 1947, Russian industrial production had reached prewar levels. Three years later, it had surpassed these levels by 40 percent. New power plants, canals, and giant factories were built, although often with little regard for the environment. Metals plants in Soviet cities, for example, spewed out noxious chemicals that polluted the land and sickened the people. New industrial plants and oil fields were set up in Siberia and Soviet Central Asia. Stalin's newly announced five-year economic plan of 1946 reached its goals in less than five years.

Although Stalin's economic policy led to growth in heavy industry, the results were chiefly for the benefit of the military. Consumer goods were scarce. The development of thermonuclear weapons (hydrogen bombs) in 1952 and the first space satellite (*Sputnik I*) in 1957 enhanced the Soviet state's reputation as a

▲ *The Soviets launched* Sputnik I *on October 4, 1957. It made a full orbit around the Earth every one and one-half hours, and it stayed up for fifty-seven days.* Sputnik II, *which carried a live dog, was launched in November 1957.*

world power abroad. At home, however, the Soviet people were shortchanged. Heavy industry grew at a rate three times that of consumer goods. Moreover, the housing shortage was severe. An average Russian family lived in a one-room apartment. A British official in Moscow reported that "all houses, practically without exception, show lights from every window after dark. This seems to indicate that every room is both a living room by day and a bedroom by night. There is no place in overcrowded Moscow for the luxury of eating and sleeping in separate rooms."[5]

When World War II ended in 1945, Stalin had been in power for over fifteen years. During that time, he had removed all opposition to his rule. He remained the undisputed master of the Soviet Union. Other leading members of the Communist Party were completely obedient to his will. Stalin distrusted competitors, and exercised sole power. He pitted his subordinates against one another. Stalin had little respect for other Communist Party leaders. He is reported to have said to members of his inner circle in 1952, "You are as blind as kittens. What would you do without me?"[6]

Stalin's paranoid suspicions added to the constantly increasing repression of the regime. In 1946, government decrees stated that all forms of literary and scientific expression must conform to the political needs of the state and the Communist Party line. An econo-

mist, for example, was condemned for suggesting that the West might have an economic boom. Along with an anti-intellectual campaign came political terror. A new series of purges— like those of the late 1930s—seemed likely in 1953 when a number of Jewish doctors were accused of plotting to kill high-level party officials. A great fear began to spread throughout the country. Only Stalin's death on March 5, 1953, prevented more bloodletting.

## The Khrushchev Era

After Stalin's death, power passed into the hands of a group of ten leaders of an executive committee known as the Presidium. A struggle for power soon arose. Lavrenti Beria, head of the secret police, was the first member of the Presidium to fall from power. Others followed as the struggle grew. Gradually, however, the new general secretary of the Communist Party, Nikita Khrushchev, became the chief Soviet leader. Khrushchev had been responsible for ending the system of forced-labor camps, a regular feature of Stalinist Russia. At the Twentieth Congress of the Communist Party in 1956, Khrushchev condemned Stalin for his "administrative violence, mass repression, and terror." Stalin, he said, "often chose the path of repression and annihilation" against both party members and individuals who had committed no crimes whatsoever. The process of eliminating the more ruthless policies of Stalin became known as **de-Stalinization.**

Once in power, Khrushchev extended the policy of de-Stalinization. He stated that "readers should be given the chance to make their own judgements" regarding controversial literature. Police measures, he said, should not be used. He allowed the publication in 1962 of Alexander Solzhenitsyn's (SOLE-zhuh-NEET-sun) *A Day in the Life of Ivan Denisovich*, a grim portrayal of life in a Siberian forced-labor camp. Each day, as Solzhenitsyn related, prisoners were marched from the prison camp to a work project through temperatures of seventeen degrees below zero: "There were escort guards all over the place, . . . their machine guns sticking out and pointed right at your face. And there were guards with gray dogs. One dog bared its fangs as if laughing at the prisoners." Many Soviets identified with Ivan as a symbol of the suffering they had endured under Stalin.

There was a limit to de-Stalinization, however. When Khrushchev's revelations about Stalin fed a spirit of rebellion in Soviet satellite countries in Eastern Europe, there was a reaction. Soviet troops crushed an uprising in Hungary in 1956 (see the next section). Khrushchev and the Soviet leaders, afraid of a further undermining of the regime, downplayed their campaign of de-Stalinization.

Khrushchev tried to place more emphasis in the economy on light industry and consumer goods. His attempts to increase agricultural output by growing corn and cultivating vast lands east of the Ural Mountains were not successful and damaged his reputation within the party. These failures, combined with increased military spending, hurt the Soviet economy. The industrial growth rate, which had soared in the early 1950s, now declined dramatically from 13 percent in 1953 to 7.5 percent in 1964.

Khrushchev's personality also did not endear him to the higher Soviet officials. They frowned at his tendency to crack jokes and play the clown. The higher members of the party bureaucracy also were not pleased when Khrushchev tried to curb their privileges. Foreign policy failures further damaged Khrushchev's reputation among his colleagues. His rash plan to place missiles in Cuba was the final straw. While he was away on vacation in 1964, a special meeting of the Soviet leaders voted him out of office (because of "deteriorating health") and forced him into retirement. A group of leaders officially succeeded him, but real power came into the hands of Leonid Brezhnev (BREZH-nef). Supposedly the "trusted" supporter of Khrushchev, it was Brezhnev who had engineered his downfall.

## Eastern Europe: Behind the Iron Curtain

At the end of World War II, Soviet military forces had occupied all of Eastern Europe and the Balkans (except for Greece, Albania, and Yugoslavia). All of the occupied states came to be part of the Soviet sphere of influ-

### CONNECTIONS
### AROUND THE WORLD

**Economic Miracles: Germany and Japan**   Both Germany and Japan were devastated by World War II. Their economies were in shambles. Their cities lay in ruins. So many German men had been killed or wounded in the war that women had to take on the backbreaking work of clearing the rubble in the cities by hand.

At the end of the twentieth century, Germany and Japan are two of the world's greatest economic powers. What explains their economic miracles?

Because of the destruction of the war, both countries were forced to build new industrial plants. For many years, thanks to American military forces, neither country had to spend much on defense. Their governments could focus on rebuilding the infrastructure (roads, bridges, canals, and buildings) that had been destroyed during the war. Both German and Japanese workers had a long tradition of hard work and basic skills. In both countries, U.S. occupation policy focused on economic recovery, a goal that was made easier by American foreign aid.

Today, Germany and Japan share many similarities in the structure of their economies. Both rely on imports of raw materials for their industries. Both depend for their prosperity on exports of manufactured goods, including machinery, automobiles, steel, textiles, electrical and electronic equipment, and ships. Both nations must import food to feed their populations.

ence. After 1945, they all had similar political developments. Coalitions of all political parties were formed to run the governments in these states. Within a year or two, however, the Communist parties in these coalitions had taken over most of the power. The next step was the creation of one-party Communist governments.

▶ *In 1955, Nikita Khrushchev, on the right, visited Belgrade, Yugoslavia, where he was welcomed by Tito and accorded full military honors. Why do you think Khrushchev is dressed in civilian clothes and Tito is wearing a military uniform?*

The timetables of these Communist takeovers varied from country to country. Between 1945 and 1947, Communist governments became firmly entrenched in East Germany, Bulgaria, Romania, Poland, and Hungary. In Czechoslovakia, where there was a strong tradition of democracy, the Communists did not achieve their goals until 1948. In the elections of 1946, the Communist Party of Czechoslovakia had become the largest party, but it was not all-powerful and shared control of the government with the noncommunist parties. When it appeared that the noncommunist parties might win new elections early in 1948, the Communists seized control of the government on February 25. All other parties were dissolved.

Albania and Yugoslavia were exceptions to this pattern of Soviet dominance. Both countries had had strong Communist resistance movements during the war, and yet the Communist parties took control when the war ended. In Albania, local Communists set up a rigidly Stalinist-type regime, but one that grew more and more independent of the Soviet Union.

In Yugoslavia, Josip Broz, known as Tito (TEE-TOE), leader of the Communist resistance movement, seemed to be a loyal Stalinist. After the war, however, he moved toward the creation of an independent Communist state in Yugoslavia. Stalin hoped to take control of Yugoslavia, just as he had done in other Eastern European countries. Tito, however, refused to give in to Stalin's demands. He gained the support of the people by portraying the struggle as one of Yugoslav national freedom. The Yugoslav Communists rejected Stalinism and followed a more decentralized economic system in which workers could manage themselves. Greater social freedom was also part of Yugoslav communism.

Between 1948 and Stalin's death in 1953, the Eastern European satellite states, directed by the Soviet Union, followed a policy of Stalinization. They instituted Soviet-type five-year plans with emphasis on heavy industry rather than consumer goods. They began to collectivize agriculture. They eliminated all noncommunist parties and established the institutions of repression—secret police and military forces.

However, communism—a foreign product—had not developed deep roots among the peoples of Eastern Europe. Moreover, the Soviets exploited Eastern Europe economically for their own benefit and made living conditions harsh for most people. The Soviets had removed factories from their defeated wartime enemies, Bulgaria, Romania, and Hungary, and shipped them to the Soviet Union. The Soviet government

# YOU ARE THERE

# Soviet Repression in Eastern Europe—Hungary, 1956

◄ In 1956, Soviet tanks manned by Soviet soldiers traveled freely in Budapest, Hungary. What do you believe were the mood and thoughts of the Hungarians who were watching these tanks move through their capital city?

*The first selection that follows is a statement by the Soviet government justifying the use of Soviet troops in Hungary. The second is a brief and tragic final statement from Imre Nagy, the Hungarian leader.*

### Statement of the Soviet Government, October 30, 1956

The course of the events has shown that the working people of Hungary, who have achieved great progress on the basis of their people's democratic order, correctly raise the question of the necessity of eliminating serious shortcomings in the field of economic building, the further raising of the material well-being of the population, and the struggle against bureaucratic excesses in the state apparatus.

However, this just and progressive movement of the working people was soon joined by forces of black reaction and counterrevolution, which are trying to take advantage of the discontent of part of the working people to undermine the foundations of the people's democratic order in Hungary and to restore the old landlord and capitalist order.

The Soviet Government and all the Soviet people deeply regret that the development of events in Hungary has led to bloodshed. On the request of the Hungarian People's Government the Soviet Government consented to the entry into Budapest of the Soviet Army units to assist the Hungarian People's Army and the Hungarian authorities to establish order in the town.

*(continued)*

## YOU ARE THERE

# Soviet Repression in Eastern Europe—Hungary, 1956, continued

### The Last Message of Imre Nagy, November 4, 1956

This fight is the fight for freedom by the Hungarian people against the Russian intervention, and it is possible that I shall only be able to stay at my post for one or two hours. The whole world will see how the Russian armed forces, contrary to all treaties and conventions, are crushing the resistance of the Hungarian people. They will also see how they are kidnapping the Prime Minister of a country which is a Member of the United Nations, taking him from the capital, and therefore it cannot be doubted at all that this is the most brutal form of intervention. I should like in these last moments to ask the leaders of the revolution, if they can, to leave the country. I ask that all that I have said in my broadcast, and what we have agreed on with the revolutionary leaders during meetings in parliament, should be put in a memorandum, and the leaders should turn to all the peoples of the world for help and explain that today it is Hungary and tomorrow, or the day after tomorrow, it will be the turn of other countries because the imperialism of Moscow does not know borders, and is only trying to play for time.

1. Which of the two accounts do you think is the most accurate description of what actually happened in Hungary? Why do you think this?

2. Based on these selections, what was Soviet policy in the 1950s toward its Eastern European satellite states?

also forced all of the Eastern European states to trade with the Soviet Union to the latter's advantage.

After Stalin's death, many Eastern European states began to pursue a new, more nationalistically oriented course. The new Soviet leaders, including Khrushchev, also interfered less in the internal affairs of these states. In the late 1950s and 1960s, however, the Soviet Union also made it clear, especially in Poland, Hungary, and Czechoslovakia, that it would not allow its Eastern European satellites to become independent of Soviet control.

In 1956, after Khrushchev had denounced Stalin, protests—especially by workers—erupted in Poland. In response, the Polish Communist Party adopted a series of reforms in October 1956 and elected Wladyslaw Gomulka as first secretary. Gomulka declared that Poland had the right to follow its own socialist path. Fearful of Soviet armed response, however, the Poles compromised. Poland pledged to remain loyal to the Warsaw Pact. The Soviets then agreed to allow Poland to follow its own path to socialism. The Catholic Church, an extremely important institution to many Poles, was also allowed to govern its own affairs.

These developments in Poland in 1956 led Hungarian Communists to seek the same kinds of reforms and independence. They chose Imre Nagy as the new Hungarian leader. Internal dissent in Hungary, however, was directed not simply against the Soviets but against communism in general, which was viewed as a creation of the Soviets. The Stalinist secret police had also bred much terror and hatred in Hungary.

The unrest in Hungary, combined with economic difficulties, led to calls for revolt. To quell the rising rebellion, Nagy declared Hungary a free nation on November 1, 1956. He promised free elections. The mood of the country soon made it clear that this could mean the end of Communist rule in Hungary. However, Khrushchev was in no position at home to allow a member of the Communist group of nations to leave. Just three days after Nagy's declaration, the Red Army attacked Budapest (see "You Are There: Soviet Repression in Eastern Europe—Hungary, 1956"). The Soviets reestablished control over the country. János Kádár, a reform-minded cabinet minister, replaced Nagy and worked with the Soviet Union to squash the revolt. By collaborating with the Soviet invaders, Kádár saved many of Nagy's economic reforms.

The developments in Poland and Hungary in 1956 did not lead to a revolt in Czechoslovakia. There the "Little Stalin," Antonin Novotny, had been placed in power in 1952 by Stalin himself and remained firmly in control. By the late 1960s, however, Novotny had alienated many members of his own party. He was especially disliked by Czechoslovakia's writers, including the playwright Václav Havel. A writers' rebellion late in 1967, in fact, led to Novotny's resignation. In January 1968, Alexander Dubcek was elected first secretary of the Communist Party. He soon introduced a number of reforms, including freedom of speech and press and freedom to travel abroad. Dubcek hoped to create "communism with a human face." A period of euphoria broke out that came to be known as the "Prague (PRAWG) Spring."

The euphoria proved to be short-lived, however. It had led many to call for more far-reaching reforms, including withdrawal from the Soviet bloc. To forestall the spreading of this "spring" fever, the Red Army invaded Czechoslovakia in August 1968 and crushed the reform movement. Gustav Husák (HYOO-SAWK) replaced Dubcek, crushed his reforms, and reestablished the old order.

▲ *In 1968, the Soviet response to Alexander Dubcek's efforts to reform Communist rule in Czechoslovakia was to send Soviet tanks into Prague to stop any possible changes. Why do you think the Czechs believed they might succeed in liberalizing Communist practices when their neighbors in Hungary had failed to thwart the Soviets?*

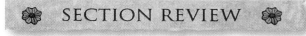

## SECTION REVIEW

1. **Locate:**
   (*a*) Soviet Union,    (*b*) Hungary

2. **Define:**
   (*a*) de-Stalinization

3. **Identify:**
   (*a*) satellite states,    (*b*) Presidium,
   (*c*) Alexander Solzhenitsyn,    (*d*) Leonid Brezhnev,    (*e*) Tito,    (*f*) "Prague Spring"

4. **Recall:**
   (*a*) Why did much of the work of rebuilding the Soviet Union after World War II fall on women?
   (*b*) What prevented even greater repression and terror from taking place in the Soviet Union during the early 1950s?
   (*c*) What failures did Khrushchev suffer that contributed to his decline from power?
   (*d*) Why didn't communism develop deep roots among the peoples of Eastern Europe?
   (*e*) Why did the Soviet Union invade Hungary but not Poland in 1956?

5. **Think Critically:** Both Yugoslavia and Albania had strong Communist parties during World War II but did not come under the direct control of the Soviet Union after the war. Other nations with

weaker Communist parties were quickly dominated by the Soviets. Why was the Soviet Union more successful in controlling nations that had weak Communist movements?

## WESTERN EUROPE: THE REVIVAL OF DEMOCRACY AND THE ECONOMY

All the nations of Western Europe faced similar kinds of problems at the end of World War II. Above all, they needed to rebuild their economies and recreate their democratic institutions. Within a few years of the defeat of Germany and Italy, an incredible economic revival brought a renewed growth to European society.

### Western Europe: Domestic Politics

The important role that Communists had played in the resistance movements against the Nazis gained them a new strength once the war was over. Communist parties did well in elections in Italy and France in 1946 and 1947, as well as in a few other countries. Communist success was short-lived, however. Once the Cold War was in full swing, Communist support of Soviet policies hurt Communist parties at home. They began to decline.

As part of their election strategies, Communist parties had often joined forces with other left-wing parties, such as the Social Democrats or the Socialists. The Socialist parties had also fared well immediately after the war as people became willing to overthrow the old order. Support for the Socialists soon waned, however. The Cold War also hurt the Socialist parties. Their working together with Communist parties in postwar coalitions cost them dearly.

By 1950, moderate political parties had made a remarkable comeback in Western Europe. Especially important was the rise of Christian Democratic parties.

The new Christian Democrats were sincerely interested in democracy and in significant economic reforms. They were especially strong in Germany and Italy, and they played an important role in achieving Europe's economic recovery.

With the economic aid of the Marshall Plan, the countries of Western Europe recovered relatively rapidly from the devastation of World War II. Between 1947 and 1950, European countries received $9.4 billion for new equipment and raw materials. By 1950, industrial output in Europe was 30 percent above prewar levels. Steel production alone expanded by 70 percent. Furthermore, this economic recovery continued well into the 1950s and 1960s. The decades of the 1950s and 1960s were periods of dramatic economic growth and prosperity in Western Europe. Indeed, Western Europe had virtually full employment during these decades.

### France: The Domination of de Gaulle

The history of France for nearly a quarter of a century after the war was dominated by one man—Charles de Gaulle (di-GOLE). He had an unshakable faith in his mission to restore the greatness of the French nation. During the war, de Gaulle had been the leader of French resistance groups. He also played an important role in establishing a French provisional government after the war. The creation of a new government called the Fourth Republic in 1946, with its return to a parliamentary system based on parties that de Gaulle considered weak, led him to withdraw from politics. Eventually, he formed the French Popular Movement, which blamed the parties for France's political mess and called for an even stronger presidency. De Gaulle finally achieved this goal in 1958.

The political stability of the Fourth Republic was badly shaken by the Algerian crisis. After suffering defeat in Vietnam in 1954, the French army was determined to resist the demands of Algerians for independence (see Chapter 15). A strong antiwar movement among French intellectuals and church leaders, however, led to bitter divisions within France. Even the possibility of civil war loomed large. The panic-stricken leaders of the Fourth Republic offered to let de Gaulle take over the government as president and revise the constitution.

In 1958, de Gaulle drafted a new constitution for the Fifth Republic that greatly enhanced the power of the president. He now had the right to choose the prime minister, dissolve parliament, and supervise both defense and foreign policy. De Gaulle had always believed in strong leadership. The new Fifth Republic under de Gaulle, while preserving the forms of democracy, lacked much of the substance of a democratic system.

As the new president, de Gaulle sought to return France to a position of great power. He did realize, however, that France was only wasting its economic strength by continuing its colonial empire. By 1962, he had granted independence to France's black African colonies and to Algeria. At the same time, the French president believed that playing an important role in the Cold War might enhance France's stature. For that reason, he pulled France out of NATO, arguing that France did not want to be an American "vassal state." With an eye toward achieving the status of a world power, de Gaulle invested heavily in the nuclear arms race. France exploded its first nuclear bomb in 1960. Despite his successes, de Gaulle did not really achieve his ambitious goals of world power. In truth, France was too small for such global ambitions.

Although the cost of the nuclear program increased the defense budget, de Gaulle did not neglect the economy. Between 1958 and 1968, the economy grew at an annual rate of 5.5 percent, faster than that of the United States. By the end of de Gaulle's era, France was a major industrial producer and exporter, especially in automobiles and weapons. However, problems remained. The expansion of traditional industries, such as coal, steel, and railroads, which were now owned by the state, led to large government deficits. The cost of living increased faster in France than in the rest of Europe.

Many French people became unhappy when de Gaulle's government failed to deal with these problems. Some even took violent action. In May 1968, a series of student protests, followed by a general strike by the labor unions, shook de Gaulle's government. Although he managed to restore order, the events of May 1968 had seriously undermined the French peo-

▲ *Charles de Gaulle, shown here in his military uniform, worked to restore France to its previous greatness as a world power. Why do you think the French people turned to a leader of the resistance to restore stability and prosperity to their nation?*

ple's respect for their president. Tired and discouraged, de Gaulle resigned from office in April 1969 and died within a year.

### West Germany: The Economic Miracle

As a result of the pressures of the Cold War, the three Western zones of Germany were unified into the Federal Republic of Germany in 1949. Konrad Adenauer (AD-un-OW-ur), the leader of the Christian Democratic Union (CDU), served as chancellor from 1949 to 1963. He became the "founding hero" of the Federal Republic. Adenauer sought respect for West Germany

▲ *Konrad Adenauer, the first chancellor of the Federal Republic of Germany, served as mayor of his hometown, Cologne, following World War I until 1933, when he was removed by the National Socialists. In 1944, he was imprisoned by the Gestapo, but in 1945 he resumed his position as Cologne's mayor. Why is it significant that West Germans elected a Nazi opponent and anticommunist as their first chancellor?*

by cooperating with the United States and the other Western European nations. He especially wanted to work with France—Germany's longtime enemy.

Under Adenauer, West Germany experienced an "economic miracle." This revival of the West German economy was largely guided by the minister of finance, Ludwig Erhard (AIR-hart). The West German economy boomed. Real wages doubled between 1950 and 1965 even though work hours were cut by 20 percent. Unemployment fell from 8 percent in 1950 to 0.4 percent in 1965. To maintain its economic expansion, West Germany even imported hundreds of thousands of guest workers from Italy, Spain, Greece, Turkey, and Yugoslavia.

The beginning of the Korean War in June 1950 had unexpected results for West Germany. The fear that South Korea might fall to Communist forces led many Germans and westerners to worry about the security of West Germany. Calls for West Germany to rearm were now being heard. Many people, afraid of a new German military machine, condemned the proposals for rearmament. Cold War tensions were decisive, however. West Germany rearmed in 1955 and became a member of NATO.

For many years, West Germany remained troubled by its Nazi past. The surviving major Nazi leaders had been tried and condemned as war criminals at the Nuremberg war crimes trials in 1945 and 1946. The victorious Allies continued war crimes trials of lesser officials as well. These declined in frequency, however, as the Cold War produced a shift in attitudes. By 1950, German courts had begun to take over the war crimes trials. Beginning in 1953, the West German government also began to make payments to Israel and to Holocaust survivors and their relatives to atone for the crimes of the Nazi Era. German president Richard von Weizsäcker (VIT-SAW-kur) reminded Germans of their responsibility "for the unspeakable sorrow that occurred in the name of Germany."

Adenauer resigned in 1963, after fourteen years of firmly guiding West Germany through its postwar recovery. Ludwig Erhard succeeded Adenauer as chancellor and largely continued his policies. An economic downturn in the mid-1960s, however, opened the door to the rise of the Social Democrats, who became the leading party in 1969.

## Great Britain: The Decline of the Empire

The end of World War II left Great Britain with massive economic problems. In elections held immediately after the war, the Labour Party overwhelmingly defeated Churchill's Conservative Party. The Labour Party had promised far-reaching reforms, especially in the area of social welfare. In a country with a tremendous shortage of consumer goods and housing, the Labour Party's platform was quite appealing. The Labour government under Clement Attlee, the new prime minister, set out to enact the reforms that created a modern **welfare state** in which the government takes responsibility for providing citizens with services and a minimal standard of living.

**Map 12.2    The Economic Division of Europe during the Cold War**

Six original members of NATO and members of the Common Market

Member of European Economic Community (Common Market), 1986

Member of Council for Economic Assistance (COMECON), founded by the Soviet Union in 1949.

FINLAND
SWEDEN
NORWAY
North Sea
UNION OF
Baltic Sea
DENMARK
SOVIET
IRELAND
GREAT BRITAIN
NETH.
GERMAN DEMOCRATIC REPUBLIC
POLAND
SOCIALIST
BELGIUM
FEDERAL REPUBLIC OF GERMANY
CZECHOSLOVAKIA
LUX.
REPUBLICS
Atlantic Ocean
FRANCE
AUSTRIA
SWITZ.
HUNGARY
ROMANIA
YUGOSLAVIA
ITALY
BULGARIA
PORTUGAL
ALBANIA
SPAIN
TURKEY
GREECE

Mediterranean Sea

0    250    500    750 Kilometers
0    250    500 Miles
AFRICA

The establishment of the British welfare state began with the **nationalization** (government ownership) of the Bank of England; the coal and steel industries; public transportation; and public utilities, such as electricity and gas. In the area of social welfare, the new government passed the National Insurance Act and the National Health Service Act, both in 1946. The insurance act provided state funds to help the unemployed, the sick, and the aged. The health act created a system of socialized medicine that forced doctors and dentists to work with state hospitals, although private practices could be maintained. This measure was very costly for the state, but within a few years 90 percent of the medical profession was taking part. The British welfare state became the norm for most European states after the war (see "Creation of the Welfare State" later in the chapter).

The cost of building a welfare state at home forced Britain to reduce expenses abroad. This meant the dismantling of the British Empire and the reduction of military aid to such countries as Greece and Turkey. Economic necessity forced Britain to give in to the demands of its many colonies for national independence.

Continuing economic problems, however, brought the Conservatives back into power from 1951 to 1964. Although they favored private enterprise, the Conservatives accepted the welfare state and even extended it by financing an ambitious building program to improve British housing.

Although the British economy had recovered from the war, it had done so at a slower rate than other European countries. Britain was experiencing a long-term economic decline caused by a variety of factors. For one thing, Britain was not willing or was unable to invest in modern industrial machinery and to adopt new methods. Underlying the immediate problems, however, was a deeper issue. As a result of World War II, Britain had lost much of its revenues from abroad, but it still had a burden of debt from its many international commitments. With the rise of the United States and the Soviet Union, Britain was no longer able to play the role of a world power.

## Western Europe: The Move toward Unity

As we have seen, the divisions created by the Cold War led the nations of Western Europe to form the North Atlantic Treaty Organization in 1949. Military unity, however, was not the only kind of unity fostered in Europe after 1945. The destructiveness of two world wars caused many thoughtful Europeans to consider the need for some form of European unity. National feeling was still too powerful, however, for European nations to give up their political sovereignty. As a result, the desire for unity was forced to focus chiefly on the economic arena, not the political one.

In 1951, France, West Germany, the Benelux countries (Belgium, the Netherlands, and Luxembourg), and Italy formed the European Coal and Steel Community (ECSC). It created a common market for coal and steel products among the six nations by getting rid of tariffs and other trade barriers. The success of the ECSC encouraged its members to do more.

In 1957, the same six nations signed the Rome Treaty, which created the European Economic Community (EEC), also known as the Common Market. The EEC eliminated all customs barriers for the six member nations and created a large free-trade area protected from the rest of the world by a common tariff. In this way the EEC encouraged cooperation among the six nations' economies. All the member nations benefited economically. By the 1960s, the EEC nations had become an important trading bloc. With a total population of 165 million, the EEC became the world's largest exporter and purchaser of raw materials.

## ❧ SECTION REVIEW ❧

1. **Locate:**
   (*a*) France,    (*b*) West Germany,    (*c*) Great Britain

2. **Define:**
   (*a*) welfare state,    (*b*) nationalization

3. **Identify:**
   (*a*) Christian Democrats,    (*b*) Charles de Gaulle,
   (*c*) the West German "economic miracle",
   (*d*) European Economic Community (EEC)

4. **Recall:**
   (*a*) How did cooperation with Communist parties hurt Socialist parties in Western Europe after World War II?
   (*b*) Why did de Gaulle pull France out of NATO?
   (*c*) What did the invasion of South Korea have to do with the decision to rearm West Germany?
   (*d*) Why did British voters become dissatisfied with the Conservative Party and Winston Churchill after World War II?
   (*e*) Why did the British experience an economic decline after World War II?

5. **Think Critically:** Why do nations, such as France under Charles de Gaulle, who try to "go it alone" often suffer economic and social problems that are greater than those of nations that cooperate with each other?

## THE UNITED STATES AND CANADA: A NEW ERA

At the end of World War II, the United States emerged as one of the world's two superpowers. Reluctantly, the United States remained involved in European affairs. As the Cold War with the Soviet Union intensified, the United States worked hard to combat the spread of communism throughout the world. American domestic political life after 1945 was played out against a background of American military power abroad.

### American Politics and Society in the 1950s

Between 1945 and 1970, the ideals of Franklin Delano Roosevelt's New Deal largely determined the patterns of American domestic politics. The New Deal had brought basic changes to American society. These included a dramatic increase in the role and power of

◄ *Following the war, the United States experienced an unprecedented baby boom and a move to the suburbs. Do scenes like this 1949 photograph of a Levittown shopping center accurately portray postwar America? Why or why not?*

the federal government, the rise of organized labor as a significant force in the economy and politics, the beginning of a welfare state, and a grudging realization of the need to deal fairly with the concerns of minorities.

The New Deal tradition in American politics was reinforced by the election of Democratic presidents— Harry S Truman in 1948, John F. Kennedy in 1960, and Lyndon B. Johnson in 1964. Even the election of a Republican president, Dwight D. Eisenhower, in 1952 and 1956 did not change the basic direction of the New Deal. As Eisenhower stated in 1954, "Should any political party attempt to abolish Social Security and eliminate labor laws and farm programs, you would not hear of that party again in our political history."

No doubt, the economic boom after World War II fueled confidence in the American way of life. A shortage of consumer goods during the war had left Americans with both extra income and the desire to buy consumer goods after the war. Then, too, the growth of labor unions brought higher wages and gave more and more workers the ability to buy consumer goods. Government expenditures also indirectly helped the American private economy. Especially after the Korean War began in 1950, funds spent on defense provided money for scientific research in the universities and markets for weapons industries. After 1955, tax dollars built a massive system of interstate highways. Between 1945 and 1973, **real wages** (actual purchasing power of

income) grew an average of 3 percent a year, the most prolonged advance in American history.

The prosperity of the 1950s and 1960s led to social changes. Work patterns changed. More and more people moved away from work in factories and fields into **white-collar** occupations. These included professional and technical workers, managers, officials, and clerical and sales workers. In 1940, **blue-collar** workers in industrial production occupations made up 52 percent of the labor force; farmers and farm workers, 17 percent; and white-collar workers, 31 percent. By 1970, blue-collar workers constituted 50 percent; farmers and farm workers, 3 percent; and white-collar workers, 47 percent. Many of these white-collar workers now considered themselves middle class.

The growth of this middle class had many repercussions. From rural areas, small towns, and central cities, people moved to the suburbs. In 1940, 19 percent of the American population lived in suburbs, 49 percent in rural areas, and 32 percent in central cities. By 1970, those figures had changed to 38, 31, and 31, respectively. The move to the suburbs also led to an imposing number of shopping malls and automobiles. Americans loved their automobiles, which carried them from suburban home to suburban mall and workplace.

Finally, the search for prosperity led to new migration patterns. The West and South experienced rapid economic growth through the development of new industries, especially in the defense field. As a result, massive numbers of people made the exodus from the cities of the Northeast and Midwest to the sunbelt of the South and West. Between 1940 and 1980, cities such as Chicago, Philadelphia, Detroit, and Cleveland lost between 13 and 36 percent of their populations. Los Angeles, Dallas, and San Diego grew between 100 and 300 percent.

A new prosperity was not the only characteristic of the early 1950s. Cold War struggles abroad led to massive fears at home. The takeover of China by Mao Zedong's (MAU zuh-DUNG's) Communist forces in 1949 and Communist North Korea's invasion of South Korea in 1950 led to the widespread fear that communists had infiltrated the United States. President Truman's attorney general warned that communists "are everywhere—in factories, offices, butcher stores, on street corners, in private businesses. And each carried in himself the germ of death for society." For many Americans, proof of this threat to the United States became more evident when thousands of American soldiers were sent to Korea to fight and die in a war against Communist aggression.

This climate of fear produced a dangerous political agitator, Senator Joseph R. McCarthy of Wisconsin. His charges that hundreds of supposed communists were in high government positions helped to create a massive "Red Scare"—fear of communist subversion. When he attacked alleged "Communist conspirators" in the U.S. Army, he was condemned by Congress in 1954. Very quickly, his anticommunist crusade came to an end.

## An Age of Upheaval: The United States from 1960 to 1970

Between 1960 and 1970, the United States experienced a period of upheaval that brought forward problems that had been glossed over in the 1950s. The 1960s began on a youthful and optimistic note. At age forty-three, John F. Kennedy became the youngest elected president in the history of the United States. His administration, cut short by an assassin's bullet on November 22, 1963, focused chiefly on foreign affairs.

Kennedy's successor, Lyndon B. Johnson, won a new term as president in a landslide victory in 1964. (As vice president, Johnson had become president upon Kennedy's assassination.) Johnson used his stunning victory to pursue the growth of the welfare state, first begun in the New Deal. Johnson's programs included health care for the elderly, a War on Poverty to be fought with food stamps and a Job Corps, a new Department of Housing and Urban Development to deal with the problems of the cities, and federal assistance for education.

Johnson's other domestic passion was equal rights for African Americans. The civil rights movement had its beginnings in 1954, when the United States Supreme Court took the dramatic step of striking down the practice of racially segregated public schools. According to Chief Justice Earl Warren, "separate educational facilities are inherently unequal." African Americans in Montgomery, Alabama, boycotted segregated buses. Soon after, the eloquent Martin Luther King, Jr. became the leader of a growing movement for racial equality. King followed the peaceful resistance style of Mohandas Gandhi.

By the early 1960s, a number of groups, including King's Southern Christian Leadership Conference (SCLC), were organizing demonstrations and sit-ins across the South to end racial segregation. In August 1963, King led a March on Washington, D.C., for Jobs and Freedom that dramatized the African American desire for equality. This march and King's impassioned plea for racial equality had an electrifying effect on the American people (see "You Are There: 'I Have a Dream'"). By the end of 1963, 52 percent of the American people called civil rights the most significant national issue. Eight months earlier, only 4 percent had done so.

President Johnson took up the cause of civil rights. As a result of his leadership, Congress passed a Civil Rights Act in 1964. This act created the machinery to end segregation and discrimination in the workplace and all public places. A Voting Rights Act the following year made it easier for African Americans to vote in southern states. Laws alone, however, could not guarantee the Great Society that Johnson talked about creating. He soon faced bitter social unrest from both the civil rights movement and a growing antiwar movement.

# YOU ARE THERE

## "I Have a Dream"

*In the spring of 1963, a bomb attack on a church killed four children and brought the nation's attention to the policies of racial segregation in Birmingham, Alabama. A few months later, on August 28, 1963, Martin Luther King, Jr., led a march on Washington, D.C., and gave an inspired speech that energized the civil rights movement.*

**Martin Luther King, Jr., A Speech Delivered August 28, 1963, in Washington, D.C.**

I am happy to join with you today in what will go down in history as the greatest demonstration for freedom in the history of our nation. . . .

I say to you today, my friends, so even though we face the difficulties of today and tomorrow, I still have a dream. It is a dream deeply rooted in the American dream. I have a dream that one day this nation will rise up and live out the true meaning of its creed, "We hold these truths to be self-evident, that all men are created equal." I have a dream that one day on the red hills of Georgia, sons of former slaves and the sons of former slave owners will be able to sit down together at the table of brotherhood. . . . I have a dream that my four little children will one day live in a nation where they will not be judged by the color of their skin, but by the content of their character. . . .

This is our hope. This is the faith that I go back to the South with. With this faith we will be able to hew out of the mountain of despair a stone of hope. With this faith we will be able to transform the jangling discords of our nation into a beautiful symphony of brotherhood. With this faith we will be able to work together, to pray together, to struggle together, to go to jail together, to stand up for freedom together, knowing that we will be free

▲ *In August 1963, Martin Luther King, Jr., traveled to Washington, D.C., to support civil rights legislation sponsored by President Lyndon B. Johnson. Nearly 200,000 people gathered at the Lincoln Memorial to hear his "I Have a Dream" speech. Despite King's inspiring message, the civil rights legislation was delayed for another year.*

one day. And this will be the day. This will be the day when all of God's children will be able to sing with new meaning, "My country 'tis of thee, sweet land of liberty, of thee I sing. Land where my father died, land of the pilgrims' pride, from every

*(continued)*

## YOU ARE THERE

# "I Have a Dream," continued

mountainside, let freedom ring." And if America is to be a great nation, this must become true. . . .

And when this happens, and when we allow freedom to ring, when we let it ring from every village and every hamlet, from every state and every city, we will be able to speed up that day when all of God's children, black men and white men, Jews and Gentiles, Protestants and Catholics, will be able to join hands and sing in the words of the old Negro spiritual: "Free at last, Free at last. Thank God Almighty, we are free at last."

1. Who was Martin Luther King, Jr.?

2. What was King's dream?

3. To what extent has his dream been realized?

In the North and West, blacks had had voting rights for many years. However, local patterns of segregation led to higher unemployment rates for blacks than for whites. Blacks often lived in huge urban ghettos. In these ghettos, the calls for action by radical black leaders, such as Malcolm X (MAL-kuh-MECKS) of the Black Muslims, attracted more attention than did the nonviolent appeals of Martin Luther King, Jr. Malcolm X's advice was straightforward: "If someone puts a hand on you, send him to the cemetery."

In the summer of 1965, race riots broke out in the Watts district of Los Angeles. Thirty-four people died, and over one thousand buildings were destroyed. Cleveland, San Francisco, Chicago, Newark, and Detroit likewise exploded in the summers of 1966 and 1967. After the assassination of Martin Luther King, Jr. in 1968, over one hundred cities had riots, including Washington, D.C., the nation's capital. The combination of riots and extremist comments by radical black leaders led to a "white backlash" and a severe division of the United States. In 1964, 34 percent of American whites agreed with the statement that blacks were asking for "too much." By late 1966, that number rose to 85 percent, a figure not lost on politicians eager to achieve political office.

Antiwar protests also divided the American people after President Johnson sent American troops to war in Vietnam (see Chapter 16). As the war progressed and a military draft started, protests grew. There were teach-ins, sit-ins, and the occupations of buildings at universities. More radical demonstrations led to violence. The killing of four student protestors at Kent State University in 1970 by the Ohio National Guard startled the nation. A reaction set in, and the antiwar movement began to decline. By that time, however, antiwar demonstrations had helped to weaken the willingness of many Americans to continue the war.

The combination of antiwar demonstrations and ghetto riots in the cities prepared many people for "law and order." This was the appeal used by Richard Nixon, the Republican presidential candidate in 1968. With Nixon's election in 1968, a shift to the political right in American politics began.

## The Development of Canada

Canada experienced many of the same developments that the United States did in the postwar years. For twenty-five years after World War II, a prosperous Canada set out on a new path of industrial development. Canada had always had a strong export economy based on its abundant natural resources. Now it developed electronic, aircraft, nuclear, and chemical engineering industries on a large scale. Much of the Canadian growth, however, was financed by capital from the United States, which led to U.S. ownership of Canadian businesses. Many Canadians did not care, as they welcomed the economic growth. Others, however, feared American economic domination of Canada.

Canadians also worried about playing a secondary role politically and militarily to its neighboring superpower. Canada agreed to join the North Atlantic Treaty Organization in 1949. It even sent military forces to fight in Korea the following year. To avoid subordination to the United States, however, Canada actively supported the United Nations.

Nevertheless, concerns about the United States did not keep Canada from having a special relationship with its southern neighbor. The North American Air Defense Command (Norad) was formed in 1957. It was based on close cooperation between the air forces of the United States and Canada for the defense of North America against missile attack. As another example of their close cooperation, in 1972, Canada and the United States signed the Great Lakes Water Quality Agreement to regulate pollution of the lakes that border both countries.

The Liberal Party dominated Canadian politics until 1957, when John Diefenbaker (DEEF-fun-BAKE-ur) achieved a Conservative Party victory. Major economic problems, however, returned the Liberals to power. Under Lester Pearson, they created Canada's welfare state by enacting a national social security system (the Canada Pension Plan) and a national health insurance program.

---

### SECTION REVIEW

**1. Define:**
(a) real wages,    (b) white-collar,    (c) blue-collar

**2. Identify:**
(a) Senator Joseph R. McCarthy,    (b) War on Poverty,    (c) John F. Kennedy,    (d) Martin Luther King, Jr.,    (e) Malcolm X

**3. Recall:**
(a) What fueled confidence in the American way of life after World War II?
(b) What migration patterns took place in the United States after World War II?
(c) What may have caused the "white backlash" that was apparent among many white Americans during the 1960s?
(d) Why did rapid growth in the Canadian economy after World War II cause some Canadians to believe the United States had too much power in their nation?

**4. Think Critically:** How may spending for defense both help and harm a nation's economy?

---

## THE EMERGENCE OF A NEW SOCIETY

After World War II, Western society witnessed rapid change. Such products of new technologies as the computer, television, and jet plane all quickly altered the pace and nature of human life. The rapid changes in postwar society led many to view it as a new society. Called a technocratic society by some and the consumer society by others, postwar Western society was marked by a changing social structure and new movements for change.

### The Structure of European Society

The structure of European society was altered after 1945. Especially noticeable were the changes in the middle class. Traditional middle-class groups were made up of businesspeople and professionals in law, medicine, and the universities. Now a new group of managers and technicians, hired by large companies and government agencies, joined the ranks of the middle class. Whether in Eastern or Western Europe, the new managers and experts were very much alike.

Everywhere their positions depended upon skills gained from some form of higher education. Everywhere they took steps to ensure that their own children would be educated.

Changes also occurred among the lower classes. First, there was a dramatic shift of people from rural to urban areas. The number of people in farming declined drastically. By the 1950s, the number of peasants throughout most of Europe had dropped by 50 percent. Nor did the size of the industrial working class grow. In West Germany, industrial workers made up 48 percent of the labor force throughout the 1950s and 1960s. Thereafter, the number of industrial workers began to decline as the number of white-collar workers increased.

At the same time, a noticeable increase in the real wages of workers made it possible for them to imitate the buying patterns of the middle class. This led to what some observers have called the **consumer society.** Buying on the installment plan, which began in the 1930s, became widespread in the 1950s. Workers could now buy such products as televisions, washing machines, refrigerators, vacuum cleaners, and stereos. The automobile was the most visible symbol of the new mass consumerism. Before World War II, most cars were owned by people in the upper classes. In 1948, there were 5 million cars in all of Europe. By 1957, the number had tripled. By the 1960s, there were almost 45 million cars.

Rising incomes, combined with shorter working hours, created an even greater market for mass leisure activities. Between 1900 and 1960, the workweek was reduced from sixty hours to almost forty hours. The number of paid holidays also increased. All aspects of popular culture—music, sports, the media—now offered opportunities for leisure activities, including concerts, sporting events, and television viewing.

Another very visible symbol of mass leisure was the growth of mass tourism. Before World War II, mostly the upper and middle classes traveled for pleasure. After the war, the combination of more vacation time, higher wages, and package tours with their low-cost rooms enabled millions to travel. By the mid-1960s, 100 million tourists were crossing European boundaries each year. Travel at home was even more widespread.

▲ By 1956, 80 percent of all American families owned a television set. Many families considered a television a necessity, not a luxury. What role do you think advertising played in changing attitudes of Americans in the consumer society?

In Sweden, three out of four people spent a holiday outside their hometowns.

## Creation of the Welfare State

One of the most noticeable social developments in postwar Europe was the creation of the welfare state. Supporters of the welfare state believed that eliminating poverty and homelessness, providing medical services for all, providing for the needs of the elderly, and giving education to all who wanted it would free peo-

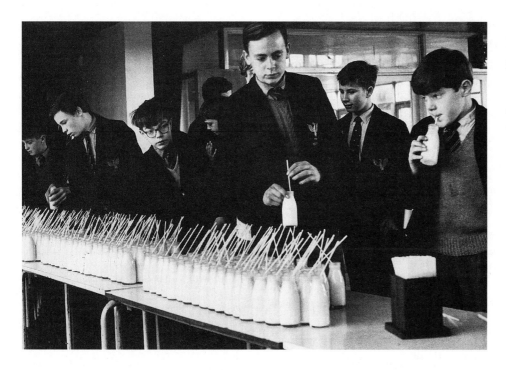

◄ *Many of the primary beneficiaries of the welfare state are children. These students at Holloway Comprehensive School in England received free milk daily as part of government aid to education.*

ple to achieve happiness by satisfying their material needs.

Social welfare schemes were not new, of course. The new postwar social legislation, however, extended earlier benefits and created new ones. In many countries, existing benefits for sickness, accidents, unemployment, and old age were simply extended to cover more people and provide larger payments. Men were generally eligible for old-age pensions at age sixty-five and women, at age sixty.

Affordable health care for all people was another goal of the welfare state. In Great Britain, Italy, and Germany, medical care was free to all people with some kind of insurance. In France, Belgium, and Switzerland, people had to pay toward the cost of their medical care. The amount ranged from 10 to 25 percent of the total cost.

Family allowances were begun in some countries to provide a minimum level of material care for children. Most programs gave a fixed amount per child. In 1964, for example, France granted $60 per month per child. Welfare states also tried to remove class barriers to opportunity by expanding the number of universities and providing scholarship aid to allow everyone to attend them.

Of course, welfare state benefits cost money. In 1967, spending on social services made up 17 percent of the gross national product of the major European countries. By the 1980s, it absorbed 40 to 50 percent. To critics, this meant that people had become overly dependent on the state. The majority of people, however, favored the benefits. Most leaders were aware that it would be political suicide to cut or lower those benefits.

## Higher Education and Student Revolt

Social change was also evident in new educational patterns and student revolts. Before World War II, it was mostly members of Europe's wealthier classes who went to universities. Even in 1950, only 3 or 4 percent of Western European young people were enrolled in a university. In addition, European higher education remained largely centered on the liberal arts, pure science, and preparation for the professions of law and medicine.

## YOU ARE THERE

# 1968—The Year of Student Protests

*The outburst of student upheavals in the late 1960s reached its high point in 1968. These two very different selections illustrate some of the issues that prompted university students to demand reforms.*

### A Student Manifesto in Search of a Real and Human Educational Alternative (University of British Columbia), June 1968

Today we as students are witnessing a deepening crisis within our society. We are intensely aware, in a way perhaps not possible for the older generation, that humanity stands on the edge of a new era. Because we are young, we have insights into the present and visions of the future that our parents do not have. Tasks of an immense gravity wait solution in our generation. . . . Much of the burden of solving the problems of the new era rests on the university. We have been taught to look to it for leadership. While we know that part of the reason for the university is to render direct services to the community, we are alarmed at its servility to industry and government as to what and how it teaches. We are scandalized that the university fails to realize its role in renewing and

vivifying those intellectual and moral energies necessary to create a new society—one in which a sense of personal dignity and human community can be preserved.

### Student Inscriptions on the Walls of Paris, May and June 1968

May 1968. World revolution is the order of the day.
To be free in 1968 is to take part.
Take the trip every day of your life.
Make love, not war.
No exams.
The mind travels farther than the heart but it doesn't go as far.
Run, comrade, the old are behind you!
Don't make a revolution in the image of your confused and hide-bound university.
Exam = servility, social promotion, hierarchic society.
Love each other.
Are you consumers or participants?
Live in the present.
Revolution, I love you.

Much of this changed after World War II. European states began to encourage more people to gain higher education by eliminating fees. As a result, universities saw an influx of students from the middle and lower classes. Enrollments grew dramatically. In France, 4.5 percent of young people went to a university in 1950. By 1965, the figure had increased to 14.5 percent. The number of students in European universities more than tripled between 1940 and 1960.

There were problems, however. Many European university classrooms had too many students. Many pro-

fessors paid little attention to their students. In addition, students often felt that the universities were not providing an education relevant to the realities of the modern age. Growing discontent led to an outburst of student revolts in the late 1960s (see "You Are There: 1968—The Year of Student Protests").

In part, these protests were an extension of the revolts in U.S. universities in the mid-1960s, which were often sparked by student opposition to the Vietnam War. In West Berlin, university students led a protest against Axel Springer, leader of Germany's

## YOU ARE THERE
# 1968—The Year of Student Protests, continued

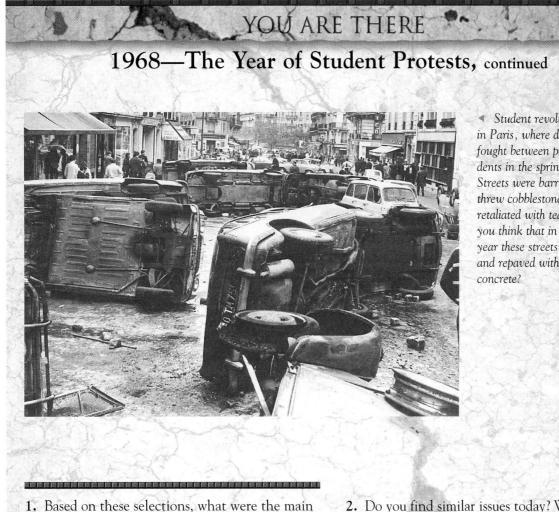

◀ *Student revolt led to extremes in Paris, where daily battles were fought between police and students in the spring of 1968. Streets were barricaded, students threw cobblestones, and police retaliated with tear gas. Why do you think that in the following year these streets were torn up and repaved with asphalt and concrete?*

1. Based on these selections, what were the main issues that generated student unrest in the 1960s?

2. Do you find similar issues today? Why or why not?

largest newspaper. Many German students wanted to destroy what they considered to be the corrupt old order. They were especially influenced by the ideas of the German American philosopher Herbert Marcuse (mar-KOO-suh). In *One-Dimensional Man*, published in 1964, Marcuse argued that a small group of students could free the masses from the control of the capitalist ruling class. However, the German students' attempt at revolutionary violence backfired as angry Berliners supported police repression of the students.

The student protest movement in both Europe and the United States reached its high point in 1968 (see "Young People in the 1960s: The Youth Protest Movement"). There were several reasons for the student radicalism. Some students truly wanted to reform the university system. Others were protesting the Vietnam War, which they viewed as a product of Western imperialism. They also expressed concern about becoming small cogs in the large and impersonal bureaucratic wheels of the modern world. Many students called for democratic decision making within the universities, a

# YOUNG PEOPLE IN THE 1960s

## The Youth Protest Movement

The decade of the 1960s witnessed a dramatic change in traditional manners and morals. The new standards were evident in the breakdown of the traditional family as divorce rates increased dramatically. Movies, plays, and books broke new ground in the treatment of once-hidden subjects. A growing youth movement also emerged in the 1960s. New attitudes toward sex and the use of drugs were two of its features. Young people also questioned authority and rebelled against the older generation. Spurred on by the Vietnam War, the youth rebellion in the United States became a youth protest movement by the second half of the 1960s. Active participants in the movement were often called "hippies."

In the 1960s, the lyrics of rock music reflected the rebellious mood of many young people. Bob Dylan (DILL-un), a well-known recording artist, expressed the feelings of the younger generation. His song "The Times They Are a-Changin'," released in 1964, has been called an "anthem for the protest movement." Some of its words, which follow, tell us why.

*This young couple enjoys the sun atop their highly decorated van. Which of the symbols used to embellish this car can you identify?*

You'll be drenched to the bone
  If your time to you
 Is worth savin'
  Then you better start swimmin'
 Or you'll sink like a stone
  For the times they are a'changin . . .'
  Come mothers and fathers
  Throughout the land
  And don't criticize
 What you can't understand
 Your sons and your daughters
Are beyond your command
Your old road
Is rapidly agin'
Please get out of the new one
If you can't lend your hand
For the times they are a'changin'

### Bob Dylan, "The Times They Are a-Changin'"

*Come gather round people*
*Wherever you roam*
*And admit that the waters*
*Around you have grown*
*And accept it that soon*

1. How does Bob Dylan's song express the feelings of the young people of the 1960s?

2. Who are the opponents in the song?

3. How relevant is this song today?

demand that reflected deeper concerns about the direction in which Western society was headed. Although student revolts fizzled out in the 1970s, the larger issues they raised have been increasingly revived in the 1990s.

## ❀ SECTION REVIEW ❀

1. **Define:**
   (*a*) consumer society

2. **Identify:**
   (*a*) Axel Springer,   (*b*) Herbert Marcuse

3. **Recall:**
   (*a*) How was the structure of European society altered after 1945?
   (*b*) How did affordable health care become available to most people in Western Europe after World War II?
   (*c*) Why was the rapid increase in the number of students in European universities important?

4. **Think Critically:** Why was it fair to say the following about post–World War II European politicians?

   "Most leaders were aware that it was political suicide to cut or lower those (social) benefits."

## Conclusion

At the end of World War II, a new conflict erupted in the Western world as the two new superpowers, the United States and the Soviet Union, competed for political domination of the world. Europeans, whether they wanted to or not, were forced to become supporters of one side or the other. This division also spread to the rest of the world. The United States fought in Korea and Vietnam to prevent the spread of communism, while the Soviet Union used its armies to prop up pro-Soviet regimes in Eastern Europe.

Western Europe also became a new community in the 1950s and 1960s as a remarkable economic recovery fostered a new optimism. Western European states became accustomed to political democracy. With the creation of the European Economic Community, many of them began to move toward economic unity. Although Western Europeans staged a remarkable economic recovery, the Cuban Missile Crisis made it clear that their future still depended on the outcome of the conflict between the two superpowers. In the Western Hemisphere, the two North American countries—the United States and Canada—built prosperous economies and relatively stable communities in the 1950s that were marred by a growing number of problems in the 1960s.

The student protests of the late 1960s caused many people to rethink some of their basic assumptions. Looking back, however, we can see that the student upheavals were not a turning point in the history of postwar Europe, as some people thought at the time. In the 1970s and 1980s, student rebels would become middle-class professionals. The vision of revolutionary politics would remain mostly a memory.

## Notes

1. Quoted in Joseph M. Jones, *The Fifteen Weeks (February 21–June 5, 1947)*, 2nd ed. (New York, 1964), pp. 140–141.
2. Quoted in Walter Laqueur, *Europe in Our Time* (New York, 1992), p. 111.
3. Quoted in Wilfried Loth, *The Division of the World, 1941–1955* (New York, 1988), pp. 160–161.
4. Quoted in Peter Lane, *Europe since 1945: An Introduction* (Totowa, N.J., 1985), p. 248.
5. R. Hilton, *Military Attaché in Moscow* (London, 1949), p. 41.
6. Quoted in Laqueur, *op. cit.*, p. 150.

# CHAPTER 12 REVIEW

## USING KEY TERMS

1. The value of a person's salary when adjusted for inflation is called _____.
2. _____ is the act of a government taking over private property either with or without payment.
3. The idea that allowing Communist aggressors to take over one country will encourage them to take over other nations as well has been called the _____.
4. The process of removing Stalin's influence from the Soviet government, economy, and social system was called _____.
5. A nation that is preoccupied with the desire to provide its people with material goods may be said to have a _____.
6. Nations with governments that intervene in the economy to assure a minimal standard of living for all people are said to have a _____.
7. The threat of both sides being destroyed during a nuclear war helped discourage such a war, and was known as the policy of _____.
8. Employees who work in industrial positions are referred to as _____ workers.
9. The attempt of non-communist world powers to prevent a further spread of communism to other states was called a _____.
10. Employees who have professional, technical, or managerial responsibilities in their jobs are referred to as _____ workers.

## REVIEWING THE FACTS

1. How was the Marshall Plan carried out and what was its purpose?
2. How did the Soviet Union make use of factories and tools from Eastern Europe to help them rebuild after World War II?
3. Why did the East Germans build the Berlin Wall?
4. What caused the Soviet Union to invade Hungary in 1956?
5. What happened during the Cuban Missile Crisis in 1962?
6. What action resulted in the first break in the united front of NATO nations?
7. What changes were made in the British government's role in their economic system after World War II?
8. What social, political, and economic movement changed the face of American society after World War II?
9. What was the primary reason for many Americans moving north and west during and after World War II?

## THINKING CRITICALLY

1. In what ways did the de-Stalinization of the Soviet Union help Nikita Khrushchev gain and maintain his control of the Soviet government?
2. What reasons might the people of Cuba have had for not supporting the Bay of Pigs invasion in 1961?
3. Why did the successful Soviet invasion of Hungary in 1956 make it more difficult for the Soviet Union to influence nations in other parts of the world?
4. How did the formation of the European Economic Community help member nations recover from World War II?
5. What are several reasons for the rapid economic growth that took place in the United States after World War II?
6. Why were many Americans willing to believe Joseph R. McCarthy during the Red Scare?
7. Why have many wealthy people been opposed to the creation of welfare states in their nations?
8. Why do some people believe the creation of welfare states in European nations reduced people's incentive to manage financial affairs carefully?

# CHAPTER 12 REVIEW

## APPLYING SOCIAL STUDIES SKILLS

1. **Government:** Identify and explain social and political forces that may have caused the people of France to choose Charles de Gaulle for their president and to approve a constitution that greatly enhanced the power he had in their government.
2. **Sociology:** Identify and describe social forces that caused many Europeans to believe that they were entitled to the benefits of a welfare state after World War II.
3. **Government:** Explain why it is difficult to achieve a smooth transfer of power in a totalitarian form of government. Use the transition of power from Stalin to Khrushchev and from Khrushchev to Brezhnev in the Soviet Union as examples.
4. **Sociology:** Identify and explain social forces that contributed to the growth of the Civil Rights movement in the United States.

## MAKING TIME AND PLACE CONNECTIONS

1. In recent years the United States and other developed nations have provided significant amounts of aid to developing nations. In general this assistance has not resulted in rapid economic expansion of these countries. Why was the assistance provided by the United States to European nations after World War II so much more successful in helping them recover from the war?
2. Identify and explain reasons for the different treatments given to Germany at the end of World War I and to West Germany at the end of World War II.
3. Identify and explain possible reasons for the comparatively slow growth of social benefits provided Americans, compared to the rapid growth of these programs in Europe, after World War II.
4. Compare and contrast Hitler's policy of creating fear and blaming problems on Jewish people in Europe with Joseph R. McCarthy's Red Scare tactics in the United States.
5. Explain how recent developments in the means of mass communication may have made it more difficult for the Soviet Union to put down revolts in eastern Europe in the late 1980s than it had been in the mid 1950s.

## BECOMING AN HISTORIAN

1. **Economics as a Key to History:** Create a graph that shows trends in American trade with Europe after World War II based on the data in the table below. Explain the probable causes and importance of the information communicated by your graph.

### The Value of U.S. Trade With Europe (in millions of dollars)

| Year | U.S. Exports | U.S. Imports |
|------|-------------|-------------|
| 1945 | $5,515 | $  409 |
| 1947 | 5,187 | 820 |
| 1949 | 4,118 | 925 |
| 1951 | 4,044 | 2,043 |
| 1953 | 2,910 | 2,335 |

*Source:* U.S. Bureau of the Census, *Historical Statistics of the United States; Colonial Times to 1957* (Washington, D.C., 1960), pp. 550, 552.

2. **Making Hypotheses and Predicting Outcomes:** In the past decade revolutions have replaced strong leaders with weak governments that have been unable to stop nationalist groups from creating chaos in many countries. This situation has often led to violence, disruption of economic systems, and a lack of personal security. Form and support a hypothesis about whether these conditions will result in a return to strong central governments in many European nations.

# THE CHANGING WORLD
# OF THE SUPERPOWERS:

**13**

Between 1945 and 1970, Europe not only recovered from the devastating effects of World War II but also experienced an economic recovery that seemed miraculous. By 1970, after more than two decades of the Cold War, Europeans had become used to a new division of Europe between West and East. A prosperous Western Europe that was allied to the United States stood opposed to a still-struggling Eastern Europe that remained largely subject to the Soviet Union. This new order seemed well established. However, within twenty years, a revolutionary upheaval in the Soviet Union and Eastern Europe would bring an end to the Cold War and would destroy the long-standing division of post-war Europe.

For years, the Berlin Wall had stood as the most visible symbol of the Cold War. In 1988, the American president Ronald Reagan, leader of the Western world, traveled to West Berlin. Facing the Berlin Wall, he challenged Mikhail Gorbachev, leader of the Soviet bloc, to "tear down this wall." During his own visit to West Germany a year later, Gorbachev responded, "The wall could disappear once the conditions that generated the need for it disappear. I do not see much of a

problem here." East Germany's Communist leaders, however, did see a problem, and they refused to remove the wall. In the summer of 1989, tens of thousands of East Germans fled their country while hundreds of thousands took to the streets to demand the resignation of the hardline Communist leader, Erich Honecker (HOE-nuh-kur). Honecker finally caved in. On November 9, 1989, a new East German government opened the wall and allowed its citizens to travel freely between West and East Berlin. The next day, government workers began to knock down the wall. They were soon joined by thousands of West and East Berliners who used sledgehammers and crowbars to rip apart the dreaded Cold War symbol. Germans were overcome with joy and celebrated. Many danced on the wall while orchestras played in the streets. Churches, theaters, and shops remained open day and night in West Germany as East Germans took advantage of their new freedom to travel. In 1990, West and East Germany became a single nation, and Berlin was once again the capital of Germany. With the destruction of the Berlin Wall, the Cold War seemed a thing of the past.

◄ *These two young people are chipping away at the remains of the Berlin Wall, just as many others did in January 1990. For how long did this wall divide East and West Berlin?*

# THE CONTEMPORARY WESTERN WORLD

## (1970 TO PRESENT)

### THE WORLD SINCE 1945

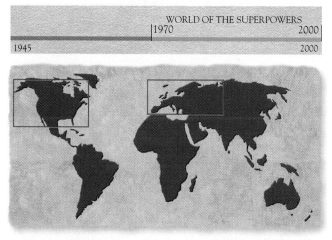

WORLD OF THE SUPERPOWERS
| 1970 | 2000 |
| 1945 | 2000 |

## QUESTIONS TO GUIDE YOUR READING

1. How and why did the Cold War end?
2. What reforms did Mikhail Gorbachev make in the Soviet Union?
3. What direction did the Eastern European nations take once Soviet control was gone?
4. What problems have the Western European nations, the United States, and Canada faced since 1970?
5. What have been the major social developments since 1970?
6. What have been the major cultural and intellectual developments since 1970?

## THE COLD WAR AND THE SOVIET BLOC

By the 1970s, American-Soviet relations had entered a new phase, known as **détente,** which was marked by a reduction of tensions between the two superpowers. Beginning in 1979, however, the apparent collapse of détente began a new period of East-West confrontation. Then, after Mikhail Gorbachev came to power in 1985, the Soviet Union began to make changes in its foreign policy, and the Cold War rapidly came to an end.

### From Cold War to Post-Cold War: Toward a New World Order?

One example of détente in the 1970s was the Helsinki (HEL-SING-kee) Agreements. Signed by the United States, Canada, and all European nations in 1975, these accords recognized all borders in central and Eastern Europe that had been set up since the end of

World War II. In doing so, they accepted the Soviet sphere of influence in Eastern Europe. The Helsinki Agreements also called for the protection of the human rights of the citizens of the nations signing the agreement.

This protection of human rights became one of the major foreign policy goals of the next U.S. president, Jimmy Carter. Hopes ran high for détente but received a setback in 1979, when the Soviet Union invaded Afghanistan. The Soviet Union wanted to restore a pro-Soviet regime there, but the United States viewed it as another example of Soviet expansion. Carter canceled American participation in the 1980 Olympic Games held in Moscow and placed an embargo on the shipment of American grain to the Soviet Union.

The Cold War intensified when Ronald Reagan was elected president in 1980. Calling the Soviet Union an "evil empire," Reagan began a military buildup and a new arms race. In 1982, the Reagan administration introduced the nuclear-tipped cruise missile, a weapon whose ability to fly at low altitudes made it difficult to detect. Reagan also became an ardent supporter of the Strategic Defense Initiative (SDI), nicknamed "Star Wars." Its purpose was to create a space shield that could destroy incoming missiles. By giving military aid to the Afghan rebels, Reagan helped to maintain a war in Afghanistan that the Soviet Union could not win. Like the Vietnam War for the United States, the war in Afghanistan showed that the power of a superpower was actually limited in the face of strong nationalist opposition. The armed forces of the mighty Soviet Union were not able to defeat rebel armies in Afghanistan, who were armed by an opposing super-power and willing to use guerrilla tactics.

The accession of Mikhail Gorbachev to power in the Soviet Union in 1985 eventually brought a dramatic end to the Cold War. Gorbachev was willing to rethink many of the basic assumptions underlying Soviet foreign policy. His "New Thinking," as it was called, opened the door to a series of stunning changes.

For one, Gorbachev made an agreement with the United States in 1987 to eliminate intermediate-range nuclear weapons (the INF Treaty). Both sides had reasons to dampen the expensive arms race. Gorbachev hoped to make far-reaching economic and internal

▲ *Mikhail Gorbachev, on the right, and Ronald Reagan were photographed in front of St. Basil's Cathedral during President Reagan's 1988 visit to Moscow. The willingness of both leaders to reduce the arms race helped end the Cold War. In light of Reagan's earlier views on the Soviet Union, do you think this meeting was ironic? Why or why not?*

reforms. The United States had its own financial problems. During the Reagan years, as the national debt tripled, the United States had moved from being a creditor nation, exporting more than it imported, to being the world's biggest debtor nation. As its imports overtook exports, the United States owed money to foreign investors. By 1990, both countries were becoming aware that their large military budgets made it difficult for them to solve their serious domestic social problems.

The years 1989 and 1990 were crucial in the ending of the Cold War. The postwar settlements that had become the norm in central and Eastern Europe came undone as a mostly peaceful revolutionary upheaval swept through Eastern Europe. A new Soviet policy made this upheaval possible. Under Gorbachev, the Soviet Union no longer gave military support to Communist governments in Eastern Europe that were faced with internal revolt.

This unwillingness of the Soviet regime to use force in Eastern Europe opened the door to the overthrow of the Communist regimes there (see "Eastern Europe: From Soviet Satellites to Sovereign States," later in the chapter). The reunification of Germany on October 3, 1990, was a powerful symbol of the end of the Cold War Era. By the end of 1991, the breakup of the Soviet Union made almost impossible any renewal of the global rivalry between the two competing superpowers. Although the United States had emerged as the world's leading military power by 1992, its role in the creation of a "New World Order" that President George Bush called for was not yet clear. After some hesitation, President Bill Clinton began to reassert American power in the world. He sent American troops to Haiti in September 1994 to restore that country's fragile democratic system. In December 1995, the United States took the lead in bringing an end to the war in Bosnia. As part of the agreement signed by the warring parties, twenty thousand U.S. troops were sent to the region as part of a NATO military presence intended to enforce the peace.

## Upheaval in the Soviet Union

Between 1964 and 1982, drastic change in the Soviet Union seemed highly unlikely. The man in charge—Leonid Brezhnev—did not want reforms. Nor did he want the states in Eastern Europe to lose their Communist governments. Brezhnev insisted on the right of

the Soviet Union to intervene if communism was threatened in another Communist state (known as the **Brezhnev doctrine**).

### The Brezhnev Era

Brezhnev benefited from the more relaxed atmosphere associated with détente. The Soviet Union was roughly equal to the United States in nuclear arms. Its leaders felt secure and were willing to relax their authoritarian rule. The regime allowed more access to Western styles of music, dress, and art. Of course, **dissidents**—those who spoke out against the regime—were still punished. Andrei Sakharov (SAW-kuh-RAWF), for example, who had played an important role in the development of the Soviet hydrogen bomb, was placed under house arrest for his defense of human rights.

In his economic policies, Brezhnev continued to emphasize heavy industry. Two problems, however, weakened the Soviet economy. The government's central planning led to a huge, complex bureaucracy that discouraged efficiency and led to apathy. Farm problems added to Soviet economic woes. Collective farmers had no incentive to work hard. Many preferred working their own small private plots to laboring in the collective work brigades. To make matters worse, bad harvests in the mid-1970s, caused by a series of droughts, heavy rains, and early frosts, forced the Soviet government to buy grain from the West, especially the United States.

By the 1970s, the Communist ruling class in the Soviet Union had become complacent and corrupt. Party and state leaders—as well as leaders of the army and secret police (KGB)—received awards and enjoyed a high standard of living. Brezhnev was unwilling to tamper with the party leadership and state bureaucracy, regardless of the inefficiency and corruption that the system encouraged.

By 1980, the Soviet Union was seriously ailing. A declining economy, a rise in infant mortality rates, a dramatic surge in alcoholism, and poor working conditions all gave rise to a feeling that the system was in trouble. Within the Communist Party, a small group of reformers emerged who knew the real condition of the Soviet Union. One member of this group was Mikhail

Gorbachev. A new era began when party leaders chose him in March 1985 to lead the Soviet Union.

### The Gorbachev Era

Mikhail Gorbachev had joined the Communist Party in 1952 and worked his way up the ranks. In 1978, Gorbachev was made a member of the party's Central Committee in Moscow. Two years later, he became a full member of the ruling Politburo and secretary of the Central Committee. In March 1985, party leaders elected him general secretary of the party, and he became the new leader of the Soviet Union.

Educated during the reform years of Khrushchev, Gorbachev seemed intent on making new reforms. By the 1980s, Soviet economic problems were obvious. Although the Soviet Union still excelled in space exploration, it fell behind the West in other new technology, especially in the use of computers. Most noticeable to the Soviet people was the actual decline in the standard of living. Ordinary citizens grew tired of standing in line for hours just to buy many basic goods.

From the start, Gorbachev preached the need for radical reforms. The basis of Gorbachev's radical reforms was **perestroika,** or "restructuring." At first, this meant only a restructuring of economic policy. Gorbachev called for the beginning of a market economy (consumers influence what is produced) with limited free enterprise (based on private ownership of businesses) and some private property. He soon realized, however, that in the Soviet system, the economic sphere was closely tied to the social and political spheres. An attempt to reform the economy without political or social reform would be doomed to failure.

One of the most important instruments of perestroika was **glasnost,** or "openness." Soviet citizens and officials were encouraged to discuss openly the strengths and weaknesses of the Soviet Union. *Pravda,* the official newspaper of the Communist Party, now

▲ *Mikhail Gorbachev was dynamic, outgoing, and determined to improve the daily lives of Soviet citizens. Do you think he initially understood where the reforms he supported would lead?*

began to report official corruption, sloppy factory work, and protests against government policy. Movies began to show the negative aspects of Soviet life. Music based on Western styles, such as jazz and rock, was performed openly.

Political reforms were equally revolutionary. In June 1987, the principle of two-candidate elections was introduced. Previously, voters had been presented with only one candidate. At the Communist Party conference in 1988, Gorbachev called for the creation of a new Soviet parliament, the Congress of People's Deputies, whose members were to be elected. It met in 1989, the first such meeting in Russia since 1918. Early in 1990, Gorbachev decreed that other political parties could now form. He also struck Article 6, which had guaranteed the "leading role" of the Communist Party, from the Soviet constitution.

At the same time, Gorbachev tried to strengthen his power by creating a new state presidency. Up to this time, the position of first secretary of the party (Gorbachev's position) had been the most important post in the Soviet Union. However, as the Communist Party became less closely tied to the state, the position of first secretary carried less and less power. In March 1990, Gorbachev became the Soviet Union's first president.

One of Gorbachev's most serious problems came from the nature of the Soviet Union. The Union of Soviet Socialist Republics was a truly multiethnic country, containing 92 nationalities and 112 different languages. Before, the iron hand of the Communist Party, centered in Moscow, had kept a lid on the centuries-old ethnic tensions. As Gorbachev released this iron grip, these tensions again came to the forefront. Nationalist movements emerged throughout the republics of the Soviet Union. Between 1988 and 1990, there were calls for independence first in Soviet

Georgia and then in Latvia, Estonia, Moldavia, Uzbekistan, Azerbaijan, and Lithuania.

During 1990 and 1991, Gorbachev struggled to deal with the problems unleashed by his reforms. He especially wanted to work more closely with Boris Yeltsin, who had been elected president of the Russian Republic in June 1991. By 1991, the conservative leaders of the traditional Soviet institutions—the army, government, KGB, and military industries—were worried. The possible breakup of the Soviet Union meant an end to their privileges. On August 19, 1991, a group of these people arrested Gorbachev and tried to seize power. The attempt failed, however, when Yeltsin and thousands of Russians bravely resisted the rebel forces in Moscow. Their actions opened the door to the final disintegration of the Soviet Union.

The Soviet republics now moved for complete independence. Ukraine voted for independence on December 1, 1991. A week later, the leaders of Russia, Ukraine, and Belarus (BELL-uh-ROOS) announced that the Soviet Union had "ceased to exist."

### The Yeltsin Era

Gorbachev resigned on December 25, 1991, and turned over his responsibilities as commander in chief to Boris Yeltsin, the president of Russia. By the end of 1991, one of the largest empires in world history had come to an end. A new era had begun in its now-independent states.

Within Russia, a new power struggle soon ensued. Boris Yeltsin was committed to introducing a free-market economy as quickly as possible, but the transition was not easy. Economic hardships and social disarray were made worse by a dramatic rise in the activities of organized crime mobs. This situation led increasing numbers of Russians to support both former Communists and hard-line nationalists who criticized Russia's loss of prestige in world affairs. Yeltsin's brutal use of force against the Chechens (CHET-chunz), who wanted to secede from Russia and create their own independent republic, also undermined his support. Despite the odds against him, however, Yeltsin won reelection as Russian president in 1996.

## SECTION REVIEW

1. **Locate:**
   (a) Soviet Georgia,   (b) Latvia,
   (c) Estonia,   (d) Azerbaijan,
   (e) Lithuania,   (f) Ukraine,
   (g) Belarus

2. **Define:**
   (a) détente,   (b) Brezhnev doctrine,
   (c) dissidents,   (d) perestroika,   (e) glasnost

3. **Identify:**
   (a) Strategic Defense Initiative (SDI),
   (b) Mikhail Gorbachev,   (c) Boris Yeltsin

4. **Recall:**
   (a) What was accomplished through the Helsinki Agreements?
   (b) What problems did the central planning system create in the former Soviet Union?
   (c) Why did Gorbachev need to be elected president to retain much of his power in 1990?
   (d) Why did Communist and military leaders try to seize power from Gorbachev in 1991?
   (e) What events caused some Russians to wish for a return to Communist leadership in the mid-1990s?

5. **Think Critically:** What benefits did both superpowers receive from the winding down of the Cold War?

## EASTERN EUROPE: FROM SOVIET SATELLITES TO SOVEREIGN STATES

As we have seen, Stalin's postwar order had set up Communist regimes throughout Eastern Europe. Few people believed that the new order could ever be undone. People in Eastern Europe, however, were never really happy with their Soviet-style regimes. After Gorbachev made it clear that the Soviet Union would not intervene militarily in their states, revolutions broke out throughout Eastern Europe in 1989. In Poland, Hungary, Czechoslovakia, Romania, Bulgaria, East Germany, and Albania, mass protests led to the overthrow of the Communist rulers. By looking at four of these states, we can see how the process worked.

## Poland

It was workers' protests that led to demands for change in Poland. In 1980, a worker named Lech Walesa (vaw-LEN-suh) organized a national trade union known as Solidarity. The rise of an independent labor movement soon became a threat to the government's control of power. Solidarity gained the support of the workers and the Roman Catholic Church, now under the leadership of Pope John Paul II, the first Polish pope. The union thus was able to win some concessions from the government. Even a period of military rule in the 1980s, when Walesa was arrested, could not stop the movement.

After new demonstrations in 1988, the Polish regime finally agreed to free parliamentary elections—the first free elections in Eastern Europe in forty years. A newly elected government ended forty-five years of Communist rule in Poland. In December 1990, Walesa was chosen as the new Polish president. Poland's new path, however, was not an easy one. Rapid free-market reforms led to severe unemployment and popular discontent. At the end of 1995, Aleksander Kwasniewski, a former Communist, defeated Walesa and became the new Polish president.

## Czechoslovakia

After Soviet troops had crushed the reform movement in Czechoslovakia in 1968 (see Chapter 12), hardline Czech Communists under Gustav Husák used a policy of massive repression to maintain their power. Only writers and other intellectuals provided any real opposition to the government. Even they had little success until the later 1980s. Mass demonstrations took place

throughout Czechoslovakia in 1988 and 1989. When the government tried to suppress them, even larger demonstrations appeared. By November 1989, crowds as large as 500,000 were forming in Prague. In December 1989, the Communist government collapsed. President Husák resigned and at the end of December was replaced by Vaclav Havel, a writer who played an important role in bringing down the Communist government. Havel proved to be an eloquent spokesperson for Czech democracy and a new order in Europe (see "You Are There: Vaclav Havel: The Call for a New Politics").

Within Czechoslovakia, the new government soon faced old problems. The two different national groups, Czechs and Slovaks, did not agree over the makeup of the new state. They were able, however, to agree to a peaceful division of the country. On January 1, 1993, Czechoslovakia split into the Czech Republic and Slovakia. Havel was elected the first president of the new Czech Republic.

## Romania

In 1965, the Communist leader Nicolae Ceausescu (NIK-oh-LIE chow-SHES-KOO) and his wife, Elena, set up a rigid and dictatorial regime in Romania. Ceausescu ruled Romania with an iron grip. He used a secret police—the Securitate—to crush all dissent. Nonetheless, opposition to his regime grew. Ceausescu's economic policies led to a sharp drop in living standards, including food shortages and the rationing of bread, flour, and sugar. His plan for rapid urbanization, especially a program that called for the bulldozing of entire villages, further angered the Romanian people.

One incident became the spark that ignited the flames of revolution. In December 1989, the Securitate murdered thousands of men, women, and children who were peacefully demonstrating in the city of Timosoara (TEE-mish-uh-WAWR-uh). News of the massacre soon led to mass demonstrations in the capital city of Bucharest (BYOO-kuh-REST). After the dictator was booed at a mass rally on December 21, the army refused to support any more repression. Ceausescu and his wife were captured on December 22 and executed on Christmas Day. A new government under Ion Iliescu was quickly formed. Questions remain, however, about the new government's commitment to democracy.

## The Reunification of Germany

After building the Berlin Wall separating West from East Berlin in 1961, East Germany developed the strongest economy among the Soviet Union's Eastern European satellites. Beginning in 1971, Erich Honecker became head of the Communist Party and used the *Stasi*, the secret police, to rule with an iron fist for the next eighteen years.

In 1988, however, popular unrest, fueled by the economic slump of the 1980s and Honecker's harsh regime, led many East Germans to flee their country. Mass demonstrations against the regime broke out in the summer and fall of 1989. By the beginning of November 1989, the Communist government was collapsing. It gave in to popular pressure on November 9, when it opened the entire border with the West. Hundreds of thousands of Germans swarmed across the border, mostly to visit and return. The Berlin Wall, long the symbol of the Cold War, became the sight of massive celebrations as thousands of people used sledgehammers to tear down the wall.

By December, new political parties had emerged. On March 18, 1990, in East Germany's first free elections ever, the Christian Democrats won almost 50 percent of the vote. The Christian Democrats supported political union with West Germany, which took place on October 3, 1990. What had seemed almost impossible at the beginning of 1989 had become a reality by the end of 1990—the country of East Germany had ceased to exist.

## The Disintegration of Yugoslavia

Although Yugoslavia had a Communist government, it had never been a Soviet satellite state. It, too, however, was affected by the revolutionary events in Eastern Europe. After World War II, its dictatorial leader, Marshall Joseph (Broz) Tito, had worked to keep together the six republics and two provinces that made up Yugoslavia. After Tito's death in 1980, Tito's responsibilities passed to a collective state presidency

▲ *This young Romanian rebel waves the national flag, but one with the Communist emblem cut from the center. What does her defiant pose suggest she is doing?*

under the leadership of the Communist Party of Yugoslavia. At the end of the 1980s, Yugoslavia was caught up in the reform movements sweeping through Eastern Europe. New parties quickly emerged, and the authority of the Communist Party collapsed.

The Yugoslav political scene was complex. In 1990, the Yugoslav republics of Slovenia, Croatia (kroe-AY-shee-uh), Bosnia-Herzegovina, and Macedonia began to lobby for their independence. Slobodan Milosevic, who became leader of the Yugoslav republic of Serbia in 1987, rejected these efforts. He believed that these republics could only be independent if new borders were drawn up to take care of the Serb minorities in

# YOU ARE THERE

## Vaclav Havel—The Call for a New Politics

*In their attempts to deal with the world's problems, some European leaders have pointed to the need for a new perspective if people are to live in a sane world. This excerpt is taken from a speech that Vaclav Havel gave to the U.S. Congress on February 21, 1990, two months after he had become president of Czechoslovakia.*

**Vaclav Havel, Speech to the U.S. Congress**

For this reason, the salvation of this human world lies nowhere else than in the human heart, in the human power to reflect, in human meekness and in human responsibility.

Without a global revolution in the sphere of human consciousness, nothing will change for the better in the sphere of our being as humans, and

▶ *Vaclav Havel was warmly welcomed when he addressed a joint meeting of the United States Congress in 1990. Standing behind him on the left is Vice President Dan Quayle and on the right is Speaker of the House Thomas Foley. What is the significance of Havel's victory gesture?*

the republics who wanted to live within the boundaries of a Greater Serbian state. Serbs made up 11.6 percent of Croatia's population and 32 percent of Bosnia-Herzegovina's population in 1981.

After negotiations failed, Slovenia and Croatia declared their independence in June 1991. Milosevic's government sent the Yugoslavian army, which it controlled, into Slovenia, but without much success. In September 1991 the Yugoslavian army began a full assault against Croatia. Increasingly, the Yugoslavian army was the Serbian army and was aided by Serbian minorities in Croatia. Before a cease-fire was arranged,

the Serbian forces had captured one-third of Croatia's territory in brutal fighting.

The recognition of Slovenia, Croatia, and Bosnia-Herzegovina by many European countries and the United States early in 1992 did not stop the Serbs from turning their guns on Bosnia-Herzegovina. By mid-1993, Serbian forces had acquired 70 percent of Bosnian territory. The Serbian policy of ethnic cleansing—killing or forcibly removing Bosnian Muslims from their lands—revived memories of Nazi atrocities in World War II. Nevertheless, despite worldwide outrage, European governments failed to take a decisive

## YOU ARE THERE

# Vaclav Havel—The Call for a New Politics, continued

the catastrophe toward which this world is headed—be it ecological, social, demographic or a general breakdown of civilization—will be unavoidable. . . .

We are still a long way from that "family of man." In fact, we seem to be receding from the ideal rather than growing closer to it. Interests of all kinds—personal, selfish, state, nation, group, and if you like, company interests—still considerably outweigh genuinely common and global interests. We are still under the sway of the destructive and vain belief that man is the pinnacle of creation and not just a part of it and that therefore everything is permitted. . . .

In other words, we still don't know how to put morality ahead of politics, science and economics. We are still incapable of understanding that the only genuine backbone of all our actions, if they are to be moral, is responsibility.

Responsibility to something higher than my family, my country, my company, my success—responsibility to the order of being where all our actions are indelibly recorded and where and only where they will be properly judged.

The interpreter or mediator between us and this higher authority is what is traditionally referred to as human conscience.

1. What is the difference between the way Vaclav Havel views politics and the way that most politicians have traditionally viewed politics?

2. Political ideas are of little value unless they can be implemented. What is your opinion—do you think that Havel's ideas could be turned into political reality? Why or why not?

3. If implemented, do you think that Havel's ideas would be successful?

4. Are you aware of a politician in the United States who exemplifies Havel's ideals for politicians? If so, describe examples of the work done by that politician that make you think he or she is practicing this type of politics.

---

and forceful stand against these Serbian activities. By 1995, 250,000 Bosnians (mostly civilians) had been killed. Two million others were left homeless, often having been driven from their homes by ethnic cleansing.

The Bosnian Serbs seemed well in control of Bosnia until 1995, when a sudden turn of events occurred. New offensives by mostly Muslim Bosnian government army forces and by the Croatian army regained considerable territory that had been lost to Serbian forces. Air strikes by NATO bombers, strongly advocated by President Bill Clinton, were launched in retaliation for Serb attacks on civilians. These attacks weakened the

Serb military positions. All sides were now encouraged by the United States to end the war and met in Dayton, Ohio, in November 1995 for negotiations.

A formal peace treaty, based on the Dayton Accords, was signed in Paris on December 14. The agreement split Bosnia into a loose union of a Serb republic (with 49 percent of the land) and a Muslim-Croat federation (with 51 percent of the land). NATO agreed to send a force of sixty thousand troops, which would monitor the frontier between the new political entities. It remained to be seen whether the agreement would bring a lasting peace to war-torn Bosnia.

▶ *The civilian casualties in the Bosnian war were staggering. Here two brothers in Sarajevo weep following the funeral of their third brother. What is the current political situation in Bosnia-Herzegovina?*

## Eastern Europe after the Fall of Communism

The fall of Communist governments in Eastern Europe during the revolutions of 1989 brought a wave of euphoria to Europe. In 1989 and 1990, new governments throughout Eastern Europe worked to introduce the democratic and market systems that they believed would give their scarred lands a new life. It was neither a simple nor an easy process, however, and the mood of euphoria had largely faded by 1992.

Most Eastern European countries had little or no experience with democratic systems. Then, too, ethnic divisions that had troubled these areas before World War II and had been forcibly submerged under authoritarian Communist rule again came to the forefront, making political unity almost impossible. Czechoslovakia resolved its differences peacefully. Yugoslavia, as we have seen, descended into the kind of brutal warfare that had not been seen in Europe since World War II. In the lands of the former Soviet Union, ethnic and nationalist problems threatened to tear some of the new states apart. The Chechens, for example, wanted

to secede from Russia and create their own independent republic. The Russians waged a brutal war against the Chechens to keep them part of Russia.

The rapid conversion of Eastern Europe to capitalist, or free-market, economies also proved painful. Many states tried to jump quickly from a system of government-run industries to private industries. The results were often disastrous and produced much suffering and uncertainty. Unemployment climbed to over 15 percent in the former East Germany and to 13 percent in Poland in 1992. Wages remained low while prices skyrocketed. Russia experienced a 2,000 percent inflation rate in 1992. At the same time, in many countries, former Communists were able to retain important positions of power or become the new owners of private property. Many people began to yearn for the "good old days," when Communist governments at least guaranteed people work of some kind. For both political and economic reasons, the new noncommunist states of Eastern Europe faced dangerous and uncertain futures. Nevertheless, by 1996, some of these states, such as Poland and the Czech Republic, were making a successful transition to both free markets and democracy.

**Map 13.1    The States of Eastern Europe and the Former Soviet Union**

## 🌸 SECTION REVIEW 🌸

1. **Locate:**
   (a) Bucharest,
   (b) Yugoslavia,
   (c) Croatia,
   (d) Bosnia,
   (e) Poland

2. **Identify:**
   (a) Solidarity,    (b) Vaclav Havel,
   (c) Nicolae Ceausescu,

(d) Erich Honecker,
(e) Slobodan Milosevic,
(f) Dayton Accords

3. **Recall:**
   (a) What is important about the way Czechoslovakia divided into the Czech Republic and Slovakia in 1993?
   (b) What caused the East German government to open its border with the West in 1989?
   (c) Why didn't European powers and the United States act sooner to end the war in Bosnia?

(*d*) What difficulties did Russia experience as it changed its economic system to one based on free enterprise?

4. **Think Critically:** Why has it been difficult for most formerly Communist nations to create democratic governments and free-market economies?

# TOWARD A NEW ORDER IN EUROPE AND NORTH AMERICA

Between 1945 and the early 1970s, Europe and North America experienced an age of prosperity. Economic growth and virtually full employment continued for so long that when economic problems arose in the 1970s, they came as a shock to many people.

## Western Europe: The Winds of Change

Between the early 1950s and late 1970s, Western Europe experienced virtually full employment. Social welfare programs—in the form of affordable health care; housing; family allowances for children; increases in sickness, accident, unemployment, and old-age benefits; and educational opportunities—helped create the modern welfare state. An economic downturn, however, occurred in the mid-1970s and early 1980s. Both inflation and unemployment rose dramatically. No doubt, the dramatic increase in the price of oil that followed the Arab-Israeli conflict in 1973 (see Chapter 15) was a major cause for the downturn. The economies of the Western European states recovered in the course of the 1980s, although problems remained. Unemployment was still high. France had a 10.6 percent unemployment rate in 1993; it reached 11.7 percent by the end of 1995. Despite their economic woes, however, the Western European states seemed quite capable of standing up to economic competition from the United States and Japan.

The Western European nations also moved toward a greater union of their economies after 1970. The European Economic Community expanded in 1973 when Great Britain, Ireland, and Denmark gained membership in what its members now began to call the European Community (EC). By 1986, three additional members—Spain, Portugal, and Greece—had been added.

The European Community was chiefly an economic union, not a political one. By 1992, the EC was comprised of 344 million people and made up the world's largest single trading bloc. It handled almost one-fourth of the world's commerce. In the 1980s and 1990s, the EC moved toward even greater economic integration. The Treaty on European Union (also called the Maastricht [MOSS-TRIKT] Treaty, after the city in the Netherlands where the agreement was reached) was an attempt to create a true economic and monetary union of all EC members. The treaty did not go into effect until all members agreed. Finally, on January 1, 1994, the European Community became the European Union. One of its first goals was to introduce a common currency, called the *euro*, by 2002.

Western Europe became used to political democracy. Even Spain and Portugal, which had kept their prewar dictatorial regimes until the mid-1970s, established democratic systems in the late 1970s. Moderate political parties, especially the Christian Democrats in Italy and Germany, played a particularly important role in achieving Europe's economic recovery. Overall, moderate Socialist parties, such as the Labour Party in Britain and the Social Democrats in West Germany, also continued to share power. Western European Communist parties declined drastically, especially after the collapse of communism in the Soviet Union and Eastern Europe.

### Uncertainties in France

The worsening of France's economic situation in the 1970s brought a shift to the left politically. By 1981, the Socialists had become the chief party in the National Assembly. The Socialist leader, François Mitterand (MEE-ter-AW[n]), was elected president. His first concern was with France's economic difficulties. In 1982, Mitterand froze prices and wages in the hope

**Map 13.2    The New Europe**

of reducing the huge budget deficit and high inflation. Mitterand also passed a number of measures to aid workers: an increased minimum wage, a mandatory fifth week of paid vacation for salaried workers, a thirty-nine-hour workweek, and higher taxes for the rich. The victory of the Socialists had convinced them that they could enact some of their more radical reforms. Consequently, the government nationalized major banks, the steel industry, the space and electronics industries, and important insurance firms.

The Socialist policies, however, largely failed to work. Within three years, a decline in support for the Socialists caused the Mitterand government to return some of the economy to private enterprise. Some economic improvements in the late 1980s enabled Mitterand to win a second seven-year term in the 1988 presidential election. Nevertheless, France's economic decline continued. In 1993, French unemployment stood at 10.6 percent. In the elections in March of that year, the Socialists won only 28 percent of the vote while a coalition of conservative parties gained 80 percent of the seats in the National Assembly. The move to the right in France was strengthened when the conservative mayor of Paris, Jacques Chirac, was elected president in May 1995.

### From West Germany to Germany

In 1969, the Social Democrats replaced the Christian Democrats as the leading party in West Germany. The first Social Democratic chancellor in West Germany was Willy Brandt (BRAWNT). He was especially successful with his "opening toward the east" (an attempt to work more closely with East Germany), for which he received the Nobel Peace Prize in 1972. On March 19, 1971, Brandt met with Walter Ulbricht (ul-BRIKT), the East German leader, and worked out the details of a Basic Treaty that was signed in 1972. This agreement called for "good neighborly" relations. As a result, it led to greater cultural, personal, and economic contacts between West and East Germany. Despite this success, Brandt was forced to resign in 1974 after the discovery of an East German spy among his advisors.

Brandt's successor, Helmut Schmidt, concentrated chiefly on the economic problems brought about by high oil prices between 1973 and 1975. Schmidt was successful in eliminating a deficit of ten billion marks in three years. In 1982, the Christian Democrats, under the leadership of Helmut Kohl (KOLE), came back into power.

Kohl was a clever politician who benefited greatly from an economic boom in the mid-1980s. Gradually, however, discontent with the Christian Democrats increased. Then the 1989 revolution in East Germany unexpectedly led to the reunification of the two Germanies, leaving the new Germany, with its seventy-nine million people, the leading power in Europe. Reunification, which was achieved during Kohl's administration, brought rich political benefits as the Christian Democrats remained in power.

However, the joy over reunification soon dissipated as new problems arose. All too soon, it dawned on Germans that the rebuilding of eastern Germany would take far more money than was originally thought. Kohl's government was soon forced to face the politi-cally undesirable task of raising taxes. Moreover, the virtual collapse of the economy in eastern Germany led to extremely high levels of unemployment and severe discontent.

One of the responses was an attack on foreigners. For years, illegal immigrants and foreigners seeking a place of refuge had found haven in Germany because of its very liberal immigration laws. In 1992, over 440,000 immigrants came to Germany seeking refuge; 123,000 came from former Yugoslavia alone. Attacks against foreigners by right-wing extremists—especially young neo-Nazis who believed in Hitler's idea of a pure Aryan race—became an all-too-frequent part of German life.

### Great Britain: Thatcher and Thatcherism

Between 1964 and 1979, the Conservative and Labour Parties alternated in power in Great Britain. Both parties had to face some very difficult problems.

One problem was the intense fighting between Catholics and Protestants in Northern Ireland. When the British government established direct rule over Northern Ireland in 1972, the Irish Republican Army (IRA) staged a series of dramatic terrorist acts. The problems in Northern Ireland have not yet been solved.

Another problem that neither party was able to deal with successfully was Britain's ailing economy. Failure to modernize made British industry less and less competitive. Moreover, Britain was hampered by frequent labor strikes, many of them caused by conflicts between rival labor unions.

In 1979, after Britain's economic problems had appeared to worsen during five years under a Labour government, the Conservatives returned to power under Margaret Thatcher. She became the first female prime minister in British history. Thatcher pledged to lower taxes, reduce government bureaucracy, limit social welfare, restrict union power, and end inflation.

The "Iron Lady," as Thatcher was called, did break the power of the labor unions. Although she did not eliminate the basic parts of the social welfare system, she did control inflation. **Thatcherism,** as her economic policy was termed, improved the British economic situation, but at a price. The south of England, for example, prospered, but old industrial areas elsewhere declined and were beset by high unemployment, poverty, and even violence.

In the area of foreign policy, Thatcher, like President Ronald Reagan, her counterpart in the United States, took a hard-line approach against communism. She oversaw a large military buildup aimed at restoring Britain as a world police force. In 1982, Great Britain went to war. Argentina had tried to take control of the Falkland Islands, one of Britain's few remaining colonial outposts, three hundred miles off Argentina's coast. The British victory in the Falklands War brought Thatcher much popular patriotic support.

Thatcher dominated British politics in the 1980s. The Labour Party, beset by divisions between moderate and radical wings, offered little real opposition. Only in 1990 did Labour's fortunes seem to revive when Thatcher's government tried to replace local property taxes with a flat-rate tax payable by every adult. Many argued that this was nothing more than a poll tax (a tax of a fixed amount per person) that would enable the rich to pay the same rate as the poor. In 1990, after antitax riots broke out, Thatcher's once remarkable popularity fell to an all-time low. At the end of November, a revolt within her own party caused Thatcher to resign as prime minister. She was replaced by John Major, whose Conservative Party continued to hold a narrow majority. His government, however, failed to capture the imagination of most Britons. In new elections on May 1, 1997, the Labour Party won a landslide victory.

## The United States: The American Domestic Scene (1970 to Present)

With the election of Richard Nixon as president in 1968, American politics made a shift to the right. Nixon ended American involvement in Vietnam by gradually withdrawing U.S. troops. Politically, he followed a "southern strategy." In other words, Nixon

*◄ Margaret Thatcher, Great Britain's first woman prime minister, dominated British politics in the 1980s. She was the first British prime minister in the twentieth century to ever win three consecutive elections. This photo was taken in May 1990, six months before she was forced to resign.*

carefully calculated that "law and order" issues and a slowdown in racial desegregation would appeal to southern whites. The South, which had once been a stronghold for the Democrats, began to form a new allegiance to the Republican Party.

The Republican strategy, however, also gained support among white Democrats in northern cities. Court-mandated busing to achieve racial integration in these cities had led to a white backlash against blacks. Nixon was less conservative on other social issues. Moreover, in a break with his own strong anticommunist past, he visited Communist China in 1972 and

*▲ Zhou Enlai, on the right, and President Richard Nixon relax for a moment over tea during their historic 1972 meeting in Beijing. Why is this trip considered to be a major foreign policy success for President Nixon?*

opened the door to the eventual diplomatic recognition of that state (see Chapter 16).

As president, Nixon was afraid of conspiracies. He began to use illegal methods to gain political intelligence on his opponents. One of the president's advisors said that the idea was to "use the available Federal machinery to screw our political enemies." "Anyone who opposes us, we'll destroy," said another aide. Nixon's zeal led to the Watergate scandal—the attempted bugging of the Democratic National Headquarters, located in the Watergate Hotel in Washington, D.C. Nixon repeatedly lied to the American public about his involvement in the affair. Secret tapes of his own conversations in the White House, however, revealed the truth. On August 9, 1974, Nixon resigned the presidency rather than face trial and possible impeachment by the Senate.

After Watergate, American domestic politics focused on economic issues. Vice President Gerald Ford became president when Nixon resigned, only to lose in the 1976 election to the former governor of Georgia, Jimmy Carter. Carter campaigned as an outsider against the Washington establishment. Both Ford and Carter faced severe economic problems. The period from 1973 to the mid-1980s was one of economic stagnation, which came to be known as **stagflation**—a combination of high inflation and high unemployment. In 1984, the median family income was 6 percent below that of 1973.

In part, the economic downturn stemmed from a dramatic change in oil prices. Oil was considered an inexpensive and abundant source of energy in the 1950s, and Americans had grown dependent on its importation from the Middle East. By the late 1970s, 50 percent of the oil used in the United States came from the Middle East. However, an oil embargo and price increases by the Organization of Petroleum Exporting Countries (OPEC) as a result of the Arab-Israeli War in 1973 quadrupled oil prices. Additional price hikes caused oil prices to increase twentyfold by the end of the 1970s. The Carter administration produced a plan for reducing oil consumption at home while spurring domestic production. Neither Congress nor the American people, however, could be persuaded to follow what they considered to be drastic measures.

By 1980, the Carter administration was faced with two devastating problems. First, high rates of inflation and a noticeable decline in average weekly earnings were causing a drop in American living standards. At the same time, a crisis abroad erupted when fifty-three Americans were held hostage by the Iranian government of the Ayatollah Khomeini (EYE-uh-TOLE-uh koe-MAY-nee) (see Chapter 15). Carter had little control over the situation, but his inability to gain the release of the American hostages led to perceptions at home that he was a weak president. His overwhelming loss to Ronald Reagan in the election of 1980 brought forward the chief exponent of right-wing Republican policies and a new political order.

The Reagan Revolution, as it has been called, consisted of a number of new directions. Reversing decades of changes, Reagan cut back on the welfare state by decreasing spending on food stamps, school lunch programs, and job programs. At the same time, his administration oversaw the largest peacetime military build-up in U.S. history. Total federal spending rose from $631 billion in 1981 to over a trillion dollars by 1986. Instead of raising taxes to pay for the new expenditures, which far outweighed the budget cuts in social areas, Reagan convinced Congress to support **supply-side economics.** Massive tax cuts would supposedly stimulate rapid economic growth and produce new revenues. Much of the tax cut went to the wealthy. Between 1980 and 1986, the income of the lower 40 percent of the workforce fell 9 percent, while the income of the highest 20 percent rose by 5 percent.

Reagan's policies seemed to work in the short run. The United States experienced an economic upturn that lasted until the end of the 1980s. The spending policies of the Reagan administration, however, also produced record government deficits, which loomed as an obstacle to long-term growth. In the 1970s, the total deficit was $420 billion. Between 1981 and 1987, Reagan budget deficits were three times that amount.

The inability of George Bush, Reagan's vice president and his elected successor, to deal with the deficit problem, as well as an economic downturn, enabled a Democrat, Bill Clinton, to be elected president in 1992. The new president was a southern Democrat who claimed to be a new Democrat—one who favored a number of the

Republican policies of the 1980s. This was a clear indication that the rightward drift in American politics was by no means ended by this Democratic victory. In fact, Clinton's reelection in 1996 was partially due to his adoption of Republican ideas and policies.

## Canada

In Canada in 1963, during a major economic recession, the Liberals were returned to power. The most prominent Liberal government was that of Pierre Trudeau (TROO-doe), who came to power in 1968. Although French in background, Trudeau was dedicated to Canada's federal union. In 1968, his government passed the Official Languages Act, which allowed both English and French to be used in the federal civil service. The Trudeau government also encouraged the growth of French culture and language in Canada.

Trudeau's government supported a vigorous program of industrialization. However, the problem of inflation, along with Trudeau's efforts to impose the will of the federal government on the powerful provincial governments, alienated voters and weakened his government. Economic recession in the early 1980s brought Brian Mulroney, leader of the Progressive Conservative Party, to power in 1984. Mulroney's government sought to return some of Canada's state-run corporations to private owners. It also made a free-trade agreement with the United States. The agreement, which was bitterly attacked by many Canadians as being too favorable to the United States, cost Mulroney's government much of its popularity. In 1993, the ruling Conservatives were drastically defeated. They received only two seats in the House of Commons.

Mulroney's government also was unable to settle the ongoing crisis over the French-speaking province of Quebec. In the late 1960s, the Parti Québécois (KAY-buh-KWAW), headed by René Lévesque, ran on a platform of Quebec's secession from the Canadian union. In 1970, the party won 24 percent of the popular vote in Quebec's provincial elections. To pursue their dream

◄ *Pierre Trudeau, photographed in June 1977, served twice as prime minister of Canada, first from 1968 to 1979, and again from 1980 until his resignation in 1984.*

of separation, some underground separatist groups used terrorist bombings and kidnapped two government officials. In 1976, the Parti Québécois won Quebec's provincial elections. Four years later, it called for a referendum that would enable the provincial government to gain Quebec's independence from the rest of Canada. In 1995, voters in Quebec narrowly rejected the plan. Debate over Quebec's status continues to divide Canada in the 1990s.

## 🌸 SECTION REVIEW 🌸

1. **Define:**
   (a) Thatcherism,
   (b) stagflation,
   (c) supply-side economics

2. **Identify:**
   (a) Maastricht Treaty,
   (b) the *euro*,
   (c) François Mitterand,
   (d) Irish Republican Army (IRA),
   (e) Organization of Petroleum Exporting Countries (OPEC),
   (f) René Lévesque

3. **Recall:**
   (a) What caused much of the joy of reunification to dissipate in Germany?
   (b) What was the apparent cause for attacks on foreign workers in Germany during the 1990s?
   (c) What policy caused Margaret Thatcher's government to lose popularity in 1990?
   (d) Why did Richard Nixon's decision to open relations with Communist China represent a change from his traditional point of view?

**4. Think Critically:**

(*a*) Why is it possible for many nations in Europe to have high rates of unemployment without also having widespread social unrest?

(*b*) Why is it unlikely that the nations of Europe will completely join together into one political and economic unit in the near future?

# NEW DIRECTIONS AND NEW PROBLEMS IN WESTERN SOCIETY

With the political and economic changes since the 1960s have come dramatic social developments. New opportunities for women have emerged, and a women's liberation movement sought to bring new meaning to the principle of women's equality with men. New problems for Western society also arose with a growing awareness of environmental dangers, a reaction against foreign workers, and the growth of terrorism.

## A Changing Society: Women since the 1960s

After World War II, a trend toward earlier marriage continued. In Sweden, the average age of first marriage dropped from twenty-six in the 1940s to twenty-three in 1970. Birthrates declined in most nations as new contraceptive devices and abortion became widely available. It is estimated that mothers need to average 2.1 children to ensure a natural replacement of a country's population. In many European countries, the population has stopped growing. By 1992, among the twelve nations of the European Community, the average number of children per mother was 1.58.

Because of early marriages and smaller families, women since World War II have had more years when they were not raising children. This has contributed to changes in the character of women's employment in both Europe and the United States. The most impor-

tant development has been the increased number of married women in the workforce. At the beginning of the twentieth century, even working-class wives tended to stay at home if they could afford to do so. In the postwar period, this is no longer the case. In the United States, for example, in 1900 married women made up about 15 percent of the female labor force. By 1990, their number had increased to 70 percent.

The increased number of women in the workforce, however, has not changed some old patterns. Working-class women in particular still earn salaries lower than those of men for equal work. Women still tend to enter traditionally female jobs. As one female Swedish guidance counselor remarked in 1975, "Every girl now thinks in terms of a job. This is progress. They want children, but they don't pin their hopes on marriage. They don't intend to be housewives for some future husband. But there has been no change in their vocational choices."[1] A 1980 study of twenty-five European nations revealed that women still made up over 80 percent of the typists, nurses, tailors, and dressmakers in these countries. Many European and American women also still face the double burden of earning income on the one hand and raising a family and maintaining the household on the other. Such inequalities have led increasing numbers of women to rebel.

The participation of women in World Wars I and II helped them achieve one of the major aims of the nineteenth-century feminist movement—the right to vote. After World War I, many governments expressed their thanks to women for their war efforts by granting them the right to vote. Sweden, Great Britain, Germany, Poland, Hungary, Austria, and Czechoslovakia did so in 1918, followed by the United States in 1920. Women in France and Italy, however, did not obtain the right to vote until 1945.

After World War II, European women tended to fall back into the traditional roles expected of them, and little was heard of feminist concerns. By the late 1960s, however, women began to assert their rights again and to speak as feminists. Along with the student upheavals of the late 1960s came renewed interest in feminism, or the **women's liberation movement,** as it came to be called. Increasingly, women argued that political and legal equality had not brought true equality with

▲ The Second Sex *was written in 1949, but it was not until the late 1960s that women began a determined fight for equal rights. At this rally in Washington, D.C., for the equal rights amendment, some young women have climbed the statue of Admiral Farragut to better display their posters. How far do you believe women have come in their struggle for equality with men?*

men. These are the words of the British Women's Liberation Workshop in 1969:

*We are economically oppressed: in jobs we do full work for half pay, in the home we do unpaid work full time. We are commercially exploited by advertisement, television, and the press; legally we often have only the status of children. We are brought up to feel inadequate, educated to narrower horizons than men. This is our specific oppression as women. It is as women that we are, therefore, organizing.*[2]

Of great importance to the emergence of the postwar women's liberation movement was the work of

Simone de Beauvoir (si-MONE de bove-WAWR). Born into a Catholic middle-class family and educated at the Sorbonne in Paris, de Beauvoir supported herself as a teacher and later as a novelist and writer. She maintained a lifelong relationship (but not marriage) with Jean-Paul Sartre (SAWRTuh).

De Beauvoir believed that she lived a "liberated" life for a twentieth-century European woman. For all her freedom, however, she still came to believe that as a woman she faced limits that men did not. In 1949, she published her highly influential work *The Second Sex*. In it she argued that as a result of male-dominated societies, women had been defined by their differences from men and, as a result, received second-class status. De Beauvoir took an active role in the French women's movement of the 1970s. Her book was a major influence on both the American and European women's movements (see "You Are There: The Voice of the Women's Liberation Movement").

Feminists in the women's liberation movement came to believe that women themselves must change the basic conditions of their lives. They helped women make these changes in a variety of ways. First, in the 1960s and 1970s, they formed "consciousness-raising" groups to make people aware of women's issues. Women also gained a measure of control over their own bodies by seeking to make both contraception and abortion legal. In the 1960s and 1970s, hundreds of thousands of European women worked to repeal the laws that outlawed contraception and abortion. They met with much success. Even in Catholic countries, where the church remained strongly opposed to laws legalizing abortion, laws allowing contraception and abortion were passed in the 1970s and 1980s.

As more women became activists, they also became involved in new issues. In the 1980s and 1990s, female faculty members in universities focused on changing cultural attitudes through the new academic field of women's studies. Other women began to try to affect the political and natural environment by allying with the antinuclear and ecological movements. As one German writer who was concerned with environmental issues said, it is women "who must give birth to children, willingly or unwillingly, in this polluted world of ours."

## YOU ARE THERE

# The Voice of the Women's Liberation Movement

*Simone de Beauvoir was an important figure in the emergence of the postwar women's liberation movement. This excerpt is taken from her book* The Second Sex, *in which she argued that women have been forced into a position subordinate to men.*

### Simone de Beauvoir, *The Second Sex*

Now, woman has always been man's dependent, if not his slave; the two sexes have never shared the world in equality. And even today woman is heavily handicapped, though her situation is beginning to change. Almost nowhere is her legal status the same as man's, and frequently it is much to her disadvantage. Even when her rights are legally recognized in the abstract, long-standing custom prevents their full expression. In the economic sphere men and women can almost be said to make up two castes; other things being equal, the former hold the better jobs, get higher wages, and have more opportunity for success than their new competitors. In industry and politics men have a great many more positions and they monopolize the most important posts. In addition to all this, they enjoy a traditional prestige that the education of children tends in every way to support, for the present enshrines the past—and in the past all history has been made by men. At the present time, when women are beginning to take part in the affairs of the world, it is still a world that belongs to men—they have no doubt of it at all and women have scarcely any. To decline to be the Other, to refuse to be a party to a deal—this would be for women to renounce all the advantages conferred upon them by their alliance with the superior caste. Man-the-sovereign will provide woman-the-liege with material protection and will undertake the moral justification of her existence;

▲ *Simone de Beauvoir, who wrote both essays and novels, was an existentialist and an ardent feminist. She published* The Second Sex *in 1949. What do you think she would have said about the state of women's affairs at the time of her death in 1986?*

thus she can evade at once both economic risk and the metaphysical risk of a liberty in which ends and aims must be contrived without assistance.

1. What is Simone de Beauvoir's basic argument?

2. Do you agree with her argument? Why or why not?

## The Environment and the Green Movements

Beginning in the 1970s, **environmentalism** (a movement to control the pollution of the Earth) became an important issue. By that time, serious ecological problems had become all too apparent. Air pollution, produced by nitrogen oxide and sulfur dioxide emissions from road vehicles, power plants, and industrial factories, was causing respiratory illnesses and having corrosive effects on buildings and monuments. Many rivers, lakes, and seas had become so polluted that they posed serious health risks. Dying forests and disappearing wildlife alarmed more and more people. The opening of Eastern Europe after the revolutions of 1989 brought to the world's attention the incredible environmental destruction of that region as a result of uncontrolled industrial pollution. In the Bohemian basin in Czechoslovakia, for example, the burning of low-quality brown coals in power stations and industries created a brown chemical haze that destroyed forests and led to high infant mortality rates, ill and malformed children, and high cancer rates.

Environmental concerns forced the major political parties in Europe to favor new regulations for the protection of the environment. In 1986, Europeans became even more aware of environmental hazards when a nuclear power reactor exploded at Chernobyl (chur-NOE-buhl), in the Soviet Union. A radioactive cloud spread over northern Ukraine and across Europe. Hundreds of thousands of people were evacuated from the area, but it was too late to avoid their contamination. Authorities believe that thousands of people will suffer serious or deadly health problems from the Chernobyl disaster. Tragic birth defects are already evident among livestock. Horses, for example, have been born with eight deformed legs.

Growing awareness of the environment also gave rise to Green movements and Green parties. These emerged throughout Europe in the 1970s. The origins of these movements were by no means the same. Some came from the antinuclear movement. Others arose out of such causes as women's liberation and concerns for foreign workers. Most started at the local level and then gradually expanded to include activities at the

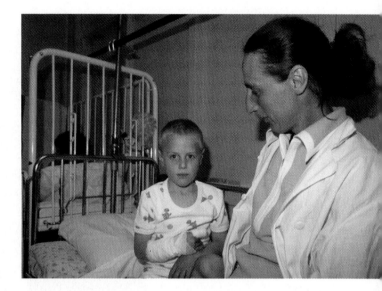

▲ *This child was being treated at a hospital in Kiev in 1992 for bone disease that resulted from the Chernobyl disaster. Five years after the explosion at the power plant, children were still being born with bone diseases and tumors. What precautions have been taken at U.S. nuclear power plants to prevent a similar disaster?*

national level, where they became organized as political parties. Most visible was the Green Party in Germany. It was officially organized in 1979, and by 1987 it had elected forty-two delegates to the West German parliament. Green parties also competed successfully in Sweden, Austria, and Switzerland.

The Green movements and parties have played an important role in making people aware of environmental problems, but they have by no means replaced the traditional political parties. For one thing, the coalitions that make up the Greens find it difficult to agree on all issues and tend to divide into factions. Then, too, traditional political parties have taken over the environmental issues of the Greens.  By the early 1990s, more and more European governments were beginning to sponsor projects to safeguard the environment and to clean up the worst sources of pollution.

## Guest Workers and Immigrants

As Western European countries made their economic recoveries in the 1950s and 1960s, a severe shortage of

▶ *Riot police in France had to force their way through crowds to reach three hundred illegal African immigrants who had occupied a church for two months, protesting their deportation. What do you think public reaction in the United States would be to such a scene?*

workers led them to import foreign workers. Scores of Turks and eastern and southern Europeans went to Germany. North Africans went to France, and people from the Caribbean, India, and Pakistan went to Great Britain. Overall, there were probably fifteen million guest workers in Europe in the 1980s. They constituted 17 percent of the labor force in Switzerland and 10 percent in West Germany.

Although these workers brought economic benefits to their host countries, socially and politically their presence created problems. Many foreign workers complained that they received lower wages. Moreover, their large numbers in certain cities, and even in certain sections of those cities, often created tensions with the local native populations. Foreign workers, many of them nonwhites, made up almost one-fifth of the population in the West German cities of Frankfurt, Munich, and Stuttgart. In the 1970s, as an economic downturn created rising unemployment, many guest workers were unwilling to leave when European countries tried to send the workers home.

In the 1980s, the problem of foreign workers was made worse by an influx of other refugees. This was especially true in West Germany, which allowed people to seek refuge for political persecution. During the 1970s and 1980s, West Germany absorbed over a million refugees from Eastern Europe and East Germany. In 1986 alone, 200,000 political refugees from Pakistan, Bangladesh, and Sri Lanka entered the country.

This great influx of foreigners to Western Europe, many of them nonwhite, strained the patience of many native residents who opposed making their countries ethnically diverse. Especially in a time of growing unemployment, antiforeign sentiment increased and was encouraged by new right-wing political parties that catered to people's complaints. Thus, the National Front in France, which campaigned with the slogan "France for the French," won 10 percent of the vote in the 1986 elections. Even more frightening, however, have been the organized campaigns of violence—especially against African and Asian immigrants—by radical right-wing groups.

## The Growth of Terrorism

Acts of terror by those opposed to governments became a regular aspect of modern Western society.

During the late 1970s and early 1980s in particular, concern about terrorism was widespread in the United States and many European countries. Small bands of terrorists used the killing of civilians (especially by bombing), the taking of hostages, and the hijacking of airplanes to draw attention to their demands or to achieve their political goals. Terrorist acts gained much media attention. When Palestinian terrorists (known as the Black September) kidnapped and killed eleven Israeli (iz-RAY-lee) athletes at the Munich Olympic games in 1972, hundreds of millions of people watched the drama unfold on television. Indeed, some observers believe that media attention has caused some terrorist groups to become even more active.

Why do terrorists commit these acts of violence? Both left- and right-wing terrorist groups flourished in the late 1970s and early 1980s. The major left-wing groups were the Baader-Meinhof (Bayder-MINE-hof) gang (also known as the Red Army Faction) in West Germany and the Red Brigades in Italy. They consisted chiefly of wealthy middle-class young people who denounced capitalism and supported acts of revolutionary terrorism in order to bring down the system. The Red Army killed prominent industrial and financial leaders in West Germany. The Red Brigades were experts in "kneecapping," or crippling their victims by shooting them in the knees. Right-wing terrorist groups, such as the New Order in Italy and the Charles Martel Club in France, used bombings to create disorder and try to bring about authoritarian regimes. These groups received little or no public support, and authorities were able to crush them fairly quickly.

Terrorist acts also came from militant nationalists who wished to create separatist states. These terrorists received much support from local populations who favored their causes. With this support, these terrorist groups could maintain their activities over a long period of time. Most prominent is the Irish Republican Army (IRA), whose goal is to unite Northern Ireland with the Irish Republic. It has resorted to vicious attacks against the ruling government and innocent civilians in Northern Ireland. Over a period of twenty years, IRA terrorists were responsible for the deaths of two thousand people in Northern Ireland.

International terrorism has remained commonplace

## CONNECTIONS
### AROUND THE WORLD

**Global Terrorism**   Terrorist acts have become a regular feature of life in the second half of the twentieth century. A growing number of groups have used terrorism as a means to achieve their political goals. Such groups exist around the world: urban guerrilla groups in Latin America; militants dedicated to the liberation of Palestine; Islamic fundamentalists fighting against Western influence in the Middle East; and separatists seeking independent states, such as the Basques in Spain, the Tamils in Sri Lanka, the Québecois in Canada, and the Sikhs in India.

International terrorists, however, did not limit their targets to their own countries. On May 30, 1972, three members of the neo-Marxist Japanese Red Army, who had been hired by the Popular Front for the Liberation of Palestine, opened fire at Tel Aviv's Lod Airport in Israel, killing twenty-four people, chiefly Christian pilgrims from Puerto Rico. The goal of the terrorists was to hurt Israel by discouraging people from visiting there.

International terrorists have been well aware that they can maximize publicity for their cause by appearing on televised newscasts. By killing eleven Israeli athletes at the Munich Olympic Games in 1972, the Palestinian Black September terrorist group gained a television audience of more than 500 million people. In 1975, rebels from the South Moluccas hijacked a Dutch train in order to publicize their demands for independence from Indonesia.

in the 1980s and 1990s. Angered over the loss of their territory to Israel by 1967, some militant Palestinians responded with a policy of terrorist attacks against Israel's supporters. Palestinian terrorists operated throughout European countries, attacking both Europeans and American tourists. In 1983, a Lebanese terrorist blew up U.S. military barracks in Lebanon, killing 241 U.S. Marines and sailors.

▶ *In July 1995, even the subways in Paris became targets for terrorist activities. A bomb exploded during rush hour, injuring fifty people. What incidents of random terrorism have occurred in the United States during the last decade?*

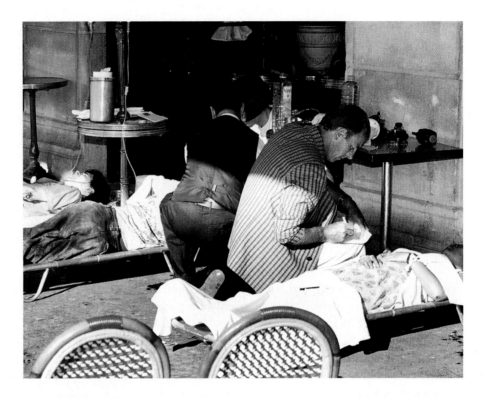

State-sponsored terrorism was often an important part of international terrorism. Militant governments, especially in Iran, Libya, and Syria, aided terrorist organizations that made attacks on Europeans and Americans. On December 21, 1988, Pan American flight 103 from Frankfurt to New York exploded over Lockerbie (LOCK-ur-bee), Scotland, killing all 259 passengers and crew members. A massive investigation finally revealed that the bomb responsible for the explosion had been planted by two Libyan terrorists. Both were connected to terrorist groups based in Iran and Syria.

Governments fought back by creating special antiterrorist units that became effective in responding to terrorist acts. The German special antiterrorist unit, known as GSG, for example, in 1977 rescued ninety-one hostages from a Lufthansa airplane that had been hijacked to Mogadishu, in Somalia. In a daring raid at Entebbe (en-TEB-uh), Uganda, in 1976, a force of Israeli paratroopers freed a group of Israeli citizens who were being held hostage by a group of Palestinian terrorists. **Counterterrorism,** or a calculated policy of direct retaliation against terrorists, also made states

that sponsored terrorism more cautious. In 1986, the Reagan administration responded to the terrorist bombing of a West German disco club that was popular with American soldiers with an air attack on Libya. Libya had long been suspected as being a major sponsor of terrorist organizations.

## ❀ SECTION REVIEW ❀

1. **Locate:**
   (a) Iran,
   (b) Libya

2. **Define:**
   (a) women's liberation movement,
   (b) environmentalism,
   (c) counterterrorism

3. **Identify:**
   (a) Simone de Beauvoir,
   (b) Chernobyl,

(c) Green movements,

(d) Baader-Meinhof gang,

(e) Red Brigades,

(f) state-sponsored terrorism

4. **Recall:**

(a) What inequalities led increasing numbers of women to demand more equal treatment in recent years?

(b) Why did the fall of communism lead to a greater realization of the need for protection of the environment?

(c) Why did many foreigners migrate to Western European nations in the 1950s and 1960s?

(d) How have some Europeans reacted to the large number of foreign workers living in their countries?

(e) Why do terrorists often act to gain media attention?

5. **Think Critically:** Why may the decline in birth-rates cause problems in the future as older people live longer lives?

# THE WORLD OF WESTERN CULTURE

Intellectually and culturally, the Western world during the last half of the twentieth century has been marked by much diversity. Many trends still represent a continuation of prewar modern developments. New directions in the last two decades, however, have led some to speak of a postmodern cultural world.

## Recent Trends in Art and Literature

For the most part, the United States has dominated the art world in the second half of this century. American art, often vibrantly colored and filled with activity, reflected the energy of the postwar United States. After 1945, New York City became the artistic center of the Western world. The Guggenheim (GOO-gun-HIME) Museum, the Museum of Modern Art, and the Whitney Museum of American Art, together with New York City's numerous art galleries, promoted modern art. They helped determine artistic taste not only in New York City and the United States but also throughout much of the world (see "Our Artistic Heritage: Modern and Postmodern Art in the Western World").

The most significant trend in postwar literature was the Theater of the Absurd. This new form of drama began in France in the 1950s. Its most famous example is *Waiting for Godot* (1952), a play written by Samuel Beckett, an Irish author who lived in France. In *Waiting for Godot*, it is at once apparent that the action on the stage is not realistic. Two men wait for the appearance of someone, with whom they may or may not have an appointment. No background information on the two men is provided. During the course of the play, nothing seems to be happening. Unlike in traditional theater, suspense is maintained not by having the audience wonder, "What is going to happen next?" but by having it wonder, "What is happening now?"

The Theater of the Absurd reflected its time. After the experience of World War II, many people felt that the world was absurd or even meaningless. This belief gave rise to a new philosophy, called **existentialism.** This philosophy was chiefly the work of two French writers, Albert Camus (KA-M[oo]UH) and Jean-Paul Sartre. The beginning point of the existentialism of Sartre and Camus was the absence of God in the universe. The absence of God meant that humans had no fixed destiny. They were utterly alone in the universe, with no future and no hope. As Camus expressed it:

> *A world that can be explained even with bad reasons is a familiar world. But, on the other hand, in a universe suddenly divested of illusions and lights, man feels an alien, a stranger. His exile is without remedy since he is deprived of the memory of a lost home or the hope of a promised land. This divorce between man and his life, the actor and his setting, is properly the feeling of absurdity.*[3]

According to Camus, then, the world is absurd and without meaning. Humans, too, are without meaning

# OUR ARTISTIC HERITAGE

## Modern and Postmodern Art in the Western World

◄ *Jackson Pollock found it easier to work with his huge canvases spread out on the ground. Here a photographer catches Jackson Pollock at work in his studio in Long Island, New York. Do you believe Pollock's paintings will be as famous two hundred years from now as those done by the impressionist painters or Picasso? Why or why not?*

World War II. The excitement of American artists with abstract expressionism is evident in the enormous canvases of Jackson Pollock (PAWL-uk). In such works as Pollock's *Lavender Mist* (1950), paint seems to explode, assaulting the viewer with emotion and movement. Pollock's swirling forms and seemingly chaotic patterns broke all the usual conventions of form and structure. His drip paintings, with their total abstraction, were extremely influential to other artists. The public, however, was at first hostile to his work.

The early 1960s saw the emergence of pop art, which took images of popular culture and transformed them into works of fine art. Andy Warhol (WAWR-HAWL) was the most famous of the pop artists. Warhol took as his subject matter images from commercial art, such as Campbell soup cans, and photographs of such celebrities as Marilyn Monroe. Derived from mass culture, these works were mass produced and deliberately "of the moment," expressing the fleeting whims of popular

Abstractionism, especially abstract expressionism, was the most popular form of modern art after

and purpose. Reduced to despair and depression, humans have but one ground of hope—themselves.

## The Revival of Religion

Existentialism was one response to the despair created by the apparent collapse of civilized values in the twen-

tieth century. The revival of religion has been another. Ever since the Enlightenment of the eighteenth century, Christianity, as well as religion in general, had been on the defensive. A number of religious thinkers and leaders, however, tried to bring new life to Christianity in the twentieth century. Despite the attempts of the Communist world to build an atheistic society

# OUR ARTISTIC HERITAGE

## Modern and Postmodern Art in the Western World, continued

▲ Andy Warhol's painting 100 Cans was done in 1962. It is a large painting, 72" × 52", and is photographic in nature. What does it reveal about American culture and civilization?

culture.

In the 1980s, styles emerged that some have referred to as postmodern. Postmodern artists believe in using tradition, whether that includes other styles of painting or raising traditional craftsmanship to the level of fine art. Weavers, potters, glassmakers, metalsmiths, and furniture makers gained respect as postmodern artists.

Another response to modernism has been a return to realism in the arts. Some extreme realists paint with such close attention to realistic detail that their paintings appear to be photographs. Their subjects are often ordinary people stuck in ordinary lives.

1. Describe the characteristics of modern and postmodern art.

2. How do modern art and postmodern art reflect the times in which they were created?

3. What is your reaction to the Warhol painting? Give specific reasons for your opinion of this work of art.

and the attempts of the West to build a secular society, religion continued to play an important role in the lives of many people.

One expression of this religious revival was the attempt by Christian thinkers, such as the Protestant Karl Barth (BART), to breathe new life into traditional Christian teachings. In his numerous writings,

Barth tried to show how the religious insights of the Reformation were still relevant for the modern world. To Barth, the imperfect nature of human beings meant that humans could know religious truth not through reason but only through the grace of God.

In the Catholic Church, attempts at religious renewal came from two popes—John XXIII and John

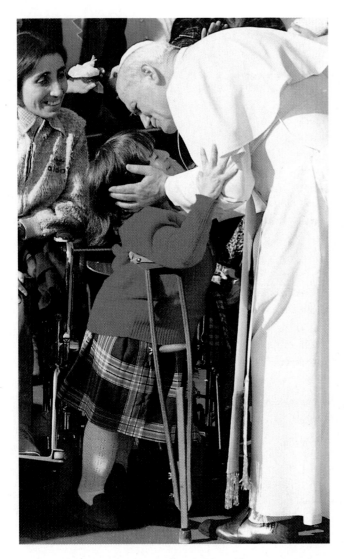

▲ *Pope John Paul II is a popular world traveler. In 1987, he visited Chile where he was greeted by this young girl at a Catholic church just outside Santiago.*

Paul II. Pope John XXIII reigned as pope for only a short time (1958 to 1963). Nevertheless, he sparked a dramatic revival of Catholicism when he summoned the twenty-first ecumenical council of the Catholic Church. Known as Vatican Council II, it liberalized a number of Catholic practices. For example, the mass could now be celebrated in the vernacular languages as well as Latin. New avenues of communication with other Christian faiths were also opened for the first time since the Reformation.

John Paul II, who had been the archbishop of Cracow in Poland before he became pope in 1978, was the first non-Italian pope since the sixteenth century. Pope John Paul's numerous travels around the world helped strengthen the Catholic Church throughout the non-Western world. Although he alienated a number of people by reasserting traditional Catholic teaching on such issues as birth control and a ban on women in the priesthood, John Paul II has been a powerful figure in reminding Catholics of the need to temper the pursuit of materialism with spiritual concerns.

## The New World of Science and Technology

Since the Scientific Revolution of the seventeenth century and the Industrial Revolution of the nineteenth century, science and technology have played increasingly important roles in world history. Many of the scientific and technological achievements since World War II have revolutionized people's lives. When American astronaut Neil Armstrong walked on the moon on July 20, 1969, for example, millions watched the event on their televisions in the privacy of their living rooms.

Before World War II, science and technology were largely separated. Pure science was the domain of university professors, who were far removed from the practical matters of technicians and engineers. During World War II, however, university scientists were recruited to work for their governments and to develop new weapons and practical instruments of war. British physicists played a crucial role in the development of an improved radar system in 1940 that helped to defeat the German air force in the Battle of Britain. German scientists converted coal to gasoline to keep the German war machine moving. They created self-propelled rockets, as well as jet airplanes, to keep Hitler's hopes alive for a miraculous turnaround in the war.

The computer, too, was a wartime creation (see "The Role of Science and Technology: The Computer"). An equally famous product of wartime scientific research was the atomic bomb, created by a team of American and European scientists under the guidance of the physicist J. Robert Oppenheimer. Obvi-

# THE ROLE OF SCIENCE AND TECHNOLOGY
# The Computer

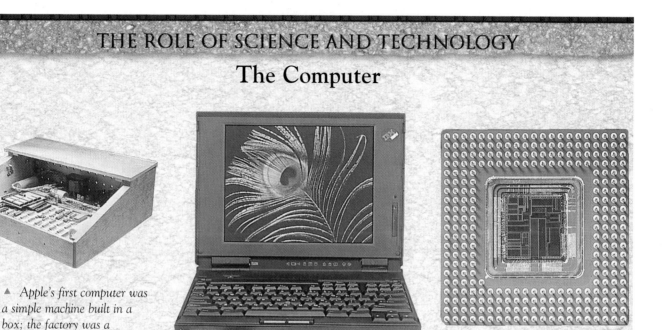

▲ Apple's first computer was a simple machine built in a box; the factory was a garage, not a high-tech, clean laboratory.

▲ The computer industry quickly developed into a highly competitive, billion-dollar business. The IBM ThinkPad, shown here, is just one of many laptop computers on the market. What do you believe will be the next major improvement in computer technology?

▲ Pentium microprocessor chips, like this one, have made it possible for computers to be both smaller and more powerful.

The computer may yet prove to be the most revolutionary of all the technological inventions of the twentieth century. The first computer was really a product of World War II. Designed by the British mathematician Alan Turing, the first electronic computer was used to crack enemy codes by doing mathematical calculations faster than any human could do them.

The first electronic computer with stored memory was made in the United States by the IBM Corporation in 1948. The IBM 1401, marketed in 1959, was the first computer used in large numbers in business and industry.

All of these early computers, which used thousands of vacuum tubes to function, were large and took up considerable room space. The development of the transistor and then the silicon chip produced a revolutionary new approach to computers. With the invention in 1971 of the microprocessor, a machine that combines the equivalent of thousands of transistors on a single, tiny silicon chip, the road was open for the development of the personal computer. It was both small and powerful.

The first personal computer was made by Steve Jobs (JOEBZ) and Steve Wozniak. They worked in a family garage to make and market their Apple computer. By the end of 1978, Apple had become one of the fastest-growing companies in the United States. Apple dominated the personal computer market until the IBM Corporation introduced its own personal computer in August 1981.

*(continued)*

## THE ROLE OF SCIENCE AND TECHNOLOGY

# The Computer, continued

The computer is a new kind of machine. Its chief function is to store and produce information, which is now considered a basic feature of our fast-paced civilization. By the 1990s, the personal computer had become a regular fixture in businesses, schools, and homes. The Internet—the world's largest computer network—provides millions of people around the world with quick access to immense quantities of information. By 2000, an estimated 500 million people will be using the Internet.

The computer not only makes a whole host of tasks much easier, such as writing this book, but it has also become an important tool in virtually every area of modern life. Indeed, other tools and machines now depend for their functioning on computers. Many of the minute-by-minute decisions used in flying an airplane, for example, are done by a computer.

1. What is the computer and what is its purpose?

2. What problems might the computer create for our civilization?

---

ously, most wartime devices were created for destructive purposes. Merely the mention of computers or jet airplanes, however, shows how wartime technology could easily be adapted for peacetime uses.

In sponsoring research, governments and the military during World War II created a new scientific model. Science had become very complex. Only large organizations with teams of scientists, huge laboratories, and complex equipment could undertake the large-scale projects that were being funded. Such facilities were so expensive, however, that they could be provided only by governments and large corporations.

Because of its postwar prosperity, the United States was able to take the lead in the development of the new science. Almost 75 percent of all scientific research funds in the United States came from the government in 1965. Unwilling to lag behind, especially in military development, the Soviet Union was forced to provide large outlays for scientific and technological research and development. In fact, the defense needs of the United States and the Soviet Union generated much of the postwar scientific research. One-fourth of the trained scientists and engineers after 1945 worked at creating new weapons systems. Universities found

their research agendas increasingly set by government funding for military-related projects.

There was no more stunning example of how the new scientific establishment operated than the space race of the 1960s. When the Soviet Union announced in 1957 that it had sent the first space satellite—*Sputnik I*—into orbit around the Earth, winning the first stage of the space race, Americans were shocked. President John F. Kennedy led the United States in a gigantic project to land astronauts and their spacecraft on the moon within a decade. Massive government funds financed the scientific research and technological creations that enabled the United States to attain this goal in 1969.

The postwar alliance of science and technology led to a fast rate of change that became a fact of life in Western society. The underlying assumption of this alliance—that scientific knowledge gave human beings the ability and right to manipulate the environment for their benefit—was questioned by some in the 1960s and 1970s. These questioners noted that some technological advances had far-reaching side effects that were damaging to the environment. The chemical fertilizers, for example, that were used for growing

◀ *Rock and roll may have originated in the United States, but its most famous band was certainly the Beatles. Television audiences throughout the United States watched the group's American debut on the* Ed Sullivan Show *in 1964.*

larger crops destroyed the ecological balance of streams, rivers, and woodlands. *Small is Beautiful*, written by the British economist E. F. Schumacher, warned about the dangers of the new science and technology. As we have seen, the spread of fouled beaches and dying forests and lakes made environmentalism one of the important issues of the 1990s.

## Popular Culture

Popular culture in the twentieth century, especially since World War II, has played an important role in helping Western people define themselves. The history of popular culture is also the history of the economic system that supports it, for it is this system that makes and sells the images that people buy as popular culture. Modern popular culture, therefore, is closely tied to the mass consumer society from which it has emerged.

The United States has been the most powerful force in shaping popular culture in the West and, to a lesser degree, in the entire world. Through movies, music, advertising, and television, the United States has spread its particular form of the American Dream to millions around the world. Already in 1923, the *New York Morning Post* noted that "the film is to America

what the flag was once to Britain. By its means Uncle Sam may hope some day . . . to Americanize the world."[4] In movies, television, and popular music, the impact of American popular culture on the Western world is obvious.

Movies and television were the chief vehicles for the spread of American popular culture in the years after World War II. American movies continued to dominate both European and American markets in the next decades. Many American movies make more money in worldwide distribution than they do in the United States. Kevin Costner's *Waterworld* is but one example of this pattern.

Although developed in the 1930s, television did not become readily available until the late 1940s. By 1954, there were thirty-two million television sets in the United States as television became the centerpiece of middle-class life. In the 1960s, as television spread around the world, U.S. networks unloaded their products on Europe and the non-Western world at very low prices. *Baywatch* was the most popular show in Italy in 1996.

The United States has also dominated popular music since the end of World War II. Jazz, blues, rhythm and blues, rap, and rock and roll have been by far the most popular music forms in the Western world—and in much of the non-Western world—during this time. All

▶ *These New York businessmen take a moment to check on the New York Mets baseball game against the Philadelphia Phillies in May, 1963. The Mets won the game 3–2, but that year the Los Angeles Dodgers went on to win the World Series against the New York Yankees.*

of these music forms began in the United States, and all are rooted in African American musical forms. American popular music later spread to the rest of the world, inspiring local artists who then transformed the music in their own way. For example, through the 1950s, American figures such as Chuck Berry and Elvis Presley inspired the Beatles and other British performers. The Beatles in turn led an "invasion" of the United States in the 1960s, sparking new American rockers.

In the postwar years, sports have become a major product of both popular culture and the leisure industry. Through television, sports became a worldwide phenomenon. Olympic games could now be broadcast across the globe from anywhere in the world. The World Cup soccer championship is the most-watched event on television. Sports became an inexpensive form of entertainment for consumers, as fans did not have to leave their homes to enjoy sporting events. In fact, some sports organizations at first resisted television because they feared that it would hurt ticket sales. Enormous revenues from television contracts, however, helped change their minds. Many sports organizations came to receive most of their yearly revenues from television contracts.

## ❀ SECTION REVIEW ❀

1. **Define:**
   (*a*) existentialism

2. **Identify:**
   (*a*) Samuel Beckett,   (*b*) Albert Camus,
   (*c*) Jean-Paul Sartre,   (*d*) Karl Barth,
   (*e*) J. Robert Oppenheimer,   (*f*) E. F. Schumacher

3. **Recall:**
   (*a*) What was Theater of the Absurd intended to force the audience to do?
   (*b*) What action did Vatican Council II take to make Catholic religious services more appealing to many people?
   (*c*) What inventions were created during World War II that also changed people's lives after the war?
   (*d*) What event caused John F. Kennedy to set a goal of landing an American on the moon before 1970?
   (*e*) What did the *New York Morning Post* mean when it printed "the film is to America what the flag was once to Britain"?

**4. Think Critically:**

(*a*) Why was the United States able to lead the world in technological advancements after World War II?

(*b*) What facts support the idea that the television has become the "centerpiece of the middle-class life"?

## Conclusion

By the end of the 1980s and the beginning of the 1990s, profound changes in the Soviet Union had brought an end to the Cold War. Mikhail Gorbachev began a new Soviet policy in which there would be no military intervention to prop up Communist regimes elsewhere. As a result, revolutions against Communist governments broke out in almost all the Eastern European satellite states at the end of 1989. Quite unexpectedly, the forces of change that had enabled Communist regimes in Eastern Europe to collapse also spread to the Soviet Union and led to its demise as well. The Soviet Union soon broke up into a number of independent states.

After 1970, the nations of Western Europe and North America faced economic challenges stemming from a dramatic increase in the price of oil in the 1970s. They also faced problems unique to each country. Great Britain, for example, had its crisis in Northern Ireland. Germany had problems connected with reunification. Canada had its problems with the desire of French Quebec to separate from the Canadian union.

A number of social and cultural developments have accompanied the political and economic changes since 1970. A women's liberation movement tried to provide new opportunities for women to achieve equality with men. Concerns about planetary pollution gave rise to environmental movements and even new political parties (the Green parties). Terrorist groups used violence to reach their goals. The United States has continued to dominate Western culture in both the arts and popular culture. Through movies and television programs, American popular culture has, in fact, spread to the rest of the world.

Western societies have also been participants in an era of rapidly changing international relationships. Between 1947 and 1962, virtually every colony of European states achieved independence and attained statehood. This process was not easy. However, as we shall see in the next three chapters, it created a new world as the non-Western states put an end to the long-held ascendancy of the Western nations.

## Notes

1. Quoted in Hilda Scott, *Sweden's "Right to Be Human"— Sex-Role Equality: The Goal and the Reality* (London, 1982), p. 125.
2. Quoted in Marsha Rowe et al., *Spare Rib Reader* (Harmondsworth, 1982), p. 574.
3. Quoted in Henry Grosshans, *The Search for Modern Europe* (Boson, 1970), p. 421.
4. Quoted in Richard Maltby, ed., *Passing Parade: A History of Popular Culture in the Twentieth Century* (New York, 1989), p. 8.

# CHAPTER 13 REVIEW

## USING KEY TERMS

1. _____ is the philosophical belief that humans are utterly alone in the universe.
2. People who protest against an existing power structure are called _____.
3. The _____ is a force that is working for greater equality and rights for women.
4. An economic condition that combines high rates of inflation and unemployment is called _____.
5. The _____ asserted that the Soviet Union had the right to intervene in any state where Communist power was threatened.
6. _____ is the period marked by a reduction of tensions between the U.S. and Russia.
7. Efforts to support the protection and preservation of the world's environment have been called _____.
8. _____ is a Russian term used to describe the open discussion of Russia's government and economic systems.
9. The theory that economic growth can be achieved through lowering tax rates to encourage greater production is called _____.
10. _____ is the organized effort to thwart the work of terrorist groups.
11. The restructuring of the Soviet economy in the late 1980s to allow limited free enterprise and greater use of the market is called _____.
12. Efforts of the British government to fight inflation during the 1980s were called _____.

## REVIEWING THE FACTS

1. What caused the leaders of the Soviet Union to establish the Brezhnev doctrine?
2. What compromise was reached between the Soviet Union and Western powers through the Helsinki Agreements?
3. What was the Solidarity organization and how did it help achieve independence for Poland?
4. What conflict was stopped, although not entirely settled, by the Dayton Accords?
5. What American president reopened relations between the United States and China?
6. Why was the Organization of Petroleum Exporting Countries an important force in world economics, particularly in the 1970s and 1980s?
7. What happened at Chernobyl that increased support for the anti-nuclear movement?
8. What nations have been accused of using state-sponsored terrorism to achieve their goals?
9. What warning did E. F. Schumacher make about the impact of development on the environment?

## THINKING CRITICALLY

1. Why does the military might of the former Soviet Union still represent a threat to global survival?
2. Why is any complex system that is centrally controlled likely to suffer from a difficulty in changing or adjusting to new circumstances?
3. Why couldn't the leaders of East Germany reasonably expect much support from the Soviet Union in the late 1980s?
4. What problems did nations in Eastern Europe experience when they converted their economies from government ownership and control to market economies with private business ownership?
5. Why has the return of many industries to private ownership in Western Europe resulted in widespread dissatisfaction among workers and labor organizations?
6. What reasons could explain why the former leaders of communist governments in Eastern Europe apparently had little or no regard for the environmental impact of their policies?
7. Why are women demanding and to an extent achieving, a greater voice in the political and economic systems of Europe?

# CHAPTER 13 REVIEW

## APPLYING SOCIAL STUDIES SKILLS

1. **Psychology:** After the Soviet Union fell, Russian soldiers who had lived in Eastern Europe were expected to return to their homeland. Some went, while others refused to go. Why did soldiers from both of these groups experience severe psychological and emotional problems in adjusting to their new living situations?

2. **Economics:** What historical reasons might there be for Germany, Poland, the Czech Republic, and Hungary having been relatively successful in converting their economic systems to capitalism while Romania, Bulgaria, Serbia, and Albania have been much less successful?

3. **Government:** Why is it difficult to exclude former Communist leaders from the new governments in Eastern Europe?

4. **Sociology:** Make a list of the social problems that need to be solved to create a lasting peace in the former Yugoslavia. Why is it impossible for the United States or any other power to impose peace on these people?

## MAKING TIME AND PLACE CONNECTIONS

1. The unemployment rate in the United States was 5.2 percent in the spring of 1997. At the same time, it was over 10 percent in many western European nations. Why were the Europeans willing to tolerate such high rates? What is likely to happen to these nations if high unemployment rates persist for many years?

2. Some people believe that the nuclear disaster at Chernobyl was also a political disaster for the leaders of the Soviet Union. It showed that they were not in control of their economy or its nuclear facilities, and it cost the nation many billions of rubles. If this is true, why was the nuclear leak at

Three Mile Island in Pennsylvania less of a political problem for U.S. leaders?

3. Compare the role of women in Western society in the past decade with their role before World War II. Identify and explain several important events that have contributed to these changes.

## BECOMING AN HISTORIAN

1. **Making Hypotheses and Predicting Outcomes:** The North Atlantic Treaty Organization has considered inviting some nations in Eastern Europe to join their organization. Russia's leaders have strongly opposed this idea. If these nations do join NATO how might Russia react? Form and explain a hypothesis of what you think might happen.

2. **Time Lines:** Create a time line of events that contributed to the decline and fall of communism in Eastern Europe and the former Soviet Union. Identify how these events were related to policies of the United States and other Western powers.

3. **Economics as a Key to History:** The table below shows the percent of national income allocated to military spending by the United States and the Soviet Union during the 1980s. At this time the value of production in the United States was roughly twice that of the Soviet Union. Study the data and use it to explain why the Soviet Union found it difficult to maintain its position in the arms race and provide sufficient consumer goods.

### Military Spending of the U.S. & U.S.S.R. as a Percent of Production

| Year | U.S. | U.S.S.R. |
|------|------|----------|
| 1980 | 5.3% | 12.9% |
| 1982 | 5.7% | 12.9% |
| 1984 | 5.6% | 12.8% |
| 1986 | 5.4% | 12.6% |
| 1988 | 5.0% | 11.9% |

# CONFLICT AND CHALLENGE

**14**

On July 26, 1953, two brothers, Fidel and Raúl Castro, led a band of 165 young people in an attack on an army camp at Moncada, near Santiago de Cuba. While a law student at the University of Havana, Fidel Castro had become a revolutionary. He was determined to overthrow the government of Fulgencio Batista, the dictator of Cuba. The attack on Moncada, however, was a disaster. Many of the troops led by the Castro brothers were killed, wounded, or arrested. Fidel and Raúl Castro escaped but were later captured and sent to prison with a sentence of fifteen years. The Castro brothers were lucky. They could easily have died in a prison where political prisoners were routinely tortured. Instead, they were released after eleven months. By freeing political prisoners, Batista hoped to win the favor of the Cuban people. He certainly did not gain the favor of the Castros, however. After his release, Fidel Castro fled to Mexico and built a new revolutionary army. Six years later, on January 1, 1959, Fidel Castro and his forces finally seized control of Cuba. Hundreds of thousands of Cubans swept into the streets, overcome with joy. One person remarked, "We were walking on a cloud." To the many Latin Americans who wanted major social and economic changes, Castro soon became a powerful model and source of hope.

Since 1945, the nations of Latin America have followed different paths of change. Many have relied on military dictators to maintain political stability while undergoing economic change. A few, like Cuba, used Marxist revolutions to create a new political, economic, and social order. Many Latin American nations have struggled to build democratic systems, especially since the late 1980s.

The Cold War also had an impact on Latin America. The two superpowers—the United States and the Soviet Union—carried on their conflicts there as well as in the rest of the world. In the process, many Latin American nations became dependent on American loans and subsidies. A few came to depend on financial support from the Soviet Union. However, the nations of Latin America also sought to free themselves from dependence on other nations, although it was not easy to do so.

◄ *On January 1, 1959, Fidel Castro and his band of revolutionary followers successfully overthrew the government of Cuban dictator Fulgencio Batista. This photo of Castro was taken at one of his hidden bases in 1957.*

# IN LATIN AMERICA

## (1945 TO PRESENT)

THE WORLD SINCE 1945

| 1945 | LATIN AMERICA | 2000 |
| 1945 | | 2000 |

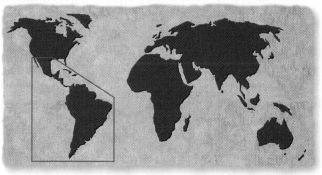

## QUESTIONS TO GUIDE YOUR READING

1. What economic and political changes did Latin America experience after 1945?

2. How did the roles of women and the Catholic Church change in Latin America after 1945?

3. What problems did Mexico and the nations of Central America face after 1945?

4. What were the chief features and impact of the Cuban Revolution?

5. What role have the military and wealthy elites played in the history of Argentina, Brazil, Chile, Colombia, and Peru since 1945?

6. What have been the major educational and cultural trends in Latin America since 1945?

## LATIN AMERICA SINCE 1945: GENERAL TRENDS

Latin America contains many nations with very different outlooks and ways of life. Despite the differences, however, some general economic, political, social, and religious trends have been noticeable throughout this region of the world since 1945.

### Economic and Political Developments

As we saw in Chapter 10, the Great Depression of the 1930s forced many Latin American countries to move to a modern economic structure. From the nineteenth century to the 1930s, Latin Americans had been dependent on an export-import economy. In other words, they had exported raw materials, especially minerals and foodstuffs, while buying the manufactured goods of the industrialized countries, particularly Europe and the United States. As a result of the Great Depression, however, the exports from Latin America

485

were cut in half. Thus, the revenues that had been used to buy manufactured goods declined. The decline in revenues led many Latin American countries to develop new industries that now made the goods they previously had imported. This process of industrial development was known as **import-substituting industrialization (ISI).**

Import-substituting industrialization was supposed to achieve greater economic independence for Latin America. By the 1960s, however, this process had begun to fail. Latin American countries were still dependent on the United States, Europe, and now Japan, especially for the advanced technology needed for modern industries. Moreover, because of the great poverty in many Latin American countries, many peo-

ple could not buy the products of their own industries. Then, too, many Latin American countries often failed to find markets abroad for their products.

The failure of import-substituting industrialization led to instability and a new reliance on military regimes. These military governments sought to curb the power of the new industrial middle class and working class—classes that had increased in size and power as a result of industrialization. Beginning in the 1960s, almost all economically advanced Latin American countries experienced domestic wars and military despotism. Repressive military regimes in Chile, Brazil, and Argentina abolished political parties.

These military regimes often returned to export-import economies financed by foreigners. They also

▼ *Argentina was one of the Latin American nations that developed a strong industrial base. The Ducilo rayon plant in Berazategui made use of modern technology, as shown in this view of a spinning bay. The company also produced cellophane and nylon.*

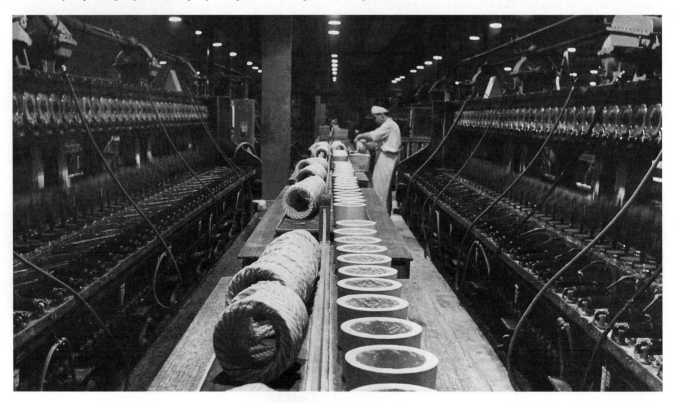

encouraged **multinational corporations** (companies that had divisions in more than two countries) to come into their countries. Those companies that did so wanted chiefly to take advantage of Latin America's raw materials and large supply of inexpensive labor. This, of course, made Latin America even more dependent on the industrially developed nations.

As their economies began to fail in the 1970s, Latin American regimes reacted by borrowing from abroad, especially from banks in Europe and the United States. Between 1970 and 1982, debt to foreigners grew from $27 billion to $315.3 billion. By 1982, a number of governments said that they could no longer pay interest on their debts to foreign banks. Their economies began to crumble. Wages fell, and unemployment and inflation skyrocketed.

To get new loans, Latin American governments were now forced to make basic reforms. Many came to believe that government had taken control of too many industries. Too fast a pace for industrialization had led to the decline of the economy in the countryside as well. Many hoped that encouraging peasants to grow food for home consumption rather than export would stop the flow of people from the countryside to the cities. At the same time, they believed that more people could now buy the products from Latin American industries.

With the debt crisis in the 1980s came a movement toward democracy. Some military leaders were simply unwilling to deal with the monstrous debt problems. At the same time, many people realized that military power without popular consent could not maintain a strong state. Then, too, there was a swelling of popular support for basic rights, as well as for free and fair elections.

The movement toward democracy was the most noticeable trend of the 1980s and early 1990s in Latin America. In the mid-1970s, only Colombia, Venezuela, and Costa Rica had democratic governments. In the mid-1980s, democratic regimes were everywhere except Cuba, some of the Central American states, Chile, and Paraguay. This revival of democracy, however, is fragile. In 1992, for example, President Alberto Fujimori (FOO-ji-MORE-ee) undermined democracy and returned Peru to an authoritarian system (see "Peru" later in the chapter).

## Society in Latin America

Latin America's economic problems were made worse by a dramatic growth in the population. Both Latin America and North America (the United States and Canada) had the same population in 1950—about 165 million people. By the mid-1980s, however, Latin America's population had exploded to 400 million. That of North America was about 270 million. Both a decline in death rates and an increase in birth rates in Latin America led to this population explosion.

With the increase in population came a rapid rise in the number and size of cities. In 1930, only one Latin American city had more than one million people. By 1990, there were twenty-nine cities with over a million people, including Mexico City, with sixteen million inhabitants, and Buenos Aires, with eight million. By the 1980s, one-half of Latin America's population lived in cities of over twenty thousand people.

Cities grew in large part because peasants fled their rural poverty to seek a better life. Rarely did they find it, however. Population growth far outstripped economic growth, and millions were left without jobs. Cities could not cope with the needs of the people, and slums, or shantytowns, became part of virtually every Latin American city (see "Young People in Latin America: The Street Kids").

The gap between the poor and the rich had always been enormous in Latin America. It remained so after 1945. Landholding and urban elites still owned huge estates and businesses. These elites were largely descendants of the Europeans who had colonized Latin America centuries before. A small but growing middle class consisted of businesspeople and office and government workers. Peasants and the urban poor, struggling just to survive, became more vocal. The peasants called for reforms that would give them more land. Urban workers joined trade unions and demanded better wages and better working conditions.

The enormous gulf between rich and poor often undermined the stability of Latin American countries. So, too, did the international drug trade. Latin America's northern neighbor, the United States, was one of the world's largest consumers of drugs. Eighty percent of the cocaine and 90 percent of the marijuana used in

▶ *This photo of a favela, or shantytown, documents the misery of Brazil's urban poor. Why do you think the government has not done more to alleviate the housing and health problems of its poverty-stricken people?*

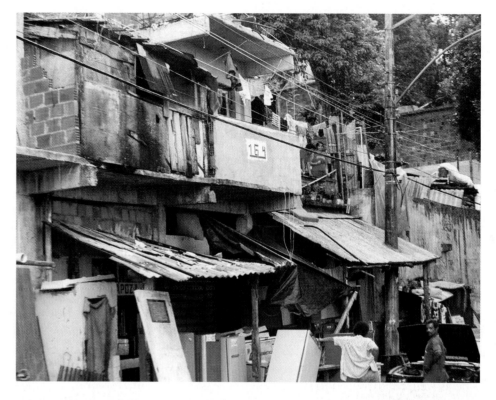

the United States came from Latin America. Bolivia, Peru, and Colombia were especially big producers. Peasants in these countries found that the growing of coca leaves and marijuana plants, from which these drugs were produced, was an important part of their economic survival.

Drug traffickers in Colombia became especially wealthy. Their leaders formed **drug cartels** (groups of drug businesses whose purpose is to eliminate competition) that bribed and intimidated government officials and police officers into protecting their activities. The United States has long sought to work with the governments of Colombia, Bolivia, and Peru to lessen the problem of drug cartels. It has had little success, however. Even when one large cartel is broken up, new ones emerge to continue the business.

The roles of women, too, have changed in Latin American society. Throughout much of Latin American history, women were expected only to be homemakers for their husbands and children. This role continues for many millions of Latin American women.

However, women have also moved into new kinds of jobs. In addition to doing farm labor, lower-class women have found jobs in industry, especially in textile mills. Women, however, are frequently paid less than men in these jobs. Women from the middle and upper classes have found even greater opportunities, and have become teachers, professors, dentists, doctors, and lawyers.

As in many other areas of the world, women have usually not played important roles in the political life of Latin America. Most countries in Latin America did not grant women the right to vote until the 1930s and 1940s. In some countries, such as Mexico and Argentina, women entered the political arena by taking part in demonstrations. In the Cuban and Nicaraguan Revolutions (see later in the chapter), women played an active role. Nevertheless, even now, only 2 or 3 percent of important political posts are held by women. The first female president in Latin America was Isabel Perón, but she came to office as a result of her husband's death.

# YOUNG PEOPLE IN LATIN AMERICA

## The Street Kids

According to the United Nations, there are 100 million young people living on the streets of the world's cities. Probably half of them live in Latin America. High birth rates have left large numbers of young people living in the shantytowns that surround Latin America's cities. Many of these young people—from families often torn by poverty, alcoholism, and despair—flee their slum homes and become street kids, or *meninos de rua* (muh-NEEN-yose day ROO-uh).

Those who live on the streets survive as best they can. They work by shining shoes, washing windshields, selling gum, and collecting cardboard. Some beg. Others pick pockets and steal purses and goods. Some work in gangs and are recruited by drug dealers to be couriers. Some kids even kill.

*Meninos de rua* have been on the streets of Brazil for decades. Beginning in the early 1990s, however, these children were increasingly blamed for rising crime rates. Death squads, often made up of police officers who seek extra work because of their low salaries, have begun to kill the street kids in ever larger numbers. According to a Brazilian congressional investigation, 4,611 children were murdered in Brazil between 1992 and 1995. The investigation also revealed that at least 180 death squads are at work in Rio de Janeiro alone. These death squads, often hired by businesspeople who worry about trade, are supposed to "clean up" commercial districts.

*Street kids like these suffer from disease, hunger, exposure, and lack even the most basic amenities associated with family life.*

Some people welcome the killings. One Brazilian said of the street kids, "Everyone is making them out to be heroes, but they were not sweet flowers." Another said, "Many of these 13-year-old kids have killed. They deserve to die."

Others are alarmed at the killings. Private groups, many of them run by churches, have organized aid societies. They try to provide jobs, housing, and education for street kids. Their funds are limited, however, and government promises to provide more money for the street kids have usually turned out to be just promises.

1. Why are so many young people living on the streets of Latin America?

2. What dangers do street kids face?

3. How would you solve this enormous social problem?

▲ *Working women often find employment in the fields, just as their ancestors did. Here a Colombian woman picks coffee beans. Who do you think will profit most from this crop?*

## CONNECTIONS
### AROUND THE WORLD

**International Women's Conferences**   As women around the world organized movements to change the conditions of their lives, an international women's movement emerged. Especially in the 1970s, much attention was paid to a series of international conferences on women's issues. Between 1975 and 1985, the United Nations celebrated the Decade for Women by holding conferences in such cities as Mexico City, Copenhagen, and Nairobi. These meetings made it clear how women in both developed and developing nations were organizing to make people aware of women's issues.

The conferences also made clear the differences between women from Western and non-Western countries. While women from Western countries spoke about political, economic, cultural, and sexual rights, women from developing countries in Latin America, Africa, and Asia focused their attention on bringing an end to the violence, hunger, and disease that haunt their lives. At the International Women's Year Tribunal in Mexico in 1974, sponsored by the United Nations, Dimitila Barrios de Chungara, a miner's wife from Bolivia, expressed her lack of patience with professional women at the conference. She said, "So, I went up and spoke. I made them see that they don't live in our world. I made them see that in Bolivia human rights aren't respected. . . Women like us, housewives, who get organized to better our people well, they [the Bolivian police] beat us up and persecute us."

## The Role of the Catholic Church

The Catholic Church had been a powerful force in Latin America for centuries. However, its hold over people declined as cities and industrial societies grew. By the beginning of the twentieth century, most Latin American governments had separated church and state. Nevertheless, the church remained a powerful social and cultural force.

Eventually, the Catholic Church pursued a middle way for Latin American society. It called for a moderate capitalist system that respected workers' rights, brought about land reform, and provided for the welfare of the poor. This policy led to the formation of Christian Democratic parties that had some successes in the 1960s and 1970s.

In the 1960s, however, some Catholics in Latin America took a more radical path to change. Influenced by Marxist ideas, they called for a **theology of liberation.** Supporters of liberation theology believed that Christians must fight to free the oppressed, even if it meant the use of violence. Some members of the Catholic clergy even teamed up with Marxist guerrillas in rural areas. Other radical priests worked in factories

alongside workers or carried on social work among the poor in the slums. Liberation theology attracted much attention, but most church leaders rejected it.

In the 1970s and 1980s, the Catholic Church continued to play a significant role in Latin America by becoming an important voice for human rights against authoritarian regimes. Priests, nuns, and archbishops

◄ *In 1989, the national elections in Panama were believed to be fraudulent, and in November the Organization of American States declared that the newly elected government lacked legitimacy. In December, the United States sent armed military forces to restore the constitutional government. How can you tell this is an American soldier?*

spoke out against injustice and crimes of the military regimes. To speak out was dangerous. Military regimes did not hesitate to murder members of the Catholic clergy. For example, Archbishop Oscar Romero was a fierce critic of El Salvador's military regime. On March 30, 1980, right-wing assassins murdered him while he was saying mass in a hospital chapel.

## The United States and Latin America

The United States has always played a large role in Latin America. For years, the United States had sent troops into Latin American countries to protect U.S. interests and bolster friendly dictators. Eventually, the United States also sought a new relationship with Latin America. In 1933, President Franklin Delano Roosevelt announced the Good Neighbor policy. This policy promised to treat Latin American states as sovereign nations and to stop the use of U.S. military action in the Western Hemisphere. In 1948, the states of the Western Hemisphere formed the Organization of American States (OAS), which called for an end to military action by one state in the affairs of any other state. The OAS encouraged regional cooperation and allowed for group action to maintain peace.

The formation of the Organization of American States, however, did not end the interference of the United States in Latin American affairs. As the Cold War between the United States and the Soviet Union developed, so, too, did the anxiety of American policy makers about the possibility of Communist regimes in Central America and the Caribbean. As a result, the United States returned to a policy of taking action when it believed that Soviet agents were trying to use local communists or radical reformers to set up governments hostile to U.S. interests.

After Fidel Castro created a Marxist state in Cuba (see later in the chapter), the desire of the United States to prevent "another Cuba" largely determined U.S. policy toward Latin America. In the 1960s, President John F. Kennedy's Alliance for Progress encouraged social reform and economic development in Latin America. It was hoped that economic growth would keep ordinary people happy and less inclined to follow radical leaders. The United States provided over $10 billion in aid to those elected governments whose reform programs it deemed acceptable.

The Alliance for Progress failed to work, however. Much of the money intended for economic development ended up in the pockets of the rich. When Cuba began to start guerrilla wars in other Latin American countries, the United States reacted by providing massive military aid to anticommunist regimes, regardless of their nature. By 1979, 83,000 soldiers from twenty-one Latin American countries had received military training from the United States. Special emphasis was placed on antiguerrilla activity so that Latin American countries could fight social revolutionaries.

In the 1980s and 1990s, the United States returned to a policy of direct intervention in Latin American affairs. In 1983, President Ronald Reagan sent U.S. Marines to the tiny island of Grenada (gruh-NADE-uh), where the United States claimed that "a brutal group of leftist thugs had violently seized power." In 1989 and 1990, during the presidency of George Bush, U.S. military forces overthrew the government of Panama. The new government was supported by U.S. troops. President Bill Clinton used U.S. forces to oust a military regime and restore democracy to Haiti in 1994 and 1995.

## ❀ SECTION REVIEW ❀

1. **Locate:**
   (*a*) Colombia,   (*b*) Venezuela,   (*c*) Costa Rica,
   (*d*) Chile,   (*e*) Paraguay,   (*f*) Bolivia,   (*g*) Peru,
   (*h*) El Salvador

2. **Define:**
   (*a*) import-substituting industrialization,
   (*b*) multinational corporations,
   (*c*) drug cartels,
   (*d*) theology of liberation

3. **Identify:**
   (*a*) debt crisis,   (*b*) Alberto Fujimori,   (*c*) Oscar Romero,   (*d*) Organization of American States (OAS),   (*e*) Alliance for Progress

4. **Recall:**
   (*a*) Why did the attempt of many Latin American countries to industrialize contribute to an emergence of new military regimes?
   (*b*) How did many Latin American countries deal with the declining value of their exports in the 1970s?
   (*c*) What is probably the most important reason for the migration of Latin American people from rural areas to cities?
   (*d*) What effect does the wide gap between the rich and poor have in Latin American countries?

(*e*) What did the Cold War have to do with American concerns about Latin America?

5. **Think Critically:** What positive and negative events may result for the people of Latin America from a renewed United States policy of direct intervention in their affairs?

# THE CARIBBEAN BASIN: REVOLUTION AND ECONOMIC CHANGE

The Caribbean Basin includes Mexico, the states of Central America, and the Caribbean islands. Since 1945, this area has witnessed revolutionary upheavals and considerable economic and political change.

## The Mexican Way

The Mexican Revolution at the beginning of the twentieth century created a political order that has remained the most stable in Latin America. The official political party of the Mexican Revolution (known as the Institutional Revolutionary Party, or PRI) came to dominate Mexico. Every six years, party bosses of the PRI chose the party's presidential candidate. He was then dutifully elected by the people, who had no other party to choose from.

During the 1950s and 1960s, Mexico's ruling party focused on a balanced program of industrial growth. Fifteen years of steady economic growth led to real gains in wages for more and more people. To many people, those years appeared to be a golden age in Mexico's economic development.

At the end of the 1960s, however, the true nature of Mexico's domination by a one-party system became apparent in the student protest movement. On October 2, 1968, university students filled Tlatelolco Square in Mexico City to protest government policies. Police forces opened fire and killed hundreds of students (see "You Are There: Student Revolt in Mexico"). Leaders

**Map 14.1   The Caribbean Basin**

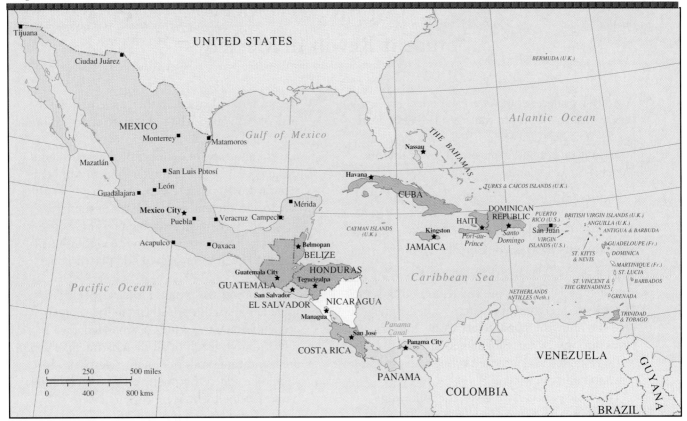

of the PRI now became concerned about the need for change in the system.

The next two presidents, Luis Echeverría (AY-chuh-vuh-REE-uh) and José López Portillo, made political reforms. New rules opened the door to the emergence of new political parties. Greater freedom of debate in the press and universities was also allowed. Economic problems, however, continued to haunt Mexico. In the late 1970s, vast new reserves of oil were discovered in Mexico. The sale of oil abroad increased dramatically, which made the government more and more dependent on oil revenues. When world oil prices dropped in the mid-1980s, Mexico was no longer able to make payments on its foreign debt, which had reached $80 billion in 1982. The government was forced to adopt new economic policies. These included the sale of companies owned by the state to private companies (a policy known as **privatization**).

The debt crisis and rising unemployment left many people unhappy with the government. This was especially evident in the 1988 election. The PRI's choice for president was Carlos Salinas. Normally, he would have been expected to win in a landslide. However, he gained only 50.3 percent, a bare majority. The new president continued the economic reforms of the previous presidents. He went even further by making a free-trade agreement with the United States and Canada, known as the North American Free Trade Agreement (NAFTA). The success or failure of these economic policies will no doubt determine the continuing ability of the PRI to dominate Mexico politically. In 1995, a new challenge appeared when a group of rebels in the extreme south of Mexico led an armed revolt against the government. Although the revolt failed, peasant unrest in the area remains a challenge to the government.

## YOU ARE THERE

# Student Revolt in Mexico

*A growing conflict between the government and university students in Mexico came to a violent and bloody climax on October 2, 1968. This excerpt is taken from an account of the events by the student National Strike Council.*

### Account of the Clash Between the Government and Students in Mexico, October 2, 1968

After an hour and a half of a peaceful meeting attended by 10,000 people and witnessed by scores of domestic and foreign reporters, a helicopter gave the army the signal to attack by dropping flares into the crowd. Simultaneously, the plaza was surrounded and attacked by members of the army and all police forces.

The local papers have given the following information about the attack, confirmed by first-hand witnesses:

1. Numerous secret policemen had infiltrated the meeting in order to attack it from within, with orders to kill. They were known to each other by the use of a white handkerchief tied around their right hands. . . .
2. High-caliber weapons and expansion bullets were used. Seven hours after the massacre began, tanks cleaned up the residential buildings of Nonoalco-Tlatelolco with short cannon blasts and machine-gun fire.
3. On the morning of October 3, the apartments of supposedly guilty individuals were still being searched, without a search warrant.
4. Doctors in the emergency wards of the city hospitals were under extreme pressure, being forced to forego attention to the victims until they had been interrogated and placed under guard. . . .
5. The results of this brutal military operation include hundreds of dead (including women and children), thousands of wounded, an unwarranted search of all the apartments in the area, and thousands of violent arrests. . . . It should be added that members of the National Strike Council who were captured were stripped and herded into a small archaeological excavation at Tlatelolco, converted for the moment into a dungeon. Some of them were put up against a wall and shot.

All this has occurred only ten days before the start of the Olympics. The repression is expected to become even greater after the Games. . . .

WE ARE NOT AGAINST THE OLYMPIC GAMES. WELCOME TO MEXICO.

## The Cuban Revolution

Until the 1960s, Marxism played little role in the politics of Latin America. The success of Fidel Castro in Cuba and his support of Marxism, however, changed that situation. Other Marxist movements then arose that aimed to gain the support of peasants and industrial workers and to bring radical change to Latin America. The United States saw these movements as communist threats and provided substantial military aid to fight them.

An authoritarian regime, headed by Fulgencio Batista, had ruled Cuba since 1934. The regime was closely tied economically to U.S. investors. A strong opposition movement to Batista's government developed, led by Fidel Castro. He was assisted by Ernesto

# YOU ARE THERE

## Student Revolt in Mexico, continued

◄ *This woman was wounded by armed federal troops during the student protest in Tlatelolco Plaza on October 2, 1968. The official government report said that Mexican authorities were fired upon, and they returned the gunfire. What other country experienced student demonstrations and riots in 1968?*

1. What was the reason for the military attack on the students?

2. Why do you think the government reacted with such violence?

3. Do you think the government handled the situation well? Why or why not?

4. What was the result of this incident? What other tragic events in history helped bring about needed changes?

Ché Guevara (gay-VAH-ruh), an Argentinian who believed in the need for revolutionary upheaval to change Latin America. Castro thought that only armed force could overthrow Batista. Castro's first direct attacks on Batista's regime brought little success. Castro, whose forces were based in the Sierra Maestra (MIE-struh) Mountains, then went over to guerrilla warfare (see "You Are There: Castro's Revolutionary

Ideals"). As the rebels gained more support, Batista's regime reacted with such brutality that it even alienated its own supporters. The dictator fled in December 1958. Castro's revolutionaries seized Havana on January 1, 1959.

The new government moved cautiously, but relations between Cuba and the United States quickly deteriorated. A land-reform law in May 1959 national-

# YOU ARE THERE

## Castro's Revolutionary Ideals

*On July 26, 1953, Fidel Castro was arrested and put on trial after he and a small band of followers failed to capture the Moncada barracks, near Santiago de Cuba. This excerpt is taken from his defense speech, in which he discussed the goals of the revolutionaries.*

### Fidel Castro, From His 1953 Defense Speech

I stated that the second consideration on which we based our chances for success was one of social order because we were assured of the people's support. When we speak of the people we do not mean the comfortable ones, the conservative elements of the nation, who welcome any regime of oppression, any dictatorship, and despotism, prostrating themselves before the master of the moment until they grind their foreheads into the ground. When we speak of struggle, the people means the vast unredeemed masses, to whom all make promises and whom all deceive; we mean the people who yearn for a better, more dignified

▲ *Fidel Castro addressed the Cuban nation by radio after the ouster of Fulgencio Batista. Do you think that the Cuban people initially believed Castro would turn Cuba into a Marxist dictatorship? Why or why not?*

ized all landholdings of more than one thousand acres. This irritated the United States. Then the Soviet Union, the Cold War enemy of the United States, agreed early in 1960 to buy Cuban sugar and provide $100 million in credits to Cuba.

On March 17, 1960, President Dwight Eisenhower directed the Central Intelligence Agency (CIA) to "organize the training of Cuban exiles, mainly in Guatemala, against a possible future day when they might return to their homeland."[1] Arms from Eastern Europe began to arrive in Cuba. The United States cut its purchase of Cuban sugar. In response, the Cuban government nationalized U.S. companies and banks. In October 1960, the United States declared a trade

embargo of Cuba, thus driving Castro closer to the Soviet Union. In December 1960, Castro declared himself a Marxist.

On January 3, 1961, the United States broke off diplomatic relations with Cuba. The new American president, John F. Kennedy, supported an attempt to overthrow Castro's government. The landing in Cuba of 1,400 Cubans, assisted by the CIA, on April 17, 1961, turned into a total military disaster (the Bay of Pigs invasion). The Soviets were now encouraged to make an even greater commitment to Cuban independence by placing nuclear missiles in the country. This act led to a showdown with the United States—the Cuban Missile Crisis (see Chapter 12). As its part of

## YOU ARE THERE

# Castro's Revolutionary Ideals, continued

and more just nation; who are moved by ancestral aspirations of justice, for they have suffered injustice and mockery, generation after generation; who long for great and wise changes in all aspects of their life; people, who, to attain these changes, are ready to give even the very last breath of their lives—when they believe in something or in someone, especially when they believe in themselves.

In the brief of this cause there must be recorded the five revolutionary laws that would have been proclaimed immediately after the capture of the Moncada barracks. . . .

The First Revolutionary Law would have returned power to the people. . . .

The Second Revolutionary Law would have granted property to all planters, sub-planters, lessees, partners and squatters who hold parcels of five or less "caballerias" [tract of land, about 33 acres] of land. . . .

The Third Revolutionary Law would have granted workers and employees the right to share

30 percent of the profits of all the large enterprises, including the sugar mills. . . .

The Fourth Revolutionary Law would have granted all planters the right to share 55 percent of the sugar production. . . .

The Fifth Revolutionary Law would have ordered the confiscation of all holdings and ill-gotten gains of those who had committed frauds during previous regimes. . . .

1. List in your own words the revolutionary laws stated here.

2. Considering the revolutionary laws, who was Castro trying to help?

3. Do you think communism was a basic ingredient of Castro's revolution, or did it become part of his regime after the revolution? Explain your answer.

the bargain to end the crisis, the United States agreed not to invade Cuba.

The Cuban Missile Crisis affected Cuba in another way as well. Castro realized that the Soviet Union had been unreliable. If the Cuban Revolution was to be secure, Cuba could no longer be surrounded by hostile states tied to U.S. interests. The Cubans would have to start social revolution in the rest of Latin America. Castro thought that Bolivia, Haiti, Venezuela, Colombia, Paraguay, and a number of Central American states were especially open to radical revolution. By launching guerrilla wars, peasants would flock to the movement and overthrow the old regimes. Guevara began a guerrilla war in Bolivia but was caught and

killed by the Bolivian army in the fall of 1967. The Cuban strategy had failed.

Nevertheless, within Cuba, Castro's Marxist revolution went on, although with mixed results. The Cuban Revolution did secure some social gains for its people, especially in health care and education. The regime provided free medical services for all citizens, and the country's health did improve. Illiteracy was nearly eliminated as new schools and teacher-training institutes that tripled the number of teachers within ten years were set up. The theoretical equality of women in Marxist thought was put into practice in Cuba by new laws. One such law was the family code, which stated that husband and wife were equally responsible for the

▶ *Sugar was one of Cuba's primary exports, but working in the cane fields was hard manual labor, as evidenced by this illustration. How did Cuba replace the income from U.S. sugar imports?*

economic support of the family and household, as well as for child care. Such laws led to improvements but were far from creating full equality for women.

Castro rejected a path of rapid industrialization and encouraged the development of mixed farming. The Cuban economy, however, continued to rely on the production and sale of sugar. Economic problems forced the Castro regime to depend on Soviet aid and the purchase of Cuban sugar by Soviet bloc countries. After the collapse of these Communist regimes in 1989, Cuba lost their support. Without the Soviet subsidies, economic conditions in Cuba have steadily declined. Nevertheless, despite the poor economy and increasing isolation from other countries, Castro manages to remain in power.

## Upheaval in Central America

There are six states in Central America: Costa Rica, Nicaragua, Honduras, El Salvador, Panama, and Guatemala. Economically, these states have depended on the export of bananas, coffee, and cotton. Prices for these products vary at times, however, which creates economic crises. An enormous gulf between a wealthy elite and a mass of poor peasants also created a climate of instability. Fear in the United States of the spread of communism often led to American support for repressive regimes in the area. American involvement was especially evident in El Salvador, Nicaragua, and Panama.

### El Salvador

El Salvador is the smallest state in Central America. By the beginning of the twentieth century, about forty families owned most of the coffee plantations and controlled both banking and trade. The gulf between this wealthy elite and the mass of poor peasants was enormous.

After World War II, the United States supported the rule of the wealthy elite and the military. The rise of an urban middle class led to some hopes for a more democratic government. This group supported the Christian Democratic Party, led by José Napoleon Duarte (DWAR-tay). The army, however, refused to allow the free elections that were planned for 1972.

In the late 1970s and the 1980s, El Salvador was rocked by a bitter civil war. Both Marxist-led guerrillas and right-wing groups used savage terror to win the struggle. During the presidency of Ronald Reagan, the United States provided weapons and training to the Salvadoran army to defeat the guerrillas. At the same time, the United States urged land reform and free elections. Even the election of the moderate José Duarte as president in 1984, however, failed to stop the killing. By the early 1990s, this brutal civil war had led to the deaths of at least 75,000 people. Finally in 1992, a peace settlement was reached that brought an end to the civil war.

### Nicaragua

The United States had intervened in Nicaraguan domestic affairs in the early twentieth century. U.S. Marines even remained there for long periods of time. The leader of the U.S.-supported National Guard, Anastasio Somoza, seized control of the Nicaraguan government in 1937. The Somoza family ruled Nicaragua for the next forty-three years. U.S. support for the Somoza family's military regime enabled the Somozas to overcome any opponents while enriching themselves at the expense of the state. Here, too, there existed a wealthy elite while most people lived in extreme poverty.

Opposition to the regime finally arose. The Somoza family and the National Guard it controlled used murder and torture to stop the opposition. At the same time, corruption was rampant in the government. By 1979, even the United States, under President Jimmy Carter, was unwilling to support the corrupt, dictatorial family. In that same year, military victories by the Marxist guerrilla forces known as the Sandinista (SAN-duh-NEES-tuh) National Liberation Front left them in virtual control of the country. They now set up a provisional government.

The Sandinistas inherited a poverty-stricken nation. Their alignment with the Soviet Union caused the Reagan and Bush administrations to believe that Central America faced the danger of another Communist state. American money was used to finance rebels, known as **Contras,** to wage a guerrilla war against the Sandinista government. The Contra war and a U.S. economic embargo damaged the Nicaraguan economy and undermined support for the Sandinistas. In 1990, the Sandinistas agreed to free elections, and they lost to a coalition headed by Violeta Barrios de Chamorro. Nevertheless, the Sandinistas remained the strongest

▲ *The Sandinistas celebrate their victory that led to the overthrow of the Somoza dictatorship in Nicaragua. Why is it symbolic that these soldiers are standing on a tank and waving guns?*

single party in Nicaragua. Nicaragua itself remained devastated by these years of bloodshed.

### Panama

A revolution in 1903 enabled Panama to free itself from Colombia and form a separate nation. However, this was done with help from the United States. The price for American aid was control of the Panama Canal, which Colombia had refused to give, and extensive influence over the government and economy of Panama. A wealthy oligarchy ruled, with American support.

After 1968, power in Panama came into the hands of the military leaders of Panama's National Guard. One of the most ruthless leaders was Manuel Noriega (NOR-ee-AY-guh), who took control of Panama in 1983. At first, Noriega was supported by the United States. His corruption, brutality, and involvement with the drug trade, however, turned American leaders against him. On December 20, 1989, President George Bush sent 24,000 U.S. troops to Panama. Noriega was arrested and sent to prison in the United States on charges of drug trafficking. Guillermo Endara, who had opposed Noriega, then became president of Panama.

## ❀ SECTION REVIEW ❀

1. **Locate:**
   (*a*) Havana,   (*b*) Haiti,   (*c*) Nicaragua,
   (*d*) Honduras,   (*e*) Panama

2. **Define:**
   (*a*) privatization,   (*b*) Contras

3. **Identify:**
   (*a*) Carlos Salinas,   (*b*) North American Free Trade Agreement (NAFTA),   (*c*) Fidel Castro,
   (*d*) Anastasio Somoza,   (*e*) Manuel Noriega

4. **Recall:**
   (*a*) Why haven't the people of Mexico had much choice in the past in determining the political leadership of their country?
   (*b*) How was Castro's Cuba affected by the collapse of communist governments in Eastern Europe?

5. **Think Critically:** Why was Castro able to maintain control of Cuba even after he lost his foreign support?

---

◆ 3 ◆

## THE NATIONS OF SOUTH AMERICA: NATIONALISM, MARXISM, AND THE MILITARY

The countries of South America shared in the political, economic, and social problems that plagued Latin America after 1945. The military in particular became the power brokers of twentieth-century South America. Especially in the 1960s and 1970s, South American armies portrayed themselves as the guardians of national honor and orderly progress, while maintaining dictatorial and often ruthless regimes.

### Argentina

Argentina is Latin America's second largest country. For years, it had been ruled by a powerful oligarchy whose wealth was based on growing wheat and raising cattle. Support from the army was crucial to the continuing power of the oligarchy. In 1943, in the midst of World War II, a group of army officers overthrew the oligarchy. The new military regime, however, was unsure of how to deal with the working classes until one of its members, Juan Perón, devised a new strategy.

Using his position as labor secretary in the military government, Perón sought to win over the workers, known as the *descamisados* (the shirtless ones). He encouraged them to join labor unions. Moreover, he increased job benefits, as well as the number of paid holidays and vacations. In 1944, Perón became vice president of the military government and made sure that people knew he was responsible for the better conditions for workers. As Perón grew more popular, however, other army officers began to fear his power, and they arrested him. An uprising by workers forced the officers to back down. In 1946, Perón was elected president, with 54 percent of the vote.

Perón followed a policy of increased industrialization in order to please his chief supporters—labor and the urban middle class. At the same time, he sought to free Argentina from foreign investors. The government bought the railways and took over the banking, insurance, shipping, and communications industries.

Perón's regime was also authoritarian. His wife, Eva Perón, organized women's organizations to support the government (see "Biography: Evita"). She also used state funds to set up foundations that helped orphans and the poor. Juan Perón, meanwhile, created Fascist gangs modeled after Hitler's Brownshirts. They used violent means to terrify Perón's opponents. More and

**Map 14.2   South American Countries**

more people were alienated, however, by the regime's methods and its corruption. After the death of the popular Eva Perón in 1953, the regime's support dropped even further. Fearing Perón's power over the masses, the military overthrew the Argentinian leader in September 1955. Perón went into exile in Spain.

# BIOGRAPHY

## Evita

▲ *Evita Perón was adored by the masses, but shunned by Argentina's upper classes. This photograph was taken in 1952, when Perón celebrated the inauguration of his second term as president. Eva Perón died less than one year after this photo was taken.*

Eva Perón, known as "Evita" to her followers, was one of five children born to a seamstress who lived in poverty in the small town of Los Toldos. As a child, Eva dreamed of being an actress. At age fifteen, she moved to Buenos Aires, Argentina's largest city, where she tried to get some kind of acting job. She worked in a few theaters and eventually gained fame as a radio soap opera actress.

On January 15, 1944, during a concert to benefit victims of an earthquake, Eva met Juan Perón, one of the army officers then running the government. She later described the meeting: "I put myself at his side . . . I spoke up as best I could: 'If, as you say, the cause of the people is your own cause, however great the sacrifice I will never leave your side until I die.' " Eva became Juan Perón's mistress and a year later, his wife.

Eva Perón was an important force in her husband's rise to power. Together, they courted the working-class poor with promises of higher wages and better working conditions. Juan Perón, who was elected president in 1946, owed much to the people's adoration of his wife.

It had been easy for the military to seize power, but it was harder for it to rule. Argentina now had a party of Perón supporters (called Peronistas), who clamored for the return of the exiled leader. In the 1960s and 1970s, military and civilian governments (the latter closely watched by the military) alternated in power. Neither was able to do much to provide economic stability. Thus, the military leaders allowed Juan Perón to come back from exile in Spain.

Perón was again elected president in September 1973. He died one year later before he could accomplish very much. His third wife, Isabel, who had run as

vice president, succeeded him, but she was not effective in dealing with the country's problems. In 1976, the military once again took over power. This new military regime was brutal. It tolerated no opposition, and the military leaders encouraged the "disappearance" of its opponents. Perhaps 36,000 people, including 600 leftists, were killed as a result.

Economic problems remained. To divert people's attention, the military regime invaded the Falkland Islands, off the coast of Argentina, in April 1982. Great Britain, which had controlled the islands since the nineteenth century, sent ships and troops to take

# BIOGRAPHY

## Evita, continued

As the wife of President Juan Perón, Eva was the first lady of Argentina from 1946 to 1952. Juan and Eva Perón made regular appearances on the balcony of the Presidential Palace, where they spoke to the adoring crowds of workers. Eva Perón became a tireless champion of the people. She went to the slums of the poor and gave them gifts. She formed a charitable foundation that built hospitals, schools, and orphanages, thus providing many services for Argentina's poor. Eva Perón also worked to benefit Argentinian women. She campaigned for women's right to vote and equal pay for equal work.

Eva Perón was also ambitious. She enjoyed her newfound power and loved to appear publicly, adorned in a new gown or jewelry. In 1951, she wanted to be her husband's vice presidential candidate. She backed down, however, after army leaders made it clear that they would never accept Eva Perón in office. Less than a year later, on July 26, 1952, she died of cancer. Her coffin was carried in a mile-long funeral procession, accompanied by government officials and hundreds of thousands of grieving Argentinians. During her illness, she promised the people she would always be with them. To this day, monuments, street names, and even the American musical and movie *Evita* continue to keep her memory alive.

1. Who was Evita, and what was her claim to fame?

2. Do you think Evita was driven to accomplish what she did by a desire to help the people or a desire for personal power? Explain your answer.

3. Why do you think the army leaders opposed Evita's desire to run for the office of vice-president?

4. Can you think of a person, either male or female, who is admired by people today in the way that Evita was? Describe the similarities between this person and Evita.

them back. When the Argentinian forces surrendered to the British in July, angry Argentinians denounced the military regime. The loss discredited the military and opened the door to civilian rule. In 1983, Raúl Alfonsín (al-fawn-SEEN), a member of the Radical Party, was elected president and tried to restore democratic practices. The Perónist Carlos Saúl Menem won the presidential elections of 1989. This peaceful transfer of power gave rise to hope that Argentina was moving on a democratic path. Reelected in 1995, President Menem has pushed to control inflation and government spending.

## Brazil

Brazil is the largest country in Latin America. As we saw in Chapter 10, the authoritarian regime of Getúlio Vargas, from 1930 to 1945, brought the first strong industrialization to Brazil. The army, fearing Vargas's power, forced him to resign in 1945.

A second Brazilian republic came into being in 1946. Four years later, Vargas himself won the election to the presidency. However, he was unable to solve Brazil's economic problems, especially its soaring inflation. In 1954, after the armed forces called upon him

▲ *This mother holds a photo of her ten-year-old son, who disappeared in January 1995 while playing near his home in Rio de Janeiro, Brazil. Every week this woman and the other Mothers of Cinelandia, named after a plaza in the city, march to draw attention to their missing children.*

▲ *Clear-cutting in the Amazon forest is causing worldwide concern. This photo shows the destruction left when a forest is clear-cut. What worldwide environmental problems are caused by clear-cutting in the South American rain forests?*

to resign, Vargas killed himself. The democratically elected presidents who followed Vargas had no more success in controlling inflation while trying to push rapid industrialization. In the spring of 1964, the military stepped in and took over the government.

This time the armed forces remained in direct control of the country—for the next twenty years. The military set course on a new economic direction. It cut back somewhat on state control of the economy and stressed free-market forces. Beginning in 1968, the new policies seemed to work. Brazil experienced an "economic miracle" as its economy grew spectacularly. Women began to participate in the labor force.

Economic growth, however, had its drawbacks and problems. Economic growth included the exploitation of the Amazon basin. The regime opened it to farming by cutting down its extensive rain forests. Some saw this as a serious threat to the ecological balance not only of Brazil but of the Earth itself. Moreover, ordi-

nary Brazilians benefited little from economic growth as the gulf between rich and poor, which had always been wide, grew even wider. In 1960, the wealthiest 10 percent of Brazil's population received 40 percent of the nation's income. In 1980, they received 51 percent. Then, too, rapid development led to an inflation rate of 100 percent a year. Combined with an enormous foreign debt, the economic miracle by the early 1980s was turning into an economic nightmare. Overwhelmed, the generals retreated and opened the door for a return to democracy in 1985.

The new democratic government faced enormous obstacles—a massive foreign debt, almost runaway inflation (it was 800 percent in 1987), and the lack of any real social unity. Presidential elections in 1990 brought a newcomer, Fernando Collor de Mello, into office. He promised to end inflation with a drastic reform program. Based on strict control of wages and prices, large reductions in public spending, and cuts in the number of government employees, his program soon led to high unemployment and a recession. Collor de Mello's efforts were also undermined by corruption in his own administration. He resigned from office at the end of 1992 after having been impeached. In new elections in 1994, Fernando Cardoso was elected president by an overwhelming majority of the popular vote.

## Chile

Another challenge to U.S. influence in Latin America came from Chile. Chile had suffered from a series of economic problems. Much wealth was held by large landowners and a select number of large corporations. Inflation, foreign debts, and a decline in the mining industry (the export of copper made up 80 percent of Chile's export income) caused untold difficulties. Right-wing control of the government failed to achieve any solutions. There was already a strong resentment against American corporations—especially Anaconda and Kennecott, which owned the copper industries.

In elections held in 1970, a split in the moderate forces enabled Salvador Allende (ah-YEN-dae), a Marxist, to become president of Chile with 36 percent of the vote. Allende tried to create a Marxian socialist society by constitutional means. A number of labor leaders, who represented the interests of the working classes, were made the ministers of labor, finance, public works, and interior in the new government. Allende increased the wages of industrial workers. He began to move toward socialism by nationalizing the largest domestic and foreign-owned corporations. Nationalization of the copper industry—which was basically carried out without paying the owners—angered the American owners and Richard Nixon, the American president. Nixon cut off all aid to Chile, which created problems for the Chilean economy. At the same time, radical workers were beginning to take control of the landed estates of the wealthy. The government made little effort to stop them.

These activities brought growing opposition from the upper and middle classes, including many women

▲ *This black-and-white photo of Salvador Allende was taken in March 1973 during a press conference. The congressional elections held two days after this photo was taken increased his hold over the country, but his victory was short-lived.*

who were organized to back the conservative cause. The forces of opposition began to organize strikes against the government (with support from the American CIA). Allende tried to stop the disorder by bringing military officers into his government. This did end the strikes. In March 1973, however, new elections increased the number of Allende's supporters in the Chilean congress. Afraid of Allende's growing strength, the Chilean army, under the direction of General Augusto Pinochet (PEE-noe-shay), decided to overthrow the government. On September 11, 1973, military forces seized the presidential palace. Allende was shot to death. His wife publicly denounced the

▶ *A small group of Shining Path guerrillas was photographed when they came across members of the press who were working in the Andes. How does this group differ from Castro's revolutionary followers or the Sandinistas?*

takeover and maintained that the United States had financed it. Contrary to the expectations of many right-wing politicians, the military remained in power and set up a dictatorship.

The Pinochet regime was one of the most brutal in Chile's history. Thousands of opponents were imprisoned. Thousands more were cruelly tortured and murdered. The regime also moved quickly to outlaw all political parties and remove the congress. It then restored many nationalized industries and landowners' estates to their original owners. The copper industries, however, remained in government hands. The regime's horrible abuse of human rights led to growing unrest against the government in the mid-1980s. In 1989, free presidential elections led to the defeat of Pinochet. A Christian Democrat, Patricio Azócur, became president and restored a somewhat democratic system.

## Colombia

On paper, Colombia has long had a democratic political system. In truth, however, a conservative elite—led by the owners of coffee plantations—has dominated the government. When Jorge Eliécer Gaitán led a movement of workers and landless peasants for land reform in the 1940s, he was assassinated. After 1950, the conservative elite ruled alone. When Marxist guerrilla groups organized the peasants and fought back, the government responded with violence. More than 200,000 peasants had lost their lives in the struggle by the mid-1960s.

Violence remained a constant feature of Colombian life in the 1980s and 1990s. Peasants who lived in poverty turned to a new cash crop—coca leaves—to satisfy the U.S. thirst for cocaine. As the drug trade increased, so, too, did the number of drug lords. They used bribes and violence to get government cooperation in the drug traffic. Despite government attempts to stop the drug traffic, both large and small drug lords continued their trade. The drug trade and the violence that goes with it continue to haunt Colombian life. Many Colombians, however, argue that they are only fulfilling a need and did not create the market for drugs in the United States.

## Peru

The history of Peru has been marked by much instability. Peru's dependence on the sale abroad of its products—such as sugar, cotton, fish meal, and copper—has led to extreme ups and downs in the economy. With these have come the rise and fall of governments. A large, poor, and landless Indian peasant population created an additional source of continual unrest.

A military takeover in 1968 led to some change. General Juan Velasco Alvarado realized the need to help the oppressed Indians. His government seized almost 75 percent of the nation's large landed estates. Ownership of the land was then put into the hands of peasant cooperatives. The government took control of foreign-owned companies and established its own form of socialism. The government also provided low food prices to help urban workers. Economic problems continued, however, and Peruvian military leaders removed General Alvarado from power in 1975. Five years later, unable to cope with Peru's economic problems, the military returned Peru to civilian rule.

New problems made the task of the new civilian governments even more difficult. A radical guerrilla group with ties to Communist China, known as **Shining Path,** waged a ruthless war by killing mayors, missionaries, priests, and peasants. Shining Path members followed the ideas of the Chinese Communist leader Mao Zedong (see Chapter 16). Their goal is to smash all authority and create a classless society. Peruvian drug traffickers, who made enormous profits from the sale of cocaine to the United States, financed Shining Path rebels in return for protection.

In 1990, fed up with their problems, Peruvians chose a political newcomer, Alberto Fujimoro, as their new president. Fujimoro, the son of a Japanese immigrant, promised reforms. Two years later, he suspended the constitution and congress, became a dictator, and began a ruthless campaign against Shining Path guerrillas. It remains to be seen whether Fujimoro's dictatorial powers will help him solve Peru's growing problems.

## SECTION REVIEW

1. **Define:**
   (a) *descamisados,*
   (b) Shining Path

2. **Identify:**
   (a) Evita Perón,   (b) Carlos Saúl Menem,
   (c) Fernando Collor de Mello,   (d) Salvador Allende,   (e) General Augusto Pinochet,
   (f) General Juan Velasco Alvarado

3. **Recall:**
   (a) How did Juan Perón seek to free Argentina from foreign investors?
   (b) Why did Argentina invade the Falkland Islands in 1982?
   (c) What is the most apparent environmental cost Brazil has paid for its economic growth?
   (d) What two economic problems did the new democratic government of Brazil face in the late 1980s?
   (e) Why have many poor Latin American farmers turned to the production of coca leaves?

4. **Think Critically:** Why is it often easier for the military to seize power in a nation than it is for the military to rule that nation effectively?

# CULTURE IN LATIN AMERICA SINCE 1945

It is difficult to speak of a single Latin American culture. Many different nations make up Latin America. Many different peoples and cultural heritages make up those nations. Mexico and Peru, for example, have rich Indian heritages (that of the Aztecs and Incas). In contrast, Argentina has no Indians, and most of its people are descendants of European immigrants. However, Latin American culture does have some common features. In this section, we will look at a few of them.

## Education

All countries in Latin America have compulsory (required by law) education for children. The number of years required varies from five to twelve. Dropout rates, however, are high. In Brazil, for example, less than 60 percent of students advanced from grade 1 to grade 2. The major reason is poverty. In many countries, parents often need their children to work for survival or cannot afford to send them to school. Those who can afford it often go to private Catholic schools. Children in some Latin American countries also miss many school days. In four countries, for example, illnesses, caused chiefly by the lack of nourishing food, caused children to miss as many as fifty days of school a year. Because many Latin American children are not receiving much education, illiteracy remains a problem in many Latin American countries.

There has been rapid growth in higher education in Latin America, however. In part, this reflects a greater investment of state funds in universities, often at the expense of primary or secondary schools. Also noticeable has been the growth in private universities. As an example, in Brazil, 63 percent of university students are enrolled at eleven Catholic universities and nine private secular schools. The remaining 37 percent of the university students attend 37 state-funded institutions.

The situation is quite different elsewhere, however. In Mexico, for example, 85 percent of university students attend state-funded schools. At the same time, the number of students in Mexican universities and colleges has risen dramatically. In 1965/1966, there were 256,000 university students. Only ten years later, the number had increased to 970,000. Unfortunately, jobs are often not available for the large numbers of university graduates.

The military regimes in Latin America have greatly affected universities. In Chile, for example, the military regime that came into power in 1973 fired 30 to 35 percent of the professors. Military governments have also hired their supporters to run the universities. These changes have led to a decline in the quality of education in many Latin American institutions of higher learning.

## Cultural Life

One constant theme in Latin American culture is the desire for a return to a lost past. To many Latin American intellectuals, the European conquest destroyed a world in which native peoples were an organic part of nature. Both artists and writers have sought to recapture this lost natural world. To them, nature frees people of the destructive habits imposed by civilized life.

Another tradition has also developed among some Latin American intellectuals—a civilizing tradition. These intellectuals believe in progress. To them, nature reduces people to primitive habits (to barbarians). Culture gives people their sensitivity and their compassion. The civilizers want a modern Latin America that includes industries and cities. They represent the majority in Latin America today.

Regardless of how they view their world, artists and writers have played important roles in Latin American society. They have been given a public status that few writers and artists have had in other countries. The poet Pablo Neruda, for example, was a Marxist presidential candidate in Chile in 1970. Another novelist and poet, José Sarney, was elected president of Brazil in 1985. Peru's greatest novelist, Mario Vargas Llosa (HOH-suh), ran for the presidency of Peru in 1990. In Latin America, writers and artists are seen as people who can express the hopes and desires of the people.

### The Arts

Before World War II, modern forms of art had been brought to Latin America by artists who had studied in Europe. Latin American artists, however, responded to modern art in their own way. For a long time, modern art was closely identified with nationalism, or a search for national identity. As we saw in Chapter 10, for many artists, this search included the desire to incorporate native traditions in their artworks. The painting of nationalist and worker-inspired murals in Mexico in the 1920s and 1930s had a strong impact on artists elsewhere in Latin America. Especially in Ecuador, Peru, and Bolivia, artists followed the Mexican artists in including elements of their native traditions in their murals.

After World War II, Latin American painting moved in new directions that were strongly influenced by international styles. Especially important was abstract painting—the most radical form of modern art. Abstract art was especially important in Argentina and Venezuela.

Modern art in Latin America was also helped by the development of a whole new set of art institutions. In the 1950s, a number of major cities built national museums, as well as museums of modern art. Large corporations also became important patrons of artists. International art exhibits, held in São Paulo, Buenos Aires, and Mexico City, came to be held regularly. These exhibitions set new standards for world art.

The use of modern international styles was also evident in architecture. Brazil, Venezuela, and Mexico led this movement, because these were the richest countries in Latin America at the time and thus were able to provide funds for buildings. Perhaps the most notable example of modern architecture can be seen in Brazil in the building of Brasília, the new capital city, in the 1950s and 1960s. Latin America's greatest modern architect, Oscar Niemeyer (NEE-mie-ur), designed some of the major buildings.

▲ *Lucila Godoy Alcayaga used the pen name Gabriela Mistral. She won her first poetry contest in 1914. Many of her poems have been translated into English by American poet Langston Hughes. Why do you think a well-known poet such as Langston Hughes would commit the time and energy needed to translate Lucila's poems into English?*

and Pablo Neruda (nay-ROO-thuh).

Gabriela Mistral was a Chilean poet and teacher. She was trained to be a teacher and became director of a secondary school for girls in 1918. She was soon asked to be the director of a new school for girls in Santiago. In 1922, she was invited by the Mexican government to introduce educational programs for the poor in that country. Later she took up residence in the United States and taught at Middlebury and Barnard Colleges. In 1945, she became the first Latin American author to win the Nobel Prize for literature.

The suicide of her fiancé when Mistral was twenty-one had a profound effect on her life and her poems. Her poems explored the many dimensions of love but were usually tinged with an element of sadness. Her first book of poetry was published in 1922. Her second collection, *Ternura (Tenderness)*, included a number of children's poems that captured the sweetness of childhood:

### Literature

In literature, Latin Americans developed a unique form of expression, which some have called **magic realism.** Magic realism brings together realistic events with dreamlike or fantastic backgrounds. This kind of fiction reflects reality, but with an element of fantasy. Magic realism is evident in the works of many of Latin America's great writers.

Since 1945, Latin American writers have received worldwide recognition. Indeed, a number of them have been awarded the Nobel Prize for literature. Among the great writers were Gabriela Mistral (mee-STRAWL), Jorge Luis Borges (BAW r-hess), Mario Vargas Llosa, Gabriel García Márquez (mahr-KEZ),

*Stars are circles of children
Looking at the earth as they play . . .
Wheat stalks are bodies of children
swaying and swaying as they play . . .
Rivers are circles of children
running off to the sea as they play
Waves are circlets of little girls
embracing this world...as they play.*[2]

Jorge Luis Borges was born in Argentina, where he spent most of his life. However, he was educated to a great extent in Europe. He wrote numerous poems and a large number of short stories. The latter contain many of the themes that make his work such a good example of magic realism. In *Fictions*, *The Aleph*, and *Labyrinths*, Borges created a fantastic world in which what seems absurd might well be true. However, who can really know? Borges chooses to stress that we know so little about the world that anything can happen.

Mario Vargas Llosa was born in Peru and educated in both Spain and France. His novels are realistic but also contain an element of fantasy. They mix time, space, and identity into a profound puzzle. His first novel, *Time of the Hero*, takes place in a military school. Here students deny the sensitive sides of their beings in order to appear tough, as society dictates. Many of Vargas Llosa's later works focus on the incredible corruption that he found in all levels of Peruvian society and government. In the 1980s, he began a search for new political values for Latin America. In *The War of the End of the World*, he gave a realistic portrayal of the crushing of a rebellion in Brazil in 1897. His message was clear: he supported the liberal principles of progress and modernization.

In the 1960s, Gabriel García Márquez was the most famous of the Latin American novelists. He was born and brought up in poverty in Colombia. Much of his early career was spent in journalism. He worked as a foreign reporter in Paris, Rome, Havana, and New York City. By the late 1950s and early 1960s, he was becoming known as a novelist. He won the Nobel Prize for literature in 1982.

The best known of his novels is *One Hundred Years of Solitude*. One critic, in fact, has called it one of the greatest novels ever written. It is the story of the development of the fictional town of Macondo as witnessed

▲ *Gabriel García Márquez continues to write. In 1996, he published a new novel,* News of a Kidnapping, *about drug-related kidnappings in Colombia. What is the most unique aspect of his writing style?*

by several generations of the Buendias, its founding family. Macondo is much like García Márquez's own hometown of Aracataca, near the Caribbean coast of Colombia. This novel is the foremost example of magic realism. The author slips back and forth between fact and fantasy. Villagers are not surprised when a local priest rises into the air and floats. However, when wandering gypsies introduce these villagers to magnets, telescopes, and magnifying glasses, the villagers are dumbfounded by what they see as magic. According to the author, fantasy and fact simply depend on one's point of view.

Pablo Neruda was a Chilean poet who won the Nobel Prize for literature in 1971. He was born in Chile but lived for a while in both Spain and Mexico. When he returned home, he entered political life, serving as a Communist deputy in the Chilean senate. In 1948, a new government forced him to leave Chile. He was not able to return until 1952. Neruda was a poet of great power. Through his poetry, he became a voice for the common people. He died in 1973, soon after the military coup that killed his friend, the Chilean president Salvador Allende.

Female writers also achieved new levels of success in Latin America. As we have seen, it was a woman—Gabriela Mistral—who was the first Latin American to win the Nobel Prize for literature, in 1945. In the 1980s, the work of Isabel Allende (niece of Salvador Allende) also achieved worldwide recognition. *The House of the Spirits* was a novel in the tradition of magic realism. It tells the history of twentieth-century Chile through four generations of women.

## ❀ SECTION REVIEW ❀

1. **Locate:**
   (*a*) Brasília

2. **Define:**
   (*a*) magic realism

3. **Identify:**
   (*a*) Pablo Neruda,   (*b*) José Sarney,   (*c*) Mario Vargas Llosa,   (*d*) Gabriela Mistral,   (*e*) *The War of the End of the World*

4. **Recall:**
   (*a*) Why is it difficult to speak of a single Latin American culture?
   (*b*) Although many more Latin American people are completing university degrees, why do they not always benefit materially from their education?
   (*c*) What is one constant theme in Latin American culture?

5. **Think Critically:** What factors combine to make it difficult to provide adequate education for most children in many Latin American nations?

## Conclusion

Since 1945, the nations of Latin America have experienced a number of common trends. Especially troublesome were economic problems. Although some Latin American nations shared in the economic growth of the 1950s and 1960s, this growth was not matched by any real political stability. Often armies overthrew democratic governments and established military regimes. Staggering debts owed to foreign banks made conditions even worse. With the debt crisis in the 1980s, however, came a movement toward democracy.

Democratic governments began to replace oppressive military regimes, and the trend continued into the 1990s.

Since 1945, a population explosion has magnified Latin America's economic and political problems. An enormous gulf between rich and poor has been a key factor in maintaining considerable social upheaval. Then, too, despite attempts to form a new relationship with Latin America, the United States continued to intervene in Latin American affairs, especially in the Caribbean Basin.

The nations of the Caribbean Basin experienced considerable upheaval after 1945. Mexico's economic problems magnified discontent with the nation's sole political party, the PRI. Successful Marxist revolutions in Cuba and Nicaragua fed U.S. fears of the spread of communism and led to active American involvement in the affairs of Caribbean Basin nations.

The nations of South America also experienced economic, social, and political problems. Strong military regimes alternated with civilian regimes in Argentina, Brazil, Chile, Colombia, and Peru. Recently, political democracy has made great strides. However, the vast gulf between rich and poor, along with the drug trade, has added to both the social and economic instability of the region.

## Notes

1. Dwight Eisenhower, *The White House Years: Waging Peace, 1956–1961* (Garden City, N.Y., 1965), p. 533.
2. Quoted in Ruth Ashby and Deborah Gore Ohrn, *Herstory: Women Who Changed the World* (New York, 1995), p. 204.

# CHAPTER 14 REVIEW

## USING KEY TERMS

1. The process of returning government owned businesses to private ownership is called

   _____.

2. The support given by some religious leaders in Latin America for violence to bring about political change has been called the _____.

3. A style of literature that combines elements of the real world with imaginary events is called

   _____.

4. Businesses that have divisions in two or more countries are called _____.

5. _____ was the name given to workers who supported Juan Perón in Argentina.

6. The anti-Communist forces that fought the Sandinistas in Nicaragua were called _____.

7. The Communist guerrilla movement in Peru is called the _____.

8. When a nation takes steps to encourage the production of products it buys from other countries it has undertaken _____.

9. _____ are organizations that work to eliminate competition for their illegal drug businesses.

## REVIEWING THE FACTS

1. What is the purpose of the Organization of American States?
2. Why have many Latin American cities experienced rapid population growth?
3. Why did many Latin American nations have difficulties in making payments on their international debts during the 1980s?
4. What is the North American Free Trade Agreement?
5. What did Fidel Castro do in 1960 that probably contributed to the decision of the United States to sponsor an invasion of Cuba at the Bay of Pigs in 1961?

6. What happened that ended Manuel Noriega's control of Panama in 1989?
7. What islands did Argentina invade in 1982?
8. Why did the armed forces of Chile overthrow and apparently kill Salvador Allende in 1973?
9. What did General Juan Velasco Alvarado do in the early 1970s that earned him the support of many of Peru's peasants?
10. What two career goals did Pablo Neruda pursue that made him famous?

## THINKING CRITICALLY

1. Why is the rapid rate of population growth in many Latin American countries a problem for their economic and political systems?
2. How may the creation of the Alliance for Progress in 1961 have been related to the conversion of Cuba to communism in the same year?
3. What caused the United States to use its military power to arrest Manuel Noriega after ignoring many other dishonest and corrupt leaders in Latin America?
4. Why did relations between the Soviet Union and Cuba become more difficult after 1962?
5. Why was the very close presidential election in Mexico in 1990 such a surprise?
6. Many Latin American nations have attempted to pay the costs of running their governments by printing money instead of collecting taxes. What problems has this policy caused?
7. Why was Evita Perón's use of government funds to help the poor probably bad for that country's political system in the long run?
8. Latin American nations have developed many high quality colleges and universities. Why hasn't this solved their problems of illiteracy and inequality?

# CHAPTER 14 REVIEW

## APPLYING SOCIAL STUDIES SKILLS

1. **Sociology:** Identify and explain several possible ways in which the social values of Latin American countries may be influenced by those of the United States.
2. **Geography/Economics:** Draw a map that indicates significant resources and products traded between the United States and Latin American nations. Identify and explain economic advantages each side has in this trade relationship.
3. **Government:** Explain why economic conditions encouraged the growth of dictatorial governments in Latin America during the 1980s.
4. **Geography/Ecology/Economics:** Study a map of the Amazon river valley and investigate the resources and uses of this region. What uses can you suggest that would preserve the Amazon's environment and at the same time provide a means of earning a living for the people of Brazil?

## MAKING TIME AND PLACE CONNECTIONS

1. Compare and contrast conditions that existed during the rapid growth of industries in Europe and the United States in the nineteenth century with those that have existed while Latin American nations have worked to industrialize.
2. Some people have compared the policies of the United States toward Latin American countries to those of the Soviet Union toward countries in Eastern Europe after World War II. Explain why you feel this is, or is not, a valid comparison.
3. What are the reasons for class distinctions that exist in the United States and in Latin American society? Explain the similarities and differences between the situations in the two countries.
4. Explain why many Latin American nations are more concerned with the influence of multinational corporations than are the United States or developed countries in Europe.

## BECOMING AN HISTORIAN

1. **Analyzing Information/Drawing Inferences:** The table below measures and projects the population of Latin America between 1940 and 2025. It also shows what percentage this population was or will be of total world population. Identify and explain the trend demonstrated by this data and what it is likely to mean for the future of Latin America.
2. **Art as a Key to History:** Ask a Spanish teacher in your school to help you identify writings by a well-known current Latin American poet or author. Write an essay that relates his or her point of view with social, political, or economic trends in Latin America.
3. **Conducting Research:** On April 22, 1997 anti-terrorist forces stormed the Japanese embassy in Lima, Peru where seventy-one hostages were held captive by members of a leftist group called Tupac Amaru. Although initial evaluations of the action were positive some people said it would only encourage reprisals from the guerrilla movement. Conduct research and write a report that describes the long-term results of this action by the Peruvian government.

### Latin American Population and Percentages of World Population (in millions of people)

| Year | 1940 | 1960 | 1980 | 2000 | 2025 |
|---|---|---|---|---|---|
| Population | 131 | 213 | 364 | 566 * | 865 * |
| % of World | 5.7% | 7.1% | 8.2% | 9.2%* | 10.6%* |

*projections
Source: United Nations, *Long Range Global Population Projections* (New York, 1992), pp. 16–17.

# CHALLENGES OF NATION BUILDING

**15**

In the 1970s, many Iranians began to grow dissatisfied with their ruler, Muhammad Reza Pahlavi, the shah of Iran. An opposition movement, led by the Muslim clergy under the guidance of the Ayatollah (IE-uh-TOE-luh) Ruholla Khomeini (KOE-MAE-nee), grew in strength. (An ayatollah is a major religious leader. The word means "the sign of God.") One observer described a political rally in the capital city of Tehran in 1978: "On Sunday, December 11, hundreds of thousands of people held a procession in the center of Tehran. . . . Slogans against the shah rippled in the wind—'Death to the Shah!' 'Death to the Americans!' 'Khomeini is our leader,' and so on. People from all walks of life could be found in the crowd." In January 1979, the shah left Iran, officially for a "period of rest and holiday." Three weeks later, the Ayatollah Khomeini returned to Iran from exile in Paris. On April 1, his forces seized control and proclaimed Iran to be an Islamic republic. Included in the new government's program was an attack on Western culture and, above all, on the United States, viewed by Khomeini as the "Great Satan." On November 4, after the shah had gone to the United States for medical help, Iranian revolutionaries seized the U.S. Embassy in Tehran, taking fifty-two Americans hostage. Not until the inauguration of a new American president in January 1981 did the Iranians free their American captives.

These revolutionary events in Iran were but one example of the upheavals that changed both the Middle East and Africa after 1945. In both these areas of the world, Europeans were forced to give up their control and allow independent states to emerge. The change from colony to free nation in both regions has not been easy, however. In Africa, the legacy of colonialism left arbitrary boundaries, political inexperience, and continued European economic domination. Combined with overpopulation and climatic disasters, this colonial legacy has made it difficult for the new states to achieve political stability and economic prosperity. In the Middle East, the problems are deep-seated ethnic and religious disputes, superpower involvement, and a gross inequality in the distribution of oil resources throughout the region. All these problems have led to a high level of tension and conflict, as well as a strong anti-Western sentiment. These two regions—Africa and the Middle East—remain among the most conflict ridden in the world.

◀ *This young Iranian armed with a machine gun stands in front of a revolutionary poster, a fitting symbol of the changes that occurred in Iran in the 1980s.*

# IN AFRICA AND THE MIDDLE EAST

## (1945 TO PRESENT)

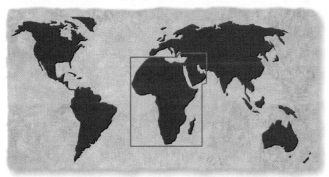

## QUESTIONS TO GUIDE YOUR READING

1. What were the backgrounds and ideas of the new African political leaders?

2. How have dreams clashed with realities in the independent nations of Africa?

3. What significant tensions exist in contemporary African society?

4. How have the tensions in contemporary African society affected African culture?

5. What political and economic problems have Middle Eastern states faced since 1945?

6. What are the major social and cultural developments in the Middle East since 1945?

## OUTLINE

1. THE ERA OF INDEPENDENCE IN AFRICA

2. CONTINUITY AND CHANGE IN MODERN AFRICAN SOCIETIES

3. CONFLICT IN THE MIDDLE EAST

4. SOCIETY AND CULTURE IN THE CONTEMPORARY MIDDLE EAST

## THE ERA OF INDEPENDENCE IN AFRICA

European colonial rule had been imposed on almost the entire continent of Africa by 1900. During the 1960s and 1970s, the Europeans finally retreated. Independent states with governments patterned after the Western model emerged across the continent.

The process of nation building has not been easy. The peoples of Africa were not well prepared for democracy. Even with political independence, they remained economically dependent upon their former European masters. The geographical shape of the new states reflected colonial interests rather than African realities. Most of the colonial boundaries had been drawn for the convenience of the European imperialists. Only rarely did the boundaries reflect the ethnic, cultural, or linguistic divisions of Africa.

African societies and their leaders have struggled for a generation to overcome these difficulties, but with only modest success. Many of the poorest nations in the world are in Africa. Several are threatened by mass starvation, and others, by the spread of AIDS. If unchecked, AIDS will devastate the populations

515

of these states early in the next century. Political stability is rare, and civil wars often erupt throughout the continent.

## Background: The Struggle for Independence

After World War II, Europeans realized that colonial rule in Africa would have to come to an end. Little had been done, however, to prepare Africans for self-rule. The political organizations that had been formed by Africans before the war to gain their rights became formal political parties. Independence was now their goal. In the Gold Coast, Kwame Nkrumah (en-KROO-

▼ *Kwame Nkrumah served as the first president of Ghana (formerly the Gold Coast) after the country gained its independence from Great Britain in 1957. Nkrumah was educated in the United States and became a strong voice in leading African opposition against colonialism.*

muh) formed the Convention People's Party, the first African political party in black Africa. In the late 1940s, Jomo Kenyatta founded the Kenya African National Union. It focused on economic issues but also sought independence or self-rule for Kenya.

For the most part, these political activities were nonviolent. They were led by Western-educated African intellectuals. The members of these parties were chiefly merchants, urban professionals, and members of labor unions. However, the demand for independence was not limited to the cities. In Kenya, for example, the **Mau Mau movement** among the Kikuyu peoples used terrorism to demand *uhuru* (freedom) from the British. Mau Mau terrorism alarmed the European population and caused the British in 1959 to promise eventual independence.

A similar process was occurring in Egypt, which had been a protectorate of Great Britain since the 1880s. In 1918, a formal political party called the Wafd was formed to promote Egyptian independence. Egyptian intellectuals, however, were opposed as much to the Egyptian monarchy as to the British. In 1952, an army coup overthrew King Farouk (fah-ROOK) and set up an independent republic.

In areas such as South Africa, where the political system was dominated by European settlers, the transition to independence was more complicated. In South Africa, political activity by local blacks began with the formation of the African National Congress (ANC) in 1912. At first, it was a group of intellectuals and had little mass support. Its goal was to gain economic and political reforms, including full equality for educated Africans, within the framework of the existing system. The ANC's efforts, however, met with little success. At the same time, by the 1950s, South African whites (descendants of the Dutch, or Afrikaans) were strengthening the laws separating whites and blacks. This activity created a system of racial segregation in South Africa known as **apartheid.** When blacks demonstrated against the apartheid laws, the white government brutally repressed the demonstrators. On March 21, 1960, for example, police opened fire on people who were leading a peaceful march in Sharpeville and killed sixty-nine. Two-thirds of the dead were found to be shot in the back. After the arrest of ANC leader Nelson Mandela in 1962, members of the ANC called for armed resistance to the white government.

In Algeria, some resistance to French rule by Arabs in rural areas had never ceased. However, a widespread rebellion broke out in the mid-1950s. At first, the French government tried to maintain its authority in Algeria. When Charles de Gaulle became president in 1958, however, he reversed French policy. Algeria was given its independence in 1962. The armed struggle in Algeria affected its neighbors as well. Both Tunisia and Morocco won their independence from France in 1956.

When both Great Britain and France decided to let go of their colonial empires in the late 1950s and 1960s, most black African nations achieved their independence. The Gold Coast, now renamed Ghana and under the guidance of Kwame Nkrumah, was first, in 1957. Nigeria, the Belgian Congo (renamed Zaire), Kenya, Tanganyika (TAN-gun-YEE-kuh) (later, when joined with Zanzibar, renamed Tanzania), and others soon followed. Seventeen new African nations emerged in 1960. Another eleven nations soon followed between 1961 and 1965. By the late 1960s, only parts of southern Africa and the Portuguese possessions of Mozambique and Angola remained under European rule. After a series of brutal guerrilla wars, the Portuguese finally gave up their colonies in the 1970s.

## Pan-Africanism and Nationalism: The Destiny of Africa

The newly independent African states faced many challenges. Most of them were chiefly traditional, agrarian societies (societies based on farming). Most African leaders, however, came from the urban middle class and had studied in either Europe or the United States. They spoke and read European languages. Most were very critical of colonial policies, but they still believed in using the Western democratic model in Africa.

The views of these African leaders on economics, however, were somewhat more diverse. Some, such as Jomo Kenyatta of Kenya and General Mobutu Sese Seko (moe-BOO-too SAY-SAY SAE-KOE) of Zaire, believed in Western-style capitalism. Others, such as

▲ *South African women unsuccessfully demonstrated in the streets of the Cato Manor Township to protest apartheid policies in 1959. They were outnumbered by the police, who prevented their entry into what had become a "whites-only" building.*

Julius Nyerere (nie-RAIR-ay) of Tanzania, Kwame Nkrumah of Ghana, and Sékou Touré of Guinea, preferred an "African form of socialism." This socialism was not like that practiced in the Soviet Union or Eastern Europe. Instead, it was based on African traditions of community in which ownership of the country's wealth would be put into the hands of the people. As Nyerere declared in 1967, "The basis of socialism is a belief in the oneness of man and the common historical destiny of mankind. Its basis, in other words, is human equality."[1]

The new political leaders in Africa were highly nationalistic. In general, they accepted the boundaries of their states, even though these had been drawn up arbitrarily by the colonial powers. Virtually all of the new states included widely different ethnic, linguistic, and territorial groups. In Zaire, for example, there were over two hundred different territorial groups speaking seventy-five different languages. In Uganda, the state radio station broadcast in twenty-four languages.

Some African leaders themselves helped to undermine the fragile sense of common identity that was needed to knit together these diverse groups in their countries. A number of them, including Nkrumah of Ghana, Touré of Guinea, and Kenyatta of Kenya, believed in the dream of pan-Africanism. This was a belief in the unity of all black Africans, regardless of national boundaries. The Organization of African Unity, founded by the leaders of thirty-two African states in 1963, was a concrete result of this belief.

Pan-Africanists believed in negritude (blackness), meaning that there was a distinctive "African personality." In their view, all black African peoples had a common identity and a common sense of destiny. Pan-Africanism was shared by several of the new African leaders, including Léopold Senghor of Senegal, Nkrumah of Ghana, and Kenyatta of Kenya. Nkrumah in particular hoped that a pan-African union could be established that would unite all of the new countries of the continent in a broader community. His dream never became a reality.

**Map 15.1   Modern Africa**

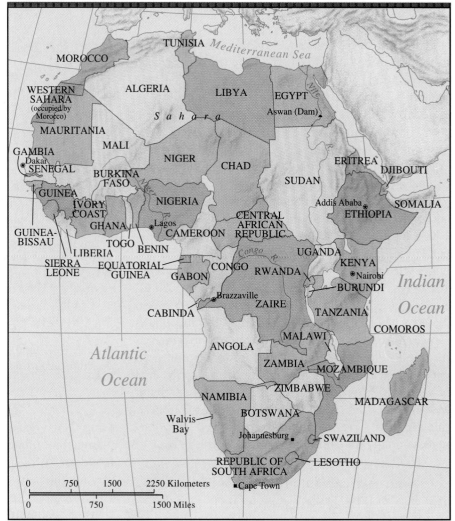

## Dreams and Realities

Other dreams failed as well in Africa. Many people had hoped that independence would lead to stable political structures based on "one person, one vote." They were soon disappointed as democratic governments gave way to a series of military regimes and one-party states. Between 1957 and 1982, over seventy leaders of African countries were overthrown by violence. In 1984, only seven of the forty-one major African states allowed opposition parties to operate legally. The rest were under single-party regimes or were ruled by the military.

Some of these military regimes were especially brutal. In 1966, President Milton Obote (oh-BOH-tay) had named Idi Amin (ee-DEE ah-MEEN) commander in chief of the Ugandan army. Five years later, Amin seized control of the country. He ruled with an iron fist and gave free rein to his secret police. Political opponents were shot, bludgeoned to death, and run over by tanks. Probably 150,000 people were murdered. Then, too, Amin ruined Uganda's economy with his lavish expenditures on luxuries and pleasures during his eight years of rule.

Hopes that independence would bring economic prosperity and equality were also crushed. Some of the problems were left over from colonial days. Most newly independent countries in Africa still relied on the export of a single crop or natural resource. Liberia, for example, depended on the export of rubber; Nigeria, on oil. When prices dropped, their economies suffered. To make matters worse, most African states had to import technology and manufactured goods from the West. The prices of those goods usually rose more rapidly than did prices of the export products.

The new states also created their own problems. Scarce national resources were spent on military equipment or expensive consumer goods rather than on building the foundations for an industrial economy. Corruption became almost a way of life in Africa. Bribery was needed to get even the most basic services.

Finally, population growth crippled efforts to create modern economies. By the 1980s, population growth averaged nearly 3 percent throughout Africa, the highest rate of any continent. Drought conditions have led to widespread hunger and starvation, first in West African countries such as Niger and Mali and then in Ethiopia, Somalia, and the Sudan. Millions are in danger of starvation and malnutrition. Countless others have fled to neighboring countries in search of food. In recent years, the spread of AIDS in Africa has caused the disease to reach epidemic proportions. According to one estimate, one-third of the entire population of sub-Saharan Africa is infected with the virus that causes AIDS.

As a result of all these problems, poverty is widespread in Africa, especially among the three-quarters of the population still living off the land. Cities have grown tremendously. In much of Africa, cities are surrounded by massive slums populated by rural people who fled to the cities to find a better life. The growth of the cities has overwhelmed transportation and sanitation systems. Pollution and perpetual traffic jams are the result. Millions are forced to live without water and

▲ *Two very wealthy Nigerian aristocrats emerge from their new Mercedes. What is the probable source of their wealth?*

electricity in their homes. In the meantime, the fortunate few (usually government officials willing to take bribes in return for favors) have lavish lifestyles. The rich in many East African countries are known as the *wabenzi,* or Mercedes Benz people.

Concern over the dangers of economic inequality (the wide gap between rich and poor) inspired a number of African leaders to limit foreign investment and nationalize the major industries and utilities. Nyerere promoted the ideals of socialism and self-reliance in Tanzania. He placed limits on income and set up village collectives to avoid government corruption. Many observers noted that levels of corruption and political instability were lower in Tanzania than in many other African countries.

The countries that opted for capitalism faced their own problems. Kenya has a strong current of African capitalism and a substantial middle class, mostly based in the capital of Nairobi. However, landlessness, unemployment, and income differences are high. Eighty percent of the population lives in the countryside. Forty percent lives below the poverty line. The result has been widespread unrest in a country formerly admired for its successful development.

Beginning in the mid-1970s, a few African nations decided to adopt Soviet-style Marxism-Leninism. In Angola and Ethiopia, Marxist parties followed the Soviet model. Economically, the results were disappointing, and both countries faced severe internal opposition. In Ethiopia, the revolt by Muslim tribal peoples in the province of Eritrea (AIR-i-TREE-uh) led to the fall of the Marxist leader Mengistu (MING-jist-oo) and his regime in 1990. A similar revolt erupted against the government in Angola.

Neither capitalism nor socialism could reverse Africa's downward spiral. According to recent statistics, eighteen of the world's twenty poorest countries are in Africa. Excluding South Africa, the gross national product in 1991 for all countries south of the Sahara, representing almost 600 million people, was roughly equivalent to that of Belgium, with a population of about 10 million.

Furthermore, Africans have been disappointed that the dream of a united Africa has not been realized. Some continue to blame the West for their problems and resent any Western interference in their affairs. One reason for the formation of the Organization of African Unity was to reduce Western influence. However, African states have had difficulty achieving a united position on many issues. Their disagreements have left the region open to outsiders and have even led to conflict. During the late 1980s and early 1990s, border disputes festered in many areas of the continent and, in some cases, flared into outright war.

Even within many African nations, the concept of nationhood was undermined by warring tribes. During the late 1960s, civil war tore Nigeria apart. When northerners began to kill the Ibo (EE-boe) peoples, thousands of Ibos fled to their home region in the eastern part of Nigeria. There, Colonel Odumegu-Ojukwu organized the Ibos in a rebellion and declared the eastern region of Nigeria an independent state called Biafra. After three years of bloody civil war, Biafra finally surrendered and accepted the authority of the central government of Nigeria.

Ethnic conflicts also broke out among hostile tribal groups in Zimbabwe (zim-BOB-way). In central Africa,

fighting between the Hutus (HOO-TOOZ) and Tutsis (TOOT-seez) has created unstable governments in both Burundi (buh-ROON-dee) and Rwanda (roo-WAWN-duh). In 1994, a Hutu rampage left 500,000 Tutsis dead in Rwanda. Many of them, including women and children, were hacked to death with machetes. Even those who sought refuge in churches were massacred. As hostilities have grown in many African nations, so too have new ways to put together armies, including the use of children as soldiers (see "Young People in Africa: The Boy Soldiers").

Not all the news in Africa has been bad, however. In recent years, popular demonstrations have led to the collapse of one-party regimes and the emergence of fragile democracies in several countries. The most notorious case was that of Idi Amin of Uganda. After ruling by terror and brutal repression, Amin was finally deposed in 1979. Dictatorships were also brought to an end in Ethiopia, Liberia, and Somalia. However, in each case, the fall of the regime was later followed by bloody civil war.

The election of Nelson Mandela to the presidency of the Republic of South Africa is one of the more remarkable events of recent African history. Mandela was sentenced to life imprisonment in 1962. However, in 1990, he was released because of the efforts of F. W. de Klerk, head of the National Party, and massive world pressure. As head of the African National Congress, Mandela continued to campaign against apartheid. In 1993, the government of President F. W. de Klerk agreed with ANC leader Nelson Mandela to hold democratic national elections—the first in South Africa's history. In 1994, Mandela became South Africa's first black president and expressed his hopes for unity. He declared in his presidential inaugural address, "We shall build a society in which all South Africans, both black and white, will be able to walk tall, without any fear in their hearts, assured of their inalienable right to human dignity—a rainbow nation at peace with itself and the world."

As Africa evolves, it is useful to remember that economic and political change is often a slow and painful process. As one African writer observed, it is easy to be cynical in Africa. Changes in political regimes have had little effect on people's livelihoods. "Still," he said,

## YOUNG PEOPLE IN AFRICA

# The Boy Soldiers

Throughout the world, wherever extreme poverty and civil strife have torn apart the normal fabric of society, young boys are being used as full-time soldiers. Between 50,000 and 200,000 are currently fighting in twenty-four conflicts. A number of these conflicts are in Africa.

In Liberia, the rebel leader Charles Taylor made regular use of boy soldiers. In fact, he gave them their own regiment, the Small Boy Unit. Their survival depended upon the ability to steal the supplies they needed on a daily basis. Boy soldiers have also been recruited in other African states, including Mozambique, Angola, the Sudan, Rwanda, and Sierre Leone.

Different methods are used to recruit and keep boys in military units. In Mozambique, the rebel movement known as Renamo recruited boys whose average age was eleven years. The group used terror to recruit the boys, including hanging them upside down from trees. Many were forced to kill their own parents. One recruit, who is now in school, said, "I killed and I robbed and I feel ashamed." Unfortunately, many no longer even feel his kind of remorse.

Other methods also are used to encourage boys to fight. In African bush wars, military leaders used drugs to keep their troops excited for battle. In Liberia, children were given Valium (a tranquilizer used to relieve anxiety and tension) before they went into combat.

What impact does being a soldier have on young children? For some, becoming a soldier is a matter of survival. One gets a uniform, shoes, reg-

▲ *This child, armed with an AK-47 assault rifle, rides his bicycle through the streets of Monrovia, Liberia. Although in 1995 to 1996 a program was established to help change the lives of these "child soldiers," the program collapsed, and half of the children involved returned to the streets, armed with high-powered weapons. What do you think the future holds for these children and for Liberia?*

*(continued)*

## YOUNG PEOPLE IN AFRICA

### The Boy Soldiers, continued

ular meals, and a gun—a symbol of power. In Uganda, hundreds of war orphans recruited into the regular army are now fed and housed.

Of course, the violence that many young people encounter can also ruin their lives. Some fully admit that they enjoy the killing. As one United Nations worker in Liberia observed, "Kids make more brutal fighters because they haven't developed a sense of judgment."

1. How are young boys recruited and kept in military units in many African nations?

2. What impact does being a soldier have on such young people?

3. What does the use of children as soldiers tell about a society?

"let us welcome the wind of change. This, after all, is a continent of winds. The trick is to keep hope burning, like a candle protected from the wind."[2]

### ✿ SECTION REVIEW ✿

1. **Locate:**
   (a) Algeria,    (b) Tunisia,    (c) Morocco,
   (d) Ghana,    (e) Nigeria,    (f) Zaire,
   (g) Kenya,    (h) Tanzania,    (i) Mozambique,
   (j) Angola,    (k) Niger,    (l) Mali,
   (m) Ethiopia,    (n) Somalia,    (o) Sudan,
   (p) Zimbabwe,    (q) Rwanda

2. **Define:**
   (a) Mau Mau movement,
   (b) apartheid

3. **Identify:**
   (a) Kenya African National Union,    (b) King Farouk,    (c) African National Congress (ANC),
   (d) Nelson Mandela,    (e) Kwame Nkrumah,

(f) Organization of African Unity,    (g) Hutus,
(h) Tutsis

4. **Recall:**
   (a) What difficulties have African societies struggled to overcome for generations?
   (b) What challenges did newly independent African states face?
   (c) What dreams of African nationalists have not been achieved?
   (d) What problems resulted from the migration of Africans from rural areas into cities?
   (e) Why are African countries that are regarded as successful, like Kenya, still experiencing many economic and social problems?

5. **Think Critically:**
   (a) Why weren't European powers able to maintain their control over their African colonies after World War II?
   (b) Why has population growth made it almost impossible for many African nations to achieve economic improvements?

# CONTINUITY AND CHANGE IN MODERN AFRICAN SOCIETIES

Africa is a study in contrasts. Old and new and native and foreign live side by side. The tension between traditional ways and Western culture is felt especially strongly by many African intellectuals. They are torn between their admiration for things Western and their desire to retain an African identity.

## The City and the Countryside

In general, the impact of the West has been greater on the urban and educated and more limited on the rural and illiterate. After all, the colonial presence was first and most firmly established in the cities. Many cities, including Dakar, Lagos, Capetown, Johannesburg, Brazzaville, and Nairobi, are direct products of colonial rule. Most African cities today look like cities elsewhere in the world. They have high-rise buildings, blocks of apartments, wide boulevards, neon lights, movie theaters, and, of course, traffic jams.

The cities are also where the African elites live and work. Wealthy Africans have been strongly attracted to the glittering consumer products of Western culture. They live in Western-style homes or apartments and eat Western foods stored in Western refrigerators. Those who can afford it drive Western cars. It has been said that there are more Mercedes Benz automobiles in Nigeria than in Germany, where they are made.

The minds of the elite have also become Western. In part, this is due to the educational system. In the precolonial era, public schools as we know them did not really exist in Africa. For the average African, education took place in the home or in the village courtyard. It stressed basic skills and being part of a community. This traditional education in Africa provided what the people needed in their communities. Society's values and customs were passed on to the young by the storytellers, often the village elders. One scholar has described the practice among the Luo people in Kenya: "Traditionally, Luo stories were told in *siwindhe*, or the house of a widowed grandmother, a circular building with a thatched cone-shaped roof. Here in *siwindhe*, in the home of a woman who could talk freely about all subjects, Luo boys and girls gathered together to be taught the ways and thinking of their people. Its basic medium of instruction was the story."[3]

◄ *Nairobi, Kenya, is located in the southern part of the country, and its population is close to two million. Nairobi serves as the East African headquarters for many multinational corporations. This modern city, whose skyline is dotted with skyscrapers, was begun in the 1890s as a railroad construction camp.*

Modern Western education was introduced into Africa in the nineteenth century by the Europeans. The French colonists set up the first state-run schools in Senegal in 1818. In British colonies, the earliest schools were set up by missionaries. At first, these schools stressed vocational training with some classes in European languages and Western civilization. Eventually, pressure from Africans led to the introduction of professional training. The first schools of higher learning were established in the early twentieth century. Most college-educated Africans, however, received their higher education abroad.

With independence, African countries set up their own state-run schools. The emphasis was on primary schools, but high schools and universities were established in major cities. The basic objectives have been to introduce vocational training and improve literacy rates. Unfortunately, both trained teachers and funding are scarce in most countries. Few rural areas have schools. As a result, illiteracy rates remain high, estimated at about 70 percent of the population across the continent.

Christianity has also been an avenue for the introduction of Western ideas. Christian missionaries spread their faith rapidly during the nineteenth century among the urban elites and in rural areas as well. By 1950, an estimated fifty million Africans were Christians.

Outside the major cities, where about three-quarters of the inhabitants of Africa live, Western influence has had less of an impact. Millions of people throughout Africa live much as their ancestors did, in thatched huts without modern plumbing and electricity. They farm or hunt by traditional methods. They practice time-honored family rituals and believe in the traditional gods.

Even in the countryside, however, change is taking place. Economic need has brought a massive movement of people. Some leave to work on plantations. Some move to the cities, and others flee to refugee camps to escape starvation. Migration is a wrenching experience, because it disrupts family and village ties.

Nowhere, in fact, is the split between the old and the new, or the rural and the urban, so clear and painful as in Africa. On the one hand, urban dwellers view the

▲ *In Mogadishu, Somalia, students gather around their teacher. List the differences between this makeshift classroom and an elementary school classroom that you remember. Do you think it surprising that the teacher is a woman? Why or why not?*

village as the storehouse of all that is backward in the African past. Rural peoples, on the other hand, view the growing urban areas as a source of corruption and of the destruction of time-honored customs and values.

## Women in Modern Africa

Independence from colonial powers had a significant impact on women's roles in African society. Almost without exception, the new governments established the principle of sexual equality. Women were allowed to vote and run for political office. However, as elsewhere, legislation was not enough to make women equals in a world dominated by men. Politics remains a world of men. A few professions, such as teaching, child care, and clerical work, are dominated by women. Most African women, however, are employed in menial positions such as farm laborers, factory workers, workers in retail trade, and servants. Education is open to all at the elementary level. However, women make up less than 20 percent of upper-level students in most African societies today.

Women have made the greatest strides in the cities. Most urban women, like men, now marry on the basis of personal choice. A significant minority, however, are still willing to accept as their spouses the choices of their parents. After marriage, African women appear to occupy a more equal position than married women in most Asian countries. In Africa, each marriage partner usually maintains a separate income. Women often have the right to possess property separate from their husbands.

Nevertheless, many wives still defer to their husbands in the traditional manner. Others, however, are like the woman in Abioseh Nicol's story "A Truly Married Woman" who, after years of living as a common-law wife with her husband, is finally able to provide the price and finalize the marriage. After the wedding, the wife declares, "For twelve years I have got up every morning at five to make tea for you and breakfast. Now I am a truly married woman and you must treat me with a little more respect. You are now my husband and not a lover. Get up and make yourself a cup of tea."[4]

In general, women in cities in contemporary Africa are sometimes held to different standards than men. African men often expect their wives to be both modern and traditional—both wage earners and housekeepers. Furthermore, women do not possess the full range of career opportunities that men do.

In rural areas, traditional attitudes toward women still prevail. In the village, polygamy is not uncommon. Arranged marriages are still the rule rather than the exception. As a father tells his son in Cyprian Ekwensi's *Iska:*

*We have our pride and must do as our fathers did. You see your mother? I did not pick her in the streets. When I wanted a woman I went to my father and told him about my need of her and he went to her father. . . . Marriage is a family affair. You young people of today may think you are clever. But marriage is still a family affair.*[5]

To villagers in Africa, African cities often look like founts of evil and corruption. Women in particular have suffered from the tension created by the conflict between the lure of the city and their village roots. As men are drawn to the cities in search of employment and excitement, their wives and girlfriends may be left behind in the native villages.

## African Culture

The tension between traditional and modern and native and foreign that has played such a large part in modern African society also affects African culture (see "Our Artistic Heritage: Art in Contemporary Africa"). Africans have kept their native traditions while also being affected by foreign influences. Wood carving, metalwork, painting, and sculpture, for example, have kept their old forms, but they are increasingly adapted to please tourists. Some African art retains its traditional purpose, however, including serving as the objects of worship.

Similar developments have taken place in music and dance, which have retained their traditional vigor. The earlier emphasis on religious ritual, however, has been replaced to some degree by a new interest in the spectator. To take advantage of the growing popularity of African dancing, several governments have sponsored traveling folk dance companies. African music has been exported to Europe, North America, and Latin America. It then has returned to Africa in a new synthesis with foreign styles, such as the samba.

No area of African culture has been so strongly affected by political and social events as literature. The most common form of fiction writing in contemporary Africa is the novel. Novels began to appear in British colonies in the decade after World War II. By the

# OUR ARTISTIC HERITAGE

## Art in Contemporary Africa

One common theme in the work of many contemporary African artists is the need to find a balance between Western techniques and training on the one hand and the rich heritage of traditional African art forms on the other. For some artists who rely on government support for their work,

*These two young women are decorating the door to their home compound. What designs are they creating for the door that you have seen in other art?*

*Sokari Douglas Camp created this 91-inch-tall sculpture, Masquerader with Boat Headdress, in 1987 from steel, pieces of mirror, wood, bells, and cloth. It is just one composition from a full set of huge pieces she made, entitled* Echoes of the Kalabari. *Douglas Camp was born in Kalabari, and most of her work celebrates her Yoruba culture. In what ways does the artist combine ancient and modern ideas?*

the governments have decided which of the two elements is more important. In Senegal under President Léopold Senghor and in Zaire under President Mobutu Sese Soso, artists were told to depict tribal masks, carvings, and scenes of traditional African life. These works are often designed to serve the tourist industry and the export market.

Some African artists have taken their own approaches to this problem. The South African artist David Koloane has argued that artists should be able to use any style they want. Others, however, have chosen to combine new forms with traditional ones. Bruce Onobrakpeya is one of Nigeria's best-known artists. He uses his own unique techniques in making prints. However, the subject

*(continued)*

## OUR ARTISTIC HERITAGE

# Art in Contemporary Africa, continued

matter or content of his prints comes from the history of his own Urhobo people and other Nigerian cultures. Sokari Douglas Camp is another Nigerian artist who has received worldwide attention for her work. Her sculptures in welded metal combine a Western approach to modern sculpture with African traditions.

A second theme in contemporary African art is the continuation of divisions between men and women. Men have traditionally created art using stone, bronze, and wood. Women, in contrast, have expressed themselves through textiles, clay, woven fiber, paint, or other material readily available in the home. The art of women is used to celebrate the gods, beautify their surroundings, and introduce their children to color and design. As seen in the illustration, two young women engage in the annual repainting of the carved door to their family meeting place in Nigeria.

1. What are the two main themes in contemporary African art?

2. What are two purposes of African art?

3. Do you think that artists who are paid and supported by a government should be required to produce art that meets the approval of that government? Why or why not?

4. There are definite differences between the art created by African men and African women. Do you think there are similar differences between the art of men and women in other cultures? If so, what are some general differences? Can you support your claim with examples?

---

1960s, they had become increasingly popular, especially in West and East Africa. To appeal to educated English-speaking readers, most of the early novels appeared in English.

African writers, perhaps more than any other group in African society, have been tortured by the tensions and dilemmas that modern Africans face. The conflicting demands of town versus country and native versus foreign were the themes of most of the best-known works of the 1960s and 1970s. These themes certainly characterize the work of Chinua Achebe (A-chay-bay), a Nigerian novelist and winner of the Nobel Prize for literature in 1989. In the 1950s and 1960s, Achebe wrote four novels that won him international acclaim. All four show the problems of Africans caught up in the conflict between traditional and Western values. Most famous of Achebe's four novels is *Things Fall Apart* (see "Our Literary Heritage: *Things Fall Apart*").

Another African author who has received world acclaim is the Nigerian Wole Soyinka. Like many other African writers, Soyinka has expressed his frustration over the failures of many of Africa's new leaders. His novel *The Interpreters* condemned corruption in Nigerian politics. Soyinka also focused on the problems of daily life in Africa, especially the great gap between the traditional rural village and the impersonal modern city. He won the Nobel Prize for literature in 1986.

In Africa, novels are read chiefly by an educated minority in the cities. Some novels have found a larger audience by being serialized in newspapers and magazines. However, they have not entirely replaced the traditional oral literature. Illiteracy rates are still high. Thus, professional storytellers entertain village audiences by telling stories about the past, much as their ancestors did before the colonial era. Even in the villages, however, modern technology has had an impact through radio and television.

## OUR LITERARY HERITAGE

# Things Fall Apart

*In* Things Fall Apart, *Chinua Achebe portrayed the complex society of the Ibo people as it came into contact with Westerners. As seen in this excerpt, Achebe sought to portray the simple dignity of traditional African village life.*

### Chinua Achebe, *Things Fall Apart*

During the planting season Okonkwo worked daily on his farms from cock-crow until the chickens went to roost. He was a very strong man and rarely felt fatigue. But his wives and young children were not as strong, and so they suffered. But they dared not complain openly. Okonkwo's first son, Nwoye, was then twelve years old but was already causing his father great anxiety for his incipient laziness. At any rate, that was how it looked to his father, and he sought to correct him by constant nagging and beating. And so Nwoye was developing into a sad-faced youth.

Okonkwo's prosperity was visible in his household. He had a large compound enclosed by a thick wall of red earth. His own hut, or *obi*, stood immediately behind the only gate in the red walls. Each of his three wives had her own hut, which together formed a half moon behind the *obi*. The barn was built against one end of the red walls, and long stacks of yarn stood out prosperously in it. At the opposite end of the compound was a shed for the goats, and each wife built a small attachment to her hut for the hens. Near the barn was a small house, the "medicine house" or shrine where Okonkwo kept the wooden symbols of his personal god and of his ancestral spirits. He wor-

▲ *The family scene described by Achebe could take place in many different areas in Africa. This 1978 photo of an African family was taken in rural Nigeria.*

shipped them with sacrifices of kola nut, food and palm-wine, and offered prayers to them on behalf of himself, his three wives and eight children.

1. What does this excerpt tell about the Ibo tribal society in Nigeria?

2. Put yourself in the place of Nwoye, the son. How would you describe your life?

## SECTION REVIEW

**1. Identify:**
(*a*) Abioshe Nicol,   (*b*) Chinua Achebe

**2. Recall:**
(*a*) Why has it been difficult to build an educational system in most African countries?
(*b*) What signs in African culture demonstrate the conflict between traditional and modern values?

**3. Think Critically:** Why doesn't the fact that many African cities look much like cities in Europe necessarily mean they are as prosperous, successful, or as stable as European cities?

3

# CONFLICT IN THE MIDDLE EAST

For the countries of the Middle East, the period between the two world wars was an age of transition. With the fall of the Ottoman and Persian Empires, new, modernizing regimes emerged in Turkey and Iran (see Chapter 10). A fiercely independent government was established in Saudi Arabia in 1932. Iraq gained its independence from Great Britain in the same year. Elsewhere in the Middle East, European influence remained strong. Great Britain and France had mandates in Syria, Lebanon, Jordan, and Palestine (see Chapter 10).

## The Question of Palestine

In the Middle East, as in other areas of Asia, World War II led to the emergence of new independent states. Syria and Lebanon had already received their independence near the end of World War II. Jordan achieved complete self-rule soon after the war. Although Egypt had gained its independence in 1922, it still remained under British control. Sympathy for the idea of Arab unity led to the formation of an Arab League in 1945, but its members could not agree on much.

The one issue on which all Muslim states in the area could agree was Palestine. As tensions between Jews

▲ *Local Arabs living in Jerusalem were stopped and searched by British soldiers in the years prior to the declaration of the Israeli state in 1948. How has the treatment of Arab residents changed since this time?*

and Arabs intensified during the 1930s, Great Britain, which had a mandate in Palestine, began to limit Jewish immigration into the area. Moreover, Great Britain firmly rejected Jewish proposals for an independent state in Palestine (see Chapter 10).

The Zionists who wanted Palestine as a home for Jews were not to be denied, however. Many people had been shocked at the end of World War II when they learned about the Holocaust, the deliberate killing of six million European Jews in Nazi death camps. Sympathy for the Jewish cause grew dramatically. As a result, when Zionists turned for support to the United States, they were well received. In March 1948, the Truman administration approved the concept of an independent Jewish state in Palestine, despite the fact that only about one-third of the local population was Jewish. When a United Nations resolution divided Palestine into a Jewish state and an Arab state, the Jews in Palestine acted. On May 14, 1948, they proclaimed the state of Israel.

**Map 15.2   The Modern Middle East**

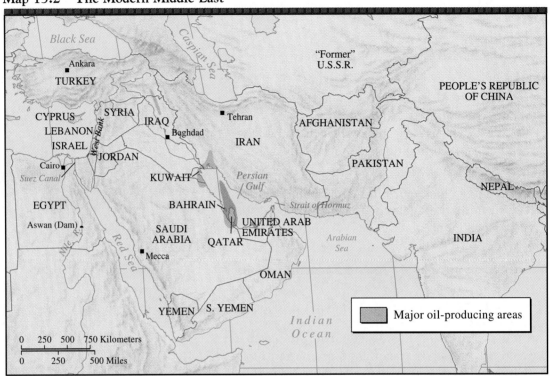

Its Arab neighbors saw the new state as a betrayal of the Palestinian people, 90 percent of whom were Muslim. Outraged at the lack of Western support for Muslim interests in the area, several Arab countries invaded the new Jewish state. The invasion failed, but both sides remained bitter. The Arab states refused to recognize the existence of Israel.

The war in 1948 had other results as well. Thousands of Palestinian refugees fled from Israel into neighboring Muslim states. Jordan, a country occupied by half a million bedouins (BED-oh-winz) (nomads), was now flooded by the arrival of almost one million urban Palestinians. To the north, the state of Lebanon had been created to provide the local Christian community with a country of its own. The arrival of Palestinian refugees, however, upset the delicate balance there between Christians and Muslims. Moreover, the creation of Lebanon had angered the Syrians, who had lost it as a result of European decisions after the war.

## Nasser and Pan-Arabism

The dispute over Palestine placed Egypt in a difficult position. Technically, Egypt was not an Arab state. However, King Farouk, who had come to power in 1936, had often declared support for the Arab cause. Farouk, in fact, had committed Egyptian armies to the disastrous war against Israel in 1948.

In 1952, King Farouk was overthrown by a military coup led by young military officers. The real force behind the scenes was Colonel Gamal Abdul Nasser, son of a minor government official. In 1953, Nasser replaced the monarchy with a republic.

One year later, Nasser took control of Egypt. His first act was to begin a land-reform program to help the peasants. While adopting a policy of neutrality in foreign affairs, he expressed sympathy for the Arab cause. Nasser was especially upset with Great Britain. Even after it had granted Egypt independence in 1922,

# YOU ARE THERE

## The Suez Canal Belongs to Egypt

▲ *Gamal Abdul Nasser, shown here, presented an eloquent defense for the Arab cause in the Middle East. He is respected for his integrity and for his attempts to improve the lives of the poor in Egypt.*

*The Suez Canal was built between 1854 and 1869, using mainly French money and Egyptian labor. It was managed by a Paris-based corporation, called the Suez Canal Company. In this excerpt from a speech, Egyptian president Gamal Abdul Nasser declared that it was time for the canal to be owned and managed by Egyptians.*

### Nasser's Speech Nationalizing the Suez Canal Company

The Suez Canal is an Egyptian canal built as a result of great sacrifices. The Suez Canal Company is an Egyptian company that was expropriated [taken away] from Egypt by the British who, since the canal was dug, have been obtaining the profits of the Company. . . . And yet the Suez Canal Company is an Egyptian limited liability company. The annual Canal revenue is 35 million Egyptian pounds. From this sum Egypt—which lost 120,000 workers in digging the Canal—takes one million pounds from the Company.

It is a shame when the blood of people is sucked, and it is no shame that we should borrow for construction. We will not allow the past to be repeated again, but we will cancel the past by restoring our rights in the Suez Canal. . . .

*(continued)*

## YOU ARE THERE

# The Suez Canal Belongs to Egypt, continued

The people will stand united as one man to resist imperialist acts of treachery. We shall do whatever we like. When we restore all our rights, we shall become stronger and our production will increase. At this moment, some of your brethren, the sons of Egypt, are now taking over the Egyptian Suez Canal and directing it. We have taken this decision to restore part of the glories of the past and to safeguard our national dignity and pride. May God bless you and guide you in the path of righteousness.

1. What was the problem President Nasser was addressing?

2. According to Nasser, why does the Suez Canal rightfully belong to Egypt?

---

Britain had kept control over the Suez Canal in order to protect its sea route to the Indian Ocean. On July 26, 1956, Nasser suddenly nationalized the Suez Canal Company, which had been under British and French administration (see "You Are There: The Suez Canal Belongs to Egypt").

Concerned over the threat to their route to the Indian Ocean, Great Britain and France decided to strike back. They were quickly joined by Israel. The forces of the three nations launched a joint attack on Egypt, starting the Suez War of 1956. Both the United States and the Soviet Union supported Nasser and forced Britain, France, and Israel to withdraw their troops from Egypt (see "You Are There: A Plea for Peace in the Middle East").

Nasser now turned to **pan-Arabism,** or a belief in Arab unity. In 1957, the Ba'ath (BATH) Party, which advocated a union of all Arab states in a new socialist society, assumed power in Syria. It opened talks with Egypt on a union between Syria and Egypt. In March 1958, Egypt formally united with Syria in the United Arab Republic (UAR). Nasser was named the first president of the new state.

Egypt and Syria hoped that the union would eventually include all the Arab states. Other Arab leaders, however, including young King Hussein of Jordan and the kings of Iraq and Saudi Arabia, were suspicious.

The kings of Iraq and Saudi Arabia particularly feared pan-Arabism. They thought that they would be asked to share their vast oil revenues with the poorer states of the Middle East.

Nasser certainly had dreams of a new kind of Middle East. Much of the wealth of the Middle East, he thought, now flowed into the treasuries of a few states or to foreign oil interests. In Nasser's view, through Arab unity, this wealth could be used to improve the standard of living throughout the Middle East. To achieve this, natural resources (including oil) and major industries would have to be nationalized. Central planning could then guarantee that these resources would be utilized efficiently, creating a new economic policy that Nasser called **scientific socialism.**

In the end, however, Nasser's desire to extend state control over the economy brought an end to the UAR. When his government announced the nationalization of a large number of industries and utilities in 1961, a military coup overthrew the Ba'ath leaders in Syria. The new leaders then withdrew Syria from its union with Egypt.

The breakup of the UAR did not end Nasser's dream of pan-Arabism. During the mid-1960s, Egypt was active in promoting Arab unity against Israel. At a meeting of Arab leaders held in Jerusalem in 1964, the Egyptians took the lead in forming the Palestine Liber-

# YOU ARE THERE
## A Plea for Peace in the Middle East

*During the Suez War in 1956, Israel quickly captured the Sinai peninsula. The United Nations, however, pressured Israel to withdraw its troops. At first, Israel refused. In March 1957, however, Golda Meir, Israel's foreign minister, announced that Israel had agreed to withdraw from the Sinai. This excerpt is taken from her statement.*

### Golda Meir Announces the Israeli Withdrawal from the Sinai

May I now add these few words to the states in the Middle East area and, more specifically, to the neighbors of Israel. We all come from an area which is a very ancient one. The hills and the valleys have been witnesses to many wars and many conflicts. But this is not the only thing which characterizes the part of the world from which we come. It is also a part of the world which is of an ancient culture. It is part of the world which has given to humanity three great religions [Judaism, Christianity, and Islam]. It is also that part of the world which has given a code of ethics to all humanity. In our countries, in the entire region, all our peoples are anxious for and in need of a higher standard of living, of great programs of development and progress. Can we, from now on—all of us—turn a new leaf and, instead of fighting with each other, can we all, united, fight poverty and disease and illiteracy? Is it possible for us to put all our efforts and all our energy into one single purpose, the betterment and progress and development of all our lands and all our peoples? I can here pledge the government and the people of Israel to do their part in this united effort. There is

▲ *Golda Meir served as Israeli minister of foreign affairs from 1956 to 1966 and as prime minister of Israel from 1969 to 1974. Do you believe it unusual that someone born in Kiev, Ukraine, and educated in the United States could become prime minister of Israel?*

no limit to what we are prepared to contribute so that all of us, together, can live to see a day of happiness for our peoples and can see again from that region a great contribution to peace and happiness for all humanity.

1. What is the single purpose Golda Meir wanted to work toward?

2. How did she suggest that the countries of the Middle East achieve that purpose?

3. Has that purpose been achieved in the Middle East?

ation Organization (PLO) to represent the interests of the Palestinians. The PLO believed that only the Palestinian peoples (and not Jewish immigrants from abroad) had the right to form a state in Palestine. A guerrilla movement called al-Fatah (al-fat-AW), led by the PLO political leader Yasir Arafat, began to launch terrorist attacks on Israeli territory. In retaliation, the Israeli government began to raid PLO bases in Jordan in 1966.

## The Arab-Israeli Dispute

The growing Arab hostility was a constant threat to the security of Israel. In the years after independence, Israeli leaders dedicated themselves to creating a Jewish homeland. The government tried to build a modern democratic state that would attract Jews from throughout the world.

It was not easy for such a tiny state to survive in the midst of hostile neighbors. Divisions among the Israeli

### Map 15.3   Israel and Its Neighbors

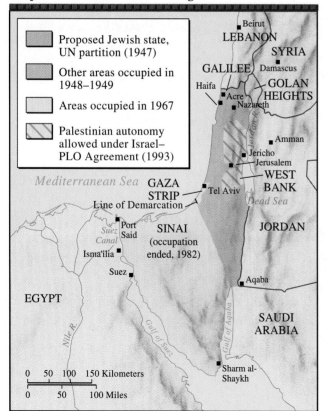

Proposed Jewish state, UN partition (1947)

Other areas occupied in 1948–1949

Areas occupied in 1967

Palestinian autonomy allowed under Israel–PLO Agreement (1993)

## CONNECTIONS
### AROUND THE WORLD

**Global Migrations**   Since 1945, tens of millions of people have migrated from one part of the world to another. There are many reasons for these migrations. Persecution for political reasons caused many people from Pakistan, Bangladesh, Sri Lanka, Eastern Europe, and East Germany to seek refuge in Western European countries. Brutal civil wars in Asia, Africa, the Middle East, and Europe have led to millions of refugees seeking safety in neighboring countries. A devastating famine in Africa in 1984–1985 caused hundreds of thousands of Africans to move to relief camps throughout the continent to find food.

Most people who have migrated, however, have done so to find jobs. Guest workers from Turkey, southern and eastern Europe, North Africa, India, and Pakistan, for example, flooded into prosperous Western European countries. Overall, there were probably fifteen million guest workers in Europe in the 1980s. Many countries adopted policies that allowed guest workers to remain in the host countries for a few years. In the 1980s and 1990s, however, foreign workers often became scapegoats when countries had economic problems. New political parties in France and Norway, for example, called for the removal of blacks and Arabs in order to protect the ethnic purity of their nations. In Asian countries, there is often a backlash against other ethnic Asian groups.

people made it even more difficult. Some Israelis were immigrants from Europe. Others came from the countries of the Middle East. Some were secular and even socialist in their views. Others were politically conservative and stressed religious orthodoxy, or a strict adherence to the traditional practices of Judaism. Israel was also home to many Muslim Palestinians who had not fled to other countries.

To balance these different interests, Israel established a parliament, called the Knesset, on the European model. Each political party received a number of

◄ *During the Six-Day War, Israeli forces destroyed oil refineries at Port Suez in Egypt. An Israeli soldier watches the fires burn from the safety of the other side of the Suez Canal.*

representatives based on how many votes each party received in the general election (a system called **proportional representation**). This system created a parliament with so many parties that no one party ever received a majority of the votes. All governments had to be formed from a coalition of several parties. As a result, moderate leaders, such as longtime prime minister David Ben Gurion, had to cater to the wishes of small parties to stay in power.

During the late 1950s and 1960s, the dispute between Israel and other states in the Middle East became more heated. Israel was basically alone except for the sympathy of the United States and a few Western European countries. It adopted a policy of quick and strong response to any hostile act by its Arab neighbors and the PLO. By the spring of 1967, Nasser had stepped up his military activities and imposed a blockade against Israeli shipping through the Gulf of Aqaba (AW-kee-bee). He declared: "Now we are ready to confront Israel. We are ready to deal with the entire Palestine question." When Nasser asked the commander in chief of the Egyptian forces if they were ready for war, the commander replied, "On my own head be it, boss! Everything is in tiptop shape."

Fearing that it was going to be attacked, on June 5,

1967, Israel suddenly launched air strikes against Egypt and several of its Arab neighbors. Israeli warplanes bombed seventeen Egyptian airfields and wiped out most of the Egyptian air force. Israeli armies then broke the blockade at the head of the Gulf of Aqaba and occupied the Sinai peninsula. Other Israeli forces seized Jordanian territory on the West Bank of the Jordan River, occupied the whole of Jerusalem, and attacked Syrian military positions in the Golan Heights area along the Israeli-Syrian border.

In this brief Six-Day War, as it is called, Israel devastated Nasser's forces and tripled the size of its territory. The new Israel aroused even more bitter hatred among the Arabs. Furthermore, another million Palestinians now lived inside Israel's new borders, most of them on the West Bank.

During the next few years, Arab states demanded the return of the occupied territories. Many Israelis, however, argued that the new lands improved their security and should be retained. In 1970, Nasser died of a heart attack and was succeeded by his vice president, Anwar al-Sadat (suh-DAWT). Sadat was more moderate than Nasser and sought to sign a peace treaty with Israel on the condition that the latter retire to its pre-1967 frontiers.

When Israel refused, Sadat tried once again to renew Arab unity through war with Israel. On October 6, 1973, Egyptian forces suddenly attacked Israeli positions in the Sinai just east of the Suez Canal. At the same time, Syrian armies attacked Israeli positions in the Golan Heights. Early Arab successes in this October War left the Israelis reeling. Golda Meir (MIE-ear), the prime minister of Israel, remarked: "The circumstances could not have been worse. In the first two or three days of the war, only a thin line of brave young men stood between us and disaster. They fought, and fell, like lions, but at the start they had no chance. What those days were like for me I shall not even try to describe." The Israelis stormed back, and a cease-fire was finally reached on October 24.

In the next few years, a fragile peace was maintained. Negotiations continued but with little success. The conflict spread to Lebanon, where many Palestinians had found refuge. The PLO now set up its headquarters in Lebanon. Heated disputes between Christians and Muslims over control of the capital city, Beirut, added to the rising tension along the border between Israel and Lebanon.

In 1976, the American president Jimmy Carter began to press for a compromise peace. He asked the Israelis to return the occupied Arab territories in exchange for Arab recognition of the state of Israel. President Sadat of Egypt, who wanted to reduce his military expenses, announced his willingness to seek peace.

In September 1978, President Sadat met with Menachem Begin (muh-NAWK-um BAE-gin [hard "g"]), Israel's prime minister, and President Carter at Camp David in the United States. Both sides agreed to the **Camp David Accords,** an agreement to sign an Israeli-Egypt peace treaty on March 26, 1979. The treaty ended the state of war between Egypt and Israel. Israel also agreed to withdraw from the Sinai, but not from other occupied territories until it was recognized by other Arab countries. Many Arab countries refused to recognize Israel, however.

During the early 1980s, Palestinian Arabs became more militant. This militancy led to rising unrest, popularly called the *intifada* (uprising), among PLO supporters living inside Israel. As the 1990s began, U.S.-sponsored peace talks opened between Israel and a number of its Arab neighbors. The first major breakthrough did not come until 1993. Israel and the PLO reached an agreement calling for Palestinian autonomy in certain areas of Israel. In return, the PLO recognized the Israeli state. Yasir Arafat became the head of the semi-independent area known as the Palestinian Authority.

Progress in making the agreement work, however, has been slow. Terrorist attacks by Palestinian militants who are opposed to the agreement have resulted in heavy casualties and have shaken the confidence of many Jewish citizens that their security needs can be protected under the agreement. At the same time, Jewish residents in the Left Bank have resisted the extension of Palestinian authority in the area. In November 1995, Prime Minister Yitzhak Rabin (ruh-BEEN) was assassinated by an Israeli opponent of the accords. National elections held a few months later led to the formation of a new government under Benjamin Netanyahu. This administration has adopted a tougher stance in negotiations with the Palestinian authority under Yasir Arafat. For the moment, future progress in implementing the agreement is in doubt.

## Revolution in Iran

The Arab-Israeli dispute also caused an international oil crisis. The Arab states had formed the Organization of Petroleum Exporting Countries (OPEC) in 1960 to gain control over oil prices. In the 1970s they used oil prices as a weapon to force Western governments to abandon their support of Israel. During the 1973 war, some OPEC nations announced large increases in the price of oil to foreign countries. The price hikes, coupled with cuts in oil production, led to an oil shortage and serious economic problems in the United States and Europe. The price increases also brought new riches to oil-exporting countries, such as Libya, now under Colonel Muammar Qadhafi (gah-DAH-fee). Qadhafi used his country's newfound oil riches to build roads, schools, and hospitals. However, he also used these resources to finance terrorist activities against Western nations and to overthrow governments he disliked. President Sadat of Egypt referred to Qadhafi as "that madman of the Mediterranean."

One of the key oil-exporting countries was Iran. Under the leadership of Shah Mohammad Reza Pahlavi, who occupied his position with the help of the American CIA, Iran had become one of the richest countries in the Middle East. During the 1950s and 1960s, Iran had become a chief ally of the United States in the Middle East. With American encouragement, the shah had tried to carry through a series of reforms to transform Iran into the most advanced country in the region.

The shah's efforts seemed to be succeeding. Per capita income increased dramatically. Literacy rates improved, and an affluent middle class emerged in the capital of Tehran. However, trouble was brewing under the surface. Many peasants were still landless, many people did not have jobs, and the urban middle class felt squeezed by high inflation. Housing costs had skyrocketed.

Some of the unrest that developed took the form of religious discontent. Millions of devout Muslims looked with distaste at the new Iranian civilization. In their eyes, it was based on greed and materialism, which they identified with Western, and especially American, influence. They opposed governmental corruption and the extension of voting rights to women. Some opposition elements used terrorism against wealthy Iranians or foreigners to provoke political disorder. In response, the shah's security police, the *Savak*, imprisoned and sometimes tortured thousands of dissidents.

Leading the opposition was the Ayatollah Ruholia Khomeini, an Iranian cleric who had been exiled to Paris because of his outspoken opposition to the shah's regime. From Paris, Khomeini continued his attacks in print, on television, and in radio broadcasts. By the late 1970s, large numbers of Iranians—students, peasants, and townspeople—began to respond to Khomeini's words.

▶ *The Ayatollah Khomeini, who served as leader of Iran from 1979 until his death in 1988, turned Iran into an Islamic state. What is Iran's current relationship with the United States?*

When workers' strikes grew in intensity in 1979, the shah left the country.

With rising public unrest, the shah's government collapsed and was replaced by a hastily formed Islamic republic. The new government, under the guidance of the Ayatollah Khomeini, immediately began to rid the country of Western influence and restore traditional Islamic law. At the same time, a new reign of terror began. Supporters of the shah were rounded up and executed.

Much of the attention of the outside world focused on the American Embassy in Tehran, where militant Iranians held a number of Americans hostage. In the eyes of the ayatollah and his followers, the United States was the "Great Satan," the protector of Israel and enemy of Muslim people everywhere. Furthermore, the United States was held responsible for the corruption of Iranian society under the shah. Now Khomeini demanded that the shah be returned to Iran for trial and that the United States apologize for acts against the Iranian people. In response, the U.S. government stopped buying Iranian oil and froze Iranian assets in the United States.

The effects of the disturbances in Iran quickly spread beyond its borders. Islamic militants called for similar revolutions in Islamic countries around the world. In July 1980, the shah died of cancer in Cairo. With economic conditions in Iran deteriorating, the Islamic revolutionary government finally agreed to free the U.S. hostages in return for the release of Iranian assets in the United States. During the next few years, the intensity of the Iranian Revolution moderated somewhat.

After the death of Khomeini in 1989, a new government, under President Hashemi Rafsanjani (RAWF-san-JAW-nee), began to loosen clerical control over freedom of expression and social activities. Rising criticism of rampant official corruption and a high rate of

▲ *Soldiers of the French Foreign Legion undertook the danger-ous task of clearing land mines the Iraqis had placed along Kuwait City beaches. The Kuwait Towers, a modern landmark of this oil-rich city, loom in the background. Why did the Iraqis place land mines along Kuwait City beaches?*

inflation, however, sparked a new wave of government repression in the mid-1990s. Newspapers were cen-sored, the universities were purged of "un-Islamic" ele-ments, and self-appointed religious militants raided private homes in search of treasonous activities. One Iranian journalist remarked, "There is deep fear and absolutely no freedom of expression."

## Crisis in the Persian Gulf

During the early phases of the revolution in Iran, the Iranians directed their anger toward the United States. However, Iran also had enemies closer to home. To the

north was the Soviet Union, long considered a threat to Iran. To the west was a militant and hostile Iraq, now under the leadership of the ambitious and ruthless Saddam Hussein. Problems from both directions ap-peared shortly after Khomeini's rise to power. Soviet military forces moved into Afghanistan in 1979 to prop up a weak Soviet-supported regime there. The follow-ing year, Iraqi forces suddenly attacked along the Iran-ian border.

Iraq and Iran had long had an uneasy relationship, fueled by religious differences. Both were Muslim nations. The Iranians, however, were largely Shi'ites, whereas the members of the ruling caste in Iraq were Sunnites (see Chapter 2). Also, Iran and Iraq had argued for years over borderlands next to the Persian Gulf, the vital waterway for the export of oil for both countries. Like several of its neighbors, Iraq had long dreamed of unifying the Arabs. Suspicion among its neighbors, however, kept Iraq from doing so.

During the 1970s, Iran had given some support to a Kurdish rebellion in the mountains of Iraq. In 1975, the Iranian government agreed to stop aiding the rebels in return for some land at the head of the Per-sian Gulf. Five years later, Iraq had crushed the Kurdish revolt. President Saddam Hussein now accused Iran of violating the earlier agreement and launched an attack on his neighbor.

The war was a brutal one. Poison gas was used against civilians, and children were used to clear mine-fields. The Khomeini government told young boys that if they died for their country, they were sure of gaining an afterlife. The war lasted for nearly ten years. The two superpowers—the United States and the Soviet Union—watched nervously in case the conflict would spread throughout the region. With both sides virtually exhausted, a cease-fire was finally arranged in the fall of 1988.

Hussein's appetite for land had not been satisfied, however. In early August 1990, Iraqi troops suddenly moved across the border and occupied the small neigh-boring country of Kuwait, at the head of the Persian Gulf. Iraq argued, without much cause, that Kuwait was legally a part of Iraq.

The Iraqi invasion of Kuwait in 1990 sparked an international outcry. The United States, under President George Bush, took the lead in amassing an international force that freed Kuwait and destroyed a large part of Iraq's armed forces. However, the allied forces did not occupy the capital city of Baghdad at the end of the war. They feared that doing so would cause the total breakup of the country, and that would only benefit Iran. American casualties would have only increased, and U.S. troops would have had to stay in Iraq longer than the Bush administration was willing to allow. The allies hoped instead that an internal revolt would overthrow Hussein. In the meantime, harsh economic sanctions were imposed on the Iraqi government. The hoped-for overthrow of Hussein, however, did not happen. Hussein's tireless efforts to evade the conditions of the cease-fire continued to vex the administration of President Bill Clinton.

 **SECTION REVIEW**

1. **Locate:**
   (*a*) Iran,   (*b*) Saudi Arabia,   (*c*) Iraq,
   (*d*) Syria,   (*e*) Lebanon,   (*f*) Jordan,   (*g*) Suez Canal,   (*h*) Gulf of Aqaba,   (*i*) Sinai peninsula,
   (*j*) West Bank of the Jordan River,   (*k*) Golan Heights,   (*l*) Persian Gulf

2. **Define:**
   (*a*) pan-Arabism,   (*b*) scientific socialism,
   (*c*) proportional representation,   (*d*) Camp David Accords,   (*e*) *intifada*

3. **Identify:**
   (*a*) Arab League,   (*b*) Gamal Abdul Nasser,
   (*c*) Palestine Liberation Organization (PLO),
   (*d*) Yasir Arafat,   (*e*) Anwar al-Sadat,
   (*f*) Golda Meir,   (*g*) Yitzhak Rabin,
   (*h*) Benjamin Netanyahu,   (*i*) Muammar Qadhafi,
   (*j*) Shah Mohammed Reza Pahlavi,
   (*k*) Ayatollah Ruholla Khomeini,   (*l*) Saddam Hussein

4. **Recall:**
   (*a*) How did Jewish and Arab people in Palestine react to the United Nations resolution that divided Palestine in 1948?
   (*b*) In addition to the military defeat of Arab forces, what resulted from the war in Palestine in 1948?
   (*c*) Why did the creation of Lebanon anger the Syrians?
   (*d*) Why did Israel launch air strikes against Egypt and its Arab neighbors in 1967?
   (*e*) Why did many Iranians oppose the shah even when their average standard of living was improving?

5. **Think Critically:**
   (*a*) Why did the United States and the Soviet Union stand together against Israel, France, and Great Britain when they tried to recover the Suez Canal from Egypt in 1956?
   (*b*) Why do some people believe it was a mistake for the United Nations and the United States not to occupy Iraq after the Persian Gulf War?

# SOCIETY AND CULTURE IN THE CONTEMPORARY MIDDLE EAST

In recent years, many developments in the Middle East have been seen in terms of a revival of traditional values in response to Western influence. Indeed, some conservative religious forces in the area have tried to replace foreign culture and values with supposedly "pure" Islamic forms of belief and behavior. This movement to apply the strict religious teachings of Islam to all aspects of political and social life is called **Islamic fundamentalism.**

## The Islamic Revival

The revival of Islam that has taken place in the contemporary Middle East has a long history. For quite some time, many devout Muslims have believed that the attempt to follow Western ways in the major cities has given birth to many evils, including the use of alcohol, pornography, and drugs.

This negative response to the West began early in the twentieth century. It grew stronger after World

▶ *Oil and its by-products have created the modern-day wealth in the Middle East. The Al-Jubail Petrochemical Company plant is a joint venture between a Saudi Arabian company and Exxon. This plant produces low-density polyethylene.*

War I, when the Western presence increased. In 1928, devout Muslims in Egypt formed the Muslim Brotherhood. Its goal was to create a new order based on a strict following of the Quran and Islamic law. Later the movement became more radical and made use of terrorism to pursue its goals.

The movement to return to the pure ideals of Islam reached its high point in Iran under the Ayatollah Khomeini. In revolutionary Iran, traditional Muslim beliefs reached into clothing styles, social practices, and the legal system. Divorce was outlawed. Women were expected to wear veils and were fined or even flogged for violating the dress code. Non-Muslims were fired from government jobs. Ancient Islamic punishments were also introduced, including stoning for adultery and cutting off hands for theft.

In turn, these Iranian ideas and practices have spread to other Muslim countries. In Algeria, the political influence of fundamentalist Islamic groups enabled them to win a stunning victory in the national elections in 1992. In Egypt, militant groups such as the Muslim Brotherhood have engaged in terrorism. Militant Muslims assassinated President Sadat. More

recently, they have attacked foreign tourists, who are considered to be carriers of corrupt Western ideas.

Throughout the Middle East, even governments and individuals who do not support the efforts to return to pure Muslim beliefs have changed the way they behave. In Egypt, for example, the government now encourages television programs on religion instead of comedies and adventure shows imported from the West. Middle-class women in Cairo tend to dress more modestly than in the past. The use of alcohol is also discouraged in Egypt.

## The Economics of Oil and Land

Millions live in poverty in the Middle East, but a fortunate few rank among the most wealthy people in the world. The annual per capita income in Egypt is about $710, but it is nearly $20,000 in the tiny state of Kuwait. The chief reason, of course, is oil. Oil reserves are distributed unevenly. All too often they are located in areas where the population density is low. Egypt and Turkey, for example, with more than fifty million people apiece, have almost no oil reserves. In contrast, the combined population of the oil-rich states of Kuwait, the United Arab Emirates (i-MIR-its), and Saudi Arabia is well under ten million people.

The growing importance of oil has been a benefit to several of the states in the region. However, oil has been an unreliable basis for an economy. The price of oil has varied dramatically in the last twenty years. So, too, has the income of the oil-producing states. During the 1970s, members of OPEC were able to raise the price of a barrel of oil from about $3 to $42. This has not happened again, however, forcing a number of oil-producing countries to scale back their economic development plans. Prices in the 1990s have varied between $15 and $25 per barrel.

The amount of land that can be farmed in the Middle East is relatively small. Nevertheless, most countries rely to a certain extent on farming to supply food for their growing populations. In some cases—for example, Egypt, Iran, Iraq, and Turkey—farmers until recently have been a majority of the population. Often, much of the fertile land was owned by wealthy landlords. Land-reform programs in several countries, especially in Egypt, have given land to more small farmers.

Lack of water, however, has been the biggest obstacle to farming, and it is reaching crisis proportions. With populations growing at high rates, several governments have tried to increase the amount of water available for irrigation. Many attempts, however, have been ruined by government mistakes or political disagreements. The best-known example is the Aswan Dam, begun in Egypt by Soviet engineers in the 1950s and completed in 1970. The project was designed to control the flow of water throughout the Nile River valley, but it has had unforeseen consequences. Because the dam does not allow the annual flooding of the Nile, farmers no longer get rich silt for growing their crops but must rely on chemical fertilizers. Then, too, if irrigation water is not drained properly, salt deposits can poison the land.

## Middle Eastern Societies and Women's Rights

At the beginning of the twentieth century, a woman's place in Middle Eastern society had changed little for

▲ *Many women in Egypt now wear veils when in public. For what reasons might this mother and her daughters have decided to dress so traditionally?*

hundreds of years. Women were secluded in their homes and had few legal, political, or social rights.

Early in the twentieth century, a modernist movement arose in several countries in the Middle East. Supporters of modernist views believed that Islamic doctrine was not inherently opposed to women's rights. During the first decades of the twentieth century, these views had a significant impact on a number of Middle Eastern societies, including Turkey and Iran. In both countries, rulers allowed greater rights for women and encouraged their education.

Modernist views had somewhat less effect in other Islamic states, such as Iraq, Jordan, Morocco, and Algeria. In these countries, traditional views of women prevailed, especially in rural areas. Most conservative by far was Saudi Arabia, where women were segregated and expected to wear veils in public. They were also restricted in education and forbidden to drive automobiles.

Until recently, the general trend in urban areas of the Middle East was toward a greater role for women. This was especially true in Israel, the most westernized state in the Middle East. Women in Israel, for example, have achieved substantial equality with men. They are active in politics, the professions, and even the armed forces. Golda Meir, prime minister of Israel from 1968 to 1974, became an important symbol of the ability of women to be world leaders.

Beginning in the 1970s, however, there was a shift toward a more traditional approach to women in many Middle Eastern societies. This shift was accompanied by attacks on the growing Western influence within the media and on the social habits of young people. The reactions were especially strong in Iran during the revolution of 1979.

The revolution caused Iranian women to return to more traditional forms of behavior. They were told to wear veils and to dress modestly in public. Films produced in the new Iran expressed the new morality. They rarely featured women. When they did, physical contact between men and women was prohibited. Still, Iranian women have many freedoms that women lacked before the twentieth century. For example, they can attend a university, receive military training, practice birth control, and write novels.

The Iranian Revolution helped to promote a revival of traditional attitudes toward women in other Islamic societies. Women in secular countries such as Egypt, Turkey, and Malaysia have begun to dress more modestly in public. Moreover, public attacks on open sexuality in the media have become more frequent.

## Contemporary Literature and Art in the Middle East

The contemporary literature of the Middle East deals with a number of new themes. The rise in national awareness has encouraged interest in historical traditions. Writers also have switched from religious to secular themes. They now discuss the problems of this world and how to fix them. Moreover, literature is no longer the preserve of the elite but is increasingly written for the broader mass of the people.

Iran has produced some of the best-known national literature in the contemporary Middle East. Perhaps the most outstanding Iranian author of the twentieth century was the short story writer Sadeq Hedayat (hay-DAW-yat). Hedayat was obsessed with the frailty and absurdity of life. He wrote with compassion about the problems of ordinary human beings. Frustrated at the government's suppression of individual liberties, he committed suicide in 1951.

Like Iran, Egypt has had a flowering of literature in the twentieth century. The most famous contemporary Egyptian writer is Naguib Mahfouz (ma-FOOZ). He was the first writer in Arabic to win the Nobel Prize for literature (in 1988). His *Cairo Trilogy*, published in 1952, is considered the finest writing in Arabic since World War II. The novel tells the story of a merchant family in Cairo during the years between the two world wars. Mahfouz is especially good at blending historical events with the personal lives of ordinary human beings. Unlike many other modern writers, his message is basically positive and reflects his hope that religion and science can work together for the betterment of humankind.

Although Israeli literature arises from a totally different tradition than that of its neighbors, it shares a concern for ordinary human beings. Israeli writers have inherited not only a long tradition of Hebrew literature but also the various traditions of the many nationalities that make up its population. As Israeli writers identify with the goals of their new nation, many try to find a sense of order in the new reality. They voice both terrors from the past and hopes for the future.

Some Israeli authors are also speaking out on sensitive national issues. The well-known novelist Amos Oz has examined problems in the **kibbutz** (a collective, or commune, in which farmers share property and work together, adults eat together, and children are raised in a separate children's home), one of Israel's most valued institutions. Other novels by Oz examine the psychological complexities of his characters, such as the emotional collapse of a housewife in *My Michael* or the collapse of a marriage in *To Know a Woman*. Oz is a strong supporter of peace with the Palestinians.

Like literature, the art of the modern Middle East has been strongly influenced by Western culture. At first, artists tended to imitate Western models. Later, however, they began to experiment with national styles and returned to earlier forms for inspiration. Some returned to the village to paint peasants and shepherds. Others followed international trends and tried to express the alienation that marks so much of modern life.

Reflecting their hopes for the new nation, Israeli painters sought to bring to life the feelings of pioneers arriving in a promised land. Many tried to capture the longing for community expressed in the Israeli kibbutz. Others searched for the roots of Israeli culture in the history of the Jewish people or in the horrors of the Holocaust. The experience of the Holocaust has attracted special attention from sculptors, who work in wood, metal, and stone.

## ❀ SECTION REVIEW ❀

1. **Define:**
   (a) Islamic fundamentalism,    (b) kibbutz

2. **Identify:**
   (a) Muslim Brotherhood,    (b) modernist movement,    (c) Sadeq Hedayat,    (d) Naguib Mahfouz,    (e) Amos Oz

3. **Recall:**
   (a) What do many devout Muslims believe has resulted from attempts to follow Western ways?
   (b) What is the greatest obstacle to farming in most Middle East countries?
   (c) What freedoms do Iranian women have that they lacked before the twentieth century?
   (d) What themes are common in the contemporary literature of the Middle East?

4. **Think Critically:** Why may attempts to return Muslims to strict Islamic lives fail in the long run?

## Conclusion

After World War II, colonial rulers began to grant independence to their African states. Many of the new African states emerged on an optimistic note. Problems, however, are rampant. Military regimes, economic problems, climatic disasters, and civil strife all have made it difficult to create stable governments and prosperous societies in Africa. Contemporary Africa is a land of contrasts between city and country and modern and traditional ways.

Nowhere in the developing world is the dilemma of continuity and change more agonizing than in contemporary Africa. What is the destiny of Africa? Some African political leaders still yearn for the dreams embodied in the program of the Organization of African Unity. Some believe that African states need democracy to survive. Other African political leaders, however, have rejected the democratic ideal and favor subordination of the individual to the community as the guiding principle of national development. Like all peoples, Africans must ultimately find their solutions within the context of their own traditions, not by seeking to imitate the example of others.

Like Africa, the Middle East is one of the most unstable regions in the world today. In part, this turbulence is due to the continued interference of outsiders attracted by the massive oil reserves of the Middle East. Oil is indeed both a blessing and a curse to the peoples of the region. Another factor contributing to the conflict in the Middle East is the tug-of-war between the sense of ethnic identity in the form of nationalism and the intense longing to be part of a broader Islamic community, a dream that dates back to the time of the Prophet Muhammad. The desire to create that broader community inspired Gamal Abdul Nasser in the 1950s and the Ayatollah Ruholla Khomeini in the 1970s and 1980s. Until the peoples of the Middle East are able to reconcile their desire for nationhood with their sense of common religious experience, it seems unlikely that they will find true peace and political stability.

## Notes

1. Julius Nyerere, "The Arusha Declaration," *Freedomways* (1970), p. 124.
2. Quoted in *World Press Review*, August 1991, p. 16.
3. Adrian Roscoe, *Uhuru's Fire: African Literature East to South* (Cambridge, 1977), p. 103.
4. Abioseh Nicol, *A Truly Married Woman and Other Stories* (London, 1965), p. 12.
5. Cyprian Ekwensi, *Iska* (London, 1966), p. 21.

# CHAPTER 15 REVIEW

## USING KEY TERMS

1. A collective farming community in Israel is called a _____ .
2. The _____ was a native terrorist group dedicated to the elimination of British control from Kenya.
3. The mob violence to protest Israeli domination of Palestine was called the _____ .
4. The peace agreement between Egypt and Israel signed in 1979 was called the _____ .
5. The former South African policy of separating races was called _____ .
6. The belief in Arab unity has been called _____ .
7. _____ is a movement to enforce strict religious teaching of Islam on all aspects of political and social life in some Arab nations.
8. There is _____ when members of an elective body are chosen based on the share of popular vote received by each political party.
9. President Nassar of Egypt called his objective of uniting and sharing resources of all Arab lands _____ .

## REVIEWING THE FACTS

1. What problems in Europe after World War II contributed to the willingness of colonial powers to grant independence to their African colonies?
2. What aspect of white rule in South Africa did many native Africans find most offensive?
3. Why was Nelson Mandela jailed by the white South African government?
4. Why are many national boundaries in Africa drawn without regard to where different tribal groups live?
5. What did Nelson Mandela achieve in 1994?
6. How do most African people earn their living?

7. Why has Israel allocated a large part of its national production to maintaining one of the most highly trained and best equipped military forces in the world?
8. Why did Shah Mohammed Reza Pahlavi of Iran lose the support of his people despite rapid growth in Iran's economy and standard of living?
9. Why did the United States support the government of Saddam Hussein through much of the 1980s?

## THINKING CRITICALLY

1. What are several reasons that have made it difficult for the people of Africa to achieve the dream of pan-Africanism?
2. Why have English and French been used as official languages of government in many African nations?
3. Why might Nelson Mandela have had a greater impact on the lives of South African blacks after he was put in jail than before?
4. Why have many well-educated Africans chosen to leave their native lands to live in Europe or the United States?
5. Although the Israelis have won every war they fought with their Arab neighbors, they must negotiate to achieve a lasting peace. Why is this statement true?
6. Why is it unlikely that a lasting peace could have been established in Iraq even if the United Nations had captured or killed Saddam Hussein?
7. Why is it possible for the United States to have good relations with some nations that are strongly Islamic and not with others?
8. Why do all Arab nations rely on imported goods to satisfy the needs of their people? Does this make them vulnerable to pressures from foreign nations? Explain your answer.

# CHAPTER 15 REVIEW

## APPLYING SOCIAL STUDIES SKILLS

1. **Government:** Often political parties in Africa are associated with a particular tribal group instead of a philosophy. Explain why this makes it difficult for African governments to be efficient, effective, fair, or widely supported.
2. **Economics:** Most African governments generate most of their revenues by taxing businesses and imported goods. Income and property taxes don't exist for most people. Why might this discourage industrialization of these states?
3. **Government:** Explain why the new government of South Africa has difficulty satisfying the desires of its black citizens, who are a majority and now hold the bulk of governmental power.
4. **Geography:** Draw a resource map of the Middle East that shows where major deposits of oil exist. Consider transportation routes used for oil exports from that part of the world. Explain why the western nations should be concerned about maintaining a steady flow of petroleum from the Middle East.
5. **Sociology:** Identify and explain conflicting social values that are likely to cause future disputes within Islamic nations.

## MAKING TIME AND PLACE CONNECTIONS

1. Many African Americans who have returned to Africa to visit or live have experienced difficulty in communicating their ideas and values to native African blacks. What situations in the United States and Africa might explain this situation?
2. The United States placed embargoes on trade with Cuba after Cuba became communist, and on South Africa to protest its policy of apartheid. Identify and explain possible reasons why the embargo against South Africa was apparently more effective than the one against Cuba.

3. Compare and contrast conflicts between Catholic and Protestant groups during the Reformation in Europe with the conflicts that have taken place between Islamic fundamentalists and more liberal Muslims in the Middle East during recent years.
4. The United States and European nations did little while massacres of civilians took place during the war in Bosnia, but many did intervene when Iraq invaded Kuwait. Explain why this involvement in the Middle East may have been more than a matter of Western powers protecting their supply of oil.

## BECOMING AN HISTORIAN

1. **Charts, Graphs, and Tables:** The table below indicates the average value of production per person in various nations in 1994. Explain what this data shows you about the greater difficulty many African nations will experience in achieving economic growth than the United States or countries in Europe.

### Gross National Product per person 1994

| Nation | GNP | Nation | GNP |
|---|---|---|---|
| United States | $25,810 | S. Africa | $2,720 |
| Germany | 25,220 | Egypt | 689 |
| Canada | 18,600 | Ghana | 309 |
| United Kingdom | 17,670 | Kenya | 232 |
| Italy | 17,330 | Zaire | 133 |

Source: U.S. Government Printing Office, *Statistical Abstract of the United States* (Washington, D.C., 1996), p. 835.

2. **Geography as a Key to History:** Study Map 15.3 on page 534 that shows the boundaries of Israel when it was originally formed and after the wars in 1948 and 1967. Explain why it is unlikely that a lasting peace can be achieved in the Middle East unless the issue of ownership of conquered lands is resolved.

# TOWARD THE PACIFIC CENTURY:

**16**

In the spring of 1989, China began to experience a remarkable series of events. Crowds of students, joined by workers and journalists, filled Tiananmen (tee-EN-uh-muhn) Square in Beijing day after day. Some students waged a hunger strike, and others carried posters calling for democracy. To China's elderly rulers, calls for democracy were a threat to the dominating role that the Communist Party had played in China since 1949. Some leaders interested in reform advised restraint in handling the protestors. Most of the Communist leaders, however, wanted to repress the movement. When students erected a thirty-foot-high statue entitled "The Goddess of Democracy" that looked similar to the American Statue of Liberty, party leaders became especially incensed.

On June 3, 1989, the Chinese army moved into action. Soldiers carrying automatic rifles fired into the unarmed crowds. Tanks and troops moved in and surrounded the remaining students in the square. At 5:30 in the morning on June 4, the mayor of Beijing announced that Tiananmen Square had been "handed back to the people." Even then the random killing of unarmed citizens continued. In all, more than five hundred civilians died in the streets of Beijing. The movement for democracy in China had come to an abrupt end.

This movement for democracy was but one of many tumultuous events that made Asia a continent in ferment after World War II. In China, a violent civil war gave way to a new China under the control of the Communists. Japan not only recovered from the devastation of World War II but went on to build an economic powerhouse. In South Asia and Southeast Asia, nations that had been dominated by Western colonial powers struggled to gain their freedom.

Throughout all of Asia, nations worked to move out of their old ways and develop modern industrialized states. Building modern industrial states was not always easy, however. Old hatreds among different ethnic groups reemerged and led to new sources of conflict. Nevertheless, the success of the Asian states in building strong economies has led many observers to see the next one hundred years as the Pacific Century—a century dominated by the Asian nations bordering the Pacific Ocean.

▶ Students marched in the streets of Beijing asking for democratic freedom, an end to the corruption in government, and the resignation of China's leadership. The gathering in Tiananmen Square with this plaster "Goddess of Democracy" proved to be too much for the government to bear. Do you believe the students understood the risks they were taking when they openly opposed the government?

# DEVELOPMENT OF THE ASIAN NATIONS

## (1945 TO PRESENT)

## THE WORLD SINCE 1945

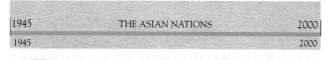

| 1945 | THE ASIAN NATIONS | 2000 |
| --- | --- | --- |
| 1945 | | 2000 |

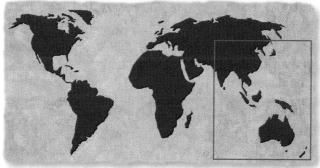

## QUESTIONS TO GUIDE YOUR READING

1. How did the Great Leap Forward and the Great Proletarian Cultural Revolution affect China?
2. What were the major economic, social, and political developments in China after the death of Mao Zedong?
3. What was the impact of Communist rule on women, marriage, and family in China?
4. What policies did Jawaharlal Nehru put into effect in India, both domestically and in foreign policy? What changes occurred after Nehru's death?
5. What problems did Pakistan face after it achieved independence?
6. What internal and external problems did the Southeast Asian nations face after 1945?
7. What important political, economic, and social changes have occurred in Japan and the "little tigers" since 1945?

## OUTLINE

1. CHINA UNDER COMMUNISM
2. SERVE THE PEOPLE: CHINESE SOCIETY UNDER COMMUNISM
3. THE EMERGENCE OF INDEPENDENT STATES IN SOUTH ASIA
4. INDEPENDENCE AND NATIONALISM IN SOUTHEAST ASIA
5. JAPAN AND THE "LITTLE TIGERS"

## 1

## CHINA UNDER COMMUNISM

At the end of World War II, two Chinese governments existed side by side. The Nationalist government of Jiang Jieshi (see Chapter 10), based in southern and central China, was supported by the United States. The Communists, under the leadership of Mao Zedong, had built a strong base in North China. By the end of World War II, twenty to thirty million Chinese were living under Communist rule. The People's Liberation Army of the Communists included nearly one million troops.

When efforts to form a coalition government in 1946 failed, full-scale war between the Nationalists and the Communists broke out. In the countryside, millions of peasants were attracted to the Communists by promises of land. Many joined Mao's People's Liberation Army. In the cities, even middle-class Chinese, who were alienated by Jiang's repressive policies, supported the Communists. Jiang's troops began to defect

547

to the Communists. Sometimes whole divisions—officers as well as ordinary soldiers—changed sides.

By 1948, the People's Liberation Army had surrounded Beijing. The following spring it crossed the Yangtze (YANG-SEE) and occupied Shanghai (SHANG-HIE). During the next few months, Jiang's government and two million of his followers fled to Taiwan (see later in the chapter). On October 1, 1949, Mao Zedong mounted the rostrum of the Gate of Heavenly Peace in Beijing and made a victory statement to the thousands gathered in the square before him. We, the Chinese people, have stood up, he said, and no one will be able to humiliate us again.

## The Great Leap Forward

In the fall of 1949, China was at peace. The newly victorious Communist Party, under the leadership of its chairman, Mao Zedong, turned its attention to ruling the country. Its long-term goal was to build a socialist society. Its leaders realized, however, that popular support for the revolution had been based on the party's platform of honest government and land reform, not the socialist goal of a classless society. Thus, the new regime moved slowly, having adopted a program known as the New Democracy.

Like Lenin's New Economic Policy, the **New Democracy** was a program of modified capitalism. Major industries were placed under state ownership, but most trading and manufacturing companies remained in private hands. To win the support of the peasants, lands were taken from wealthy landlords and given to poor peasants. About two-thirds of the peasant households in China received land under the new program.

The New Democracy worked as the economy began to grow. However, there was a darker side to the picture. Thousands, if not millions, of landlords and rich farmers lost their lands, and sometimes their lives. Many of those who died had been tried and convicted of "crimes against the people" in people's courts set up in towns and villages around the country. Some were innocent of any crime. In the eyes of the Communist Party, however, their deaths were necessary to destroy the power of large landowners in the countryside.

The New Democracy was never meant to be permanent. In 1955, the Chinese government launched a new program to build a socialist society. Virtually all private farmland was collectivized. Peasant families were allowed to keep small plots for their private use, but they worked chiefly in large collective farms. In addition, most industry and commerce was nationalized.

The Chinese leaders had hoped that collective farms would increase food production, which would allow more people to work in industry. Food production, however, did not increase. In 1958, Mao began a

**Map 16.1    The People's Republic of China**

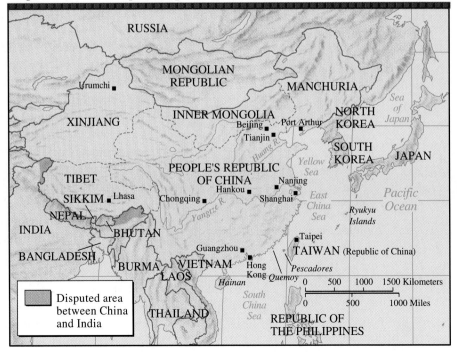

more radical program, known as the **Great Leap Forward.** Existing collective farms, normally the size of the traditional village, were combined into vast **people's communes.** Each contained more than thirty thousand people.

Mao Zedong hoped this program would mobilize the people for a massive effort to speed up economic growth and reach the final stage of communism—the classless society—before the end of the twentieth century. The party's official slogan promised the following: "Hard work for a few years, happiness for a thousand." However, the Great Leap Forward was a disaster. Bad weather and the peasants' hatred of the new system combined to drive food production downward. Over the next few years, as many as fifteen million people may have died of starvation. Many peasants were reportedly reduced to eating the bark off trees and, in some cases, to allowing infants to starve. In 1960, the people's communes were abandoned and a return was made to the collective farms.

▲ Mao Zedong was born in 1893 in the Hunan province. He helped found the Chinese Communist Party in 1921 and became its leader in 1936. He was the dominant leader in China until his death in 1976.

## The Great Proletarian Cultural Revolution

Despite his failures, Mao was not yet ready to abandon his dream of a totally classless society. In 1966, he returned to the attack and unleashed the **Red Guards.** These were revolutionary units composed of unhappy party members and discontented young people (see "Young People in Communist China: The Red Guards"). They were urged to take to the streets to cleanse Chinese society of impure elements guilty of taking the capitalist road. Schools, universities, factories, and even government ministries were all subject to the scrutiny of the Red Guards. In June 1966, all schools and universities were closed for six months to prepare for a new system of education based on Mao's ideas. Supported by his wife Jiang Qing (jee-ONG SHING) and other radicals in the party, Mao launched China on a new forced march toward communism.

Mao's so-called Great Proletarian Cultural Revolution (the Chinese name literally meant "great revolution to create a proletarian culture") lasted for ten years, from 1966 to 1976. Mao was convinced that Communist Party and government officials had lost their revolutionary zeal. Only an atmosphere of constant revolutionary fervor **(permanent revolution)** could enable the Chinese to overcome the past and achieve the final stage of communism.

Mao's supporters were now in power, and the party carried out vast reforms. A new school system stressed "Maozedong Thought." Mao's famous *Little Red Book,* a collection of his thoughts, was hailed as the most important source of knowledge in all areas. Red Guards set out across the nation to eliminate the **"four olds"** (old ideas, old culture, old customs, and old habits). The Red Guards destroyed temples, books written by foreigners, and jazz records. They tore down street signs and replaced them with ones carrying revolutionary names. At one point the city of Shanghai even ordered that the meaning of colors in stoplights be changed. Red (the revolutionary color) would indicate that traffic could move, not stop.

Destruction of property was matched by vicious attacks on individuals who had supposedly deviated from Mao's thought. Those so accused were humiliated at public meetings, where they were forced to admit their "crimes." Many were brutally beaten, often to death. Intellectuals and artists, who were accused of being pro-Western, were especially open to attack. Red Guards broke the fingers of one pianist for the "crime" of playing the works of Frédéric Chopin, the nineteenth-century European composer.

## YOUNG PEOPLE IN COMMUNIST CHINA

# The Red Guards

The Red Guards were revolutionary units formed by Mao Zedong, beginning in 1966. Many of the Red Guards were young people between the ages of fifteen and twenty, often without any job opportunities. The task of the Red Guards was to root out all aspects of the former capitalist system.

With the energy of the young, the Red Guards carried out their activities with great zeal. They believed Mao's message and even were devoted to him as a god. Liang Heng (LEE-un HUNG), who wrote an account of his activities called *Son of the Chinese Revolution*, describes the ecstasy he felt when he first saw the Chinese leader:

> *Chairman Mao's car was first, a Beijing-brand army jeep. As in a dream, I saw him. He seemed very tall to me, magnificent, truly larger than life. He waved his hat as the jeep drove slowly through the throng. The soldiers forming the passageway stood at attention, but the tears poured down their faces. . . . I was bawling like a baby, crying again and again: "You are our hearts' reddest sun." My tears blocked my vision, but I could do nothing to control myself.*

In his enthusiasm, Liang Heng at first helped friends organize groups of Red Guards: "I thought it was a great idea. We would be following Chairman Mao just like the grownups, and Father would be proud of me. I suppose I too resented the teachers who had controlled me and criticized me for so long, and I looked forward to a little revenge."

Later, Liang Heng had reason to repent. His sister ran off to join the local group of Red Guards. Before she left, she denounced her mother and the rest of her family as enemies of the revolution. Their home was regularly raided by the Red Guards. Their father was beaten and tortured for having three neckties and "Western shirts." Books,

▲ *Chinese Red Guards gather in Beijing to see Mao Zedong. The little red book they are waving is* Thought of Chairman Mao, *which describes his views of the Chinese way to attain a Marxist society. Why do you think so many young men and women eagerly joined this group, whose primary goal was to change the Chinese view of tradition and obedience?*

paintings, and writings were piled in the center of the floor and burned before his eyes. On leaving, a few of the Red Guards helped themselves to his monthly salary and his transistor radio.

1. Who were the Red Guards?

2. What was the purpose of the Red Guards?

3. What kind of activities did they carry out in order to fulfill their purpose?

4. What groups in other countries in the twentieth century carried out similar activities?

Mao found that it is not easy to maintain a permanent revolution, or constant mood of revolutionary enthusiasm. Key groups, including Communist Party members, urban professionals, and many military officers, did not share Mao's desire for permanent revolution. Many people were disgusted with the actions of the Red Guards. People began to turn against the movement.

## China after Mao

In September 1976, Mao Zedong died at the age of eighty-three. A group of practical-minded reformers, led by Deng Xiaoping (DUNG SHOU-PING) (who had himself been in prison during the Cultural Revolution), seized power from the radicals and brought the Cultural Revolution to an end. Mao's widow, Jiang Qing, and three other radicals (called the **gang of four)** were placed on trial and sent to prison for life. The policies of the last ten years were halted, and a new program was put in place.

Under the leadership of Deng Xiaoping, the government created a new policy called the **four modernizations**—in industry, agriculture, technology, and national defense. Deng had opposed Mao's Cultural Revolution and had been punished for his beliefs. Deng, however, took a practical approach to change. He once said, "Black cat, white cat, what does it matter so long as it catches the mice?" Under the program of four modernizations, people were encouraged to work hard to benefit both themselves and Chinese society.

Crucial to the success of the new program was the government's ability to attract foreign technology and capital. For over twenty years, China had been isolated from the technological advances taking place elsewhere in the world. To make up for lost time, the government now invited foreign investors to China. Moreover, thousands of students were sent abroad to study science and technology, as well as modern business techniques.

By adopting this practical approach, China began to make great strides in ending its problems of poverty and underdevelopment. Per capita income doubled during the 1980s. Housing, education, and sanitation

▲ *During the Cultural Revolution, many professional people lost their jobs and were subjected to constant harassment. Red Guards seem to enjoy humiliating one of their public enemies by placing a tall dunce cap on his head and marching him through the crowded streets.*

improved. Both agriculture and industrial output skyrocketed. Clearly, China had begun to enter the Industrial Age.

However, many people, both inside and outside China, complained that Deng Xiaoping's program had failed to achieve a fifth modernization—that of democracy. It soon became clear that the new leaders would not allow any direct criticism of the Communist Party. Those who called for democracy were suppressed. Some were sentenced to long terms in prison.

The problem began to intensify in the late 1980s. More Chinese began to study abroad. More information about Western society reached educated people inside the country. The economic improvements of the early 1980s led to pressure from students and other city residents for better living conditions and more freedom to choose jobs after graduation.

In the late 1980s, rising inflation led to growing discontent among salaried workers, especially in the cities. At the same time, corruption and special treatment for senior officials and party members led to increasing criticism. In May 1989, student protestors carried signs calling for an end to official corruption and the resignation of China's aging Communist Party leadership. These demands received widespread support from people in the cities. They also led to massive demonstrations in Tiananmen Square in Beijing.

Chinese leaders were divided over how to respond. Some, led by Communist Party general secretary Zhao Ziyang (JOO ZEE-YANG), were sympathetic to the protestors. Older leaders, such as Deng Xiaoping, however, saw the student demands for democracy as a call for an end to the Communist Party. The government sent tanks and troops into Tiananmen Square to crush the demonstrators. Chinese leaders insisted that economic reforms could take place only with political stability. Democracy remained a dream.

## SECTION REVIEW

1. **Locate:**
   (*a*) Taiwan

2. **Define:**
   (*a*) New Democracy,    (*b*) Great Leap Forward,
   (*c*) people's communes,    (*d*) Red Guards,
   (*e*) permanent revolution,    (*f*) four olds,
   (*g*) gang of four,    (*h*) four modernizations

3. **Identify:**
   (*a*) Great Proletarian Cultural Revolution,
   (*b*) *Little Red Book*,    (*c*) Deng Xiaoping,
   (*d*) Tiananmen Square

4. **Recall:**
   (*a*) What caused many peasants to support the Communist side when war broke out in China in 1946?
   (*b*) Why was the Great Leap Forward an economic disaster for China?
   (*c*) What help did China require to improve its economy after the Cultural Revolution?
   (*d*) What did economic improvements in China lead many students and urban residents to demand?

5. **Think Critically:** Why has it not been easy to maintain a constant mood of revolutionary enthusiasm in China or any other nation?

## SERVE THE PEOPLE: CHINESE SOCIETY UNDER COMMUNISM

Enormous changes have taken place in Chinese society since the Communist rise to power in 1949. No longer an agrarian society, China today is in the midst of its own Industrial Revolution. Beneath the surface of rapid change, however, there are hints of the survival of elements of the old China.

### Economics in Command

During the late 1950s, Mao Zedong began to maintain that political considerations were more important than economic ones in building a socialist society. After 1976, in contrast, Deng Xiaoping and other party leaders were hoping that rapid economic growth would satisfy the Chinese people and prevent them from demanding political reforms.

To stimulate the growth of industry, the new leaders allowed local managers in the state-owned factories to have more say over prices, salaries, and quality control. Bonuses could now be paid to workers for extra effort. The regime also permitted a small private sector to emerge. People could set up restaurants or handicraft shops on their own. Foreign firms were also now invited to build factories in China.

The new leaders abandoned the system of education begun during the Cultural Revolution. They opened new schools that were based on the Western model. Merit examinations determined who could go to universities. Courses in science and mathematics were now given priority.

Under Deng Xiaoping, a new agricultural policy also came into being. Collective farms could now lease land to peasant families. The families paid a rent (in the form of a percentage of their goods) to the collective. Anything produced on the land above the amount of that payment could be sold on the private market. Sideline industries were also allowed. For example, peasants raised fish and made consumer goods they could sell to others.

The reform program had a striking effect on farm production. Farm income doubled during the 1980s. However, the reforms also caused problems. By 1970, the government had launched a strict family planning program. All families were supposed to limit themselves to one child. Those with more than one child would be fined. The new farm program led many peasant families to pay the penalties for having more than one child. They believed that the labor of these extra children would increase family income and make it worthwhile to pay the penalties. Sons, however, continued to be valued more highly than daughters. Thus, female infanticide did not entirely disappear.

Overall, economic modernization worked well for many people in China. The standard of living improved for most people. The average Chinese citizen in the early 1980s had struggled to earn enough to buy a bicycle, radio, or watch. By the 1990s, however, many were beginning to buy refrigerators and color television sets. The government stressed the idea that all Chinese would prosper, although not at the same rate.

## Daily Life and Women's Rights

From the start, the Chinese Communist Party intended to create a new citizen free from the ideas of the past. These new citizens would have racial and sexual equality. They would also be expected to contribute their utmost for the good of all. In the words of Mao Zedong, the people "should be resolute, fear no sacrifice, and surmount every difficulty to win victory."

During the 1950s, the government took a number of steps to end the old system in China. Women were allowed to take part in politics. At the local level, an increasing number of women became active in the Communist Party. In 1950, a new Marriage Law was passed, guaranteeing women equal rights with men (see "You Are There: The Correct Viewpoint toward Marriage"). The law also allowed women to initiate divorce proceedings against their husbands. Within a year, nearly one million divorces had been granted.

The new regime also tried to destroy the influence of the traditional family system. To the Communists, loyalty to the family, an important element in the Confucian social order, undercut loyalty to the state. For Communist leaders, family loyalty was against the basic principle of Marxism—dedication to society at large.

During the Great Leap Forward, children were encouraged for the first time to report to the authorities any comments by their parents that criticized the system. These practices continued during the Cultural Revolution. Red Guards expected children to report on their parents, students on their teachers, and employees on their superiors.

At the time, many foreign observers feared that the Cultural Revolution would transform the Chinese people into robots spouting the slogans fed to them by their leaders. However, this did not happen. After the death of Mao Zedong, there was a noticeable shift away from revolutionary fervor and a return to a practical approach to nation building. For most people, the shift meant better living conditions and a return to family traditions. Married couples who had been given patriotic names such as "Protect Mao Zedong" and "Build the Country" by their parents chose more elegant names for their own children.

The new attitudes were also reflected in people's physical appearances. For a generation after the civil war, clothing had been restricted to a baggy "Mao suit" in olive drab or dark blue. Today, young Chinese people crave such Western items as jeans, sneakers, and sweat suits. Cosmetic surgery to create a more Western

# YOU ARE THERE

## The Correct Viewpoint toward Marriage

*One of the major goals of the Communist government in China was to reform the tradition of marriage. In this excerpt, a writer with the magazine* China Youth Daily *describes the ideal socialist marriage.*

### A Chinese Writer Describes the Perfect Socialist Marriage

Now then, what is our viewpoint? Is it different from that of the exploiting bourgeois class?

For one thing, our basic concept on marriage is and must be that we build our happiness upon the premise that happiness should be shared by all. We advocate equal rights for man and woman, equal rights for husband and wife. We oppose the idea that man is superior to woman or that the husband has special prerogatives over his wife. We also oppose any discrimination against or ill treatment of the wife.

We believe that marriage should be based solely upon mutual consent. We oppose the so-called arranged marriage, or the use of any deceitful or compulsory method by one of the parties in this matter. We uphold the system of monogamy. Hus-

*A happy bride and groom celebrate their wedding vows in Lanzhou, China, in 1994. As weddings grow more and more lavish, it is not uncommun for weddings to cost up to four or five times a family's monthly income. What signs of Westernization do you see in this photo?*

band and wife ought to have pure and exclusive love toward each other.

We believe that the very basic foundations for love between man and woman are common political understanding, comradeship in work, mutual help, and mutual respect. Money, position, or the so-called prettiness should not be taken into consideration for a right marriage, because they are not reliable foundations for love.

We also believe that solemnity and fidelity are important elements for a correct relationship between husband and wife, and for a happy family life. To abandon one's partner by any improper means is to be opposed. In our society, those who intend to pursue their happiness at the expense of others run contradictory to the moral principle of Communism and will never be happy.

1. What is the ideal marriage according to the Chinese Communist Party?

2. How is this "socialist" ideal of marriage different from marriage in capitalist countries?

3. Is the "socialist" ideal of marriage a realistic one? Why or why not?

facial look is increasingly common among wealthy young women in the cities.

Religious practices and beliefs have also changed since the Cultural Revolution, when the official belief was atheism. Some Chinese have been returning to the traditional Buddhist faith. Buddhist and Taoist temples are once again crowded with worshipers. Christianity has also become increasingly popular, because many view it as a symbol of success.

Such changes are much more common among urban dwellers and China's small middle class than among rural folk, who still make up more than half of the population. Most peasants have been little affected by the events that have occurred since Mao's death. The gap that has always divided town and country in China still remains. Such practices as arranged marriages and mistreatment of females continue in rural areas. Many parents in the countryside reportedly have killed female infants in the hope of having a son to fulfill the expectation of only one child per family.

## China and the World: The Cold War in Asia

In 1949, the Cold War spread from Europe to Asia when the Chinese Communists won the Chinese civil war and set up a new Communist regime. American fears about the spread of communism intensified, especially when the new Chinese Communist leaders made it clear that they supported "national wars of liberation"—or movements for revolution—in Africa, Asia, and Latin America. When Communist China signed a pact of friendship and cooperation with the Soviet Union in 1950, some Americans began to speak of a Communist desire for world domination.

### The Korean War

The outbreak of war in Korea helped bring the Cold War to Asia. Korea had once been under the control of China. In 1905, however, Korea became a part of the Japanese Empire and remained so until 1945. In August 1945, the Soviet Union and the United States agreed to divide Korea into two zones at the thirty-eighth parallel. The plan was to hold elections after

**Map 16.2   The Korean Peninsula**

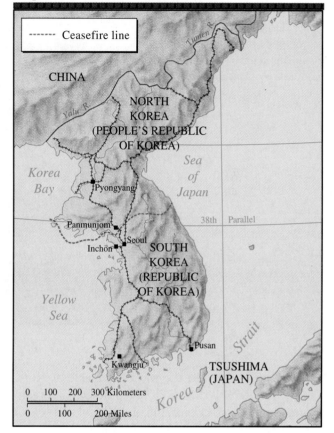

the war to reunify Korea under an independent government. As American-Soviet relations grew worse, however, two separate governments emerged in Korea—a Communist one in the north and an anti-Communist one in the south.

Tensions between the two governments ran high. On June 25, 1950, with the approval of Joseph Stalin, North Korean troops invaded South Korea. U.S. president Harry Truman, seeing this as yet another example of Communist aggression, gained the support of the United Nations and sent American troops to turn back the invasion. By September 1950, UN forces (mostly American soldiers) marched northward across the thirty-eighth parallel with the aim of unifying Korea.

The Chinese, greatly alarmed as U.S. forces approached the Yalu (YAW-LOO) River border with

▶ *A U.S. Tandem helicopter delivers battle-ready American troops in Korea. The U.S. entered the war as part of a UN police action and fought it as a limited war. What were the worldwide consequences of this war?*

China, then came into the war on the side of North Korea. Hundreds of thousands of Chinese "volunteers" swarmed into North Korea and pushed UN forces back across the thirty-eighth parallel. When three more years of fighting produced no final victory, an armistice was finally signed in 1953. The thirty-eighth parallel remained the boundary line between North and South Korea. Western fears of China now led to China's isolation from the major Western powers. China was forced to rely almost entirely on the Soviet Union for both technological and economic aid. Even that became more difficult as relations between China and the Soviet Union began to deteriorate in the late 1950s.

### The Shifting Power Balance in Asia

Several issues divided China and the Soviet Union in the 1950s. For one thing, the Chinese were not happy with the economic aid provided by the Soviet Union. More important, however, was their disagreement over the Cold War. The Chinese wanted the Soviets to go on the offensive to promote world revolution. Specifi-

cally, China wanted Soviet aid in retaking Taiwan from Jiang Jieshi. The Soviet Union, however, was trying to improve its relations with the West and thus rejected the Chinese demands.

By the end of the 1950s, the Soviet Union had begun to remove its advisors from China. In the 1960s, the dispute between China and the Soviet Union broke into the open. Military units on both sides of the frontier clashed on a number of occasions. Faced with internal problems and a serious security threat on its northern frontier from the Soviet Union, some Chinese leaders decided to improve relations with the United States. In 1972, President Richard Nixon made a state visit to China. The two sides agreed to improve relations. China's long isolation from the West was coming to an end.

After the Cultural Revolution, China further sought to improve relations with the Western states. Diplomatic ties were established with the United States in 1979. In the 1980s, Chinese relations with the Soviet Union also gradually improved. By the 1990s, China emerged as an independent power and was playing an increasingly active role in Asian affairs.

## SECTION REVIEW

1. **Locate:**
   (a) Yalu River

2.

3.

4. **Think Critically:** Why were urban Chinese more likely to abide by their government's call for only one child per family than rural Chinese?

## THE EMERGENCE OF INDEPENDENT STATES IN SOUTH ASIA

For over a century, the peoples of the Indian subcontinent had been ruled by Great Britain. After World War II, they finally gained their independence. Ethnic and religious differences, however, made the process both difficult and violent.

### Independence for India

At the end of World War II, Great Britain negotiated with both the Indian National Congress, which was mostly Hindu, and the Muslim League. British India's Muslims and Hindus were bitterly divided and unwill-

ing to accept a single Indian state. Great Britain soon realized that British India would have to be divided into two countries, one Hindu (India) and one Muslim (Pakistan). Pakistan would actually consist of two regions separated by over a thousand miles. One part was to the northwest of India (West Pakistan) and the other (East Pakistan), to the northeast.

Among Congress leaders, only Mohandas Gandhi objected to the division of India. A Muslim woman criticized him for opposition to partition, asking him, "If two brothers were living together in the same house and wanted to separate and live in two different houses, would you object?" "Ah," Gandhi replied, "if only we could separate as two brothers. But we will not. It will be an orgy of blood. We shall tear ourselves asunder in the womb of the mother who bears us."[1]

On August 15, 1947, India and Pakistan became independent. However, Gandhi had been right. The flight of millions of Hindus and Muslims across the new borders led to violence, and more than a million people were killed. One of the dead was especially well known. On January 30, 1948, a Hindu militant assassinated Gandhi as he was going to morning prayer. India's new beginning had not been easy.

### Independent India: An Experiment in Democratic Socialism

With independence, the Indian National Congress was renamed the Congress Party, and it began to rule India. It was not an easy task. Most of India's nearly 400 million people were poor and illiterate. There were many religions, ethnic groups, and languages. In fact, fourteen major languages were spoken throughout the country. Congress leaders spoke bravely of building a new nation, but Indian society was badly divided.

The new nation did have one advantage. The Congress Party had some experience in government. The leaders of the party were self-confident and fairly united. Jawaharlal Nehru (ju-WAW-hur-LAWL NAE-roo), the new prime minister, was a popular figure who was respected and even revered by millions of Indians.

India's new leaders had strong ideas about the future of Indian society. Nehru admired Great Britain's political institutions, but he had also been influenced by the socialist ideals of the British Labour Party. Nehru's vision of the new India combined democratic political institutions with a moderate socialist economic structure.

Under Nehru's leadership, the new Republic of India adopted a political system based on the British model. There was a figurehead president and a parliamentary form of government led by a prime minister. There were many political parties, but the Congress Party, with its enormous prestige, was dominant at both the national and the local levels. The Congress Party claimed to represent all Indians, from rich to poor, from Hindus to Muslims and other minority religious groups.

Economic policy was modeled roughly after the program of the British Labour Party (see Chapter 12). The state took over the ownership of major industries, transportation, and utilities. Private enterprise was permitted at the local levels. Farmland remained in private hands. The Indian government also sought to avoid dependence on foreign investment and technological aid. All business enterprises were required by law to be owned primarily by Indians.

Nehru was fully convinced that in order to succeed, India must industrialize. In this respect, he departed sharply from Gandhi. Gandhi had believed that material wealth was morally corrupting. Only simplicity and nonviolence, he said, could save India, and the world itself, from self-destruction. Nehru, however, had little fear of material wealth (see "You Are There: Gandhi and Nehru—Two Visions of India"). He complained that Gandhi "just wants to spin and weave," referring

**Map 16.3    Modern South Asia**

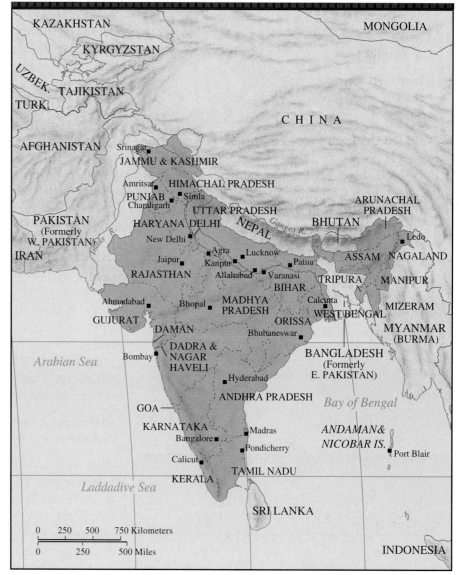

to Gandhi's practice of making his own cloth and garments.

Nehru actively pursued a policy of industrialization. He set up a series of five-year plans, which achieved some success. India developed a large industrial sector centered on steel, vehicles, and textiles. Industrial production almost tripled between 1950 and 1965.

Nehru also tried to bring about reforms in agriculture. In 1948, farming techniques were still primitive.

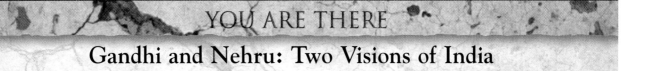

## YOU ARE THERE

# Gandhi and Nehru: Two Visions of India

*Whereas Jawaharlal Nehru saw socialism as the answer for India's ills, Mohandas Gandhi found the answer in the traditional village. Nehru favored industrialization to achieve material wealth, whereas Gandhi praised the simple virtues of manual labor. The first excerpt is from a speech by Nehru; the second is from a letter written by Gandhi to Nehru.*

### Nehru's Speech to the Indian National Congress

I am convinced that the only key to the solution of the world's problems and of India's problems lies in socialism. Socialism is, however, something even more than an economic doctrine; it is a philosophy of life and as such also it appeals to me. I see no way of ending the poverty, the vast unemployment, the degradation and the subjection of the Indian people except through socialism. That involves vast and revolutionary changes in our social structure, the ending of vested interests in land and industry. That means the ending of private property, except in a restricted sense, and the replacement of the present profit system by a higher ideal of cooperative service. In short, it means a new civilization, radically different from the present capitalist order. Some glimpse we can have of this new civilization in the territories of the U.S.S.R. Much has happened there which has pained me greatly, but I look upon that great and fascinating unfolding of a new order and a new civilization as the most promising feature of our dismal age.

### Gandhi's Letter to Nehru

I believe that if India, and through India the world, is to achieve real freedom, then sooner or

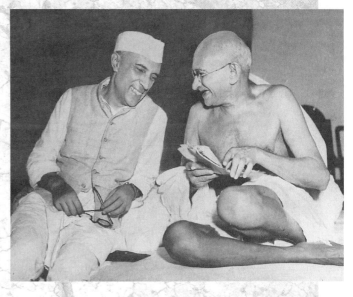

▲ *Mahatma Gandhi, on the right, shares a happy moment with Jawaharlal Nehru, on the left. The differences in their dress serve as a reminder of their sharply contrasting views for the future of India. Why was it particularly tragic that Gandhi was assassinated?*

later we shall have to go and live in the villages—in huts, not in palaces. Millions of people can never live in cities and palaces in comfort and peace. Nor can they do so by killing one another, that is, by resorting to violence and untruth. I have not the slightest doubt that, but for the pair, truth and non-violence, mankind will be doomed. We can have the vision of that truth and non-violence only in the simplicity of the villages. . . . The sum and substance of what I want to say is that the individual person should have control

*(continued)*

# YOU ARE THERE

## Gandhi and Nehru: Two Visions of India, continued

over the things that are necessary for the sustenance of life. . . . You will not understand me if you think that I am talking about the villages of today. . . . In the villages of my dreams the villager will not be dull—he will be all awareness. . . . Men and women will live in freedom, prepared to face the whole world. . . . Nobody will be allowed to be idle or to wallow in luxury. Everyone will have to do body labour.

1. What vision did Nehru have for the future of India?

2. What vision did Gandhi have for the future of India?

3. What did Gandhi mean when he said "to achieve real freedom . . . we shall have to go and live in the villages—in huts, not in palaces"? How could living in huts make people free?

4. Gandhi says "Nobody will be allowed to be idle or to wallow in luxury. Everyone will have to do body labour." How do you think this statement would be received if it were made by a politician in the United States? Explain.

India had few tractors, and fertilizer was rarely used. Most farms were small because of the Hindu tradition of dividing the land equally among all male children. Nehru realized that a more efficient farming system was needed if industrial growth were to continue.

First, the government tried to limit the size of land-holdings, thereby forcing a redistribution of land to the poor. Second, it encouraged farmers to form voluntary cooperatives. Both programs, however, ran into severe opposition. Landlords simply evaded the new laws, and farmers refused to form cooperatives. As one farmer said, many feared that "everyone will leave it to the others to do the work and shirk his own responsibility."

Under Nehru's guidance, India adopted a neutral posture in the Cold War. It also sought to provide leadership to all newly independent nations in Asia, Africa, and Latin America. This neutral and independent stance quickly placed India in opposition to the United States. During the 1950s, the United States was trying to mobilize all nations against what it viewed as the menace of international communism. India tried to remain friendly with both the United States and the Soviet Union. The country also worked to maintain good relations with the new People's Republic of China, although the two nations did have border disputes.

India did not hesitate, however, to fight for what it considered its own self-interests. Tension between India and Pakistan increased during the early 1960s, which led to war in 1965. India won a quick victory, but hostilities remained. When riots against the Pakistani government broke out in East Pakistan in 1971, India intervened on the side of East Pakistan. The latter declared its independence as the new nation of Bangladesh (see later in the chapter).

### The Post-Nehru Era in India

The death of Nehru in 1964 caused widespread concern about India's future. In 1966, the leaders of the Congress Party selected Nehru's daughter, Indira Gandhi (who was not related to Mohandas Gandhi), as the new prime minister. Indira Gandhi had had little experience in politics, but she quickly showed that she could lead her nation.

Indira Gandhi basically followed her father's policies, continuing democratic socialism and maintaining neutrality in foreign affairs. In some ways she took an even more active stance than her father. She was especially worried about poverty in the countryside and launched a major program to reduce it. The government nationalized the banks, provided loans to peasants on easy terms, built low-cost housing, and distributed land to the landless.

Indira Gandhi was especially worried by India's growing population. Even in 1948, the country was not able to support its population of nearly 400 million. In the 1950s and 1960s, the population increased at a rate of more than 2 percent per year. To curb the rate of population growth, Gandhi adopted a policy of monetary rewards and enforced sterilization. Males who had fathered too many children were sometimes forced to have vasectomies. Despite these efforts, India has made little progress in holding down its growing population, now estimated at over 900 million.

The Green Revolution of the 1970s at least made the population problem more bearable. The **Green Revolution** was the work of researchers who introduced new strains of rice and wheat that were more productive and resistant to disease, but which required more fertilizer and water. Grain production increased from about 50 million tons per year in 1950 to 100 million in 1970.

India paid a price for the Green Revolution, however. Only wealthy peasants could afford to buy the necessary fertilizer. Therefore, even more poor peasants were now driven off the land. Millions fled to the cities, where they lived in vast slums. They worked at menial jobs or even begged for a living. Almost 40 percent of Calcutta's 8.4 million people live in slum dwellings, while hundreds of thousands remain homeless and sleep in the city's streets every night. Open sewers that drain into the water system have been a major factor in making Calcutta the "cholera capital of the world."

Indira Gandhi's population policy made her unpopular. Growing corruption in her government, as well as her censorship of the press and restriction of civil lib-

▲ Indira Gandhi tried to help India's poor by providing low-cost loans, building low-cost housing, and giving land to those who owned none. She also helped extend voting rights. In what ways did she carry on her father's legacy?

erties (begun in 1975), also turned Indians against her. As a result, she was defeated in the general elections in 1977. It was the first time the Congress Party had failed to win a majority at the national level since independence. Three years later, however, Gandhi was back in power after the Congress Party won new national elections. She soon faced a new challenge in the rise of ethnic and religious strife.

The most dangerous situation was in the Punjab (PUHN-JAWB), a province of India that was heavily populated by Sikhs (SEEKS). The Sikhs are followers of a religion founded in the fifteenth century that is based on both Hindu and Muslim ideas. Militant Sikhs demanded independence for their province from India. Gandhi refused and used military force against Sikh rebels hiding in Amritsar (um-RIT-sur) in their Golden Temple, one of the Sikhs' most revered shrines. More than 450 Sikhs were killed. In revenge in 1984, two Sikh members of Gandhi's personal bodyguard assassinated her in her garden.

Indira Gandhi's son Rajiv (raw-JEEV), an airline pilot with little interest in politics, was now persuaded to replace his mother as prime minister. Rajiv Gandhi was not an effective leader, however. His government was criticized for inefficiency and corruption, as well as for not caring for the poor.

Rajiv Gandhi's government, however, did move in new directions. Foreign investment was encouraged. So, too, was private enterprise. Moreover, since Rajiv Gandhi's assassination in 1991, his successors have continued to transfer state-run industries into private hands and to rely on the free market. This has led to a noticeable growth in India's new prosperous middle class, now estimated at more than 100 million, or 11 percent of the population.

In the years after the assassination of Rajiv Gandhi, the Congress Party remained the leading political party. However, its powerful hold over the Indian people was now gone. Rising new parties competed with the Congress Party for control of the national and state governments. At the same time, rising tensions between Hindus and Muslims continued to disturb India's stability.

Further problems came from economic growth. For one thing, India has experienced incredible environmental damage. Water and air pollution, as well as the leakage of chemicals, have led to illness and death for many people. Not all the environmental damage is due to industrialization, however. The river Ganges (GAN-JEEZ) is so polluted by human overuse that it is risky for Hindu believers to bathe in it. (Hindus believe the sacred water of the Ganges washes away evil.)

Moreover, not all Indians have benefited from the new prosperity. Nearly one-third of the Indian people live below the national poverty line. Millions continue to live in rural slums, such as the "City of Joy" in Calcutta. Thousands of families there live in primitive shacks and lean-tos, sharing water and toilet facilities.

Indeed, India has been described as two nations: an educated urban India of 100 million people surrounded by 800 million poverty-stricken peasants living in the countryside.

### Daily Life in India

One of the major changes introduced in the newly independent India was the official elimination of caste distinctions. The constitution of 1950 guaranteed equal treatment and opportunity for all people, regardless of caste. Discrimination against the Untouchables was specifically outlawed. Of course, prejudice is hard to eliminate. Especially in the villages, the Untouchables are still denied basic human rights (see "Focus on Everyday Life: The Indian Village"). In the cities, however, material wealth rather than caste is increasingly beginning to define status. The days when upper-class Indians refused to eat in a restaurant unless they knew the caste of the cook are gone.

The position of women has also improved. In few societies was the life of women more restricted than in traditional India. Males were dominant in virtually all aspects of life. Females received no education and had no inheritance rights. They were expected to remain at home and were tied to their husbands for life.

After independence, India's leaders sought to give women equality with men. The constitution of 1950 forbade discrimination based on sex and called for equal pay for equal work. Child marriage and the payment of a dowry by the bride's family were outlawed. Women were encouraged to attend school and enter the labor market.

The lives of many Indian women have changed. Middle-class women in urban areas are much more likely to have jobs outside the home. Many hold managerial and professional positions. However, many, if not most, young Indians still accept the idea of arranged marriages. Moreover, an Indian woman is often expected to be a professional executive at work and a dutiful wife and mother at home.

In the countryside, the changes are not as noticeable. Female children are much less likely to receive an education or even to survive. According to a recent study, one-quarter of the female children born in India

# FOCUS ON EVERYDAY LIFE
## The Indian Village

In the cities in India, the rise of a middle class has changed many of the traditional ways of life. This is not necessarily true in the villages of India. The rural poor appear to live in conditions little changed from past generations. Nearly 80 percent of the Indian people still live in traditional rural villages.

Although some progress in education has been made in India, in the countryside education has been neglected. Thousands of villages remain without schools. The graduation rate from primary school is only 37 percent, compared with more than 60 percent for all Asia.

In Indian villages, housing styles, customs, and methods of farming have changed little since they were first described by Portuguese travelers in the sixteenth century. According to recent statistics, nearly 40 percent of people in rural areas live below the poverty level. The vast majority live in mud-and-thatch dwellings without running water or electricity, without education, and often without hope. Their lives have been affected only slightly by the changes taking place in the cities or in the world beyond.

A visitor described one such village in the state of Uttar Pradesh (prah-DESH) in the upper Ganges valley:

*I went inside every single cottage in the village. They are small mud huts with tiled roofs. The entrance is very low and many have no doors. Inside is a small walled-in yard, lined on one side with a little verandah, and one or at the most two rooms. In each room lives a whole family. Inside the room there is usually an earthen silo for storing grain, but no other furniture. The chula [a brick or earthen stove used for cooking] is in the veran-dah; straw lies scattered in the yard; in some a little*

▲ *Despite some improvements and attempted reforms, almost 80 percent of India's population continues to live in primitive villages without running water, paved roads, or electricity.*

*grain is drying on the floor. In the corner near the chula are piled neatly, face downward, the cooking utensils, earthen pots and a rare piece of brass.*

That description was written in 1961, but could easily apply to thousands of Indian villages today.

1. What do the majority of the rural population in India live without?

2. What percentage of Indians in villages graduate from primary school?

3. Compare your home to the home described here. How are they similar? How are they different?

die before the age of fifteen because of neglect or even infanticide by their parents.

## Pakistan since Independence

Unlike its neighbor India, Pakistan was in all respects a new nation when it attained independence in 1947. Pakistan, which consisted of two separate territories over a thousand miles apart, was unique. West Pakistan was always short of water. East Pakistan, comprising the eastern parts of the old Indian province of Bengal, was made up of the marshy deltas of two rivers and was densely populated with rice farmers. People in East and West Pakistan spoke different languages.

From its beginnings, the new state was a product of the Muslims' wish to have their own state. However, from the start, Pakistan's leaders made it clear that they were not extremists. Muhammed Ali Jinnah, leader of the Muslim League, which had been the chief force for a separate Muslim state, had a broad vision. A united India, he said, would have been a "terrific disaster." Jinnah also insisted that now that Pakistan was independent, it must put aside its past grievances with the new India. Pakistan, he said, must assure freedom of religion and equal treatment for all.

However, there were Muslim extremists who wanted a state based solely on Islamic principles. As a result, Muhammed Ali Jinnah's vision of a democratic society based on equal treatment for all citizens was only partly realized. His death in 1948 left his nation without a strong leader. The constitution of 1956 described Pakistan as an "Islamic Republic, under the sovereignty of Allah." Even though Pakistan was an essentially Muslim society, its first years were marked by intense internal conflicts. Most dangerous was the growing division between East and West Pakistan.

Many people in East Pakistan felt that the government, based in West Pakistan, ignored the needs of the eastern section of the country. In 1958, a military coup led by General Ayub Khan overthrew the civilian government. Khan believed that Pakistan was a badly divided nation. The only answer to the disunity, he thought, lay in a greater emphasis on law and order and less on democracy. His regime dissolved the constitu-

▲ *Benazir Bhutto, shown here, proved to be a dynamic leader. Why do you think both India and Pakistan have had women prime ministers, but the United States has never had a woman president?*

tion and set up a strong central government with a small group of 100,000 voters. His military government, however, was unable to curb the growing division between the eastern and western parts of the country. In March 1971, negotiations between representatives of East and West Pakistan broke down. East Pakistan now declared its independence as the new nation of Bangladesh. After a brief struggle, the Pakistan government gave in and recognized Bangladesh.

The breakup of the union between East and West Pakistan also led to the collapse of the military regime in West Pakistan. A new civilian government under Zulfikar Ali Bhutto (BOO-toe) took over, but the military was not yet ready to give up power. In 1977, a new military government under General Zia Ul Ha'q (ZEE-uh ul HAWK) seized power. It was committed to making Pakistan a truly Islamic state. Islamic law became the basis for the legal system and social behavior. Laws based on strict Muslim beliefs outlawed alcohol and governed the position of women. Also introduced was the practice of publicly whipping people with a cane, leather whip, or tree branch for breaking the law.

General Zia's death in a plane crash led to a restoration of democracy in 1988. Benazir Bhutto, educated in the United States and daughter of Zulfikar Ali Bhutto, was elected prime minister. She, too, was removed from power by the military in 1990 on charges of corruption. Reelected in 1993, she tried to crack down on opposition forces but was removed once again by the military on renewed charges of official corruption.

## ❀ SECTION REVIEW ❀

1. **Locate:**
   (a) Bangladesh,   (b) Punjab,   (c) Ganges River

2. **Define:**
   (a) Green Revolution

3. **Identify:**
   (a) Jawaharlal Nehru,   (b) Indira Gandhi,
   (c) Sikhs,   (d) Rajiv Gandhi,   (e) Muhammed Ali Jinnah,   (f) General Ayub Khan,
   (g) Zulfikar Ali Bhutto,   (h) Benazir Bhutto

4. **Recall:**
   (a) Why was the former British colony of India divided into two new nations when it achieved its freedom?
   (b) What two programs were begun in India in 1948 that slowed the growth of agricultural production?
   (c) What position did India try to maintain in relation to Communist and non-Communist powers in the Cold War?
   (d) Why was Indira Gandhi particularly concerned with the rapid rate of population growth in India?
   (e) What price did India pay for the Green Revolution?

(f) Why did Pakistan separate into two nations?

5. **Think Critically:**
   (a) Why may the decision to require all businesses in India to be more than half owned by Indians have slowed economic growth in that nation?
   (b) Why didn't the legal elimination of the caste system in India eliminate prejudice and discrimination?

# INDEPENDENCE AND NATIONALISM IN SOUTHEAST ASIA

The Japanese occupation of Southeast Asia during World War II had shown that an Asian power could defeat Europeans. Moreover, the Allied governments themselves had promised self-determination for all peoples at the end of the war. After 1945, those promises began to become a reality. The United States was the first to act when, in July 1946, it granted total independence to the Philippines.

Great Britain, too, was willing to end its colonial rule in Southeast Asia. The Labour government under Clement Attlee moved rapidly to grant independence to those colonies prepared to accept it. In 1948, Burma became independent. Malaya's turn came in 1957, after a Communist guerrilla movement had been crushed.

Other European nations—particularly France and the Netherlands—were less willing to abandon their colonial empires in Southeast Asia. Both regarded their colonies as symbols of national grandeur. The Dutch returned to the East Indies and tried to suppress a new Indonesian republic that had been set up by Sukarno, leader of the Indonesian Nationalist Party. When the Indonesian Communist Party began its own attempt to seize power, the United States pressured the Netherlands to grant independence to Sukarno and his non-Communist forces. In 1949, the Netherlands recognized the new Republic of Indonesia.

The situation was different in Vietnam. The leading force in the movement against the colonial French rule

▲ *Sukarno led the movement for Indonesian independence and became president of the new republic in 1950. Sukarno was a charismatic leader, but his ambitious policies led to his political downfall in 1966.*

there was the local Indochinese Communist Party led by Ho Chi Minh (HOE CHEE MIN). In August 1945, following the collapse of the Japanese occupation, an alliance of patriotic forces (the Vietminh) under Communist leadership seized power throughout most of Vietnam. Ho Chi Minh was elected president of a new provisional republic in Hanoi (ha-NOY). France, however, refused to accept the new government and seized the southern part of the country. War between France and Ho Chi Minh's forces broke out in 1946.

## The Era of Independent States

Many of the leaders of the newly independent states in Southeast Asia admired Western political principles and economic practices. They, too, hoped to form democratic, capitalist states like those in the West. Only in Vietnam, where the Communist Party came to

power, did local leaders choose the Soviet Leninist model.

By the end of the 1950s, hopes for rapid economic growth had failed. Internal disputes within the new countries weakened the new democratic governments. Ethnic conflicts were especially troublesome. In Burma, for example, one-third of the population was made up of ethnic groups not related to the majority Burmese people. Some of these ethnic groups launched a rebellion against the government. In Malaysia, the majority Malays—most of whom were farmers—feared domination by the local Chinese minority, who were much more active in industry and commerce. In 1969, tensions between Malays and Chinese erupted into violent battles on the streets of Malaysian cities.

As the experiments in democracy failed, both military and one-party autocratic regimes appeared. In Burma, a modern parliamentary government gave way to a military government. In Thailand, too, a constitutional monarchy was replaced by military rule. In the Philippines, an American-style two-party presidential system survived, but the power of a strong landed elite undermined democratic practices.

The most serious threat to democracy in the region arose in Indonesia. President Sukarno dissolved the democratic political system and tried to rule on his own through what he called **Guided Democracy.** Highly suspicious of the West, Sukarno nationalized foreign-owned enterprises and sought economic aid from China and the Soviet Union. However, Sukarno faced opposition to his rule, especially from the army and from Muslims. The Muslims were especially upset by Sukarno's refusal to make Indonesia an Islamic state. Sukarno was forced into retirement after a military coup in 1966. The new military government also found it difficult to placate the Muslims.

In recent years, some Southeast Asian societies have shown signs of moving again toward more democratic forms. Malaysia, for example, is a practicing democracy. The most spectacular example, however, is the Philippines. The regime of Ferdinand Marcos was overthrown by a massive public uprising in the 1980s. After the assassination of her husband by government forces in 1983, Corazon Aquino (uh-KEE-noe) became leader of the opposition to the Marcos government. After Marcos fled the country, Aquino became presi-

**Map 16.4   Modern Southeast Asia**

dent of a government that tried to establish democratic procedures and improve conditions for the poor.

In addition to their internal problems, Southeast Asian states also became involved in conflicts with each other. Cambodia, for example, fought with both Thailand and Vietnam over mutual frontiers—disputes that have not yet been resolved. Sukarno of Indonesia unleashed a policy of confrontation against Malaysia, arguing that the Malay peoples were part of Indonesia. The people of the Malay peninsula, however, had no desire to be part of Indonesia. In the end, Indonesia dropped its claim.

## The Vietnam War

The most important conflict in Southeast Asia immediately after independence was the war in Vietnam. The struggle of Ho Chi Minh's Vietminh Front against the French after World War II had begun as an anticolonial struggle. In the 1950s it became part of the Cold War. China began to provide military aid to the Vietminh to protect its own borders. The Americans supported the French.

At the Geneva Conference in 1954, France agreed to a peace settlement with Ho Chi Minh's Vietminh.

▲ *The war in Vietnam inflicted heavy civilian damages and destroyed many villages and homes. A fire is spreading quickly through this village market along the Saigon River. The boys quickly gather up their baskets in their attempts to save their meager belongings.*

Vietnam was divided into a northern Communist half based in Hanoi and a non-Communist southern half based in Saigon. Both sides agreed to hold elections in two years to create a single government. Cambodia and Laos were both declared independent states under neutral governments.

The United States, opposed to any further spread of communism, then began to provide aid to South Vietnam. Under the leadership of Ngo Dinh Diem (NYOE DIN DEE-em) and with the support of the United States, South Vietnam refused to hold the national elections called for by the Geneva Conference. It was widely expected that the Communists would win such elections. Disappointed, Ho Chi Minh in 1959 returned to a policy of revolutionary war in the south.

By 1963, South Vietnam was on the verge of collapse. Diem's autocratic methods and widespread corruption in his government had caused him to lose the support of most of the people. Revolutionary forces known as the National Liberation Front, or the **Viet Cong** (Vietnamese Communists), expanded their influence throughout much of the country. In November 1963, the American government supported a military coup that killed Diem and established a military regime. However, the new military leaders were able to do no better than Diem's regime. The situation in South Vietnam grew worse.

By early 1965, the Viet Cong, supported by military units from North Vietnam, were on the verge of seizing control of the entire country. In March, President Lyndon Johnson decided to send U.S. troops to South Vietnam to prevent a total victory for the Communists. The Communist government in North Vietnam responded by sending more of its forces into the south. By the end of the 1960s, the war had reached a stalemate. With American public opinion sharply divided on the issue, President Richard Nixon reached an agreement with North Vietnam in 1973 that allowed the United States to withdraw its forces. Within two years, Vietnam had been forcibly reunited by Communist armies from the north.

## ASEAN and the Issue of Regional Integration

The reunification of Vietnam under Communist rule had an immediate impact on the region. By the end of the year, both Laos and Cambodia had Communist governments. In Cambodia, a brutal revolutionary regime under the leadership of the Khmer Rouge (ku-ME[uh]R ROOZH) (Red Khmer) dictator Pol Pot carried out the massacre of more than one million Cambodians. However, the Communist triumph in Indochina did not lead to the "falling dominoes" that many U.S. policy makers had feared.

One reason was that the political and economic situation in Indochina had gradually stabilized during the 1960s and early 1970s. In Indonesia, Sukarno was forced from office in 1966 and replaced by a military government under General Suharto. The new government restored good relations with the West and sought foreign investment to repair the country's ravaged economy. Meanwhile, other countries in the region, such as Malaysia, Thailand, and the island state of Singapore, were experiencing relative political stability and rapid economic growth.

With political stability and improving economies came mutual cooperation. A new regional organization, known as the Association of Southeast Asian Nations (ASEAN), was formed in 1967. Composed of Indonesia, Malaysia, Thailand, Singapore, and the Philippines, ASEAN worked to resist further Communist growth in the region. When Vietnam invaded Cambodia in December 1978, ASEAN supported resistance troops. This action forced Vietnam to withdraw its forces.

Although some countries today, such as Myanmar (formerly Burma), the Indochinese states (Vietnam, Laos, and Cambodia), and the Philippines, continue to face serious political and economic problems, most of the members of ASEAN have entered a stage of steady economic growth. For the first time, the people of Southeast Asia are trying to control their own destinies.

## Daily Life: Town and Country in Contemporary Southeast Asia

Like much of the non-Western world, most Southeast Asian countries today can still be seen as dual societies. Their modern cities are often congested and polluted. Their villages in the countryside are peaceful rural scenes of palm trees and rice paddies. In Bangkok, Manila, and Jakarta, broad boulevards lined with skyscrapers mingle with muddy lanes passing through neighborhoods packed with wooden shacks.

Millions of Southeast Asians in recent years have fled from the peaceful rice fields to the urban slums. To many Southeast Asians, villages mean boredom and poverty. Cities mean jobs that, even if they are menial, pay more than people can earn in the villages.

Perhaps the greatest changes in lifestyle have taken place within the middle class and the small financial and professional elites. Western values, tastes, and customs are common in the lives of the wealthy urban minority. Western films, novels, food, alcohol, and

### CONNECTIONS
### AROUND THE WORLD

**Cities and Cars**   Since the beginning of the Industrial Revolution in the nineteenth century, the growth of industrialization has been accompanied by the growth of cities. In both the developed and developing countries, congested and polluted cities have become a way of life. In recent years, as more people have been able to afford to buy cars, traffic jams have also become a regular feature of life.

In São Paulo, Brazil, for example, traffic jams in which nobody moves last for hours. There are 4.5 million cars in São Paulo, twice the number as in New York City, although the cities have about the same population (sixteen million people). Workers in auto factories in Brazil work around the clock to meet the demand for cars.

São Paulo's situation is also evident in other cities around the world. In Cairo, a city of fourteen million people, pollution from stalled traffic erodes the surface of the Sphinx outside the city. In Bangkok, the capital city of Thailand, it can take six hours to reach the airport. (Clever merchants sell small personal toilets for car use.) In many cities in developing nations around the world, it is reported that the use of leaded gasoline is already affecting children's mental development.

A major cause of traffic congestion is a lack of roads. As more and more poor people have fled the countryside for the city, many cities have tripled in population in just twenty years. At the same time, few new roads have been built.

such luxury goods as expensive automobiles have become common among the wealthy. Most speak English, and many have been educated abroad.

Less wealthy urban dwellers are less affected by Western values. However, their lifestyles are changing, too. Television programs (including American programs such as *Dallas, Kojak,* and *Baywatch*) and the spread of literacy are having an impact. The literacy rate is well above 80 percent in Singapore, Thailand,

# BIOGRAPHY

## Aung San Suu Kyi: A Study in Courage

Suu Kyi was born in 1945 to Khin Kyi and Aung San. Her father—Aung San—was leader of the movement that led to Burma's independence from British rule on January 4, 1948. In 1989, the country's name was changed to Myanmar.

Suu Kyi barely knew her father, because he was assassinated when she was three years old. Only later did she learn more about the man who was called the Father of Modern Burma. She said: "It was only when I grew older that I conceived an admiration for him as a patriot and statesman. . . . It is perhaps because of this strong bond that I came to feel such a deep sense of responsibility for the welfare of my country."

Aung San Suu Kyi was educated abroad. She first studied in India, where she was influenced by the nonviolent teachings of Mahatma Gandhi. She then studied in Great Britain. She married a British educator and settled in Britain.

In 1988, Suu Kyi returned to Burma to take care of her ailing mother. Soon, she became aware of the repressive tactics used by the military government of General Ne Win. She was appalled by the regime's brutal murder of political opponents. She said, "As my father's daughter, I felt I had a duty to get involved." Suu Kyi became leader of a movement for democracy and helped to organize the National League for Democracy.

Despite the military repression, Suu Kyi toured her country. Everywhere she went, this champion of democracy was received with great joy and respect. Fearing her growing popularity, General

◄ *Aung San Suu Kyi first left Burma when she was just fifteen years old and did not return to live there until she was forty-three. One year later, the name of the country was changed to Myanmar.*

Ne Win ordered her assassination, an attempt that just barely failed.

Thanks to the efforts of Suu Kyi, General Ne Win resigned in 1988. However, another military regime took power. The new regime agreed to national elections in 1990. The National League for Democracy emerged as the clear winner. Nevertheless, the military government refused to step down. Suu Kyi was arrested and confined to her house, where she remained until July 10, 1995. In 1991, she won the Nobel Peace Prize for her efforts to end military rule in Myanmar by nonviolent methods. Her courageous efforts to bring democracy to her people continue to this day.

1. Who was Aung San Suu Kyi's father, and why was he important?

2. Why did General Ne Win order the assassination of Suu Kyi?

3. How would the phrase "like father, like daughter" apply to Suu Kyi?

◄ *Modern skyscrapers loom over an historic mosque in downtown Kuala Lumpur, the capital of Malaysia. Do you think it is possible to retain a cultural heritage in face of such modern advances?*

and the Philippines. Although the Western way of life is less noticeable in Vietnam, Laos, and Cambodia, even here one can find Coca-Cola, Western sneakers, and sweatshirts for sale in the shops.

In contrast, little has changed in rural areas. Most peasants still live in traditional housing and live their lives according to the annual harvest cycle. Travel is by cart or bicycle or on foot. Telephones are rare. Through the spread of electricity, radio, and television, however, changes are coming to the countryside as well.

In general, women in Southeast Asia traditionally have enjoyed a higher status than women elsewhere in Asia. Nevertheless, they were not the equal of men in every respect. After independence, the trend toward liberating Southeast Asian women continued. Virtually all of the newly independent states granted women full legal and political rights with men, including the right to work. In some respects, that promise has been fulfilled. Women have new opportunities for education and have entered new careers previously reserved for men. Women also have become more active in politics. In the Philippines in 1986, Corazon Aquino was the

first woman to be elected president of a country in Southeast Asia.

Women are not truly equal to men in any country in Southeast Asia, however. In Vietnam, where women are legally equal to men, no woman has served on the Communist Party's ruling committee. In Thailand, Malaysia, and Indonesia, women rarely hold senior positions in government or in major corporations. Similar limitations apply in Myanmar (formerly Burma), although Aung San Suu Kyi, the daughter of one of the country's heroes in its struggle for liberation, is the leading figure in the democratic opposition movement. (See "Biography: Aung San Suu Kyi: A Study in Courage.")

## ❀   SECTION REVIEW   ❀

1. **Locate:**
   (*a*) Philippines,   (*b*) Burma,   (*c*) Malaysia,
   (*d*) Indonesia,   (*e*) Cambodia

2. **Define:**
   (*a*) Guided Democracy,   (*b*) Viet Cong

3. **Identify:**
   (*a*) Clement Attlee,   (*b*) Sukarno,   (*c*) Vietminh,
   (*d*) Ferdinand Marcos,   (*e*) Corazon Aquino,
   (*f*) Ngo Dinh Diem,   (*g*) Khmer Rouge,
   (*h*) Pol Pot

4. **Recall:**
   (*a*) What problems emerged in the newly free countries of Southeast Asia in the 1950s?
   (*b*) What population groups show the dual societies that exist in Southeast Asian countries?
   (*c*) How have Western values begun to reach into even the most rural areas of Southeast Asia?

5. **Think Critically:** What factors contributed to the United States' lack of success in defeating the Viet Cong?

## JAPAN AND THE LITTLE TIGERS

In August 1945, Japan was in ruins. Its cities were destroyed, its vast Asian empire was in ashes, and its land was occupied by a foreign army. Half a century later, Japan was the second greatest industrial power in the world, democratic in form and content. How did it happen?

▲ *General Douglas MacArthur, on the left, posed for a formal photograph with Emperor Hirohito, on the right. What differences do you think are expressed by their body language and by their dress?*

### The Allied Occupation

For five years after the end of the war in the Pacific, Japan was governed by an Allied administration under the command of U.S. general Douglas MacArthur. The occupation regime was controlled by the United States. As commander of the occupation administration, MacArthur was responsible for destroying the Japanese war machine, trying Japanese civilian and military officials charged with war crimes, and laying the foundations of postwar Japanese society.

Under MacArthur's firm direction, Japanese society was remodeled along Western lines. A new constitution replaced the Meiji (MAE-jee) Constitution of

1889. It was designed to change Japan into a peaceful society that would no longer be capable of waging war. The constitution renounced war as a national policy. Japan agreed to maintain armed forces at levels that were only sufficient for self-defense. The constitution also established a parliamentary system, reduced the power of the emperor (the emperor was forced to announce that he was not a god), guaranteed human rights, and gave women the right to vote.

The rise of the Cold War in the late 1940s had an impact on American foreign relations with Japan. On September 8, 1951, the United States and other nations (but not the Soviet Union) signed a peace

**Map 16.5   Modern Japan**

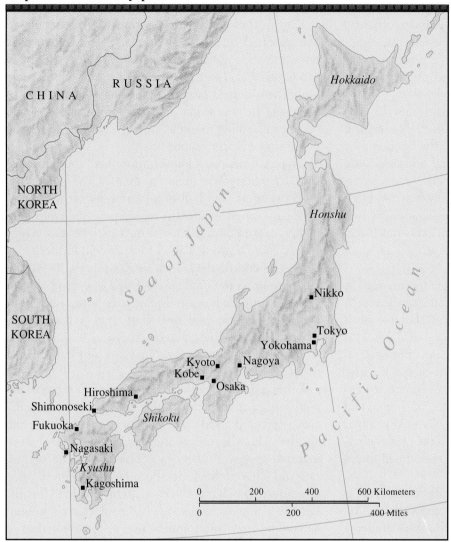

one of the most stable and advanced democracies in the world today. It has also become the second largest economy in the world.

Japan's achievements in the area of human services are especially noteworthy. The infant mortality rate is only five per thousand, the lowest in the world. The literacy rate is almost 100 percent. Crime rates are low. On an average day, according to a recent statistic, 4,584 crimes are committed in Japan, compared with 93,474 in the United States.

Japan's rapid emergence as an economic giant has often been described as the "Japanese miracle." Whether or not this description is accurate, Japan has made a dramatic recovery from the war. To understand modern Japan fully, we must examine not just the economy but also the changes that have occurred in recent years throughout Japanese society.

## Politics and Government

The concepts of universal suffrage and a balance of power among the executive, legislative, and judicial branches of government that were embodied in Japan's new constitution have held firm. Japan today is a stable and mature democratic society. However, the current Japanese political system carries over some of Japan's traditional political culture. Japan has a multiparty system with two major parties—the Liberal Democrats and the Socialists. In practice, however, there was a "government party" and a permanent opposition. The Liberal Democrats were not voted out

treaty restoring Japanese independence. On the same day, Japan and the United States signed a defensive alliance and agreed that the United States could maintain military bases on the Japanese islands.

## The Japanese Miracle: The Transformation of Society in Modern Japan

As the world would soon discover, the Japanese quickly adapted to the new conditions. It has developed into

of office for thirty years. Decisions on key issues, such as who should become prime minister, were decided by a small group within the party. A dramatic change, however, did occur in 1993, when the Liberal Democrats were defeated on charges of government corruption. Mirohiro Hosokawa was elected prime minister and promised to clean up the political system.

The current political system also continues the centralizing tendencies of the Meiji period. The central government plays an active role in the economy. It establishes price and wage policies and subsidizes vital industries. This government role in the economy is widely accepted in Japan. Indeed, it is often cited as a key reason for the efficiency of Japanese industry and the emergence of the country as an industrial giant. Japan's economic system has been described as "state capitalism."

Some problems remain, however. Corruption in government has shaken Japanese self-confidence in recent years. Two recent prime ministers have been forced to resign over improper financial dealings with business associates. Japan is also experiencing a rise in nationalist sentiment. Especially noticeable are the growing demands for a more assertive stance toward the United States. Moreover, critics at home and abroad have charged that the textbooks used in Japanese schools do not adequately discuss the crimes committed by the Japanese government and armed forces during World War II.

The issue of Japan's behavior during World War II has been especially sensitive. A U.S. professor teaching for a year in Japan reports that many of his students said they had learned about Pearl Harbor and the massacre of Chinese civilians in World War II "from my uncle, from my grandfather, from TV, from books, from family talk," but not from their classes. Asked why such things were not taught in school, the students always say, "Because the Government, or the Education Ministry, does not want us to know."[2]

### The Economy

Nowhere are the changes in postwar Japan so visible as in the economic sector. Japan has developed into a major industrial and technological power in the space of a century.

During their occupation of Japan, Allied officials had planned to break up the large conglomerations known as the *zaibatsu* (see Chapter 7). With the rise of the Cold War, however, the policy was scaled back. Only the nineteen largest companies were affected. In addition, the new policy did not keep Japanese companies from forming looser ties, which basically gave rise to another *zaibatsu* system.

The occupation administration had more success with its land-reform program. Half of the population lived on farms, and half of all farmers were tenants of large landowners. Under the reform program, lands were sold on easy credit terms to the tenants. The reform program created a strong class of independent farmers.

At the end of the Allied occupation in 1950, the Japanese gross national product was one-third that of Great Britain or France. Today, it is larger than both put together and well over half that of the United States. Japan is the greatest exporting nation in the world. Its per capita income equals or surpasses that of most advanced Western states.

What explains the Japanese success? Some analysts point to cultural factors. The Japanese are naturally group oriented and find it easy to cooperate with one another. Hardworking and frugal, they are more inclined to save than to buy. This boosts the savings rate and labor productivity. Because the Japanese value education, the labor force is highly skilled. Finally, Japan is a homogeneous society. People share common values and respond in similar ways to the challenges of the modern world.

Other analysts have cited more practical reasons for the Japanese economic success. Because its industries were destroyed in World War II, Japan was forced to build entirely new factories. Japan spends little on defense. Japanese workers spend a substantially longer period of time at their jobs than do workers in other advanced societies. Corporations reward innovation and maintain good management-labor relations. Finally, some charge that Japan uses unfair trade practices—that it dumps goods at prices below cost to break into a foreign market and restricts imports from other countries.

## Social Changes and the Role of Women

Allied planners during the occupation tried to change Japanese society. They thought they could eliminate the aggressiveness that had characterized Japanese behavior before and during the war. The new educational system removed all references to patriotism and loyalty to the emperor. At the same time, it stressed individual values. The new constitution gave women the right to get a divorce and hold a job. Women were guaranteed the right to vote and were encouraged to enter politics.

Such efforts to remake Japanese behavior through laws were only partly successful. Many of the distinctive characteristics of traditional Japanese society have persisted into the present day, although in altered form. Emphasis on the work ethic, for example, remains strong. The tradition of hard work is stressed at a young age within the educational system (see "Young People in Japan: Education and Growing Up").

The subordinate role of women in Japanese society has also not been entirely eliminated. Women are now legally protected against discrimination in employment, yet very few have reached senior levels in business, education, or politics. Japan has had no female prime ministers and few female cabinet ministers. Women now make up nearly 50 percent of the workforce, but most are in retail or service occupations. Their average salary is only about half that of males. Most women in Japan consider being a homemaker the ideal position. Only 15 percent of the women surveyed in a poll taken during the 1980s wanted a full-time job.

In the home, however, a Japanese woman has considerable responsibility. She is expected to be a "good wife and wise mother." She manages the family finances and raises the children with intense interest in their performance at school. Japanese husbands do little housework and share few leisure activities with their wives. Both in and out of the family, differences in gender roles and power remain much greater than in the West.

*Haruki Murakami, whose novels have become best-sellers, is known for his contemporary style, characters, and his irreverent attitude toward traditional social conventions.*

## Culture

After the Japanese defeat in World War II, many of the writers who had been active before the war resurfaced. However, their writing was now more sober. This "lost generation" described its anguish and piercing despair. Several writers committed suicide. For them, defeat was made worse by fear of the Americanization of postwar Japan.

Since the 1970s, increasing wealth and a high literacy rate have led to a massive outpouring of books. In 1975, Japan already produced twice as much fiction as the United States. This trend has continued into the 1990s. Much of this new literature deals with the common concerns of all the wealthy industrialized nations. Many current Japanese authors were raised in the crowded cities of postwar Japan, where they soaked up movies, television, and rock music. These writers speak the universal language of today's world.

Haruki Murakami (MUR-uh-KAWM-ee) is one of Japan's most popular authors today. He was one of the first to discard the somber style of the earlier postwar period and to speak the contemporary language. *A Wild Sheep Chase*, published in 1982, is an excellent example of his gripping, yet humorous, writing.

## The "Little Tigers"

A number of Asian nations have imitated Japan in creating successful industrial societies. Known as the "little tigers," they are South Korea, Taiwan, Singapore, and Hong Kong. Along with Japan, they have become economic powerhouses. These four states rank among the world's top seventeen trading nations.

# YOUNG PEOPLE IN JAPAN
## Education and Growing Up

▲ *The emphasis on conformity is clearly mirrored in this photograph of middle school students who are on a field trip with their teacher. In what ways is such conformity an advantage and a disadvantage?*

Young people in Japan grow up in a much stricter environment than do children in the United States. The Japanese school year runs for 240 days, compared with 180 days in the United States. Work assignments outside class are more demanding. A Japanese student averages about five hours of homework per day. Competition for acceptance into universities is intense. Many young Japanese students take cram courses to prepare for the "examination hell" that lies ahead. The results are impressive: The literacy rate in Japanese schools is almost 100 percent. Japanese schoolchildren earn higher scores on achievement tests than do children in other advanced countries.

At the same time, this devotion to success has often been due to bullying by teachers. One Japanese writer has observed: "Many Japanese incorrectly believe that our education has been a success because there aren't as many dropouts as in

## South Korea

While the world was focused on the economic miracle in Japan, another miracle of sorts was taking place in South Korea. In 1953, the Korean peninsula was exhausted from three years of bitter war. Two heavily armed countries now faced each other across the thirty-eighth parallel.

North of this line was the People's Republic of Korea (North Korea), a police state under the dictatorial rule of the Communist leader Kim Il-sung. To the south was the Republic of Korea (South Korea), under the dictatorial president Syngman Rhee. South Korea was now under American military protection, but the

U.S. troops there could not save Rhee from the anger of the South Koreans. After several years of harsh rule and government corruption, demonstrations broke out in the capital city of Seoul in the spring of 1960. Rhee was forced to retire.

A coup d'etat in 1961 put General Chung Hee Park in power in South Korea. Two years later, Park was elected president and began to strengthen the South Korean economy. The government played an active role in the process by putting in motion a series of five-year plans. Land reform provided land for ordinary peasants, and new industries were promoted.

South Korea gradually emerged as a major industrial power in East Asia. The key areas for industrial devel-

## YOUNG PEOPLE IN JAPAN

# Education and Growing Up, continued

the United States. But in fact Japanese schools are akin to prisons ruled by fear, where kids must constantly be looking around to make sure they're behaving exactly like everyone else."

This sense of conformity is reinforced by strict rules of behavior. Most Japanese schoolchildren, for example, wear black and white uniforms to school. The following rules were adopted by middle school systems in various parts of Japan:

1. *Boys' hair should not touch the eyebrows, the ears, or the top of the collar.*
2. *No one should have a permanent wave, or dye his or her hair. Girls should not wear ribbons or accessories in their hair. Hair dryers should not be used.*
3. *Wear your school badge at all times. It should be positioned exactly.*
4. *Going to school in the morning, wear your book bag strap on the right shoulder, in the afternoon on the way home, wear it on the left shoulder.*

5. *When you raise your hand to be called on, your arm should extend forward and up at the angle prescribed in your handbook.*
6. *After school you are to go directly home.*
7. *Before and after school, no matter where you are, you represent our school, so you should behave in ways we can all be proud of.*

Parental pride often becomes a factor in the motivation to succeed. Mothers pressure their children to work hard and succeed for the honor of the family.

1. In your own words, describe the Japanese system of education for young people.

2. Compare the Japanese system of education to the American system with which you are familiar. How are they similar? How are they different?

opment were chemicals, textiles, and shipbuilding. By the 1980s, South Korea was moving into automobile production. The largest Korean corporations, such as Samsung, Daewoo (DA-WOO), and Hyundai (HUN-DAY), became massive conglomerates. Taking advantage of low wages and a high rate of saving, South Korean businesses began to compete actively with Japanese businesses for export markets throughout the world.

Like many other countries in the region, South Korea was slow to develop democratic principles. Park ruled by autocratic means and suppressed any opposition. Park was assassinated in 1979, and another military government seized power in 1980. However, opposition to military rule began to develop under the leadership of Kim Dae Jung. College and high school students, as well as many people in the cities, protested government policies. Finally, new elections in 1992 brought Kim Young Sam to the presidency. He selected several women for his cabinet and promised that he would make South Korea "a freer and more mature democracy."

### Taiwan: The Other China

South Korea is not the only rising industrial power besides Japan in East Asia. To the south, on the island of Taiwan, the Republic of China is joining the other industrial forces.

After retreating to Taiwan after their defeat by the Communists, Jiang Jieshi and his followers established a capital at Taipei (TIE-PAY). They then set out to build a strong and prosperous nation based on Chinese traditions. The government continued to call itself the Republic of China. It maintained that it was the legitimate government of the Chinese people and would eventually return in triumph to the mainland.

Protection by American military forces enabled the new regime to concentrate on economic growth without worrying about a Communist invasion. Making good use of foreign aid and the efforts of its own energetic people, the Republic of China built a modern industrialized society.

A land-reform program, which put farmland in the hands of working tenants, doubled food production. With government help, local manufacturing and commerce expanded. At first, relatively small firms engaged in exporting textiles and food products. The 1960s, however, saw a shift to heavy industry—including shipbuilding, steel, and machinery—with a growing emphasis on exports. During the 1960s and 1970s, industrial growth averaged well over 10 percent a year. By the mid-1980s, over three-quarters of the population lived in urban areas. Throughout the industrializing process, the Republic of China actively maintained Chinese tradition.

Prosperity, however, did not lead to democracy. Under Jiang Jieshi, the Nationalists ruled by emergency decree and refused to allow the formation of new political parties. After the death of Jiang in 1975, the Republic of China slowly began to evolve toward a more representative form of government. By the end of the 1980s, democratic elections and opposition parties had come into being. A national election in 1992 resulted in a bare majority for the Nationalists.

A major issue for Taiwan is whether it will become an independent state or be united with mainland China. The United States continues to provide military aid to the Taiwanese military forces and clearly supports self-determination for the people of Taiwan. The United States also believes that any final decision on Taiwan's future must be by peaceful means. Meanwhile, the People's Republic of China remains committed to eventual unification.

### Singapore and Hong Kong

The smallest, but by no means the least successful, of the little tigers are Singapore and Hong Kong. Both are city-states with large populations densely packed into small territories.

Singapore, once a British colony and briefly a part of the state of Malaysia, is now an independent state. Under the leadership of Prime Minister Lee Kuan-yew (GWAWN-yoo), Singapore developed an industrial economy based on shipbuilding, oil refineries, tourism, electronics, and finance. Singapore has become the banking center of the entire region.

As in the other little tigers, in Singapore an authoritarian political system has created a stable environment for economic growth. The prime minister once stated that the Western model of democracy was not appropriate for Singapore. Its citizens, however, are beginning to demand more political freedoms. There is reason to believe that a more democratic political system will gradually emerge.

Like Singapore, Hong Kong, too, has become an industrial powerhouse with standards of living well above the levels of its neighbors. The future of Hong Kong is not so clear-cut, however. In negotiations with China, Great Britain returned control of Hong Kong to mainland China in 1997. China, in turn, promised that for fifty years, the people of Hong Kong would live under a capitalist system and be self-governing. Recent statements by Chinese leaders, however, have raised questions about the degree of freedom Hong Kong will receive under Chinese rule. The shape of Hong Kong's future remains in doubt.

### ❀ SECTION REVIEW ❀

1. **Locate:**
   (*a*) Singapore

2. **Identify:**
   (*a*) General Douglas MacArthur,   (*b*) Japanese miracle,   (*c*) Mirohiro Hosokawa,   (*d*) *zaibatsu* system,   (*e*) work ethic,   (*f*) Haruki Murakami, (*g*) Kim Il-sung,   (*h*) Syngman Rhee

3. **Recall:**

(*a*) What impact did the beginning of the Cold War have on United States relations with Japan?

(*b*) Why do many people believe the Japanese political system was not particularly democratic after the war?

(*c*) Why are the writers in Japan at the time of the war sometimes referred to as the "lost generation"?

(*d*) Why do some people believe the "little tigers" of Asia owe a debt of gratitude to Japan?

(*e*) How did promises of military protection from the United States help Taiwan develop its economy?

(*f*) What happened to Hong Kong in 1997?

4. **Think Critically:**

(*a*) One way Japan has maintained its homogeneous society is by accepting few immigrants from other countries. In what ways has this policy probably helped and harmed Japan?

(*b*) Both North and South Korea were governed by dictators for many years. What made the two countries develop so differently?

## Conclusion

Since 1945, Asia has witnessed the growth of two world powers—Communist China and capitalist Japan. The two nations were enemies in World War II and took sharply different paths after the war. Today, both nations play significant roles in world affairs: China for political and military reasons; Japan, for economic reasons.

In 1949, the Chinese Communists took control of all of China. During the next thirty years, Mao Zedong and the Chinese government tried a number of radical programs to bring about a socialist society. They mostly failed. After Mao's death, more moderate party leaders took control and used modified capitalist techniques to encourage growth in industry and farming. These moderates met with considerable success in economic modernization but so far have refused to allow any significant political changes. By crushing the movement for democracy in 1989, China's aging leaders signaled

their unwillingness to give up the Communist Party's rigid control of China.

Japan's history after 1945 is a remarkable success story. Under American occupation, Japan's economy and society were modernized. Subsequently, Japan developed a stable and mature democratic society. At the same time, it emerged as one of the world's economic giants.

Elsewhere in Asia, nations have struggled to build stable societies. The people of British India were given their independence on August 15, 1947, when two states—the largely Hindu India and the largely Muslim Pakistan—were formed. India tried to create a system of democratic socialism. However, ethnic and religious divisions, as well as overpopulation and rural poverty, continue to plague Indian society. Pakistan began with a democracy but has been ruled largely by military regimes.

After World War II, most of the states of Southeast Asia received independence from their colonial rulers. Many began with democratic regimes, but military regimes often replaced them. France's refusal to let go of Indochina led to a long war in Vietnam that ultimately involved other Southeast Asian nations in a widening spiral of conflict. After more than thirty years of violence and war, however, there are promising signs of increasing political stability. A number of states in Southeast Asia have joined the steadily growing ranks of flourishing Asian industrial societies, including Japan and the "little tigers" (South Korea, Taiwan, Singapore, and Hong Kong). Indeed, the growing economic strength of Asian nations bordering the Pacific Ocean has led many observers to speak of the next century as the Pacific Century.

## Notes

1. Quoted in Larry Collins and Dominique Lapierre, *Freedom at Midnight* (New York, 1975), p. 252.
2. Bernard K. Gordon, "Japan's Universities," *Far Eastern Economic Review*, January 14, 1993.

# CHAPTER 16 REVIEW

## USING KEY TERMS

1. The program of modified capitalism used in the first years that Communists controlled China was called _____.
2. The _____ were values Communists tried to eliminate from China's society that included old ideas, culture, customs, and habits.
3. President Sukarno dissolved Indonesia's democratic political system in order to rule on his own through a policy called _____.
4. _____ refers to the development of new seeds and farming methods to increase the amount of food that can be grown.
5. The _____ were units of young Communists who tried to cleanse Chinese society of impure elements.
6. Massive collective farms created in China's Great Leap Forward were called _____.
7. The _____ were leaders of the Cultural Revolution in China who were eventually jailed for their political excesses.
8. The policy created to improve China's industry, agriculture, technology, and national defense during the 1980s was called the _____.
9. The _____ was a plan to combine small land holdings into massive collective farms in China.
10. An idea supported by Mao that a constant state of revolution could create perfect communism was called _____.
11. Vietnamese Communists were revolutionary forces also known as the National Liberation Front, or the _____.

## REVIEWING THE FACTS

1. Why was the Great Leap Forward an economic disaster for China?
2. What was the *Little Red Book* that was carried by most people in China during the Cultural Revolution?
3. Why has the government of China tried to limit each family to having only one child?
4. What happened in Tiananmen Square in 1989?
5. What events led to the creation of the nation of Bangladesh?
6. Why is it difficult to create a stable government in India?
7. What nations fought for control of Vietnam before the United States became involved in fighting there?
8. What policy did the Khmer Rouge follow toward the people they regarded as enemies after they gained control of Cambodia?
9. Why was United States military presence in the Far East helpful to the Japanese in rebuilding their nation?
10. What nations are called the little tigers?

## THINKING CRITICALLY

1. How does the fact that the average Chinese citizen is less than thirty years old make it more difficult for China's leaders to maintain their people's revolutionary enthusiasm?
2. Why is it difficult to wipe out values people have held for generations in only a few years?
3. Although the people of China are not all satisfied with their government, they appear to be willing to tolerate the political situation in their nation because their standard of living has been improving. Why might they not tolerate the political situation in the long run?
4. Why will there continue to be rapid population growth in China for many years even if each family has only one child?
5. Why do some people believe the efforts to provide a minimum standard of living and health care to all people in India are doomed to failure?

6. Why didn't the increased ability of India to produce food as a result of the Green Revolution permanently eliminate its food shortages?
7. Why did the United States support the Vietnamese Communists in the 1940s, only to fight them in the 1960s?
8. Why do the Japanese still feel vulnerable to foreign pressures even when they have one of the richest economies in the world?
9. Why have many wealthy people left Hong Kong in recent years?

## APPLYING SOCIAL STUDIES SKILLS

1. **Ecology:** During the Great Leap Forward the leaders of China instituted a program in the countryside that had the slogan, "get the birds." Birds seemed to be eating lots of grain in the fields so they thought that killing the birds would increase harvests. Write an essay that describes the ultimate result of this program in terms of China's environment and harvests.
2. **Geography:** Explain why India's geographic location almost forced it to remain neutral in international politics.
3. **Economics:** Recently Vietnam has aggressively sought political recognition by the United States. Identify and explain reasons why this former enemy may be so interested in establishing diplomatic relations with the United States.
4. **Geography:** Consider the location of the Philippine Islands. Explain why the United States absolutely insisted on maintaining its right to use military bases on these islands until the late 1980s.

## MAKING TIME AND PLACE CONNECTIONS

1. Compare the decline of the Ottoman Empire with the fall of the Nationalist Chinese government.

How was the new government that came to power in China different from the political systems that emerged from the Ottoman Empire?
2. In 1959 differences between China and the Soviet Union became apparent to the world. Three years later France withdrew from NATO. Identify and explain ways in which these events were similar and how they were different.
3. Explain why it is unlikely that there will ever be a two-party system in India as there is in the United States.
4. Compare and contrast social, economic, and political problems facing Vietnam after it was united under Communist rule in 1975 with those of former colonies of European nations that have gained their independence in Africa.
5. Explain why Japan didn't need to create an extensive welfare state after World War II similar to those established in many western European countries at that time.

## BECOMING AN HISTORIAN

1. **Conducting Research:** Investigate the status of individual rights in Singapore. Compare these with the rights guaranteed to American citizens by the Bill of Rights. Identify and explain possible reasons why the people of Singapore are willing to be regimented by their government. What would probably happen if the government of the United States attempted to impose similar requirements on U.S. citizens?
2. **Map Interpretation:** Consider Map 16.4 on page 567. Identify and explain reasons why this region is vital to world trade and why the physical geography of the area makes it difficult for foreign nations to dominate these island and peninsular nations.

# EPILOGUE: TOWARD A GLOBAL

On Friday, April 25, 1986, plant managers at the nuclear power plant at Chernobyl, in Ukraine, ordered a series of tests to determine the capability of Reactor Four. A string of bad decisions quickly led to disaster. At 1:24 the next morning, a massive explosion rocked the site. Clouds of radioactive material raced into the sky and quickly began to spread over the Soviet Union and across Europe. In Sweden, scientists detected radiation levels that were 20 percent above normal. In Reactor Four, a radioactive fire burned out of control. Workers in the immediate vicinity of the explosion died quickly and painfully from the intense radiation.

For thirty-six hours, nothing was done to warn people nearby of the danger. Finally, more than 300,000 people were ordered to leave the area while firefighters dumped tons of concrete on the radioactive inferno. Deadly radiation, however, had immediate effects. More than three hundred people died within a short time in hospitals in the nearby city of Kiev. Many of the workers who fought the blaze, including the pilots of the planes that dropped load after load of concrete onto the fire, died within a year. It is estimated that thousands of people in all will experience physical problems from the disaster. Birth defects are common among people and animals who lived in the surround-

ing area. Even in other European countries, meat products were found to be contaminated with radiation.

On the eve of the twenty-first century, human beings are coming to understand that destructive forces unleashed in one part of the world soon affect the entire world. More and more people are becoming aware of the political and economic interdependence of the world's nations, as well as of the global nature of our current problems. The spread of nuclear weapons makes nuclear war an ever-present possibility. Nuclear war would mean radioactive fallout and widespread destruction for the entire planet.

Pollution from factories in one nation can produce acid rain in another. Oil spills and dumping of wastes in the ocean have an impact on the shores of many nations. The consumption of drugs in the world's wealthy nations affects the stability of both developed and developing nations. As food, water, energy, and natural resources crises increase, solutions of one nation often affect other nations.

◄ *This stunted tree has been killed by acid rain, a combination of sulfuric and nitric acids mixed with moisture in the air. Entire forests of trees killed by acid rain are becoming common sights in Canada, the United States, and Northern Europe.*

# CIVILIZATION—CHALLENGES AND HOPES

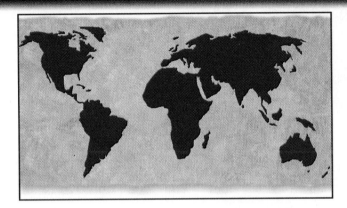

## 1

## THE CHALLENGES OF OUR WORLD

The challenges that seem to threaten human existence itself at the beginning of the twenty-first century are global challenges. As a Soviet physicist and an American engineer jointly concluded in 1988, "The emergence of global problems and the recognition of their importance is perhaps the greatest accomplishment of contemporary thought."[1]

### The Crisis of the Environment

In 1962, American scientist Rachel Carson published a book entitled *Silent Spring*. Carson argued that the use of pesticides, or chemicals sprayed on crops to kill insects, was having deadly, unforeseen results. Not only insects, but also birds, fish, and other wild animals were being killed by the buildup of these pesticides in the environment. Moreover, the pesticide residue on food, Carson maintained, was harmful to human beings as well. Carson's warnings alarmed many scientists and gave rise to a new field of science called **ecology,** the study of the relationship between living things and their environment. Many people became more aware of the dangers to the environment on which they depended for their survival.

These dangers to the environment have many different sources. A rapid increase in world population

## QUESTIONS TO GUIDE YOUR READING

1. What environmental challenges does the world now face?

2. What are the promises and perils of the Technological Revolution?

3. What economic and social challenges does the world now face?

4. What political challenges does the world now face?

5. What new global visions have arisen since World War II to deal with the world's problems?

has led to new fears that Earth's resources simply cannot keep up with the number of human beings. By 1990, there were more than five billion people on Earth. An estimated 1.3 billion are so poor that their basic needs for food and water cannot be met. Many people in less developed nations flee the countryside and move to cities in search of jobs. In 1950, the city of Cairo, Egypt, had one million people; today, it has more than thirteen million. Cities such as Cairo simply cannot keep up with basic needs such as food, water, and the disposal of garbage.

◀ *This view of the Earth shows the Mediterranean Sea, Africa, and Antarctica. Seen from space, Earth is an incredibly beautiful planet; however, recent satellite views show the human-made problems that Earth is facing.*

**Deforestation** (the clearing of forests) is another by-product of the growing population. Large forests and jungles have been cut down to provide new farmland and firewood for the growing number of people on Earth. As forests are cut down to provide land for roads, farms, houses, and industry, natural dwelling places for plants and animals are destroyed. An alarming number of species of plant and animal life have become extinct or barely survive due to deforestation. At the same time, the deliberate killing of animals for their by-products also creates new endangered species. The making of ivory products from the tusks of elephants, for example, has led poachers in Africa to kill vast numbers of these animals. As a result, the African elephant is in danger of becoming extinct. Many scientists worry about the long-term impact to life on Earth of the loss of so many plant and animal species.

Especially worrisome is the destruction of tropical rain forests near Earth's equator. Although the tropical rain forests cover only 6 percent of Earth's surface, they support 50 percent of the world's species of plants and animals. Moreover, the tropical rain forests are crucial to human survival. They remove carbon dioxide from the air and return oxygen to it. Fifty percent of the world's tropical rain forests are now gone forever. Every second of every day, an area of rain forest the size of a

football field is burned or bulldozed. Once cut down, a rain forest never recovers.

Another danger to the environment is chemical wastes. Many scientists warn that the release of chlorofluorocarbons (gases used in aerosol cans, refrigerators, and automobile air conditioners) is destroying the **ozone layer,** a thin layer of gas in the upper atmosphere that shields Earth from the sun's ultraviolet rays. Other scientists fear the **greenhouse effect,** or Earth's warming because of the buildup of carbon dioxide in the atmosphere. If this warming were sufficient, sea levels could rise and cause flooding of coastal areas. The amount of desert land could increase, which would make it even more difficult to grow enough food for the world's people. Some scientists have wondered whether recent extreme weather patterns, including the heat wave that claimed almost five hundred lives in Chicago in the summer of 1995, are the result of the greenhouse effect. Finally, **acid rain,** the rainfall that results when sulfur spewed out by industrial factories mixes with moisure in the air, has been held responsible for killing large forested areas in North America and Europe.

Major ecological disasters have also occurred during the last twenty years. As we have seen, a 1986 explosion at a nuclear power plant at Chernobyl, in Ukraine, spread enormous quantities of radioactive gases over large areas of Europe. In 1984, a chemical plant at Bhopal, India, released toxic fumes into the air, killing

▲ *As humans continue to cut down the majestic trees of the rain forest, deforestation is quickly becoming a reality of the twentieth century. The destruction has a far reaching impact on animal life, on human population, and on the Earth's atmosphere and climate.*

2,000 people and injuring another 150,000. In 1989, the oil tanker *Exxon Valdez* ran aground in Alaska. Thousands of birds were killed, fishing grounds were polluted, and the local environment was devastated.

These ecological disasters made people more aware of the need to deal with environmental problems. In 1987, representatives of forty-six nations met in Montreal and agreed to protect Earth's ozone layer by reducing the use of chlorofluorocarbons. In 1992, an Earth Summit in Rio de Janeiro examined the challenges to the environment and proposed new solutions. Individual nations have reacted to environmental problems

with the enactment of recycling programs, the curbing of dumping toxic materials, and salt and water conservation measures. Whether these global and national efforts will be sufficient to save the environment and keep Earth habitable will no doubt be one of the major questions of the early twenty-first century.

## The Technological Revolution: Promises and Perils

Since World War II, a stunning array of technological changes have created a Technological Revolution that has transformed the world in which we live. The lives of people in highly industrialized societies have been most affected by these developments. However, developing nations, too, continue to feel the impact of these changes. Especially spectacular developments have occurred in transportation, communications, space, medicine, and agriculture.

Since the 1970s, jumbo jet airliners have moved millions of people around the world each year. In 1945, a flight from London to New York took at least fifteen hours. Now a jet airplane takes between five and six hours to fly the route. The development of the Concorde has reduced the time even more—to three hours—but it has also raised issues about damage to the atmosphere.

Global communication systems are transforming the world community. The use of satellites, cable television, facsimile (fax) machines, cellular telephones, and computers makes it possible for people to communicate with other people anywhere in the world in minutes. Events happening in one part of the globe are seen a few hours later on news reports in other parts of the world.

The **Internet**—the world's largest network of computers—provides people around the world with quick access to enormous quantities of information. On the Internet, people can exchange messages (known as electronic mail, or E-mail) anywhere in the world in a matter of minutes. The Internet also provides access to the **World Wide Web.** The Web, as it is called, is an immense number of "pages" of information connected to one another around the world. Each "Web page" can

▶ *The World Wide Web was developed by an English computer scientist in 1989. Today, a great deal of research is conducted via the Internet, and most schools throughout the United States have computer labs such as the one pictured, where students learn to use Internet resources effectively.*

combine text, pictures, and video and audio clips. Each page is linked to other pages, thus enabling one person to connect to sources of information anywhere in the world.

The Internet has also created new questions about the right to privacy. Typing on a keyboard in the privacy of our homes gives us the illusion that what we send or receive is private. However, information that is sent from computer to computer offers others the chance to look at what is being sent. Company officials, for example, might read their employees' E-mail to see what they are doing on company time. Thus, the Internet, which has opened a whole new world of global communications, has also raised serious issues of privacy that have not yet been completely resolved.

Another technological development that has changed the world is space exploration. Ever since Neil Armstrong and Buzz Aldrin landed on the moon in 1969, the exploration of space has continued. Space stations and **space shuttles,** or reusable spacecraft that return to Earth under their own power, are first steps in developing space-based manufacturing. Space probes have increased our understanding of distant planets. Satellites in orbit provide information about weather

on Earth. Other satellites transmit signals for radio, television, and telephone communications.

New medicines enable doctors to treat both physical and mental illnesses. New technologies that include the use of computer-aided imaging have enabled doctors to provide better health care and to perform "miracle" operations. Mechanical valves for the heart, as well as organ transplants such as heart and kidney transplants, have allowed people to live longer and more productive lives. **Genetic engineering** is a new scientific field that alters the genetic information of cells to produce new variations—from cells as simple as yeast cells to those as complex as mammal cells.

Technological changes in the field of health have raised new questions and concerns and have had some unexpected results. For example, some scientists have questioned whether genetic engineering might accidentally create new strains of deadly bacteria that could not be controlled outside the laboratory. The overuse of antibiotics has created "supergerms" that no longer respond to treatment with available antibiotics. New diseases, such as AIDS—a disease that destroys the body's immune system and leaves it unable to fight infection—have spread rapidly and have not yet been

▲ *Takeoffs and landings of the U.S. space shuttles have become common events, making us forget how fantastic these flights really are. Here, the space shuttle* Columbia *lifts off from the Kennedy Space Center in Florida. What do you think the future holds for the U.S. space program?*

controlled. In 1995, the United Nations World Health Organization estimated that fourteen to fifteen million adults worldwide were infected with the virus that causes AIDS. This number includes eight million males and over six million females.

In agriculture, the Green Revolution has promised immense returns. The Green Revolution refers to the development by scientists of new strains of rice, corn, and other grains that have greater yields. It was touted as the technological solution to feeding the world's ever-growing population. However, immense quantities of chemical fertilizers are needed to grow the new

strains, which many farmers cannot afford. The new crops have also been subject to insect infestation. Thus, they require the use of pesticides and create additional environmental problems. Then, too, it has been the larger agricultural producers, rather than poor peasants, who often have benefited the most from the Green Revolution. These producers often use the new seeds and fertilizers to grow sunflower seeds, cotton, and peanuts for export rather than foods to help feed poor peasants in their own countries.

The Technological Revolution has also led to the development of more advanced methods of destruction. Most frightening have been nuclear weapons. The end of the Cold War in the late 1980s reduced the chances of a major nuclear war. However, nuclear weapons continue to spread, making a regional nuclear war even more likely. At the present time, twelve nations have nuclear weapons, and another fifteen are close to making their own. Another concern is whether any nuclear materials—bombs or radioactive matter—can end up in terrorist hands. One U.S. Central Intelligence Agency (CIA) official reported that in their bid for independence from Russia, Chechen fighters used the threat of bombs that could spread radioactive materials among Moscow residents. Other officials have worried that nuclear materials smuggled out of the former Soviet Union could be used by terrorists for crude bombs that could kill massive numbers of people.

## The Economic and Social Challenges of Our World

Since World War II, the nations of the world have developed a **global economy,** or an economy in which the production, distribution, and sale of goods are done on a worldwide scale. About 20 percent of the food and goods produced in the United States, for example, are sold abroad. Almost 40 percent of the profits of American businesses come from the sale of goods abroad or investments in foreign nations.

### The Gap between Rich and Poor Nations

One of the most noticeable features of the global or world economy is the wide gap between rich and poor

▶ *This shantytown built on the hillsides of Rio de Janeiro serves as a reminder of the desperate poverty in which many people are forced to live. What steps do you think national and local government agencies should take to improve living conditions for their citizens?*

nations. The rich nations are the **developed nations.** They are mainly in the Northern Hemisphere and include countries such as the United States, Canada, Germany, and Japan. Developed nations have well-organized industrial and agricultural systems, make use of advanced technologies, and have strong educational systems. The poor nations are **developing nations.** These nations are located mainly in the Southern Hemisphere and include many nations in Africa, Asia, and Latin America. Developing nations are primarily farming nations with little technology or education. In developing nations, students on average attend school for only three years. For many young people, the school experience may last only a few months.

A serious problem in developing nations is an explosive population growth. The world's population today is 5.6 billion. According to United Nations projections, by 2050, the world's population could reach 10 billion. Much of that rapid growth is taking place in developing nations, which can least afford it. Growing enough food for more and more people is a severe problem in many developing countries. Oftentimes, rich landowners in these countries grow such cash crops as coffee, sugar, or cocoa for sale abroad. Little land is left

to meet the needs of poor peasants. Countryside villages that had once grown the food they needed are now often forced to import food. At the same time, they themselves are unable to afford to buy the food they need to survive.

Then, too, rapidly growing populations have caused many people to flee the countryside and move to cities to find jobs. In developing countries, the size of some cities has exploded as a result. Saó Paulo, Brazil, for example, had 8.1 million people in 1970; today, it has over 16 million. There, as in many other cities in developing countries, millions of people rarely find jobs and struggle to survive. They live in slums or shantytowns. These shantytowns consist of groups of one- or two-room shacks that are built of any material—wood, plastic, scrap metal, cardboard—that is nearby and cheap. Living conditions in these slum dwellings are often horrendous. These shacks are stifling hot in summer and cold in winter. Few have running water, regular sewers, or electricity. Disease often spreads rapidly. The shantytowns are often the scene of prostitution, gambling, and other forms of crime.

The need to survive has also led many poor peasants to grow illegal drugs for sale abroad. Peasants in

Colombia and Peru in Latin America, as well as in Myanmar and Thailand in Asia, have found that the growing of coca leaves and marijuana plants, from which cocaine and marijuana are produced, is important to their economic survival. At the same time, such a lucrative trade has given rise to drug cartels (groups of drug businesses whose purpose is to eliminate competition) that bribe government officials and police officers into protecting their activities. Developed nations, such as the United States, have been the world's largest consumers of these drugs. Despite the efforts of the American government to aid nations in lessening the power of drug cartels, there has been little success. Thus, for different reasons, illegal drug traffic has become a serious problem for both developed and developing nations.

Hunger has also become a staggering problem in many developing nations. Of course, the problem of hunger is not unique to developing nations. It has been estimated that one billion people worldwide suffer from hunger. Every year thirteen to eighteen million people die of hunger, many of them children under five years of age. No doubt, poor soil, rapidly growing populations, and natural catastrophes contribute to the problem of hunger in developing nations. In North Korea, for example, drought, floods, and tidal waves that destroyed rice fields led to serious famine in 1996 and 1997. Some authorities have estimated that between 500,000 and 2 million people have died so far from starvation in North Korea.

Economic and political factors, however, have been even more important in many areas in causing widespread hunger. The growing of crops for sale abroad, for example, might lead to enormous profits for large landowners, but it leaves many ordinary peasants with little land on which to grow food for basic needs. Civil wars have been especially devastating in helping to create massive food shortages. In Sudan, for example, a civil war broke out in the 1980s between rebels in the south, who were largely Christians, and a mostly Arab-Muslim government in the north. Both sides used food as an instrument of war by not allowing it to be sent to their enemies. Government troops even blocked attempts by the United Nations to deliver food to starving people. By the early 1990s, an estimated 1.3 million people had died in Sudan from starvation.

▲ *Hunger and starvation is a daily reality in many countries. As shown in this photo taken in Somalia, international relief agencies provide some help in alleviating the suffering. Do you think prosperous nations, such as the United States and Canada, should take a more active role in providing aid to victims of famine?*

To improve their economic situations, developing nations sought to establish industrial economies. These nations have not found this goal easy to reach, however. Rapidly growing populations place enormous burdens on the economies of developing nations and make it difficult or even impossible to create a new industrial order. The populations of developing nations such as Kenya, for example, double every eighteen years. Overused soil, lack of water, and diseases add to the economic problems.

Another problem in the developing nations is raising capital, or money, to industrialize. Many developing nations rely on the sale of raw materials to raise money. They often find, however, that developed nations pay low prices for raw materials while charging high prices for their own manufactured goods. Many developing nations have tried to raise capital by borrowing, either from the World Bank and the International Monetary Fund (financial organizations whose goal is to provide funds for international trade) or from private banks. These loans, often at high interest rates, can lead to incredible burdens of debt for developing nations. For example, in the 1980s, Brazil owed almost $110 billion to foreign lenders. These massive debts have often made economic development impossible and have even led to declining living standards.

Some developing countries, however, have had remarkable success in creating industrial economies and in joining the ranks of the developed nations. Some nations along the Asian Pacific rim—including South Korea, Taiwan, Hong Kong, and Singapore, for example—have created prosperous export industries and built nations with high standards of living. Some observers have even spoken of the twenty-first century as the Pacific Century, proving that industrial capitalism is by no means a monopoly of the West.

It should also be kept in mind that the global economy today is highly dependent upon the continued economic prosperity of the industrialized countries. A global economic turndown could put a serious dent in the pace of economic development in many parts of the world. That, in turn, could lead to serious political instability and a crisis in the global economy.

No matter how the current economic situation evolves, it has clearly taken on a truly global character.

▲ *These two futuristic skyscrapers are located in the central business district of Hong Kong. Just two among the many soaring buildings that create a sensational skyline for this bustling city, these skyscrapers are a symbol of the economic progress and prosperity of the Pacific Rim countries. Can you name some of the many products you and your family use that are produced in Pacific Rim countries? How many multinational corporations that have major industrial factories in these nations can you identify?*

A fitting symbol of that global character is the multinational corporation (a company that has divisions in more than two countries). The growing number of multinational corporations (including banks, computer companies, airlines, and fast-food chains) that do business around the world increasingly tie one country to another in a global economy. In fact, today we live not only in a world economy but also in a world society. An economic downturn in the United States can create stagnant conditions in Europe and Asia. A revolution in Iran can cause a rise in the price of oil in the United States. The collapse of an empire in Russia can send shock waves as far as Hanoi and Havana. We live in an interdependent world.

### The Gender Gap

The gap between rich and poor nations is also reflected in the gap between men and women. In the social and economic spheres of the Western world, the gap that once separated men and women has been steadily narrowing. The number of women in the workforce continues to increase. In the 1990s, women make up half of the university graduates in Western countries. In the 1950s, they made up only 20 percent. Many countries have passed laws that require equal pay for women and men doing the same work, as well as laws that prohibit promotions based on gender. Nevertheless, in most Western countries, women still have not been elected to the top political offices, nor do they hold the top positions in business and industry.

Women in developing nations continue to face considerable difficulties. Women usually remain bound to their homes and families and subordinate to their fathers and husbands. Women in poor nations often are unable to obtain education, property rights, or decent jobs. The difficult conditions women face were described well by Dimitila Barrios de Chungara, a miner's wife from Bolivia, in an interview in 1981: "But women like us, housewives, who get organized to better our people well, they beat us up and persecute us. . . . [People do not know] what it's like to get up at four in the morning and go to bed at eleven or twelve at night, just to be able to get all the housework done, because of the lousy conditions we live in." De Chungara's words remind us of the global problems of poverty and the struggles for equality that go on throughout the world.

## Political Challenges and Possibilities

The leaders of African and Asian countries after World War II were concerned with creating a new political culture that met the needs of their citizens. For the most part, they accepted the concept of democracy as the defining theme of that culture. Within a decade, however, democratic systems throughout the developing nations of Africa, Asia, and Latin America were replaced by military dictatorships or one-party governments. It was clear that many of these leaders had underestimated the difficulties of building democratic political institutions in developing societies.

Establishing a common national identity has in some ways been the most difficult of all the challenges facing the new nations of Asia and Africa. Many of these new states were composed of a wide variety of ethnic, religious, and linguistic groups that found it difficult to agree on common symbols of nationalism. Establishing an official language and determining territorial boundaries after the colonial era were difficult in many countries. In some cases, these problems were made worse by political and economic changes. The introduction of the concept of democracy sharpened the desire for a separate identity for individual groups within larger nations. Furthermore, economic develop-

ment often favored some people or groups at the expense of others.

The introduction of Western ideas and customs has also had a destabilizing effect in many areas. Such ideas are often welcomed by some groups and resisted by others. When Western influence undermines traditional customs and religious beliefs, it sparks tension and even conflict within individual societies. To some people, Western customs and values represent the wave of the future and are to be welcomed as a sign of progress. Others see the Western influences as being destructive of native traditions and as a barrier to the growth of a genuine national identity based on history and culture.

In recent years, there have been signs of a revival of interest in the democratic model in various parts of Asia, Africa, and Latin America. The best examples have been the free elections in South Korea, Taiwan, and the Philippines. Similar developments have taken place in a number of African countries and throughout Latin America. It is clear that in many areas, democratic institutions are fragile. Many political leaders in Asia and Africa are convinced that such democratic practices as free elections and freedom of the press can destroy other national objectives. A good example is China, where official tolerance of free means of expression led ultimately to the demonstrations in Tiananmen Square and the bloody crackdown that brought them to an end. Many people still do not believe that democracy and economic development necessarily go hand in hand.

The collapse of the Soviet Union and its satellite states in Eastern Europe between 1989 and 1991 brought new hopes for democracy and for international cooperation on global issues. In fact, the collapse of the Soviet empire has had almost the opposite effect. The disintegration of the Soviet Union has led to a general atmosphere of conflict and tension throughout much of Eastern Europe. Regional and ethnic differences continue to exist, not only in Eastern Europe but also worldwide.

In the Middle East, the conflict between Israelis and Palestinians over the land of Palestine continues to produce terrorist acts and seemingly endless conflict between the two peoples. In Europe, Yugoslavia was torn apart by ethnic divisions as Slovenians, Croatians, Bosnian Muslims, and Serbs fought over territory and

▶ *The bombing and terrorist activities have lasted in Belfast, Ireland, for more than twenty-five years. An entire generation of children and adults have become accustomed to such sights as these burned-out vehicles. What steps do you believe Great Britain and the IRA could take to establish a lasting peace?*

the right to establish their own states. The Serbian policy of "ethnic cleansing"—killing of Bosnian Muslims—caused worldwide outrage and finally led the U.S. and European governments to impose a peace on the area. Ethnic conflicts among hostile tribal groups in Africa have led to massacres of hundreds of thousands of innocent men, women, and children. In Indonesia, the government since 1975 has killed 200,000 people in East Timor to keep it part of Indonesia.

Longstanding religious differences have also added to the ongoing conflicts around the world. In the Middle East, Islamic fundamentalists have often resorted to terrorist acts to overthrow governments that do not meet their strict religious standards. In Northern Ireland, the conflict between a Protestant majority and Catholic minority gave rise to the Irish Republican Army. This radical group began a terrorist campaign against Protestant civilians and British soldiers to gain more rights for the Catholic minority in Northern Ireland. The conflict is not yet settled, and innocent civilians continue to die.

New regional organizations have also sometimes served to magnify regional differences. In 1960, the Arab states of the Middle East formed the Organization of Petroleum Exporting Countries (OPEC). Its purpose was to gain control over oil prices. In the 1970s, OPEC used oil prices as a weapon to force Western governments to abandon their support of Israel. In 1967, a number of Southeast Asian nations formed the Association of Southeast Asian Nations (ASEAN). Its goal was cooperation in a number of social and economic endeavors. It also worked to resist further Communist growth in the region. The Organization of African Unity was founded by the leaders of thirty-two African states in 1963. Its founders believed in the unity of all black Africans, regardless of national boundaries. The European Economic Community, first founded in 1957, has expanded to create a single trading bloc of 344 million Europeans. Through the North American Free Trade Agreement (NAFTA), the United States, Canada, and Mexico worked to create a similar trading bloc. It remains to be seen in what ways these regional organizations will shape world history.

❀    SECTION REVIEW    ❀

1. **Define:**
   (*a*) ecology,   (*b*) deforestation,   (*c*) ozone layer,
   (*d*) greenhouse effect,   (*e*) acid rain,
   (*f*) Internet,   (*g*) World Wide Web,   (*h*) space
   shuttles,   (*i*) genetic engineering,

(j) global economy, (k) developed nations,
(l) developing nations

2. **Identify:**
   (a) Rachel Carson, (b) Bhopal, (c)*Exxon Valdez,* (d) World Bank and the International Monetary Fund

3. **Recall:**
   (a) What fear has the rapid increase in the world's population created?
   (b) What international agreement was reached in Montreal in 1987?
   (c) What did the Earth Summit in Rio de Janeiro accomplish in 1992?
   (d) Why hasn't the Green Revolution benefited all people?
   (e) Why do developing nations rely on the success of developed nations?
   (f) What has happened to the difference between opportunities available to men and women in the developed Western world relative to the gap in developing nations?
   (g) What problem appears to be the most difficult challenge facing new nations of Asia and Africa?
   (h) What new threats to world peace have emerged from the fall of the former Soviet Union?

4. **Think Critically:**
   (a) Why is it unlikely that any country will be able to keep and use technological advances just for itself?
   (b) Why will advances in genetic engineering force people to make new ethical and moral decisions in the future?

# THE EMERGENCE OF NEW GLOBAL VISIONS

As people have become aware that the problems humans face are global—not national—they have responded to this challenge in different ways. The United Nations has been one of the most visible symbols of the new globalism of the last half of the twentieth century.

## The United Nations

The United Nations was founded in 1945 in San Francisco, when representatives of the Allied forces worked out a plan for a new organization. U.S. president Franklin Delano Roosevelt had been especially eager to create a new international organization to help maintain the peace after the war. At the Yalta Conference in February 1945, Joseph Stalin of the Soviet Union had agreed to join the new organization. In the original charter, the members pledged "to save succeeding generations from the scourge of war, which twice in our lifetime had brought untold sorrow to mankind, and to reaffirm faith in fundamental human rights, in the dignity and worth of the human person, in the equal rights of men and women and of nations large and small, and to promote social progress and better standards of life in larger freedom." The United Nations, then, has two chief goals: peace and human dignity.

The General Assembly of the United Nations is composed of representatives of all member nations. It was given the power to discuss any question of importance to the organization and to recommend action to be taken. The day-to-day administrative business of the United Nations is supervised by the secretary-general, whose offices are located at the permanent headquarters in New York City.

The most important organ of the United Nations is the Security Council. It is composed of five permanent members—the United States, the Soviet Union (now Russia), Great Britain, France, and China—and ten members chosen by the General Assembly. The Security Council decides what actions the United Nations should take to settle international disputes. Because each of the permanent members can veto the council's decision, a stalemate has frequently resulted.

A number of specialized agencies function under the direction of the United Nations. These include the United Nations Educational, Scientific, and Cultural Organization (UNESCO), the World Health Organi-

▶ *At the UN headquarters in New York City, votes are recorded on an overhead electronic board so that all can see the results. How effective do you believe the UN has been in establishing worldwide peace?*

zation (WHO), and the United Nations International Children's Emergency Fund (UNICEF). All these agencies have been successful in providing aid to help lessen the world's economic and social problems. The United Nations has also performed a valuable service in organizing international conferences on important issues such as population growth and the environment.

The United Nations has also managed to provide peacekeeping military forces drawn from neutral member states to settle conflicts. Until recently, however, the basic weakness of the United Nations was that throughout its history, it had been subject to the whims of the two superpowers. The rivalry of the United States and the Soviet Union during the Cold War was often played out at the expense of the United Nations. The United Nations had little success, for example, in reducing the arms race between the two superpowers. With the end of the Cold War, the United Nations has played a more active role in keeping alive a vision of international order and peace. Missions in Somalia and Bosnia, however, have still raised questions about the effectiveness of the United Nations in peacekeeping.

The United Nations also took the lead in affirming the basic **human rights** of all people. On December 10, 1948, the General Assembly adopted the Universal Declaration of Human Rights. According to the declaration, "All human beings are born free and equal in dignity and rights. . . . Everyone is entitled to all the rights and freedoms set forth in this Declaration, without distinction of any kind, such as race, color, sex, language, religion, political or other opinion, national or social origin, property, birth or other status. . . . Everyone has the right to life, liberty, and security of person."

## New Global Visions

One approach to the global problems we face has been the development of social movements led by ordinary citizens, including environmental, women's and men's liberation, human potential, appropriate-technology, and nonviolence movements. Hazel Henderson, a British-born economist, has been especially active in founding public interest groups. She believes that citizen groups can be an important force for greater global unity and justice. In *Creating Alternative Futures*, Henderson explained: "These aroused citizens are by no means all mindless young radicals. Well-dressed, clean-shaven, middle-class businessmen and their suburban wives comprise the major forces in California fighting against nuclear power. Hundreds of thousands of middle-class mothers are bringing massive pressure to ban commercials and violent programs from children's television."[2] "Think globally, act locally" is frequently the slogan of these grassroots groups.

Related to the emergence of these social movements is the growth of **nongovernmental organizations (NGOs).** NGOs are often represented at the United Nations and include professional, business, and cooperative organizations; foundations; religious, peace, and disarmament groups; youth and women's organizations; environmental and human rights groups; and research institutes. According to the American educator Elise Boulding, who has been active in encouraging the existence of these groups, NGOs are an important instrument in the cultivation of global perspectives. Boulding states: "Since NGOs by definition are identified with interests that transcend national boundaries, we expect all NGOs to define problems in global terms, to take account of human interests and needs as they are found in all parts of the planet."[3] The number of international NGOs increased from 176 in 1910 to 18,000 in 1990.

Global approaches to global problems, however, have been hindered by political, ethnic, and religious disputes. The Palestinian-Israeli conflict keeps much of the Middle East in constant turmoil. Religious differences between Hindus and Muslims help to inflame relations between India and Pakistan. Pollution of the Rhine River by factories along its banks often provokes angry disputes among European nations. The United States and Canada have argued about the effects of acid rain on Canadian forests. The collapse of the Soviet Union has led to the emergence of new nations in conflict and a general atmosphere of friction and tension throughout much of Eastern Europe. The bloody conflict in the lands of the former Yugoslavia clearly indicates the dangers in the rise of nationalist sentiment among various ethnic and religious groups in Eastern Europe. Even as the world becomes more global in culture and more interdependent in its mutual relations, disruptive forces still exist that can sometimes work against efforts to enhance our human destiny.

Many lessons can be learned from the study of world history. One of them is especially clear: a lack of involvement in the affairs of one's society can easily lead to a sense of powerlessness. An understanding of our world heritage and its lessons might well give us the opportunity to make wise choices in an age that is often crisis laden and chaotic. We are all creators of history. The choices we make in our everyday lives will affect the future of world civilization.

## ❀ SECTION REVIEW ❀

1. **Define:**
   (*a*) human rights,   (*b*) nongovernmental organizations (NGOs)

2. **Identify:**
   (*a*) United Nations Educational, Scientific, and Cultural Organization (UNESCO),   (*b*) World Health Organization (WHO),   (*c*) United Nations Children's Emergency Fund (UNICEF), (*d*) Hazel Henderson

3. **Recall:**
   (*a*) What are the two chief goals of the United Nations?
   (*b*) What position is responsible for the day-to-day administration of United Nations activities?
   (*c*) What is required for the Security Council to approve a resolution?

4. **Think Critically:**
   (*a*) Why is it difficult for the United Nations to intervene with military force?
   (*b*) What lessons have you learned from studying this text that will help you make wise choices and help create a better future for the world?

### Notes

1.  Sergei Kapitza and Martin Hellman, "A Message to the Scientific Community," in *Breakthrough—Emerging New Thinking: Soviet and Western Scholars Issue a Challenge to Build a World beyond War,* ed. Anatoly Gromyko and Martin Hellman (New York, 1988), p. xii.
2.  Hazel Henderson, *Creating Alternative Futures* (New York, 1978), p. 356.
3.  Elise Boulding, *Women in the Twentieth Century World* (New York, 1977), p. 186.

# CHAPTER 17 REVIEW

## USING KEY TERMS

1. People, working in groups to define and/or support a particular cause, form _____.
2. _____ are countries that rely primarily on farming to support their people and that have a limited industrial and technological base.
3. The United States sends astronauts on missions in reusable vehicles called _____.
4. The _____ is the world's largest network of computers.
5. _____ is the study of the relationship between living things and their environment.
6. Countries with well-organized, technologically advanced industries and agriculture are called _____.
7. The basic individual rights that were affirmed by the United Nations in 1948 are called _____.
8. _____ is the destruction of large forests and jungles that may affect the world's climate.
9. An immense number of "pages" make up what is called the _____.
10. The interdependency of all nations' economic systems shows that there is a _____ in our world.
11. The ability of scientists to alter cells to produce new life forms is _____.
12. Sulfuric emissions mixing with moisture in the atmosphere results in _____.
13. The warming of the atmosphere that results from the accumulation of carbon dioxide in the air is called the _____.
14. The _____ is a thin layer of gas in the upper atmosphere.

## REVIEWING THE FACTS

1. What environmental message was the theme of *Silent Spring?*

2. What chemical has been identified as a danger to the Earth's ozone layer?
3. In what ways are economies of developing nations dependent on those of developed nations?
4. When and where did nations of the world meet to discuss environmental issues?
5. Why are nongovernmental organizations (NGOs) taking greater responsibilities in the fight to protect the world's environment?
6. Why is it often difficult for the United Nations Security Council to make decisions?
7. What new issue has been raised with the introduction of the Internet and why is it an issue?
8. What is the purpose of the United Nations Children's Emergency Fund?

## THINKING CRITICALLY

1. Why isn't an agreement among developed nations to protect the world's environment likely to be effective by itself?
2. What possible benefits and ethical problems may result from developments in genetic engineering?
3. Explain why it may be hypocritical for people in developed nations to condemn developing nations for abusing their environments by gathering raw materials to sell to earn money to pay debts and buy imported goods.
4. In the early 1990s, developed nations took a series of steps through a program called the Brady Plan to help developing nations make payments on their international debts. How did the developed nations benefit from providing this help?
5. Why must the United Nations have a respected military capacity if it is to be effective in maintaining the peace in many parts of the world?
6. Why might the fall of the Soviet Union have decreased the likelihood of a major nuclear war between superpowers while increasing the potential for relatively small regional wars?

# CHAPTER 17 REVIEW

## APPLYING SOCIAL STUDIES SKILLS

1. **Ecology:** Identify several activities in your life that are harmful to the environment. Describe steps you could take as an individual to help protect the world's environment.
2. **Economics:** A suggestion was made in the late 1980s to have each developed nation contribute a share of its annual income to developing nations to be used to protect their environments because they could not afford to do this on their own. State whether you would have supported this idea and explain the reasons for your point of view.
3. **Government:** Identify and explain several reasons why it is unlikely that there will be a true world government at any time in the near future.

## MAKING TIME AND PLACE CONNECTIONS

1. Why does the birth of another American baby have a greater impact on the world's environment than does the birth of a baby in a developing nation?
2. In the nineteenth century, vast forests in North America were cut for lumber and other products. What right then does the United States or other developed nations have to tell developing nations that they should protect their forests?
3. What events in Africa have increased the need for services of the United Nations Children's Emergency Fund? Why should Americans care what happens to people who are poor in developing nations?

## BECOMING AN HISTORIAN

**Charts, Graphs, Tables:** Study the data below and use it to explain why population density is not a good indicator of a nation's prosperity. What would probably be a better way of predicting what makes a nation's people prosperous?

**Population Density and Production Per Person**

| Country | People per square mile (1990) | Annual production per person (1989) |
| --- | --- | --- |
| U.S.A. | 69 | $20,910 |
| France | 267 | 17,000 |
| Switzerland | 424 | 27,510 |
| Germany (West) | 570 | 19,520 |
| India | 669 | 321 |
| Philippines | 570 | 697 |
| Bangladesh | 2,130 | 180 |
| Zaire | 40 | 258 |

*Source: Statistical Abstract of the United States,* U.S. Government Printing Office (Washington, D.C., 1993), p. 840.

**Writing Research Papers:** Write a thesis statement about your opinion of the ability of the United Nations to resolve international disputes. Choose a recent example and explain what happened that caused the United Nations to become involved. Describe the actions the United Nations took and the results. Explain the impact the situation had on the people who were directly involved, and on the world in general. Finally, explain how these events support the thesis of your report. Be sure to provide appropriate documentation for your statements.

# HISTORICAL ATLAS

## CONTENTS

# World Political Map
## (Inset: Western Europe)

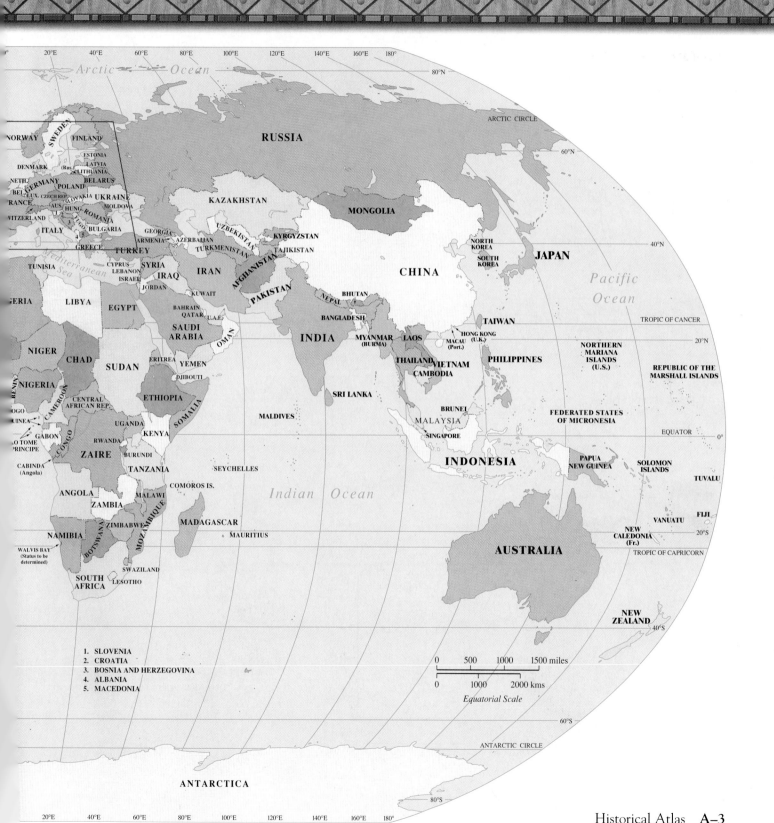

1. SLOVENIA
2. CROATIA
3. BOSNIA AND HERZEGOVINA
4. ALBANIA
5. MACEDONIA

0   500   1000   1500 miles

0   1000   2000 kms

*Equatorial Scale*

Historical Atlas   **A–3**

# World Physical Map

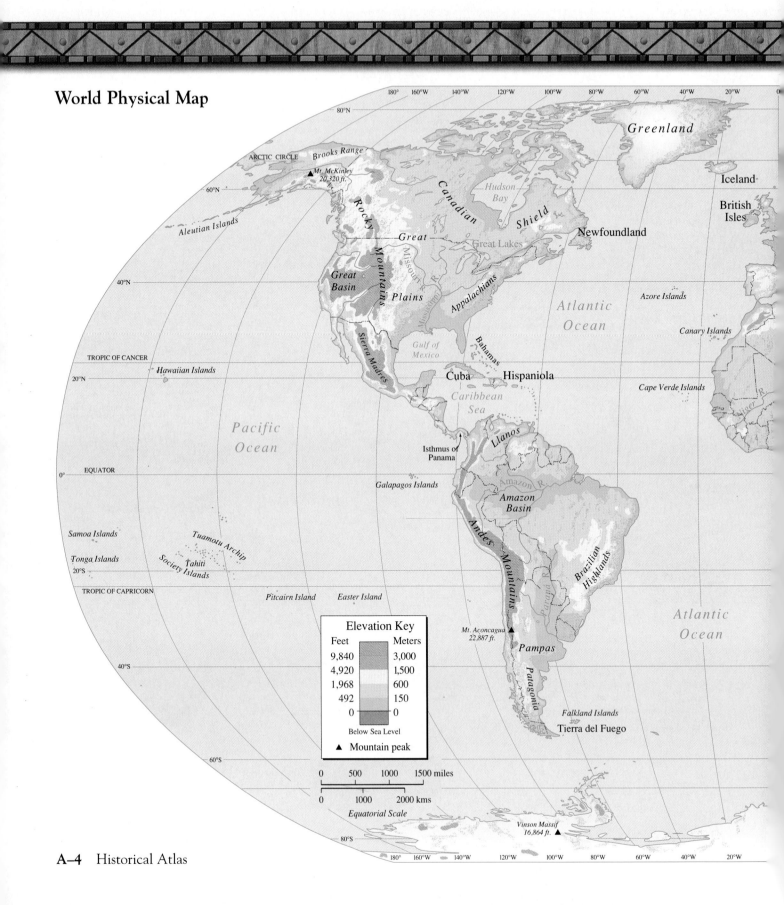

80°N

ARCTIC CIRCLE

Greenland

Iceland

British Isles

Brooks Range

▲ Mt. McKinley
20,320 ft.

60°N

Aleutian Islands

Canadian

Shield

Hudson Bay

Newfoundland

Rocky

Mountains

Great

Great Lakes

40°N

Great Basin

Missouri R.

Plains

Appalachians

Atlantic
Ocean

Azore Islands

TROPIC OF CANCER

Sierra Madres

Gulf of
Mexico

Mississippi

Canary Islands

20°N

Hawaiian Islands

Bahamas

Cuba

Hispaniola

Cape Verde Islands

Caribbean
Sea

Pacific
Ocean

Llanos

Niger R.

Isthmus of
Panama

0° EQUATOR

Galapagos Islands

Amazon R.

Amazon
Basin

Samoa Islands

Tuamotu Archip.

Andes

Paraná R.

Brazilian
Highlands

Tonga Islands

20°S

Tahiti
Society Islands

Mountains

TROPIC OF CAPRICORN

Pitcairn Island

Easter Island

Atlantic
Ocean

## Elevation Key

| Feet | Meters |
|------|--------|
| 9,840 | 3,000 |
| 4,920 | 1,500 |
| 1,968 | 600 |
| 492 | 150 |
| 0 | 0 |

Below Sea Level

▲ Mountain peak

Mt. Aconcagua
22,887 ft. ▲

Pampas

Patagonia

40°S

Falkland Islands

Tierra del Fuego

60°S

0    500    1000    1500 miles

0    1000    2000 kms

Equatorial Scale

Vinson Massif
16,864 ft. ▲

80°S

180°  160°W  140°W  120°W  100°W  80°W  60°W  40°W  20°W

Arctic Ocean

Norwegian Sea

Scandinavian Peninsula

Baltic Sea

North Sea

North European Plain

Alps

Ural Mountains

Ob River

West Siberian Plain

Central Siberian Plateau

Lena R.

ARCTIC CIRCLE

80°N

60°N

Kamchatka Peninsula

Sea of Okhotsk

Volga R.

Aral Sea

Caspian Sea

Tian Shan

Gobi Desert

Lake Baikal

Sea of Japan

40°N

Japanese Archipelago

Mt. Elbrus 18,510 ft.

Black Sea

Mediterranean Sea

Central Plateau of Iran

Hindu Kush

Tibetan Plateau

Mt. Everest 29,028 ft.

Himalaya Mtns.

Yangtze R.

Pacific Ocean

Sahara

Nile R.

Arabian Peninsula

Red Sea

Ganges R.

Bay of Bengal

Mekong R.

TROPIC OF CANCER

20°N

Arabian Sea

Sri Lanka

Philippine Islands

Mariana Islands

Marshall Islands

Lake Chad

African Horn

Maldive Islands

South China Sea

Caroline Islands

EQUATOR 0°

Zaire R.

Congo Basin

Lake Victoria

Mt. Kilimanjaro 19,340 ft.

Seychelles

Borneo

Sumatra

New Guinea

Mt. Puncak Jaya 16,500 ft.

Solomon Islands

Tuvalu

Comoros Islands

Indian Ocean

Java

Vanatu

Fiji Islands

Madagascar

Mauritius

Great Sandy Desert

Great Dividing Range

New Caledonia

20°S

Kalahari Desert

TROPIC OF CAPRICORN

AUSTRALIA

New Zealand

40°S

Cape of Good Hope

Tasmania

60°S

ANTARCTIC CIRCLE

ANTARCTICA

80°S

20°E 40°E 60°E 80°E 100°E 120°E 140°E 160°E 180°

# World Population Density Map

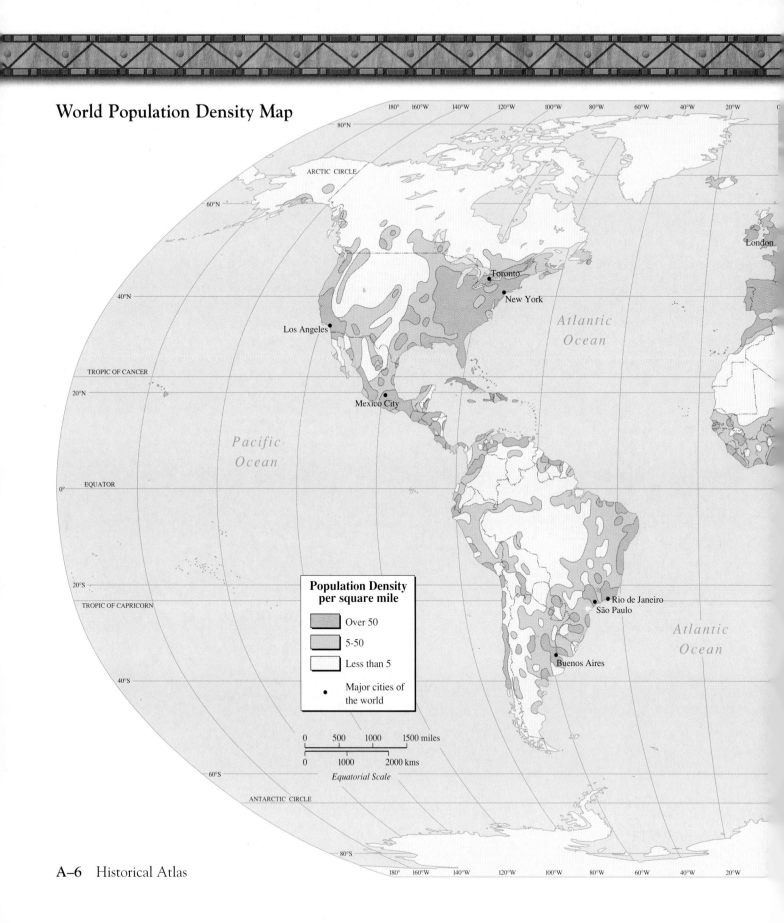

Population Density per square mile

- Over 50
- 5-50
- Less than 5
- Major cities of the world

0   500   1000   1500 miles
0   1000   2000 kms
*Equatorial Scale*

Arctic Ocean

80°N

ARCTIC CIRCLE

60°N

•Moscow

40°N

Paris•

Beijing•
•Seoul
•Tokyo
Osaka-Kobe

•Shanghai

Mediterranean Sea

Tehran•

TROPIC OF CANCER

Cairo•

20°N

•Delhi

Karachi•
Calcutta•

Bombay•

Manila•

Lagos•

Pacific Ocean

EQUATOR
0°

Nairobi•

Jakarta•

Indian Ocean

20°S

Johannesburg•

TROPIC OF CAPRICORN

Cape Town•

•Sydney

Melbourne•
40°S

60°S

ANTARCTIC CIRCLE

80°S

20°E  40°E  60°E  80°E  100°E  120°E  140°E  160°E  180°

## The Beginnings of Civilization

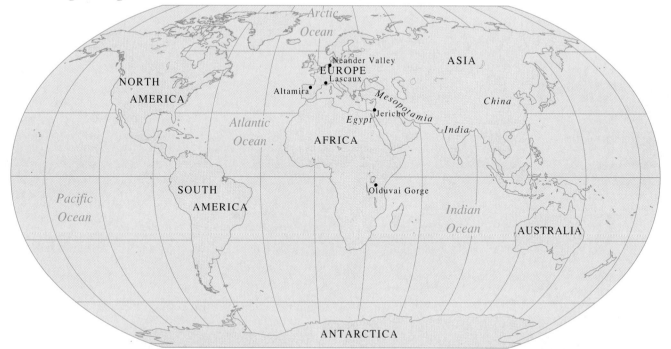

## Ancient Civilizations, 100–500

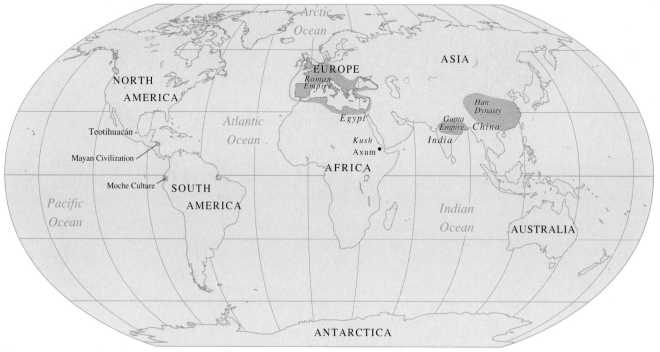

## New Patterns of Civilization, 500–1500

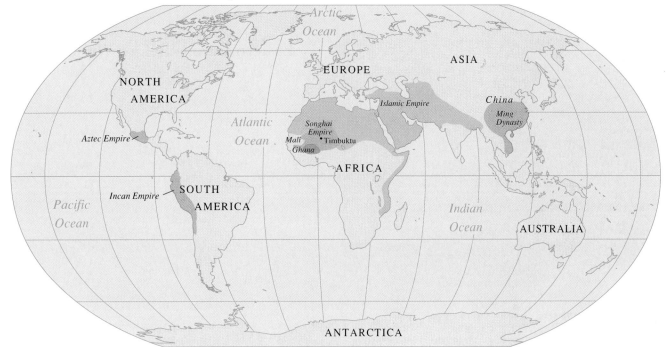

## Modern Patterns of World History, 1900

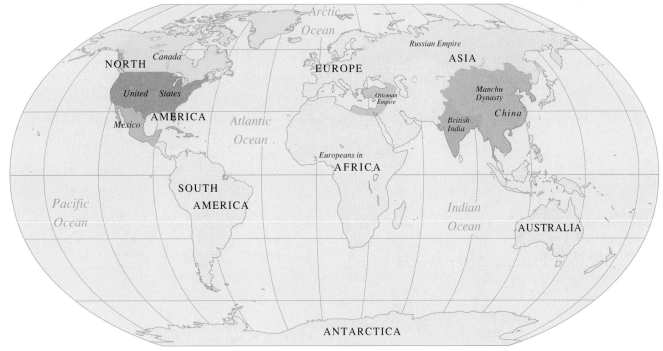

# 1. Eastern Europe Before World War I

# 2. Eastern Europe After World War I

## 3. Eastern Europe After World War II

## 4. Modern Eastern Europe

# GLOSSARY

## A

**abolitionism**   a movement to end slavery (147)

**absolutism**   a form of rule where ultimate authority was in the hands of a monarch who claimed to rule by divine right (62)

**acid rain**   rainfall that results when sulfur spewed out by industrial factories mixes with the moisture in the air (responsible for killing large forested areas in North America and Europe) (584)

**acropolis**   usually the upper fortified part of a city or town, which served as a refuge during attack and sometimes as the religious center for temples and public buildings (20)

**agora**   an open space below an acropolis that was used for citizen assembly and a market (21)

**Anschluss**   refers to Hitler's union of Germany and Austria (374)

**anti-Semitism**   hostility toward or discrimination against Jews as a religious group (322)

**apartheid**   a system of racial segregation in South Africa (516)

**appeasement**   Great Britain's policy (prior to World War II) based on the belief that if European states satisfied the reasonable demands of dissatisfied powers, the latter would be content, and stability and peace would be achieved in Europe (374)

**Aryan racial state**   a nation consisting solely of a hypothetical homogeneous ethnic type descended from early Indo-European peoples (Hitler considered Germans the supreme group of Aryans) (374)

**Atman**   according to Hindu belief, the individual self whose duty it was to seek to know Brahman (15)

**Ausgleich**   the Compromise of 1867, which created the dual monarchy of Austria-Hungary (146)

## B

**balance of power**   the idea that states should have equal power in order to prevent any one state from dominating the others (93)

**banana republics**   small countries dependent on large, wealthy nations (363)

**Blitzkrieg**   "lightning war," a war conducted with great speed and force (380)

**blue-collar**   of, relating to, or constituting the class of wage-earners whose duties call for the wearing of work clothes or protective clothing—industrial production occupations (435)

**bourgeois**   a person of the middle class (130)

**bourgeoisie**   the middle class (164)

**Brahman**   according to Hindu belief, a force in the universe, a form of ultimate reality or God (15)

**Brezhnev doctrine**   Leonid Brezhnev's insistence on the right of the Soviet Union to intervene if communism was threatened in another Communist state (451)

**brinkmanship**   threatening to go to war to achieve one's goals (274)

## C

**Camp David Accords**   an agreement to sign an Israeli-Egyptian peace treaty on March 26, 1979 (the meeting was held at Camp David, Maryland, and attended by Jimmy Carter, Menachim Begin, and Anwar al-Sadat) (536)

**caudillos**   strong leaders who ruled the new independent nations of Latin America chiefly by military force; they were usually supported by the landed elites (232)

**centuriate assembly**   the most important assembly of the Roman Republic; it was organized by classes based on wealth, where the wealthiest citizens always had the majority (29)

**collective bargaining**   the right of unions to negotiate with employers over wages and hours (312)

**collectivization**   many small holdings brought together into a single unit for joint operation under governmental supervision (319)

**conscription**   a military draft (274)

**conservatism**   an ideology that favored obedience to political authority and the belief that organized religion was crucial to order in society (134)

**consulate** a new form of French republic proclaimed in 1799, which was entirely controlled by Napoleon Bonaparte (114)

**consuls** chief executive officers of the Roman Republic, two of which were chosen every year; they ran the government and led the army into battle (29)

**consumer society** a preoccupation with and the inclination toward the buying of goods that directly satisfy human wants (440)

**Contras** American-financed rebels who waged a guerrilla war against the Sandinista provisional government in Nicaragua (499)

**cottage industry** the production of goods from one's home (84)

**council of the plebs** a popular assembly of the Roman Republic created for plebeians only, founded in 471 B.C. (30)

**counterterrorism** a calculated policy of direct retaliation against terrorists (radicals who commit violent acts, such as killing civilians, taking hostages, and hijacking planes, in order to achieve their goals) (472)

**covenant** a contract made by God with the tribes of Israel (12)

**creole elites** locally born descendants of the Europeans who became permanent inhabitants of Latin America (228)

# D

**deficit spending** the spending of government funds raised by borrowing rather than taxation (312)

**deforestation** the process of cutting down trees in forests and jungles to provide wood products and new farmland (584)

**deism** a system of thought that denies the interference of the Creator with the laws of the universe (75)

**democracy** rule of the many (21)

***descamisados*** "the shirtless ones," the working classes in Argentina (500)

**de-Stalinization** Nikita Khrushchev's process of eliminating the more ruthless policies of Stalin (424)

**détente** a relaxation of strained relations or tensions (as between the United States and the Soviet Union in the 1970s) (449)

**developed nations** rich nations, located mainly in the Northern Hemisphere, which have well-organized industrial and agricultural systems, make use of advanced technologies, and have strong educational systems (588)

**developing nations** poor nations, located mainly in the Southern Hemisphere, which are primarily farming nations with little technology or education (588)

**Diet** the Japanese legislature (260)

**diplomatic revolution** the forming of new alliances without resorting to war (93)

**direct rule** the form of rule that occurred when local elites were removed from power and replaced with a new set of officials brought from the mother country (205)

**dissidents** those who speak out against or disagree with the status quo (for example, those who opposed the regime in the Soviet Union) (451)

**divine right of kings** the belief that kings receive their power directly from God and are responsible to no one except God (64)

**domino theory** the argument that if the Communists succeeded in one country (that is, South Vietnam), the neighboring countries would likewise fall to communism (422)

**drug cartels** groups of drug businesses whose purpose is to eliminate competition (488)

**Duma** a legislative assembly, or representative council, in Russia (184)

# E

**ecology** the study of the relationship between living things and their environments (583)

**emancipation** the act of setting free from bondage (147)

**enlightened absolutism** a type of late eighteenth-century European monarchy, which was influenced by the philosophes (88)

**enlightened ruler** according to the philosophes, a ruler who allowed basic human rights; nurtured arts, sciences, and education; and obeyed the laws and enforced them fairly (88)

**environmentalism** a movement begun in the 1970s to control the pollution of the Earth (469)

**ethnic cleansing** the practice of genocide during the Bosnian War (1993–96) (343)

**existentialism** a twentieth-century philosophy based on the concept of the absence of God in the universe—meaning that humans were utterly alone and responsible for their actions with no certain knowledge of right or wrong; reduced to despair and depression, their only ground of hope was themselves (473)

**export-import economy** an economic system based on exporting raw materials while importing manufactured goods (364)

**extraterritoriality** a practice (during the 1800s) whereby Europeans lived in their own sections in Chinese ports and were subject not to Chinese laws but to their own (241)

## F

**feminism**   the movement for women's rights (76)

**feudal system**   a political practice whereby landed aristocrats or nobles dominated political, economic, and social life in Europe (54)

**fez**   the brimless cap worn by Turkish Muslims (345)

**fiefs**   grants of land made to vassals (54)

**Final Solution**   the physical extermination of the Jewish people by the Nazis during World War II (391)

**four modernizations**   modernization in regard to industry, agriculture, technology, and national defense—a policy set up by Deng Xiaoping in which people were encouraged to work hard to benefit both themselves and Chinese society (551)

**four olds**   old ideas, old culture, old customs, and old habits—which the Red Guards set out to eliminate by violent means during China's Cultural Revolution (549)

**functionalism**   a theory of design that places great emphasis on how an object will be used (333)

## G

**gang of four**   Jiang Qing—the widow of Mao Zedong—and three other radicals of the Cultural Revolution who were put on trial and sent to prison for life by reformers led by Deng Xiaoping (551)

**genetic engineering**   a new scientific field that alters the genetic information of cells to produce new variations—from cells as simple as yeast cells to as complex as mammal cells (586)

**genocide**   the deliberate mass murder of a group of people (343)

**glasnost**   "openness," an important instrument of Mikhail Gorbachev's perestroika—Soviet citizens were encouraged to discuss openly the strengths and weaknesses of the Soviet Union (452)

**global economy**   an economy, developed by the nations of the world since World War II, in which the production, distribution, and sale of goods are done on a worldwide scale (587)

**Great Leap Forward**   a program begun by Mao Zedong in China in 1958 in the hopes of speeding up economic growth and obtaining a classless society; existing collective farms, normally the size of the traditional village, were combined into vast people's communes (549)

**Green Revolution**   the work of researchers in India in the 1970s who introduced new strains of rice and wheat that were more productive and resistant to disease but that required more fertilizer and water (561)

**greenhouse effect**   Earth's warming because of the buildup of carbon dioxide in the atmosphere (584)

**Guided Democracy**   the government of President Sukarno, who dissolved Indonesia's democratic political system in order to rule on his own; he nationalized foreign-owned enterprises and sought economic aid from China and the Soviet Union (566)

## H

**heresy**   the holding of religious doctrines different from the orthodox teachings of the church (73)

**human rights**   the just claims of all people, outlined in the Declaration of Human Rights, which was adopted by the UN General Assembly in 1948 (594)

## I

**imperialism**   the extension of one nation's power over other lands (201)

**import-substituting industrialization**   the development of new industries to make goods that previously had been imported (as was done in Latin America after the Great Depression because of a decline in revenues) (486)

**impressionism**   a theory or practice of painting (which began in France in the 1870s) in which the natural appearances of objects were depicted by dabs and strokes of primary unmixed colors in order to simulate actual reflected light (193)

**indemnity**   a large sum of money (248)

**indirect rule**   rule that occurred when local rulers were allowed to maintain their positions of authority and status in a new colonial setting (205)

**insurrection**   the act of revolting against an established government (249)

**Internet**   the world's largest network of computers (585)

*intifada*   "uprising," a rising unrest created by Palestinian Arab militancy (536)

**Islamic fundamentalism**   a movement by conservative religious forces in the Middle East to replace foreign culture and values with supposedly "pure" Islamic forms of belief and behavior (539)

## K

**kamikaze**   "divine wind," a member of the Japanese air attack corps that was assigned to make suicidal attacks on targets (that is, U.S. ships) during World War II (401)

**karma**  the force of a person's actions in this life in determining rebirth in a next life  (15)

**kibbutz**  a collective, or commune, in Israel in which farmers share property and work together; adults eat together, and children are raised in a separate children's home  (542)

# L

**liberalism**  the idea that people should be as free from restraint as possible; a belief in the protection of civil liberties, or the basic rights of all people  (135)

**lineage group**  African community formed by combining extended family units  (47)

**Luftwaffe**  the German air force  (381)

# M

**magic realism**  a form of Latin American literature that brings together realistic events with dreamlike or fantastic backgrounds  (509)

**Mahatma**  "Great Soul," the name Indians used to refer to Mohandas Gandhi  (350)

**Mau Mau movement**  an organized effort among the Kikuyu peoples of Kenya who used terrorism to demand uhuru (freedom) from the British  (516)

**Meiji**  "Enlightened Rule," the reign of the Japanese emperor Mutsuhito  (258)

**mestizos**  the offspring of Europeans and native American Indians  (96)

**militarism**  glorification of the military  (143)

**ministerial responsibility**  the idea that the prime minister is responsible to the popularly elected legislative body and not to the executive officer (a crucial principle of democracy)  (181)

**mirs**  village communes or communities of peasants in tsarist Russia that were responsible for land payments to the government  (147)

**mobilization**  the process of assembling and making both troops and supplies ready for war  (276)

**modernism**  changes produced by writers and artists (between 1870 and 1914) rebelling against the traditional literary and artistic styles dominating European cultural life since the Renaissance  (190)

**monotheism**  the belief that there is only one God for all peoples  (12)

**mulattoes**  the offspring of Africans and Europeans  (96)

**multinational corporations**  companies that have divisions in more than two countries  (487)

**multinational state**  a collection of different peoples  (137)

**mutual deterrence**  the policy based on the belief that an arsenal of nuclear weapons prevents war by ensuring that even if one nation launched its weapons in a first strike, the other nation would still be able to respond and devastate the attacker  (418)

# N

**nationalism**  loyalty and devotion to a nation  (117)

**nationalization**  government ownership  (433)

**naturalism**  a literary style where the material world is accepted as real, and therefore, literature is written in a realistic manner  (190)

**natural selection**  "survival of the fittest"— organisms most adaptable to their environment pass on the variations that enabled them to survive until a new, separate species emerges  (155)

**New Democracy**  a modified version of capitalism put into effect by Mao Zedong in China in 1958; major industries were placed under state ownership, but most trading and manufacturing companies remained in private hands  (548)

**New Economic Policy**  a modified version of capitalism put into effect by Vladimir Lenin in Russia in 1921; heavy industry, banking, and mines remained in government hands, but peasants could sell their produce openly, and retail stores and small industries (less than twenty employees) could be privately owned and operated  (317)

**nongovernmental organizations (NGOs)**  interest groups (related to the emergence of grass-roots social movements) that transcend national boundaries; they are often represented at the United Nations  (595)

# O

**oligarchy**  rule by the few  (21)

**orders**  social groups, also known as *estates* (divisions of society in Europe, first established in the Middle Ages and continuing well into the eighteenth century)  (87)

**organic evolution**  Charles Darwin's principle that each kind of plant and animal evolved over a long period of time from earlier and simpler forms of life  (155)

**ostracism**  a practice devised in ancient Athens whereby members of the assembly wrote the name of a person who was considered harmful on a pottery fragment *(ostrakon)*; if 6,000 votes were recorded, the person was banned from the city for ten years  (25)

**ozone layer**  a thin layer of gas in the upper atmosphere that shields Earth from the sun's ultraviolet rays  (584)

# P

**pan-Africanism**   a movement that stressed the need for the unity of all Africans  (350)

**pan-Arabism**   a belief in Arab unity  (532)

**patriarchal**   a society dominated by men  (8)

**patricians**   great landowners who became Rome's ruling class  (29)

**peninsulars**   Spanish and Portuguese officials who resided temporarily in Latin America for political and economic gain and then returned to their mother countries  (228)

**people's communes**   the result of collective farms being combined during the Great Leap Forward in China  (549)

**perestroika**   "restructuring," a term applied to Mikhail Gorbachev's radical economic, political, and social reforms in the Soviet Union  (452)

**permanent revolution**   constant revolutionary fervor  (549)

**philosophes**   members of the Enlightenment, an eighteenth-century movement of intellectuals who believed in reason, or the application of the scientific method to the understanding of life  (74)

**philosophy**   an organized system of thought  (26)

**planned economies**   systems directed by government agencies  (287)

**plebeians**   Rome's less wealthy landholders, craftspeople, merchants, and small farmers  (29)

**pogroms**   organized massacres of helpless people  (190)

**policy of containment**   U.S. diplomat George Kennan's plan to keep communism within its geographical boundaries and prevent further aggressive moves  (417)

**polis**   a Greek city-state  (20)

**Politburo**   a committee that was the leading policymaker of the Communist Party  (318)

**polytheistic**   having many gods  (42)

**post-impressionism**   an artistic movement (which began in France in the 1880s) where artists were especially interested in color, believing it could act as its own form of language  (194)

**praetors**   chief executives of the Roman Republic; they were in charge of civil law as it applied to Roman citizens  (29)

**prefectures**   Japanese territories, governed by the former daimyo owners  (258)

**principle of intervention**   the right of great powers to send armies into countries where there were revolutions in order to restore legitimate monarchs to their thrones  (135)

**principle of legitimacy**   a guideline used by Prince Klemens von Metternich during the Congress of Vienna in 1814, which meant that lawful monarchs were restored to their positions of power in order to keep peace and stability in Europe  (134)

**privatization**   the act of changing state-owned (or public-owned) companies to private control or ownership  (493)

**proletariat**   the working class  (164)

**prophets**   religious leaders believed to have been sent by God to his people  (12)

**proportional representation**   a system where the number of representatives assigned per political party is based on the number of votes each party received during the general election  (535)

**protectorate**   a political unit that depends on another state for its protection  (204)

**psychoanalysis**   a method devised by Sigmund Freud by which a psychotherapist and patient could probe deeply into the memory of the patient in order to retrace the chain of repressed thoughts  (189)

**puddling**   a process developed by Henry Cort where coke, derived from coal, was used to burn away impurities in pig iron (crude iron) to make high-quality iron  (125)

# R

**realpolitik**   the "politics of reality," or politics based on practical matters rather than theory or ethics  (144)

**real wages**   the actual purchasing power of income  (435)

**Red Guards**   Mao Zedong's revolutionary units organized during the Cultural Revolution to cleanse Chinese society of impure elements guilty of taking the capitalist road  (549)

**Reichstag**   the German parliament  (323)

**Reign of Terror**   a system devised by the National Convention and the Committee of Public Safety in France (1793–94) whereby revolutionary courts were set up to protect the revolutionary republic from its internal enemies by conducting mass executions  (113)

**reincarnation**   the belief that the individual soul is reborn in a different form after death  (15)

**relics of feudalism**   obligations of peasants to local landlords (or the privileges of aristocrats) that had survived from an earlier age (for example, the payment of fees by peasants for the use of local facilities)  (104)

**reparations**   financial compensation  (301)

**revisionists**   Marxists who rejected the revolutionary approach and instead argued for workers to organize in mass political parties (and work with other parties) to gain reforms  (167)

**ricksha**   a small, covered, two-wheeled vehicle, usually for one passenger, that is pulled by one man (used originally in Japan) (361)

## S

**scientific socialism**   Gamal Abdul Nasser's plan to improve the standard of living throughout the Middle East by nationalizing major industries and using central planning to guarantee that resources would be used efficiently (532)

**secular state**   a state that rejects any church influence on its policies (345)

**self-strengthening**   the idea that China should adopt Western technology while keeping its Confucian values and institutions (243)

**Senate**   a select group of about 300 landowning Roman males who served for life, and whose advice to government officials had the force of law by the third century B.C. (29)

**separation of powers**   a system of government in which the executive, legislative, and judicial powers are separate (thereby providing checks and balances among the powers) (75)

**sepoys**   Indian soldiers hired by the British East India Company in the 1800s to protect its interests in India (220)

**Shining Path**   a radical guerrilla group in Peru with ties to Communist China (507)

**Social Darwinism**   a social order that was based on Charles Darwin's principle of organic evolution (189)

**Socialist**   a member of the Socialist Party; an advocate of collective or governmental ownership and administration of the means of production and distribution of goods (164)

**Socratic method**   a form of teaching that uses a question-and-answer format to lead pupils to conclusions by using their own reasoning (26)

**soviets**   Russian councils composed of deputies from workers and soldiers (291)

**space shuttles**   reusable spacecraft that return to Earth under their own power (586)

**spheres of influence**   areas in China where foreign nations were granted exclusive trading rights or railroad and mining privileges by warlords in exchange for money (244)

**squadristi**   bands of black-shirted armed Fascists organized by Benito Mussolini to attack Socialist offices and newspapers and break up Socialist strikes (315)

**stagflation**   the economic stagnation that occurred from 1973 to the mid-1980s in the United States (it was characterized by high inflation and high unemployment) (464)

**supply-side economics**   Ronald Reagan's policy of massive tax cuts that would supposedly stimulate rapid economic growth and produce new revenues (464)

**symbolists**   a group of French writers and artists (after the 1880s) who believed an objective knowledge of the world was impossible since the external world was made up of only symbols; they dealt in general truths instead of actualities, exalting the metaphysical and mysterious; they believed that art should exist for art itself (192)

## T

**Tennis Court Oath**   a promise made by the Third Estate in 1789 to meet until they produced a French constitution (the oath was sworn during a meeting that took place at a tennis court) (106)

**Thatcherism**   the economic policy of Margaret Thatcher, Britain's first female prime minister (462)

**theology of liberation**   Latin American Catholics in the 1960s who were influenced by Marxist ideas and believed that Christians must fight to free the oppressed, even if it meant the use of violence (490)

**totalitarian state**   a government that aims to control the political, economic, social, intellectual, and cultural lives of its citizens (314)

**total war**   war involving a complete mobilization of resources and people (286)

**trench warfare**   fighting from ditches protected by barbed wire (as in World War I) (278)

**tribunes of the plebs**   Roman officials who were given the power to protect the plebeians (30)

## U

**Uncertainty Principle**   German physicist Werner Heisenberg's statement that one cannot determine the path of an electron because the act of observing with light affects the electron's location (in a larger sense, he suggested that at the bottom of all physical laws was uncertainty) (337)

**unconditional surrender**   absolute, unqualified surrender (385)

**universal male suffrage**   the right of all adult men to vote (137)

**utopian socialists**   a movement of idealistic intellectuals—begun in the first half of the nineteenth century—who believed in the equality of all people and in replacing competition with cooperation in industry (labeled as such by later socialists) (132)

# V

**viceroy** the governor of a country or province who rules as a representative of his king or sovereign (British viceroys carried out Parliament's wishes in India in the 1800s) (221)

**Viet Cong** Vietnamese Communists—also known as the National Liberation Front (568)

# W

**war of attrition** war based on wearing the other side down by constant attacks and heavy losses (280)

**war communism** a policy used to ensure regular supplies for the Red Army during the Russian Civil War (1918–21), which included government control of banks and most industries, seizing grain from peasants, and the centralization of state administration under Communist control (295)

**welfare state** a nation in which the government takes responsibility for providing citizens with services and a minimal standard of living (432)

**westernization** conversion to or adoption of western traditions or techniques (354)

**white-collar** of, relating to, or constituting the class of employees whose duties do not require the wearing of work clothes or protective clothing—such as professional and technical workers, managers, officials, and clerical and sales workers (435)

**women's liberation movement** a renewed interest in feminism in the late 1960s that called for political and legal equality with men (466)

**World Wide Web** an immense number of "pages" of information connected to one another around the world (585)

# Z

**zaibatsu** in Japan, a concentration of various manufacturing processes within a single enterprise—a large financial and industrial corporation (265)

**Zionism** an international movement originally for the establishment of a Jewish national or religious community in Palestine and later for the support of modern Israel (190)

# SPANISH GLOSSARY

## A

**absolitionism/abolicionismo** un movimiento para poner a un fin la esclavitud (147)

**absolutism/absolutismo** una forma de regla donde la autoridad última estaba en las manos de una monarca que sostuvo gobernar por derecho divino (62)

**acid rain/lluvia ácida** lluvia que resulta cuando azufre arrojado de fábricas industriales se mezcla con la humedad en el aire (responsable por la matanza de grandes áreas selváticas en Norteamérica y Europa) (584)

**acropolis/acropolis** usualmente la parte de arriba, fortificada de una ciudad o pueblo que sirvió como un refugio durante ataques y a veces como el centro religioso para templos y edificios públicos (20)

**agora/ágora** un espacio abierto debajo de un acropolis que fue usado para la asamblea de la ciudad y para un mercado (21)

**Anschluss/Unión política de Austria con Alemania en 1938** se refiere a la unión de Hitler de Alemania y Austria (374)

**anti-Semitism/antisemitismo** hostilidad hacia los judíos o discriminación contra los judíos como un grupo religioso (322)

**apartheid/segregación racial** un sistema de segregación racial en Sudáfrica (516)

**appeasement/apaciguamiento** la póliza de Gran Bretaña (antes de la Segunda Guerra Mundial) basada en la creencia que si estados europeos satisficieron las demandas razonables de poderes no satisfechos, el segundo sería contento, y se lograría estabilidad y paz en Europa (374)

**Aryan racial state/estado racial ario** una nación que consiste sólo de tipo étnico homogéneo hipotético descendido de antiguos indo-europeos (Hitler consideró que los alemanes eran el grupo supremo de los arios) (374)

**Atman/Atmn** según la creencia hindú, el individuo mismo cuyo deber era buscar y conocer a Brahmán (15)

**Ausgleich/Ausgleich** el Compromiso de 1867 que creó la monarquía dual de Austria-Hungría (146)

## B

**balance of power/equilibrio de poder** la idea que los estados deben tener poder igual para prevenir que un estado domine los otros (93)

**banana republics/país de la América Latina que está bajo la excesiva influencia económica de los Estados Unidos** países pequeños dependientes de naciones grandes y ricas (363)

**Blitzkrieg/Guerra Relámpago** una guerra conducida con gran rapidez y fuerza (380)

**blue-collar/obrero** relacionando a, o constituyendo de la clase de ganadores de sueldos cuyos deberes requieren que usen ropa de trabajo o ropa protector—ocupaciones de producción industrial (435)

**bourgeois/burgués** una persona de la clase media (130)

**bourgeoisie/burguesía** la clase media (164)

**Brahman/Brahmán** según la creencia hindú, un fuerza en el universo, una forma de realidad última o Dios (15)

**Breshnev doctrine/doctrina de Breshnev** la insistencia de Leonid Breshnev sobre el derecho de la Unión Soviética de intervenir si el comunismo fue amenazado en otro estado comunista (451)

**brinkmanship/práctica de llevar las cosas muy cerca de la línea fronteriza de peligro o al borde de una guerra** amenaza de empezar una guerra para lograr las metas de alguien (274)

## C

**Camp David Accords/Acuerdos de Camp David** un acuerdo para firmar un convenio de paz entre Israel y Egipto en 26 de Marzo, 1979 (la reunión ocurrió en Camp David, Maryland, y fue asistido por Jimmy Carter, Menachim Begin, y Anwar al-Sadat) (536)

**caudillos/caudillos** líderes fuertes que dominaron las nuevas naciones independientes de Latinoamérica principalmente por fuerzas militares; usualmente fueron apoyados por la nobleza provinciana (232)

**centuriate assembly/asamblea centurión** la asamblea más importante del Repúblico Romano; fue organizado por clases basadas sobre la riqueza, donde los ciudadanos más ricos siempre tenían la mayoría (29)

**collective bargaining/contrato colectivo** el derecho de sindicatos de negociar con empleadores sobre sueldos y horas (312)

**collectivization/colectivización** muchas pequeñas posesiones unidas en una sola unidad para operación conjunta bajo supervisión gubernamental (319)

**conscription/conscripción** reclutamiento militar (274)

**conservatism/conservatismo** una ideología que favoreció obediencia a la autoridad política y la creencia que religión organizada era crucial para la orden en la sociedad (134)

**consulate/consulado** una nueva forma de república francesa proclamada en 1799, que fue totalmente controlada por Napoleón Bonaparte (114)

**consuls/cónsules** los directores ejecutivos oficiales del Repúblico Romano, dos que eran elegidos cada año; dirigieron el gobierno y guió el ejército en batalla (29)

**consumer society/sociedad del consumidor** una preocupación con, y la inclinación hacia la compra de bienes que directamente satisfacen los deseos humanos (440)

**Contras/Contras** rebeldes financiados por los Estados Unidos que empezaron una guerra guerrillera contra el gobierno provisional sandinista en Nicaragua (499)

**cottage industry/industria de casa de campo** la producción de bienes en el hogar de uno (84)

**council of the plebs/consejo de los plebeyos** una asamblea popular del Repúblico Romano creada solamente para los plebeyos, fundada en 471 a. de J.C. (30)

**counterterrorism/contraterrorismo** una política calculada de venganza directa contra terroristas (radicales que comiten actos violentos, como matar a civiles, tener como rehenes, y asaltar aviones, para lograr sus metas) (472)

**covenant/alianza** a un contrato establecido entre Dios y las tribus de Israel (12)

**creole elites/élites criollos** descendentes localmente nacidos de los europeos que llegaron a ser habitantes permanentes de Latinoamérica (228)

# D

**deficit spending/gastos deficitarios** los gastos de fondos gubernamentales ganados prestando en vez de por impuestos (312)

**deforestation/desforestación** el proceso de cortar árboles en bosques y selvas para proveer productos de madera y nuevos terrenos para cultivo (584)

**deism/deísmo** un sistema de pensamiento que deniega la interferencia del Creador con las leyes del universo (75)

**democracy/democracia** poder de la mayoría (21)

*descamisados/descamisados* "los sin camisas", las clases obreras en Argentina (500)

**de-Stalinization/de-Estalinización** el proceso de Nikita Khrushchev de eliminar las políticas más crueles de Stalin (424)

**détente/disminución** un relajamientop de relaciones o tensiones tenas (como entre los Estados Unidos y la Unión Soviética durante la década de 1970) (449)

**developed nations/naciones desarrolladas** naciones ricas, localizadas primordialmente en el Hemisferio Norte, que tienen sistemas industriales y agrícolas bien organizados, usan tecnologías avances, y tienen sistemas educativos fuertes (588)

**developing nations/naciones desarrollándose** naciones pobres, localizadas primordialmente en el Hemisferio Austral, que son primordialmente naciones agrícolas con poca tecnología o educación (588)

**Diet/Diet** la legislatura japonesa (260)

**diplomatic revolution/revolución diplomática** la formación de nuevas alianzas sin recurrir a guerra (93)

**direct rule/dominio directo** la forma de regla que ocurrió cuando élites locales fueron removidos de poder y reemplazados con una nueva serie de oficiales traídas de la madre patria (205)

**dissidents/disidentes** aquellos que dan su opinión contra el statu quo o no están de acuerdo con él (por ejemplo, aquellos que opusieron el régimen en la Unión Soviética) (451)

**divine right of kings/derecho divino de reyes** la creencia que los reyes reciben sus poderes directamente de Dios y están responsable a nadie sino Dios (64)

**domino theory/teoría dominó** el argumento que si los comunistas sucedieron en un país (es decir, Vietnam del Sur), los países vecinos también caerían al comunismo (422)

**drug cartels/carteles de drogas** grupos de negocios de drogas cuyo propósito es eliminar la competencia (488)

**Duma/Duma** una asamblea legislativa, o consejo representativo, en Rusia (184)

# E

**ecology/ecología** el estudio de la relación entre cosas vivas y sus ambientes (583)

**emancipation/emancipación** liberar de cautiverio (147)

**enlightened absolutism/Absolutismo Ilustrado** tipo de monarquía europca de fines del siglo dieciocho, influenciada por los filósofos (88)

**enlightened ruler/gobernante ilustrado**   según los filosofes, un gobernante que permitió derechos básicos; las artes fomentadas, las ciencias, y la educación; y obedeció las leyes y las obligó justamente (88)

**environmentalism/ambientalismo**   el movimiento empezado durante la década de 1970 para controlar la polución de la Tierra (469)

**ethnic cleansing/purificación étnica**   la práctica de genocidio durante la Guerra de Bosnia (1993–1996) (343)

**existentialsim/existencialismo**   una filosofía del siglo veinte basada en el concepto de la ausencia de Dios en el universo—que significa que humanos eran completamente solos y responsables por sus acciones sin cierto conocimiento de lo correcto y lo malo; reducidos a desesperación y depresión, la única base de esperanza era sí mismos (473)

**export-import economy/economía de exportación-importación**   un sistema económico basado en la exportación de materias primas mientras importando bienes manufacturados (364)

**extraterritoriality/extraterritorialidad**   la práctica (durante los años de 1800) donde los europeos vivieron en sus propias secciones en puertos chinos y no eran sujetos a las leyes chinas sino a sus propias leyes (241)

# F

**feminism/feminismo**   el movimiento para los derechos de mujeres (76)

**feudal system/sistema feudal** (or **fuedal, sistema**)   agregar este término al nuevo glosario, usando la definición previa de feudalismo (54)

**fez/fez**   el gorro sin ala usado por musulmanes turcos (345)

**fiefs/feudos**   poner en plural el término y las definiciones, en ambos glosarios (54)

**Final Solution/Solución Final**   la exterminación física de la gente judía por los Nazis durante la Segunda Guerra Mundial (391)

**four modernizations/cuatro modernizaciones**   modernización tocante a industria, agricultura, tecnología, y defensa nacional—una política desarrollada por Deng Xiaoping donde se animaron que la gente trabajara duro para beneficiar tanto sí mismos como la sociedad china (551)

**four olds/cuatro antiguos**   ideas antiguas, cultura antigua, costumbres antiguas, y hábitos antiguos—que las Guardias Rojas trataron de eliminar usando maneras violentas durante la Revolución Cultural en China (549)

**functionalism/funcionalismo**   una teoría de diseño que pone gran énfasis en cómo se usará un objeto (333)

# G

**gang of four/banda de cuatro**   Jiang Qing—la viuda de Mao Zedong—y tres otros radicales de la Revolución Cultural que fueron enjuiciados y mandados a la cárcel por reformadores guíados por Deng Xiaoping (551)

**genetic engineering/ingeniería genética**   un nuevo campo científico que cambia la información genética de células para producir nuevas variaciones—de células de tan simples como células de gérmenes a tan complejos como células de mamíferos (586)

**genocide/genocidio**   la matanza deliberada de un grupo de gente (343)

**glasnost/glasnost**   "franqueza", un instrumento importante de la perestroika de Mikhail Gorbachev—los ciudadanos soviéticos fueron animaron para discutir francamente las fuerzas y debilidades de la Unión Soviética (452)

**global economy/economía global**   una economía, desarrollada por las naciones del mundo desde la Segunda Guerra Mundial, donde la producción, distribución, y venta de bienes están hechas en una escala mundial (587)

**Great Leap Forward/Gran Avance Adelante**   un programa empezado por Mao Zedong en China en 1958 con la esperanza de adelantar rápidamente el crecimiento económico y obtener una sociedad sin clase; combinaron granjas colectivas existentes, normalmente el tamaño del pueblo tradicional, con vastas comunidades de la gente (549)

**Green Revolution/Revolución Verde**   el trabajo de investigadores en la India durante la década de 1970 que introdujeron nuevos estilos de arroz y trigo que eran más productivos y resistentes a enfermedades pero que requisieron más fertilizante y agua (561)

**greenhouse effect/efecto invernadero**   la calentura de la Tierra a causa del aumento de bióxido de carbono en la atmósfera (584)

**Guided Democracy/Democracia Guiada**   el gobierno de Presidente Sukarno, que disolvió el sistema político democrático de Indonesia para dominar él solo; nacionalizó empresas poseídas por extranjeros y buscó ayuda económica de China y la Unión Soviética (566)

# H

**heresy/herejía**   el mantenimiento de doctrina religiosa diferente de las enseñanzas ortodoxas de la iglesia (73)

**human rights/derechos humanos**   los derechos justos de todo el mundo, delineados en la Declaración de Derechos Humanos, que fue adaptada por la Asamblea General de las Naciones Unidas en 1948 (594)

# I

**imperialism/imperialismo**  la extensión del poder de una nación sobre otras tierras (201)

**import-substituting industrialization/industrialización por substitución de importaciones**  el desarrollo de nuevas industrias para hacer bienes que previamente habían sido importados (como fue hecho en Latinoamérica después de la Gran Depresión a causa de una reducción de ingresos) (486)

**impressionism/impresionismo**  una teoría o práctica de pintar (que empezó en Francia en la década de 1870) donde se retrataron las apariencias naturales de objetos por toques suaves y rasgos de colores primarios no mezclados para estimular luz reflejada actual (193)

**indemnity/indemnidad**  una gran cantidad de dinero (248)

**indirect rule/dominio indirecto**  domino que ocurrió cuando fue permitido que gobernantes locales mantuvieran sus posiciones de autoridad y nivel social en una nueva colocación colonial (205)

**insurrection/insurrección**  el hecho de rebelarse contra un gobierno establecido (249)

**Internet/Internet**  La red de computadoras más grande en el mundo (585)

*intifada/intifada*  "insurrección", una intranquilidad aumentada creada por la militancia palestino árabe (536)

**Islamic fundamentalism/fundamentalismo islámico**  un movimiento por fuerzas religiosas conservativas en el Oriente Medio para reemplazar cultura y valores extranjeros con, de modo supuesto, formas "puras" islámicas de creencia y conducta (539)

# K

**kamikaze/kamikaze**  "viento divino", un miembro del cuerpo japonés de ataques por aire que fue asignado para hacer ataques suicidas en objetos (es decir, barcos de EE.UU.) durante la Segunda Guerra Mundial (401)

**karma/karma**  la fuerza de las acciones de una persona en esta vida que determina el renacimiento en una próxima vida (15)

**kibbutz/kibbutz**  una comunidad, o colectiva, en Israel donde los granjeros comparten propiedad y trabajan juntos, los adultos comen juntos y los niños están criados en hogares de niños separados (542)

# L

**liberalism/liberalismo**  la idea que gente deben estar tan libre de restricción como sea posible; una creencia en la protección de libertades civiles, o los derechos básicos de todo la gente (135)

**lineage group/linaje**  poner en singular el término y las definiciones en ambos glosarios (47)

**Luftwaffe/Fuerza Aérea alemana (Nazi) durante la Segunda Guerra Mundial**  la fuerza aérea alemana (381)

# M

**magic realism/realismo mágico**  una forma de literatura latinoamericana que une eventos realísticos con fondos como sueños o fantásticos (509)

**Mahatma/Mahatma**  "Gran Alma", el nombre que los indios usaron refiriéndose a Mohandas Gandhi (350)

**Mau Mau movement/movimiento Mau Mau**  un esfuerzo organizado entre la gente Kikuyu de Kenya que usó terrorismo para demandar uhuru (liberación) de los británicos (516)

**Meiji/Meiji**  "Dominio Iluminado", el reino del emperador japonés Mutsuhito (258)

**mestizos/mestizos**  la progenie de europeos e indios americanos nativos (96)

**militarism/militarismo**  glorificación de las fuerzas armadas (143)

**ministerial responsibility/responsabilidad ministerial**  la idea que el primer ministro está responsable al elegido cuerpo legislativo popular y no al oficial ejecutivo (un principio crucial de democracia) (181)

**mirs/mires**  comunes o comunidades de pueblos de campesinos en Rusia zarista que eran responsables por pagos de tierras al gobierno (147)

**mobilization/movilización**  el proceso de asemblar y hacer tanto las tropas como las ofertas listas para la guerra (276)

**modernism/modernismo**  cambios producidos por escritores y artistas (entre 1870 y 1914) rebelándose contra los estilos literarios y artísticas tradicionales dominando la vida cultural europea desde el Renacimiento (190)

**monotheism/monoteísmo**  creencia de que existe sólo un Dios para toda la gente (12)

**mulattoes/mulatos**  la progenie de africanos y europeos (96)

**multinational corporations/corporaciones multinacionales**  compañías que tienen divisiones en más de dos países (487)

**multinational state/estado multinacional**  una colección de diferentes personas (137)

**mutual deterrence/refrenamiento mutuo**  la póliza basada en la creencia que un arsenal de armas nucleares previene guerra asegurando que si aun una nación lanzara sus armas en un primer ataque, que la otra nación todavía podría responder y devastar él que atacó (418)

# N

**nationalism/nacionalismo** lealtad y devoción a una nación (117)

**nationalization/nacionalización** posesión gubernamental (433)

**naturalism/naturalismo** un estilo literario donde se acepta el mundo material como verdadero y, entonces, la literatura está escrita en una manera realista (190)

**natural selection/selección natural** "supervivencia del más apto"—organismos más adaptables a sus ambientes pasan las variaciones que les encapaticen sobrevivir hasta que una nueva especie separada emerge (155)

**New Democracy/Democracia Nueva** una versión modificada de capitalismo puesto en efecto por Mao Zedong en China en 1958; industrias mayores fueron puestos bajo la posesión del estado, pero la mayoría de compañías manufactureras y de intercambio permanecieron en las manos privadas (548)

**New Economic Policy/Política Económica Nueva** una versión modificada de capitalismo puesto en efecto por Vladimir Lenin en Rusia en 1921; industria pesadas, bancario, y minería permanecieron en las manos del gobierno, pero los campesinos podrían vender sus productos agrícolas sin restricciones, y las tiendas de ventas al por menor e industrias pequeñas (menos de veinte empleados) podrían ser privadamente poseídas y operadas (317)

**nongovernmental organizations (NGOs)/organizaciones no gubernamentales** grupos de interés (relacionados a la emergencia de movimientos sociales de orígenes populares) que transcienden fronteras nacionales; frecuentemente están representados en las Naciones Unidas (595)

# O

**oligarchy/oligarquía** control por la minoría (21)

**orders/órdenes** grupos sociales, también conocidos como *estados* (divisiones de la sociedad en Europa, establecidas durante la Edad Media y continuando hasta más que la mitad del siglo dieciocho) (87)

**organic evolution/evolución orgánica** el principio de Charles Darwin que cada tipo de planta y animal evolucionó sobre un período de tiempo largo de formas de vida simples y más antiguas (155)

**ostracism/ostracismo** una costumbre concebida en Atenas antigua donde los miembros de la asamblea escribieron los nombre de una persona que se consideran dañosa en un fragmento de alfarería (*ostrakon*); si habían 6.000 votos registrados, la persona fue proscrita de la ciudad por diez años (25)

**ozone layer/ozonosfera** una capa delgada de gas en la parte de arriba de la atmósfera que protege la Tierra de los rayos ultravioletos del sol (584)

# P

**pan-Africanism/pan-africanismo** un movimiento que enfatizó la necesidad para la unidad de todos los africanos (350)

**pan-Arabism/pan-Arabismo** una creencia en la unidad árabe (532)

**patriarchal/patriarcal** una sociedad dominada por hombres (8)

**patricians/patricios** grandes propietarios que llegaron a ser la clase gobernadora de Roma (29)

**peninsulars/peninsulares** oficiales españolas y portugueses que vivieron temporariamente en Latinoamérica para la ganancia política y económica y luego volvieron a su madre patria (228)

**people's communes/comunidades de la gente** la resulta de la combinación de granjas colectivas durante el Gran Avance Adelante en China (549)

**perestroika/perestroika** "reestructurar", un término puesto a las reformas económicas, políticas, y sociales radicales de Mikhail Gorbachev en la Unión Soviética (452)

**permanent revolution/revolución permanente** fervor revolucionario constante (549)

**Philosophes/filósofos** miembros de la Ilustración, un movimiento de intelectuales del siglo dieciocho que creía en la razón, o la aplicación del método cientifico al entendimiento de la vida (74)

**philosophy/filosofía** un sistema de pensamiento organizado (26)

**planned economies/economías planeadas** sistemas dirigidos por agencias gubernamentales (287)

**plebeians/plebeyos** los terratenientes, artesanos, comerciantes, y pequeños granjeros menos ricos de Roma (29)

**pogroms/pogromos** masacres organizados de gente indefensa (190)

**policy of containment/política de contención** el plan de diplomático EE.UU. George Kennan de mantener comunismo dentro de sus bordes geográficos y prevenir futuros movimientos agresivos (417)

**polis/polis** una ciudad-estado griego (20)

**Politburo/Politburó** un comité que era el constructor principal de las pólizas del Partido Comunista (318)

**polytheistic/politeístico** el tener muchos dioses (42)

**post-impressionism/post-impresionismo** un movimiento artístico (que empezó en Francia en la década de 1880) donde los artistas eran especialmente interesados en colores, creyendo que podría servir como su propia forma de idioma (194)

**praetors/pretores**   directores ejecutivos del República Romano; se encargaron de la ley civil como fue aplicada a los ciudadanos romanos (29)

**prefectures/prefecturas**   territorios japoneses, gobernados por los antiguos dueños daimyo (258)

**principle of intervention/principio de intervención**   el derecho de grandes poderes para mandar ejércitos a países donde habían revoluciones para restaurar monarcas legítimas a sus tronos (135)

**principle of legitimacy/principio de legitimidad**   una guía usada por el Príncipe Klemens von Metternich durante el Congreso de Viena en 1814, que significó que monarcas legítimas eran restauradas a sus posiciones de poder para mantener la paz y estabilidad en Europa (134)

**privatization/privatización**   el acto de cambiar compañías poseídas por el estado (o el público) a control o posesión privada (493)

**proletariat/proletariado**   la clase obrera (164)

**prophets/profetas**   ciertos maestros religiosos que se creía había enviado Dios para difundir su palabra entre la gente (12)

**proportional representation/representación proporcional**   un sistema donde el número de representativos asignados por partido político está basada en el número de votos que cada partido recibió durante la elección general (535)

**protectorate/protectorado**   una unidad política que depende de otro estado para su protección (204)

**psychoanalysis/psicoanálisis**   un método desarrollado por Sigmund Freud donde el psicoterapista y paciente podrían inquirir profundamente en la memoria del paciente para retrasar la cadena de pensamientos reprimidos (189)

**puddling/pudelación**   un proceso desarrollado por Henry Cort donde el coque, derivado de carbón, fue usado para quemar las impurezas en hierro en bruto (hierro crudo) para hacer un hierro de alta calidad (125)

## R

**realpolitik/realpolitik**   las "políticas de realidad", o las políticas basadas en asuntos prácticos en vez de en teoría o ética (144)

**real wages/salarios reales**   el poder adquisitivo actual de ingresos (435)

**Red Guards/Guardias Rojas**   las unidades revolucionarias de Mao Zedong organizadas durante la Revolución Cultural para purificar la sociedad china de los elementos impuros culpables de tomar el sendero capitalista (549)

**Reichstag/Reichstag**   el parlamento alemán (323)

**Reign of Terror/reinado de terror**   un sistema concebido por la Convención Nacional y el Comité de Seguridad del Público en Francia (1793–1794) donde las cortes revolucionarias fueron establecidas para proteger el república revolucionario de sus enemigos internos conduciendo ejecuciones en muchedumbre (113)

**reincarnation/reencarnación**   la creencia que el alma del individuo se vuelve a nacer en una forma diferente después de la muerte (15)

**relics of feudalism/reliquia de feudalismo**   obligaciones de campesinos a propietarios locales (o los privilegios de aristócratas) que han sobrevividas de una edad antigua (por ejemplo, el pago de honorarios por los campesinos para el uso de facilidades locales) (104)

**reparations/reparaciones**   compensación financiera (301)

**revisionists/revisionistas**   Marxistas que rechazaron el método revolucionario y en su lugar argumentaron que los trabajadores organizaran en partidos políticos en grupo (y trabajara con otros partidos) para ganar reformas (167)

**ricksha/ricksha**   un pequeño vehículo cubierto de dos ruedas, usualmente para un pasajero, halado por un hombre (usado originalmente en Japón) (361)

## S

**scientific socialism/socialismo científico**   el plan de Gamal Abdul Nasser para mejorar el nivel de vida a través del Oriente Medio nacionalizando industrias mayores y usando planificación central para garantizar que se usarían recursos eficientemente (532)

**secular state/estado secular**   un estado que rechaza cualquiera influencia de la iglesia sobre sus pólizas (345)

**self-strengthening/fortalecimiento propio**   la idea que China debe adoptar tecnología occidental mientras que mantiene sus valores e instituciones confucianos (243)

**Senate/Senado**   un grupo selecto de alrededor de 300 hombres romanos propietarios que sirvieron toda la vida, y cuyos consejos a oficiales gubernamentales tenían la fuerza de la ley para el tercer siglo a. de J.C. (29)

**separation of powers/separación de poderes**   un sistema de gobierno donde los poderes ejecutivos, legislativos, y judiciales son separados (entonces proveyendo un sistema de equilibrio de poderes entre los poderes) (75)

**sepoys/sepoys**   soldados indios contratados por la Compañía Bretaña de India Oriental en los años de 1800 para proteger los intereses en India (220)

**Shining Path/Sendero Brillante**   un grupo guerrillero radical en Perú con obligaciones a China comunista (507)

**Social Darwinism/Darvinismo Social** una orden social que fue basada sobre el principio de Charles Darwin de evolución orgánica (189)

**Socialist/Socialista** un miembro del Partido Socialista; advoca posesión colectiva o gubernamental y administración de las maneras de producción y distribución de bienes (164)

**Socratic method/método socrático** una forma de enseñanza que usa un formato de preguntas-y-respuestas para guiar a los alumnos a conclusiones usando su propio razonamiento (26)

**soviets/soviéticos** consejos rusos compuestos de diputados de trabajadores y soldados (291)

**space shuttles/transbordadores especiales** astronaves para uso repetido que regresan a la Tierra bajo su propio poder (586)

**spheres of influence/esféricos de influencia** áreas en China donde naciones extranjeras fueron dadas derechos de intercambio exclusivos o privilegios de ferrocarriles y minería por jefes militares en cambio por dinero (244)

**squadristi/squadristi** bandas de fascistas armadas con camisas negras organizadas por Benito Mussolini para atacar oficinas y periódicos socialistas y interrumpir huelgas socialistas (315)

**stagflation/stagflation** el estancamiento económico que ocurrió desde 1973 hasta la mitad de la década de 1980 en los Estados Unidos (fue caracterizado por alta inflación y alto desempleo) (464)

**supply-side economics/economía de lado de oferta** la póliza de Ronald Reagan de reducciones impositivas que de modo supuesto estimularía crecimiento económico rápido y produciría nuevos ingresos (464)

**symbolists/simbolistas** un grupo de escritores y artistas franceses (después del año 1880) que creyó que un conocimiento objetivo del mundo era imposible porque el mundo externo fue hecho sólo de símbolos; trató con verdades generales en vez de actualidades, exaltando el metafísico y misterioso; creyó que el arte debe existir por el arte mismo (192)

## T

**Tennis Court Oath/Juramento de Cancha de Tenis** una promesa hecha por el Tercer Estado en 1789 para reunirse hasta que produjeran una constitución francesa (el juramento fue jurado durante una reunión que tuvo lugar en una cancha de tenis) (106)

**Thatcherism/Thatcherismo** la política económica de Margaret Thatcher, la primera primer ministro femenina de Bretaña (462)

**theology of liberation/teoría de liberación** católicos de Latinoamérica en la década de 1960 que fueron influenciados por ideas marxistas y creyeron que los cristianos deben pelear para liberar el oprimido, aun si significó el uso de violencia (490)

**totalitarian state/estado totalitario** un gobierno que trata de controlar la vida política, económica, social, intelectual, y cultural de sus ciudadanos (314)

**total war/guerra total** guerra envolviendo una movilización completa de recursos y personas (286)

**trench warfare/guerra de trinchera a trinchera** pelear de trincheras protegidas por alambre de púas (como en la Primera Guerra Mundial) (278)

**tribunes of the plebs/tribunos de los plebeyos** oficiales romanos que fueron dado el poder para proteger a los plebeyos (30)

## U

**Uncertainty Principle/Principio de Incertidumbre** la declaración de físico alemán Werner Heisenberg que uno no puede determinar el sendero de un electrón porque el acto de observar con luz afecta la localidad del electrón (en un sentido más grande, sugirió que en la base de todas leyes físicas era incertidumbre) (337)

**unconditional surrender/rendición incondicional** rendición absoluta, ilimitada (385)

**universal male suffrage/derecho al voto masculino universal** el derecho de todos los hombres adultos al voto (137)

**utopian socialists/socialistas utópicas** un movimiento de intelectuales idealistas—que empezó en la primera mitad del siglo diecinueve—que creyó en la igualdad de toda la gente y en el reemplazo de la competencia con la cooperación en industrias (nombrado así por futuras socialistas) (132)

## V

**viceroy/virrey** el gobernador de un país y provincia que domina como representativo de su rey o soberanía (los virreyes bretañas cumplieron los deseos del Parlamento en India en los años de 1800) (221)

**Viet Cong/Vietcong** comunistas vietnamitas—también conocidos como el Ejército de Liberación Nacional (568)

## W

**war of attrition/guerra de agotamiento** guerra basada en el agotamiento del otro lado por ataques constantes y demasiadas pérdidas (280)

**war communism/comunismo de guerra**    una política usada para asegurar ofertas regulares para el Ejército Rojo durante la Guerra Civil Rusa (1918–1921), que incluyó control gubernamental de bancos y la mayoría de las industrias, tomando granos de campesinos, y la centralización de administsración estatal bajo el control comunista (295)

**welfare state/estado benefactor**    una nación donde el gobierno toma la responsabilidad de proveer a los ciudadanos con servicios y un nivel de vida mínimo (432)

**westernization/hacerse occidental**    conversión a, o adopción de tradiciones o técnicas occidentales (354)

**white-collar/oficinista**    relacionando a, o constituyendo de la clase de empleados cuyos deberes no requieren que usen ropa de labor o ropa protector—como trabajadores profesionales y técnicos, gerentes, oficiales, y trabajadores clericales y de ventas (435)

**women's liberation movement/movimiento de liberación de mujeres**    el interés renovado en feminismo al final de la década de 1960 que insistió en igualdad política y legal con hombres (466)

**World Wide Web/El World Wide Web**    Un número inmenso de páginas de información conectado uno al otro alrededor del mundo (585)

# Z

**zaibatsu/zaibatsu**    en Japón, una concentración de varios procesos manufactureros dentro de una sola empresa—una grande corporación financiera e industrial (265)

**Zionism/sionismo**    un movimiento internacional originalmente para el establecimiento de una comunidad judía nacional o religiosa en Palestino y luego para el apoyo de Israel moderno (190)

# INDEX

**PHOTO ACKNOWLEDGMENTS** (*continued from page iv*)

**Chapter 1**  4 ©Nik Wheeler; 7 Reproduced by Courtesy of the Trustees of the British Museum; 9 Babylonian, Stele of Hammurabi, Musee du Louvre, ©Photo R.M.N.; 13 The Israel Museum, Jerusalem; 16 ©John Elk; 16 Robert Harding Picture Library; 18 (left) Ontario Science Centre; 18 (right) Corbis-Bettmann; 22 ©Michael Holford; 24 ©Michael Holford, London; 25 Reproduced by Courtesy of the Trustess of the British Museum; 27 Scala/Art Resource, NY; 28 British Museum, Photo Michael Holford, London; 29 Erich Lessing/Art Resource, NY; 31 Scala/Art Resource, NY; 33 Scala/Art Resource, NY; 35 Bridgeman/Art Resource, NY.

**Chapter 2**  40 North Wind Picture Archives; 42 Photograph by Mark Gulezian ©Smithsonian Institution; 43 ©Lee Boltin, Boltin Picture Library; 44 ©1997 Suzanne-Murphy-Larronde; 45 Bibliotheque Nationale, Paris; 47 ©Robert Aberman/Art Resource, NY; 50 ©Nigel Cameron/Photo Researchers; 52 ChinaStock; 54 Giraudon/Art Resource, NY; 55 Victor R. Boswell, Jr. ©National Geographic; 57 The Pierpont Morgan Library/Art Resource, MS399, f.5v, c. 1515, Bruges; 58 Bibliothèque Nationale, Paris; 59 (left) ©Sylvain Grandadam/Photo Researchers, Inc.; 59 (right) Sonia Halliday Photographs; 62 (left) Scala/Art Resource, NY; 62 (right) Hyacinthe Rigaud, *Louis XIV*, Musee du Louvre, Photo R.M.N.; 65 The National Galleries of Scotland, By permission of the Earl of Rosebery; 66 Peter Hoadley, *William III and Mary Stuart*, Rijksmuseum, Amsterdam; 68 By courtesy of the Board of Trustees of the Victoria and Albert Museum; 70 Corbis-Bettmann; 72 Courtesy of William J. Duiker; 74 Giruadon/Art Resource, NY; 75 Mary Evans Picture Library.

**Chapter 3**  82 Corbis-Bettmann; 84 Joseph Vernet, *Port of Diepp*, Depot du Louvre au Musee de la Marine, ©Photo R.M.N.; 85 Corbis-Bettmann; 87 Giovanni Michele Graneri, *Market in Piazza San Carlo*, 1752, Museo Civico di Torino; 89 Giraudon/Art Resource, NY; 90 Giraudon/Art Resource, NY; 92 Scala/Art Resource, NY; 95 Benjamin West, *The Death of General Wolfe*, Transfer from the Canadian War Memorial, 1921, Gift of the second Duke of Westminster, Eaton Hall, Cheshire, 1918, National Gallery of Canada, Ottawa; 99 (top) © O. Louis Mazzatenta/National Geographic Society Image Collection; 99 (bottom) Art Resource, NY; 102 John Trumbull, *The Declaration of Independence*, 4 July 1776, Yale University Art Gallery, Trumbull Collection; 103 Yale University Art Gallery; 105 Giraudon/Art Resource, NY; 107 Anonymous, *Fall of the Bastille*, Musee National des Chateau de Versailles, Giraudon/Art Resource, NY; 108 Corbis-Bettmann; 109 Giraudon/Art Resource, NY; 112 Giraudon/Art Resource, NY; 113 Giraudon/Art Resource, NY; 115 Antoine Jean Gros, *Napolean Crossing the Bridge at Arcola*, Musee du Louvre, ©Photo R.M.N.; 118 Giraudon/Art Resource, NY.

**Chapter 4**  122 North Wind Picture Archives; 124 (left and right) North Wind Picture Archives; 126 & 127 ©Ann Ronan at Image Select; 128 Library of Congress; 130 Gustave Dore, *Over London by Rail*, from *London, A Pilgrimage*; Bill Rose Theatre Collection, The New York Public Library at Lincoln Center; Astor, Lenox and Tilden Foundations; 131 ©Ann Ronan at Image Select; 132 Culver Pictures, Inc.; 135 Austrian Information Service; 136 Lecomte, *Battle in the rue de Rohan*, 1830, Giraudon/Art Resource, NY; 138 Historisches Museum der Stadt Wein; 142 Stock Montage, Chicago; 144 *Proclamation of the German Empire at Versailles*, 1871, Anton von Werner, Photo Bildarchiv Preussischer Kulturbesitz, Berlin; 146 Flandrin, *Napolean III*, Musee National des Chateau de Versailles, ©Photo R.M.N.; 148 ©Ullstein Bilderdeinst, Berlin; 149 Library of Congress; 151 ©David H. Endersbee/Tony Stone Worldwide; 152 North Wind Picture Archives; 153 Caspar David Friedrich, *Man and Woman Gazing at the Moon*, Nationalgalerie SMPK Berlin, Photo: Jorg P. Anders, ©Bildarchiv Preussischer Kulturbesitz, Berlin; 154 Eugene Delacroix, *Women of Algiers*, Musee du Louvre, ©Photo R.M.N.; 155 Gustave Courbet, *The Stonebreakers*, Foto Marburg/Art Resource, NY.

**Chapter 5**  160 Corbis-Bettmann; 162 The Fotomas Index; 163 ©Tom Burnside/Photo Researchers, Inc.; 166 Verein fur Geschichte der Arbeiterbewegung, Vienna; 170 Bettmann/Hulton; 172 Musee de la Poste, Paris, photo J.L. Charmet; 173 William Powell Frith, *Many Happy Returns of the Day*; Harrogate Museums and Art Gallery/Bridgeman Art Library, London; 174 Giraudon/Art Resource, NY; 176 Snark/Art Resource, NY; 178 Corbis-Bettmann; 183 Corbis-Bettmann; 184 David King Collection. London; 186 E.T. Archive, London; 189 Bild-Archiv der Osterreichischen Nationalbibliothek, Vienna; 191 (left) Phillips collection, Washington, DC; 191 (right) Art Resource, NY; 193 (top) Scala/Art Resource, NY; 193 (bottom) Erich Lessing/Art Resource, NY; 194 Vincent Van Gogh, *The Starry Night*, (1889), Oil on canvas, 29 × 36 1/4", Collection, The Museum of Modern Art, New York, Acquired through the Lillie P. Bliss Bequest; 195 Vasily Kandinsky, *Painting with White Border*, May 1913; Collection, the Solomon R. Guggenheim Museum, New York; 196 Photo ©E. Louis Lankford.

**Chapter 6**  200 Image Select/Art Resource, NY; 202 North Wind Picture Archives; 204 Collections of the Bibliotheque Nationale, Paris, Photo: ©Giraudon/Art Resource, NY; 206 Sipahioglu, Gamma-Liaison; 207 North Wind Picture Archives; 210 The Opening of the Suez Canal, Photo ©Bildarchv Preussischer Kulturbesitz, Berlin; **211** North Wind Picture Archives; **213** Aberdeen University Library; **214** Hulton Deutsch Collection/ Corbis; **217** North Wind Picture Archives; **220** North Wind Picture Archives; **222** By permission of the British Library, London, Oriental and India Office Collections, WD.2443; **224** ©The Hulton Getty Picture Collection, Limited/Rischgitz Collection/Tony Stone Images; **225** Reproduced by Courtesy of the British Library, Oriental and India Office Collections; **226** Brown Brothers; **227** Brown Brothers; **229** Corbis-Bettmann; **231** ©G. Dagli Orti; **234** Brown Brothers.

**Chapter 7** **238** James P. Blair, ©National Geographic Image Collection; **240** Peabody Essex Museum, Salem, Mass. Photo by Mark Sexton; **242** National Maritime Museum, London; **243** Harper's Weekly/Corbis; **245** Courtesy of the Freer Gallery of Art, Smithsonian Institution, Washington, DC; **246** Corbis-Bettmann; **250** Camera Press/Globe Photos; **251** ChinaStock; **253** Corbis-Bettmann; **255** ChinaStock; **258** Courtesy of the United States Naval Academy Museum; **261 (left)** Corbis-Bettmann; **261 (right)** Mary Evans Picture Library; **262** The Metropolitan Museum of Art, Gift of Lincoln Kirstein, 1959 (JP 3276), photograph by Otto E. Nelson; **265** Culver Pictures, Inc.

**Chapter 8** **272** Tony Stone Images; **275** Archive Photos; **276** Bilderdienst Suddeutscher Verlag, Munich; **277** Corbis-Bettmann; **279** ©Roger-Viollet, Paris; **282 (top)** Librairie Larousse, Paris; **282 (bottom)** Express News/Archive Photos; **283** Archive Photos/American Stock; **286** Corbis-Bettmann; **287** E.T. Archive, London; **288** ©Ullstein Bilderdienst; **291** Archive Photos; **292** Archive Photos; **295** Brown Brothers; **296** David King Collection, London; **297** Corbis-Bettmann; **300** Bettmann/Hulton.

**Chapter 9** **306** Archive Photos; **310** Corbis-Bettmann; **311** ©Roger-Violett; **313** Ellis Herwig/Stock Boston; **315** ©Popperfoto; **316** Corbis-Bettmann; **318** David King Collection, London; **320** ©The Hulton Getty Picture Collection, Limited/Tony Stone Images; **324** Hugo Jaeger, Life Magazine, ©Time Warner, Inc.; **327** Hugo Jaeger, Life Magazine, ©Time Warner, Inc.; **328** The National Archives/Corbis; **329** Snark/Art Resource, NY; **331** ©The Hulton Getty Picture Collection, Limited/Tony Stone Images; **332** Archive Photos/Popperfoto; **334** Salvador Dali, *The Persistence of Memory*, 1931, Oil on canvas, 9 1/2 × 13:, Collection, The Museum of Modern Art, New York, Given Anonymously; **336** Corbis-Bettmann.

**Chapter 10** **340** Hulton Deutsch Collection/Corbis; **342** Tate Gallery, London/Art Resource, NY; **344** ©The Hulton Getty Picture Collection, Limited/Tony Stone Images; **345** ©The Hulton Getty Picture Collection, Limited/Tony Stone Images; **347**

Corbis-Bettmann; **351** ©The Hulton Getty Picture Collection, Limited/Tony Stone Images; **352** Hulton Deutsch Collection/ Corbis; **353** Archive Photos; **356** Corbis-Bettmann; **359 (left)** ©The Hulton Getty Picture Collection, Limited/Tony Stone Images; **359 (right)** ©Earl Leaf/Rapho; **360** ChinaStock; **364** Charles O'Rear/©Corbis; **366** ©The Hulton Getty Picture Collection, Limited/Tony Stone Images; **367** Schalkwijk/Art Resource, NY; **368** Nik Wheeler/Corbis.

**Chapter 11** **372** Corbis-Bettmann; **376** Hugo Jaeger, Life Magazine, © Time Warner Inc.; **377** National Archives (#306-NT-1222E); **379** Paul Dorsey, Life Magazine, © 1938, Time, Inc.; **382** Archive Photos/Imperial War Museum; **383** © The Hulton Getty Picture Collection, Limited/Tony Stone Images; **384** The National Archives/Corbis; **387** ©The Hulton Getty Picture Collection, Limited/Tony Stone Images; **389** National Archives (#111-C-273); **392** UPI/Corbis-Bettmann; **395** Main Commission for the Investigation of Nazi War Crimes, courtesy of the United States Holocaust Memorial Museum; **396** Courtesy of the Simon Wiesenthal Center Beit HaShoah Museum of Tolerance Library/Archives, Los Angeles, CA; **399** ©The Hulton Getty Picture Collection, Limited/Tony Stone Images; **400** ©The Hulton Getty Picture Collection, Limited/Tony Stone Images; **402** The Herald & Evening Times Picture Library ©Caledonian Newspapers Ltd.; **403** Snark/Art Resource, NY; **405** J. R. Eyerman, Life Magazine, ©Time Warner, Inc.; **408** E. T. Archive.

**Chapter 12** **414** Hulton Deutsch Collection/Corbis; **416** AP/Wide World Photos; **417** Corbis-Bettmann; **418** Corbis-Bettmann; **419** Hulton Deutsch Collection/Corbis; **421** Corbis-Bettmann; **426** UPI/Corbis-Bettmann; **427** Corbis-Bettmann; **429** ©Prache-Lewin/Sygma; **431** ©1990 Pierre Boulat-Cosos/Woodfin Camp and Associates; **432** Hulton Deutsch Collection/Corbis; **435** Corbis-Bettmann; **437** ©Bob Adelman/Magnum Photos; **440** Corbis-Bettmann; **441** ©The Hulton Getty Picture Collection, Limited/Tony Stone Images; **442** ©C. Raimond-Dityvon/Viva, Woodfin Camp and Associates; **444** AP/Wide World Photos.

**Chapter 13** **448** AP/Wide World Photos; **450** Courtesy Ronald Reagan Library; **452** AP/Wide World Photos; **455** Georges Merillon/Gamma-Liaison; **456** AP/Wide World Photos; **458** Reuters/Bettmann; **463 (top)** ©Mark Stewart/Camera Press, London; **463 (bottom)** AP/Wide World Photos; **465** Hulton Deutsch Collection/Corbis; **467** AP/Wide World Photos; **468** Hulton Deutsch Collection/Corbis; **469** Jim McDonald/Corbis; **470** Agence France Presse/Corbis-Bettmann; **472** AP/Wide World Photos; **474** ©Hans Namuth/Photo Researchers, Inc.; **475** The Andy Warhol Foundation, Inc./Art Resource, NY;

Excerpt from *The French Revolution* edited by Paul Beik. Copyright © 1971 by Paul Beik. Reprinted by permission of Harper-Collins Publishers, Inc.

**DECLARATION OF THE RIGHTS OF WOMAN AND THE FEMALE CITIZEN 109**
From *Women in Revolutionary Paris 1789–1795* by Darleen Gay Levy, Harriet Branson Applewhite, and Mary Durham Johnson. Copyright © 1979 by University of Illinois Press. Used with permission of the publisher.

**Chapter 4**
**REVOLUTIONARY EXCITEMENT 138**
From *The Reminiscences of Carl Schurz* by Carl Schurz (New York: The McClure Co. 1907), vol. 1, pp. 112–113

**EMANCIPATION—Serfs and Slaves 148**
From *U.S. Statutes at Large* (Washington, D.C., Government Printing Office, 1875), vol. 12, pp. 1268–1269

**Chapter 5**
**MARX AND ENGELS PROCLAIM THE CLASSLESS SOCIETY 166**
From *The Communist Manifesto* by Karl Marx and Friedrich Engels (Penguin Classics, 1985) pp. 105, 120–121.

**A DOLL'S HOUSE—ONE WOMAN'S CRY FOR FREEDOM 191**
From *Roots of Western Civilization* by Wesley D. Camp. Copyright © 1983 by John Wiley & Sons. Reproduced with permission of McGraw-Hill, Inc.

**Chapter 6**
**A CALL TO ARMS 207**
from *The Vietnamese Response to Foreign Intervention*, Truong Buu Lam, ed., (New Haven, Conn.: Yale University Southeast Asian Series, 12967), pp. 76–78.

**THE POETRY OF TAGORE 227**
From *The Poetry of Tagore from Amiya Chakravarty*, ed. A Tagore Reader (Boston, 1961), p. 300

**Chapter 7**
**A PROGRAM FOR A NEW CHINA 251**
Excerpt from *Sources of Chinese Tradition* by William Theodore de Bary, Copyright © 1960 by Columbia University Press. Reprinted with permission of the publisher.

**BA JIN AND THE CHINESE NOVEL 255**
Excerpt from *Family* by Ba Jin. Copyright © 1964 Foreign Language Press, 24 Baiwanzhuang Road, Beijing 100037, P.R. China. Used with permission.

**A LETTER TO THE SHOGUN 258**
Excerpt from *Commodore Perry in Japan*, Robert L. Reynolds (New York: Harper & Row, 1963), p. 68.

**Chapter 8**
**THE EXCITEMENT OF WAR 279**
From *The World of Yesterday* by Stefan Zweig, translated by Helmut Ripperger, Translation copyright 1943 by The Viking Press, Inc. Used by permission of Viking Penguin, a division of Penguin Books USA, Inc. Publication rights for Stefan Zweig, by permission of Williams Verlag AG, Zuerich ©1976, and Atrium Press Ltd. London © 1980

**THE REALITY OF WAR—TRENCH WARFARE 283**
*All Quiet on the Western Front* by Erich Maria Remarque. "Im Westen Nichts Neues", copyright 1928 by Ullstein A. G.; Copyright renewed © 1956 by Erich Maria Remarque. "All Quiet on the Western Front", copyright 1929, 1930 by Little, Brown and Company; Copyright renewed © 1957, 1958 by Erich Maria Remarque. All Rights Reserved.

**TEN DAYS THAT SHOOK THE WORLD 294**
From *Ten Days That Shook the World* by John Reed. Copyright © by Signet Books. Reprinted with permission of the publisher.

**Chapter 9**
**THE FORMATION OF COLLECTIVE FARMS 320**
*The Formation of Collective Farms* from Sidney Harcave, *Readings in Russian History* (New York: Thomas Crowell and Co., 1962), pp. 208–210

**MASS MEETINGS IN NAZI GERMANY (Speech at Nuremburg) 326**
From Norman Baynes, ed., *The Speeches of Adolf Hitler* (New York: Oxford University Press, 1942), 1:206–207

**MASS MEETINGS IN NAZI GERMANY (Adolf Hitler *Mein Kampf*) 326**
Excerpt from Mein Kampf by Adolf Hitler, translated by Ralph Manheim. Copyright © 1943, renewed 1971 by Houghton Mifflin Co. Reprinted by permission of Houghton Mifflin Co. All rights reserved.

**THE NOVELS OF HERMANN HESSE 336**
From *The Novels of Hermann Hesse* by Hermann Hesse, Demian (New York: Bantam Books, 1966), p. 30

**Chapter 10**
**IF AFRICANS WERE LEFT IN PEACE 351**
From Jomo Kenyatta, *Facing Mount Kenya* (London: Secker and Warburg, 1959), p. 318